HISTORY OF EARLY CHILDHOOD EDUCATION

SOURCE BOOKS ON EDUCATION
VOLUME 55
GARLAND REFERENCE LIBRARY OF SOCIAL SCIENCE
VOLUME 982

HISTORY OF EARLY CHILDHOOD EDUCATION

V. CELIA LASCARIDES and BLYTHE F. HINITZ

FALMER PRESS
A MEMBER OF THE TAYLOR & FRANCIS GROUP
NEW YORK & LONDON
2000

Published in 2000 by
Falmer Press
A member of the Taylor & Francis Group
29 West 35th Street
New York, NY 10001

10   9   8   7   6   5   4   3   2   1

Library of Congress Cataloging-in-Publication Data
Lascarides, V. Celia
  History of Early Childhood Education/ V. Celia Lascarides and Blythe F. Hinitz.
    p. cm.-- (Garland reference library of social sciences ; 982. Source books on
  education ; 55)
  Includes bibliographical references and index.
  ISBN 0-8153-1794-8- (alk. paper)
    1.Early childhood education--History. 2. Early childhood education--United
States--History. I. Hinitz, Blythe Simone Farb, 1944- II. Title. III. Garland reference
libraryof social science ; v. 982. IV. Garland reference library of social science. Source
books on education ; vol. 55.

LB1139.23 .L39 2000
372.21'09--dc21
                          00-021691

Between the time of research and the date of publication, World Wide Web sites may
unexpectedly close or change addresses. The web sites listed in the references of this
encyclopedia are the most recent known to the publisher.

Printed on acid-free, 250-year-life paper
Manufactured in the United States of America

DEDICATIONS

To our husbands, William and Herman

V. Celia Lascarides dedicates this book to the memory of her parents Joseph and Sevasti Lascarides for instilling in her the joy of learning and a sense of responsibility.

Blythe F. Hinitz dedicates this book to the memory of her mother Gertrude A. (Nachitowitz) Farb who modeled dedication to teaching and advocacy for children and families.

CONTENTS

List of Figures

PREFACE

Contrary to popular opinion, early childhood education did not begin in January 1965 when Lady Bird Johnson held a White House tea to announce federal funding for preschool classes that would "break the vicious cycle of poverty." This national program, which soon became known as Head Start, brought into focus the idea of child care and early education as a public responsibility and an entitlement. It illustrates the complicated interaction between political strategy and children's programs, with public funding having to meet the test of public advantage. As a consequence of this interaction, issues related to early education were discussed in the public press and "everybody" became aware of this lowest level of the educational ladder.

The desire to orient their offspring to the needs of a society seems to be an innate mammalian characteristic, as anthropologists and biologists have shown through the years. However, there have been many ideas about how this can best be done so that young humans will grow up to fill the patterns designed by their elders. Should they be ignored? Should toddlers be beaten upon any provocation to "break their will" so that they are prepared to enter the Heavenly Gates? Can any useful learning be acquired before the age of six or seven? Are children like little plants in a garden, needing only tender attention so that they will blossom naturally? Is it possible for adults, so far from their own early childhoods, to understand what is going on in the minds of youngsters? Should authority be imposed from above, or should children recognize that their own initiative and creative thought are of primary importance? Throughout this history of early childhood education, V. Celia Lascarides and Blythe F. Hinitz will trace questions as these that have been discussed for centuries.

From the mid-nineteenth century onward, philosophers and historians have discussed and written about established and theoretical educational systems, including Froebelian kindergarten, but women and children have been largely ignored by historians of the past. Only recently have we had women historians or historians who have written about women. Serious attempts to discover and systematize the antecedents of today's beliefs about *early* education have proliferated since the 1970s. One indication of increased interest is the popularity of history seminars held during conferences of the National Association for the Education of Young Children. The first, in 1977, had one presentation and an audience of about a dozen. During the 1990s, there have been about a dozen presentations and an audience of over a hundred. The International Standing Working Group for the History of Early Childhood

Education has held annual meetings at European universities each August since 1984. Participants often base their research papers upon previously unknown primary sources and archival collections. Both Hinitz and Lascarides have presented significant papers at these conferences and at other national and international meetings.

Why is history important? Most of us have dismal recollections of our history classes, which seemed to focus on military men and their battles. In our contemporary lives, it is easier to reject the past because it is about things that are irrelevant and utterly out of date. We become involved with today's problems and decisions affecting the immediate future without recognizing that the *historical perspective* can aid in the decision process by showing how situations of the past developed and were dealt with. Understanding the past helps us escape short-range perspectives and understand the origins of the present. Perhaps the most important contribution is to help define early childhood education. Establishing is one prerequisite of a profession. A profession's historical knowledge provides pride and a shared memory for its members and helps establish the respect of those in other professions. This comprehensive and scholarly volume makes a solid contribution to public knowledge and to the profession of early childhood education.

Dorothy W. Hewes, Ph.D.
La Mesa, California
November, 1999

Acknowledgments

Many persons, groups, and institutions have helped along the way in the preparation of this book, and we would like to take this opportunity to acknowledge and thank them. Deserving special mention are: Dorothy Hewes for her professional mentoring, kindness, and generosity and for permitting us to use her material on education in the Japanese internment camps; Philip Herbst's astute editing was appreciated; our editors at Garland Publishing, Marie Ellen Larcada, Michael Spurlock, Karita France Dos Santos, Seema Shah, and Alexis Skinner for their expert guidance and patience; and Chuck Bartelt, Director of Resources at Garland Publishing, for her gracious and masterful assistance; the members of the NAEYC history seminar; our students; and any person whom we failed to acknowledge by name.

Blythe Hinitz expresses her thanks to the following individuals, who have provided original sources or expert opinion during the development of this manuscript: Professor Lesley Abbott, Dr. Kevin J. Brehony, Dr. Harriet Cuffaro, Dr. Mary Ann Fowlkes, Dr. Harlene Galen, Dr. Barbara J. Harned, Dr. Keith L. Miller, Dr. Edna Ranck, John Siraj-Blatchford, Valentina K. Tikoff, Henk van Setten; and the members of Division F of the American Educational Research Association for their responses to Internet inquiries; and to the librarians and staffs of the following library and archival centers for their assistance: the British and Foreign School Society Archive Centre, London, England, Brian Seagrove, Archivist, Dr. G. Collins, Associate Archivist; the Tuttleman Library of Gratz College, Philadelphia, Pennsylvania, Robert Manstein, Librarian; the Association for Childhood Education International Archives, Archives and Manuscripts, Special Collections, Maryland Room, University of Maryland at College Park Libraries, Lauren Brown, Curator, Anne S. K. Turkos, Associate Curator; The University of London Library, London, England; the Margaret Naumburg Papers, Department of Special Collections, Van Pelt–Dietrich Library Center, University of Pennsylvania, Philadelphia, Pennsylvania, Nancy M. Shawcross, Curator of Manuscripts; The William Torrey Harris Papars and the Jennie Wahlert papers, The Missouri Historical Society, St. Louis, Missouri; Special Collections, The Millbank Memorial Library of Teachers College, Columbia University, New York, New York, Bette Weneck, Manuscripts Curator; the Modern Records Centre, University of Warwick, Coventry, England; the Froebel Archive for Childhood Studies, Roehampton Institute, London, Jane Read, Archivist; and especially to the Roscoe L. West Library, The College of New Jersey, Ewing, New

Jersey, particularly Mrs. Janice Kisthardt, Librarian for Education, Curriculum, Children and Youth; the Interlibrary Loan Librarians, and all the reference librarians. Acknowledgment is given to the Faculty and Institutional Research Committee, Trenton State College, for its support of the initial stages of this work; to the Information Management staff and to Dr. Alex Pan of the College of New Jersey for their contributions to the computer and technological aspects of this work; and to Marilia Barrows Oliver for expert transcription services. Most of all grateful appreciation is given to Dr. Herman J. Hinitz for contributing his computer expertise to this project, creating Figures 9.1, 13.1, 13.2, 20.1, and 20.2, and for his unfailing support, motivational inspiration, and forbearance.

V. Celia Lascarides expresses many thanks: to the Boston Athenaeum: Trevor Johnson, Archivist, for securing hard-to-find materials through interlibrary loan, Stephen Nonack, Reference Librarian, Catharina Slautterback, Curator of Prints and Photographs, for her help to locate and select photographs, and all the staff for their many kindnesses; the Boston Public Library, Ms. Katherine Dibble, Supervisor of Research Library Services, and all the staff for locating and bringing materials out of storage, John Dorsey, for photographs, Mrs. Dorothy Keller, Head Reference Librarian, William Grealish, Curator of Humanities, and all the staff for their assistance; the Social Science librarians, Boston University, Mugar Library, all the Reference Librarians, too many to name individually, and Paula Langley of the circulation desk; Dr. Ann G. DePlacido, University of Massachusetts at Boston, for providing early editions of books, advice and encouragement, and for reviewing the manuscript at various stages of development; Dr. Joan Herwig, Director of Child Development Lab School, Iowa State University at Ames; The Massachusetts State Library, Eva Murphy, Librarian, for locating materials on Horace Mann; Massachusetts Historical Society, for early issues of kindergarten periodical literature; The Mattapoisett Historical Society, Ms. Bette Roberts, Curator, for making it possible to examine their collection of New England Primers and children's books, and for providing photographs; the Merrill-Palmer Institute at Wayne State University; The Museum of Fine Arts, Boston, Ms. Karen L. Otis; Radcliffe College, Schlesinger Library, Abigail Adams Eliot Papers, Eva Moseley, Curator of Manuscripts, and Sylvia McDowell, director's office; University of Massachusetts at Boston, Peggy Adlum, Reference Librarian; Pat Spahr, Director of Information and Development at NAEYC; Everett Carlson for his expert computer assistance, Victoria Casana for proofreading, and Carrie Levine for typing earlier drafts. Last but not least, to my husband William F. Manley, J.D., for his patience, sustained material and moral support, and encouragement throughout this endeavor, many thanks.

INTRODUCTION

This book is designed to bring the history of education, childhood education, and child development closer to our lives. The early education programs of today stand on a strong historical foundation. This work examines the impact of history on current practice by focusing on the history of early childhood education within the historical context of each time period. The content of this volume is selective rather than exhaustive.

The genesis of the book goes some years back (1987) when the authors did a survey in selected institutions of higher education, to find out how much history students receive as part of their early childhood education undergraduate[1] teacher training. Among the findings were that: (1) there was not a separate course teaching early childhood education history to the undergraduates; (2) whatever historical information they received was incidental and part of other courses; and (3) there was not a coherent, clearly defined historical content. The students received an eclectic mix of information. One of the conclusions was that undergraduates were lacking in historical knowledge that is important for developing a professional identity. The results of the survey were presented to the history seminar of the National Association for the Education of Young Children (NAEYC) (1987–1989). Subsequently, the study was published in Moscow as a chapter in *Why Should We Teach History of Education?* (1993).[2]

The age span of children covered in this book is birth though eight years. This span has been defined as the early childhood period in the contemporary United States, by the NAEYC since 1986.[3]

The book includes: descriptions of child-rearing practices in specific societies; brief biographies, description of work, and selected writings of creators of educational programs who have been influencing early childhood education over the years; and descriptions of selected examples of early childhood education programs.

Part I (Chapters 1–6) looks at childhood, child rearing, and education in antiquity, and selected European pedagogues, their biographies, philosophies, and programs they developed, which form the European roots of early childhood education, and which have influenced American practices.

Part II (Chapters 7-13) details the evolution of programs and ideas after they reached the United States. It includes the beginnings of child care and early education in different geographical sections of the country. The kindergarten, nursery school, child care movements, and the involvement of the federal government in programs for young children are described.

Part III (Chapters 14–19) presents four of the diverse cultural and ethnic populations and traditions that are part of the American society and which have contributed their richness to the panoply of early education diversity, in this country. This part begins with Native American society, and includes descriptions/presentations of Black, Asian, and Hispanic American children. It concludes with chapters on bilingualism in America, and on recent influences from other lands.

Part IV (Chapters 20) describes the evolution of some professional organizations that foster and shape the field.

We acknowledge that current professional literature uses egalitarian terminology. However, the majority of historical writings reviewed use the masculine form generically. Therefore, masculine pronouns are used throughout this book for the sake of consistency.

Names of individuals, cities, and other names are left as they appear in the reviewed texts.

The figures and photographs were chosen for their relevance to the topics covered in the text.

V. Celia Lascarides had responsibility for chapters 1, 4, 12, 14, 15, 18, and 21, and four of the appendices, and for putting the final manuscript together; Blythe F. Hinitz for 3, 5, 6, 11, 13, 16, 17, and 19 and the Abbreviations. Chapters 2, 7, 8, 9, 10, and 20, and the Introduction were written jointly.

Searching though books, journals, and other materials of earlier eras, and discovering nuggets to include, generated much excitement. The overwhelming mass of information made it difficult to decide what to include and what to leave out. The authors hope that the book will stimulate others to pursue further topics presented here.

Every care has been taken to give credit to the authors and editors of the books and resources we reviewed. However, when one has been studying a particular subject for a long period of time, it becomes difficult to attribute all the ideas one possesses to a specific source. Each subject studied contains numerous sources, which, when combined with personal knowledge, creates a whole picture of the topic under investigation. Any errors in the text are the sole responsibility of the authors.

The authors have been working together for a number of years. They have presented jointly and individually in the history seminar of the National Association for the Education of Young Children (NAEYC) annual conference; the National Association of Early Childhood Teacher Educators (NAECTE) annual meeting; and at the International Standing Group for the History of Early Childhood Education (ISCHE).

NOTES

1. At the time of the study, this was the terminology used. Now it is refered to as initial teacher training.

2. V. Celia Lascarides and Blythe Hinitz, "Survey of Important Historical and Current Figures in Early Childhood Education," in *Why Should We Teach History of Education?*,

ed. Kadriya Salimova and Erwin V. Johanningmeir (Moscow: International Academy of Self-Improvement, 1993), 264–277.

3. Sue Bredecamp and Carol Copple, eds. *Developementally Appropriate Practice in Early Childhood Programs,* rev. ed. (Washington, D.C.: National Association for the Education of Young Children, 1997), 3.

ABBREVIATIONS

AAAS	American Association for the Advancement of Science
AAMTE	Association for the Accreditation of Montessori Teacher Education
AAUW	American Association of University Women
ABC	Act for Better Child Care
ACCESS	American Associate Degree Early Childhood Teacher Educators
ACE	Association for Childhood Education (now ACEI)
ACEI	Association for Childhood Education International (formerly IKU, ACE)
ACYF	Agency for Children, Youth, and Families
AFDC	Aid to Families with Dependent Children
AMA	American Missionary Association
AMI	Association Montessori Internationale (The International Montessori Association)
AMS	American Montessori Society
APEA	American Physical Education Association
APHA	American Public Health Association
ASPCA	American Society for the Prevention of Cruelty to Animals
ASSA	American Social Science Association
ATE	Association of Teacher Educators
BEE	Bureau of Educational Experiments
BFSS	British and Foreign Schools Society
BIA	Bureau of Indian Affairs
CAP	Community Action Program
CAP	Center Accreditation Project
CCDBG	Child Care and Development Block Grant
CDF	Children's Defense Fund
CDGM	Child Development Group of Mississippi
CEC	Council for Exceptional Children
CETA	Comprehensive Employment and Training Act

CFRP	Child and Family Resource Program
COCE	Community Organization for Cooperative Education Incorporated
CWLA	Child Welfare League of America
DCCDCA	Day Care and Child Development Council of America
DEC	Division for Early Childhood (of the Council for Exceptional Children)
DHEW	Department of Health, Education and Welfare
DHHS	Department of Health and Human Services
DVAEYC	Delaware Valley Association for the Education of Young Children
EDC	Educational Development Center (Newton, Mass.)
EEPCD	Early Education Program for Children with Disabilities
ENS	Emergency Nursery School
EOA	Educational Opportunity Act of 1964
EPSDT	National Early and Periodic Screening, Diagnosis, and Treatment Program
ESEA	Elementary and Secondary Education Act
FERA	Federal Emergency Relief Administration
GEB	General Education Board
HCEEP	Handicapped Children's Early Education Program
HSPV	Head Start Planned Variation Study
HSST	Head Start Supplementary Training
ICWRS	Iowa Child Welfare Research Station
IDEA	Individuals with Disabilities Education Act
IEP	Individualized Education Plan
IFSP	Individualized Family Service Plan
IKU	International Kindergarten Union (now ACEI)
ILP	Independent Labour Party
IQ	Intelligence Quotient
JOBS	Jobs Opportunities and Basic Skills
LCKA	Louisville Colored Kindergarten Association
LEA	Local Education Authority (U.K.)
LEP	limited-English-proficient
LFKA	Louisville Free Kindergargarten Association
Lit. and Phil.	Manchester Literary and Philosophical Society
NACW	National Association of Colored Women

NAECP	National Academy of Early Childhood Programs
NAECTE	National Association of Early Childhood Teacher Educators
NAEP	National Assessment of Educational Progress
NAEYC	National Association for the Education of Young Children (formerly NANE)
NANE	National Association for Nursery Education (now NAEYC)
NBCDI	National Black Child Development Institute
NBPTS	National Board for Professional Teaching Standards
NCATE	National Council for the Accreditation of Teacher Education
NCBE	National Council for Bilingual Education
NCPE	National Council for Parent Education
NEA	National Education Association
NGO	Non-governmental Organization
NNEB	National Nursery Examination Board (U.K.)
NUEA	National Universities Extension Association
NYPSS	New York Public School Society
OBEMLA	Office for Bilingual Education and Minority Language Affairs
OCD	Office of Child Development
OEO	Office of Economic Opportunity
OERI	Office of Educational Research and Improvement
OMB	Office of Management and Budget
OMEP	World Organization for Early Childhood Education (Organisation Mondiale pour l'Education Prescolaire) (OMEP-USNC, United States National Committee of OMEP)
OSPRI	On-Site Program Review Instrument
PCC	Parent Child Center
PCDC	Parent and Child Development Center
PCPI	Parent Cooperative Preschools International
PDC	Project Developmental Continuity
PEA	Progressive Education Association
PEA	Public Education Association
PIR	Program Information Report
PTA	Parent Teacher Association (also PTO, Parent Teacher Organization)
RAP	Resource Access Projects
RTO	Regional Training Officer
SACUS	Southern Association for Children Under Six (now SECA)

SECA	Southern Early Childhood Association
SPG	Society for the Propagation of the Gospel in Foreign Parts
SRCD	Society for Research in Child Development
SSBG	Social Services Block Grant
SSI	Supplemental Security Income (a supplement to Social Security)
STO	State Training Officer
TADS	Technical Assistance and Development System
Title XX	Title XX of the Social Security Act of 1974
UCLA	University of California, Los Angeles
UNESCO	United Nations Educational, Scientific and Cultural Organization
USOE	U.S. Office of Education (also Office of Education)
WCCA	Wartime Civilian Control Administration
WCTU	Women's Christian Temperance Union
WEA	Women's Education Association of Boston
WIN	Work Incentive Program
WPA	Works Progress Administration
WRA	Civilian War Relocation Authority
WTUL	Women's Trade Union League

PART I

The Beginnings of Early Childhood Education

CHAPTER 1

Antiquity

For we are lovers of the beautiful, yet simple are our tastes,
and we cultivate the mind without loss of manliness.
—The Funeral Oration *of Pericles*

In antiquity the family was the center of the child's early education. Education proper, *paideia,* did not begin until the child was seven and was sent to school. Until then, he was "brought up" at home by women, primarily by his mother, and in well-to-do families also by his "nanny." She was different from the one who might have nursed the child. Usually a slave stayed with the family until she died and was tenderly regarded by the child. During these early years, the child was introduced into social life, shown how to behave and be well mannered and polite, and given some of moral discipline. The early years were devoted to learning the language and something about his own culture. He was introduced to music by listening to cradle songs, and to literature through his "nanny's" tales, Aesop's fables, and the myths and legends of gods and heroes. In addition to parents and nurses, many other adults contributed to child rearing: tutors, "companions" (slaves of the same sex as the child), physicians, academic teachers, athletic trainers, and military instructors. The laws of many city-states in antiquity had substantial provisions regulating the ways children were to be reared. Child rearing was an important sociopolitical aspect. The family was the primary unit of social and economic organization in ancient Greece and Rome. Political life was an extension of the family into the public realm.[1]

Several themes have been identified to give cohesiveness to this chapter and to lead the reader from one historical period to the next, to monitor continuity and change, to make comparisons between the past and the present, and to draw some conclusions. The themes are: (1) the importance of children; (2) differentiation between children and adults, stages of development; (3) education: its aim or goal, location, persons responsible for teaching children and content taught; gender differences; and (4) play and its importance.

Sparta and Athens were city-states.[2] Rome was first a city-state, then a republic, and later an empire. City-states distinguished between citizens and noncitizens. City-states and empires needed different classes of citizens to sustain themselves. In both, only citizens could own land and participate in government.

ANCIENT GREECE

The ancient Greek civilization was influenced by the cultures around it. This fact does not diminish, however, the contributions the Greeks have made. The goal of ancient Greek education was to produce citizens able to take their places in the civic community regardless of the political system. The educational system started from a concept of what form the state ought to have, and it was designed to fit that concept.

Sparta and Athens were chosen because they represent two different ideas about education. The government of the first was totalitarian, of the second democratic. Both have influenced subsequent educational systems throughout the Western world and beyond.[3] The eras described were at the height of both communities, having evolved for several hundred years before they reached their pinnacle.

SPARTA[4] (600 B.C.)

Sparta was a settlement of five neighboring unwalled villages in a fertile valley on the banks of the river Eurotas in the southeast Peloponnesus ruled by the Spartans, a small group of conquerors among a large subject population. The land was divided equally among the Spartan citizens. Spartan society was composed of the Spartan citizens, the *Helots* or state serfs, who were not barbarian slaves who could be sold. They were subjugated Greeks of "sturdy and prolific stock" who were compelled to work the land they did not own and were not allowed to leave. The rising numbers of *Helots* were a constant threat to the Spartans. The third class in the society was the *Perioikoi* or "dwellers around." They were landed gentry, who were allowed to keep their personal freedom and to manage their village governments had to follow the Spartans to war, but did not share Spartan rights. Sparta was an oligarchy, ruled by a council of thirty men, all over the age of sixty, elected for life. No citizen had the right to make proposals to the council. Sparta's national existence depended on the military excellence of its citizens. Their whole life was organized to this end. The cost of security was the loss of individualism.[5]

Spartan citizens were supported by a hereditary allotment produced for them by the state serfs. The citizens spent their lives hunting, in military exercises, at the yearly festivals, and in their clubs. A Spartan took all his meals at his club and regularly contributed to it a specified amount and type of food produced on his share of the land. In addition to their military training, the chief occupation of the adults was the education of the younger generation. Spartan education was almost identical with Spartan life. It produced individuals completely subject to the state. The Spartan ideal was physical bravery, power, and endurance. Patriotism and sacrifice of the individual to the common welfare were inculcated in the individual throughout life.[6]

Importance of Children/Infanticide

Spartan law was interested in children from birth. Sparta had a highly developed system of eugenics. Every newborn baby had to be inspected by a committee of elders, and if the infant did not meet the Spartan physical standards, it was exposed to die. Sometimes the abandoned infant was lucky and was rescued and raised by the *Helots* or the *Perioikoi*.

If the infant was approved, it was taken back home to be brought up by its mother until the age of seven years. During this period, the parents acted as the guardians of the child on behalf of the state. At home, children were taught the epics of Homer: the Iliad and the Odyssey, and other songs of heroic acts. Spartans did not swaddle their infants. They believed that full use of their limbs would make children strong. Spartan parents were not allowed to interfere in their child's training, even at the earliest stages. Discipline was an important aspect of the children's education. Mothers or nurses enforced rules that taught the children not to be afraid of the dark, not to be afraid when left alone, and not to have temper tantrums.

The boys went with their fathers to their clubs until they were seven. At the club, they sat on the floor near their fathers and learned how to play with their peers and how to engage in rough playing without flinching. Any adult could stop the game if it became too rough. The boys were introduced into the Spartan way of life by seeing the hardships their fathers endured and by listening to their discussions.[7]

Differentiation between Children and Adults/Stages of Development

The Spartans acknowledged that children develop through several stages and are different from adults. They divided these stages into two segments: the preschool years, from birth to seven; and the years of formal education, from seven to twenty. When a boy reached seven years, the state took him over and he was state property until the day he died.

According to Marrou,[8] the years from eight to twenty were divided into: the little boy (8–11 years), the adolescent (12–15 years), and the *ephebe* (16–20 years). Each stage was divided into substages and named individually.[9]

EDUCATION OF BOYS

When the boys became seven years old, they left their homes and went to live in the barracks or boarding schools for a collective education. Early in their lives, future Spartan citizens were instilled with the spirit of war. Being brought up in boarding schools eliminated the individualizing tendencies of family and hereditary instincts. The ideal character of the Spartan was instilled in all boys.[10]

The Spartan boarding schools were organized in some ways like today's Boy Scouts. They were divided into packs and divisions, and the older boys were in charge of the younger ones. In other ways, they were organized like the youth programs of totalitarian regimes where the youth eat, sleep, and train together. Education was entirely physical, with boys exercising and exposing themselves to all kinds of weather so they could be hardened. The process was progressive. During the first four years, the little boys met for games and exercises. The adolescents had to become tougher and started military training, and the *ephebes* were totally in military training. They learned how to move in formation, how to handle arms, how to fence and throw the javelin, and to look for food to survive when left in the countryside for long periods of time.[11]

Discipline was an important aspect of education and was taught by the perpetual presence of authority, the *paidonomos*—superintendent of boys. The child owed obedience to older children, to all adult citizens, and to *paidonomos*. The *paidonomos* by law had "whip carriers" next to him ready to carry out his punishment for idleness or other infractions. The training of the young was the job of every "freeman." The training was aimed to produce self-control in action and speech, endurance, reverence, and self-sacrifice. A Spartan was not allowed to leave the barracks, even if he married, until he was thirty years old, when he was admitted to citizenship.[12]

There was neither commerce nor accounting in Sparta, and literary instruction was minimal. Rhetoric was forbidden. Sparta had a few written laws that had to be memorized. Spartans memorized the epics of Homer so that they might remember examples of heroism in their battles, and sang the praises of past victories as they marched into battle. Spartan education included music, gymnastics, and dancing.[13]

Education of Girls

There were gender differences in Spartan education because of the sexes' adult roles. Spartan girls were trained to be mothers of soldiers. All female education was subordinated to the duty of producing as many healthy babies as possible, like women in some totalitarian systems.[14] Girls ate all their meals at home, but they lived an outdoor life like their brothers, and had to train their bodies in order to bear strong children. They took part in contests of strength and speed, sharing the gymnasium and the musical training with their brothers. Among their sports were wrestling, running, and swimming.[15] Girls danced and sang on certain festival days in the presence of young men, so they might meet and marry.

Sparta's educational system resulted in a rigid society, which became the victim of itself. Spartan society in the fifth century B.C. numbered about 8,000, but declined to 700 in the year 244 B.C.[16]

CLASSICAL ATHENS (FIFTH–FOURTH CENTURY B.C.)

Athenian society by the fifth century B.C. had evolved from an aristocratic to a democratic society. It consisted of four classes: (1) those with an annual income of 500 bushels of produce; (2) the "knights," who either had a horse or an income of 300 bushels, to support a horse; (3) the "teamsters," who owned a team of oxen and had income of 200 bushels; and (4) the laborers, the remaining citizens. They were governed by an elected assembly, to which all citizens, even the landless, could be admitted.

While Athens was perfecting its democratic way of life, it fought and won a series of battles with the Persians along with the other city-states.[17] Athens reached its cultural pinnacle (drama, art and architecture, philosophy) following the Persian wars. This Golden Age ended in 431 B.C. with the Peloponnesian Wars. Athens and Sparta fought over which one of them should lead the other city-states. Athens was starved into surrendering to Sparta in 405 B.C. Athens, however, remained an educational center during the Roman period, although other centers such as Rhodes, Tarsus, and Alexandria became strong rivals.[18]

Importance of Children/Infanticide

All Greeks since Homer's time (1000–750 B.C.) felt that a family without children was incomplete. The Athenians saw themselves linked to the future through their children, both at the familial and the community levels. If a father did not have a natural son, he would adopt one to continue the family line. All citizens, regardless of class, saw children as the future bearers of their culture and civilization. Philosophers and law givers devoted significant attention to the education and training of the young. Children were valued as family members. They were a source of pleasure, joy, and comfort to their parents. Adult children supported parents in their old age.[19]

Children were so important to the Athenians that during wars they were evacuated for their safety. For example, during the Peloponnesian War children were sent to Pontus on the Black Sea.[20]

In spite the fact that children were a source of pleasure and joy for their parents and the state was concerned about their well-being, these two conditions did not prevent the Athenians from practicing infanticide. Infanticide, the willful "exposure" of newborns, reflected an attempt to regulate the size and quality of the population and to eliminate children too weak or malformed to survive. Those lucky enough to be rescued from "exposure" were adopted by childless families, as is evidenced by funerary epitaphs by grateful children honoring their adoptive parents. Others less fortunate were sold as slaves to be used as household servants, as child prostitutes in brothels, or as deliberately maimed street beggars.[21] It appears that more girls than boys were victims of exposure.[22]

Being born was not sufficient to make a child a member of the family. Children had to be accepted by the household head, the father, and his decision was based on a complex number of factors including cultural constructs such as gender and the optimum size of the family.[23] Ceremonies of naming and accepting a child in the family took place during the first week of the child's life. Once the newborn was accepted into the family, the family was obliged to rear it, and the infant's safety and position in the family were secure. Athenians had no family names or surnames. Their identification

included the personal name, the father's name or patronymic, and the name of
the township or *demos* to which the family belonged.[24]

Differentiation of Children and Adults/Stages of Development

The Athenians differentiated between the characteristics of children and those
of adults and were aware of the changes that occurred from one stage to
another. Some of these characteristics were physical—the plasticity of the
limbs, and swaddling was recommended. Physical helplessness of infants and
young children meant that they needed nursing and additional protection.
Other characteristics were behavioral, such as an "unformed character"
(capable of being molded); helplessness, being unable to speak; fearfulness; an
affectionate nature; and an ability to imitate. Medical writers of the time provided additional knowledge of differences between children and adults. They
identified childhood diseases and treated them differently from those of the
adults.[25]

The belief that the child's mind as well as his body can be trained underlies the whole system of Athenian education.

STAGES OF DEVELOPMENT

The earliest stages of development were identified by Hippocrates (460–377
B.C.), the father of medicine. Hippocrates divided man's life into seven stages:
infant (birth to seven years), *child* (7 to 14 years), *adolescent* (14 to 21 years),
youth (21 to 28 years), *man* (28 to 49 years), *elderly man* (49 to 56 years),
and *old man* (between 56 and death).[26]

Plato and Aristotle took special interest in childhood and gave the fullest
account of it in their writings. Plato [27] (427–347 B.C.), who was concerned
with knowledge as the key to ethical development, gives a list of children's
shortcomings. He claimed that children know little, and are gullible and easily
persuaded (*Laws*, 2.664A and 2.663B); they lack understanding except for
the simplest things (*Laws*, 11.929E); and their lack of judgment, makes them
unreliable judges (*Laws*, 4.720A).

Following are the three stages of development described by Plato in the
Laws. The first stage was from birth to three years. He recommended that a
baby be swaddled from birth until the age of two and be carried about by his
nurse until he was three (7.789E). During the first three years, the child makes
many noises but does not understand language, so the nurse has to judge what
he wants only from his crying (7.791E–7.792E).[28] Infants and toddlers, were to
be catered to through special equipment such as feeding bottles, potty chairs,
cradles, and rattles to amuse them. Excavations in the Mediterranean area have
unearthed a wide and impressive variety of childhood equipment and toys.[29]

The second stage, according to Plato, was from three to six years. During
this stage, children needed to play games with other children. Punishment was
to be used to prevent children from getting pampered (*Laws*, 7.793E), but it

should neither be of a degrading kind nor to enrage the children (*Laws*, 6.777D and E). Plato pointed out that the child grew more quickly in height during the first five years of his life than during the next twenty years (*Laws*, 7.788D). Until the age of six, boys and girls lived together at home under the care and supervision of their mother and/or the family nanny.

The third stage was from six to fourteen years (puberty).[30] Boys and girls began to live separate lives, and formal education began outside the home. The boys went to teachers, and a few girls were also included (*Laws*, 7.794C).

Aristotle (384–322 B.C.) in *Politics*[31] also described stages of development. He delineated four stages and said the critical ages are two, five, seven, and fourteen years. Until the age of two, children were to drink plenty of milk but little wine, to exercise as much as possible, and to become accustomed to the cold (7.1336a2–24, 1336b36). From two until five years of age, children were to continue to exercise and through play to prepare themselves for adult activities. Ideally, both play and stories told to children of this age should be supervised by officials, the *paidonomoi* (7.1336a24–40). Aristotle continued that children are to be reared at home until the age of seven and protected as much as possible from indecent talk and images. Children should not be allowed to attend comedies or dramas with indecent language (7.1336b1–36). At seven years of age, children should start formal education, outside the home, for a period divided into two halves, before and after *puberty*, at fourteen (7.1336b36–1337a7). The final stage, according to Aristotle, was "adolescence," from fourteen years (puberty) until the child reached the late teens or early twenties (7.1336b).

The importance accorded the ages five, six, and seven finds parallels in many cultures studied by anthropologists, for it is commonly the time that the child's attributes and social roles change.[32] Plato and Aristotle justly stressed the importance of proper training and environment from the moment of birth for the development of good citizens (*Laws*, 7.788D–490A; *Politics*, 7.1334b29–1335b20).

The ancient Athenians believed that nature and nurture worked together, each playing a significant role in child rearing. They did not create a nature versus nurture controversy over the primacy of one or the other, as often happens in our times. The Athenians accepted children for what they saw them to be (nature) and provided appropriately for their support, development, and education (nurture).

Play and Its Importance

The Greek idea of childhood is interwoven with play. The Greek word for child is *pais*, and the word for *I play* is *paizo*, both having the same root. Play characterized the life of children, whereas adults were involved in the serious matters of running the *deme*, the township. Evidence of children at play is found on Greek vases, which regularly depict children playing with wagons, rattles, pets, balls, see-saws, swings, and toys on wheels.[33]

Plato saw play and games as a vital part of children's nature. Because of his concern for education, he wanted to make children's games an introduction to the professions (*Laws*, 6.793E), and even to science (*Laws*, 8.819C). He saw a connection between children's play and the way they would think and act in their later roles as adults. Games are needed for the child between three and six years old, to form its character. Games come to children by natural instinct. They invent games whenever they come together. All children from three to six must meet together in the same place and Plato proposes the village temple. Nurses must watch over the children's behavior whether it is orderly or disorderly. After the age of six, each sex shall be kept separate, boys spending time with boys, and girls with girls (*Laws*, 7.794A, B).

Plato, however, considered it irresponsible to allow children to play as they like. He cautioned that "lawless" games make the children unruly, unlikely to mature into serious, law-abiding citizens. He thought that constant "chopping and changing" and love for novelty might threaten the established order (*Laws*, 7.797A–798C). He recommended children's enthusiasm for play to be used to identify aptitudes. Toys should prepare the child for his future role in life and skills should be taught with the help of games. For example, the man who is to become a good builder must play by constructing toy houses. Plato recommended that "those in charge of child rearing must provide each child with toys modeled on real implements, and children should have elementary instruction in all subjects" (*Laws*, 1.643B, C, D). These are the seeds for the content of contemporary early childhood education. Aristotle agreed with Plato's thinking about play (*Politics*, 7.1336a29–34).

When boys became seven years of age, they put away childish things. They dedicated their toys to Hermes, one of the gods.[34] The girls dedicated their toys to Artemis—the divinity protecting young children—before they were married. This ceremony was a great event in one's life and continued to be practiced during the first century A.D.[35]

Education

The aim of education was to develop the male child's moral character to become a good citizen, for his future participation in the life of the community. Understanding both how to rule and how to be ruled justly was important (*Laws*, 1.644A). Education was an end in itself. The well-rounded life was the justification for human existence. To an Athenian, education meant the training of character and taste: the symmetrical development of body, mind, and imagination. It began when the child turned seven and went to school.[36]

It took Athenian education a thousand years to evolve and crystallize its elements before it reached its pinnacle between 450 and 350 B.C., and continued for another thousand years. During the first millennium, it was transformed from a military education to a civilian one, from a privilege of the aristocracy to a democratic right. This new education, intended for all free men, was collective in character out of necessity and led to the creation and development of the school. It was a paramount importance in the whole of the subsequent history. It became universal education at the primary level.[37]

Plato suggested that those teaching the young should be selective of the content and leave out items that may have a bad influence on the child, like violence and immorality (*Laws,* 7.811A, D). Learning through games was important because the child learned to work within a set of rules. This learning would be crucial to citizens of a democracy.[38] The Athenians were among the first to be concerned about age appropriateness and content appropriateness for the children.

Education of Boys and Its Content

There were gender and class differences in educating boys in Athens. When they became seven, school began. Plato wanted children to start school earlier, at the age of six instead of seven (*Laws,* 7.794C). Aristotle said five years (*Politics* 7.1336a; b). Schools were important areas of peer interaction. This interaction took place under the strict supervision of the teacher and each boy's *paidagogos,* who went into the classroom with the boy and never let him out of his sight.[39] Elementary education was neither compulsory nor free. Parents had to pay for it, but it was supervised by the state. In contrast to the Spartans, Athenian adults were not involved with the education of the children unless they were teachers or *paidagogoi.* Wealthy children began school at a younger age and attended for a longer period.[40]

The content consisted of three and sometimes four subjects: *grammar, gymnastics,* and *music,* each taught by a separate teacher.[41] These three subjects were considered to be a complete education in virtue. To these subjects, *painting* and *drawing* were added. Teachers were employed to teach specific skills.

Grammar learning included *reading, writing,* and *arithmetic.* The children began with the alphabet. They learned the twenty-four letters one after the other, by their names from A to Ω. After that, they were given a written alphabet with capital letters that they would recite in chorus. Having learned the alphabet, the students went on to learn syllables. No words were attempted until all the syllables had been combined in every possible way. The simplest came first. The child first named each individual letter and then pronounced them as joined together. The children then passed to three-syllable words made up of different combinations of letters. When the syllables were mastered, the children went on to words. After that, they were allowed to read short continuous passages, and then selected poetry. Closely associated with reading was recitation. It was both read aloud and learned by heart.

Writing was taught the same way as reading. There was the same progression from the simple to the complex, from monosyllables to words, to short sentences, and to longer passages. Greek letters were used both as numerals and as musical notes. *Arithmetic* was limited to counting, learning to say and read numbers. The numbers were taught at the same time as the syllables.

After whole numbers came a list of fractions of a drachma, which again the children learned first as names and then as symbols. This passing from pure arithmetic to systems of measurement indicates an introduction to practical matters of life rather than to mathematics proper. After this came more complex calculations.[42]

The purpose of *gymnastics* was to develop a sound physique, not simply to make a warrior. The Athenian ideal was the symmetrical development of body and mind.[43] The physical training was done by the *paidotribes*, a trainer. Athenian exercises consisted of running, discus and javelin throwing, and wrestling. They were less rigid than those of the Spartans, and were taught in the *gymnasium* or the *palaistra*.[44]

The *music master*, the *kitharistes*, taught students how to play the lyre and the poetry that was sung to it. The learning of the poetry was important for two reasons; for "the training of character," it taught reverence, loyalty, and temperance in word and deed, and for its usefulness, "it contained both the wisdom of the race and practical knowledge." The Athenians tried to develop the individual instead of suppressing it as the Spartans did.[45]

METHODS OF TEACHING AND TEACHING AIDS

To make learning attractive, there were metrical alphabets and alphabetical riddles by which to teach letters and a dance drama used to teach spelling. The metrical alphabet was the prologue to a spelling drama, in which the whole process of learning to spell was expressed in choral songs.[46] Methods of instruction were primarily mimicry and memory, which tend to stifle originality and self-expression. Boys learned to write by following the furrows of an inscribed alphabet, tracing letters lightly sketched in wax, and memorizing texts. The children used slates—wooden boards with a waxed surface. The student used a *stylus* or pricker to write. Its opposite end was rounded and was used to smooth the surface.[47]

Good behavior was as important as progress in letters. There was emphasis on discipline. Punishment was in the form of beatings. The typical implement for punishment was a sandal; it was used at home by both parents and at school by the teacher. Teachers also used a stick and involved other children in the punishment.[48]

Athenian schools brought together boys of varied social and economic backgrounds who lived in the same section of the city. Athenians regarded equality in education for rich and poor as a mark of democracy. (Aristotle, *Politics*, 4.1294b21).

DAILY SCHEDULE, ATTENDANCE, AND CALENDAR

The school day began very early, after daybreak. The first lesson was letters, followed by gymnastics, then by a bath and a meal at home, then by letters again in the afternoon before the child returned home for the evening.[49] Children attended school seven days a week all year round. There were no school vacations except for the various civic, religious, municipal, and national festivals celebrated by the city. School attendance was a matter between the boy's father or guardian and the teacher. One of the methods to motivate students to learn was emulation through the competitions in the festivals; the other was discipline and punishment, many times severe.[50]

Greek schools did not have examinations. They had state-sponsored *competitions* in all fields of academic, musical, and physical achievements, which served as a motivation for students to emulate. They were a more rigorous assessment than we know today.

The competitions served many purposes: compared one student's performance with another, facilitated the task of student promotion, tested the teacher's efficiency, and gave proof to parents, who paid the fees of the value of the instruction their children received. Competitions provided opportunities to display the child's individual talent and a way to get attention and acclaim. Boys met and matched each other through musical and athletic competitions at a city's major religious festivals and in all four Pan Hellenic Games.[51] The competitions gave boys a chance to locate their place in their community, winning glory and/or material rewards. There were separate prizes for different ages.[52]

THE PAIDAGOGOS, OR PEDAGOGUE, AND HIS FUNCTION

The Athenians had created in their households a special position, that of the *paidagogos,* the leader or conductor of children. Although a slave, he was regarded as a member of the family. There was a mutual loyalty between a boy and his *paidagogos.* The *paidagogos* took the boy to school and brought him back each day, protected him from dangers they might meet in the streets, and trained him in good manners and helped mold his character. The *paidagogos* was entrusted with the actual moral education of the boy, as distinct from the technical instruction he received from the various masters. He made sure that the boy learned his lessons, supervised his conduct, and helped him with his homework. Each family had only one *paidagogos,* regardless of the number of male children in the family. He was with the boy all day long, from earliest childhood to the end of adolescence. Since the *paidagogos* was with the boy all day, he made a much greater impression on the boy's character than a teacher who only imparted lessons. He provided the boy with continuity between his home, the school, and the gymnasium.[53]

Education of Girls

In Athens, women's education was essentially a training in domestic duties, even though Plato (*Laws* 7.794D) suggested that girls, if they agreed to, should share in the lessons available to the boys. If they did not share the lessons with the boys, they should have their own system of education (*Laws* 7.805D). Girls were lifelong minors. Marriage marked the biggest break in a girl's life. However, it did not involve any change in the legal or political status, because wives were as subordinate as daughters. The control of the husband replaced that of

Figure 1.1 Woman Cooking with Young Girl Looking On. 5th century B.C., Greece, Boeotian, Tanagra. Terracota. H: 0.107 m. *Courtesy, Museum of Fine Arts, Boston.*

the father. Fathers or guardians had the right to determine whom their daughter should marry in order to preserve the family property, as is evidenced by a fragment of a comedy from Athens, fourth/third century B.C., in which a daughter tries to persuade her father not to make her marry a man richer than the one she has already married.[54] Young girls of fourteen or fifteen years of age were given in marriage, had to leave their family, and to join another family in a separate house. Even though her dowry provided the bride an ongoing connection with her parental family, there was the trauma of separation, the moving from one part of the community to another, and the shift in her role. There was substantial age difference between husbands and wives. Men did not marry until they were thirty years old.[55]

Within the home, women and girls had a special place, the *gynaikonitis*, women's quarters, where they spent much of their time and carried on their responsibilities. The *gynaikonitis* was also shared by the young boys of the family. One may conclude that much of the child care took place there.

The girls learned domestic arts to prepare for their future role as wives.[56] Unlike the Spartan girls, the Athenian girls neither competed in athletic festivals in other Greek cities nor in public contests within the city. There is some evidence that Athenian girls could read and that they attended school to receive literary education. Among the evidence is a gravestone of a young girl named Albeita, who is reading with her pet dog sitting at her feet, and an Attic cup, with a girl carrying a writing tablet by a strap (like boys do on other vases).[57]

In later years, when Greek women wanted intellectual equality, it came at a sacrifice. They lost the secure position they had held in the home. Greek women were not equal to their husbands.[58]

ROME (1000 B.C.–A.D. 476)

Roman history can be divided roughly into three eras: the old Roman, the Graeco-Roman, and the Christian. Rome started as a peasant society about 1000 B.C. It grew from a small local power into a world power. Around 528 B.C. it became a republic and began warring with its Mediterranean neighbors, conquering them and expanding. By 200 B.C., Rome was the strongest power in its world but continued to be aggressive in the east. Rome developed laws providing an administrative structure of a state beyond that of a city-state, which allowed it to govern efficiently its vast geographic area. By the first century B.C., it had become an empire that stretched from the Atlantic through North Africa to the Caspian Sea. In the process it became a very wealthy nation. The rich became richer, spending their wealth on luxuries, and could not be restrained by democratic movements of protest for a more equitable distribution of the wealth, while the majority became steadily poorer.

Rome conquered all of mainland Greece and most of its colonies and territories by the year 146 B.C. The Roman Empire became a bilingual state that included within its boundaries all the cities in which Greek was the spoken language. The Imperial Chancellery had two separate departments for correspondence, one in Latin and one in Greek.[59]

Rome had its own traditions and culture but had been exposed to Greek culture since the third and second centuries B.C. through the Greek colonies in Sicily and Italy. After Rome conquered Greece, the Greek culture was freely adopted. The Roman poet Horace (65 B.C.–8 B.C.) remarked, "Captive Greece took captive her conqueror, and brought civilization to barbarous Latium."[60] Gradually the societies and cultures of Greece and Rome became intertwined and inseparable, and known as Graeco-Roman.

During the Augustan era, a new religion appeared, Christianity, which challenged the pagan culture. After centuries of persecutions of Christians by the Romans, it became the official religion of the Roman Empire when Constantine I the Great (A.D. 306–337) identified himself with it. In A.D. 364, the Roman Empire was divided into the East and West Roman Empire. The Eastern Roman Empire became the Byzantine Empire and lasted until A.D. 1453, when its capital, Constantinople, fell to the Ottomans. The Western Roman

Empire collapsed in A.D. 476, as a result of the barbarian invasions and the disappearance of the political framework of the Empire, and the Middle Ages began in Europe.[61] When Constantinople fell, many scholars from the East migrated to the West and the Renaissance began first in Italy and later in the rest of Western Europe.

Roman society underwent several changes during these historical periods. These changes are reflected in the Roman descriptions of children and in their education.

Importance of Children

The Romans differed from the Greeks in two aspects: the absolute, total control of the father over his children and the family, *patria potestas,* the absolute paternal power; and the continued struggle of the upper classes to replenish themselves.

In classical Athens, the father had the power of life or death over all new-born children, but once the infant was accepted into the family, the father's legal right to decide life or death ended. In Roman society the father, *paterfamilias,* retained the legal right to kill his children, even when they had attained adulthood. This power applied both to natural and to adopted sons. The *patria potestas* ended only with the father's death; neither marriage nor holding high office in the state made the son independent of his father in private life.[62] Gradually the father's power was curtailed. In the 2nd century A.D. Hadrian declared that if a father killed his child, he would be banished. It was completely abolished by A.D. 374 under the Christian influence.[63]

Rome, a militaristic society, relied heavily on its men to fight the wars for its survival and prosperity. Many parents, however, especially those of the upper classes, did not want to have any children killed in war. In 18 B.C. the Emperor Augustus became concerned that luxury and adultery were widespread. Marriage was infrequent among the upper classes, and those who married did not have children. Augustus, seeing the danger in such behavior, sought to raise both the morals and the numbers of the upper classes in Rome, and to increase the population of native Italians. He enacted laws to encourage marriage and having children. Augustus laid heavier assessment on the unmarried men and women and offered prizes for marriage and the begetting of children. He allowed any citizen who was not a senator to marry freed women and decreed that children of such marriages be legitimate. He granted seniority to senators who were fathers of three children and levied penalties on the unmarried.[64]

Birth was an important event for the Romans. Female relatives, neighbors, and midwives assisted in the delivery. After the delivery, the baby was laid on the ground. The father owned it as his own by picking it up, a thanksgiving meal was prepared, and the door of the house was decorated with flowers.[65] The birth and naming of a Roman child was attended by ceremony and ritual. In addition, the Romans had a number of gods and goddesses to protect the children: Three presided over a baby's eating and drinking; three more looked over his walking; and one each over the baby's sleeping, speaking, fearfulness, crying, and growth of bones. This array of deities safeguarding the baby shows the Romans' awareness of the difficulties and dangers of the growing child.[66]

The week immediately after birth, when an infant actually loses weight until it learns to suck properly, was the most critical for the infant's survival. Girls tended to have a better chance to survive than boys. The *dies lustricus*, the day on which the Romans named a child, was the eighth day for girls and the ninth for boys.[67]

Roman mothers were expected to nurse their own children, but in the event they had to hire a wet nurse, there were specific instructions for her selection, among which were that she be clean, be modest, have enough milk, be of good temperament, be practical, and be Greek. There was one example of a woman's parent (sex not specified) who offered to pay for a wet nurse so that the daughter would not have to breast-feed her infant.[68]

A sense of reciprocity existed between parents and children. Roman adult children were expected to look after their parents in old age in return for the sustenance they had given them as infants.[69]

Infanticide[70]

Roman law allowed or even encouraged the exposure of infants. Romulus (753–716 B.C.), the legendary founder of Rome, obliged the citizens to raise every male child and the firstborn female and forbade them to put to death any child below the age of three years unless it was crippled. He did not prevent the parents from exposing such children, provided they had displayed them first to five neighbors and had secured their approval.[71] Later, *The Twelve Tables* allowed the killing of deformed children. *The Twelve Tables*, adopted in 451–450 B.C. were the basis of Roman civil law and have their origins in what the Romans called *mos maiorum*, the traditions of their ancestors. Although some of the laws became outdated, the code was never abolished until the adoption of the Justinian code one thousand years later, about A.D. 430.[72]

According to Harris (1994),[73] there were four reasons for Roman child exposure: (1) the deformity or other physical inadequacy of the newborn infant, (2) illegitimacy, (3) perceived economic need, and (4) evil omens and despair. It is also possible that the real reasons for infanticide may have been concealed (11).

The exposure of infants was widespread in many parts of the Roman Empire. It was inflicted on large numbers of children who were neither physically handicapped nor illegitimate. Many, however, disagreed with the practice, especially the Stoic moralists and the Jews, who insisted that all infants should be kept alive (1).

There were two kinds of exposure. Those who exposed infants for economic reasons left them in a prominent place to be found and rescued. Some parents even left tokens with the infants in hopes they could recognize them later on in life. The other exposure, where death was the expected result, was for the illegitimate and the physically handicapped babies. Of those who were rescued, many were raised as slaves, often for the purpose of prostitution; a small number became "changelings" (replacing another child); and some were adopted (9).

Whether an exposed infant survived depended on the following: (1) the infant's initial physical condition; (2) how much those exposing the infant helped it to survive; (3) whether the community included persons willing to invest in bringing up the child as a slave (in Egypt, Asia Minor, Syria, and Italy it was common to collect exposed infants); (4) the level of demand for slave labor; and (5) gender—boys were more likely to be rescued than girls. Romans relied heavily on child exposure to control population. It allowed them to choose the sex of the child, which neither contraception nor abortion did (11).

Christian emperors were the first to take steps to prevent child exposure. These actions were in response to religious concerns and worry about depopulation. From the Jews, the Christians had inherited the view that infanticide was murder. By A.D. 312, emperors had taken measures to encourage the bringing up of children in the form of imperial aid to indigent parents, but child exposure was not a crime. In 374, Valentian issued an edict stating that parents who exposed their children would be punished by death (19–21).

Roman law treated abortion as a crime against the father, not against the mother or the child. Men condemned their wives if they suspected that they were unwilling to have children, yet the fathers insisted on their legal right to decide whether the child his wife gave birth to would live or not. The mother had nothing to say about whether her child lived or died after she bore it.[74]

Differentiation between Children and Adults/Stages of Development

The Romans clearly identified the differences between children and adults. In Rome, as in Athens, the adult male was the center of activity. Those who were not adult male citizens were in the margin of community life. The first function of the citizen was to fight to protect his community in war. Children, women, old men, and slaves were different because they were incapable of joining in the fighting. The relative physical weakness of the children, women, and old men meant that they required particular support from the supernatural, especially the children who were seen as imperfect and vulnerable.[75]

This marginality gave children certain advantages. They should neither be killed in wars nor taken hostage by the victors, and should be protected by those more fortunate. As a marginal being, the child was only a partial member of the adult society, a condition which implied that the child was closer to the world of gods than that of the adult male. The Romans saw the child as physically and mentally weak, unable to think or to plan rationally. The child's inability to communicate in the way adults do made him a symbol of nonparticipation in the rational world of the adult citizen. Lack of judgment and not being able to distinguish right from wrong or to follow duty rather than pleasure were considered characteristics of a child. To call someone *boy* was the ultimate insult because *boy* was a quality of a nonadult. *Child* was also a term used to address a slave, another individual who could not share in the community of adult citizens.[76]

STAGES OF DEVELOPMENT

The Romans had several approaches for categorizing children and youth that reflected the evolution of their society. First was the terminology set in the *Twelve Tables*, which had immediate and practical impact on the young Romans. The law was concerned with wardship and delinquency below the age of puberty. Roman males went on military campaigns, and many did not return, leaving orphans in need of custody. The legal definition, for example, of "children" meant "nonadults." Other definitions, those of Varo and Tubaro, were attempts to measure the various stages in which life was more or less divided, and loose categories that did not attempt to define in years the limits of each stage.[77]

Roman law identified the following stages of development: *infans*, one who could not speak, a newborn; *infantia proximus*, "next beyond infancy," which meant the young child who could speak but who lacked the developed vocabulary or mental capacity to make meaningful decisions; *impubes*, all the children under puberty; *pubertate proximus*, "very near puberty," a child who was able to speak, had the vocabulary, and could make decisions but who had not reached puberty. All those over the age of puberty were called *puberes*. Both sexes between puberty and age twenty-five were called *minores*. Puberty, in addition to physical growth, brought the ability to reason. When a girl reached puberty, she was *viripotens* (had the ability to bear a man's weight); she was marriageable. Girls could marry as early as the age of twelve.[78] The Roman stages stated what a person was not, rather than what a person was, suggesting incompleteness.

Roman law distinguished children below the age of seven years as not able to answer for their actions, and girls and boys below twelve and fourteen, respectively, not capable of undertaking the responsibilities of marriage. The crucial division between child and adult was age seventeen, the age when a male could learn to fight and his name was put in the census list.[79]

A later description of childhood stages is from Quintilian's (A.D. 35–100) *Institutes of Oratory (Institutio Oratoria)*.[80] More like Plato's and Aristotle's, Quintilian's stages refer both to physical and psychological aspects of the child and what should be done with the child. Quintilian identified three stages of development. The first, birth to three years, is the time when the child has learned to speak. During this stage the child is "highly impressionable," and therefore the nurse "must speak properly" and set good moral examples (*Institutes of Oratory*, 1.1.5–11). The second, three to seven years, the child is still at home, but education should begin (*Institutes of Oratory*, 1.1.15–19); the child needs to be amused and to be praised (*Institutes of Oratory*, 1.1.20);

tasks assigned to the child should fit the child's ability (*Institutes of Oratory*, 1.1.22); and the child should not be pushed too hard (*Institutes of Oratory*, 1.1.32–33). The third, seven years until adolescence, boys should be sent out to school (*Institutes of Oratory*, 1.2.1–13); instruction should be tailored to the individual pupil (*Institutes of Oratory*, 1.3.6); character formation is crucial before boys learn deceit (*Institutes of Oratory*, 1.3.12); and flogging and abusive punishment should be avoided (*Institutes of Oratory*, 1.3.13–17). Quintilian also introduced the idea for parents to be educated (*Institutes of Oratory*, 1.1.6).

A third description is by St. Augustine of Hippo (A.D. 354–430), a theologian and a bishop, from his *Confessions*.[81] By now Christianity had taken root in the Roman Empire. To the Christian God, everyone was equal. He cared for women, slaves, children, and barbarians as much as for adult males.

St. Augustine's stages are personal, based on his recollection of his own childhood. It is the earliest literary work to take the writer's own childhood seriously. He tried to analyze the habits that had molded his personality since his birth and which he found difficult to reform. St. Augustine observed other babies to describe his *infantia*, but he relied on his own experiences to describe *pueritia*. He identified three stages of development and their characteristics. The first was birth to three years. During this stage, the infant at first only sucks and cries, then begins to smile and laugh (*Confessions*, 1.6); the infant is frustrated at being unable to communicate, cries more, is easily angered and often sullen, and is jealous of other infants (*Confessions*, 1.7). The second was three to seven years. The child remains at home (*Confessions*, 1.8); he is learning to speak, learning one word at a time, and is disobedient (*Confessions*, 1.9). The third was seven years to adolescence. Beatings played a major part in Augustine's memories of his schooldays; he loved to play (*Confessions*, 1.9–10), but did not like to study (*Confessions*, 1.9, 1.12); he had irrational likes and dislikes (*Confessions*, 1.13); Augustine concluded that curiosity leads to learning and that frightful punishment hampers learning (*Confessions*, 1.14).

A number of authors gave advice on how to rear infants. Like some present-day experts on child development, Roman writers were divided on the relative significance of *Nature* and *Nurture*. Cicero (106–43 B.C.), the orator and writer, insisted on the primary importance of the child's nature and just as often proclaimed the saving virtues of upbringing and education. Quintilian, on the other hand, gave paramount importance to what was learned in infancy.[82]

Play and Its Importance

The Latin word for play was *ludus*. The same word applied to adult games, including religious ceremonies, and the word was also used for "school." From this application, it appears that the Romans saw play primarily as practice, perhaps as similar to the contemporary concept of play as role-learning. Quintilian suggested that "games are useful for sharpening the children's intellectual capacities, such as playing with riddles" (*Institutes of Oratory* 1.3.11). Play, like school, prepares the child for adult life, mainly by imitation.[83]

Babies had rattles made of metal or pottery; older children played with gender-specific toys such as a rag doll and wooden horse found in Egypt.[84] Roman dolls found in the catacombs were made of bone or ivory.[85] Quintilian observed that how a child played pointed toward his behavior as an adult, but not to the extent of determining it. If the child's behavior suggested moral imperfections, it was not too late for the parents to do something about it (*Institutes of Oratory* 1.3.12).

Education

The old Roman education was a training process in moral and practical aspects. The fundamental idea of that education was respect for the old customs and tradition. There was little concern for the development of intellectual attainment. The first thing was the development of the child's conscience. It was obvious to Romans that the place for children to grow and be educated was within the family.[86] Roman mothers considered it an honor to raise their own children, even in the richest families. The mother's influence lasted for a lifetime. An example is Cornelia, the mother of the Gracchi, who supervised not only her sons' studies and serious duties but also their recreation and games, and said of her sons, "these are my jewels." The aim of this upbringing was to teach the child morals, the practice of virtue. Regardless of whether he would become a soldier, a jurist, or an orator, he should devote all his energy to duty.[87]

Education of Boys

From the age of seven, the boy's education was taken over by his father. The father was the son's real teacher. He taught him reading and writing as well as physical skills like swimming, riding, and throwing the javelin. If the father was a senator, the son went with his father to the senate, where he learned from what he saw and what he heard. This parental training continued until the son was sixteen years old. The home education ended when the son became sixteen. He took off the child's toga edged in purple, *praetexta*, and the *bulla*, the amulet he wore around his neck to indicate the citizen status of children, and put on the *toga virilis*, the adult toga. He was now a Roman citizen.[88]

Roman schoolboys had to memorize the *Twelve Tables* as part of their education. The Laws were used to teach reading and writing. They expressed the ideals that dominated the education during this period.[89]

Education of Girls

Even though Roman women were more equal to their husbands and had more freedom than the Athenian women were allowed, their education was essentially a home training. Some girls attended the *ludus*, where reading and writing were learned. But if they aspired to literary education without losing their reputation and their influence in the home, they had to get it through tutors. Girls tended to remain at home with their mothers.[90]

There is a contrast between the old Roman education and the new Graeco-Roman that gradually replaced it. On the one side was a tradition of family life and national custom, and on the other an ideal of culture that included Greek literature, rhetoric, and philosophy all depending on instruction. This change was inevitable once Rome became the center of a world empire. The Roman aristocrats were the first to introduce Greek tutors beginning in the second century B.C. and continuing until the fall of the empire, to teach their sons literature, rhetoric, and philosophy, and to bring up their children in the Greek manner. Soon the tutors found that the *Twelve Tables* were not enough of a literary textbook and began to translate the *Odyssey* and other works into Latin. By the middle of the second century B.C., the Hellenistic ideal of a culture based on the study of literature, rhetoric, and philosophy was fully accepted in Rome. The Romans, did not incorporate either music or athletics into their education.[91]

The Latin Primary School

Along with this Graeco-Roman (foreign) education, a parallel course of study was provided, modeled exactly on the Greek system but taught in Latin, so that side by side with the Greek schools, in which Greek subjects were taught, arose a parallel series of Latin schools: primary, secondary, and higher. Primary schools were known in Rome before the fourth century B.C. The Romans took their alphabet from the ancient Etruscans, who had taken it from the Greeks.[92]

In Rome there were three successive stages of education run by three different specialists. Children went to the primary school when they were seven, then to the *grammaticus* when they were eleven or twelve. When they wore the adult toga, sometimes as early as fifteen, they went to the *rhetor*. The primary school taught reading and writing. Like the Athenian children, the Roman children started learning the alphabet from A to X (the letters Y and Z were omitted, for they were used only in Greek words) and then backward from X to A. Then they learned it in pairs: AX, BV, CT, DS, ER; then jumbled in different combinations. After the letters came the syllables with all their combinations, and then the single names.

The Latin teachers followed exactly the same methods as the Greeks did in teaching reading and writing to the smallest detail. The Roman teaching methods were passive. The most highly prized qualities were a good memory and powers of imitation. Competition was encouraged, for it made up for the moral dangers inherent in communal education. The main stimulation for learning was through coercion, reprimands and punishment. Latin schools were as bad as Greek schools when it came to *discipline*.[93] They used the same method, the rod, which came to symbolize the master's authority over his illogical (lacking the ability to reason) child pupils. The association between beating and schooling remained constant until the end of the second century A.D., when educators, orators, and others began to question the legitimacy and the efficacy of these brutal methods. They began to rely more on competitions and prizes to motivate the pupils to like their lessons.[94]

Because of the bilingual nature of the education, bilingual manuals were published to facilitate the learning of the two languages. They were probably written for the Greeks to learn Latin, but they were arranged in such a way that they could also be used to learn Greek. They were found all over Western Europe throughout antiquity and into the Middle Ages. They began with the Greek-Latin vocabulary arranged first in alphabetical order and then under various headings, such as names of gods and goddesses, vegetables, fish, birds, and maritime and medical words. Then came short, simple passages. The passages were presented in two columns, on one side the Greek and on the opposite side the Latin.[95]

CHAPTER SUMMARY

The family had the exclusive responsibility of educating the child until the age of seven, when education outside the home began. Sparta, Athens, and Rome identified and named stages of childhood development beginning at birth. Play was an important part of the child's development. Children had age-appropriate equipment and furniture and gender-related toys. The Athenians identified some content for early childhood education and introduced the idea of children getting in groups under adult supervision. The content for elementary education was divided into subjects in Athens and Rome. Education and training were organized developmentally. Students had learning tools and teaching aids. The Romans used the stages of development to protect the child legally.

The educational systems of Sparta and Athens started with a concept of what form the state ought to have. Each state designed an educational system to achieve that concept. In Sparta, the state took over the education of the boys when they became seven years old, and trained them to become warriors. The girls were trained to be mothers of warriors. Athenian education aimed at developing the male child's moral character to become a good citizen in a democratic society. They believed in the symmetrical development of mind and body. The *paidagogos* was in charge of the moral development of the boy. Women were lifelong minors. Athenians saw *Nature* and *Nurture* working together, complementing each other.

Infanticide was practiced by all three societies. In Sparta it was called eugenics. In Rome it was practiced even when the child was neither handicapped nor illegitimate. It was abolished in the fourth century A.D. as a result of the influence of the Christian religion.

In Roman society, the father had absolute power over his children, including killing them in adulthood. Roman mothers raised their own children. Women were more equal to their husbands. The goal of Roman education was to teach the practice of virtue and devotion to duty regardless of what profession the boy would choose.

The Romans practiced bilingualism and developed materials for teaching it. They introduced the *Nature-Nurture* controversy in child rearing and the need for the parent to be educated.

The controversy created by Phillippe Aries'[96] interpretation that children were seen as miniature adults does not apply at all to antiquity. Children were viewed as incomplete nonadults.

COMMENT

Some problems in obtaining historical evidence about children arise from the fact that in almost any society the primary responsibility for the young (birth through seven years) has been exclusively in the hands of women. Most of this evidence, literary and artistic, as well as legal codes had been produced by men. Some of the information has been reconstructed by later writers. We do not know what actual contact these men had with children. Although child rearing was done exclusively by women, all of the sources from antiquity were written by male authors, and perhaps by the elite.

NOTES

1. Henri I. Marrou, *The History of Education in Antiquity*, trans. George Lamb (New York: Sheed and Ward, 1956), 142.

2. The city-state grew up by the successive amalgamation of patriarchal families into village communities, of village communities into *phratries* or brotherhoods, of *phratries* into tribes, and of tribes into cities. Lewis H. Morgan, *Ancient Society*, with a foreword by Elizabeth Tooker (Henry Holt, 1877; reprint, Tucson: University of Arizona Press, 1985), 215–234 (page citations are to the reprint edition).

3. The most recent example was the establishment of a Department of Classics in Malawi. The chieftain wanted to educate his people for democracy. Caroline Alexander, "An Ideal State," *The New Yorker*, 67, no. 43 (Dec. 16, 1991): 53–88.

4. These are brief descriptions of the context in which each educational system was found. For a comprehensive history, see Chester G. Starr, *Origins of Greek Civilization, 1100–650 B.C.* (New York: Knopf, 1961).

5. T. R. Harley, "The Public Schools of Sparta," *Greece and Rome* 3, no. 9 (May 1934): 129–139.

6. Michael Grant, *The Founders of the Western World* (New York: Charles Scribner's Sons, 1991), 31–34. The epitaph on the memorial in honor of the three hundred Spartan soldiers who died at the Battle of Thermopylae in 480 B.C. says it all: "Go tell the Spartans, thou that passes by, that here, obedient to their laws, we lie." This battle allowed the other Greek city-states to regroup their armies on the plain of Marathon and defeat the invading Persians. (One of the authors has visited the site.)

7. Kenneth J. Freeman, *Schools of Hellas* (London: Macmillan, 1907), 11–17.

8. Marrou, *History of Education in Antiquity*, 20.

9. *Ephebe* means legal maturity, when the boys leave puberty and enter the adult world.

10. Boarding schools impose a certain similarity of manners, values, and attitudes upon all who pass through them. A more recent historical example is the boarding schools for Native Americans presented in Chapter 14 of this volume.

11. Freeman, *Schools of Hellas*, 18–25.

12. Marrou, *History of Education in Antiquity,* 19–21; Freeman, *Schools of Hellas,* 25–29.

13. Freeman, *Schools of Hellas,* 20; Sparta had no written laws, as Athens did. Judges and rulers acted on their own discretion. This practice was possible only if a particular stamp of character, a particular attitude, was impressed upon every citizen. As a result, education was the most important thing in Sparta and was exactly the same for all its citizens.

14. The most recent example was Romania under the Soviet regime.

15. Freeman, *Schools of Hellas,* 29–30; Marrou, *History of Education in Antiquity,* 23.

16. Harley, "The Public Schools of Sparta," 130.

17. The most famous were Marathon, 490 B.C.; Thermopylae, 480 B.C.; and Plataea, 479 B.C. Grant, *Founders of the Western World,* 56–59. See also David Eggenberger, *An Encyclopedia of Battles* (New York: Dover Publications, 1985), 262, 379.

18. Grant, *Founders of the Western World,* 66, 71.

19. Freeman, *Schools of Hellas,* 42–50.

20. Mark Golden, *Children and Childhood in Classical Athens* (Baltimore: Johns Hopkins University Press, 1990), 143.

21. Valerie French, "Birth Control, Childbirth, and Early Childhood," *Civilization of Ancient Mediterranean,* 3 volumes, eds. Michael Grant and Rachel Kitzinger (New York: Charles Scribner's Sons, 1988), 3: 1362. A complete history of infanticide, Lloyd deMausse, *The History of Childhood* (New York: Harper & Row, 1974), 503–575.

22. Mark Golden, "Demography and the Exposure of Girls at Athens," *Phoenix* 35 (1981): 316–331.

23. Ibid., and C. Patterson, " 'Not Worth the Rearing': The Causes of Infant Exposure in Ancient Greece," *Transactions of the American Philological Association* (TAPA) 115 (1985): 103–123.

24. Mark Golden, "Names and Naming at Athens: Three Studies," *Classical Views/Échos du monde classique* (EMC) 30 (1986): 245–269.

25. George F. Still, *The History of Paediatrics* (Oxford: Oxford University Press, 1931; reprint, London: Dawsons of Pall Mall, 1965), 6–12, 18–20, 28–31.

26. Ibid., 6. These stages are reminiscent of Shakespeare's Ages of Man from his play, *As You Like It,* Act 2, Scene 7.

27. All quotations in this text are from Plato's *Laws,* 2 vols., The Loeb Classical Library, ed. E. Capps, trans. R. G. Bury (London: William Heinemann, 1926). The first number indicates the number of the Book, the second number refers to the verse(s) quoted, and the letters refer to the sections of the verses.

28. The baby's inability to express his needs and wants was frustrating for the Greeks. One of the words used to this day to describe a young child is *nepeios,* which means "not yet speaking."

29. Dorothy B. Thompson, *An Ancient Shopping Center: The Athenian Agora* (Princeton: American School of Classical Studies at Athens, 1971): high chair (illustration 39), a potty chair (illustration 40), toy animals (illustration 42), dolls and doll dishes (illustration 43); Metropolitan Museum of Art, *The Daily Life of the Greeks and Romans,* 6th ed. (New York: Metropolitan Museum of Art, 1941): a terracotta feeding bottle (fig. 55, p. 46), a toy horse on wheels (fig. 56, p. 47); Anita E. Klein, *Child Life in Greek Art* (New York: Columbia University Press, 1932): cradle with mattress (plate I B), rattle with handle (plate III E).

30. Puberty was an important time for the Athenian boy because of its characteristics: the change in the voice, the appearance of down on the chin and hair in various parts of the body. It was also considered the beginning of legal maturity.

31. All the quotations in this text are from Aristotle's *Politics,* The Loeb Classical Library, ed. T. E. Page, trans. H. Rachman (London: William Heinemann, 1926). See note 27.

32. See B. Rogoff et al., "Age of Assignment of Roles and Responsibilities to Children: A Cross-Cultural Survey," *Human Development* 18 (1975): 353–369.

33. Klein, *Child Life in Greek Art,* provides both descriptions (9–22) and illustrations of a toy horse on wheels (plate VIII B), a child with hare (plate XIII E), and dolls (plate XVI A, B, and C). Dolls A and C were jointed; Frederick A. G. Beck, *Album of Greek Education: The Greeks at School and at Play* (Sydney: Cheiron Press, 1975): boy with rattle

(plate 56, no. 286), boy with go-cart (plate 54, no. 278), girls on seesaw and girl on swing (plate 57, no. 295 and no. 293), two boys playing *passe-boule* (plate 61, no. 313), and boy throwing ball (plate 62, no. 318). Children also enjoyed theatrical presentations and puppet shows (*Laws*, 2.658C).

34. D'Arcy W. Thompson, "Games and Playthings," *Greece and Rome*, 2 (February 1933): 73–79.

35. French, "Birth Control, Childbirth, and Early Education," 3:1361; Kate McK. Elderkin, "Jointed Dolls in Antiquity," *American Journal of Archeology* 24, no. 4 (1918): 455.

36. Freeman, *Schools of Hellas*, 46; Frederick A. G. Beck, *Greek Education, 450–350 B.C.* (London: Methuen and Co., 1964), 71–105.

37. Marrou, *History of Education in Antiquity*, 36, 39.

38. Ibid., 142.

39. Beck, *Greek Education, 450–350 B.C.*, 106–141.

40. Freeman, *Schools of Hellas*, 42–78. The most famous and complete school scenes of all the subjects and school room objects are depicted on a cup painted by Douris about 485 B.C.: the flute lesson, the writing lesson with a writing-roll, a folded tablet, a ruling square (plate I. A); the lyre lesson and the poetry lesson with an ornamental manuscript basket (plate I. B). Ibid., plates between pages 52 and 53. Beck, *Album of Greek Education*, music lesson (plate 10, nos. 53 and 54) adds *paidagogoi* to the scene.

41. The *grammatistes*, *paidotribes*, and *kitharistes*, Freeman, *Schools of Hellas*, 50.

42. Marrou, *History of Education in Antiquity*, 150–153, 157.

43. Freeman, *Schools of Hellas*, 118–120.

44. The *gymnasium*, usually public, was larger and had a running track, while the *palaistra*, often private, was less elaborate and did not have a running track.

45. Beck, *Greek Education, 450–350 B.C.*, 119.

46. Freeman, *Schools of Hellas*, 88–89.

47. Illustrations of teaching aids, Beck, *Album of Greek Education*, bronze and ivory styluses (plate 7, no. 34a and no. 34b), fragment of syllabic reading exercise (plate 7, no. 37), schoolboy's wax table: multiplication table on left and column of words showing stem and endings, at right (plate 7, no. 39).

48. Beck, *Album of Greek Education*, 44–46, man beating boy with sandal (plate 52, no. 271); boy, held in the air by playmates, receives a whipping (plate 53, no. 275).

49. Freeman, *Schools of Hellas*, 93.

50. Marrou, *History of Education in Antiquity*, 148, 158.

51. The most famous competitions, the Olympic games, were founded in 776 B.C. In times of war, fighting ceased for their duration. Other games were the Isthmiam, the Nemean, and the Pythian.

52. Freeman, *Schools of Hellas*, 62–65, lists the names of the students; their respective cities; the festivals in which they competed; the types of competitions they participated in and the awards they received; Marrou, *History of Education in Antiquity*, 115; Beck, *Album of Greek Education*, literary and dramatic competitions (plate 43), musical competitions (plates 44 and 45), and athletic competitions (plate 47).

53. Beck, *Greek Education, 450–350 B.C.*, 105–109; Marrou, *History of Education in Antiquity*, 143–144. The concept of the tutor goes back to Homer. Phoenix was Achilles' tutor. Homer Iliad, 9. 485–595.

54. Mary R. Lefkowitz and Maureen B. Fant, *Women's Life in Greece and Rome*, 2nd ed., (Baltimore: Johns Hopkins University Press, 1992), 14. The volume is a translation of surviving texts describing the lives of women; a few of the texts were written by women.

55. For more about the family in Classical Greece, see Walter K. Lacey, *The Family in Classical Greece* (Ithaca, NY: Cornell University Press, 1968).

56. There is a statuette in the Museum of Fine Arts, Boston. It shows a woman teaching a girl to cook (MFA 01.7788).

57. Beck, *Album of Greek Education*, the dead girl Albeita reading (plate 71, no. 359); girl carrying writing tablet, accompanied by older girl (plate 69, no. 350).

58. Paul Monroe, *Source Book of the History of Education for the Greek and the Roman Periods* (New York: Macmillan, 1906), 36–37.

59. Grant, *Founders of the Western World,* 142–174, 176–207; Marrou, *History of Education in Antiquity,* 243, 256. This is a very brief overview; for more details see Michael Grant, *History of Rome* (London: Weidenfeld and Nicholson, 1978).

60. Horace, *Epistles,* II, 1, 156, quoted in Marrou, *History of Education in Antiquity,* 242.

61. Grant, *Founders of the Western World,* 208–223.

62. John Crook, "Patria Potestas," *Classical Quarterly,* 17, no. 1 (May 1967): 113; Aubrey Gwynn, *Roman Education: From Cicero to Quintilian* (n.p., 1926; reprint, New York: Russell & Russell, 1964), 13 (page citations are to the reprint edition).

63. Michael J. G. Gray-Fow, "The Nomenclature and Stages of Roman Childhood" (Ph.D. diss., University of Wisconsin—Madison, 1985), 12.

64. Ibid., 108; Lefkowitz and Fant, *Women's Life,* 102–103.

65. French, "Birth Control, Childbirth, and Early Childhood," 3: 1357; Walton McDaniel, *Conception, Birth and Infancy in Ancient Rome and Modern Italy* (Coconut Grove, FL: n.p., 1948), 23–24.

66. French, "Birth Control, Childbirth, and Early Childhood," 3: 1361; see also J. P. V. D. Balsdon, *Life and Leisure in Ancient Rome* (New York: McGraw-Hill, 1969).

67. Thomas Wiedemann, *Adults and Children in the Roman Empire* (New Haven: Yale University Press, 1989), 17.

68. Lefkowitz and Fant, *Women's Life,* 187–189.

69. Wiedemann, *Adults and Children in the Roman Empire,* 39.

70. Rome's foundation myth had as an integral part the exposure of Romulus and Remus, who were subsequently raised by a she-wolf. As a result, Roman society took for granted a certain amount of child exposure. The most massive infanticide occurred when Herod Antipas sent his soldiers to Bethlehem and the surrounding areas when Jesus was born to kill all the male children under two years of age. Matthew 2:16 Revised Standard Version.

71. Lefkowitz and Fant, *Women's Life,* 94.

72. Ibid., 95; Gray-Fow, "Roman Childhood," 82; Monroe, *History of Education,* 330.

73. W. V. Harris, "Child-Exposure in the Roman Empire," *Journal of Roman Studies* 84 (1994): 1–22. It is a comprehensive treatment of infanticide during the Roman period. The numbers in parentheses refer to pages in Harris.

74. Wiedemann, *Adults and Children in the Roman Empire,* 35.

75. Wiedemann, *Adults and Children in the Roman Empire,* 17–25.

76. Ibid., 176–177.

77. For more on these descriptions, see Gray-Fow, "Roman Childhood," 19–37. The Romans also had terminology to describe the unborn child. Gray-Fow, "Roman Childhood," 56–71.

78. Ibid. 10–11, 18, 209.

79. Wiedemann, *Adults and Children in the Roman Empire,* 114.

80. Quintilian's, *Institutes of Oratory: or Education of an Orator,* 2 vols., trans. Rev. John Selby Watson (Covent Garden: Henry G. Bohn, 1856). The first number refers to the book, the second to the chapter, and the third to the sections within the chapter.

81. St. Augustine, *The Confessions of St. Augustine,* 2 vols., The Loeb Classical Library, ed. T. E. Page, trans. William Watts (London: William Heinemann, 1912). The first number refers to the book, the second to the chapter.

82. Gray-Fow, "Roman Childhood," 92.

83. D'A. W. Thompson, "Games and Playthings," 71.

84. British Museum, *A Guide to the Exhibition Illustrating Greek and Roman Life* (London: Printed by the Order of the Trustees, 1929), 198. Unfortunately, there is no work comparable to Klein's for Roman children in Roman art.

85. Elderkin, "Jointed Dolls in Antiquity," 472.

86. Gwynn, *Roman Education,* 17; Marrou, *History of Education in Antiquity,* 232, 234. For more on the Roman family, see Beryl Rawson, *The Family in Ancient Rome* (Ithaca, NY: Cornell University Press, 1986).

87. Lefkowitz and Fant, *Women's Life,* 191; Gwynn, *Roman Education,* 14; Marrou, *History of Education in Antiquity,* 247.

88. Gwynn, *Roman Education,* 15–17; Marrou, *History of Education in Antiquity,* 233.

89. Monroe, *History of Education,* 331.

90. Ibid., 394.

91. Gwynn, *Roman Education,* 34–35, 39, 40–41.

92. Marrou, *History of Education in Antiquity,* 250. There is an ivory writing tablet from about 600 B.C. Engraved on the top border of the frame is a complete archaic alphabet that was meant to be copied by the pupil practicing on the wax part of the tablet below. Ibid.

93. Ibid., 265, 269–270. The Latin word for teaching, *disciplina,* also means punishment. Wiedemann, *Adults and Children in the Roman Empire,* 28.

94. Marrou, *History of Education in Antiquity,* 272.

95. Ibid., 263. Comenius used the same method as it will be seen in Ch. 2 of this volume.

96. Phillippe Aries, *Centuries of Childhood* (New York: Vintage Books, 1965).

CHAPTER 2

European Roots

> Under no circumstances should parents postpone the
> commencement of education and the strict insistence on
> proper conduct; . . . they should refrain from pampering
> children.
>
> —Shulamith Shahar[1]

INTRODUCTION: THE MIDDLE AGES AND THE RENAISSANCE

During the early part of the Middle Ages, known as the "Dark Ages," wars
and internal strife made survival difficult. The society was poor in resources,
and its hierarchical structure led to the concentration of assets in the hands of
the overprivileged few. It was a violent civilization, yet it was impotent against
disease and epidemics. Religion, as interpreted by the church, provided not only
moral norms, but also a sanction for extremism, with all that it entailed.[2] the
period from 400 to 1400 was an arduous one for children. In the years 400 to
900, many children did not live past their first days on earth. Between 900 and
1400, a child's fate often depended upon his station in life. Although their
birthrate was approximately the same, the upper classes left more heirs than
the lower classes. Only one child out of every two or three lived to maturity.[3]

Little information is available regarding child life in the early part of the
Middle Ages. Spoiled food, polluted water, and the bone-chilling dampness of
all-stone houses made the young child their particular target. In the country
and the city, there was the ever-present threat of fire and famine. Hanawalt's
research indicates that 54 percent of children under the age of one year who
perished in fires, died in their cradles or in house fires. This suggests accidental
death rather than murder. Disease epidemics devastated whole populations.
Girl children were born into an especially precarious position, for, not only
were they unable to carry on the family name, they required a dowry for their
teenaged betrothal. Infanticide and abandonment were common practices,
whether intentional or unintentional.

In the eleventh century, the European economy began to expand. New
wealth was created, and with it came renewed interest in the refinements of
life, including painting and the fine arts.[4] Artists of the Middle Ages often
depicted children as small figures in adult dress. Ariès, in his controversial
book *Centuries of Childhood*, stated that "in medieval society the idea of
childhood did not exist . . . which is why, as soon as the child could live without the constant solicitude of his mother, his nanny or his cradle-rocker, he
belonged to adult society."[5]

Shahar's research, reported in *Childhood in the Middle Ages*, found that not only did a concept of childhood exist in the central and late Middle Ages, but it was perceived as a distinct stage in the life cycle. Parents invested both material and emotional resources in their offspring. The high mortality rate among infants and children was the consequence of limited medical skills and not the absence of emotional involvement. The child was viewed as a fragile, vulnerable, naive being. Shahar found that educational theories and norms formulated by theologians, secular and ecclesiastical legislators, jurists, the authors of medical and didactic works, and preachers existed. Some norms were depicted as general and universal, and some were presented as educational goals in the second stage of childhood in accordance with social standing and gender.[6]

Lloyd de Mause, another opponent of Ariès' theories, has demonstrated that the farther back in history one looks, the more physical, mental, and sexual abuse of children one finds. The attitudes regarding the whipping of children found expression in Locke's writings.[7]

According to Shahar, several concepts that originated prior to or during the Middle Ages have been ascribed to later time periods, they include:

1. The concept of childhood innocence, which is found in medieval Christian scriptural commentary.
2. The belief that children are ruled solely by their drives, which is also found in medieval Christian scriptural commentary and was later extended by Freud.
3. The childhood years are a basis for the development of the future adult, although the period of dependence is longer in human beings than in any animal.
4. Children need both physical nurturing and affection and contact with adults in order to develop normally.
5. Childhood is divided into stages, a concept later embraced by Erikson and Piaget.[8]

Childhood existed in the context of other relationships. Hanawalt posits a two-way, dynamic relationship between parents and children. Adults did take responsibility for children, even though there were neither civil nor church laws requiring parental or community care. The community began to play an oversight role as the child became more mobile. This "culture of oversight" was important, because little if any assistance was provided by foundling hospitals, and neither orphanages nor child assistance programs existed during this time period.[9]

During the twelfth century, medieval city-states and provinces were reaching a zenith of prosperity. From that time on there was a rise in the number of nation-states, and also the influence of the Papal State. England and France entered a period of relative peace and unity. In Spain, the marriage of Ferdinand and Isabella and the discoveries of Columbus unified the monarchy.

Constantinople was captured by the Turks in 1453. The fate of children during this time period was not very much improved over previous eras.

During the Renaissance, a "cultural surge" that began in thirteenth-century Italy, there were many scientific and artistic innovations. For the most part, the period's great intellectual ferment did not engender any new consideration of children.[10] The period of Enlightenment, the Age of Reason, created the rationalist, liberal, humanitarian, and scientific trends of later Western thought. The enormous strides made in the seventeenth and eighteenth centuries by Locke, Rousseau, and others fostered the belief in natural law and universal order, promoted a scientific approach to political and social issues, and gave rise to a sense of human progress and belief in the state as its rational instrument. It also contributed to a new awareness of the child. Later, the romantics "seized upon the child as a symbol of all they believed in: nature, goodness, joy in living, human progress, instinct and original innocence," and they created the "Cult of Childhood."[11]

The Child

In medieval times, during infancy through the first seven year of life, most children were left almost exclusively in the care of women. The image of children during the Middle Ages was generally positive. Up to the age of seven, they generally enjoyed freedom, and boys and girls were not separated from each other, even in the castles of the nobility and the urban homes of the merchant class. In general, children were permitted to behave in accordance with their nature, through play. They were involved in adult society and were not shielded from its pleasures, coarseness, or tragedies. The majority of them were not forced to begin studying, unless they were in a monastery school, until they reached seven or eight years of age.

The advice of Francesco of Barbaro to wet nurses would be probably accepted today. He

> prescribes diversion instead of head-on clashes with the child. A small child should not be shown something which cannot be given to him; and, if he happens to glimpse it, his attention should be diverted through offering him some other object. If he asks for something which is permissible and is not harmful, it should be given to him. If he receives an injury, the wet nurse, when binding his wound should pretend to be taking revenge against the object which hurt him and should console him with small gifts. When the child is a little older, he should be allowed to go out and play with his peers.[12]

This view of the child holds that he was born innocent and is corrupted by adults. He was perceived as "incapable of committing an unpardonable sin on the one hand, and as lacking the understanding and capacity for choice between good and evil, on the other." The small child should therefore be treated with tenderness and not burdened with excessive demands for discipline and self-restraint.[13]

During the Enlightenment, a special costume was assigned to young people. In medieval times, all ages within the same social class had worn the same outfits. From the late 1500s on, wealthy and middle-class parents no longer dressed their children in miniature replicas of their own clothes. Instead, they put them in special dress reserved for their age group alone. Since a great deal of importance was attached to clothing as a barometer of social standing, the children's costume proclaimed to all that childhood—at least among the upper classes—was now a separate entity.[14]

Although the primary nurturing was done by females during the medieval period, affection was shown to children by both parents. There appear to have been few instances of infanticide or abandonment during this time. The community was involved in the oversight of the child, because of concern for making "as much out of this scarce population of youth as possible." It was felt that discipline was important, because the child and young adult needed to learn self-sufficiency. By the fifteenth century, there was an enormous explosion of books of advice for training children, which assisted parents and community members in this difficult task.[15]

Education

The first education of upper-class children, which usually began when they were around age five or six, was provided in the home by the father or a private tutor. Sometimes small neighborhood schools were available. Those who recommended beginning to teach reading at this young age stressed that learning should be gradual and gentle, and that the child should not be forced to study long hours each day. "Literary games" were advocated, with small prizes, or new shoes, an inkstand, or a slate as the reward. Some recommended that the adult form letters in fruits and sweetmeats and give the letters to the child to eat if he could recognize them. When a boy turned seven, it was his father's task to educate him, while the mother continued the education of daughters. She oversaw their religious education and prepared them for their roles as mothers and housewives. Some approved of giving girls a basic education, while others opposed teaching them to read and write (with the exception of those who were destined to take the veil), since such knowledge could acquaint them with sin. A few said that reading and writing would help girls to manage landed property or their household accounts.[16] Mothers and nurses also transmitted popular female culture to girls. In many societies the education of female children was not given serious attention.[17]

Few peasant children received any education. Those who did were schooled by the village priest or at a monastic house or a secular school in the nearby town. The great majority of these children became clerks or monks. The few literate laymen became the scribes of the manorial courts, the functionaries of manors, or the earliest civil servants. Some considered poor children "more intelligent and beautiful than the offspring of the rich," because the latter were indulged by their parents and often became stubborn and rebellious. Parents and teachers were cautioned to provide good models, because children tend to imitate the acts of adults. Education was thus to be achieved through prevention of the detrimental impact of a corrupt society and of literature, or through reprimand, and whipping.[18]

During the Middle Ages and for a long time thereafter, every child entered an apprenticeship. Children were expected to learn through practice while at the same time making a contribution to society at large. Boys of the middle classes had more choice of career than either their noble or peasant counterparts. In addition to becoming monks or priests, they might become lawyers, mechanics, or tradesmen. Schooling in the mercantile society consisted of learning to read and do accounting and then apprenticeship in a bank or shop. Statements about the need to develop the potential of every individual and the selection of a vocation that enabled utilization of talents referred exclusively to boys.[19]

Although some accounts describe children being sent to school at four or five years of age, most middle class children first encountered formal instruction at the age of seven, in the common schools. In these overcrowded places, only a small minority learned to read, and an even smaller proportion learned to write, or received a proper education. There was no idea that certain subjects—the easier ones—should be studied before other subjects. Nor was there a set curriculum; the student could start with any subject and follow it up with any other. As a result of this system, the more competent student was distinguished from the less competent not by the courses he took, for they were the same, but by the number of times he had repeated them.[20]

Shahar's account of the educational methods of the Middle Ages states that for those of "good parentage" and "noble origin," it was widely acknowledged that the curriculum should be graded and adapted to the stages in the child's intellectual development. All writers agreed that in the early years, children were capable of learning only simple things. In the period in which a more or less formulated curriculum was evolving for boys, no parallel curriculum evolved for girls. Universities were closed to them, as were the merchant schools and the law schools. Those girls who received schooling attended only the lowest schools.[21]

There were few differences in the studies of the "reading school" or the "song school," which children attended from age seven to ten or twelve years. The "song school" placed more emphasis on studying religious hymns, while the "reading school" had more emphasis on study as such. In the twelfth century, Latin was the basis of elementary education, and from the thirteenth century, reading in the vernacular was taught first. All pupils learned their alphabet, and reading, mathematics, writing, prayers and liturgical hymns, and the "tenets of the faith." Children destined for both the church and the secular world were placed in the "song schools."[22]

Many of those destined for knighthood were separated from their mothers at the age of seven to nine years, when they were sent to the court of other nobles to be "educated." The page boys had almost no academic study and were not separated from adult society.[23]

Girls of this social class were sent away only to the home of their betrothed. Sometimes they became "bower girls" at ages as young as four years.[24] Some daughters stayed at home and were instructed by a tutor or mistress, by an anchoress, or at a private school for children of the nobility. If they were from urban noble families, the girls could attend elementary schools in the town. There they studied reading and sometimes even writing in the vernacular, arithmetic, excerpts from the Scriptures and from the *Lives of the Saints,* as well as prayers and psalms in Latin. They were instructed in folk medicine and read narrative poetry and courtly romances. They learned embroidery and weaving. The young noblewoman who received a good education was also expected to know how to ride, to raise and train falcons, to play chess and other social games, to tell stories, to recite, to riddle, to sing and play a stringed instrument, and to dance. They learned about "the running of a household or even an estate from practical observation of the lady of the castle and through helping her."[25]

In the fifteenth and sixteenth centuries, education became more important. Middle-class parents were more anxious to have their children obtain it, because it was an avenue to upward mobility and to securing important government posts. English Puritans and reform French Catholics both saw education as a way to remove the child from this "depraved world" and prepare him for the next purer one. Philosophers promoted it as the road to universal moral improvement. More grammar schools with a rigorous classical curriculum were created for their aristocratic clients.

A Littell Dictionarie for Children was probably used for four-year-olds, since students were expected to know their ABCs before acceptance at grammar school or being apprenticed. Four was the usual age for entry to the ABC or petty school, which preceded entry to the grammar school at age six or seven. Girls still benefited less from the academic excitement, because their lives continued to revolve around the home.[26] The English thought education was necessary to develop the gentleman/woman. Their quest was aided by the tremendous expansion of the British school system, which placed a grammar school within twelve miles of almost every family.

After the idea took hold that education was for the young exclusively, age groupings gradually became more and more homogeneous within the school setting. At first, the students were grouped according to "age and development," but "development" or capabilities still counted most. Children learned the alphabet through rhymes, read a hornbook, and studied their lessons in Latin, the language of the church. Etiquette books were used to teach reading, writing, and good manners, and singing was an important part of the curriculum.[27] In seventeenth-century France, the world of children under seven was governed by customary practice and oral traditions. English Puritan schools began at 6:00 A.M. and lasted through most of the day.[28]

In summary, education during this time period was based on religious teachings. Its foremost aim was to raise a Christian human being, in whom Christian morals took precedence over worldly knowledge and vocational skills. However, it was conceded that another goal was to develop the intellectual ability of the individual and to prepare him to fulfill his role in society. Modesty and chastity were to be fostered in both sexes, but were given greater emphasis where girls were concerned. Training of girls in obedience was also considered of greater importance than the disciplining of boys, since a woman, unlike a man, was destined to be obedient all her life. Another aim of education was to teach the child to accept the social order and to respect it, since the existing order was considered both good and proper. The standing of parents determined the type of education their children received, because different outcomes were expected for the education of children from different social classes.[29]

The following sections present short biographies, significant contributions, and writings on early childhood education of selected European pedagogical reformers.

JAN AMOS KOMENSKY (1592–1670) (BOHEMIA)

> There is nothing in the intellect that has not first existed in the senses.
>
> —Comenius, *Orbis Pictus*[30]

In the sixteenth century the Continent was divided into Protestant and Catholic camps. This division had come about by circumstances. Martin Luther (1483–1546) protested against the Catholic Church, in 1529, first to reform the church as a whole and later the German church. He failed, and Germany was split into two camps. He had not planned to divide Europe along religious lines—Catholic and Protestant. Throughout the rest of Europe, religious Reformation likewise proved divisive. One of the causes was that the interests of the rising nations conflicted with those of the Roman Catholic Church and the Hapsburg Empire. The Religious Peace of Augsburg of 1555, which legalized the division, left the choice of selecting one of the two religious divisions in the Empire to the princes. This arrangement satisfied no one except the princes themselves, who profited by it. There was nothing very religious about the peace, and it was not so much a peace as a truce. The Protestants could neither leave the decision of religion in the hands of the princes, nor could they be satisfied with the meager degree of freedom they won, for it was restricted to the Lutherans only. The Calvinists and other Reformation groups were left out. The Catholics were not content, either. After all, what were gains for the Protestants were losses for the Catholics.

Competition and rivalry between nations of Protestants and Catholics led to wars such as the Thirty Years' War (1618–1646). The Reformation also marked the transfer of responsibility for education from church to laity. Latin remained, however, the language of culture and of the schools even though after Reformation it was banished from the church services of the Protestants. As soon as the child was considered sufficiently mature—between the sixth and the ninth years—he was introduced to the Latin language, beginning with Latin grammar, which he memorized. This concept of education was held by both Protestants and Catholics. There was no study of the mother tongue preliminary to the study of Latin. It monopolized the curriculum.

The invention of printing, which occurred in Holland and Germany about 1425 by more than one inventor, spread to other countries. The use of printing throughout Western Europe and its influence in informing people about issues created a large and active public who favored reforming all aspects of life. Printing had an important influence on popular education and facilitated the spread of knowledge. Books became available at a lower cost and in uniform editions. Spelling began to be standardized in printed books, a development that was a great improvement over the chaotic spelling of the many local dialects of the Middle Ages.[31]

Biographical Portrait (1592–1628)

Jan Amos Komenský (Latin: Comenius) was born in Moravia on March 28, 1592, when America was one hundred years old. His name derives from Komné the place of his birth. Sixteenth-century Moravia, part of the kingdom of Bohemia, had been ruled by the Hapsburgs since 1526. At the end of World War I, it became the Czechoslovak Republic. It fell to the Communists in 1948, and became the Czech Republic in 1989.

Comenius was the youngest of five children and the only son. His father owned a mill and an estate. His family were members of the Unity of Brethren (*Unitas Fratrum*), a Protestant church. They lived a simple life in accordance with the Scriptures. When Comenius was ten years old, his parents and two of his sisters died. Comenius and his two surviving sisters went to live with an aunt in a nearby town. She used his inheritance and neglected his schooling.[32] Comenius attended the local school for four years. He found the curriculum narrow, the teaching poor, and the discipline harsh and brutal. He had to learn many rules by rote before he had understood them and translated Latin authors without suitable dictionaries or commentaries. Comenius deplored the destruction of childhood happiness that resulted from the inhuman conditions of these schools and the aversion they created toward learning.[33] Because of his early experiences, Comenius later pleaded for more humane treatment of pupils and tried to develop new methods of instruction.

When Comenius was sixteen years old, he attended for two years the Latin school at Přerov, managed by the Unity of Brethren. There, inspired by the rector of the school, he developed a love for learning, especially of the Scriptures. It was during these years that he Latinized his name to Johannes

Amos Comenius, as was the custom of the time for members of the educated classes. He decided to devote his life to promoting the Christian faith. After Přerov, Comenius entered the Herborn Academy—favored by the Brethren for its Calvinist leanings—determined to prepare for the ministry. At Herborn, Comenius met Johann Heinrich Alsted, a distinguished theologian and educator of the day. He was especially attracted to Alsted's *Encyclopædia Scientorium Omnium,* which outlined Alsted's ideas about school reform and educational methods. Among them were: teach only one subject at a time; reserve corporal punishment for moral offenses; and teach Latin through the medium of the mother tongue. The *Encyclopædia* also directed Comenius toward one of the fundamental principles of his own educational writings—the unity and integrity of all knowledge.

In 1613, Comenius entered the University of Heidelberg, a major institution of Reformed learning. There he completed his theological studies under David Pareus, the biblical scholar, who was committed to uniting the Protestant sects. Comenius was influenced by Pareus's irenic ideas, and later tried to keep them in the forefront of his thoughts as a pastor and an educator. He matriculated and returned to Prague in the spring of 1614, having walked the distance to save his meager means.

Being too young to be ordained minister, Comenius returned to Přerov to teach at the school he attended. This experience made him face problems of methodology and classroom discipline. It also provided him with an opportunity to apply some of his theories he had formulated while studying at Herborn. Aware of the ineffective methods used to teach Latin, Comenius began to write a Latin book for beginners and a Czech-Latin dictionary.

In 1616, at the age of twenty-four, he was ordained a minister in the Unity of Brethren and continued to teach at Přerov. Two years later he was appointed pastor in Fulneck, near the Moravian-Silesian border—where he moved with his wife, Magdaline Visovská, a Hungarian—and was elected rector of the local school. Comenius ministered to the spiritual and educational needs of the Fulneck Moravians for three years, and displayed a deep interest in community affairs. He wrote a number of works on religious and social issues, published a short history and map of Moravia, and a study of the doctrinal differences that had separated the Protestant and Catholic churches since the Reformation.[34]

With the outbreak of the Thirty Years' War (1618–1648), Bohemia was immersed in turmoil. It could not escape the conflict between the major powers of Europe. The Thirty Years' War had a drastic impact on Bohemia and on Comenius's life and work. It ended freedom of religion for the Protestants and any hope for the national independence for Bohemia. In 1621, Fulneck was plundered and burned by Spanish troops. Comenius lost all his property. His library, which contained manuscripts of several educational treatises, was burned by the Capuchin friars. From this time on, Comenius and his Church (*Unitas Fratrum*) were persecuted. He became a political and a religious fugitive, separated from his wife and children, and went into hiding. While in hiding, his wife and children died in 1622 during the plague, and he was left alone. Comenius found relief from his sorrow in literary work.

In 1624, Comenius and the other pastors had to leave the estate of Count Zorotin, where they had taken refuge. The authorities pressured the count to expel them. For a time they took refuge in the Bohemian mountains in the estate of Baron Sadowsky, but this did not last. The edict of 1627 put an end to further protection of the Moravian clergy by the nobles. In 1628, Comenius went to Leszno (Lissa), Poland, never to see his country again.[35]

Educational Reformer (1628–1656)

Comenius and his compatriots found refuge in Leszno. The Brethren had maintained a congregation there since the second half of the sixteenth century. During the twelve years Comenius stayed there he was actively involved in educational reform. In addition to writing three of his most important books—the *Janua*, in 1631, *The Great Didactic* (1628–1632), and the *School of Infancy*, in 1633—he also taught. As co-rector of the Brethren Gymnasium, he took the opportunity to put into practice some of his pedagogic theories. One of his reforms at Leszno was the careful grading of the school, and the foundation of a course of study for the successive grades. The principle of this organization was that each grade should pave the way for the next higher one. These reforms were revolutionary and far reaching. They made possible the modern graded school. Soon, most of Europe was discussing these reforms.

Comenius wanted also to change the method of teaching Latin grammar, the chief subject of the curriculum and the center of all learning in the schools. He devoted three years preparing a textbook for beginners, the *Janua Linguarum Reserata* (The Gate of Languages Unlocked). It was published in 1632 by the Leszno press that the Brethren had founded with the equipment they had brought from Moravia. Comenius maintained that all language learning should be based on experience. The method of the *Janua* was to promote linguistic proficiency through the comprehension of words and phrases related to the experiences of everyday life in the mother tongue. It contains a thousand sentences. The sentences, simple at first and gradually becoming complex, are arranged in two columns, one in Latin and the other in the vernacular or mother tongue. Comenius stressed that the growth of linguistic fluency should go hand in hand with the full understanding of the "things" signified by the language. The *Janua* became the standard textbook for teaching Latin throughout Europe and America immediately following its publication and remained so for several centuries. It was translated in Polish, German, Swedish, Greek, English, French, Spanish, Italian, and Hungarian. The publication of the *Janua* and its success brought Comenius in contact with many of the influential men of this day, among them Samuel Hartlib of England. Comenius was elected bishop of the Unity of Brethren in 1632 and senior bishop in 1648. He ministered to the many needs of the exiles and tried to improve the relations among the various Protestant sects.[36]

Philosophy of Education: The Great Didactic

As the reality for an independent Bohemia became less and less attainable, Comenius turned his vision and efforts to the wider aim of education and to pedagogic reform. He envisioned education for all nations and for all people, a universal education, which he called *pampaedia*. Comenius hoped that universal education would promote social harmony.

The Great Didactic (1628–1632) is the method of teaching all things to all people. The purpose of *The Great Didactic* is stated at the beginning of the text:

> Let the main object of this, our Didactic, be as follows: To seek and to find a method of instruction, by which teachers may teach less, but learners may learn more; by which schools may be the scene of less noise, aversion, and useless labor, but of more leisure, enjoyment, and solid progress; and through which the Christian community may have less darkness, perplexity, and dissension, but on the other hand more light, orderliness, peace, and rest.[37]

Following are some of the ideas Comenius advanced in *The Great Didactic*. Education is necessary for all young people of all classes of society, for both sexes, including those who are backward, mentally weak, and of limited intelligence to help them overcome their shortcomings, as no mind can be so poor that it cannot be improved through education, because God had made everyone in His image. Children should be educated together in classes, since better results and more pleasure are obtained when they are taught together and interact.[38]

During the sixteenth century, society began to develop an interest in the study of nature, observation of her laws, imitation of her methods in education, and denouncement of the existing harsh and severe discipline of the students for the sake of learning.

Comenius looked to nature for guidelines for his pedagogy and used examples from nature to illustrate his points. The basis of the reform Comenius was advocating is an application of the principle of order he found in nature. (1) Nature, he claimed, observes a suitable time; (2) prepares the material before attempting to give it form; (3) chooses a fit subject to act upon; (4) advances with precision from one point to another; (5) develops from within; (6) begins with the universal and ends with the particular; (7) makes no leaps, but proceeds step by step; (8) does not leave the process incomplete; and (9) avoids all obstacles that are likely to interfere with her operations.[39]

Comenius's idea of education was a lifelong process. Therefore he developed an educational system of four levels: infancy, childhood, boyhood, and youth, each lasting for six years. For infancy, a Mother School should exist in every house, a Vernacular School in every hamlet and village, a Gymnasium or Latin school in every city, and a University in every kingdom or in every province. The various subjects were not to be separated but taught concurrently. The same subjects were to be taught at all four levels, but the degree of difficulty of each subject was to be adapted to each pupil's stage of development and progress.

The main objectives of the Mother School were character training, the development of the senses, and fostering the mother tongue. In the Vernacular School, the processes of imagination and memory were to be developed in combination with their related organs through reading, writing, painting, singing, counting, measuring, weighing, and memorizing. The Vernacular School was to be universal, compulsory, free for all children of both sexes regardless of their social class or religious affiliation, and divided into definite classes. The Latin School provided a classical curriculum of dialectic, grammar, rhetoric, and other sciences and arts that are based on principles of causation. Through these courses, the student was to be trained to understand and to judge the information he has collected. Finally, the University, through the faculties of theology, philosophy, medicine, and jurisprudence, provided professional training.[40] Comenius initiated a school system that was developmentally appropriate.

Comenius devotes a whole chapter in *The Great Didactic* on school discipline. He protests against the severe and inhuman discipline of his day. He pleads for gentle discipline, free from personal elements such as anger or dislike, and exercised with frankness and sincerity. Teachers should administer punishment just as physicians prescribe medicine—to improve the condition of the individual. Severe discipline should not be used for studies, only in the case of moral delinquencies such as: (1) impiety of any kind; (2) premeditated misbehavior, or neglect of duty; and (3) pride, disdain, envy, and idleness. Corporal punishment is not useful to inculcating a love for schoolwork, but it is very likely to create an aversion to learning. He suggests praise, encouragement, and emulation as better methods of discipline.[41]

School of Infancy

Comenius wrote several guides and schoolbooks for the use of the teachers and pupils in the various grades of his educational scheme. The first of these was the *Informatorium Skoly Materske*, or *Informatory of the Mother School*, written in Czech between 1628 and 1630, during the time Comenius was pastor in Leszno, but it was not published in Czech until 1858. A German translation was issued at Leszno in 1633. It was also translated into Polish and Latin.[42]

Since the education of the child must begin at birth, mothers must assume the teacher's role. The mothers of the seventeenth century, according to Comenius, were not prepared to undertake this mission due to lack of training.[43] The *School of Infancy* outlines definite instructions for mothers. It lays the foundation for all that the child is to learn. Comenius advised that children should stay with their mothers and not be given to teachers before the age of six. Among the reasons he gives is that young children require more attention and care than a teacher can give, who has the responsibility for many children.

According to Comenius, the purpose of educating the child is threefold: (1) faith and piety, (2) uprightness in respect to morals, and (3) knowledge of language and of arts. This order must not be inverted. Parents, therefore, do not fully perform their duty when they merely teach their children to eat, drink, walk, and talk. These things are subservient to the body. Greater care must be taken for the soul, which is the highest part of the child's nature.[44]

Comenius does not ignore the physical care of the child. Bodily vigor influences mental development. He counseled mothers to take care of themselves during pregnancy; nurse their own children—giving them to strangers to nurse them, is "hurtful"; gradually introduce them to solid foods; allow them to move and play; and provide some stimulation for the senses. The body and soul of the child should be trained from birth, as ought to be throughout his life.[45]

For the mental training of the child, he outlined two groups of studies: (1) those providing the materials for thought such as nature study, geography, household economy and (2) those supplying the symbols of thought, such as drawing, writing, and language. Comenius described the content and examples of educational activities for young children, which he divided into: things young children should know, things they should be able to do, and things they should be able to say. Children under six should have knowledge of: (1) natural things—the differences between plants and animals; the names of fruits; the names of the external parts of their bodies and their uses; (2) optics—the difference between light and darkness; (3) astronomy—distinguish between sun, moon, and stars; (4) geography—knowledge of where the child was born, and where he lives, village, town, or city; (5) chronology—what is an hour, a day, a week, or a month; (6) the beginning of history—ability to remember what he did yesterday; (7) household affairs—ability to distinguish who belongs to the family and who does not; and (8) politics—knowing that there is a state, a ruler, ministers, and legislators. These form the basis of the early childhood education curriculum today. Many of the activities of the contemporary preschool education curriculum in the United States are Comenian in scope and content.

Comenius recommended stories and fables, particularly those about animals that contain some moral principle. By age six, children should be able to distinguish between a question and answer, express themselves understandably, count to twenty, and understand the difference between even and odd numbers. Additional activities were related to music, health, cleanliness, justice, patience, and industriousness. Comenius believed that instruction should be individualized because children learn to speak and reach their developmental milestones at different ages.[46]

Comenius called attention to the importance of children's play. Beginning in infancy, parents should provide toys for the child's enjoyment, and equipment to help him move about. Parents are to encourage play, and to provide a safe place for it. Play must not be left to chance, but provided for. Because children try to imitate what they see adults do, they should be permitted to have all things except those that might cause injury to themselves. When this is not convenient, they should be given toys in place of real implements. With these toys, children will amuse themselves, and exercise their bodies and minds. Children are delighted to construct houses and erect walls of clay, wood, or stone to display their skills. Whatever children delight playing with, it should be gratified rather than restricted. Inactivity is more injurious to both mind and body of the child. Most of all, children need to play with other children of the same age. The free interaction requires all the powers of invention, sharpens their wits, and cultivates their manners and habits.[47]

Comenius recognized the importance of early childhood education and saw it as the key to equality of opportunity, long before Froebel, Pestalozzi, and others became concerned with the early years.

Orbis Sensualium Pictus
(The World of Senses in Pictures)

Orbis Pictus (The world in pictures) is the result of Comenius's experimentation with language teaching. After he published the *Janua*, he decided to create a text for beginners that would give equal attention to both Latin and the mother tongue or vernacular. The book was in preparation for several years and was not completed until 1658 because he had to overcome great technical problems before his plans for extensive visual illustrations could be realized. The book has 151 illustrations, many of which required a high level of visual detail. The success of this book was even greater than that of the *Janua*.[48]

Comenius states in the preface his philosophic principle that guided him in writing this book. "There is nothing in the intellect that has not first existed in the senses" (xiv). He maintained that the material of knowledge is derived through the senses. Therefore training the senses is fundamental to learning. Knowledge acquired through the senses becomes permanent. When dealing with objects in the classroom, it is easy to point them to the beginner, but when the pupils' vocabulary becomes more extensive, the process of learning can be effected by means of a picture-book.

Orbis Pictus is the best known of Comenius's books. Its popularity is attributed to the inclusion of pictures and how they were used to teach language. According to Murphy, Bohemia had a tradition of illustrated books before Comenius began writing *Orbis Pictus*, which influenced his belief of the value of visual aids. Comenius was also influenced by Eilhard Lubinus, a German theologian, who recommended the use of pictures side by side with the prose text to enable reading competence to develop more rapidly.[49] This innovation has subsequently revolutionized the whole process of language

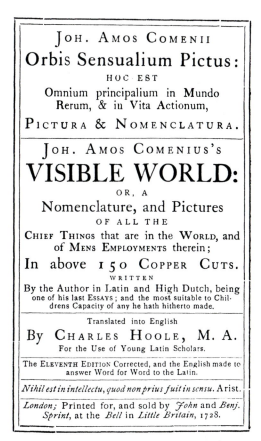

Figure 2.1 Title page of the 1728 edition of *The Orbis Pictus*, reproduced in W. C. Bardeen's 1887 edition, and page 3 from Bardeen's edition. From *The Orbis Pictus* of John Amos Comenius. *Syracuse, New York: C. W. Bardeen, Publisher, 1887. Courtesy of the Boston Public Library.*

teaching and has contributed significantly to achieving mass literacy in the years that followed the book's publication.

Orbis Pictus contains 151 topics ranging from flowers, to birds, to shoemaking, to body parts, to world religions, to morality.[50] Each topic is presented as a separate lesson illustrated by a small engraving. The text below the engraving is in parallel columns, one in Latin and the other in English or any other vernacular language into which it was translated. Everything named in the text has a corresponding number in the engraving. These numbers help the child link the word with the pictured object. The visual image is especially effective when the words or concepts are new to the child because they reinforce understanding through visual recognition. This process makes learning pleasant. *Orbis Pictus* embodies Comenius's belief that a textbook should aim to provide the pupils with the widest range of knowledge while also teaching language competence. Comenius provided also the methodology of how to use *Orbis Pictus* with children (xviii–xix).

According to Čapková, Comenius's goal was to develop the children's *cognitive* abilities, the abilities to reason and to communicate, and eye-hand coordination.[51]

Comenius's ideas, principles about education, and teaching methods came to America via his books. Comenius was admired by the colonials. His *Janua* was used as a textbook at Harvard College during the Colonial years[52] and the early grammar schools of New Engand.[53] His dreams about universal education are today reflected in the American schools because they are attended by all children of all peoples.

Comenius's Later Years

During the years 1641–1642, Comenius was invited by a group representing both of the Houses of Parliament, through his friend Samuel Hartlib, to go to London to establish a pansophic college. Comenius went to England and was received well, but the plan did not materialize for many reasons: England went to war with Ireland, his wife did not want to relocate away from friends and family, and she did not speak English.[54]

There is some evidence that in 1642, Comenius was offered the presidency of Harvard College, founded in 1636. Cotton Mather reported:

> That brave Old Man, *Johannes Amos* COMENIUS, the Fame of whose Worth hath been *Trumpetted* as far as more than *Three* Languages (whereof every one is Endebted unto his *Janua*) could carry it was indeed agreed withall, by our Mr. *Winthrop* in his Travels through the *Low Countries,* to come over into *New-England,* and Illuminate this *College and Country,* in the Quality of a *President:* But the solicitations of the *Swedish* Ambassador, diverting him another way, that Incomparable *Moravian* became not an *American.*[55]

Comenius was invited in 1642 by the Swedish government to prepare textbooks. He accepted the invitation in the hope that Protestant Sweden, then at war with the Hapsburgs, would provide support for the Brethren to return to Bohemia and to restore its national independence. These hopes, which had been kept alive for twenty-five years, were dashed by the terms of the Peace of Westphalia (1648), which ended the Thirty Years' War but did not give back the lands of Bohemia. Therefore, the exiles were prevented from returning to their homeland. As a result, Comenius settled in Elbing, Sweden, where he worked on the reformation of the Swedish schools and textbooks from 1642 to 1648.[56]

In 1650 Comenius went to Sáros Pátak, Hungary, at the invitation of the prince and his mother, to organize a school system according to his views. They offered him a good salary and a press for the publication of the required textbooks. Comenius developed a sketch for a seven-grade school—which was later published as *Plan of a Pansophic School*. It had specific directions to be used by the teachers. One of the directions explains the danger of over-working the children and recommends a rest of half an hour after each hour's instruction for free, spontaneous play.

The *Plan* required that each grade meets in a separate room with a separate teacher. In each class, the textbooks must be adapted to the abilities of the children. Over the door of each classroom there is a motto. The room is decorated with pictures illustrating the subjects to be taught in this grade, and by means of these illustrations the senses are trained. Teachers were reminded that their position is one of dignity and importance. Comenius's work at Sáros-Pátak ended in the fourth year with only the first three grades of the *Plan* implemented.

The Sáros-Pátak *Plan* became a model for educators in many lands. It introduced the graded scheme of instruction. Not only the subjects were graded according to the laws of child development but the textbooks were graded as well.[57] Comenius understood that the best way to teach children was through objects, pictures, and the use of the mother tongue and implemented them at Sáros-Pátak.

Comenius returned to Leszno in 1655, but his stay was brief. Poland was invaded by the Swedes, and he had to flee again. He spent his last years in Amsterdam as a guest of the son of his friend and patron Laurence De Geer, joined by his wife, children, and son-in-law and collaborator, Peter Fingulus. Young de Geer had a profound affection for the aged Comenius and an enthusiastic interest in all his educational reform. Through his generosity, all of Comenius's educational writings were published in four volumes as *Opera Didactic Omnia* in 1657.

Although Comenius worked very hard to finish his pansophic work, it was not completed by the time of his death. He requested that his son, Daniel, and a friend prepare it for publication after his death. The seven manuscript volumes, known as the *Consultatio,* were entrusted to a German scholar at the University of Halle, where it remained for almost three centuries. It was discovered in 1935, and given for publication to the Comenius Pedagogical Institute in Prague. All seven volumes were published by the Czech Academy of Sciences in 1966.

Comenius died in Amsterdam on November 4, 1670, and was buried in Näarden.[58] On the two-hundredth anniversary of Comenius's death (1870), a monument was erected in Näarden at the place of his burial. The same year, in Leipzig, Germany, a national pedagogical library with over 66 thousand volumes was founded in his memory. Many German cities had Comenian societies whose object was the study of his educational theories and practices.[59]

Comenius's goal for a panharmonious world through universal education still has not been attained, but because of his lifelong efforts and dedication, the educational goals of today are clearer.

A conference commemorating the four hundredth anniversary of Comenius's birth was held in Prague, in March 1992. The theme was: *Comenius'*

Heritage and Education of Man in the 21st Century. One of the authors presented a paper.

THE SEVENTEENTH CENTURY IN ENGLAND

The political and religious climate in seventeenth-century England was quite tumultuous.[60] This was the century that saw a parliamentary war with Charles I, the death of Oliver Cromwell, and, in May 1660, the restoration of the monarchy and the established church, with a promise of religious toleration. The Clarendon Code and related laws were overthrown with the flight of James II. The return of William of Orange early in November 1688, and his queen, Mary, in 1689, impacted the life of John Locke.[61]

The "Squirarchy" had little moral resistance; however, the middle class was still uncorrupted, interested in trade, and habituated to Bible reading and family prayers. The economic problem of the seventeenth century was the shift in emphasis from land to industry and commerce as the main source of national wealth. The Elizabethan voyages had opened up ocean trade routes and had begun to plant colonies. The church settlement was not a permanent solution to the struggle among the dissenters, the established church and its parties and the Roman Catholic Church. The intellectual problem of Locke and his friends in the Royal Society "(such as Newton, Sydenham, and Boyle) was to establish on a lasting foundation the habitual attitude to thought and knowledge which we know as the scientific method."[62] Locke's life covered the Civil War period, the Bloodless Revolution, the Restoration, and the early years of the Whig Settlement in England.

JOHN LOCKE (1632–1704) (ENGLAND)

John Locke was born August 29, 1632, the eldest of three boys, at Wrington, Somerset, near Bristol, England. As often happened during that time, the other brothers died at a young age. His father was a lawyer and small landowner, and his mother, the daughter of a local tanner. The Locke family belonged socially to the middle rank of the countryside. Locke's education followed the standard pattern for a middle-class child, with a private tutor for his early years, followed by admission to Westminster School, as a result of his father's political work on behalf of the Parliament during the Civil War. In 1647, Westminster was presided over by Dr. Richard Busby, who was headmaster for fifty-seven years (1638–1695), until he was nearly ninety. Busby was a dramatically effective teacher.[63]

In 1652, at the age of twenty, Locke "went up" to Christ Church, Oxford, with a scholarship. It apparently was exceptional in those days to enter the university so late, because many undergraduates "went up" at age fourteen. Locke wrote verses in both English and Latin praising Cromwell, and received both his bachelor's (1656) and master's degrees (1658) from Oxford. He was elected to a Senior Studentship (fellowship) and later became a Lecturer in Greek (1660), and Rhetoric (1662). He resisted the normal requirement of those days for Oxford dons to take Holy Orders, and instead he studied medicine.[64]

In 1660, Locke inherited his father's property, lost his surviving brother, and at thirty-one, was alone in the world. He became the secretary to Sir Walter Vane, accompanying him on a fruitless mission to the Elector of Brandenburg in 1665. When he returned to Oxford in 1666, he continued his medical and scientific studies. He applied for the degree of doctor of medicine, hoping that his political connections would facilitate his request. After being refused twice, he settled for a bachelor of medicine degree with a license to practice as a physician, granted in 1674, and was briefly in private practice.

Lord Ashley, the Earl of Shaftsbury, became his close friend and patron. As Shaftsbury's personal secretary and medical advisor, Locke saved his life by draining an abscess. Shaftsbury held several important political posts that enabled him to assist Locke in obtaining minor public offices. In this way, Locke became Secretary of Presentations of Benefices at £500 a year, and joined the Board of Trade and Plantations, in 1672. In 1673, when Shaftsbury was dismissed as Chancellor, and Locke lost his posts, Shaftsbury gave him an annuity of £100 per year. After traveling, tutoring, and studying in France, Locke returned to Shaftsbury's employ when he became President of the Privy Council. Later Shaftsbury was accused of conspiracy, and he escaped to Holland. Locke also went into exile, for six years, because Shaftsbury's patronage proved embarrassing. While he was in Holland, Locke was expelled from Christ Church, Oxford; however, he resumed his scientific studies, and kept up his political connections from a distance. As mentioned earlier, he returned to England after the Revolution, in 1688, and was given the office of Commissioner of Appeals at £200 year.

Locke became a member of the Royal Society, and transcribed Sydenham's scientific notes between 1679 and 1683. Descartes, and the work of the Royal Society, affirmed the empirical method of modern science, which was "destined to bring new life to philosophy" and dispel superstition. Locke first met Sir Isaac Newton in 1689, through the Royal Society.[65] Although he began writing prior to his days in Holland, none of his work was published until after his return to England.

Locke's life was unpretentious, "a quiet and respectable life—substantial, but not outwardly impressive" (vii). The outstanding features of Locke's character were modesty, common sense, humor, and loyalty to the truth. "He also had a warm and ready sympathy, especially toward children (possibly because he had none of his own). He spared himself nothing in order to complete a task thoroughly" (viii).[66] He is considered the intellectual leader of Whiggism. Locke also had some less admirable qualities. He did not always recognize his debt to thinkers who influenced him, and he had a passion for secrecy.[67]

Locke was a teacher, physician, scholar, administrator, and behind-the-scenes politician. "For students of education there is significance in the fact that Locke was a man of many interests, who explored many fields of knowledge. Standing on the threshold of the modern world of scientific inquiry, he still belonged to an age before the fragmentation of human knowledge into many self-contained and mutually unintelligible departments."[68]

Locke's Educational Thought and Writings

An Essay Concerning Human Understanding, which appeared in 1690, was drafted twenty years earlier, as the outcome of informal discussions between friends. An abstract of this essay was published in Leclerc's *Bibliotheque Universelle* in 1688. The full essay was completed before Locke left Holland for England in February 1689. *The Conduct of Understanding,* which was published after his death on October 28, 1704, was an extension of this essay. *Two Treatises on Government* and *Letters on Toleration,* published in 1690, were written before 1688. The substance of *Some Thoughts Concerning Education,* published in 1693, was in letters written from Holland to his friend Edward Clarke in 1684.[69]

Teaching was not a reputable profession in the seventeenth century. Men used it as a stepping-stone. There was little or no systematic study of education or of children. Locke was "a keen and shrewd observer, with a natural liking for children, and much practical wisdom." In his educational writings, he emphasized planning children's education on the basis of observation.[70] He considered the senses as "doorways through which knowledge entered the mind. He never went as far as Rousseau in valuing aesthetic experience and in urging the importance of doing rather than knowing."[71] Locke wrote that children must have the freedom to grow, play, experiment, and make mistakes.[72]

He wrote to Clarke that curiosity in children is a good sign. It demonstrates that the child seeks knowledge, and therefore ought to be encouraged. Among his recommended methods for encouraging inquisitiveness were:

1. Answer questions according to the child's age and knowledge. Do not check or laugh at the questions.
2. Take them seriously, and commend the child for asking them.
3. Take great care that they never receive deceitful or elusive answers, because children can easily perceive when they are slighted or deceived.[73]

Locke stated that

> great care must be taken with children to begin with that which is plain and simple and to teach them as little as can be at once and settle that well in their heads before you proceed to the next or anything new in that science. Give them first one simple idea and see that they take it right and perfectly comprehend it before you go any further, and then add some other simple idea which lies next in your way to what you aim at; and so proceeding by gentle and insensible steps, children without confusion and amazement will have their understandings opened. . . . And when anyone has learned anything

himself, there is no such way to fix it in his memory and to encourage him to go on as to set him to teach it others.[74]

Locke also believed that "example and practice are better than precept," and that, "children should not be wearied with lectures."[75]

In his letters, general teaching methods and the teaching of reading and writing are specifically addressed. One letter to Clarke suggests, "When he can talk 'tis time he should begin to learn. . . . There may be dice and play-things with the letters on them to teach children the alphabet by playing." "Quintilian and Plato before him recommended that lessons should take the form of play."[76] Locke commends the practice of using apples, raisins, and almonds to teach alphabet letters, as was done during the Middle Ages. He suggests using *Æsop's Fables* to draw the child into reading, saying that if Clarke cannot get a book with pictures, "get him what pictures of animals you can with the names to them which at the same time will encourage him to read and afford him matter of enquiry and knowledge."[77]

Among the subjects suggested for the child's science education are anatomy, botany, and astronomy. Locke emphasized the importance of learning geography and history at an early stage. He indicated that it would give the child pleasure and pride to teach his father, mother, or sister what he knows. Other suggestions included learning to speak French and engaging in gardening and woodworking as a "laudable manual art" (344–345). Locke placed a great deal of emphasis on physical care and the establishment of good physical habits, as preventive measures.[78]

Discussions of discipline techniques were included in his letters. In this regard, he said: "Let therefor your rules to your son be as few as possible, and rather fewer than more than seem absolutely necessary" (91). Locke did, however, state that children must acquire disciplined habits, including "the acceptance of authority; strict authority is needed to prevent wrong development. The balance of freedom and authority should be proportionate to age and maturity; and to maintain a proper balance is 'the true secret of education'" (51).[79] "Locke's insistence upon habit formation rather than the multiplication of rules led him naturally to an appreciation of forming these habits early" (114–115). "Learning for him was receptive rather than active; and in this respect he was not in line with modern educational thought" (55).[80]

Locke was quite specific with regard to his thoughts on the education of girls, writing to Mary Clarke that girls' education should differ from boys' education. He says girls should be restricted in their play outdoors in all weather to take care of their beauty (686), suggests they should have a dancing master "at home early" (689), and that "the father [ought] to strike very seldom, if at all to chide his daughters. Their governing and correcting, I think, properly belongs to the mother" (688).[81]

Several of Locke's revolutionary proposals were not followed, for example, his suggestion that a gentleman's son should learn a trade. He believed in "working schools" for the children of the "labouring classes." Although it was not adopted in his day, this idea may have influenced the charity school movement of the eighteenth century.[82] According to Jeffreys, Locke is entitled to be numbered among the originators of *child-centered education*, although he sometimes did not see the remoter implications of his own ideas.[83]

BRITISH INFANT SCHOOLS

Robert Owen is generally acknowledged to have opened the first infant school in Britain, in the Scottish town of New Lanark. Oberlin's knitting school, in the remote mountain region of Ban-de-la-Roche, France, preceded Owen by some forty years. Oberlin included some of the same concepts as Owen's school, such as storytelling, looking at pictures, and natural history. Oberlin did not influence Owen's work, but the ideas of Rousseau and Pestalozzi did influence the expansion of the infant school movement into the British Isles. Richard Lavel Edgeworth (in Ireland) wrote a book with his daughter Maria, titled *Practical Education,* in 1798. Edgeworth was strongly influenced by Rousseau's educational ideas and enunciated the general principle that we should associate pleasure with whatever we wish that our pupils should pursue, and pain, with whatever we wish that they should avoid. Edgeworth also described children's play as active work. This was one of the first times that a British publication had made this distinction. The middle class also had preparatory schools that were opened by those who admired Pestalozzi.

JEAN-JACQUES ROUSSEAU (1712–1778) (FRANCE)

Jean-Jacques Rousseau was born on June 28, 1712, in Geneva, Switzerland. His mother died on July 7, shortly after his birth. When Jean was ten, his father, a watchmaker, fled Geneva. He was cared for by an aunt and uncle. He had fragmentary formal schooling but acquired a "passion for literature" along the way. He was baptized a Catholic, and developed a system of musical notation that he published himself in January 1743. In 1758, he became the tutor to family of Jean Bonnet de Mably.

He met a peasant girl named Thérèse, by whom he had five illegitimate children who were left on the steps of the foundling hospital. He later married Thérèse. In 1745, after setting up house with Thérèse, he came into contact with the Encyclopédistes, including Didérot, who asked him to contribute to the *Encyclopédie* section on music. He discovered a competition sponsored by the provincial Academy of Dijon, and in 1750, he was awarded the prize for his essay. *Discourse on the Sciences and the Arts* defended the position that progress in the arts and the sciences has been damaging to man's well-being (ix).[84] He penned numerous works thereafter, including letters to the Archbishop of Paris defending *Emile*, which were also published.[85]

Rousseau wrote that the problem for the political thinker is to simulate the freedom, independence, equality, and happiness of the natural state through education. He believed that through a thorough and continuing commitment to education the natural goodness, independence, self-love, compassion, and equality of human beings can be brought out. He said that children should be treated as children (not little adults), acknowledging the stages through which they go, and adjusting their education to what the children are capable of at the various levels.[86]

Rousseau believed that at all stages of education, children must never desire what they cannot themselves provide in their immediate environment; they must be "protected against the seductive illusions of society—books, plays, social roles, imaginative speculation." The way to do this is to keep them busy with practical projects and constant exercise, and away from interaction with people, unless those people are "carefully rehearsed players in the planned environment" (11 of 15). All education of the child must be through experience only. What the teacher thinks the child should learn must be delivered to the child in a carefully controlled environment. Rousseau believed that "our mature sense of ourselves, and our ability to function as independent moral beings is decisively shaped by the way we are treated as children" (13 of 15).[87]

From the 1760s on, Rousseau was tormented by persecution mania, which caused him to live in seclusion in his later years. He completed his *Confessions* volume in 1765, but it remained unpublished until three years after his death. He believed that he was writing a unique work. While he had many imitators, Rousseau did create a new, intensely personal style of autobiography.[88]

Rousseau died on July 2, 1778, in Ermonville, and in 1794 his remains were transferred to Paris.[89]

Educational Thought and Writings

Rousseau published a series of books relating to education. He began with a novel, *Julie, ou la Nouvelle Héloïse*, which "records his dreams of love and his sentimental concept of virtue." In this novel we find his often quoted statement: "Nature would have children be children before they are men. If we attempt to pervert that order, we produce only forward fruit, which has neither richness nor flavor, and will soon decay."[90]

Emile

In 1762 both *The Social Contract* and *Emile ou de l'éducation* (On education) were published. *The Social Contract,* which was intended to follow *Emile,* appeared first, strengthening the misconception that the two works were independent of each other. The purpose behind writing *Emile* was to counter challenges to his *Discourse* argument by showing that "man" is not originally evil *and* that it is the teaching and utilization of the sciences, not the possession of knowledge, that is at fault when an increase in knowledge corrupted a man. *Emile* is "intended to provide an alternative basis for society, free of the flaws afflicting the present one, which mishandled the sciences and the arts to blunt and twist the searching soul of man."[91]

Rousseau had no special credentials to dispense educational advice. Initially he discounted education "as a manipulative device of an evil society." After he was asked to write a tract on education, he suddenly began to say that the right kind of education could be used to better society (62). Few people recognized how revolutionary was his thesis that the child was important as himself, and should be considered a self-active soul. Rousseau saw the primary purpose of education as identifying and drawing out the special nature of childhood. Emphasis was placed on *learning about* children rather than on controlling them through physical and psychological abuse. He encouraged interest in the *process* of growing up rather than just in its end product (63).[92] Kessen quotes a series of Rousseau postulates in agreeing with Claparède that Rousseau's work marked the beginning of child study as a field of knowledge.[93]

Claydon says the main point of Part I is to substantiate robbing the child of innocence, and the abandonment of maternal duties such as care and sustenance of a baby by its own mother (related to Rousseau's own experiences, and what he did to his children, according to some). In citing the high rate of mortality in France, in children younger than eight years old, Rousseau said that children who were "delicately reared" were more likely to die than those not so carefully protected. Claydon points out this was not because of the "ministrations of a medical charlatan."[94]

An important point is made by Rousseau in his series of statements about the three places from which education comes: nature, men, and things. "The inner growth of our organs and faculties is the education of nature, the use we learn to make of this growth is the education of men, what we gain by our experience of our surroundings is the education of things." The only one we control is the education of men "and even here our power is largely illusory."[95]

Rousseau believed that the child engages his environment, using it to suit his interests. He actively solves problems through play, by testing and exploring in order to construct knowledge. The child can grow with little adult supervision, because knowledge "is not an invention of adults poured into willing or unwilling vessels." The characteristics of childhood include "the notion of unfolding patterns of nature within us."[96] By stating that children should be allowed to develop at their own rate and through their own experiences at their own speed, to develop a sturdy sense of self-identity, Rousseau became a "founding father" of "progressive" education. His discussion of the importance of sense experiences anticipates their inclusion in the educational recommendations of Dewey, Pestalozzi, and Froebel. In speaking of creative arts experiences, Rousseau said, "I would wish him to have no other master than nature, no other model than the thing itself." This is quite different from what was occurring in schools of that time period and later.[97]

Rousseau did not believe in habit formation. He wanted to avoid all rigidity, including schedules for eating and sleeping, and rules about the use of a specific hand or arm. He encouraged development of the child's self-control, as opposed to domination by adults. His "concept of negative education is based on the statement that "one should do nothing and await signs of interest rather than have a pupil who is neither disciple nor scholar." However, we are reminded that "indiscriminate questioning of grown-ups is to be encouraged; it takes knowledge to ask good questions; children are not able to ask many that are worth while."[98]

Rousseau's opinion about the education of girls formed the foundation for Book V of *Emile*. The volume depicts both the treatment of females as property rather than persons, and the education and marriage of girls. He said that a woman's education must be planned in relation to men. During the eighteenth century, growing numbers of affluent middle-class daughters received an education that made them both literate and acquainted with philosophy and politics. For these intelligent, articulate women, there was no acceptable alternative to marriage, for formal education and entrance to the professions were denied.[99]

Rousseau's view of education for boys was innovative, while his views on girls' education were quite conservative.[100] The education of girls has become an important issue in our own day, and was the subject of the World Organization for Early Childhood Education (OMEP) focus on the girl child during the 1995–1998 triennium.

According to Cleverly and Phillips, "the child, rescued by physicians and reformers, liberated from inane ideas by Locke and Hume, is brought to the center of human affairs by Rousseau." The bridge between *Emile* and the community of educators was built by Pestalozzi.[101] Rousseau's work was studied and incorporated by such diverse educators as Robert Owen, Montessori, Dewey, and Hall, as well as others of the twentieth century.

JOHANN HEINRICH PESTALOZZI (1746–1827) (SWITZERLAND)

Johann Heinrich Pestalozzi was born in Zurich on January 12, 1746. His ancestors were Italian Protestants who had come from Italy during the Counter Reformation. He was the second of three children, having a brother and a sister. His father, a surgeon, died when Pestalozzi was about five years old, leaving his family and a faithful servant, Barbara Schmid, affectionately known as Babeli, in difficult financial circumstances.

His widowed mother devoted her thoughts and energies to the education of her three children. In her devotion she was supported by Babeli. The devotion of his mother and Babeli had a profound impact on Pestalozzi. Babeli did not allow him to play with other children in the street—in order to preserve his clothes and shoes. Consequently, Pestalozzi did not learn their games, their ways, and their secrets. When he met the other children by chance, he was awkward and they made fun of him. The influence of his home was never forgotten by Pestalozzi, and to him, the mother was the ideal educator. As he was growing up in the security of his home, he became aware of the generosity and dignity displayed by Babeli, the poor maid, who had the power to bring out the same qualities in others. Perhaps here are the origins of Pestalozzi's belief in the innate goodness of man and his dedication to the poor.[102] Pestalozzi spent his summers with his grandfather Andrew Pestalozzi, the pastor at the village of Höngg, near Zurich. Here he learned to love nature and the work in the fields, and realized the dissimilarity between country and town conditions.

Pestalozzi completed elementary and grammar school, which he found dull and mechanical. Learning for the most part was memorizing words, long passages to be understood later. Teachers flogged. The cruel treatment of the young was the result of the prevailing belief of total depravity. According to this belief, children were seen as innately bad and opposed to learning, a condition to be remedied by beatings. Pestalozzi then attended the Collegium Humanitatis in Zurich, which offered theology, medicine, and law. The Collegium at that time had some very distinguished professors, among them Bodmer, who taught history and politics. The professors advanced the utopian ideas in vogue at the University of Zurich at the time. They had a great influence on their students, who came to despise wealth, luxury, and material comfort, and cared only for the mind and the soul, and the pursuit of justice and truth.

At the Collegium, Pestalozzi joined the Helvetic Society, a historical-political association. Now he took an active part in the life of a community of like-minded persons. His closest friends were the members of the Society. Its aim was to raise the country's moral standards. The Society published a weekly journal, *The Monitor*, which publicized its views. Because of the strict censorship in Zurich, Pestalozzi stated his criticisms as "wishes."[103]

In the fall of 1767, on the recommendation of a friend, Pestalozzi went to Tschiffeli's experimental farm in the canton of Bern to learn modern farming methods. Tschiffeli, in addition to being a knowledgeable farmer, was also interested in the welfare of his farm workers. Pestalozzi learned much from Tschiffeli and decided to become a farmer himself, thinking that he would be as successful as his mentor. He had not realized that Tschiffeli had financed his farm from his private income.

Neuhof (1768–1770)

In 1768, with a loan, Pestalozzi bought a farm in the canton of Bern and began to cultivate vegetables and madder. He called his farm Neuhof, mean-ing "new farm." His intention was to repay the loan in a few years. He mort-gaged it heavily to build a house on it. From the beginning, the project had difficulties. Pestalozzi did not have good business sense, and the land was poor. In 1769, Pestalozzi married Anna Schulthess, a beautiful, well-educated, and well-to-do woman, seven years older than Pestalozzi, who approved of his plans for a country life. For fifty years she shared his successes and fail-ures. Immediately after their marriage, Anna started a diary, which she kept regularly, and in which Pestalozzi wrote often. In 1770, they had their only child, a son, whom they named Jacob but called Jacobli.[104]

After the agricultural experiment failed, Pestalozzi decided to turn Neuhof into an educational institution for the poor. He wanted to rescue these children from poverty and adverse conditions and give them a simple education. Pestalozzi believed that agriculture could improve the plight of the people. He organized an experimental farm school where the children of the very poor might be trained physically, morally, and intellectually to live self-respecting lives. During 1774–1775, Pestalozzi and his wife began their work at Neuhof with twenty-five poor, abandoned children—six to sixteen years old—some of whom he had found in the streets. Many of the children had survived by begging or being involved with vice. The children worked in the fields; performed domestic tasks such as spinning, weaving, and household chores; and were instructed in reading, writing, and arithmetic, as well as in religion. The educational experiment was a success, and it was talked about far and wide. Money was offered to Pestalozzi to carry on with it, and he was advised to appeal to the friends of the humanity for help to extend his work.

In 1776, Isaac Iselin—the editor of the newspaper *Ephimerides of Humanity*, in Basel, and an admirer and supporter of Pestalozzi—published Pestalozzi's first of several appeals: *Appeal to the Friends and benefactors of humanity to support an institution intended to provide education and work for poor country children.* Iselin kept Pestalozzi's cause alive through the newspaper. Pestalozzi, hoping that he could improve the financial condition of the school, enrolled more children, which had the opposite effect. Parents wanted to be compensated for sending their children to school. Many children ran away during the night, taking their Sunday clothes that Pestalozzi had given them. The institution had to close in 1780 when the resources and the credit had been exhausted. However, the failure at Neuhof did not change Pestalozzi's belief that he could raise the standard of people's lives through education and that he could save children by educating them.[105]

When there was illness and misery in Neuhof, and no one to sow the fields, help came from Elizabeth Naef (1762–1836). She had heard about Pestalozzi's philanthropic work and offered her services to him. In no time, Elizabeth restored order, cleanliness, and productivity in the neglected farm. She cared for the family, and her common sense impressed Pestalozzi so much that he came to rely on her advice in practical matters. Elizabeth served as a model for the character of the brave, active, clever, gentle and devoted woman in *Leonard and Gertrude*.[106]

PESTALOZZI THE FATHER

While Pestalozzi was at Neuhof, he also tried to raise his son Jacobli. Pestalozzi had read Rousseau's *Emile* and tried to apply Rousseau's ideas to educate Jacobli. According to De Guimps, every step Pestalozzi took experimenting with Rousseau's system, he would stop and turn to his own observations, and he would compare his experiences with those of Rousseau's and the methods that his own mother had used to educate him. Rousseau, however, had neither a son to educate nor a mother to remember.

Pestalozzi kept a journal of his observation on his son's education. Through these personal experiences he discovered some of the faults of Rousseau's system and at the same time developed his own ideas. The journal is the first record of Pestalozzi's educational principles and shows how they evolved, and the first of a father recording his son's progress.[107] Following are a few excerpts from the journal: "Let yourself be governed by the child's love of imitation!" (42). "Do not overload the child." "Father or schoolmaster, avoid, above all things, hurry and excitement; let your work be done quietly and in order" (43). "Make the first step sound before moving; in this way you will avoid confusion and waste" (44). "Lead your child out into Nature, teach him on the hill-tops and in the valleys." "A father who guides wisely and blames justly must be obeyed by his child, but no unnecessary command must be given" (45). "Alternate his lessons with his games, and not curtail his liberty unnecessarily" (46).

Pestalozzi's son's education was unorthodox. Jacobli, who could neither read nor write by age eleven, composed a poem for his father's birthday. His mother wrote it from his dictation (49). Jacobli had received little preparation for practical life. He was not sent to school until he was fourteen years old. Later, Pestalozzi sent his son to live with his friend Felix Battier's family in Basel. He sent Jacobli to a school in Mulhouse and later apprenticed him to his business. He did not succeed either in his studies or his apprenticeship. Jacobli, a sickly child, became very sick while in Basel and returned to Neuhof in 1790. Pestalozzi was very upset and blamed himself for the illness. In 1791, Jacobli married Anna Madeleine Froehlich, the daughter of a family friend. Their first three children died in infancy, but Gottlieb (1797–1863) was the father of Colonel Pestalozzi, who became a professor at the Zurich Polytechnic. Jacobli became gravely ill in 1797 and died in 1800.[108]

Pestalozzi the Writer, Reformer, and Educator (1780–1825)

After the collapse of the educational experiment at Neuhof, Pestalozzi continued his belief in the possibility of raising the people by education. Iselin, who still believed in the soundness of Pestalozzi's ideas, offered to help him to bring his ideas to the public and encouraged him to write. Now Pestalozzi turned all his energies to writing.[109]

Illegitimacy, infanticide, and its punishment had occupied Pestalozzi's mind since his student days in Zurich, when two young girls had been condemned to death for infanticide. He had become very upset and would not believe that an expectant mother could commit such a crime against nature. He also felt compassion for the offenders. After a long study to determine the causes of infanticide, Pestalozzi wrote, in 1780, *On Legislation and Infanti-*

cide; Facts and Fancies, Investigations and Portraits, which was published in 1783.

In the book, Pestalozzi discusses the damage done by legislation and its powerlessness to prevent infanticide. In his opinion the best means to prevent infanticide is education. He suggests some form of marriage guidance. Pestalozzi would have parents, teachers, clergymen, and magistrates take every opportunity to use their influence to reform the manners, opinions, and conduct of people of all ages. Pestalozzi said that a girl resorts to infanticide because she wants to hide her disgrace. He raises the question if infanticide would be prevented if the girl is helped, and would society gain or lose? He recommends that the state ought to take over the child and be father to the orphans and educator to illegitimate children. Pestalozzi also makes suggestions for future legislation derived from the specific causes of infanticide.[110]

Pestalozzi's publications during this period present *his* ideas as he wrote them, free from outside influences. Afterward, at Burgdorf and later at Yverdon, things were no longer the same. Pestalozzi, too busy to write everything himself, entrusted much of the work to his collaborators, particularly Hermann Krüsi and Joseph Schmidt, who not only wrote but also interpreted Pestalozzi's work.

Stanz (1799–1800)

After the French Revolution (1789), the French, who wanted to spread their ideas to the rest of Europe, tried to control their neighboring countries through a series of invasions. This unprovoked French aggression resulted in the beginning of cultural nationalism in many of the attacked nations.[111] Pestalozzi, like the majority of his countrymen dreaded the French intervention in Swiss affairs, but by 1798 it was an accomplished fact. Swiss resistance to the French troops going through their mountainous villages on their way to Austria resulted in the killing of hundreds of men and women who fought the French. Stanz, the capital village of the district, was burned, including the church where the old and the infirm had assembled with the priest. Many children were left homeless and orphaned. The federal government shocked by these events took steps to repair the damage done and opened a school at Stanz for the children, of both sexes, over five years of age. Citizen Pestalozzi was named the director.

At Stanz, Pestalozzi put into practice all the educational ideas that occupied him for a long time. The children were gradually to participate in all the work necessary to carry on and support the institution. The time of the children was to be divided between work in fields, housework, and study. At Stanz, Pestalozzi developed the principles for a natural and logical method of elementary education. The institution was closed in 1800 because of the differing religious views between Pestalozzi and the local people.[112]

Stanz served as a model for the Pestalozzi Children's Village that was established in Appenzell right after World War II (1946) to care for the thousands of homeless orphans wandering all over Europe. It protected thousands of boys and girls six to eighteen years old. It followed Pestalozzi's belief: Give the children love and keep them busy.[113]

Burgdorf (1800–1804)

After Stanz, Pestalozzi went to Burgdorf, where he became a teacher at an infants' school, with twenty-five boys and girls from four to eight years old. Pestalozzi was given a free hand in running the school. He organized the children according to their abilities, a method that resulted in success for all the children. The inspector's report was favorable, and Pestalozzi was then appointed master of a boys' school at Burgdorf. At this school there were about sixty children from six to sixteen years of age. The curriculum included Bible history, geography, Swiss history, arithmetic, and writing. Pestalozzi resumed his educational experiments. All teaching started from three elements: language, number, and form. Pestalozzi was more successful with the younger than with the older students.[114] This was the result of the experiences he had gained from teaching and observing his son.

Pestalozzi's Educational Theories and Practices

As the Burgdorf school prospered, Pestalozzi explained his process and techniques in *How Gertrude Teaches Her Children: An Attempt to Help Mothers to Teach Their Own Children* (1801).[115] Pestalozzi had introduced something new in the field of education—the principle of *self-activity* in acquiring and using knowledge. He had said, "Everything I am, everything I will, and everything I ought to do has its origin within my self."[116] The application of this concept revolutionized the method of school instruction. *How Gertrude* describes a system of education as consisting of three equal parts—intellectual, physical, and moral. The central point of *How Gertrude* is that all truly human activity must be self-generated. The presentation of Pestalozzi's ideas is complicated, but *How Gertrude* contains important principles for the *new* method of teaching that have been widely accepted and have influenced subsequent teaching methods. The book's success attracted numerous visitors from the United States who observed Pestalozzi's method in practice.

How Gertrude consists of fourteen letters addressed to H. Gessner, Pestalozzi's publisher, written in the first person singular. Gessner, without Pestalozzi's knowledge, gave it the title in hopes to repeat the success of the earlier book *Leonard and Gertrude. How Gertrude* is abundant in rich ideas but is also repetitious. The following are highlights of some of the letters.

In the *Sixth* letter (83–90), Pestalozzi comments that the traditional subjects for instruction—reading, writing, and arithmetic—could not be regarded as the starting points of learning because their "elements" for understanding—language, line (form), and number—are formed in the child's own mind in order to understand the world. He therefore demanded that these "elements" should be developed in the child before he was taught the traditional subjects. These three elements were the instruments of turning perceptions into knowledge.

Letters *Seven* through *Eleven* (90–163) deal with elementary education and its subjects: the teaching of form, of numbers, and of language. For Pestalozzi, form and number are categories of thought, the foundations of the mathematical sciences. The first stage of geometry, or as Pestalozzi refers to it, the alphabet of form, consisted of the straight line and the square, which provide an elementary groundwork to which the plane dimensions of any object can be related. The next stage is the verification of the observed spatial relations, which is done by measuring. Measuring requires a high degree of accuracy. From the measuring of geometrical forms the child proceeds to their imitation by drawing; and only after drawing does he go on to writing (116–118, 122–126).

Number is the element of arithmetic, or counting in its simplest form. It is adding one unit to another. Teaching arithmetic must begin with the use of real objects and proceed via substitute objects (pebbles, dots) to abstract numbers. According to Pestalozzi, the aim of teaching elementary arithmetic is to raise the child's natural power of reasoning into an art (133).

In the *Twelfth* letter (170–181), he points out that his method is independent of the opinions dividing man (religion and politics). Therefore, it can be applied and be beneficial to all nations regardless of their religious beliefs or their form of government. The *Fourteenth* letter (190–199), which concludes the book, is devoted to the moral and religious training of the child.

The Years at Yverdon (1805–1825)

Pestalozzi spent the last twenty years of his career as an educator and schoolmaster at Yverdon. Some of the young instructors who had been students at Burgdorf now taught the elementary subjects under Pestalozzi's guidance, slept in the dormitories, and participated in the students' games. The children's tasks were firmly prescribed. They had ten lessons daily, starting at six o'clock in the morning. The primary educational principle was to encourage the development of the child's natural gifts and talents. In addition to reading and writing, geography, history, mathematics, and the natural sciences were taught. Music, gymnastics, handwork, and religious instruction were added to the curriculum, and later the classics.

The age span of the students was from about six to twelve years. Most of the boys came from middle-class families, but a number of nonpaying students were also admitted. Many European nationalities were represented among the 250 students. The program's objectives were "order and regularity, exertion without overstraining, alteration between lessons and games, and between lessons and games, and between one subject of learning with another." Because there were numerous French-speaking children, all lessons were taught in both French and German. The different grades of each subject were taught at the same time of the day so that the children could move from one level to another according to their abilities and their progress.[117]

The cornerstone of Pestalozzi's teaching method for all subjects was *observation (Anschauung)* and *language*. The students were guided to discover things for themselves. They were taught to observe correctly, to recognize the relation of things, and to express clearly what they thought they understood. Each course was taught by a specialist in the subject, who had developed it according to Pestalozzi's principles.[118] Yverdon became the center for educational experimentation to such an extent that almost every method found in modern elementary education had at least an embryonic beginning there.

Many visitors from all over Europe and America came to observe at Yverdon. From Germany came the philosopher Fichte, who made every effort to make Pestalozzi known in his country. In his *Addresses to the German Nation*, Fichte advocated for the Pestalozzian method of instruction of self-activity as the starting point for the new national education necessary after the collapse of the German nation, which was the result of the Napoleonic wars.[119] Froebel (1782–1852), another visitor from Germany, spent two years at the school (1808–1810) with his two pupils. He sent literature about the new method both to his brother Christoph and to the reigning Princess Sophia of Schwarzburg-Rudolstadt, urging them to introduce the method in their country. Froebel's theory was influenced by Pestalozzi's ideas, but Froebel disassociated himself from Pestalozzi in his theory as well as personally by stressing the differences between them rather than their similarities.[120] From America among those who visited Pestalozzi were William Maclure, Horace Mann, and Henry Barnard.[121]

After all these successes at Yverdon, things took a turn for the worse. The school began to decline due to dissension among Pestalozzi's coworkers. Pestalozzi's wife died in 1815. The school closed in 1825, and Pestalozzi died destitute in 1827.[122]

Letters on Early Education Addressed to J. P. Greaves

Like Comenius, Pestalozzi wrote a book on early childhood education, *Letters on Early Education Addressed to J. P. Greaves,* during the years 1818–1819.[123] The *Letters* illustrate Pestalozzi's ideas about the relationship between mother and child in their most developed form. Pestalozzi maintains that education should begin at birth, proclaiming the most important period in the child's development is from birth to the end of the first year. He concedes that both the infant's reaction to his mother's care and the mother's response to the infant's needs are instinctive. A mother's love is the most formative influence on a child's development. He also says that the mother's fitness for educating her child depends on her will to educate herself (10).

There are thirty-four *Letters*. Following are some highlights of the topics covered in the *Letters*. Education during this period has been universally overlooked (*Letter I*, 9). The mother is qualified by the Creator, to be the first teacher. She needs to be wise and firm and resist the child's selfishness. His moral nature must be developed as early as possible (*Letter II*, 12–15). The child's faculties are to be cultivated equally (*Letter IV*, 20). Pestalozzi appeals to mothers to develop in the child the innate principle of love and faith (*Letter V*, 29). The mother is the principal agent in the cause of humanity. Affection is the primary motive in early education (*Letter VII*, 37). Kindness is the agent of education (*Letter XI*, 57). Fear of punishment is not a restraining power. Severity makes the child timid and encourages aggression and cowardice (*Letter XIII*, 68–69).[124] Morality is the result of developing in the child the sentiments of love and affection (*Letter XV*, 74–78). Children should be encouraged to draw first from nature and later from objects from their surroundings (*Letter XXIV*, 111–123). Children should not memorize anything without understanding it (*Letter XXVIII*, 14–145). Let the child be an *agent* in intellectual education. Encourage self-activity (*Letter XXIX*, 146–150).

In spite of his successes, Pestalozzi did not escape opposition. According to Silber, there are several explanations for the opposition to his *method*. Some was due to envy of Pestalozzi's success and fame; other opposition was due to the anxiety of religious and political orthodoxies who wanted to preserve the existing practices.[125]

Although Pestalozzi's educational system was primarily developed to rescue poor children, it also became popular with well-to-do parents. Some of Pestalozzi's assistants and students opened private Pestalozzian schools for upper-class children in many European countries, such as Anton Gruener in Frankfurt. The many visitors helped spread Pestalozzi's ideas to all parts of the world, including the United States.

Pestalozzianism in the United States

Joseph Neef and Herman Krüsi, two of Pestalozzi's associates, came to the United States and introduced his educational reforms. William Maclure who had visited Pestalozzi at Yverdon in 1804 and in 1805, wanted Pestalozzi to come to America to help with a school he planned to establish in Philadelphia. Pestalozzi was sixty years old then and did not speak English. He recommended that Maclure contact Neef, who was directing a Pestalozzian school in Paris. While in Paris on a business trip, Maclure met Neef and engaged him to start a Pestalozzian school in Philadelphia, which he funded. Thus, the first Pestalozzian school in the United States was opened in a suburb of Philadelphia in 1809.[126]

Horace Mann (1796–1859), an ardent admirer of the Pestalozzian institutions he observed in Europe, tried to implement some of Pestalozzi's ideas in the American schools around 1830. He proposed to have children observe nature, question their parents, review their own experiences, read books, and report to the class what they had learned. Henry Barnard (1811–1900), another Pestalozzi admirer, urged teachers to deal with concrete things, to teach orally and visually, to avoid the tyranny of the textbook. He urged schools to have cabinets of real objects as subjects of oral instruction in the field of the pupils' everyday observation and experience. The Massachusetts normal schools at Westfield and Bridgewater began to build science collections and to employ demonstration and object teaching.[127]

When Barnard became superintendent of the Connecticut school system (1838), for the first time ever, he conducted a six-week teachers' institute for about thirty men. He presented the life, character, and teaching methods of Pestalozzi. Barnard, first as editor of the *Connecticut Common School Journal* (1838–1842) and later as publisher of the *American Journal of Education* (1856–1881), published several articles on Pestalozzi.[128]

William T. Harris (1835–1909) was another proponent of Pestalozzi. As a superintendent of the St. Louis public schools (1868–1880), he introduced the teaching of *natural sciences* in the elementary schools according to the methods of Pestalozzi, which included detailed observation and descriptions by the children. He summarized these activities in his annual reports.[129]

One of the first teacher-training institutions in the United States was Westfield Normal School (1839), in Westfield, Massachusetts. Object teaching was a feature of the normal school since it was established. It was the first to introduce Pestalozzian methods to both teacher training and to public schools. All subjects in the normal school were taught by the object method. The subjects required to be taught in the public schools were also taught by the object method. In order that the students of the normal school have an opportunity to observe the application of their methods to real children, the town provided them with a school for observation, where they could add experience to their theories.[130]

The highly formalized object teaching that was developed and spread by the State Normal School at Oswego, New York, was introduced from England. Because the object teaching had become formal—not what Pestalozzi had developed and wrote about—it was easily transmitted by means of outlines, lesson plans, and manuals. Object teaching became a fad. Barnard became annoyed with this fad and remarked that educators for twenty-five years were urging schoolwork to be based on pupils' observations and experiences, but now (1860–1861) a lot of model object-lesson books were being published. The danger, he said, is that teachers will copy the methods of some manual without understanding the principles, without considering the ages of the pupils, and object teaching can be made as mechanical and monotonous as the teaching it was originally to replace.[131]

CHAPTER SUMMARY

Comenius and Pestalozzi advocated that education should begin at birth with the mother as the first teacher. They wrote books with definitive plans to guide the mother in that role. They encouraged the education of women. Neither Comenius nor Pestalozzi indicated that children should participate in group education before the age of six. Comenius advised that children less than six years should not be removed from their mothers and given to teachers. Among his reasons is that the young child requires more supervision and care than a teacher can provide. Pestalozzi said that "mother's love is the first agent in education."[132]

Comenius introduced pictures into children's books and identified specific content for the mental development of children. Pestalozzi introduced observation of child behavior, made observation the basis for all knowledge, and advocated that education can raise the standard of people's lives. Both recognized the importance of geography, universal education, graded elementary schools, and reformed teaching methodology.

Locke and Rousseau each addressed parental and home education. Locke's letters presented teaching methods, discussed the importance of good physical care for the child, and suggested discipline techniques. Rousseau believed in natural education. His work marked the beginning of child study as a field of knowledge.

All of these men's ideas about the education of the young were influenced by their own experiences within their families and the world and its events surrounding them. In turn their ideas influenced subsequent generations of philosophers/educators and practitioners.

NOTES

1. Shulamith Shahar, trans. Chaya Galai, *Childhood in the Middle Ages* (London: Routledge, 1992), 171–172.

2. Shahar, *Childhood in the Middle Ages*, 2, 121–144; see also: Lloyd deMause, "The Evolution of Childhood," in *The History of Childhood*, ed. Lloyd deMause (New York: Psychohistory Press, 1974), 25–39.

3. Barbara A. Hanawalt, "Narratives of a Nurturing Culture: Parents and Neighbors in Medieval England," *Essays in Medieval Studies* 12 (1995) <http://www.luc.edu/publications/medieval/vol12/hanawalt.html>, 5–6 of 12; and Barbara Kaye Greenleaf, *Children through the Ages: A History of Childhood* (New York: Barnes & Noble Books, 1978), 26.

4. Greenleaf, *Children through the Ages*, 27–28.

5. See: Philippe Ariès, *Centuries of Childhood: A Social History of Family Life*. Trans. Robert Baldick (New York: Vintage Books, 1962).

6. Shahar, *Childhood in the Middle Ages*, 1, 3.

7. Lloyd deMause, "The Evolution of Childhood," 7–8, 9–21; John Cleverly and D. C. Phillips, *Visions of Childhood: Influential Models from Locke to Spock*, rev. ed. (New York: Teachers College Press, 1986), 7; Shahar, *Childhood in the Middle Ages*, 109–111; and John Locke, *Some Thoughts Concerning Education*, 159, in Ilse Forest, *Preschool Education: A Historical and Critical Study* (New York: Macmillan, 1927), 117.

8. Shahar, *Childhood in the Middle Ages*, 6.

9. Jerome Kroll, "The Concept of Childhood in the Middle Ages," *Journal of the History of the Behavioral Sciences* 13, no. 4 (October 1977), 384–393, passim; and Hanawalt, "Narratives of a Nurturing Culture," 1, 5, 6. See also: James A. Schultz, *The Knowledge of Childhood in the German Middle Ages, 1100–1350* (Philadelphia, University of Pennsylvania Press, 1995).

10. E. H. Gwynne-Thomas, *A Concise History of Education to 1900 A.D.* (Lanham, MD: University Press of America, 1981), 68; and Greenleaf, *Children through the Ages*, 41, 42.

11. Institute for Learning Technologies, "Enlightenment," "Empiricism," "Social Contract," "John Locke," "Jean Jacques Rousseau" in *Concise Columbia Encyclopedia* (New York: Columbia University Press, 1991); available from <http://www.ilt.columbia.edu/academic/digitexts/notes/enlightenment.html>;   <http://www.ilt.columbia.edu/academic/

digitexts/notes/empiricism.html>; <http://www.ilt.columbia.edu/academic/digitexts/notes/locke/bio_JL.html>; <http://www.ilt.columbia.edu/academic/digitexts/notes/rousseau/bio_rousseau.html>; Internet accessed 18 May 1997; and Greenleaf, *Children through the Ages,* 45, 62. [For artists' depictions of children of the 1700s, see: *The New Child: British Art and the Origin of Modern Childhood:* An exhibition at the University Art Museum/Pacific Film Archive, University of California at Berkeley, 23 August–19 November, 1995. Online: Available from <http://www.uampfa.berkeley.edu/exhibits/newchild/learns.html>; Internet accessed 26 April 1997.]

12. Shahar, *Childhood in the Middle Ages,* 99.

13. Ibid., 100.

14. Greenleaf, *Children through the Ages,* 46; and Ariès, *Centuries of Childhood,* 50.

15. Hanawalt, "Narratives of a Nurturing Culture," 9.

16. Shahar, *Childhood in the Middle Ages,* 174, 175.

17. James Bruce Ross, "The Middle-Class Child in Urban Italy, Fourteenth to Early Sixteenth Century," in *The History of Childhood,* ed. Lloyd deMause (New York: Psychohistory Press, 1974), 211; Shahar, *Childhood in the Middle Ages,* 105, 174, 175; and Cleverly and Phillips, *Visions of Childhood: Influential Models from Locke to Spock,* 9.

18. Shahar, *Childhood in the Middle Ages,* 242, 173, 172.

19. Greenleaf, *Children through the Ages,* 32, 35; Ross, "The Middle-Class Child in Urban Italy, Fourteenth to Early Sixteenth Century," 212; and Shahar, *Childhood in the Middle Ages,* 175.

20. Ross, "The Middle-Class Child in Urban Italy, Fourteenth to Early Sixteenth Century," 211–212; Shahar, *Childhood in the Middle Ages,* 106; and Greenleaf, *Children through the Ages,* 38.

21. Shahar, *Childhood in the Middle Ages,* 177, 175.

22. Ibid., 187, 225.

23. Ibid., 209, 211; and Greenleaf, *Children through the Ages,* 33.

24. Greenleaf, *Children through the Ages,* 33; and Shahar, *Childhood in the Middle Ages,* 220.

25. Shahar, *Childhood in the Middle Ages,* 220, 222.

26. M. J. Tucker, "The Child as Beginning and End: Fifteenth and Sixteenth Century English Childhood," in *The History of Childhood,* ed. Lloyd deMause (New York: Psychohistory Press, 1974), 245, 246, 256; and Greenleaf, *Children through the Ages,* 52.

27. Greenleaf, *Children through the Ages,* 53–56.

28. Elizabeth Wirth Marvick, "Nature versus Nurture: Patterns and Trends in Seventeenth Century French Child-Rearing," in *The History of Childhood,* ed. Lloyd deMause (New York: Psychohistory Press, 1974), 260; and Joseph Illick, "Child-Rearing in Seventeenth Century England and America," in *The History of Childhood,* ed. Lloyd deMause (New York: Psychohistory Press, 1974), 322–323, 329.

29. Shahar, *Childhood in the Middle Ages,* 166–167.

30. John Amos Comenius, *The Orbis Pictus* (Syracuse, NY: W. C. Bardeen, 1887), xiv. The engravings and the Latin text are from the first edition printed in Nuremberg, 1658. The English text is from the English edition of 1727. For the first time, the English words were arranged to stand opposite their Latin equivalents. Ibid., iv. The idea for a book combining pictures with text is first mentioned by Comenius in *The Great Didactic, Setting forth The whole Art of Teaching all Things to all Men,* trans. and ed. C. W. Keatinge (London: Adam and Charles Black, 1896), 416–417. *The Great Didactic* is divided into Biographical (1–101), Historical (103–152), and the text (155–454). It is not indexed.

31. H. G. Good, *A History of Western Education,* 9th print. (New York: Macmillan, 1957), 158, 145; Will S. Monroe, *Comenius and the Beginnings of Educational Reform* (New York: Charles Scribner's Sons, 1900; reprint, New York: Arno Press & The New York Times, 1971), 2–12 (page citations are to the reprint edition).

32. Matthew Spinka, *John Amos Comenius: That Incomparable Moravian* (Chicago: The University Press, 1943), 24; Jan Jakubek, *Johannes Amos Comenius* (New York: Arno Press, 1971), 13.

33. *The Great Didactic,* 3. Comenius's recommendations for school reform are in Chapter XII. Ibid., 233–244. *The Great Didactic* was written in Czech (1632). Comenius

postponed its publication until his expected return to Bohemia, which was never fulfilled. The Czech version was published in Prague in 1849. A Latin version with additional chapters was published at Amsterdam in 1657, became part of the *Opera Didactica Omnia*. Ibid., 14.

34. Ibid., 4–12; Monroe, *Comenius and the Beginnings of Educational Reform*, 43–46; Daniel Murphy, *Comenius: A Critical Reassessment of His Life and Work* (Dublin: Irish Academy Press, 1995), 8–11.

35. Spinka, *John Amos Comenius*, 36–38; *The Great Didactic*, 7–8.

36. Murphy, *Comenius*, 16–17, 18; *The Great Didactic*, 103–104, 25.

37. *The Great Didactic*, 156.

38. *The Great Didactic*, 206–212, 213–217, 218–221.

39. Ibid., Chapter XVI, Universal Principles of Instruction, 264–278.

40. Ibid., 16, and Chapter XXVII, Fourfold Division of Schools, 407–410.

41. Ibid., Chapter XXVI, School discipline, 401–406.

42. Johann Amos Comenius, *School of Infancy: An Essay on the Education of Youth during the First Six Years*, ed. with introduction and notes by Will S. Monroe (Boston: D. C. Heath, 1896), v, xi; *The Great Didactic*, 15. *School of Infancy* is an elaboration of Chapter XXVIII, Sketch of the Mother-School. Ibid., 411–417. Did Comenius introduce parent education after the Middle Ages?

43. Comenius was not the first one concerned with the education of women. Juan Luis Vives (1492–1540), a Spanish humanist who taught at Oxford, wrote *On the Education of a Christian Woman* in 1523, commissioned by Queen Catherine of England (Catherine of Aragon), first wife of Henry VIII. Lawrence a Cremin, *American Education: The Colonial Experience, 1607–1783* (New York: Harper Torchbooks, 1970), 88.

44. *School of Infancy*, 10–11, 16, 80. Did Comenius predict Froebel's kindergarten when he said: "Whoever has within his house youth . . . possesses a garden in which celestial plantlets are sown, watered, bloom and flourish"? Ibid., 11.

45. *School of Infancy*, 23–34. Does Comenius imply some "bonding" between mother and infant through nursing?

46. Ibid., 35–43; 44–49. Comenius was the first of the early educators to recognize the importance of geography as a study subject. Ibid., 39. For Comenius's influence on the early education curriculum, see V. Celia Lascarides, "Comenius's Reflections in Selected U.S.A. Preschools," in *Comenius' Heritage and Education of Man for the 21st Century*, ed. Vera Mišurcová (Prague: Charles University, Comenius Institute of Education, 1992), 245–248; and idem, "John Amos Comenius: Reflections in the New World," in *History of International Relations in Early Childhood Education*, ed. Vera Mišurcová and Jaroslav Kota (Prague: Charles University, 1991), 121–135.

47. *School of Infancy*, 32–34, 42, 45. There is a similarity of Comenius's ideas about play and those of Plato presented in Chapter 1 in this volume.

48. *Orbis Pictus*, iii–v.

49. Murphy, *Comenius*, 197.

50. The list of the topics is in "An Index of the Titles," n.p. There is a similarity of methods teaching the alphabet by Comenius and by the Romans discussed in Chapter 1 in this volume.

51. Dagmar Čapková, "J. A. Comenius's *Orbis Pictus* in Its Conception as a Textbook for the Universal Education of Children," *Paedagogica Historica* 10, 1 (1970): 12.

52. Paul H. Hanus, *Educational Aims and Educational Values* (New York: Macmillan, 1899), 209. Houghton Library at Harvard University has a 1649 copy of the *Janua*, signed in two places at the end leaf by a "Goell Iacoomis." Copy examined February 20, 1999.

53. Joseph Needham, *Teacher of Nations* (Cambridge, Eng.: Cambridge University Press, 1942), 40.

54. Robert F. Young, *Comenius in England* (Oxford: Oxford University Press, 1932), 39. The book has ten documents written by Comenius while in London—September 1641 to June 1642—translated by Young.

55. There is some confusion about the identity of Mr. Winthrop whom Mather mentioned. No record indicates that Governor John Winthrop of Massachusetts was in England at that time. His son, later the governor of Connecticut, was in England at that time, and may have extended the invitation to Comenius. Cotton Mather, *Magnalia Christi Americana*

(New Haven, 1820), II, iv, 10, quoted in Albert Matthews, "Comenius and Harvard College," *Publications of the Colonial Society of Massachusetts*, vol. XXI (1919): 146.

56. Spinka, *John Amos Comenius*, 98–99.

57. Monroe, *Comenius and the Beginnings of Educational Reform*, 63–68.

58. Ibid., 72–74; Murphy, *Comenius*, 41–44.

59. *School of Infancy*, xiv. A complete list of Comenius's writings is in the appendix of *The Great Didactic*, 461–468. Those written in Czech are marked.

60. M. V. C. Jeffreys, *John Locke: Prophet of Common Sense* (London: Methuen, 1967), 3.

61. E. S. de Beer ed., *The Correspondence of John Locke: Introduction, Letters Nos. 1–461* (London: Oxford University Press, 1976), #1128, 13 April 1689, I: 601–604.

62. Jeffreys, *John Locke: Prophet of Common Sense*, 5–7.

63. John Locke, *Two Treatises of Government*, with an introduction by Thomas I. Cook (New York: Hafner Publishing Company, 1947), vii; Jeffreys, *John Locke: Prophet of Common Sense*, 20, 21; and de Beer., *The Correspondence of John Locke*, I: xvii.

64. F. W. Garforth, ed., *John Locke: Some Thoughts Concerning Education* [Abridged with an Introduction and Commentary] (Woodbury, NY: Barron's Educational series, Inc., 1964), 2; and Jeffreys, *John Locke: Prophet of Common Sense*, 23.

65. Jeffreys, *John Locke: Prophet of Common Sense*, 5.

66. Locke, *Two Treatises of Government*, vii, viii.

67. Jeffreys, *John Locke: Prophet of Common Sense*, 33.

68. Ibid., 35.

69. Ibid., 32.

70. Ibid., 60; Jeffreys, *John Locke: Prophet of Common Sense*, 50–51; and Garforth, *John Locke: Some Thoughts Concerning Education*, 10.

71. Jeffreys, *John Locke: Prophet of Common Sense*, 55.

72. Ibid., 51.

73. de Beer, *The Correspondence of John Locke*, August 1685, I: 829, 729–734, 22; and Jeffreys, *John Locke: Prophet of Common Sense*, 86.

74. Garforth, *John Locke: Some Thoughts Concerning Education*, 178; and Jeffreys, *John Locke: Prophet of Common Sense*, 86.

75. Jeffreys, *John Locke: Prophet of Common Sense*, 61, 86; and Garforth, *John Locke: Some Thoughts Concerning Education*, 91.

76. de Beer, *The Correspondence of John Locke*. I: 807, 681–682, 24; and Jeffreys, *John Locke: Prophet of Common Sense*, 99.

77. de Beer, *The Correspondence of John Locke*. January 1685? I: 845, 788–791, 5; March 1686, I: 790.

78. Ibid., 19 April [1687], I: 929, 183; 943, 219–225, 5 July 1687, 222; 6 February 1688, I: 999, 344–345; and Ilse Forest, *Preschool Education: A Historical and Critical Study* (New York: Macmillan, 1927), 117.

79. Garforth, *John Locke: Some Thoughts Concerning Education*, 91; Jeffreys, *John Locke: Prophet of Common Sense*, 51, 86; and de Beer, *The Correspondence of John Locke*. 18 January 1689, I: 1098, 534–553.

80. Forest, *Preschool Education: A Historical and Critical Study*, 114–115; and Jeffreys, *John Locke: Prophet of Common Sense*, 55.

81. de Beer, *The Correspondence of John Locke*. 28 January 1685? I: 809 to Mary Clarke, 686–689.

82. Jeffreys, *John Locke: Prophet of Common Sense*, 55, 58.

83. Ibid., 51.

84. Jean Jacques Rousseau, *The Social Contract and Discourses*, trans. with an introduction by G. D. H. Cole (New York: E. P. Dutton, 1950), ix.

85. Leslie F. Claydon, ed., *Rousseau on Education* (London: Collier-Macmillan, 1969), 3; Jean Jacques Rousseau, *The Creed of a Priest of Savoy*, trans. with an introduction by Arthur H. Beattie (New York: Frederick Ungar, 1956), ix; Jean Jacques Rousseau, "An Expository Letter from Jean Jacques Rousseau, Citizen of Geneva. To Christopher De Beaumont, Archbishop of Paris," in *The Miscellaneous Works of Mr. J. J. Rousseau in Five Volumes*, vol. III (New York: Burt Franklin, 1972), originally published by (London: T. Becket and P. A. De Hondt, MDCCLXVII), 209–234; and Jean Jacques Rousseau, *The*

Mandate of the Archbishop of Paris in *The Miscellaneous Works of Mr. J. J. Rousseau in Five Volumes*, vol. III (New York: Burt Franklin, 1972) originally published by (London: T. Becket and P. A. De Hondt, MDCCLXVII), 209–234.

86. Ian Johnston, *Introduction to the Eighteenth Century and Rousseau's Emile* (British Columbia, Canada: Malaspina University-College, 1996); available from: <http://www.mala.bc.ca/~mcneil/m31ecla.html>; <http://www.mala.bc.ca/~mcneil/emile.txt>; Internet accessed 18 May 1997, 10 of 15.

87. Johnston, *Introduction to the Eighteenth Century and Rousseau's Emile*, 10–11 of 15; and Jean Jacques Rousseau, *Émile*, trans. by Barbara Foxley introduction by André Boutet de Monvel (New York: Everyman's Library, 1966).

88. For further information on Rousseau's life, consult Maurice Cranston, *Jean-Jacques* (1983), *The Noble Savage* (1991), *The Solitary Self: Jean Jacques Rousseau in Exile and Adversity* (1997) (Chicago: University of Chicago Press).

89. Institute for Learning Technology, "Jean Jacques Rousseau," passim.

90. Beattie, *The Creed of a Priest of Savoy*, x; and Jean Jacques Rousseau, *Julie, ou la Nouvelle Héloïse* (Paris: Garnier, 1759), 478, quoted in Forest, *Preschool Education: A Historical and Critical Study*, 126.

91. Claydon, *Rousseau on Education*, 8, 12–13.

92. Greenleaf, *Children through the Ages*, 62, 63.

93. In 1912, on the bicentennial of Rousseau's birth, Claparède wrote that *Emile* contained explicitly or by clear implication all that was current and good in child psychology. William Kessen, *The Child* (New York: John Wiley, 1965), 72, 74, 75.

94. Claydon, *Rousseau on Education*, 15–16.

95. James William Noll and Sam P. Kelly, *Foundations of Education in America: An Anthology of Major Thoughts and Significant Actions* (New York: Harper & Row, 1970), 132, 133.

96. Claydon, *Rousseau on Education*, 27.

97. Johnston, *Introduction to the Eighteenth Century and Rousseau's Emile*, 15, 25.

98. Forest, *Preschool Education: A Historical and Critical Study*, 128, 134.

99. Johnston, *Introduction to the Eighteenth Century and Rousseau's Emile*, 1 of 12, 3 of 12.

100. Ana-Isabel Aliaga-Buchenau calls him reactionary. "Even in the context of his time Rousseau emerges as a very conservative voice among contemporaries such as Fénélon and Madame de Maintenon who propagated a more emancipated view of women." Ana-Isabel Aliaga-Buchenau, "The Education of Rousseau's Sophie and Goethe's Lotte: Could Romanticism Be Reactionary?" (Chapel Hill, NC: University of North Carolina at Chapel Hill, 1996); available from <http://prometheus.cc.emory.edu/panels/4D/A.Aliaga-Buchenau.html>; <http://prometheus.cc.emory.edu/panels/4D/A.Aliaga-Buchenau_fn.html>; Internet accessed 27 April 1997.

101. Cleverly and Phillips, *Visions of Childhood: Influential Models from Locke to Spock*, 72; and Kessen, *The Child*, 97.

102. Henry Holman, *Pestalozzi: An Account of His Life and Work* (New York: Longmans, Green, 1908), 19–20; Roger De Guimps, *Pestalozzi: His Aim and Work*, trans. Margaret Cuthbertson Crombie, from the edition of 1874 (Syracuse, NY: C. W. Bardeen, 1889), 1–4.

103. Holman, *Pestalozzi: An Account of His Life and Work*, 27–28; De Guimps, *Pestalozzi: His Aim and Work*, 5–6.

104. Holman, *Pestalozzi: An Account of His Life and Work*, 32–33; De Guimps, *Pestalozzi: His Aim and Work*, 12–13.

105. De Guimps, *Pestalozzi: His Life and Work*, trans. J. Russell, authorized translation from the 2nd French ed. (New York: Appleton, 1890), 52–68; pages 55–58 are Pestalozzi's *Appeal* to raise money; pages 63–66 describe the institution, the children with names and ages, how long they stayed, in what condition they arrived, and their accomplishments to date; idem, *Pestalozzi: His Life and Work*, 69–70.

106. In 1801, Elizabeth married Krüsi, the brother of Pestalozzi's colleague, and from 1805 was the housekeeper at Yverdon. Ibid., 71; idem, *Pestalozzi: His Aim and Work*, 37–38; Kate Silber, *Pestalozzi, The Man and His Work*, 3rd ed. (London: Routledge, 1973), 28.

107. De Guimps, *Pestalozzi: His Aim and Work*, 20–24; Silber, *Pestalozzi, The Man and His Work*, 27.

108. De Guimps, *Pestalozzi: His Life and Work*, 50–51.

109. Among Pestalozzi's writings during that period are: *Leonard and Gertrude* (4 volumes), *The Evening Hour of the Hermit*, and *The Causes of the French Revolution*. For a list and commentary on his writings, see De Guimps, *Pestalozzi: His Life and Work*, 74–116; a list of his writings in chronological order, see De Guimps, *Pestalozzi: His Aim and Work*, 295–297.

110. De Guimps, *Pestalozzi: His Life and Work*, 88–89, 116; Silber, *Pestalozzi, The Man and His Work*, 54. Many authors at the time were concerned about infanticide, including Goethe and Schiller, who used the plight of the unfortunate girl as subject of their plays and/or poems.

111. Peter Stearns, *Modern Europe, 1789–1914* (Glenview, IL: Scott, Foresman, 1969), 58–60, 87, 88.

112. De Guimps, *Pestalozzi: His Life and Work*, 125, 130–131, 132–133, 148. Pages 136–137 describe some of the boys and girls attending Stanz; Silber, *Pestalozzi, The Man and His Work*, 111–118.

113. Robert B. Downs, *Heinrich Pestalozzi* (Boston: Twayne Publishers, 1975), 43.

114. Silber, *Pestalozzi, The Man and His Work*, 119–132; De Guimps, *Pestalozzi: His Life and Work*, 174–178, 187.

115. Johann H. Pestalozzi, *How Gertrude Teaches Her Children: An Attempt to Help Mothers to Teach Their Own Children*, trans. Lucy E. Holland and Francis C. Turner, ed. with introduction and notes by Ebenezer Cooke (Syracuse, NY: C. W. Bardeen, 1894; reprint, New York: Gordon Press, 1973) (page citations are to the reprint edition). Even the subtitle is misleading; the book is too difficult for that purpose. Holman said that *How Gertrude*, in addition to explaining Pestalozzi's theories, is autobiographical. There is no Gertrude other than Pestalozzi himself, and there are no specific children other than all children. Holman, *Pestalozzi: An Account of His Life and Work*, 83.

116. Pestalozzi quoted in Silber, *Pestalozzi, The Man and His Work*, 133.

117. De Guimps, *Pestalozzi: His Life and Work*, 251–253, 267–269; Holman, *Pestalozzi: An Account of His Life and Work*, 104.

118. Silber, *Pestalozzi, The Man and His Work*, 207.

119. De Guimps: *Pestalozzi: His Life and Work*, 257.

120. Friedrich W. A. Froebel, *Autobiography*, trans. and annotated Emilie Michaelis and H. Keatley Moore (Syracuse, NY: C. W. Bardeen, 1908), 53–57, 78–80. Cf. Silber, *Pestalozzi, The Man and His Work*, 216.

121. Will S. Monroe, *History of the Pestalozzian Movement in the United States* (Syracuse, NY: C. W. Bardeen, 1907; reprint, New York: Arno Press and the New York Times, 1969), 39, 163, 164 (page citations are to the reprint edition). Chapter XI is a bibliography of the Pestalozzian movement in the United States.

122. Holman, *Pestalozzi: An Account of His Life and Work*, 118; Pestalozzi's Epitaph is on page 119.

123. Johann H. Pestalozzi, *Letters on Early Education Addressed to J. P. Greaves* (Syracuse, NY: C. W. Bardeen, 1898), 1–3. The German originals have been lost.

124. Pestalozzi has the same thought about punishment as Plato and Comenius did.

125. Silber, *Pestalozzi, The Man and His Work*, 157.

126. Monroe, *Pestalozzian Movement in the United States*, 39, 44, 97, 110–111.

127. H. G. Good, *A History of Western Education*, 9th print. (New York: Macmillan, 1957), 463, 464.

128. Monroe, *Pestalozzian Movement in the United States*, 164–168.

129. Ibid., 195–203.

130. Ibid., 137–139.

131. Good, *A History of Western Education*, 466–467. For more on Pestalozzianism at Oswego, see Monroe, *Pestalozzian Movement in the United States*, 169–185.

132. Comenius, *School of Infancy*, 81; Pestalozzi, *Letters on Early Education*, 9.

CHAPTER 3

The Industrial Revolution (1700–1850)

> I do not speak too harshly of the early
> Industrial Age; it is impossible to speak too
> harshly.
>
> —Louis Mumford [1]

The Industrial Revolution, which took place in Britain between 1700 and 1850, brought dramatic changes into the lives of children, families, cities, and entire nations. The problems engendered by the Industrial Revolution were the result of the confluence of theory and the practical realities of living in the time period following the Napoleanic Wars and the French Revolution. Prior to 1700, families produced the goods they needed at home using a domestic system of manufacture. Several innovations, such as the opening of the coke furnaces to smelt iron ore in 1709, and the silk factory in Derby in 1719, led to the employment of women and children as cheap labor in industry. Inventions such as the flying shuttle, the roller spinner, and the spinning jenny revolutionized the textile industry, causing many cotton factories to be built.[2]

The pronouncements of several theorists influenced the occurrences during the early and middle Industrial Revolution. The theories of the Manchester economists were exemplified by David Ricardo. He said that economic prosperity required that profits be reinvested in capital expansion to earn still more profits, even at the expense of workers. Adam Smith stated that government should not interfere with the natural laws of supply and demand. Malthus believed that plague, famine, and war would check population growth. He felt that interference with this process would cause the population to exceed the earth's potential for feeding it. The result of these socioeconomic theories (called "oppression through economics") and the changes they wrought was havoc in Britain. Small-scale business and petty bourgeois suffered at the hands of the capitalists. The vast majority of the population were dissatisfied with their lot and ready for disorder and violence.[3] Unemployed laborers and revolutionary crowds took to the streets.

There was a lack of social planning and coordination in early nineteenth-century Britain. Cities mushroomed in an unplanned and haphazard manner. The laissez-faire policies of liberal politicians left desperately needed social and educational reforms undone. The migration of the rural population to cities caused social change. Women and children met the factories' need for cheap labor. This changed family patterns, and the education of poor children became almost nonexistent. The tenements in which workers resided were crowded, poorly heated and ventilated, vermin infested, with totally inadequate water and sewage systems. Rudimentary government services, such as hospitals and schools, were totally inadequate for the burgeoning population.[4]

The unregulated exploitive industrialism led to the alienation of the industrial workers. They took no pride in craftsmanship, because the assembly line worker made only one part of the finished item. Not only were they separated from involvement with the product they were manufacturing, but they labored in social isolation. Increasing exploitation of child labor caused deformities in many children under the age of ten. They worked long hours, with unsafe machines, in poorly ventilated factories. There were no sanitary facilities and little food. The children worked steadily for twelve to sixteen hours a day without a break. At night they were locked fifty in a room to sleep. Eventually, there were parliamentary inquiries into the harsh conditions of child labor and laws were passed.[5]

Robert Owen was a utopian thinker, a social theorist, and an educational practitioner. He believed that many of the problems caused by the early Industrial Revolution resulted from a misreading of events by economic and social theorists. He said that industrialism benefited only a few, and privatism led to human exploitation and class conflicts. Owen envisioned a social order based on cooperation rather than competition, a utopian communist society. He wanted to humanize the factory system by eliminating its negative consequences on the health and welfare of human beings. He believed machine power could create a new social and economic system, because goods could be mass produced, labor could become more efficient, and this would create material abundance that should be shared equally by all. Owen envisioned total involvement by community agencies in human life, and nonviolent social change. The life story of Robert Owen bears testimony to what one person can do to enrich the lives of children and families.[6]

ROBERT OWEN (1771–1858)

Robert Owen was born on May 14, 1771, at Newtown, in Montgomeryshire, central Wales. In 1776, at the age of five, he was sent to a small private school, where the master taught him to read and write. At nine, he was sent out as an assistant in a country shop. He became a draper's apprentice in 1781, and the next year an assistant draper. At the age of fifteen, he moved to Manchester. He was invited to join the Manchester Literary and Philosophical Society (Lit. and Phil.) when he was twenty-two. This informal discussion group had been founded in 1781 by Dr. Thomas Perceval, the inventor of the water-closet. The Lit. and Phil. held weekly meetings where the members read papers to one another, and then the committee on papers decided which of them were worth publishing in whole or part. Owen was interested in science, his own technique of management, and the possible development of humanity by means of a rational system of education.[7]

In 1794, Owen formed his own company, the Chorlton Twist Company. He later met David Dale, an industrialist, who had mills in New Lanark, Scotland, which used the Falls of Clyde for the necessary power. Owen married Dale's daughter, Caroline, on September 30, 1799. Shortly after the marriage, Owen and several partners purchased the New Lanark mills. At the age of twenty-eight, Robert Owen became the managing director, and began the social and industrial experiments that would be spread over the next twenty-five years.[8]

Owen found that the children and families who worked in the mills were living under extremely poor conditions of housing and schooling. Dale had been compelled to resort to the usual methods of obtaining labor for his factories, including inducing families to settle near the mills, and importing children from poorhouses and public charities. Press gang methods obtained shipwreck survivors to work in the mills. Additional sources of labor were Irish immigrants, peasants displaced from the land because of the Enclosure Movement, and labor from the Highlands and Glasgow. Dale conducted his mills in a civilized manner. He was warmly welcomed on his visits to the factory, especially by the children, to whom he brought little presents. The New Lanark factory was praised in the *Annual Register* and by Professor Garnet of the Royal Institution as a model for the times, but it did have harsh conditions. The suffering of the children, who were forced to work in a temperature of eighty degrees for the good of the cotton, has been attributed to the general attitude of the age toward them.[9]

The forced labor of pauper children swelled the ranks of factory workers. Dale received children as young as six, seven, or eight years of age along with the nine- and ten-year-olds. The result of their work in the factory was deformity of body and little education. The children were required to work a twelve-hour day at the mill and then, following the evening meal, their education began. One can see that it would be difficult to concentrate after hours of arduous labor. Between the ages of thirteen and fifteen, the apprentices were released from their contract and most were anxious to get away from the mill.

When Owen took over the mill, he encouraged permanent settlers with large families to move into the comfortable houses he built. No longer were children of six, seven, or eight years employed in the mills. The parents were advised "to allow them to acquire health and education until they were ten years old."[10] Owen actually wanted the children to stay in school until the age of twelve; however, that was not practical because the parents were unconvinced of the necessity to lose the two years of pay that their children would bring home. In 1802, Parliament passed the Health and Morals of Apprentices Act, the beginning of factory legislation. Two Parliamentary inquiries done between 1814 and 1816 substantiated the conclusion that young children were being employed as factory workers and rarely were being educated.[11]

In his earliest days as the owner of the New Lanark mills, Owen was interested in the monitorial system invented by Dr. Andrew Bell and publicized and

disseminated by Joseph Lancaster. Bell employed older children as monitors to
teach the younger ones, using sand instead of writing paper. Lancaster
founded a nondenominational society in 1808 to foster the work of the monitorial schools, which became the British and Foreign Schools Society (BFSS) in
1814. Bell and his associates from the Church of England (the Anglican
Church) founded the National Society for the Education of the Poor in the
Principles of the Established Church. In the schools of both societies, the
monitorial system, which was economical, was utilized. Owen gave money to
both societies. He supported Lancaster with £1,000; however, when Bell and
his associates refused to eliminate doctrinal tests, Owen cut his contribution
to Bell's society in half, tendering £500.[12]

In 1812, Owen chaired a public dinner on the occasion of Lancaster's visit
to Glasgow. In his speech, Owen stated that "the primary source of all the
good and evil, misery and happiness, which exist in the world," is education.
Owen's educational assumptions were detailed in his short speech, which
stated that the differences between man and man are due to differences in
environment. The conditions of the environment are directly under human
control. These basic assumptions were later elaborated in his book *A New
View of Society*. Although Owen considered education valuable, he considered books of little value. According to his son, he confined himself to the
reading of newspapers and periodicals. Owen's educational philosophy was
derived from second-hand knowledge of the work of Rousseau in France, and
a personal visit to the schools of Fellerberg, Gerard, and Pestalozzi on a trip to
the Continent.[13]

Educator and Writer

Robert Owen opened the Institution for the Formation of Character at New
Lanark on January 1, 1816. With the assistance of his three new Quaker partners, in particular William Allen, a well-known scientist and fellow of the Royal
Society, Owen built a large new building to house the school and the community
lectures, classes, concerts, and recreation. When his partners either decided
that they cared more about dividends than children, or decried the lack of religious training, Owen received support from some members of the BFSS.[14]

The community school building had two floors. The upper floor contained two rooms, one ninety feet long, the other fifty feet long. Both had a
breadth of forty feet and a height of twenty feet. The larger room was used as
a lecture room, chapel, and the principal schoolroom for the older children
between six and ten years of age. On the lower floor, there were three rooms
of equal size. The middle one was designed for the youngest children to play
and amuse themselves in severe weather. At other times, the young children
would occupy an enclosed area at the front of the building. This was designed
to keep them in the open air as much as possible. The school included such
other amenities as a garden, a large outdoor paved area, and a ground-floor
nursery.

Children were admitted to the infant school from the age of two and began to learn dancing from that early age. The younger children learned a little reading, some natural history, and geography. The schoolroom for infant instruction contained natural objects from the garden, the fields, and the woods. Owen wrote that the examination and explanation of these objects always excited the children's curiosity and created an animated conversation between the children and their instructors.

The principal classroom for the older children contained desks arranged in the Lancastrian plan, with a free passage down the center of the room. There was a pulpit for the lecturer and galleries in which the children were to sit. The rooms used by the six- to ten-year-olds had pictures of zoological and mineralogical specimens on the walls. There were also basic maps that depicted the two hemispheres, each separate country, as well as seas, and islands. No names were attached to any of these geographic drawings. Singing lessons were given on a daily basis. Most of the instruction of the older students consisted of lectures to groups of forty or fifty children.[15]

In his *Essays on the Principle and the Formation of the Human Character and the Application of the Principle to Practice (A New View of Society)*, Owen wrote that children are liable to be impressed by the habits and beliefs held by their parents and guardians. These are only modified by the circumstances in which the children are placed, and to some extent the particular organization of each child. Owen believed that if a child were instructed rationally from infancy, he would be able to readily discover the sources of and reasons for his associates' habits and opinions. Owen's school was designed to foster these rational principles.

Owen hired James Buchannan to be the master of the infant school and Molly Young to be the nurse. According to the narrative of Buchannan's granddaughter Barbara, he marched the children around the room to the strains of his flute, marched them through the village to the riverbank, let them play there, and marched them back. Gymnastic exercises, clapping and counting movements, simple object-lessons, easy arithmetic, storytelling, children's prayers and hymns were taught.[16]

Buchannan later left New Lanark to become the master at a school opened by Lord Henry Brougham and James Mill, in 1818. Owen's description of his visit to this school was less than complimentary. Buchannan did not seem to have internalized the instructions given to him at the beginning of the New Lanark infant school. In his autobiography, Owen states that the first instruction given to his staff was that they were never to beat or threaten any child in any manner of word or action. They were not to use abusive terms and were always to speak to them with a pleasant face, in a kind manner, and tone of voice. The adults were directed to assist infants and children in making their "play-fellows" happy, with an emphasis on four- to six-year-olds taking special care of their younger peers. According to Owen, his instructions were readily received by Buchannan and Young, who faithfully adhered to them as long as they were in his employ. Owen said that because the children were trained and educated without punishment or fear of punishment, they were the happiest human beings he had ever seen.[17]

As previously discussed, children were instructed by real things, models, and paintings. They were also taught by the method of conversations. Parents were encouraged to come and see the children at any of their lessons or during their daily physical exercises. Robert Dale Owen, in *An Outline of the System of Education at New Lanark,* which was published in Glasgow, in 1824, stated that neither rewards nor punishments were countenanced, except those meted out by nature. Children were pitied rather than blamed for their misdeeds, on the principle that their environment and upbringing were responsible, not they themselves.[18]

Robert Owen wrote in his third essay, published in 1813 (before the school was built), that the child would be removed as far as practicable, from erroneous treatment by their untrained and untaught parents. Owen believed that the parents would be relieved from the anxiety occasioned by caring for children who were younger than school age, because they could now go into a situation of safety with their future school companions and learn the best habits and principles at the same time. At mealtimes and at nighttime, the child would return to its parents; therefore, the family would be able to spend pleasant, quality time together. Also, such an arrangement would lessen parents' absence from the mill. Owen charged the parents three pence per month or three shillings a year for each child so that New Lanark would not be considered a pauper school. He states that they paid this amount most willingly.[19]

Owen distrusted the system of teaching by rote. This is the reason visitor John Grisham, a professor of chemistry, was able to note in March 1818 that he saw "a great number of children, from one to three or four years of age. They are assembled in a large room, under the care of a judicious female, who allows them to amuse themselves with various selected toys, and occasionally collects the oldest into a class and teaches them their letters."[20]

Owen, a follower of Rousseau, would have preferred to defer instruction in reading until children learned about written language; however, he acquiesced to the wishes of the parents, and children learned reading at a very early age. Since finding books for young readers was difficult, accounts of voyages and travels, illustrated by maps, were used. The children were questioned on what they had read. The study of writing began with the children copying from models. Soon they were able to make up sentences on their own. They wrote many sentences that referred to their other studies, so that their interest would be retained. Arithmetic at the infant school followed a plan using Pestalozzi's system of mental arithmetic. The lectures on natural science, geography, and history were quite short, and the students were questioned by their lecturer. The children were also encouraged to ask questions, a practice unusual for that time period. A visitor from New York in November 1825 recounted that the recitations in botany were taught by means of transparent plates.[21] Girls in the school learned to knit and sew but not to cook.

The school intrigued and interested distinguished visitors from all over the world. The fact that philanthropy could be combined with the usual economic motives of a business concern was a novel idea that commended itself to people who were upset with the inhuman aspects of the Industrial Revolution. Although most of these people did not approve of Owen's political and religious views, they thought very highly of his system of training young children.

In 1824, Robert Owen purchased a tract of land from the Harmonists. He started an infant school at New Harmony, and when he left in June 1825, there were 130 children enrolled in that school. Robert Dale Owen tells us that these members of the preliminary society were boarded, clothed, and educated at the public expense. Owen and philanthropist William Maclure gathered scholars, scientists, and educators and brought them on the "boatload of knowledge" to New Harmony in January 1826. Maclure, who had founded a Pestalozzian school in Philadelphia, was in charge of the Education Society schools. In a July 4, 1826, letter to the editor of the *Review Encyclopedic,* Maclure stated that the Society had purchased the farm and buildings from Owen and that there were children between two and five years of age in the school. They were under the direction of Madame Marie Duclos Fretageot (the girls' teacher) and M. Phiquepal d'Arusmont (the boys' teacher), who had come from Philadelphia with Maclure. D'Arusmont taught "the useful arts" and mathematics. Professor Neef, his four daughters, and his son, all pupils of Pestalozzi, taught the children between the ages of five and twelve years. Pestalozzi's natural method of education, espoused by Jane Dale Owen, was used. In 1827, disagreements over education and finances caused Owen and Maclure to part company.[22] According to Johnson, New Harmony succeeded in chalking up a catalog of firsts in American cultural history, which included the first infant school and the first kindergarten.[23]

Robert Owen was invited to speak before the Congress of the United States in February and March 1825 and delivered two talks entitled *A Discourse on a New System of Society.* He also published his Fourth of July oration containing a declaration of mental independence, which he delivered at the celebration held at the public hall in New Harmony, Indiana, in 1826.[24]

Owen returned to Great Britain in the late 1820s and became a socialist, an "infidel," and a spiritualist. He died at his birthplace, Newton in Montgomeryshire, on November 17, 1858. Owen published two books, *A New View of Society* (1813) and *The New Moral World* (1836). Although neither of these is a pedagogical treatise, Owen did make many statements in these books regarding his philosophy and views of education.

Impact of the Industrial Revolution on Children and Families

The Industrial Revolution had an enormous impact on children and families, particularly those from the lower socioeconomic roots in society. Prior to the beginning of the Industrial Revolution, it was generally assumed that children younger than six years of age would be at home with their mothers. However, it was often the case that these young children were sent to school with their older brothers and sisters, or left with child minders. The origin of nursery infant education in Great Britain was in the babies classes of the elementary schools.[25]

In the rural society that preceded the Industrial Revolution, very young children assisted with farm work, household chores, and domestic crafts. When society shifted from an agricultural to an industrial focus, poor children, particularly those in the workhouses, were the victims. The "poor law guardians of child labor" apprenticed children as young as five, six, or seven from urban areas to factories and mills around the country. Under the terms of the Factory Act of 1802, the children were not supposed to work more than twelve hours a day. They were to be given some instruction in reading, writing, and arithmetic on weekdays, and religious instruction on Sundays. The provisions were often ignored.

Throughout the eighteenth century, charity schools had been founded to teach the children of the poor to read and write. The buildings could accommodate only a fraction of those who needed schooling. There was no one to make the teaching attractive; therefore, children would not stay in school very long. The fact that parents were unwilling or unable to forego their earnings propelled these young children into the factories. As a result, a large proportion of the children in Great Britain could neither read nor write.[26]

The Dame Schools held by elderly or disabled women in their crowded, unsanitary tenement apartments or cellars were often the recourse for children of working mothers. From the 1820s, the infant school movement provided an alternative to these ad hoc child arrangements.

The Role of Infant Education

Owen's infant school at New Lanark was based on two crucial principles that invited replication by others during the 1820s. The first principle stated that a person's character is formed of his constitution or organization at birth plus the effect of external circumstances acting upon that organization. Owen believed that both nature and nurture influenced the child. The second fundamental principle, stated in Owen's book *The New Model World,* is that the constitution of every infant, except in the case of organic disease, is capable of being formed either into a very inferior or a very superior being, according to the qualities of the external circumstances which influence that constitution from birth.

The New Lanark infant school, founded on these principles, attracted the attention of many prominent persons. Their school visits were one of the factors leading to the Parliamentary Committee on the Education of the Lower Orders in the Metropolis, chaired by Lord Henry Brougham, in 1816. As a result of the research done by this committee, Brougham and his colleagues decided to open an infant school. Liberals and nonconformists vied to found infant schools that represented their own point of view. The radicals sponsored the first English infant school, which opened in 1818 at Brewer's Green in Westminster with James Buchannan as master. Samuel Wilderspin became the master of the second school, opened by Joseph Wilson at Spittlefields in 1820. This school was sponsored by the Society of Friends.[27]

All of these infant schools were in the poorest urban environments, which may account for the rigid model of instruction and discipline they adopted. Wilderspin, in his book *Infant System for Developing the Physical, Intellectual, and Moral Powers of All Children from One to Seven Years of Age*, proposed the infant school as a remedy for juvenile delinquency. He wrote about opening and conducting an infant school; rewards and punishments; and teaching the alphabet and the rudiments of arithmetic and geometry. In his section on methodology, Wilderspin discussed teaching by objects, the aid of pictures, and conversation. He also discussed methods of giving children exercise, singing, grammar, and the elliptical plan of teaching.

When the school opened on July 24, 1820, Wilderspin discovered that he had to become a facilitator, because the children were strangers to each other and few of them knew their letters. He formed them into classes and selected two children from each class to act as monitors. He attempted to adapt elementary instruction to the capacities of very young children, by utilizing books, lessons and apparatus, and rote learning. Wilderspin's classes included instructional rhymes and rules, and a good deal of verbal repetition. He invented the tiered infant gallery, so that little children could sit where they could see and be seen by the teacher as the teacher instructed them by practical demonstration. He decided that infants should spend half the school time in an outdoor playground equipped with large motor equipment and wooden building blocks. The playground should have flower beds and trees for the children to learn about nature.

Wilderspin rejected the new developmental approach introduced by Owen, as well as the linking of education and social change. He also did not accept the reformist conservatism of the traditional philanthropists. Religious teaching had a prominent place in Wilderspin's school. His book *Early Discipline Illustrated* stated that corporal punishment is a last resort that might have been avoided if the child had come under previous positive influences. This is one of his few areas of agreement with Owen. The majority of infant schools, including the one run by Buchannan, used whipping and other forms of physical punishment of children.[28]

On July 16, 1824, the Infant School Society was founded in London. One purpose was promoting the establishment of Asylums for the Children of the Poor aged two to six years. The proposed infant schools were designed to teach children in large groups, using pictures and other lessons to pique their curiosity and "develop their capacities without imposing any strain on their faculties." Wilderspin felt that moral culture, the development of habits of self-governance, and feelings of mutual kindness were of greater value than the acquisition of useful knowledge.[29] Although the Society did much to promote the founding of infant schools until the early 1830s, it ceased its activities by 1835. Local infant school societies were formed in several industrial towns in the late 1820s and early 1830s.[30]

Lack of infant teacher training in England was a major problem. The Infant School Society had proposed a School of Practice Teaching, but a site was never found. In 1836, the Home and Colonial Infant School Society was formed. On June 1 of that year, the Society opened a training college in Holborn. Among the leading figures of the Society were Charles and Elizabeth Mayo, who wrote manuals on Pestalozzian methodology and lectured in courses at the new training college. In 1838, the college moved to Gray's Inn Road, and by 1843 it was training one hundred infant teachers a year.[31]

The age of steam power, which precipitated the second phase of the Industrial Revolution, occurred in the mid-1830s. Steam power was used for both factories and the new railways, which connected new factory towns near the coalfields to the urban centers of Great Britain. By the 1840s, the urban population was double that of the rural population. Thirty six hundred miles of railway line were opened, and there was increased Irish immigration. There was a substantial rise in the number of children as the birthrate rose. There was no significant fall in the death rate. One quarter of the population was under ten years of age. The living conditions of the working class worsened in the overcrowded and unsanitary slums around each new factory. When workers' real wages began to rise, they sought improved facilities for the care of their young children. Pressure was increased on the monitorial schools to admit children under seven years of age. The Factory Act of 1833, the first effective child labor law, prohibited employment of children less than nine years old. In 1842, this provision was extended to children under ten years of age in the coal mines. By 1867, it was extended to industries such as pottery works, match factories, and all factories employing more than fifty workers.[32]

The mechanization of industry meant that there were fewer tasks for which child labor could be used. However, if a working mother wanted to send her child (seven to ten years old), to school, she was left with a problem of what to do with the younger children. The easiest solution was to send them along also. This caused the elementary schools to open babies classes for children under the age of seven. It kept the older children in school, for if the young children were turned away, the older ones would have had to stay home to care for them.[33]

The infant school movement had convinced many school inspectors of the value of a separate infant stage of schooling. For this reason some new school buildings included an infant school and playground added to the schoolrooms for children above the age of six years. The idea of learning through play had won general acceptance. The infant school curriculum included drawing, music, physical exercises, sewing, knitting, and gardening. Some rudiments of reading, writing, and Pestalozzian lessons on natural objects and domestic utensils were also included. By 1861, the Royal Commission investigating elementary education found that "if two children enter an elementary school at the age of seven, one coming from a good infant school, the other uneducated, the child from the infant school will make as much progress by the age of ten as the other will by the age of twelve."[34]

Although the Newcastle commission of 1861 had declared that infant school was an important part of a national education system, the revised code of 1862 proved a serious setback for the movement. The code stipulated that twice as much money be given to a school or a teacher for an older child as for a younger one. School inspectors were required to ensure that the teaching of infants did not interfere with instruction of the other children. This forced teachers of five- and six-year-olds to begin preparing them for the standard examinations, firmly entrenching rote learning in the infant schools. It meant that infant schools were providing the benefit of a protective environment and Pestalozzian methods mainly for children of the more prosperous, skilled, working-class parents who could afford to pay the fees.

Owen's work caused a shift in beliefs during the 1870s and 1880s. Owen regarded children under the age of five as the most important part of his school at New Lanark. He also believed that the employer has the moral responsibility to treat employees well by paying them adequate wages, demanding only reasonable hours of labor, and ensuring provision for the education of children. Along with his work in the United States, Owen carried on a determined struggle in England to reduce child labor. While he was attempting to get Parliament to pass a bill to regulate child labor, children as young as five or six years were working summer and winter, fourteen to sixteen hours a day in the mills. The Education Act of 1880 was beneficial to the younger children because it made five the compulsory age for starting school. The subsequent expansion of infant schools did away with the need for the Dame Schools and allowed under-fives to attend general elementary schools. This provision continued in effect until the turn of the century.[35]

Infant Schools in the United States

Infant schools flourished in the United States between 1700 and 1840. Their purpose was to serve the children of working-class parents in the factories. Humanitarian factory owners, and reformers who feared for the morality and manner of their employees' progeny, furnished infant schools for children as young as eighteen months of age. This provided a program of periodic daily infusions of instruction in the three R's and morals.

In 1826 the New York City Infant School Society, the first philanthropic infant society in the United States, was founded. It had many socially prominent and influential men and women as patrons and members of its advisory councils. By the Jacksonian era, educators had changed their minds and now frowned on such early exposure to schooling. Some stressed the sensitivity of the very young and emphasized the importance of the mother in educating the toddler. Others, agreeing with Pestalozzi, said that young children needed a balanced, graduated education. Still others believed that early intellectual training might actually cause insanity. Although parents did not quickly accept these new theories, gradually they were forced by law to remove their very young sons and daughters from the public schools.

Amos Bronson Alcott pointed out in 1829 that infancy is a time of great and rapid change, and one of his contemporaries said that the child can and does learn a great deal more before the age of six than he can learn after that time. It was felt that poor children could make up for their disadvantages with early learning that would set them on the path to success in school and in life.[36] Youcha states that Owen's infant school at New Harmony, Indiana, was the direct ancestor of the Lanham Act Child Care Centers.

The early infant schools, which made it possible for women to work in factories, evolved from simple caretaking institutions to those that took advantage of the young child's interest in learning. Thus, the infant school idea flourished in the United States, sponsored first by churches and charitable organizations, then absorbed in some places into the public school system. New York City had fifty-eight infant schools when they were turned over to the public schools in 1853. The schools were seen as a way to counteract some of the deadening effects of poverty, and give poor children a head start before they entered primary school. The New York Public School Society (NYPSS) said that the infant mind is capable of receiving instruction at the age of two or three years. They said that it was a good idea to provide a place in which the younger children of the poor could pass the day comfortably while their parents were working, instead of wandering the streets, exposed to contamination of vice.[37]

Amos Bronson Alcott, a teacher and philosopher (and father of Louisa May Alcott), was also interested in infant schools. Alcott visited schools in New York and Philadelphia prior to accepting a position at a Boston infant school. Alcott's revolutionary theory of infant instruction was compatible with those of Pestalozzi and Owen. Alcott's essay "Observations on the Principles and Methods of Infant Instruction" called for the education of the "whole child" and praised play as the center of the curriculum.[38]

The "trickle-up" effect soon made itself felt. Infant schools were becoming available to children in privately sponsored facilities. In 1829, *The Ladies Magazine* commented that the topic of infant schools was becoming more and more popular, and "we have been told that it is now in contemplation, to open a school for the infants of others besides the poor. If such a course be not soon adopted, at the age for entering primary schools those poor children will assuredly be the richest of scholars. And why should a plan which promises so many advantages, independent of merely relieving the mother from her charge, be confined to the children of the indigent?"[39]

The decline of the infant schools, in the late 1820s and early 1830s, is more difficult to explain. Kaestle and Vinovkis examined school records and found that expert opinion began to turn against the idea of the intellectual force feeding of young children. Therefore, they suggested, people were returning to Pestalozzi's idea that the child should be allowed to develop at his own rate. The fact that a child *can* learn to read when it is three or four does not mean it is a good idea to teach him.[40, 41]

CHAPTER SUMMARY

Robert Owen influenced the education of young children in Europe and the United States in several ways. His schools at New Lanark and New Harmony demonstrated both the enlightenment of an industrialist and the social and philosophical ideas of a progressive. They incorporated many of the ideas about play and developmentally appropriate practices that are still in use today. Owen's ideas about avoiding abuse and punishment of children and treating them in a kind manner and with respect were novel for his time. Many of the practices he advocated were used in infant schools in the United States in the 1800s and continue to be used in quality child-care programs today. Owen's community education ideas formed the foundation for later adult and continuing education programs. His social policies and community ideas find expression today in educational and social communities around the world. Robert Owen built the bridge from the Industrial Revolution to the post–Industrial Revolution period.

NOTES

1. Lewis Mumford, *The Story of Utopias* (New York: Viking Press, 1962) quoted in Oakley C. Johnson, *Robert Owen in the United States* (New York: Humanities Press, 1970), 5.

2. D. Keith Osborn, *Early Childhood Education in Historical Perspective,* 3d ed. (Athens, GA: Daye Press, 1991), 31–32.

3. Gerald L. Gutek, *Historical and Philosophical Foundations of Education: A Biographical Introduction* (Upper Saddle River, NJ: Merrill/Prentice-Hall, 1997), 219, 221; and John Siraj-Blatchford, *Robert Owen: Schooling the Innocents* (Nottingham, England: Educational Heretics Press, 1997), 3–4.

4. Gutek, *Historical and Philosophical Foundations of Education,* 219–220; and Osborn, *Early Childhood Education in Historical Perspective,* 31.

5. Gutek, *Historical and Philosophical Foundations of Education,* 220; Siraj-Blatchford, *Robert Owen: Schooling the Innocents,* 3; Osborn, *Early Childhood Education in Historical Perspective,* 31; and Nanette Whitbread, *The Evolution of the Nursery-Infant School: A History of Infant and Nursery Education in Britain, 1800–1970* (London: Routledge and Kegan Paul, 1972), 4–5.

6. Gutek, *Historical and Philosophical Foundations of Education,* 218–220; and Siraj-Blatchford, *Robert Owen: Schooling the Innocents,* 2–3.

7. Margaret Cole, *Robert Owen of New Lanark, 1771–1858* (New York: Augustus M. Kelly Publishers, 1969), 5, 18, 27; and T. Raymont, *A History of the Education of Young Children* (London: Longmans, Green, Land Co., 1937), 69.

8. Cole, *Robert Owen of New Lanark,* 30, 43, 35; and Frank Podmore, *Robert Owen: A Biography* (London: George Allen and Unwin Ltd., 1906; reprint, New York: Augustus M. Kelly Publishers, 1968), 48, 53.

9. Raymont, *A History of the Education of Young Children,* 72; and Cole, *Robert Owen of New Lanark,* 44, 45–47, 48.

10. Raymont, *A History of the Education of Young Children*, 74.

11. Cole, *Robert Owen of New Lanark*, 47; and Whitbread, *The Evolution of the Nursery-Infant School*, 5.

12. Cole, *Robert Owen of New Lanark*, 77; Podmore, *Robert Owen: A Biography*, 105; and Robert Owen, *The Life of Robert Owen Written by Himself*, vol. I (London: Effingham Wilson, Royal Exchange, 1857; reprint, New York: Augustus M. Kelly Publishers, 1967), 191–192.

13. Owen, *The Life of Robert Owen Written by Himself*, 106–107, 249–252; and Podmore, *Robert Owen: A Biography*, 107, 109–110.

14. Podmore, *Robert Owen: A Biography*, 130; and Raymont, *A History of the Education of Young Children*, 75–76.

15. Podmore, *Robert Owen: A Biography*, 130–132; Raymont, *A History of the Education of Young Children*, 75–76; Cole, *Robert Owen of New Lanark*, 81; Owen, *The Life of Robert Owen Written by Himself*, 140; and Elizabeth Bradburn, "Britain's First Nursery-Infant School," in *A Point in Time: Readings in Early Childhood Education*, ed. Paula W. Smith and Verl M. Short (New York: MSS Information Corporation, 1973), 34.

16. Owen, *The Life of Robert Owen Written by Himself*, 287–288; Raymont, *A History of the Education of Young Children*; Podmore, *Robert Owen: A Biography*, 133; Cole, *Robert Owen of New Lanark*, 87; and Robert R. Rusk, *A History of Infant Education* (London: University of London Press, Ltd., 1933), 135–141.

17. Owen, *The Life of Robert Owen Written by Himself*, 139–140.

18. Raymont, *A History of the Education of Young Children*, 86–87; and Bradburn, "Britain's First Nursery-Infant School," 36.

19. Owen, *The Life of Robert Owen Written by Himself*, 289.

20. Podmore, *Robert Owen: A Biography*, 129.

21. Ibid., 143–144.

22. Raymont, *A History of the Education of Young Children*, 84–88; Podmore, *Robert Owen: A Biography*, 312; Alan R. Pence, "Infant Schools in North America, 1825–1840," in *Advances in Early Education and Day Care: A Research Annual*, Vol. 4, ed. Sally Kilmer (Greenwich, CT: JAI Press, Inc., 1986), 10–11; Vicky L. Grocke, "Education in New Harmony, Indiana;" available from <http//sun1.isub.edu/edweb01/newharm.html>; Internet accessed 25 May 1997; and Johnson, *Robert Owen in the United States*, 13.

23. Johnson, *Robert Owen in the United States*, 3.

24. Ibid., 21–64, 67–75.

25. Whitbread, *The Evolution of the Nursery-Infant School*, 24.

26. Podmore, *Robert Owen: A Biography*, 103.

27. Whitbread, *The Evolution of the Nursery-Infant School*, 9–10; and Podmore, *Robert Owen: A Biography*, 103.

28. Whitbread, *The Evolution of the Nursery-Infant School*, 13; and Forest, *Preschool Education*, 85.

29. Samuel Wilderspin, *Infant System for Developing the Physical, Intellectual and Moral Powers of All Children from One to Seven Years of Age* (Hall Court, England: Simpkin and Marshall Stationers, 1832), 86–87.

30. Whitbread, *The Evolution of the Nursery-Infant School*, 11.

31. Ibid., 21–22.

32. Ibid., 24.

33. Ibid.

34. Ibid., 26.

35. Ibid., 25–27; Johnson, *Robert Owen in the United States*, 5; Bradburn, "Britain's First Nursery-Infant School," 36; National Union of Teachers, Working Party on Educational Provision for the Pre-School Child, *The Provision of Preschool Education in England and Wales: A Report by the National Union of Teachers* (London: National Union of Teachers, [1941]); and *The Provision of Preschool Education in England and Wales* (London: The National Union of Teachers, 1984).

36. Priscilla Ferguson Clement, "The City and the Child, 1860–1885," in *American Childhood: A Research Guide and Historical Handbook*, ed. Joseph M. Hawes and N. Ray Hiner (Westport, CT: Greenwood Press, 1985), 245, 246; and Geraldine Youcha,

Minding the Children: Child Care in America from Colonial Times to the Present (New York: Scribner, 1995), 320.

37. Youcha, *Minding the Children,* 319, 320.

38. Pence, "Infant Schools in North America, 1825–1840," 13.

39. Youcha, *Minding the Children,* 320.

40. Ibid., 321; and Pence, "Infant Schools in North America, 1825–1840," 18–22.

41. The author of this chapter is indebted to Dr. Keith L. Miller for sharing his unpublished paper "An Educational Idea: New Harmony, Indiana in Its Pioneer Period," presented at the Annual Meeting of the History of Education Society, Philadelphia, Pennsylvania, October 25, 1997; to John Siraj-Blatchford for his book, *Robert Owen: Schooling the Innocents* (Nottingham, England: Educational Heretics Press, 1997), which addresses the relevance of Robert Owen's social improvement and community education ideas to current early childhood education practice; and to Valentina K. Tikoff for sharing her unpublished 1993 seminar paper "Infant Education at New Harmony: Parents and Teachers in a Community, But Was It Utopia?" TMs, History of Childhood Seminar Paper (Indiana University, August 19, 1993), especially pages 14–18, 30–32.

CHAPTER 4

Friedrich Wilhelm Froebel (1782–1852)

> Kommt, lasst uns unsern Kinder leben.
> (Come, let us live with our children.)
> —Froebel, *The Education of Man*[1]

The political revolutions in America (1776) and France (1789) had an impact on all aspects of life, including education, both in the countries experiencing them and elsewhere.

The traditional German schools and teaching methods did not include children below the age of seven. Learning in these schools was by rote, along with the formation of a few abstract notions. In this type of teaching, the children were expected to give back to the teachers the information in the same words that they had received. The child's faculties often were not stimulated. This passive way of teaching inhibited children's natural curiosity to explore and to learn.

Froebel, like many of his contemporaries, had become dissatisfied with the existing educational system and the rote teaching method used at all levels. He believed that this system was depriving the students of real knowledge and truth acquired through the student's observation and inquiry. Froebel wanted "to educate man in his true humanity, to educate man in his absolute being, according to the universal laws of development."[2]

Froebel was somewhat of a Pestalozzi disciple. Pestalozzi (1746–1827) introduced teaching by observation, *Anshauung,* and like Comenius, wrote books to educate mothers on how to educate their children. Although Froebel studied Pestalozzi's methods and was influenced by his ideas and recommended them to the reigning princess of his state, he distanced himself from Pestalozzi. Froebel wanted to develop a comprehensive educational system that would regenerate mankind and the German nation.[3] He believed that through his all-encompassing education of man, the whole German people would be united into a true community. He dedicated his entire life to the cause of education. He wanted children to be better understood than he was as a child. He also wanted to direct their activities in appropriate ways so that they might become useful to themselves and to others. Froebel wanted to contribute to the welfare of mankind by educating the mother for her role in her family.[4]

Froebel had been experimenting with different teaching methods and with school-age children at the Universal German Education Institute in Keilhau, for approximately twenty-five years before he created the kindergarten to provide for the younger child. Froebel is best known for the *kindergarten,* which was the work of his later years, after time, thought, suffering, and labor had matured in his mind and harmonized the results of his experiences. Froebel's belief in the supreme importance of early education led him to the creation of a method that was simple and philosophical, scientific, and religious.

His life is divided into the following periods: childhood and youth, 1782–1797; preparation for life and a profession, 1797–1816; the Keilhau years, 1816–1836; the kindergarten's establishment and development, 1836–1848; and Froebel's later years, 1849–1852.

FROEBEL'S CHILDHOOD AND YOUTH (1782–1797)

According to his *Autobiography,* Friedrich Froebel was born April 21, 1782, in the small town of Oberweissbach, a few years before the French Revolution (1789). He was the youngest of five sons[5] of a Lutheran pastor. His mother's death when he was only nine months old "conditioned his whole future development," Froebel wrote. For the next four years, Froebel was left to the care of servants. His father was too busy ministering to five thousand parishioners to supervise him or to direct his development. One wonders if the deprivation that he felt during these early years was the source of his commitment to maternal education and to the development of the kindergarten. His father, a theologian of the "old school," believed more in faith than in knowledge and science but tried to keep up with the times by subscribing to periodicals and carefully examined the information they provided.[6]

When Froebel was four years old, his father remarried. The stepmother became indifferent to him and created a psychological barrier as soon as her own son, Karl Poppo Froebel (1786–1824), was born. She started using the polite "Thou" instead of the familiar "you" when speaking to him. "You" is the form that is typically used among family members and especially appropriate when addressing children. Froebel felt isolated and became estranged from his father, who had no time for family issues. He developed a close relationship with his brother Christian, which lasted throughout their lives. Christian always interceded on his behalf.

As soon as Froebel was able to read, he was sent to the village school. Church and school had a mutual relationship at that time. The schoolchildren were obliged to attend church on Sundays and had their special places to sit. On Monday, each child had to recite to the teacher, at a special class, a suitable passage for children from the Scriptures used by the minister in his sermon on Sunday. Froebel attended his father's services and listened to his father's sermons. He found, however, the language of his father's hymns and sermons mystical and symbolic, "a style of speech, I should call a stone-language." Observing his father carrying out his pastoral activities and counseling his parishioners, Froebel saw the "inharmonious life of man." Many questions arose in his mind, but he could not go to his father for answers. His brother Christian provided him with some answers learned from his observation of nature. Froebel also began to integrate the lessons learned from nature into his ideas about religious life.[7]

Froebel became introspective at an early age. He was fully aware that things would have been different if his mother had lived. He turned to nature, which surrounded him, for solace and for answers to his questions. He concluded that the opportunities for growth and for self-expression that had been given or denied him were the result of personal relationships within the family. He felt that the motivation of many of his youthful actions had been misunderstood by his parents, especially his stepmother, and that his busy father never asked him for his side of the story.[8]

At the age of ten (1792), Froebel went to live with his mother's brother, Pastor Hoffmann, also a clergyman (44). He remained there until his confirmation. This household was the complete opposite of his father's. Here, Froebel found guidance from sympathetic adults, kindness, and liberty. He joined the town school taught by a clergyman and found companionship with boys of his own age. He studied reading and writing, and excelled in mathematics and religion. One is astonished by young Froebel's astuteness of what constituted effective teaching. This is how he described his two teachers: "One was pedantic and rigid, the other was large-hearted and free. The first never had any influence over the class, frequently scolding and ordering us about. The second led us with a glance, could do whatever he pleased with us but was not aware of his power. He was mild, gentle and kind hearted."[9]

PREPARATION FOR LIFE AND A PROFESSION (1797–1816)

After his confirmation, Froebel had to be prepared for some profession, as was the custom. His older brothers, Christoph and Traugott, were studying at Jena University. His stepmother had determined that he would not attend the university because of the financial burden, for she wanted her own son to be educated. It was very hard for Froebel that the stepmother was allowed to prevail and to fix his future at a lower level than his brothers.[10]

Froebel wanted to become an agriculturist and was apprenticed to a forester at the age of fifteen. He stayed with him for two years (1797–1799). The forester was too busy and lacked the skills to teach others. Froebel, wanting to learn, studied geometry and forestry from books he found in the forester's library. Nature provided him with examples of what he read. He studied plants and trees, became very interested in natural growth, and searched for the connectedness and unity of plan in the natural world and its significance for men. This sense of order and continuity that he found in nature began to dominate his thinking about education, and later was reflected in his educational practice (25).

At the age of seventeen (1799), Froebel went to the university of Jena, to deliver an allowance to Traugott, a medical student there. When Froebel reached Jena, he "was seized by the stirring intellectual life of the place and wanted to remain for a while" and gain practical knowledge. Traugott got their father's permission for Froebel to stay.[11] Froebel was thirsty for knowledge. He immersed himself attending lectures in geometry, botany, and natural history. The lectures in botany and natural history sharpened his observational skills. He became impressed by two principles: (1) the concept of evolution and continuity of plan, "the mutual relationship of all animals, extending like a network in all directions," and (2) "the skeleton of fishes, birds, and men was one and the same in plan." Now Froebel had the theoretical knowledge of what he had observed, the "inter-connection and unity of phenomena"—"Nature as one whole"(31).

Froebel left Jena two years later after having spent nine weeks in the student jail for debt. While in jail, Froebel studied Latin, hoping it would help him in his scientific studies; read Winckelman's *Letters on Art;* and read a translation of the *Zendavesta,* the ancient Persian scriptures, which broadened his ideas of religion. He also wrote a treatise on geometry, hoping to get a job. After Froebel was released from jail, he returned to his father's house, where he read German literature—Schiller, Goethe, and Wieland—and "Mappe du Monde littéraire." This book gave him a general view of all the sciences and fine arts in their various ramifications. It provided him with a general outlook of the whole human knowledge. With his father's help Froebel secured a farming job, but a few months later he was called home to help his ailing father. This gave Froebel the opportunity he was looking for to reestablish a better relationship with his father, who died later in 1802.[12]

In 1805, Froebel received the money he had inherited from his uncle. After consulting with his brother Christoph, he decided to go to Frankfurt to pursue architecture. A friend introduced Froebel to Anton Gruener (1778–1844), the headmaster of the Frankfurt Model School. Gruener, a student of Pestalozzi, had founded the school (actually two schools, one for boys and one for girls) to carry out the educational principles of Pestalozzi. Gruener was looking for a teacher and convinced Froebel to "give up architecture . . . become a teacher" (51). Initially, Froebel hesitated but accepted Gruener's offer as Providential when he learned that his papers from Jena had been lost. Pestalozzi was at the forefront of teaching and education at that time, and Froebel remembered having read about him in a paper in his father's house.[13]

In August 1805, Froebel went to Yverdon to meet and study with Pestalozzi for two weeks. He was well received by Pestalozzi and his associates. What Froebel observed at Yverdon was close to what he had figured education should be, a realization that made him "feel at once elevated and depressed" (53). The basic principle of all teaching was observation (*Anshauung*) and language. The training in Pestalozzi's school was based on a clear and firmly settled plan of teaching. Froebel was impressed by the method of teaching: The different grades of each subject were taught at the same time of the day so that the children could move from one level to another according to their abilities and their progress. The whole student body was redistributed for each subject taught. Froebel kept the plan and the methodology for his teaching (54). Froebel was inspired by Pestalozzi's ideas and resolved to return.[14]

Upon his return to the Model School in Frankfurt, Froebel was assigned to teach arithmetic, drawing, physical geography, and German to the middle classes. After his first lesson to a class of thirty or forty boys aged nine to eleven years, he wrote to his brother that he found something he had never known but had always longed for. At the public examination at the end of the school year, Froebel taught a lesson in geography to his students. He received the unanimous approval of their parents and the special commendation of his superiors. In the girls' school, he taught orthography in one of the elementary classes and preparatory drawing in another class. Now he wanted to learn more about the nature of teaching. Froebel was careful never to puzzle his pupils with anything he had not first thoroughly understood himself.[15]

In 1807, Froebel left Gruener's school to become a tutor, "to instruct and educate" three boys of a Frankfurt family. The education of minds other than his own, something beyond schoolteaching, presented a challenge to Froebel. Education as development, which was previously subjective for Froebel, now became objective. Froebel was to teach arithmetic and German. For arithmetic, he chose Pestalozzi's *Tables of Units,* and for language, Pestalozzi's *Mother Book.* He and the boys also spent time tilling the land that the boys' father had given them. Froebel tried to understand the boys by comparing their experiences to his. "All my thoughts and work were now directed to the subject of the culture and education of man."[16]

During the winter months, Froebel realized that the boys needed activities. He recalled impressing figures and forms, by properly arranging simple strokes on smooth paper. From these forms on paper, he made forms out of paper and progressively produced them in pasteboard and wood.[17] He introduced the activity to the boys. Probably this was the beginning of creating the occupations.

In 1808, Froebel and the boys went to Yverdon, where he supervised their studies and learned more about the Pestalozzian methods. They stayed until 1810. Pestalozzi's school was at the height of its success.[18]

Froebel's recent experiences as a teacher had convinced him that education was to be his life work and that he needed to be prepared for it. In addition to teaching methodology, he felt that a teacher needed to know a wide breadth of subjects. He also began to consider becoming a founder, principal, and manager of an educational establishment of his own. Regardless of which path he would follow, he needed to continue his university studies.[19]

In 1811, after a nine-year interval, Froebel went to the University of Göttingen to prepare himself to become an educator. Rather unexpectedly, he inherited from his aunt, his mother's sister, the means to pursue his much-desired studies. His goals were to find a scientific way to educate man and to find one law that applied to both man and nature.[20] In 1812, Froebel went to Berlin to hear Professor Weiss lecturing in natural history and mineralogy. Through these lectures, Froebel saw "the unity of the universe" (89). He found that all life, development as a whole, was founded on one law, the law of unity, and that this unity must be the basis of all principles of human development and of education. He decided to devote his time to education and its methods. While in Berlin, he supported himself by teaching in an upper grade of a Pestalozzian school.[21]

Froebel has been criticized that he never stayed long enough at any one of the universities he attended or in any of his employment situations.[22] According to Bell (1881), university education differed greatly between the United States and Germany. German universities neither attempted to draw students nor to retain them. They presented the best opportunities for study and investigation. Moving from one university to another allowed a student to hear all the best professors in Germany. Students learned something of their methods of teaching and were thoroughly drawn into the various scientific and literary currents of the day. The professors were there to further science and the national culture. They did not prescribe books. The essence of the German university was in making "self thinking and not merely receptive scholars."[23]

In 1813, everyone was called to arms to resist Napoleon's invasion of Prussia. French domination would have meant the death of all German nationality. Froebel joined the army "out of a feeling and consciousness of the ideal Germany." He could not think of not bearing arms and becoming a teacher of children without having defended his country.[24] He enlisted in the infantry division of Count Lützow. The company leader introduced him to Heinrich Langenthal (1792–1882), who introduced Froebel to his friend Wilhelm Middendorff (1793–1853). Both men were ten years younger than Froebel. Attracted to his character and his ideas, they became his lifelong friends, colleagues, and disciples. With the Peace of Paris (1814), the corps were dismissed. Froebel returned to Berlin, to resume his preparation to become an educator.[25]

Froebel's goal was soon fulfilled. The widow of his brother Christoph consulted him about the education of her three orphaned sons: Julius, Karl, and Theodor.[26] Froebel assumed the responsibility of educating his nephews and took the opportunity to put his educational ideas into practice. He abandoned his position in Berlin to organize a school "to educate man in his true humanity, to educate man in his absolute being, according to the universal laws of development."[27] His brother Christian (1770–1851), who was familiar with Froebel's ideas and had always supported and encouraged him, trusted Froebel with the education of his two sons, Ferdinand and William, six and eight years old, respectively.[28] Froebel devoted the rest of his life to educating children. He endured many hardships and many times lived in poverty.

TEACHER AND EDUCATIONAL REFORMER: THE KEILHAU YEARS (1816–1836)

In November 1816, in a peasant cottage, in Griesheim (the town where his brother Christoph was pastor), Froebel organized the Universal German Educational Institute, where he tried to apply his educational ideas, "to train up free, thinking, independent men."[29] The children were of various ages. Froebel intended the school to be a model for the nation and for all mankind. A year later the Institute was moved to Keilhau and became the center of Froebel's educational work. Here he created a circle of teachers, friends, and pupils whom he involved in the evolution of his philosophy and practice. Keilhau became the mother institution, as Froebel created other institutions.

Middendorff joined Froebel in April 1817, bringing with him Langenthal's eleven-year-old brother. His tuition was paid by the family; the older Langenthal was tutor. Langenthal joined them in September.[30] At Keilhau, Froebel tried to implement his idea of the unity of life, *Lebenseiningung*: to interconnect all parts of education and all parts of knowledge used in education. Froebel wanted to develop the character of the child as well as his intellect by uniting the child's faculties of feeling, thinking, willing, and doing.[31]

Froebel tried to develop each boy according to his nature, in a familylike atmosphere. All teaching was based on the *self-activity* of the pupils. As far as possible, the knowledge they gained was their own. He gave children *experiences* instead of instruction. He put *action* in the place of abstract learning. Froebel's teaching was based on the principle that the starting point of all that we see and know is *action*. Therefore, human development and education must begin with action, *self-activity*. He defined self-activity in the *Education of Man* as activity that the whole being of the child is involved in and that the child gets some enjoyment out of.[32] It is the educational process. The child is at once receiving, creating, and "giving out." This "giving out," which Froebel called making the "inner outer," is related to creativity. Froebel valued creative activity and constantly looked for ways to keep it from degenerating into destructiveness. He never allowed the children to destroy an old form they had built in order to make a new one with the same materials. He insisted that new forms be made by making suitable changes to the old ones. He tried to awaken thoughtfulness and patience and to inspire respect of existing things.[33] Froebel had always regarded man not only as a receptive being, but as a creative, and especially as a productive, one.[34]

In 1818, Froebel married Mlle. Henrietta Wilhelmine Hoffman, daughter of War-councilor Hoffman of Berlin. A remarkable woman, from a socially prominent family, highly educated, and very cultivated, she became his wife because of her enthusiasm for Froebel's educational ideas. She was deeply loved and most tenderly treated by Froebel.[35] Her willingness to sacrifice and her cheerfulness under privations set an example for others. She brought with her Ernestine Crispine, her adopted daughter, who married Langenthal in 1826.[36] In 1820, Froebel's brother Christian gave up his manufacturing business and, with his wife and family[37] and all his assets, joined Froebel in Keilhau. They all helped Froebel to promote his educational ideas throughout their lives.[38] In 1823, Johann Arnold Barop, Middendorff's nephew, joined Froebel and the Keilhau Circle.[39]

A glimpse of Keilhau at its height, before the political and financial troubles, comes from Colonel Hermann von Arnswald. Arnswald was a pupil in the school for three years (1824–1826), when Froebel was teacher and director. According to Arnswald's account, when he arrived, Froebel introduced him to the other boys, who made him feel at home. Strict order was observed in the domestic life of the school, and personal cleanliness was a must. Pupils were inspected daily before breakfast. Any boy responsible for property damage was required to personally make repairs. Implicit obedience was blended with individual liberty. "At the end of three years, I went home to my parents, healthy in soul and body."[40]

As an educational experiment, the school was successful. It provided a rich program for the boys to prepare for university studies. The Congress of Philosophers, which met in Praha (Prague) in 1868, appointed a committee to inquire into the ultimate results for individuals of the education they had received at the boys school in Keilhau. The committee reported the following year that the pupils had been looked up at the universities and elsewhere and had been found to be of "exceptional intelligence" and they themselves ascribed it to their "Froebel education."[41]

Difficult Times

Ever since the defeat of Napoleon at the Battle of Leipzig (1813), there had been unrest in Germany. The men who fought Napoleon and the university students wanted a united Germany. Some students at Jena formed a Students' Club; others followed. Then an agent of the Prussian government was killed by a student, and the government took strong measures against the students and their professors. The school at Keilhau did not escape. It became suspect for revolutionary activity. Pressure was brought on the Prince of Schwarzburg-Rudolstadt to break up the community. The prince appointed Superintendent Zeh in 1824 to inspect Keilhau and report on its activities. Zeh spent two days at the school and was very impressed by the teaching he saw and by the way the children responded and behaved. The report[42] did not find any fault with the Institute, but pressure from Berlin continued. The language teacher joined the opposition by attacking Froebel's work and caused the departure of Froebel's three nephews and their mother (1824), which saddened Froebel. Some parents, particularly the nobles, became terrified and took their children out. Enrollment began to decline, the Institute was crippled, and by 1829, Keilhau had only five pupils.[43]

Froebel wrote extensively throughout the years and reported regularly about the Institute at Keilhau in an effort to get attention for it and for his idea of "education as development." His success was limited. His writings, published privately at Keilhau, were a heavy drain on the Institute's finances, and they could not reach a broader audience outside of his immediate educational circle and provide him with the support for which he was looking.[44] Froebel's ideas were novel and in opposition to old, established methods. Misinterpretation and envy of the work at Keilhau almost contributed to its demise. His stiff and convoluted writing style made his work difficult to understand.

In 1826, Froebel published *The Education of Man,* his philosophical work on education. He also founded the weekly *Family Journal of Education.*[45]

FROEBEL'S PHILOSOPHY

Froebel's philosophy evolved during many years of teaching and observing children, discussing with colleagues, and reflecting on everything he did. It was also influenced by his schooling and education and his early experiences within his family, as well as by the prevailing idealistic philosophy,[46] the scientific spirit of his time, and the educational ideas of Pestalozzi.

The Education of Man (1826)[47] was published fourteen years before the naming of the kindergarten. It states what Froebel thought education should be, beginning at birth, and what he and his colleagues were trying to do at Keilhau.

The theme in *The Education of Man* is the application of the theory of evolution[48] (development) to education. It discusses how to develop the whole human being from birth through childhood, boyhood to manhood. Froebel was the first to apply the theory of evolution to education and to translate it into practice. He saw a correspondence between the evolution in nature and the evolution of mankind, which was happening according to a divine plan.[49] He regarded man as constantly and ever developing, self-evolving, progressing from one stage to another.[50]

Evolution means that each successive generation and each individual must traverse in its own experience the whole previous development of mankind; otherwise it would fail to appreciate the earlier stages and the contemporary phase. Such recapitulation must involve active participation of the individual. Although each individual reflects the whole history of mankind, the individual nevertheless preserves the integrity of his own unique personality.[51] This principle of recapitulation, or the parallelism of racial and individual development, complements Froebel's view of development from within. Froebel used this concept thirty years before *On the Origin of Species* was published (1859).

Froebel's concept of God and the concept of unity of life pervaded his entire philosophy. All life, according to Froebel, was based on what he called the "eternal unity," or the interconnection of all things in life. God was the "Divine Unity" and the source of all subsequent unity. Education was the process of leading man to a conscious appreciation of this principle by helping him become "a thinking, intelligent being." To be *wise* is the highest aim of man, is the most exalted achievement of human self-determination.[52] Froebel rejected the religious strictness of his childhood and spoke of religion in a broad nonsectarian sense, of a spirit of a "practical Christianity."[53] He wanted the child to learn to appreciate God through his own observations, not through dogmatic religious teaching.[54]

Froebel saw education as a continuous whole, each part related to every other part, each element helping and advancing every other element. The interconnection of all parts of education, and of all parts of knowledge used in education, he called *connectedness*. Like nature, education should advance with an orderly and continuous growth. Isolated, unrelated facts do not become knowledge until they are compared, classified, organized, and connected.[55]

The spiritual development of man was Froebel's highest priority in education. He wanted, however, to develop it in harmony with man's physical and intellectual growth. Froebel felt that his emphasis on interconnection and unity of life *(Lebenseiningung)*, which stemmed from his view of divine unity, distinguished his educational system from all others.[56] This unity of life means harmony in feeling, thinking, willing, and doing and is reflected in the gifts and occupations, games, and songs. Two implications result from the unity of man with God. Every child is born good; therefore the child must be treated as an individual and left free to develop in unhindered fashion. If a child shows evil traits in character or behavior, it is because serious mistakes were made in the child's very important first years. Because of Froebel's[57] belief in the innate goodness of man, early education should be "passive, protective," following the child's development, and "not prescriptive, categorical, interfering."[58]

Manhood could not be reached unless the fullest appropriate development had been reached in all the preceding stages. The child, from the time of his birth, should be viewed in accordance with his nature, treated correctly, and given the free "all-sided" use of his power. "The child, boy, man indeed should know no other endeavor but to be at every *stage* of development wholly what this stage calls for." One stage builds on the previous one. Every stage must be fully reached before moving to the next one. Each stage of development is essential for the proper development of later stages. Froebel assigned the greatest importance to the earliest stages.[59]

Stages of Development

According to *The Education of Man*, in *infancy* the child takes in everything (23). The child's primary concern is the use and exercise of his body, senses, and limbs for the sake of using them. The child is neither interested nor aware of the effects such activity has on his mother. Infancy is the time for nurture. Froebel, recognizing that the infant's activity exists for its own sake (48), continued that children, from this period on, should not be left too long by themselves in their cradles without some object to stimulate them. He advised "to suspend in a line within the child's vision a swinging cage with a live bird." Later he substituted it with the balls of the first gift (49).

The stage of *childhood* begins when the child is able to use his physical and sensory activity to show his thoughts and feelings. As speech develops, the child begins to organize his mind, and strives to express his ideas; "the inner become outward." The education of man begins at this stage. The child's education is "intrusted" to the mother and the father, who together with the child form a unity (50).

Froebel regarded infancy and the preschool years as the most significant period of education, and the time most neglected in conventional educational practices. The child is entirely under his mother's care during this period of his life; she is the most important of educators; the child imitates the mother. Therefore, the mother, according to Froebel, needs to be appropriately trained (educated) to fulfill her role—to do consciously for her child what she does instinctively (64). One of the things Froebel did to help the mother fulfill her role was to develop *Mutter-und Kose-Lieder*.

Froebel maintains in *The Education of Man* that *childhood* is significant, for it is the period when the child develops his first connections with his environment. It is important for the developing child whether he regards the *outer world* "as good or evil, ennobling or degrading, as a thing to be used, consumed, destroyed or having a destiny of its own." Therefore the child's surroundings should be clearly and correctly presented to him (51). A characteristic of the period of childhood is that the child cannot separate the word he speaks from the object which it describes. This is especially noticeable in his play. Childhood lasts from about the third year until formal schooling begins, about the seventh year (54).

Boyhood begins when the child learns to separate the name from the object and the object from its name, the speech from the speaker and vice versa. When language is externalized and materialized in writing, the child enters *boyhood*. *Boyhood* is predominantly the period of learning, for making the *external internal*. Instruction is carried on, not according to the child's nature, but according to fixed and definite conditions existing *outside* the child (94). As a *school boy*, he learns about external things and about their nature. School is "the conscious communication of knowledge, for a definite purpose and in definite inner connection" (95).

Froebel and Play

Froebel found in *play*[60] the instinctive activity of the child, the impulse and the method for the child's development, "from within outwards." In *The Education of Man,* he encouraged mothers to "cultivate and foster it," "fathers to protect and guard it," because through play a child reveals the future of his mind to anyone who has insight into human nature (56). Play is "the highest level of child development," the spontaneous expression of the child's thought and feeling (83).

Froebel encouraged parents to foster the play impulse by providing children with space to play and by allowing them to participate in adult occupations instead of refusing them. He exhorted the parents: "Let us live with our children" (89). He continues that play needs to be in harmony with the nature and the ability of the child. (Today it is called developmentally appropriate.) Through play, the child learns to use his body, learns how to achieve his goals and master the conventions of his mother language; he learns about the external world and the qualities of physical objects; he forms associations, recognizes moral relations, learns about the rights of others and that he is part of the community (54–56).

Froebel believed that play develops the child's mind and connects the child to the wider world. In play, the child ascertains what he can do, discovers his possibilities of will and thought, and reveals his original power. The best way is to begin with an activity which is easy and attractive that will lead the child forward, developing all his abilities and making him master of himself. For the child to develop and achieve his maximum potential, he needs activity arising from within himself. The child also needs freedom to move and act without unnecessary interference or restrictions. If the whole human being is to be developed, the entire being must be exercised through his own activity. This activity must arise from within the individual child and be in harmony with the child's nature. Froebel called this activity *self-activity*.[61]

Froebel did not advocate, however, allowing the child total self-direction that would lead to lawless behavior.[62] He recommended that the teacher observe the child and provide for his developing needs both in terms of materials for the child to experiment with and by adjusting the surroundings so that the child may be free from temptations and have ample opportunities to explore.

In addition to the kindergarten that Froebel devised for the preschool years, he also introduced the Connecting School to mediate between the kindergarten and the school proper, for he regarded the school as opposite to the kindergarten.[63]

After the publication of *The Education of Man,* things got worse, and Froebel decided to travel to advance his educational cause. In the fall of 1828, Froebel and Middendorff went to Göttingen to meet with the philosopher Carl C. F. Krause (1781–1832), who was also interested in educational reform. A friendship developed between the two men. Krause received them cordially and introduced Froebel to the whole learned society of Göttingen. He drew Froebel's attention to *Scola Materske,* Comenius's (1592–1670) treatise on early childhood education.[64] It is probable that Krause influenced Froebel to turn his mind to the younger child.

When things were really bad, in 1829, Froebel got an invitation from the Duke of Meinengen to submit a plan for a people's school that the duke wanted to establish. Froebel gave the duke a model plan for an Educational Institute and Orphanage in Helba (1829), fully developed by all of his colleagues at Keilhau. School time was to be equally divided between academic and technical instruction (weaving, carpentry, bookbinding, gardening). The duke was impressed with Froebel's plan, and offered him his estate in Helba and an annual grant of 1,000 gulden to proceed. He also consulted Froebel about the education of his only son and heir. Froebel recommended the young prince be educated with other boys. This suggestion, and the duke's interest in Froebel's work, created jealousy among the duke's advisors. The duke withdrew his support (1831), and the plan was never implemented.[65]

THE SWITZERLAND YEARS

Froebel left Keilhau and went to Frankfurt (1831) to win friends to his views. A friend influenced him to go to Switzerland, a place more attuned to educational reform, and offered him his castle in Wartensee to found a school for girls. The local Catholic clergy[66] considered the school and the teachers "heretics," and the teachers feared for their lives. Froebel moved the school to nearby Willisau at the invitation of some local businessmen, and returned briefly to Keilhau (1832) to visit his wife. Shortly after his arrival, William, his beloved nephew, who was teaching at Keilhau, died in an accident (not specified).[67] Barop, who had to return to Keilhau in 1832, managed to revive the school and eventually became its director. The University of Jena made Barop a doctor, and the Prince of Rudolstad named him his minister of education.[68]

Froebel opened the school at Willisau in 1833. His wife joined him and did all the housekeeping. The school grew in spite of conflicts created by the local Catholic clergy. Ferdinand—his nephew—succeeded Froebel at Willisau when Froebel was asked by the government of Bern to give the annual teacher-training course to sixty teachers at Burgdorf and to organize an orphanage there. Middendorff and Elise went to Willisau from Keilhau to help Froebel and continue Froebel's work. Adolph Frankenberg, a friend and teacher at Keilhau, also went to Willisau to help. The school at Willisau was given up when the Jesuits came to power in 1839; Middendorff returned to Keilhau.[69]

Langenthal joined Froebel and his wife in Burgdorf. The two men became directors of the orphanage (1835). Froebel and his wife returned to Berlin (1836) because of her mother's death and her own poor health. Ferdinand joined Langenthal as director. Langenthal left the orphanage and the Froebel Circle in 1841 to become director of a girls' school in Bern. Ferdinand continued as director until his sudden and early death (no specifics as to the cause of his death). He was given a public funeral that demonstrated his accomplishments and the general appreciation of the value of his work.[70]

Mme. Froebel died in May 1839.[71] Froebel was inconsolable for a while but eventually returned to hard work to advance the cause of the kindergarten.[72]

FOUNDER OF THE KINDERGARTEN (1836–1848)

Froebel had been baffled for many years as to why it was impossible to teach a boy during the many years spent in school all that was needed for "after school" success. First he thought the problem was the fault of the school, and he had tried in Keilhau to reform and improve the existing teaching methods, but he was not satisfied. After years of careful observation, Froebel concluded that it was either the undeveloped condition in which some children came to school or that they had been erroneously educated before they came to school. He had also learned that whatever he did could not offset the deficiencies of these early years. Froebel began to consider how to educate the child before school.and revised his earlier position; he had maintained in *The Education of*

Man that the mother should be the sole educator of the child until the age of seven. He realized that no mother had either the leisure or the strength to do for her child all that was needed in its first seven years within the confines of a single family and without some additional help. The child's social and moral development between three and seven years required a larger circle of equals. The family narrowed the child's experience. A different education was needed for the period between the end of infancy and the child's entering school.[73]

In a series of letters between 1829 and 1836, Froebel's idea for the education and training of children from three to seven years of age became clearer and culminated in the founding of "an institution for the education of little children" in Blankenburg near Keilhau in 1837. There he began to implement his ideas and to develop the gifts and occupations. Froebel wanted an institution for young children where they could *develop* freely according to their individual nature, using play as a tool, not the custodial institution that already existed.[74] The institution had been in existence for at least three years before Froebel found an appropriate name for it. One evening in 1840 as he was walking from Keilhau to Blankenburg with Middendorff and Barop, he shouted with delight *"Eureka! kindergarten* shall be the name of the new Institution!"[75]

Froebel's experiment in Blankenburg at first was received with skepticism. When the parents and others saw the joyful children, their involvement in games and sports, the guidance they received, the sewing and weaving articles they brought home, and their voluntary involvement in their own activities, the parents began to understand and appreciate the institution and doubt became interest.[76] In 1838, Froebel put an announcement in the *Sunday Journal (Sontagsblatt)*, a public request, that families should unite to carry out the motto of the paper, "Come let us live with our children."[77]

DEVELOPMENT AND EXPANSION OF THE KINDERGARTEN

Froebel used several approaches to develop and expand kindergartens. One was to go and live in a city; another was through correspondence and through his publications.

After 1837, Froebel and his associates made frequent trips from Blankenburg to various parts of Germany to promote his educational plan and the kindergarten. (He had not named his institution "kindergarten" as yet.) Froebel and Frankenberg went to Dresden from January 1838 to February 1839.[78] Froebel demonstrated his "games" (the gifts) to families and their children. Once the parents saw that both their children and themselves enjoyed the games, they formed groups and visited each other's families to continue using the games.[79] One such family was that of Privy Councilor von Schaarschmidt. He had twelve children and a "wife of rare motherly qualities." After several conversations with Froebel, he allowed his children to play with Froebel's games. Froebel used the first four games with five of the children, aged from one and a half to eight years, and got some "astonishing answers" from a six-year-old girl. (Froebel did not say what the answer was.) The games "won the heart of the children," the parents were satisfied, and promised to support Froebel's cause. The father offered Froebel all of his children to try the games.[80]

Froebel gave lectures and demonstrations explaining his system of education and the purpose of the games. One was in the Natural History Hall before five hundred people and was attended by the Queen of Saxony, to whom he was introduced.[81]

Parents began to form small family associations to get together and use the games. By the time Froebel left Dresden, there were twelve or more families with twenty-four children, who decided to continue their meetings for games.[82] Froebel told his wife that he was concerned about leaving Frankenberg in charge of what he had developed, in Dresden. Frankenberg "does not appear strong and thorough enough for the work in Dresden," and his inclination is to go to America.[83] Froebel applied to the superintendent "for the license to teach children up to the end of the sixth year." Frankenberg stayed in Dresden to carry on the family circles,[84] and later he became the director of an "Institution for the Care of Little Children."[85] Froebel went to Leipzig, where he started the process all over again.

Froebel wrote voluminous letters to friends, former students, and relatives to clarify his thinking about his system, to encourage them to start kindergartens, to "walk" them through the process of organizing kindergartens, and to get feedback and comments about his ideas—the gifts, occupations, games, and songs—that he continued to develop and modify. Constantly, Froebel reminded his correspondents the purpose of the kindergarten and the role women had to play in it. One example was his correspondence with his cousin, Mme. Schmidt. Through these letters Froebel guided her to operate a kindergarten in her town, to train assistants, and to test some of the gifts and occupations, soliciting her "severest criticism." He also asked her to involve other women in her circle, and to publish the description of the kindergarten, in the local paper.[86] Another example was his correspondence with Mlle. Luise Frankenberg, his former pupil.[87]

WOMEN AS TEACHERS

Froebel considered women his natural allies. He recognized women as the natural educators of children and considered "woman's work as the first and most essential link in the chain of human life."[88] Froebel wanted to win the German women over to his cause and rouse them to a sense of a holy mission for all women. As early as 1839, Froebel addressed the Wives and Mothers of Blankenburg when he tried to unite them in an association "for the training of healthy-minded and brave-hearted maidens into the first real nurses."[89] Froebel tried to combine the women's interest in emancipation and their capabilities as mothers with the needs of childhood. He raised the status of motherhood as he approached women first to be educated to become better mothers and later to become *kindergarterins*. He also gave unmarried women the opportunity to be "mothers through their work." Educating women to become teachers was an unusual move, for up until now the teachers were primarily men. Women flocked to listen to him. Many took up his cause; some became *kindergarterins*.

As Froebel worked in Blankenburg, the concept of the kindergarten and its purposes grew clearer.

On the occasion of the four hundredth anniversary of the invention of printing, celebrated in all German states, Froebel tried to link the advent of a new institution, the kindergarten, with the discovery that had a great impact on all education. In his appeal to "German Wives and Maidens,"[90] Froebel articulates the kindergarten and its purposes. (157, 160). He proposes to *educate female and male "gardeners" who will be able to understand the earliest care and education of childhood* (162). Froebel asked those present to spare a few pennies a day to buy a subscription of ten dollars each to found the kindergarten. The women will be in charge of the shares (165). For the first time, Froebel stated the twofold purpose of the kindergarten: to develop the child in all aspects "by a genuine encouragement of the spontaneous activity of children" . . . and "to establish an institution for the training of nursery governesses and teachers in the early education of children . . . the two institutions make a complete system under the name KINDERGARTEN" (166).

The audience was moved, and before leaving, seventy subscriptions were bought to advance the spread of the kindergarten.[91] Thus Froebel established the first German Kindergarten as a joint stock company. He chose the name "German Kindergarten" for he wanted all children to be part of it, and for it to be a "Model Institution" of its kind.[92]

No one before Froebel had organized a continuous and connected system of education equally applicable to young children of all classes and of all nations, where "Every child, regardless of rank or condition will be able to develop his real nature, character, and vocation in life; educating himself as well as being educated, and to train 'kindergartners' who will in turn educate the children."[93] Many responded to his call and came to be trained by him.

MATERIALS AND CURRICULUM: GIFTS AND OCCUPATIONS

The gifts and occupations are the content and the method of the kindergarten. Together with gardening and nature study,[94] and music, they were used to develop the child according to his nature. The purpose of the gifts was to facilitate from the very first months of life the perception of outward objects.

The inspiration for the ball to become the first *gift* came to Froebel while observing a group of children playing ball in a meadow near the school.[95] He created the *gifts and occupations* between 1837 and 1850, tested them with children in family settings (Dresden), and used them with the children in the Blankenburg kindergarten. The child used the gifts in his play and thus was introduced to concepts of the larger world. These gifts were part of a total curriculum and were combined with dance and music. They became an indispensable part of Froebel's educational system. The gifts and occupations were illustrated by lithographs, had directions, and were packaged in individual boxes by "the work-people at the kindergarten factory."[96] They were available commercially and found their way to the children and their families.[97] Froebel justified his decision to produce the gifts and occupations himself "as the surest means for securing the unity of the whole, its self-dependence and inter-dependence."[98]

Froebel would send newly developed gifts with their instructions to the children of friends or relatives to test them, and he would solicit their comments and the children's reactions in using each gift. He would then use these comments to modify the gift. Here is an example: "In each construction the whole of the materials must be used up, or at least each separate piece must be arranged so as to stand in some actual relation to the whole."[99]

The descriptions of the gifts and the accompanying games and songs, which were written by Froebel and his colleagues, appeared in the three periodicals he published: the *Sunday Journal* (1838–1840), the *Weekly Journal of Education* (1850), and the *Journal for Friedrich Froebel's Educational Aims* (1851–1852).[100]

Description of the Gifts

The gifts progress in descending order from three-dimensional objects, to flat surfaces, to sticks, to the point. They are basic forms designed to show the general qualities of things. For Froebel, all development began with what is simple and progressed to more and more complicated forms. Education is the systemic development of human nature. The gifts reflect this sequence from the simple to the more complex, following each other in a natural evolutionary order. Learning one gift was preparation for the next. Each gift was to be congruent with the child's development. The gifts were to be used first by the mother during infancy and later by the teacher. Goldammer identified sixteen gifts.[101]

The first gift. Six small wool balls: three in primary colors and three in secondary colors (1). Froebel wanted the first plaything to be something complete in itself and yet as simple as possible, so that the infant could easily perceive it and be able to grasp it (4). The ball is the simplest of the forms representing unity.[102]

The second gift. A ball, a cylinder, and a cube, all made of wood (28). The second gift is the basis of the kindergarten system. All the other gifts are derived from it. Froebel used this gift to introduce opposites, contrasts, and connections to the child. The ball and the cube are contrasts. They represent motion and rest, curved and straight surfaces. They find their connection in the cylinder, which has one curved surface on which it moves and two straight surfaces on which it rests (30–48).

The *third* through the *sixth* gifts become building blocks, thus creating an interest in number, relation, and form.

The third gift. The cube is divided into eight equal cubes (49). It was Froebel's answer to every child's desire to pull things apart and to put them together again. The cube is divided once lengthwise, breadthwise, and heightwise, giving the dimensions of length, breadth, and thickness. It introduces the whole/part concept by contrasting the whole to the part, and the parts to one another (51).

The fourth gift. The cube is divided by one vertical and three horizontal cuts into eight oblong bricks. The whole and its parts differ only in size, cut into eight rectangles this time (70). The rectangles have new possibilities for the child. He could make a square, and by sliding the rectangles inward and outward, he could create patterns such as stars. The possibilities are infinite.

The fifth gift. The cube is divided by two cuts in each direction—horizontally, vertically, and diagonally—resulting in twenty-seven pieces. It introduces the triangle (85). The use of this gift should be continued into the school years.

The sixth gift. The cube is first divided into twenty-seven oblong bricks (105). Six are halved transversely and three are halved longitudinally (105).

Gifts *seven* through *eleven* introduce the child to flat surfaces. They offer many opportunities for the invention of symmetrical patterns and artistic designs.

The seventh gift. There are forty-eight square tablets, representing the surfaces of the cube and its various divisions (120).

The eighth gift has sixty-four right-angled isosceles triangles obtained by halving the square diagonally (125); *gift nine* has sixty-four right-angled scalene triangles formed from the oblong brick of the fourth gift by halving it diagonally (139); *gift ten* has fifty-four equilateral triangles (equal-sided) (146); and *gift eleven* has fifty-four obtuse-angled isosceles triangles. They serve almost exclusively for the construction of artistic forms (152).

The twelfth gift. A packet of slats for interlacing. They are the transition from the surface to the line (154).

Gift thirteen has twelve laying sticks. The sticks also come from the cube.

After the sticks, Froebel introduced curved and circular lines made of tinned wire.

The fourteenth gift has twelve whole and twenty-four half rings or circles. According to Froebel, children are fascinated by the property of the ring, which has neither beginning nor end (173). The sticks combined with the circles could be laid out to form letters, thus beginning the learning of reading and writing. They are also used to introduce drawing, which "should be cultivated for its own sake" (168).

The fifteenth gift is the thread, which does not have a definite place in Froebel's system for the kindergarten child (179).

The sixteenth gift is a box of small pebbles or shells. From solid bodies, surfaces and lines, the *point* is reached, the corner of the cube. It has no independent existence and cannot be detached from a body (182). Children can line the pebbles or shells horizontally or vertically on the table.

Figure 4.1 Froebel's Monument, from *Froebel Letters* by Arnold Heinemann. Boston: Lee and Shepard Publishers, 1893, page 181. *Courtesy of the Boston Public Library.*

Through the use of the gifts, order, neatness, economy, and exactness are encouraged. Each child uses only his own blocks. When the child finished playing, he was expected to return the cubes into the box and put it away as he had found it (53–54).

It is obvious that Froebel built his entire system of gifts upon mathematical principles and forms. The child is unaware of the mathematical significance of his playthings. His eyes unconsciously become accustomed to correct mathematical forms, and the child develops a sense of form, proportion, and harmony. Froebel viewed the gifts not as ready-made playthings but as materials for the children to use and create.

In themselves, the "gifts" form an elaborate sequence of solids, plan surfaces, and points, not all of the forms meant for the young child. The kindergarten was to be the starting point of a new education to be continued in the school proper. Froebel clarified the use of the gifts shortly before he died in a letter from Marienthal (May 25, 1852) to one of his students, Emma Bothmann. He differentiates the stages of instruction: "In the kindergarten, the question is of intuition, of conception, of doing, of the exact designation of a small number of objects by the appropriate word but not yet by recognition and cognizance, detached from the object."[103] Froebel constantly modified the gifts and his system. He looked at his system as evolving and adaptable, not stationary and stereotyped, to be handed from one person to another and reproduced mechanically. He was aware that if the gifts were imposed on children, they could become oppressive.

The Occupations[104]

In addition to the "gifts," Froebel devised a sequence of "occupations" that trained children in such activities as drawing, modeling in clay, and using paper and pliable materials in a multiplicity of ways. The occupations require greater manual dexterity.

The difference between the *gifts* and the *occupations,* though never clearly formulated by Froebel, is important. The *gifts* were intended to teach the child universal aspects of the external world appropriate to a child's development. The *occupations,* on the other hand, provided materials for practice in certain skills. Anything can be an occupation, provided it is sufficiently plastic and within the child's ability to control it.[105]

MUTTER-UND KOSE-LIEDER

Music was an important part of the kindergarten and was closely related to the occupations and the games. Froebel had been collecting materials for his mother-songs long before he had established the kindergarten. Mme Froebel had tested the songs and games with Middendorff's children. A small collection of nursery songs set in music by Robert Kohl was printed in 1841. The work was expanded from the experiences in the kindergartens of Blankenburg, Rudolstadt, and Gera and became the *Mutter-und Kose-Lieder* or *Mother-Play and Nursery Songs,*[106] published in 1843. Froebel dedicated the book to the memory of his wife.

There are fifty songs and games in the *Mutter-und Kose-Lieder,* which are somewhat stiff. Each has a motto for the mother's guidance and a verse for her to sing to her child. Each game or song is an exercise for some part of the child's body. At the end of the book, Froebel's commentaries provide additional guidance to mothers using the book. The illustrations are not always perfect as works of art, especially the faces. The book is unique as the expression of motherly feeling and spiritual truth. Froebel tried to perpetuate and further develop the playful ways of children on the one hand and the mothers' methods on the other.

The introductory song is "The Mother in Unity with Her Child," followed by "Mother's Self-Communings," poems designed for mother-infant interaction and attachment. They include rhymes on observing, playing with the infant, talking, and nursing. They offered mothers a guide for the first stage of the infant's development. Froebel's aim was to persuade the mothers that a child's education (development) begins at birth and during infancy they might lay the foundation for intellectual and moral growth.

Mothers were to sing in order to entertain and occupy the child (from birth to two years) while caring for the child; "to assist in the physical development of the child, training his body, limbs and senses, as well as his soul, his mind and his whole inner nature."[107]

Mutter-und Kose-Lieder are divided into four groups of finger play and songs, each representing a stage in the child's development. The first deals with experiences of movement, sense discrimination, imitation, and the perception of various objects. The second group broadens the child's experience of life. They include songs dealing with family relationships. The third group was to introduce the child to unfamiliar distant objects such as stars. The fourth group was to introduce moral themes and some professions such as carpenter. Froebel's view of interconnection is reflected in the four stages of games and songs, with each stage progressing in logical order from the preceding one.

The book includes Froebel's ideas about play. Although intended for mothers, many kindergartners used it also. The plays are accompanied by pages of complex illustrations, introductory remarks in rhyme, and long prose explanations of the purpose and the symbolic meaning of the activities. Woodcuts of children, baby animals, farm scenes, and diagrams of how the mother is to use her hands in order to perform the finger plays are also included.

FROEBEL'S LATER YEARS AT LIEBENSTEIN (1849–1852)

By 1844, Keilhau was flourishing again. By 1848, there were "sixteen genuine and recognized Kindergartens" in various cities and towns of Germany.[108] The influence of Froebel's educational ideas was not limited to Germany. His ideas spread to most European countries, including Austria, England, Greece, Japan, Switzerland, Russia, and to the United States.[109]

Teacher-Trainer

In 1849, Froebel settled in Liebenstein to devote all his time to personally training kindergartners of both sexes. They would carry on his work. He established a training institution in a castle donated by the local prince in nearby Marienthal. The content and aim of his teacher training is described in "Plan for the Training School for Children's Nurses and Educators" (1847).[110] According to this plan, the aim of the institution was to train young women "to tend, develop, and educate the child from its birth up to the time it is prepared to begin its school life" (229). Those in training could become "educational helpers" for the house and the family or educators of children in kindergartens and schools, or directors (231). Their qualifications included being graduates of a public or a girls' school; between the ages of seventeen and twenty years; possessing "love for children, capacity and disposition for play with children, purity of character, modesty, religious feeling toward God, liking and capacity for singing" (232). Students were expected to develop the "correct understanding of the impulses to activity of their *own* lives and of their laws," so that later on they could foster "such impulses and their laws of development *in the child*" (233–234).

The Daily Schedule

The day began at seven o'clock. Students participated in morning prayer followed by religious instruction. It was important that the students obtain firm religious opinions and clear insight in the nature of religion, its development in mankind, and in childhood. They also needed to gain insight for their own benefit and for later use with the children in their care (234). Breakfast was from eight to nine. From nine to ten came observation of the laws of human development and of the child. There was reflection on the nature of the child, and the need for care and education. From ten to twelve was direct work with the child, learning the right kind of interaction, learning the "suggestive talk," and the "suggestive" child songs. Froebel's book *Mother-Play and Nursery Songs* was used. From twelve to two o'clock, were dinner, free time, free play with the children, and review by each student of what was learned earlier in the day (235). During the spring months of the training course, the time between two and three o'clock was devoted to gardening (237). From two to four, students made objects (not specified) for play, to be used with the children in conjunction with Froebel's various gifts. Supper and free time were between four and five o'clock. From five to six, students participated in the games of the children. Students spent from six to seven practicing in using the gifts (236). It appears that in order for a kindergartner to do the intellectual work in the kindergarten, it was necessary to play with the gifts as children do, in an orderly rather than in an accidental manner. This is the earliest description of kindergarten teacher training. Did Froebel view the teacher as an instrument as well as an agent for education?

Meeting the Baroness and Diesterweg

At Liebenstein, Froebel met and became friends with the Baroness Bertha von Marenholtz-Bülow (1810–1893). She was very interested in promoting education and was impressed when she observed Froebel interacting with children and their response to him. The Baroness knew most of the powerful people of the time and most of the noted educators. It was at her insistence that F. A. W. Diesterweg (1790–1866)—the famous pedagogue and Pestalozzian—visited Froebel, studied the kindergarten, and became Froebel's staunch supporter. He was a champion of liberal elementary education for all people, and recognized master of instruction and its methods. As the publisher of the *Reinesche Blätter,* Diesterweg's articles promoting and supporting the kindergarten and Froebel attracted the attention of the pedagogical circles in Germany, despite the disfavor of the court.[111] The Baroness became Froebel's most famous and indefatigable disciple especially after his death. She took upon herself to explain and interpret Froebel's basic principles through extensive traveling and lecturing to European countries, and through her writings. In 1861, she founded the periodical "Die Erziehung der Gegenwart" (The education of the present), where she published a series of articles on the kindergarten. Among her books are *Die Arbeit* (1866) (Work and the new education according to Froebel's method), *Reminiscences of Friedrich Froebel* (1877) and *Child and Child Nature* (1878).[112]

In July 1851, Froebel married Luise Levin. They seemed very happy together, and all his friends rejoiced because he had found someone with whom to spend the rest of his life. Frau Luise Froebel, like his first wife, had been interested in Froebel's work for many years. She had been trained by Froebel (1847–1849), and in 1849 had been appointed directress of the kindergarten training in Liebenstein by him.[113] Frau Froebel had developed a deep understanding of Froebel's work. In a letter to Luise Frankenberg, Froebel said that Luise Levin, who would be writing Frankenberg directly, "is taking every possible pain to put herself in thorough harmony with her work, both as to the spirit of her life and as to her technical proficiency." And if a job opportunity appears in the future, Frankenberg could recommend her wholeheartedly.[114]

Prohibition of the Kindergarten

In August 1851, the Prussian government issued a decree closing the Froebel kindergartens in its territory.[115] This action was a great shock for Froebel. Everyone was surprised, including the prince's family. They thought that there had been some mistake. The announcement in the newspaper referred to a pamphlet, "High Schools and Kindergartens," written by Karl Froebel, Froebel's nephew. Karl was known for his socialistic leanings, and the minister who issued the decree decided erroneously that the kindergartens were teaching atheism. The confusion was evident, but the minister would not admit that he was wrong. Froebel wrote directly to the minister, without results. This act was a departure for Froebel, for he did not respond to his critics. He also petitioned the king, who was friendly toward the kindergarten, through the baroness, but he did not succeed in repealing the decree. What hurt Froebel most, a truly religious man, was the accusation that he was an atheist. The prohibition lasted until 1860.[116]

Teachers' Convention

During September 27–29, 1851, Froebel organized a Teachers' Convention in Liebenstein. Froebel had organized such meetings over the years for kindergarten teachers and others interested in his system. They reported on existing kindergartens and exchanged views on the practice of the kindergarten. The prohibition gave greater importance to the examination of the Froebelian method by specialists. Froebel had hoped that the Convention would demonstrate his real work to the public and spread it further among the women of Germany. The majority of the participants were convinced that educational reform was necessary and that the new foundation needed for the reform was provided by Froebel's method.

The Convention was attended by ministers, clergymen, many teachers from near and far, and by Froebel's former students. Diesterweg chaired the first day and reported on several kindergartens. He also spoke about the establishment by the Women's Education Union of the first kindergarten in Berlin, in connection with the Pestalozzi-Froebel House.[117] The participants heard reports from founders of kindergartens like Adolph Frankenberg, and Director Marquard of Dresden. Marquard, a founder and director of a kindergarten, had adapted and introduced the kindergarten principles to the teaching of the transition and higher classes. He demonstrated what a good preparation for the higher grades the kindergarten was if it was carried out as Froebel intended it.[118]

The children of the Liebenstein kindergarten presented plays, which were received with applause and enthusiasm by those attending the Convention. Froebel's students, under the guidance of Frau Froebel, demonstrated some of the games, and many of those present joined in and played and sang like children. Great quantities of articles "plaited, folded, pricked, cut, and drawn with and upon paper and other materials" were displayed. The children demonstrated some of the games under Frau Froebel's direction.[119]

At the conclusion of the Convention, there was a "Declaration" that was made public and signed by men like Diesterweg. It stated that

> Froebel's educational system was far removed from all partisanship; that it must be looked at as a foundation of both theoretical and practical education; that it promised to advance school culture; and that it had proved itself particularly fitted to improve family education through the culture of women for their educational calling, which it involved.[120]

The Convention also proposed that Froebel should write an essay on his system, publish a "Kindergarten Guide" for teachers, and establish a new periodical, the *Journal for Friedrich Froebel's Educational Aims,* with Director Marquard as its editor. Froebel agreed to work toward these ends, and the meeting was ended. Through the cooperation of everyone, the journal was published before the end of the year. Froebel was unable to fulfill his promises because he died in the next year.[121]

In April 1852, Froebel was invited for the first time to participate in the German Teachers' Convention in Gotha by its president, Dr. Theodor Hoffmann. When Froebel entered the Convention, the whole assembly rose and cheered him. Froebel was touched. He had the joy of universal recognition. He thanked them with a few simple words and proceeded with his presentation, "Instruction in the Natural Sciences," to which the audience listened attentively. On the whole, this Convention was cheering and encouraging for

Froebel. Shortly after, Froebel became ill and did not recover. He received visits from the teachers and the children, and his cheerfulness never left him.[122]

Froebel died on June 21, 1852, with a broken heart. The distress he felt about the Prussian prohibition and the opposition that he had encountered throughout the years finally took their toll. He was buried at Liebenstein. A large part of the community came to pay their respects: parents, young people, and many children who brought wreaths and flowers. Friends and pupils came. Among the mourners was Ernst Luther, a descendant of Martin Luther, who had been educated gratuitously at Keilhau by Froebel, thirty-five years earlier, out of regard of his ancestor.[123] A monument, made out of sandstone, depicting the second gift was erected over Froebel's grave by the Baroness and Mme. Middendorff. The motto of the kindergarten was inscribed on the cylinder. During Froebel's centenary of his birth, all his friends in all the countries had been asked to contribute to replace it with a more permanent material.[124]

After Froebel's death, the training school was moved to Keilhau under Middendorff and Frau Froebel. She devoted all her energy to advancing the kindergarten, interpreting Froebel's ideas, organizing Froebel's papers for publication, and visiting kindergartens. One such visit Frau Froebel made, was in the spring of 1871 to the "Musical Kindergarten" and music training school founded by Frau Caroline Wiseneder in Brunswick, Germany. Frau Froebel had used the games and songs of Wiseneder in her kindergarten in Hamburg, as they had been published for some years.[125] Frau Wiseneder had, among other things, a children's orchestra of toy instruments, which were carefully tuned to harmonize together, and produced effects in this manner, which were not only extremely charming, but truly educational.[126]

Frau Froebel's financial means apparently were limited, for Emperor Frederick, a supporter of the kindergarten, saw that "the aged widow of the illustrious German educationist" received a pension for the rest of her life.[127]

FROEBELIAN LITERATURE

Many books were written about Froebel and the kindergarten system after his death by his friends, students, and others of both sexes. These volumes further advanced the kindergarten. In addition to the Froebelian literature, kindergartens also expanded after Froebel's death. There were kindergartens for the higher classes and national kindergartens; there were kindergarten belonging to private individuals, to committees and companies, to parishes, and to states; and there also were normal kindergartens for practice-teaching for young teachers of both sexes.[128]

CHAPTER SUMMARY

Froebel was concerned with the spiritual as well as the intellectual development of the child. He attempted to organize a system of education that would unfold the rational self and control the irrational. He tried to cultivate self-hood and repress selfishness, an action that must be done by the child itself under guidance. If the child does not control the irrational form within, some external constraint will do it for the child. For Froebel, self-conquest was the only basis of true freedom. His insights into the unfolding of the child's rational selfhood enabled Froebel to organize his early education philosophy and method into an institution for children below the age of seven, which he, in 1840, named *kindergarten*—"child garden."

Froebel's innovative idea was that education should develop the individual according to the peculiar tendencies of each child's nature, not according to any arbitrary standard. He believed that the child's tendencies were manifested early in his life, thus the mother's knowledge of how to work with her child was an important factor in the development of the child. He believed that the maternal instinct enabled a mother to identify and appreciate these differences in each child. It is to this maternal instinct, enlightened by knowledge and aided by systematic discipline, that Froebel trusted the destiny of the child.

Froebel started educating women to become teachers. Until this time, teaching was a male profession. He organized and implemented teacher training for kindergartners.

COMMENT

Most of the books used in this chapter were translations from the German by English and/or American educators. Many of the books did not have indexes. Some translators retained Froebel's convoluted language, while other interpreted his writings. The German word for *child* is neuter in German. The translators used the masculine *he* in English instead of *it*. Jobs and titles, whole words in capitals or words capitalized and italicized, seeming inappropriate in this text, were left as found in the reviewed materials.

NOTES

1. Friedrich Froebel, *The Education of Man (Erziehung der Mench): The Art of Education, Instruction and Training aimed at the Educational Institute at Keilhau,* trans. and ann. William N. Hailmann (New York: D. Appleton and Co., 1887; International Education Series, New York: D. Appleton and Co., 1911), 89. Hailmann, in a note, explains why he prefers "live *with*" instead of "live *for*" and we agree with his view. In the second translation, there is lack of mutuality between parents and children. This phrase became the motto for the kindergarten.

2. *Autobiography of Friedrich Froebel,* trans. and ed. Emilie Michaelis and H. Keatley Moore (Syracuse, NY: C. W. Bardeen, 1908), 113. It was translated on the occasion of the centenary of Froebel's birth. It includes Froebel's "Letter to the Duke of Meinengen" (1827), 3–101; a letter to philosopher Karl Krause (1828), 102–125; and Johann Arnold Barop, "Critical Moments in the Froebel Community" (1862), 127–139.

3. Two centuries earlier, Comenius had the same concept for the revival of his nation, Bohemia, Chapter 2 of this volume.

4. *Froebel's Letters on the Kindergarten,* ed. and ann. Emilie Michaelis and H. Keatley Moore (Syracuse, NY: C. W. Bardeen, 1896), 1–3.

5. August, a businessman died young; Christoph, a pastor at Griesheim, died in 1813 of typhus after the battle of Leipzig. He was the father of Julius, Karl, and Theodor. Christian started as a manufacturer and later (1820) joined Froebel in his educational work. Traugott studied medicine at Jena, and became a physician and burgomaster of Stadt-Ilm. *Autobiography,* 3–4. There were no sisters.

6. Ibid., 32, 7.

7. Ibid., 10, 11–12.

8. Ibid., 14–15.

9. Ibid., 44, 17–21.

10. Ibid., 23.

11. Jena at the turn of the nineteenth century had become the center of German intellectual life. It was a center for math and sciences and for Kantian studies; Schiller and Schelling were lecturing there, and Goethe was nearby at Weimar, *Autobiography,* 28. The theory of evolution was not finalized yet. Darwin's *On the Origin of Species* was published in 1859. Froebel expands the theme of interconnection and unity in *The Education of Man* (1826).

12. *Autobiography,* 35–37, 39-42.

13. Ibid., 51–53.

14. The children were from six to twelve years old. For a full account of what Froebel saw and learned at Yverdon and his interpretation, see "Letter to the Princess-Regent of Schwarzburg-Rudolstadt, April 27, 1809," in Henry Barnard, ed., rev. ed., *Kindergarten and Child Culture Papers: Papers on Froebel's Kindergarten, with Suggestions on Principles and Methods of Child Culture in Different Countries* (Hartford, CT: Office of Barnard's Journal of American Education, 1884), 49–68.

15. *Autobiography,* 58, 61, 62. The description of the public examination is similar to the public examinations in Classical Athens, Chapter 1 of this volume.

16. Ibid., 59–60.

17. Ibid., 75.

18. Ibid., 110–111.

19. Ibid., 68.

20. Ibid., 86–88. The natural sciences were being advanced in Germany at that time.

21. Ibid., 98–100.

22. Irene M. Lilley, *Friedrich Froebel* (Cambridge, England: Cambridge University Press, 1967), 7.

23. James W. Bell, "German Universities," *Education* 2, no. 1 (September 1881): 51.

24. Barnard, *Papers on Froebel's Kindergarten,* 44.

25. *Autobiography,* 96. For Middendorff's commitment and contribution to Froebel and the kindergarten, see Barnard, *Papers on Froebel's Kindergarten,* 131–144; Baroness Bertha von Marenholz-Bülow, *Reminiscences of Friedrich Froebel,* trans. Mrs. Horace Mann (Boston: Lee and Shepard Publishers, 1891), 35–49.

26. Julius, after Keilhau, studied natural sciences at Munich and wrote several publications. He studied at Jena and Berlin, became a professor at the Polytechnic School in Zurich, and was chosen deputy to the National Assembly in Frankfurt in 1848. When it was dissolved, he was condemned to death. He escaped to Switzerland and fled to New York. Later he was allowed to return to Germany and was appointed consul to Smyrna. Karl also went to Jena. He successively took a tutorship in England, and then became director of the public schools in Zurich. He founded a lyceum for young ladies in Hamburg. He returned to England, where he founded a school in Edinburgh. There is no information about Theodor. *Autobiography,* 114.

27. Ibid., 112–113.

28. Ibid., 121; Ferdinand studied philosophy and at the time of his death was director of the orphanage founded by Froebel in Burgdorf; William, Froebel's favorite, stayed to teach at Keilhau, but died young of an accident. Ibid., 113.

29. Ibid., 114–115.

30. Barnard, *Papers on Froebel's Kindergarten,* 77; *Autobiography,* 122.

31. *Autobiography,* 58.

32. *The Education of Man,* 11. Self-activity is exemplified in the kindergarten.

33. Ibid., 31–32.

34. *Autobiography,* 129.

35. We get a sense of their caring relationship from Froebel's letters to his wife during the time he lived in Dresden and Leipzig (January 17, 1838, to February 18, 1839) to establish kindergartens. Emily Shirreff, *A Short Sketch of the Life of Friedrich Froebel,* new ed. (London: Chapman and Hall, 1887), 31–109.

36. *Autobiography,* 123.

37. He had three daughters—Albertine eighteen years, who married Middendorff in 1826; Emilie, fifteen years, who married Barop in 1831; and Elise, six years, who married Dr. Siegfried Schaffner, in 1850, another member of the Keilhau Circle. *Autobiography,* 124. 142 Christian's two sons were already at Keilhau.

38. Barnard, *Papers on Froebel's Kindergarten,* 19, 78.

39. *Autobiography,* 124.

40. *Froebel Letters,* ed. Arnold H. Heinemann, with explanatory notes and additional matter (Boston: Lee & Shepard Publishers, 1893), 11–13, 19. The fourteen letters were written between February 6, 1845, and January 19, 1848. Another of Froebel's correspondents.

41. Barnard, *Papers on Froebel's Kindergarten,* 9.

42. The full text of Zeh's report is in Barnard, *Papers on Froebel's Kindergarten,* 107–110.

43. *Autobiography,* 128.

44. Ibid., 117.

45. Ibid., 123–124.

46. Idealism contends that the ultimate principle of the explanation of the universe is a spiritual one. It regards the physical world as merely one aspect of reality, which manifests itself likewise in the moral sphere and in the realm of beauty.

47. It was published in Keilhau when the school had difficulties. The book was to be the first volume of a series; no other volumes were written. *The Education of Man,* xi.

48. Elements of the theory of evolution existed before Darwin, who proved it.

49. *The Education of Man,* 2.

50. Ibid., 17.

51. Ibid., 40.

52. Ibid., 2–4.

53. *Froebel's Letters on the Kindergarten,* 286–287.

54. *Autobiography,* 74.

55. *The Education of Man,* 30, 27.

56. *Autobiography,* 53–57.

57. *The Education of Man,* 120.

58. Ibid., 7.

59. Ibid., 21, 30.

60. Froebel was not the first to see the educational value of play. He was the first to make play an essential part of learning. The value and importance of play has concerned educators/philosophers from ancient times. Froebel, however, organized and used it to educate the child.

61. Hermann Goldammer, *The Kindergarten: A Guide to Froebel's Method of Education, Gifts, and Occupations, with an Introduction by the Baroness von Bülow,* 2nd ed., trans. William Wright (London: Williams & Norgate, 1895), 156–170; *The Education of Man,* 11.

62. This line of thought is reminiscent of Plato's concerns, Chapter 1 of this volume.

63. For a full description see "The Connecting School," in Friedrich Froebel, *Education by Development,* the second part of the *Pedagogics of the Kindergarten,* trans. Josephine Jarvis (New York: D. Appleton and Co., 1899) 269–305.

64. *Autobiography,* 102.

65. Johann Barop, "Critical Moments in the Froebel Community," in *Autobiography of Froebel,* 129, 130.

66. Ibid., 131. The clergy reacted to Froebel because he was educating the child below the age of seven, the age of reason, by using play; the child-centered education was a challenge to their adult authority.

67. Barnard, *Papers on Froebel's Kindergarten*, 79–80.

68. Barop, "Critical Moments in the Froebel Community," in *Autobiography of Froebel*, 138.

69. Ibid., 132–137.

70. Ibid., 137; *Froebel's Letters on the Kindergarten*, 165. After Froebel died, Langenthal returned to Keilhau, where he spent his last years.

71. *Autobiography*, 123.

72. Froebel to Mme. Schmidt, September 19, 1843, in *Froebel's Letters on the Kindergarten*, 127–129.

73. *The Education of Man*, 64. Froebel differed from Pestalozzi, who thought the mother, as the natural educator of the child, ought to retain the sole charge up to the seventh year.

74. Froebel letters: to Barop, February 18, 1829, and to Keilhau Circle, March 1, 1836, quoted in Barnard, *Papers on Froebel's Kindergarten*, 82; to Langenthal, April 1835, July 23, 1836, and December 1, 1836, quoted in *Froebel's Letters on the Kindergarten*, 29–30. Many German states had institutions established by private charity to keep the young children of working or poor parents. Barnard, *Papers on Froebel's Kindergarten*, 19, 20.

75. *Froebel's Letters on the Kindergarten*, 31; *Autobiography*, 137. The metaphor of the child-garden has a long history in education. It can be found as early as Plato's *Republic*, paragraph 491.

76. Barnard, *Papers on Froebel's Kindergarten*, 83.

77. Froebel used this publication to explain the meaning, and use of his gifts, and to introduce the new institution. Barnard, *Papers on Froebel's Kindergarten*, 85.

78. The trip is recorded in Froebel's letters to his wife in Blankenburg. Shirreff, *A Short Sketch*, 31–109.

79. Froebel to his wife, December 14, 1838, in *A Short Sketch*, 36, 38, 41.

80. Froebel to his wife, December 12, 1838, and December 14, 1838, in *A Short Sketch*, 36, 38, 44–45.

81. "Address by Froebel before the Queen of Saxony," in *Education by Development*, 242–268.

82. Froebel to his wife, February 3, 1839, in *A Short Sketch*, 93.

83. Froebel to his wife, February 4, 1839, in *A Short Sketch*, 99.

84. Froebel to his wife, February 7, 1839, in *A Short Sketch*, 100.

85. *Froebel's Letters on the Kindergarten*, 176.

86. "Twenty Letters of Froebel to Madame Schmidt, in Gera," June 5, 1840, to February 7, 1848, in *Froebel's Letters on the Kindergarten*, 43–71, 144–147, 153–155.

87. "Seven Letters of Froebel to the Kindergarten Teacher, Mlle, Luise Frankenberg," November 13, 1846, to January 29, 1852, in *Froebel's Letters on the Kindergarten*, 236–247. For more about this correspondence, see Chapter 9 in this volume.

88. *Froebel's Letters on the Kindergarten*, 71; von Bülow, *Reminiscences of Friedrich Froebel*, 4.

89. "To the Wives and Mothers of Blankenburg," in *Froebel's Letters on the Kindergarten*, 218.

90. "Appendix to Letter I to Mme. Schmidt, in Gera, 1st May, 1840," in *Froebel's Letters on the Kindergarten*, 156–171. There were two more addresses to women: "Appeal to German Wives and Maidens" (1844) and "Appeal to German Women" (1848), in *Froebel's Letters on the Kindergarten*, 220–231 and 262–269.

91. Froebel to Mme, Schmidt, July 19, 1840, in *Froebel's Letters on the Kindergarten*, 44, 45.

92. *Froebel's Letters on the Kindergarten*, 220.

93. Ibid., 221.

94. For Froebel's thoughts on gardening and nature, see "The Children's Gardens in the Kindergarten" in Froebel *Education by Development*, 217–228. A diagram for the garden arrangement and the crops to be raised is on page 226.

95. *The Education of Man*, 285.

96. *Froebel's Letters on the Kindergarten*, 175.

97. *Froebel Letters*, 29.

98. Froebel to Mme. Schmidt, September 5, 1840, in *Froebel's Letters on the Kindergarten*, 50.

99. Froebel to Mme. Schmidt, December 19, 1840, in *Froebel's Letters on the Kindergarten*, 72. He sent several of the gifts to be tested by her three sons; and later to the kindergarten she established. Froebel did not name the gifts.

100. *Froebel's Letters on the Kindergarten*, 175–176.

101. Goldammer, *The Kindergarten: A Guide to Froebel's Method of Education, Gifts, and Occupations*, First Part, 1–184. Beginning with the third gift, there is a list of "forms of life or object forms" the child could create, followed by drawings of the structures. See also Margaret A. Trace, *Block Building* (Springfield, MA: Milton Bradley Co., 1928). Book presents the stages of development a child goes through in block building, and their educational possibilities with the other areas of the curriculum; and Harriet M. Johnson, *The Art of Block Building* (New York: The John Day Co., 1933), block building in the nursery school.

102. Froebel and his colleagues had created "A Hundred Songs for the Ball-Games of the Blankenberg Kindergarten." *Froebel's Letters on the Kindergarten*, 220.

103. Barnard, *Papers on Froebel's Kindergarten*, 362. Froebel divided schooling into: kindergarten, intermediate class or school, school of instruction and reasoning, school of vocation and life, and professional school. Ibid.

104. The descriptions of the occupations are also from Goldammer's *The Kindergarten*, Second Part, 16–149. Each part of the book is separately paginated.

105. *The Education of Man*, 287.

106. Friedrich Froebel, *Mother-Play and Nursery Songs*, trans. Fannie E. Dwight and Josephine Jarvis, ed. Elizabeth P. Peabody (Boston: Lothrop, Lee & Shepard, 1878).

107. *Froebel's Letters on the Kindergarten*, 250.

108. For a complete list of names and places, see *Froebel's Letters on the Kindergarten*, 176–178, 180–191.

109. For all the countries that adopted the kindergarten, see *Froebel's Letters on the Kindergarten*, 192–209. A great-great-aunt of one of the authors brought the kindergarten to Greece, cf. *Froebel's Letters on the Kindergarten*, 200.

110. "Plan for the Training School for Children's Nurses and Educators" in Froebel, *Education by Development*, 229–241. There are two more versions of this plan: in Miss Howe's letter, April 18, 1847, in *Froebel's Letters on the Kindergarten*, 248–256; and in a letter to von Arnswald, October 30, 1847, in *Froebel Letters*, 71–76.

111. von Bülow, *Reminiscences*, 2–27, 34. Diesterweg's "Guide for German Teachers" was the best existing manual, for both elementary and secondary teachers. It is dedicated to Froebel. Barnard, *Papers on Froebel's Kindergarten*, 149–160.

112. A biography of the Baroness, in Barnard, *Papers on Froebel's Kindergarten*, 149–160.

113. von Bülow, *Reminiscences*, 173–174.

114. Froebel to Luise Frankenberg, Keilhau, February 13, 1848, in *Froebel's Letters on the Kindergarten*, 242.

115. *Froebel's Letters on the Kindergarten*, 178. Until unification (1871), Germany was divided into many independent principalities. It had the advantage that if someone was persecuted in one principality, he could go to another.

116. von Bülow, *Reminiscences*, 198–200.

117. Barnard, *Papers on Froebel's Kindergarten*, 151, A full account of the Pestalozzi-Froebel House in Berlin and its activities is given in *Froebel's Letters on the Kindergarten*, 35–43.

118. von Bülow, *Reminiscences*, 256–259, 265, 275.

119. Ibid., 259–263.

120. Ibid., 264.

121. Ibid.

122. von Bülow, *Reminiscences*, 188–290.

123. Barnard, *Papers on Froebel's Kindergarten*, 120–121; Shirreff, in *A Short Sketch*, stated, "Luther was the officiating minister in Froebel's funeral," 134. For a detailed

account of Froebel's funeral, see von Bülow, *Reminiscences,* 292–303. She stated that Ernst Luther was present at the funeral, not that he officiated (296).

124. Barnard, *Papers on Froebel's Kindergarten,* 135. Elizabeth Peabody, "Origin and Growth of the Kindergarten" *Education* 2, no. 5 (May 1852): 516n.

125. Frau Froebel's visit is recounted by a teacher in the musical kindergarten. Marie Heinemann, "Frau Luise Froebel, Personal Reminiscences" in *Froebel Letters,* 149–151. There is no mention however, as to when the "Musical Kindergarten" was established.

126. *Froebel's Letters on the Kindergarten,* 187n2.

127. Ibid., vi.

128. Ibid., 31–32. Among those who wrote books were sixteen physicians, eight theologians, eight lawyers, eleven masters of grammar schools and commercial schools, seventeen masters of Normal Schools, eighty-six masters of National Elementary Schools, six principals of Idiot Asylums, seventy-four teachers of the actual kindergarten methods, forty-seven literary men, eight editors of journals, forty-six ladies, and thirty-two others (not specified).

CHAPTER 5

Post–Industrial Revolution (1860–1980)

> "Education by life" is the only true description of Nursery
> School education, for formal instruction has no place in it.
> —Grace Owen[1]

The inhumane conditions of child life continued into the post-industrial age, particularly for the children of working-class families. The end of the nineteenth century and the first third of the twentieth century was a period in which the standard of living in most working-class families in England declined. The Web site for the City of Bradford, England, states that the Luddites, hand weavers from Yorkshire, smashed or burned power machinery to show their opposition to industrialization. In spite of this, the pace of the Industrial Revolution continued to quicken. By 1841, there were over one hundred mills in the city of Bradford and the surrounding borough. Margaret McMillan spent eight years learning about the deplorable housing and unsanitary conditions of children there. This information was later utilized in assisting both the children of Bradford and the children of the Deptford slum section of London.

Day nurseries and free kindergartens were opened for the children of the working class in some British cities and towns. The work of Dr. Maria Montessori became known through the publication of her book *The Montessori Method*. The work of Froebel and that of Dr. Montessori influenced the early childhood education movement in Great Britain. (For a discussion of the work of Froebel see Chapter 4 and for a discussion of the work of Dr. Montessori see Chapter 6.)[2]

GRACE OWEN (1873–1965)

Grace Owen was born in 1873, in England, and trained in Froebelian methods at the Blackheath Kindergarten Training College. She attended Teachers' College of Columbia University between 1900 and approximately 1905, graduating with a bachelor of science degree. Owen attended one of the first lecture courses given by Patty Smith Hill at Teachers' College.[3] While she was in New York City, her impressions of American kindergartens were published in *Child Life*.[4] Grace Owen became the sister-in-law of Dr. James McKeen Cattell, a professor of psychology at Teachers' College, when he and her sister married.

Owen held a progressive view of the kindergarten movement. In a 1906 article, she cited the works of Froebel himself, Wilhelm Middendorff and

Baroness von Bülow, in differentiating between the original Froebel kindergartens and the structured kindergartens espoused by conservatives. Owen
pointed out that there were approximately twenty-five children in Froebel's
multi-age kindergartens. The work was based on the interests and experiences
of each child. Owen claimed that order and unity in the kindergarten program
was provided by the regularity of the daily morning circle, united prayers, and
a formal march to the playground each day. Although there was little systematic curriculum planning, a portion of the program was allocated to directed
work, such as the folding or cutting of forms from paper (209). Competitive
games and vigorous physical exercises were derived from the free, undirected
play of children, which later led to cooperative play (210). Gardening allowed
the children to learn from nature. The role of the Froebelian teacher, according to Owen, was to encourage the child's spontaneous self-expression and
individuality. The teacher was to present symbolic ideas through experience
alone. Appropriate methods included undirected play, suggestion, imitation,
and discovery by experiment (213).[5]

Upon her return to England, Owen joined the faculty of the University of
Manchester, where she was a lecturer and demonstrator until 1910.[6] In 1908
Owen testified before the Board of Education, giving evidence that contributed to the publication *Report of the Consultive Committee upon the
School Attendance of Children Below the Age of Five.* This report resulted
from a decade of previous educational events.[7] There were many uncompli-
mentary reports by Board of Education inspectors about the inclusion of
under-fives in the elementary schools. The inspectors' opinion was that children under the age of five got practically no intellectual advantage from being
in the schools. From the 1890s on, younger children were excluded physically
and monetarily. The 1905 Code of Regulations for Public Elementary Schools
officially refused "under-fives" admission to the schools. Three years later,
Owen's testimony supported the need for nursery schools for children
between the ages of three and five years. The nursery school was envisioned as
a social and medical, not an educational, institution.[8] By 1918, the twelve
existing voluntary nursery schools, and eight new nursery schools, were supported monetarily by the Board of Education.

Between 1910 and 1929, Owen lectured at institutions in Reading and
Leeds, and at the City of Manchester Training College. Owen's nursery school
was visited by Abigail Adams Eliot on her 1921 trip to England. Eliot found
Grace Owen to be "scientific and 'broad minded' and [she] enjoyed their conversations enormously."[9] During the summer of 1922, Owen taught a nursery
school course at Teachers' College of Columbia University, and was inter-
viewed for *Mother and Child Magazine.*[10] In 1924 she became the principal of
the Mather Training College in Manchester.[11]

Grace Owen's best known publication is her edited book *Nursery School
Education,* which first appeared in 1920.[12] Owen was one of the three
founders of the Nursery School Association in 1923, along with Margaret
McMillan and Lady Nancy Astor. She remained a leader in the Association

for the rest of her life. The prefatory note to the 1929 publication of the Education Enquiry Committee of 1929 thanks her, along with a handful of others,
for their contribution to the inquiry. Owen apparently made a very strong
case for nursery schools.[13]

Grace Owen lived a full life as a proponent of the nursery school, a
teacher, and a teacher educator. Although little is known of her work between
1930 and the time of her death in 1965, she will be remembered for her
staunch support of the nursery school movement in England, and her leadership of the Nursery School Association.

MARGARET MCMILLAN (1860–1931) AND RACHEL MCMILLAN (1859–1917)

Rachel McMillan was born on March 25, 1859, and Margaret on July 19,
1860, in Westchester County, New York. They and their sister Elizabeth, who
died at an early age, were the children of James and Jane Cameron McMillan.
The parents, who had been born in Scotland, headed a large household that
included eight servants. James McMillan died in July 1865 and the widow
took her two remaining children back to Scotland to live with their maternal
grandparents. Both sisters attended school until the death of their mother in
July 1877. At that time Rachel was called home to take care of her grandmother, and Margaret went away to school and became a governess. After the
death of their grandparents, Rachel decided to train to become a sanitation
inspector. When she completed the training, Margaret joined her in the
Bloomsbury section of London.[14]

Margaret did volunteer work for the labour movement and then was
employed as a companion to Lady Meux of Park Lane, London. Margaret
began to attend meetings of the socialist Fabian Society with Rachel. Some of
the members, including Margaret, made speeches on a platform in a corner of
Hyde Park. When Lady Meux heard that Margaret had made a speech, she
forced her to choose between socialism and the possibility of inheriting a considerable fortune. Margaret left Park Lane to become a founding member of
the Independent Labour Party (ILP).

Margaret first visited Bradford in 1892, when she spoke at the Labour
Church. In 1893, she and Rachel decided to accept the Bradford socialists' invitation to volunteer. However, Rachel's training as a sanitary inspector took
precedence over her volunteer work. During the summer of 1894, Margaret
was invited to become an ILP candidate for the Bradford School Board. She was
elected. On December 6, 1894, she attended her first meeting and joined the
Education Committee, the School Attendance Committee, and the School
Management Committee. She made frequent visits to the schools, where she
discovered a high level of disease and malnutrition among the children.[15]

Margaret had learned in her study of socialism that good health was the only
capital most working men possessed. Margaret maintained that the children's
low resistance to disease was caused by foul air, uncleanliness, insufficient

exercise, and severe malnourishment, which she believed was related to the low wages of their parents.[16]

Margaret and Rachel fought for children's causes on the local and national levels. Through Margaret's writing and through her work in the ILP, a number of relief orders and other laws were passed in the early 1900s. The first school baths in Britain were opened at the Wapping Street School in Bradford in 1897, and nutritious school meals for the poor and regular medical inspections for pupils were also a result of her work. One of Margaret's biographers, G. A. N. Lowndes, called her the "Albert Schweitzer of the Bradford slums."[17]

Margaret resigned from the Bradford School Board in 1902 and moved to London. Between 1908 and 1910, she established a school health clinic in the Bow section of London, with the support of soap magnate Joseph Fels. Although the clinic was not financially successful, it was the keystone of her later work in Deptford. In 1911, Deptford had a higher population density and infant mortality rate than many of the neighboring boroughs. Margaret opened a school clinic and medical home in a Deptford school. Then she turned her attention to night camps and a camp school. The girls arrived at the camp in the late afternoon, played in the garden, and participated in all of the domestic jobs connected with running the camp. They set the tables for the evening meal, and the older girls looked after the younger ones. As the tuberculosis scare in the Deptford area increased, it was decided to open a companion camp for boys. Photographs depict the children sleeping on cots in the open air covered by blankets. This was the first time many of the children had seen the sky, flowers, or butterflies. The fresh air, and nutritious food, caused the children to put on weight and get visibly stronger and healthier. Then Margaret opened a camp school for boys and girls aged six to fourteen years whose curable diseases had certified them as unfit to attend regular public schools. Classes were conducted by paid schoolteachers, in the open air.[18]

Margaret discovered that there was a gap in the supervision of the health and nutrition of children. The 1837 Notification of Birth Act insured that there was some supervision of children up to their first birthday. The existing wealthier centers looked after the health of babies from birth to approximately two years of age. When children entered the infant school at age five and above, they were cared for by the school doctors. For the majority of children aged two to five, there were great dangers from infectious diseases, and little supervision by the medical or education professions.

The Rachel McMillan Nursery School

Margaret decided to open the Baby Camp in 1911. In 1913, industrialist Fels, the maker of Naphtha Soap, wrote to the London City Council about land for the McMillan nursery school. He pointed out to the Council that the Stowage, an acre of vacant land in front of the Deptford clinic, could be used by the McMillan sisters. The Council agreed to let them rent the land at the rate of one shilling a year on the condition that the agreement could be terminated at a day's notice. However, from 1913 on, the land was used for the open-air nursery school.[19]

The Consultative Committee of the English Board of Education realized that the infant schools were unsuitable for very young children and suggested the development of a new institution. The establishment of nursery schools began during the second stage of the infant school movement, the "individual work" stage. It was believed that an infant teacher who had devoted much time and thought to careful preparation of the educational environment could provide for children in the large class to be busily and purposefully occupied, while the teacher remained in the background helping children individually.

McMillan's nursery school met some of the aims of the Consultative Committee. Its foundation was the work of Darwin, Plato, Rousseau, and Froebel. Margaret was also familiar with the work of Robert Owen and of Seguin on mental deficiency. The school was founded during the fourth stage of the infant school movement, which encouraged free play. Teachers were encouraged to take note of things done by children that were worthy of further expansion during the day. The ideas could then be enriched with stories, talks, apparatus, and visits. Margaret believed that schools should help children form good habits of personal hygiene, use sense-training, and support play as a vehicle for education. The McMillans believed that each child was a child of God, a unique being, a person of infinite worth and one to be respected and reverenced.[20]

Margaret had three major goals for her nursery school work. First, she wanted to give nurture to all children whose parents wished them to have it. Her definition of the term "nurture" was, "the all-round loving care of individuals" (54). Her second goal was to assist parents in improving their child-rearing practices, and to develop their own potentialities (61–62). Margaret's third goal was to make both a blueprint and a working model that others could use as an observation center (75). She wanted the school to be a laboratory for research, which would draw together doctors, nurses, social workers, and women of different classes. Margaret's statement was that she wanted to make the open-air nursery school she founded in 1913 "an object lesson which would be progressive in its influence," and thus people could accept, reject, or use it as a basis for their own thinking. McMillan also made a contribution to the primary school curriculum, by drawing attention to the importance of aesthetics in the curriculum.[21] With the death of her sister in 1917, the school was renamed the Rachel McMillan Nursery School.

In 1918, due in large measure to the work of the McMillans, and Grace Owen, the Fisher Act was passed. This education act made possible the establishment of nursery schools throughout Great Britain. It gave the local education authorities the power to provide nursery schools or nursery classes for children between the ages of two and five years old. The act required the nursery school to attend to the health, nourishment, and physical welfare of children attending the nursery schools. Standards for the mental and social education of children, the administrative details, and the staffing of the institution were established. Three classes of nursery staff, superintendents, adult assistants and nurses, and probationers, and their duties, were defined and discussed in the Act. The Board of Education was directed to pay, out of money provided by Parliament, grants-in-aid to the nursery school. In order to receive the grant, the school must be open to inspection by the Local Education Authority. This made the nursery school a part of the national school system in Great Britain.[22]

In 1928, Owen deplored the fact that though ten years had passed since the nursery school clause in the Education Act of 1918 was accepted, there were no more than twenty-six recognized nursery schools in England. In *Nursery School Education*, Owen stated that it was preferable to provide for a few well-equipped and adequately staffed nursery schools within each district or area. As a member of the National Administrative Council of the ILP, Margaret McMillan wanted to create a model environment that would lengthen the period of working-class children's education, and "enrich and refine the nervous system in the formative period."[23]

In the spring of 1923, Grace Owen and Mrs. Evelegh visited Margaret McMillan at the Rachel McMillan Nursery School to enlist her participation in the formation of the Nursery School Association. The main objectives of this association were to secure the effective work of the Education Act of 1918, to become a forum for discussion, and to form and focus public opinion on matters relating to the nursery school movement. The Association, renamed the British Association for Early Childhood Education in 1973, was a focus of Margaret's work from the time of its establishment until her death. She was the Association's first president, and held the office for the next six years. She chaired meetings, gave lectures, and led delegations to the Board of Education, to further the idea of nursery schools for all.[24]

The Training Centre

McMillan had difficulty in finding appropriate teachers for her nursery school during World War I. She saw a need for change in the initial and in-service training of teachers, and made her nursery school into a training school. The training center was called "The College," and began with a few students, so that they could have individual tutoring. The center functioned as a part of the nursery school, without a specific building. Students lived in four dilapidated houses, which had few amenities. The Rachel McMillan Training Centre workers were designated as "teacher-nurses."

The training center offered a program for those who wanted to work with disadvantaged children, placing nursery school work in a sociological context. Margaret believed in the sustained involvement of the home, and viewed teachers and parents as partners in a common task of preparing children for life. Both Abigail Adams Eliot and Edna Nobel White worked and studied with McMillan in London.[25] The course began with practical work and added academic work in the second year of the three-year course. In the last year, students focused exclusively on theoretical work.[26] McMillan worked outside the state system from 1914, when she first began training teachers, until she gained the Board of Education's recognition for the center in 1919.

The students' school-based course was arduous. The hours were long and included home visiting in the evenings. Despite the disadvantages, there were many applicants. Some were attracted by the size of the task Margaret had undertaken with such slender resources, some by her idealism, and others by her lofty vision of the teaching profession.

The training emphasized the relationship of physical development and health to cognitive and affective development. The college curriculum included: instruction and clinical experience in dental hygiene; experience in a general clinic for children's diseases; physical training; music (including dancing, dramatization, and instrumental music); a course in psychology especially planned to help the students understand the child of nursery age; a course in history given mainly in connection with dramatization; handwork; art; and gardening. Extensive opportunity was provided for observation and practice in the care of children. Among the distinctive features of the training course at the time of its inception were its focus on understanding children's behavior through observation, and its practical, school-based training. McMillan arranged visits outside of the training center in order to help students develop their own powers of observation, and also to prepare them for the time when they would take children for walks.[27]

To improve living and working conditions of the students at the center, McMillan envisioned a "purpose built" college alongside the nursery school. She set up a building fund to raise the money for it. The college building, completed in 1930, was opened by Queen Mary. The college exemplified McMillan's belief that *"preschool children should have appropriately trained well-qualified teachers."*[28]

McMillan's philosophy of teacher education included nurturing children. She was adamant about the fact that the nursery school teacher is "helping to make a brain and nervous system," a philosophy that finds its current expression in brain-based research. Students learned through their observations of the children. McMillan believed that a teacher of very young children must have "a finer perception and a wider training and outlook than is needed by any other kind of teacher." The student "teacher-nurses" had to learn how to bathe, dress, feed, and take care of the children. They lived in the community, near the school, so they became friendly with the mothers, and familiar with their lifestyles. They learned about service to the poorest children in the city, long before the term "compensatory education" was coined.[29]

Margaret McMillan wrote extensively about early childhood education. Her most important book was *The Nursery School*, originally published in 1919. This was one of the first books about the nursery school, and it served as the model for nursery schools both in Europe and in the United States. Between 1917 and 1931, she was awarded several British government honors for her war and nursery school work. She died in Bowden House in Harrow-on-the-Hill, on March 29, 1931, at the age of seventy. She was buried with her sister Rachel at Brockley Cemetery, in London, on March 31.[30]

In 1976, the Rachel McMillan College of Education, which had been founded by Margaret McMillan in 1930, amalgamated with Goldsmith's College and became part of the University of London. According to its Web site, Goldsmith's College focuses on the study of creative, cultural, and social processes, with a commitment to lifelong learning. It values its tradition of working with and for the people of South East London. The Rachel and Margaret McMillan papers are housed in the Special Collections Library at Goldsmith's College.[31]

In the foreword to the 1921 edition of *The Nursery School,* Patty Smith Hill wrote that McMillan presented a most convincing study in the power of early environment. She had proven that not only could the children of poverty be saved, but "that they may be worth while to themselves and society in their survival." Hill said McMillan had demonstrated that the development and education of young children cannot be left to chance. The healthy, happy children of McMillan's Nursery School had opportunities "which should be the birthright of all the children of all nations and races." They developed habits that formed the foundation of good character and citizenship. Hill warned that "if we wait until the child is three years old it may be too late."[32]

JEAN PIAGET (1896–1980)

Jean Piaget was born on August 9, 1896, in Neuchâtel, Switzerland, a small university town. His father, Arthur, was a historian and professor of medieval literature at the University of Neuchâtel. According to Pulaski, the father passed down his habit of systematic thinking to his son. His mother was Rebecca Jackson Piaget, a dynamic, intelligent, religious woman. Because of the mother's poor mental health, Jean Piaget later became intensely interested in psychopathology and the theories of Freud.[33]

The young Piaget showed an early interest in nature, observing birds, fish, and animals in their natural habitat, and publishing an article when he was ten years old.[34] He was still in high school when he assisted the director of the Neuchâtel Natural History Museum in classifying and labeling the extensive collection of shells. He did this for four years, and the director, a specialist in mollusks, taught Jean and gave him rare specimens for his own collection. Piaget learned enough from his mentor to publish a series of articles on mollusks. One of these articles, penned at the age of fifteen, earned him the offer of the directorship of the Geneva Museum of Natural History, which he had to turn down because he was still in school. Piaget vacationed with his godfather, Samuel Cornut, a Swiss scholar, during his adolescent years. Cornut introduced him to Henry Bergson's philosophy of creative evolution, because Cornut felt Jean was too restricted in pursuing the direction of the biological sciences. Piaget broadened his readings to include philosophy, religion, logic, and sociology. He became especially interested in epistemology (the branch of philosophy concerned with the study of knowledge). He developed a curiosity about answers to such questions as: What is knowledge? How is it acquired?[35]

Piaget became a student of natural sciences at the University of Neuchâtel, completing his undergraduate studies, with a focus on biology, in 1916. By the age of twenty-one, he had presented his Ph.D. dissertation in malacology (study of mollusks), and had also completed all the requirements short of the dissertation for another Ph.D. in philosophy.[36] During this time period, he published two philosophical essays that were important for the general orientation of his thinking.[37]

He then moved to Zurich, where he worked in two psychological laboratories. In addition, he worked at the Psychiatric Institute of Eugen Bleuler, where he learned the art of clinical interviewing, and published an article on the relationship between psychoanalysis and child psychology.[38] In 1919, he went to Paris for two years of study at the Sorbonne. During his time in Paris, he worked for a year at the Ecole de la rue de la Grange-aux-Belles boys' institution (school), created by Alfred Binet as a laboratory. This laboratory was later directed by Théophile Simon.[39] Simon suggested that Piaget standardize Englishman Cyril Burt's reading tests, which were used as part of the Binet scale. Simon wanted these tests to be standardized on French children. When Piaget began to work with the Parisian children, he became more interested in why children "failed" the tests than establishing "norms" for success. He began to study the reasoning of the children by presenting them with open-ended questions.[40]

From this initial work with children, Piaget made three basic findings. First, he looked at incorrect answers and found that the same wrong answers occurred frequently in children of about the same age. He decided that the problem of intelligence must be defined in terms of discovering children's ways of thinking. He said that the thought of younger children was qualitatively different from that of older children. He therefore sought a less structured questioning method, and modified psychiatric interview techniques. He had learned these techniques in his study of abnormal children at the Salpetrière Hospital in Paris. Piaget discovered that the verbal methods employed at the Binet laboratory did not work here, because the children's verbal abilities were deficient. Piaget developed a new procedure in which the child was required to both answer a question and manipulate certain materials. Although this method was not immediately applied to work with normal children, he later found the clinical method useful in his study of children's thought patterns. In carrying out his own work, he permitted the child's answers to determine the course of questioning. His reading in the area of logic led him to study why children younger than eleven years of age are unable to carry out certain elementary logical operations, for example, deduction. His goal was to determine how closely thought approximates logic. He determined that logic, rather than imprecise natural language, might be an efficient way of describing thought.[41]

Piaget was attempting to build a bridge between biology and psychology. He believed, for example, that intelligence could be viewed in terms of an organism's adaptation to its environment. He also believed that psychology should focus on the process of intellectual growth in the individual, by studying its formation and evolution in childhood.[42]

In 1921, Sir Edouard Claparède and P. Bovet offered him the post of Director of Research at the Jean-Jacques Rousseau Institute in Geneva (a school formed for the scientific study of the child and the training of teachers).[43] Between 1923 and 1932, he wrote a series of articles and published his first five books on children based on his study of the children at the Maison des Petits (preschool) at the Rousseau Institute.

He married one of his Institute students, Valentine Châtenay, and had three children. Jacqueline was born in 1925, Lucienne in 1927, and their only son, Laurent, in 1931. He and his wife studied their children's cognitive development in great detail, and Piaget published a number of books based on these observations done during the first years of life (from the children's infancy to their development of language).

Piaget held a number of academic posts in France and Switzerland. In 1929, he was first appointed a professor at the University of Geneva. He was the director of the Rousseau Institute, which was attached to the university, between 1940 and 1971. He was reportedly the only Swiss to be invited at the University of Paris, the Sorbonne, between 1952 and 1963. Piaget was also active in international venues. He was the chairman of the International Bureau of Education on which he served between 1929 and 1967. He headed the Swiss delegation to UNESCO, and was a member of its Executive Council for many years.

Piaget criticized the views which tried to justify war by citing biology. He was critical of both neo-Darwinism and Lamarckism. Piaget stated that "the more one examines the mechanism of life the more one discovers that love and altruism—that is, the negation of war—are inherent in the nature of human beings. Only later complications due to environmental inertia, and thus, competition, force living creatures to a restricted assimilation . . . in the human species, war. To struggle against war is therefore to act according to the logic of life against the logic of things, and that is the whole of morality."[44] In a 1934 bulletin of the League of Nations, Piaget stated that even during the years when the teaching of international cooperation was approved everywhere, it was exceedingly superficial. He felt that the aim was to provide students with ready-made opinions regarding the League of Nations rather than foster the intellectual and moral tendencies conducive to true collaboration. He thought that really effective education for peace should be related to the national education practiced in each country. This would lead to internationalism and peaceful collaboration. He said that education for peace is possible, if it is "situated in the realistic present," and is part of a global readjustment. He recommended a detailed study of the pedagogical techniques to be employed.[45]

During his later years, he made several trips to the United States, speaking before child development groups. One of those was an appearance before the Jean Piaget Society, the group founded by Dr. Lois Macomber of Temple University, which was meeting in Philadelphia. The Society, which was founded in 1970, has an international interdisciplinary membership of scholars, teachers, and researchers who are interested in exploring the nature of the developmental construction of human knowledge. In 1989, at the annual symposium, the Society's name was changed to Jean Piaget Society: Society for the Study of Knowledge and Development.[46]

A major milestone was the 1956 opening of the interdisciplinary international Center for Genetic Epistemology, an institute within the Faculty of Science of the University of Geneva. Each year a number of eminent scholars in such fields as biology, psychology, mathematics, physics, language and linguistics, and education would combine their efforts to study a given problem. Each member of the "Geneva group" would address the problem from the point of view of his or her specialty, but the research was coordinated through regular discussions. In June of each year, the researchers would discuss their conclusions on the topic selected for the year by Piaget in a final symposium. These deliberations were published in a monograph series entitled *Studies in Genetic Epistemology.*[47]

Jean Piaget died on September 16, 1980, in Geneva, Switzerland, at the age of eighty-four years. A tribute to him written by Dorothy Hewes shortly thereafter speculates on what a conversation between Piaget and Froebel would be like. Both were concerned about followers who adamantly accepted their theories as completed systems. Neither ever felt that his system was complete. In the United States, Froebel's system was distorted more by those who revered him than by those who were critical. With the improved communication of the mid-twentieth century, it was even easier to take simple tasks that explored the way children learn to reason logically and turn them into rote exercises intended to force learning. Piaget would talk about "The American Disease" in which adults push children into activities before they are ready. Both men would muse about why learning through play must be repeatedly justified. A major problem presented by Hewes is the teaching of cognitive tricks that give the illusion of learning. Piaget and Froebel would agree that if children have not yet reached mastery stages, the logical processes probably are not understood. Froebel called these processes, "making the inner outer and the outer inner," and Piaget described them as, "assimilation and accommodation."[48]

Publications

Jean Piaget published more than three hundred papers, book chapters, and introductions. His books in French, which were translated into English and numerous other languages, numbered more than fifty. The books in his early period[49] studied language, logic, and the morality of the preoperational child.

Piaget's structuralist period lasted from the 1940s through the 1960s. This denoted a shift in emphasis to structural analysis. The books upon which most of Piaget's reputation is based came out of this period. The writing detailed the nature of the logicomathematical structures that underlie cognitive development.[50] He wrote a number of books describing the logicomathematical formulations of the development of operational thinking. Piaget collaborated extensively with Bärbel Inhelder, and on two books with Alina Szeminska.

The 1960s marked a period of transition in Piaget's theoretical formulations. From 1970 until his death a decade later, he returned to the dominance of functionalism, albeit a "new functionalism." According to Beilin, "in the last period, there is an intellectual struggle apparent in Piaget, to bring these two major strains in the theory [structuralism and functionalism] into some kind of equilibrium. This final synthesis was intended to be achieved in the last of Piaget's books, that he co-authored with Rolando Garcia."[51] These books summarized the work Piaget was engaged in at the end of his life, which has been carried on by his associates.[52]

Piaget's Work in Historical Context

Prior to the 1920s, when Piaget began his investigations, there had been very little research on intelligence. Piaget wanted to avoid premature restrictions; therefore, he offered several definitions of intelligence, all couched in general terms. These definitions dealt with content of thought (what the individual is thinking about and what interests him at the moment, as well as in what terms he contemplates a given problem); the specific heredity (role of biological factors in the development of intelligence); and general heredity (adaptation and organization). In the course of his work at the Binet Laboratory, he came to the conclusion that psychology might provide the link between biology and epistemology.[53] Piaget's major interests were the study of life (biology) and the study of knowledge (epistemology). He decided to study the evolution of knowledge in the child. The theory that evolved from Piaget's studies was based on "the confluence of the logical and the biological models in the study of natural thought . . . a view of developmental epistemology from the perspective of learning."[54]

The early Piagetian writings dealt only sketchily with equilibration and reflexive abstraction and the concept of conflict as a spark of reorganization of thinking, all of which later became an important part of the theory.[55] Piaget's four stages, the sensorimotor, preoperational, concrete operational, and formal operational, followed each other in invariant order. However, according to Piaget, each stage must represent a qualitative change in the child's cognition. Each stage includes the cognitive structures and abilities of the preceding stage. At each stage, the child's schemas and operations form an integrated whole. Learning takes place through the process of construction. Children alter their perceptions gradually over a period of time.

The Genevan research method (*Method Clinique*) used questioning as a technique for information gathering. Open-ended questions encouraged problem-solving behavior. The researchers questioned the children about how they would approach a problem and how they arrived at their answers. Both correct and incorrect responses were recorded. The researchers probed and requestioned each child, allowing him to clarify, and amplify his thinking.[56] According to Forman and Kuschner, "Ideally, a theory of knowledge leads to a theory of development, which in turn leads to a theory of learning, which in turn leads to a theory of teaching. . . . A theory of teaching that does not derive from a theory of development represents a split between theory and practice." These authors further define the purpose of early childhood education as "the construction of knowledge in order to improve the quality of life."[57] They believe that knowing how to use knowledge is the overarching purpose of education.

Piaget's basic law of development stated that the child constructs his own intelligence and knowledge through play. Children begin with "exercise play," and then move to "symbolic play." During the preoperational stage, between ages two and seven years, pretend play has an important role in the life of the child because he is not yet capable of logical reasoning. The ability to play games with rules, when the child reaches the age of six or seven years, indicates cognitive and sociomoral development in a later play stage. Piaget believed that work develops out of play interests; therefore as symbolic play becomes more and more reflective of reality, symbolic play leads to "games of construction." The games "are initially imbued with play symbolism but tend later to constitute genuine adaptations . . . or solutions to problems and intelligent creations."[58] Play becomes the basis for self-initiated activity from which the young child constructs characteristic ways of acting and thinking. It is also "the manifestation of the developing semiotic function. . . . The ability to transform objects, roles, and situations [which] is thought to be central to the growing ability to use symbols."[59] According to Monighan-Nourot, "Play is thought to support the development of such cognitive qualities as curiosity; exploration; divergent thinking; symbolic transformation; representation of physical, logicomathematical, and social knowledge; temporal sequencing; conservation; spatial reasoning; seriation; classification; and perspectivism."[60]

Elkind, agreeing with Freud and Piaget, stated that the distinction between work and play in early childhood should be maintained. This distinction is important "because it provides the necessary tension for the kinds of integration that we call science and art."[61] In supporting the Piagetian conception of the child, Elkind reminds us that the child is potentially self-regulational—capable of learning in a directed, organized, and self-correcting way, as a logical thinker. A child thinks and uses language differently than adults do, but has the same needs and feelings as those of adults.[62] Piaget felt that play was primarily assimilation, for example, the child makes the world fit into his own schemas rather than accommodating to the demands of the world. Play serves as a reinforcer of ideas and patterns of behavior, provides an imaginative outlet, and is used by some older children to facilitate the process of adaptation.[63]

Piaget's Work in Educational Context

Beginning in the 1960s, attempts were made to apply the Genevan developmental theory directly to curriculum and instruction. Among the factors responsible for this were the direct application of Skinnerian theory and the marketing of educational materials that could be manipulated in very direct attempts to teach concepts of learning or change existing learning patterns. Piaget's research tasks became marketable kit materials to "sell" cognitive development. Materials to teach conservation found their place on the shelf next to the teaching machine and the programmed-instruction books of the stimulus-response school of learning.[64] One example of such a kit was developed by Celia Stendler Lavatelli to accompany her book *Piaget's Theory Applied to an Early Childhood Curriculum.*[65] Kamii, DeVries, Gallagher, and Reid agreed with those who said "that teaching the tasks reduces the theory to the content of the tasks themselves and results in an obvious distortion."[66]

Another problem was that many of Piaget's works had not been translated from French into English, and therefore those who studied Piagetian theory in English were "naturally drawn to what was most obvious in the then translated works—tasks and stages." Piaget was focused on the process of thinking and what the child's answers revealed about the underlying thought processes.[67] By using the method of critical exploration, and questioning children about how they approach a problem, teachers could determine the level of cognitive functioning of individual children, and then fit the program of instruction more adequately to those individuals. Teachers were also advised that the learning environment should support the activity of the child, that children's interactions with their peers are an important source of cognitive development, and that instructional strategies that make children aware of conflicts and inconsistencies in their thinking should be adopted.[68]

Educators were encouraged to adopt a child-centered point of view, and to remember that the child's experience or modes of learning are not the same as their own. They were enjoined to improve their own capacity to watch and listen, and to avoid generalizing from their experience to that of the child.[69] Ginsburg and Opper believe that Piaget's theory provides some general principles for the conduct of education, as well as the development of specific mathematical and physical concepts. Therefore they support the use of Piagetian principles in the development of curriculum and teaching practices. They caution, however, that curriculum should build on forms of thought that the child is capable of. Limitations on children's learning should be taken into consideration.[70]

Constance Kamii wrote in 1973 that the first principle of education drawn from Piaget's theory is the view that learning has to be an act of process because knowledge is constructed from within.[71] Piaget himself noted that programmed instruction is not conducive to constructing, unless the child can do the programming.[72] Kamii's second principle deals with the importance of social actions among schoolchildren. Piaget believed that cooperation among children is as important as the child's cooperation with adults, in order to further their intellectual development.[73] Kamii's third principle relates to giving priority to intellectual activity based on actual experiences rather than language. Corry cites "nurturing reflexivity, . . . the ability of students to be aware of their own role in the knowledge construction process," as another condition for learning.[74]

The Sputnik crisis of 1957 and the ferment of the 1960s, as well as the civil rights crisis of the 1960s and 1970s led to educational reform propositions. Bruner and others viewed Piagetian theory as a basis for reform. Bruner said that any academic subject can be taught to any child of any age in some intellectually honest form. This led to the so-called "spiral curriculum" approach. The reforms of the early 1960s "inadvertently left out—or deliberately ignored—poor children and children from minority groups."[75] The interest in Piaget's work, generated by the appearance of a handful of books in English, led to American research that replicated or extended Piaget's work. This research coincided with "the focus of national concern and federal resources on early cognitive education of 'deprived' or 'disadvantaged' children from poor families. It is thus not surprising that among those who responded to the challenge to develop preschool programs were psychologists and educators impressed with Piaget's work as the best available, research-based theory of cognitive development. They sought to develop a theory of educational practice based on this theory."[76] Piaget did not discuss the educational significance of his theory in detail; therefore, educators were challenged with the task of deriving a practical significance for Piaget's work. His theory was relatively insensitive to cultural and social differences; therefore, it held the promise of assisting children who had not profited from traditional schooling.[77]

The focus on what a child *could* do led to the formulation of curriculum models based on Piaget's theory. Kohlberg grouped diverse learning theories into categories, the *maturationist,* the *environmentalist,* and the *interactionist* points of view. *Maturationist* programs emphasized the part played by the child including views of unfolding and developmental maturation. The *environmentalist* point of view emphasized the impact of the outside environment, while the *interactionist* point of view stated that the organism and the environment interact in complex ways. Later the three streams were renamed *romanticism, cultural transmission,* and the *cognitive-developmental* school of thought. The *romanticists* believed that educational thought is phenomenological, and emphasized spontaneity, creativity, and self-confidence. The psychological theories of Freud and Gesell are exemplified by these programs. The *cultural transmission* stream assumed that knowledge resulted from information coming from outside the individual through the senses. Locke, Thorndike, and Skinner's theories, and Engelmann's programmed learning are examples of cultural transmission. The *cognitive-developmental* viewpoint is exemplified by Piaget's constructivist theory. It is based on the work begun by Plato and carried on by Hegel. It was formed into an educational philosophy by John Dewey. This stream is often called "interactionist," which means that there is both a psychological interchange between the individual and the environment and an interaction within the individual of multiple aspects of what is "known."[78]

The *cognitive-developmental/interactionist* theories formed the basis for a number of planned variation Head Start and Follow Through models.[79] The program descriptions sent out by the Office of Education in 1968 and 1969 included the High/Scope Cognitively Oriented Curriculum developed by David Weikart and his associates in Ypsilanti, Michigan; the Lavatelli Early Childhood Curriculum; and the Kamii-DeVries Curriculum, which were all grounded in Piagetian theory. The Bank Street approach is considered by DeVries and Kohlberg to be "the closest relative to the constructivist, cognitive-developmental approach," because of its roots in John Dewey's progressivism.[80] The degree to which children are disadvantaged apparently affects which program they will benefit from most. The verbal-didactic and verbal-cognitive programs "tend to be most effective with the *most* disadvantaged of lower-class children or to be equally effective with all lower-class children, while the child development programs tend to be most effective with the *least* disadvantaged of lower-class children."[81] In the late 1960s and early 1970s several authors compared the planned variation curriculum and program models of the 1960s. The programs that utilized Piagetian theory to undergird program and curriculum development were variously classified as child-development, child-centered, verbal-cognitive, developmental-interaction, or constructivist programs.

The Bank Street Model is based on a "whole child" approach. During the 1960s, it was one of the programs designed to "find the way out of a major social disfunctioning—the stunted life opportunities of those born into the centers of population that are dominantly poor or subject to negative discrimination on the basis of ethnicity."[82] Biber notes that in 1959 the faculty reexamined the basic assumptions of the Bank Street program and provided a firmer theoretical base for practice by utilizing both psychodynamic theory of personality and cognitive theories of learning. During the mid-1960s, the rationale was more clearly defined, and in addition to the psychodynamic theory of Freud and Erikson, the Bank Street program drew on Gestalt theory and such developmental theorists as Lewin and Piaget.[83, 84]

Bank Street College's Early Childhood Center believes that programs for disadvantaged children should be geared to the same developmental goals set for all children. However, they modify the methods for reaching the goals by adapting them to the children's "developmental deficits." Biber cites deficiencies in verbal-conceptual functioning and in "how to connect with the world of things and people" as "behavioral manifestations of fundamental faults in the developmental process." "An understanding of what is behind his inadequacy is necessary in order to help a child with language and thinking, and to initiate the child into many different kinds of experiences."[85] The Bank Street "process orientation conceives of the school as a place to foster children's psychological development in the broadest possible sense."[86] Day points out that

> minority children who have been called culturally disadvantaged are simply culturally different. They have a culture of their own and may have learned to perform quite adequately within that culture. Their culture is simply not that of mainstream, white middle-class children. . . . Accepting this argument, one can see that judgments of the competence of various cultural groups require a greater respect for cultural pluralism. Clearly, everyone can be considered disadvantaged with respect to some standard or criterion. If the middle-class, white culture and the skills and processes it fosters are taken as the standard, then children of other cultures and subcultures may be considered disadvantaged. . . . This type of "disadvantage" is not informative with respect to the child's ability to learn.

Day discusses the relation between performance in a specific context and cognitive competence, stating that if children are seen as culturally different rather than disadvantaged, different expectations and interactions may be seen in the classroom. "The focus may turn from trying to teach entirely new skills to trying to transfer or extend existing skills to new contexts and to using the children's cultural strengths to help them acquire the skills needed within the context of the dominant culture."[87]

In describing the Ypsilanti Early Education Program (now known as High/Scope), Constance Kamii stated that its aim was to enable the child to develop his total cognitive framework in order to be able to apply it to any task including "classification, seriation, conservation, arithmetic, and reading."[88] According to Kamii, cross-cultural replications of Piaget's research have shown consistently that children all over the world are able to conserve without having been taught to conserve, become able to seriate without having been taught to seriate; however, there is a difference in their rates of development. Generally, children in a more developed culture or in a city within a particular culture developed faster than those living in a less-developed culture, or in the country, or as part of a less-advantaged socioeconomic group. Kamii cites biological factors, experiences with physical objects, social factors, cultural transmission, educational transmission, and equilibration as factors necessary for cognitive development. She then describes the method by which the Perry Preschool Project, the Ypsilanti Early Education Program (and later High/Scope) address these issues.[89] When the High/Scope Program became a part of planned variation, it utilized a curriculum framework based on "key experiences." Teachers planned an environment and curriculum which encouraged active involvement by children. The curriculum was matched to each child's cognitive stage and was sequenced to allow the children to experience learning through actions and through representational activities in order to construct new concepts.[90]

Celia Stendler Lavatelli viewed Piagetian tasks as "valuable cognitive supplements to the traditional child-development . . . nursery school with which she was closely identified during most of her career. 'The objective is not to change drastically those preschool practices which have stood the test of time, but to provide a cognitive underpinning that will make the preschool more intellectually challenging.'"[91] Lavatelli's curriculum objectives included the child's development of intellectual competence through self-activity and responses to teacher questioning. The program includes activities for classification, space, number, measurement, and seriation. Language training took place through systematic modeling and "eliciting of syntactic structures relevant to logical thinking."[92] Lavatelli developed kits of manipulative materials and wrote a teacher's manual for the program. She "advocated that teachers carefully guide children to practice operational thought. . . . The role of Lavatelli's teacher is heteronomous. The child has little opportunity for self-regulation when the teacher follows Lavatelli's principles of teaching," according to DeVries.[93] Cuffaro says that Lavatelli's curriculum consisted "of materials and a large range of activities and lessons."[94]

The Kamii-DeVries program was built on a shift in Kamii's view of Piagetian theory in 1969. After a visit by one of Piaget's collaborators, Professor Hermina Sinclair, who pointed out that Piaget never intended his tasks to be instructional models, Kamii began to distinguish between logicomathematical and physical knowledge. This foreshadowed the later shift to constructivist aims. The Kamii-DeVries program was based upon the epistemological meaning of Piaget's theory, for example, the study of the nature of knowledge and how it is acquired by the child.[95] Kamii and DeVries explored Piaget's epistemological perspective, biological perspective, and his constructivism.[96] They analyzed the cognitive possibilities of the typical nursery school curriculum activities from the point of view of physical knowledge, logicomathematical knowledge, spatio-temporal knowledge, representation, and arbitrary social knowledge, prior to the revision of their own curriculum program.[97] The new approach was based on the child's construction of three different kinds of knowledge from which representations in thought and language are built: physical knowledge, social knowledge, and logicomathematical knowledge. Kamii and DeVries did not aim to teach Piagetian tasks or to move children to the stage of concrete operations.[98] They applied the four basic principles of teaching in the context of children's play, encouragement and acceptance of "wrong answers," giving instructions according to the three kinds of knowledge, and emphasis upon both content and process in learning in their work. Piaget's theory was accepted as final in developmental curriculum planning, and Kamii and DeVries provided a relatively informal, but consciously arranged set of activities for young children which involved a lot of physical movement and object manipulation.[99]

The 1970s saw many new conceptualizations of Piaget's theory. For example, Mayer, in writing of the relationship between social-emotional and cognitive development, stated that the child development position is one in which "social-emotional development feeds cognitive development." In the case of the verbal-cognitive position, Mayer stated that the arrows go in both directions.[100] Weber notes that Kohlberg and Mayer designate cognition and affect as parallel developments, while Shapiro and Biber blend these theories in the developmental-interaction approach.[101]

There have been many critiques of Piagetian theory and the programs and curricula derived from the theory. Various scholars addressed contradictions and inconsistencies within the theory itself. Other critiques deal with individual differences and cultural environments. Some have criticized the use to which Piagetian theory is put in specific curricula. However, one of the most interesting critiques is found in *The Oxford Companion to the Mind*, which states, "recent research to train children on various concepts has been more successful than the theory would predict. Piaget's account also underestimates social interaction and cultural transmission as constituents of education."[102]

Comparative analysis of the curriculum models of the 1960s began with the dawn of the decade of the 1970s. Rochelle Mayer compared child-child, teacher-child, and child-material interactions. She looked at individual versus small group instruction and the sequencing of content, in her 1971 essay.[103] Mary Carol Day's comparative analysis of 1977 looked at the theoretical foundations, cultural and ethnic differences, use of psychological theories and models, goals and objectives, classroom organization, teacher autonomy, parental involvement, evaluation methods, and exportability to different sites of a variety of preschool models.[104] Ellis Evans surveyed program content, the timing or sequential management of developmental experiences, the validity of methodology, qualifications and standards for staff, and the physical facility for early education programs. Sigel, writing in the 1972 *NSSE Yearbook* complements Evans on his six questions of *What, When, How, Who, Where,* and *Why,* which provide the guides for program analysis. Sigel says that "analysis guided by these questions can reveal that the conceptualizations pervade every phase of the program from teaching strategies to the nature of the subject population. In this way the determination of the degree to which the program components interlock becomes possible. An explicit framework also facilitates evaluation of the program."[105] Gordon and Soar and Soar utilized two different approaches to the analysis of selected early education programs. Gordon used an instructional theory approach to analyze six Follow Through programs, including that of Bank Street College of Education. Soar and Soar utilized observations of actual classroom behavior in a process approach to empirical analysis.[106]

Murray said that in the 1980s "the nation could no longer ignore the fact that performance on the Scholastic Aptitude Test had been declining steadily each year since the end of 1963. This led to the report entitled *A Nation at Risk*. American students performed poorly on the National Assessment of

Educational Progress (NAEP), particularly on those items that required the student to use higher levels of cognitive functioning. The proliferation of reports led to reform that Murray characterizes as the American educational system's assimilation of major new ideas and an accommodation or restructuring of the schools. Murray believed that Piaget's theory "has strong claims to make about the intellectual competence of schoolchildren and how that competence can be expected to vary by age and grade level."[107] In discussing post-Nation-at-Risk waves of reform, Murray states that Piagetian theory can influence the time needed for learning as well as the quality of instruction. "Piagetian theory's greatest role in the current 'crisis' may well be in the field of teacher education insofar as the study of *genetic epistemology* could provide the prospective teacher with precisely the kind of understanding that educational reformers imagine when they point out that pedagogical techniques is domain specific. . . . In this approach the student learns the relevant developmental constraints upon the pupil's acquisition of the curriculum and also learns, as an unavoidable part of the discussion, the nature of the subject itself."[108] Murray recounts the influence of teachers and mothers on Genevan theory. He discusses an implication of Piagetian theory in the 1960s that a young child was incapable of taking the cognitive point of view of somebody else. Teachers and mothers who worked with young children were able to devise experiments showing that young children were able to take the point of view of others in many situations. "These experiments led to substantial modifications in the prevailing interpretations of the child's cognitive competence that in turn supported the invention of pedagogical techniques, such as cooperative learning and reciprocal teaching, that now presuppose the young pupil's competence to take the point of view of another pupil."[109] Murray concludes with the hope that modifications in Piagetian theory will provide "both an improved developmental psychology and a truly professional teaching force of reflective practitioners who can carry out the next stages in the development of teaching. A true profession of teaching, in other words, awaits a pedagogy that has formal operational properties."[110]

CHAPTER SUMMARY

Through their work, Grace Owen, Margaret McMillan, and Jean Piaget have had a profound effect upon early childhood education, not only in their own countries, but around the world. Owen and McMillan were teachers of children and teacher educators. They passed on their beliefs and theories through both academic lectures and demonstrations of practice. Although Piaget was a scholar, and not an early childhood educator, his theories have been utilized by his students and colleagues, and early educators all over the globe, in the formulation of many new early childhood program models. These giants of the post–Industrial Revolution period paved the way for the early childhood education programs of today.

NOTES

1. Grace Owen, B. Sc., "Nursery School Education," in *Nursery Schools: A Practical Handbook* [editor not listed] (London: John Bale, Sons & Davidson Ltd., 1920), 3.

2. "Industrial Revolution!" available from <http://merlin.legend.org.uk/~nmyork/bfdhist2.html#industry>; Internet accessed 7 September 1997.

3. Ilse Forest, *Preschool Education: A Historical and Critical Study* (New York: Macmillan Company, 1927), 267; Kevin J. Brehony, Personal Communication, 18 September 1997 and 19 September 1997; and Kevin J. Brehony, "The Froebel Movement in State Schooling, 1880–1914: A Study in Educational Ideology" (Ph.D. diss., Open University, 1987).

4. Grace Owen, "An English Student's Impressions of American Kindergartens," *Child Life* II, no. 6 (1900): 97–102.

5. Grace Owen, "A Study of the Original Kindergartens," *The Elementary School Teacher* VII, no. 4 (December 1906): 205, 209, 210, 213.

6. Owen contributed to the first *Demonstration Schools Record*, a periodical published by the University of Manchester Demonstration School under the direction of Professor J. J. Findlay. Professor Findlay's school was a British version of John Dewey's progressive school at the University of Chicago. Dora Walford, Grace Owen, and Michael Sadler, "Handwork in History Teaching," *Demonstration Schools Record* no. 1, ch. VII (1908) in Kevin J. Brehony, "The Froebel Movement in State Schooling."

7. Nanette Whitbread, *The Evolution of the Nursery-Infant School: A History of Infant and Nursery Education in Britain, 1800–1970* (London: Routledge and Kegan Paul, 1972), 61–68; and Grace Owen, ed., *Nursery School Education* (New York: E. P. Dutton and Company Publishers, 1920), 12; (1928), 14.

8. This parallels the development of the day nurseries and nursery schools in the United States. It led to decreasing numbers of child-minders in the United Kingdom, as it led to a decrease in the number of tenement family day care homes in the United States.

9. Barbara Beatty, *Preschool Education in America: The Culture of Young Children in the Colonial Era to the Present* (New Haven, CT: Yale University Press, 1995), 143.

10. Orline Foster, ["Interview with Miss Grace Owen in the Summer of 1922,"] *Mother and Child Magazine* (January 1923) in Forest, *Preschool Education*, 295n.

11. The Mather Training College was named for Sir William Mather, who founded a free kindergarten in Salford, England. This kindergarten was a large facility for children of two to seven years of age. The kindergarten was in operation from 1871 to 1880, and is considered to be the first free kindergarten in England. Owen, *Nursery School Education*, 12.

12. Owen, *Nursery School Education*, 1920/1928 eds.

13. Brehony, "The Froebel Movement in State Schooling"; and The Education Enquiry Committee [R. F. Cholmbley], *The Case for Nursery Schools* (London: George Philip and Son, 1929), vi–vii.

14. Elizabeth Bradburn, *Margaret McMillan: Portrait of a Pioneer* (London: Routledge, 1984), 4–5, 7, 12, 13; and "Famous Bradfordians: Margaret McMillan," available from <http://merlin.legend.org.uk/~nmyork/mcmillan.html>; Internet accessed 7 September 1997, 1.

15. Bradburn, *Margaret McMillan: Portrait of a Pioneer*, 47–48; and Carolyn Steedman, *Childhood, Culture, and Class in Britain: Margaret McMillan, 1860–1931* (New Brunswick, NJ: Rutgers University Press, 1990), 38–39.

16. Bradburn, *Margaret McMillan: Portrait of a Pioneer*, 49.

17. Bradburn, *Margaret McMillan: Portrait of a Pioneer*, 1; and "Famous Bradfordians: Margaret McMillan," 1.

18. Bradburn, *Margaret McMillan: Portrait of a Pioneer*, 125, 138–145.

19. Steedman, *Childhood, Culture, and Class in Britain*, 83–87.

20. Forest, *Preschool Education*, 266; Dorothy E. M. Gardner and Joan E. Cass, *The Role of the Teacher in the Infant and Nursery School* (Oxford, England: Pergamon Press, 1965), 2–6; D[orothy] E. M. Gardner, *The Education of Young Children* (New York: Philosophical Library, 1957), 6–7; and Elizabeth Bradburn, *Margaret McMillan: Frame-*

work and Expansion of Nursery Education (Surrey, England: Denholm House Press, 1976), 52, 53.

21. Bradburn, *Margaret McMillan: Framework and Expansion of Nursery Education,* 54, 61–62, 75; and Whitbread, *The Evolution of the Nursery-Infant School,* 62.

22. Owen, *Nursery School Education,* 14–15; and Forest, *Preschool Education,* 290–291.

23. Owen, *Nursery School Education* (1928), 5, 17; and Beatty, *Preschool Education in America,* 134.

24. Bradburn, *Margaret McMillan: Portrait of a Pioneer,* 202–203.

25. Abigail Adams Eliot, "Nursery Schools 50 Years Ago," *Young Children* XXVII, no. 4 (April 1972): 210–211; and Steedman, *Childhood, Culture, and Class in Britain,* 184–185.

26. Steedman, *Childhood, Culture, and Class in Britain,* 185.

27. Bradburn, *Margaret McMillan: Framework and Expansion of Nursery Education,* 118–119, 128–129; Bradburn, *Margaret McMillan: Portrait of a Pioneer,* 183, 194, 207–208, 217–218; Forest, *Preschool Education,* 287; and Steedman, *Childhood, Culture, and Class in Britain,* 185.

28. Elizabeth Bradburn, "Margaret McMillan, 1860–1931," *International Journal of Early Childhood* 27, no. 2 (1995): 72.

29. Margaret McMillan, *The Nursery School* (London: J. M. Dent & Sons, Ltd., 1919), 184, 287–290; Steedman, *Childhood, Culture, and Class in Britain,* 184; and Forest, *Preschool Education,* 287–290.

30. Steedman, *Childhood, Culture, and Class in Britain,* 61; and Bradburn, *Margaret McMillan: Portrait of a Pioneer,* 221.

31. Steedman, *Childhood, Culture, and Class in Britain,* 147, 193–194, 314–321; and Goldsmith's homepage, <http://www.gold.ac.uk/about/gcl.html>.

32. McMillan, *The Nursery School,* with a foreword by Patty Smith Hill (1921 ed.), v, vi, viii, x, xi. For further information on the life and work of the McMillan sisters see: Margaret McMillan, *The Camp School* (London: George Allen and Unwin, 1917) and Margaret McMillan, *The Life of Rachel McMillan* (London: Dent, 1927).

33. Mary Ann Spencer Pulaski, *Understanding Piaget: An Introduction to Children's Cognitive Development* (New York: Harper & Row Publishers, 1971), 1, 3.

34. "Biography of Jean Piaget," in Jean Piaget Archives [data base on-line] available from <http://www.unige.ch/piaget/biog.html>; Internet accessed 25 May 1997, 1 of 2.

35. Herbert Ginsburg and Sylvia Opper, *Piaget's Theory of Intellectual Development,* 2d edition (Englewood Cliffs, NJ: Prentice Hall, Inc., 1979), 2.

36. "Jean Piaget's Biography," available from <http://education.indiana.edu/~cunningh/piagbio.html>; Internet accessed 25 May 1997, 1 of 1.

37. "Biography of Jean Piaget," in Jean Piaget Archives [data base on-line] available from <http://www.unige.ch/piaget/biog.html>; Internet accessed 25 May 1997, 1 of 2.

38. Ginsburg and Opper, *Piaget's Theory of Intellectual Development,* 3.

39. Binet and Simon co-authored the first intelligence test.

40. Ginsburg and Opper, *Piaget's Theory of Intellectual Development,* 3; and Pulaski, *Understanding Piaget,* 3.

41. Ginsburg and Opper, *Piaget's Theory of Intellectual Development,* 3–5.

42. Ibid., 5.

43. Pulaski, *Understanding Piaget,* 4.

44. Jean Piaget, "Piaget on Biology and War," in *Piaget on Peace and War: The Genetic Epistemologist,* Vol. XVII, no. 3, 1989, 4.

45. Jean Piaget, "Is An Education for Peace Possible?," translated from the French "Une Éducation Pour La Paix Est-Elle Possible?" by Hans G. Furth in *Piaget on Peace and War: The Genetic Epistemologist,* Vol. XVII, no. 3, 1989, [original article was published in *Bulletin Del'Enseignement de la Société des Nations,* no. 1, December 1934], 5–9.

46. The Jean Piaget Society: Society for the Study of Knowledge and Development Web site; available from <http://vanbc.wimsey.com/~chrisl/JPS/index.html>; Internet accessed 25 May 1997, 1 of 4. [current: <http://www.piaget.org>; Internet accessed 12 January 2000.]

47. Piaget was also the co-director of the Institute of Educational Science at the University of Geneva. Jeanette McCarthy Gallagher and D. Kim Reid, *The Learning Theory of Piaget & Inhelder* with a foreword by Jean Piaget and Bärbel Inhelder (Monterey, CA: Brooks/Cole Publishing Co., 1981), 14; and Pulaski, *Understanding Piaget,* 5.

48. Dorothy Hewes, "Speculation on a Conversation between Piaget and Froebel," *Delta Phi Upsilon Winter Bulletin* (December, 1980) [unpaged reprint], 1–2.

49. According to Beilin, Montangero says that the books published between 1923 and 1932 are part of Piaget's first period (which dealt with social explanation). Three books written in the 1930s constitute Piaget's second period (development of the theory of adaptation). Both of these periods represent Piaget's sympathy with Claparède's functionalism. Montangero, *Genetic Epistemology: Yesterday and Today* (New York: CUNY, Graduate School and University Center, 1985) in Harry Beilin, "Piaget's New Theory," in *Piaget's Theory: Prospects and Possibilities,* ed. Harry Beilin and Peter Pufall (Hillsdale, NJ: Lawrence Erlbaum Associates, 1992), 2.

50. Ibid., 3.

51. Ibid. This collaborative work was published posthumously as: Jean Piaget and Rolando Garcia, *Psychogenesis and the History of Science* (New York: Columbia University Press, 1989) and Jean Piaget and Rolando Garcia, *Toward a Logic of Meanings (*Hillsdale, NJ: Lawrence Erlbaum Associates, 1991).

52. Ibid., 7–8. Piaget wrote two books that deal with education: Jean Piaget, *The Science of Education and the Psychology of the Child* (New York: Penguin/Orion Press, 1970) and Jean Piaget, *To Understand Is to Invent: The Future of Education* (New York: Grossman Publishers, 1973).

53. Ginsburg and Opper, *Piaget's Theory of Intellectual Development,* 13, 15, 16, 17, 24.

54. Gallagher and Reid, *The Learning Theory of Piaget & Inhelder,* x.

55. Ibid., 149.

56. Barry J. Wadsworth, *Piaget's Theory of Cognitive and Affective Development,* 3d ed. (New York: Longman, 1984), 185; Janie Dyson Osborn and D. Keith Osborn, *Cognition in Early Childhood* (Athens, GA: Education Associates, 1983), 187–188; Gallagher and Reid, *The Learning Theory of Piaget & Inhelder,* 150; and Michael Corry, "Jean Piaget's Genetic Epistemology" prepared for Dr. Donald Cunningham, Spring 1996; available from <http://copper.ucs.indiana.edu/~cunnigh/corry2.html>; Internet accessed 5 October 1997, 2 of 4.

57. George E. Forman and David S. Kuschner, *The Child's Construction of Knowledge: Piaget for Teaching Children* (Monterey, CA: Brooks/Cole Publishing Co., 1977), 3.

58. Rheta DeVries and Lawrence Kohlberg, *Constructivist Early Education: Overview and Comparison with Other Programs* (Washington, DC: National Association for the Education of Young Children, 1987), 26–28.

59. Patricia Monighan-Nourot, "The Legacy of Play in American Early Childhood Education," in *Children's Play and Learning: Perspectives and Policy Implications,* ed. Edgar Klugman and Sara Smilansky (New York: Teacher's College Press, 1990), 76.

60. Ibid., 77.

61. David Elkind, "Work Is Hardly Child's Play," in *Images of the Young Children: Collected Essays on Development and Education* (Washington, DC: National Association for the Education of Young Children, 1993), 29.

62. David Elkind, "Piaget and Montessori in the Classroom," in *Images of the Young Children: Collected Essays on Development and Education* (Washington, DC: National Association for the Education of Young Children, 1993), 20.

63. J. D. Osborn and D. K. Osborn, *Cognition in Early Childhood,* 17.

64. Gallagher and Reid, *The Learning Theory of Piaget & Inhelder,* 148.

65. Celia Stendler Lavatelli, *Piaget's Theory Applied to an Early Childhood Curriculum* (Boston: Center for Media Development, Inc. Book, American Science and Engineering, Inc., 1970), 53–145.

66. Gallagher and Reid, *The Learning Theory of Piaget & Inhelder,* 148.

67. Ibid., 149.

68. Corry, "Jean Piaget's Genetic Epistemology," 2 of 4.

69. Ginsburg and Opper, *Piaget's Theory of Intellectual Development*, 223.

70. Gallagher and Reid, *The Learning Theory of Piaget & Inhelder*, 231–232.

71. Constance Kamii, "Pedagogical Principles Derived from Piaget's Theory: Relevance for Educational Practice," in *Piaget in the Classroom*, ed. Milton Schwebel and Jane Ralph (New York: Basic Books, Inc., Publishers, 1973), 199.

72. Gallagher and Reid, *The Learning Theory of Piaget & Inhelder*, 52. See also Richard L. Gregory, ed. with the assistance of O. L. Zangwill, *The Oxford Companion to the Mind* (New York: Oxford University Press, 1987), 622.

73. Kamii, "Pedagogical Principles Derived from Piaget's Theory," 200; and Michael Corry, "Constructivism and Technology" prepared for Dr. Donald Cunningham, Spring 1996; available from <http://copper.ucs.indiana.edu/~cunnigh/corry3.html>; Internet accessed 5 October 1997, 1 of 4.

74. Corry, "Constructivism and Technology," 2 of 4.

75. Frank B. Murray, "Restructuring and Constructivism: The Development of American Educational Reform," in Harry Beilin, "Piaget's New Theory," in *Piaget's Theory: Prospects and Possibilities,* ed. Harry Beilin and Peter Pufall (Hillsdale, NJ: Lawrence Erlbaum Associates, 1992), 287–288.

76. DeVries and Kohlberg, *Constructivist Early Education*, 42.

77. Murray, "Restructuring and Constructivism," 288.

78. Constance Kamii, "Piaget's Interactionism and the Process of Teaching Young Children," in *Piaget in the Classroom*, ed. Milton Schwebel and Jane Ralph (New York: Basic Books, Inc., Publishers, 1973), 216–217; and DeVries and Kohlberg, *Constructivist Early Education*, 3–10.

79. Sue C. Wortham, *Childhood, 1892–1992* (Washington, DC: Association for Childhood Education International, 1992), 51–52; Rochelle Selbert Mayer, "A Comparative Analysis of Preschool Curriculum Models," in *As the Twig Is Bent: Readings in Early Childhood Education,* ed. Robert H. Anderson and Harold G. Shane (Boston: Houghton Mifflin, Co. 1971), 286–314; and Bernard Spodek, "Early Childhood Curriculum and Cultural Definitions of Knowledge," in *Issues in Early Childhood Curriculum, Yearbook in Early Childhood Education,* Vol. 2, ed. Bernard Spodek and Olivia N. Saracho (New York: Teacher's College Press, 1991), 11.

80. DeVries and Kohlberg, *Constructivist Early Education,* 299.

81. Joan Bissell, "The Cognitive Effects of Pre-School Programs for Disadvantaged Children," Ph.D. Thesis, Harvard University, 1970, in Mayer, "A Comparative Analysis of Preschool Curriculum Models," in *As the Twig Is Bent,* ed. Anderson and Shane, 312.

82. Barbara Biber, "A Developmental-Interaction Approach: Bank Street College of Education," in *The Preschool in Action: Exploring Early Childhood Programs,* 2d ed., ed. Mary Carol Day and Ronald K. Parker (Boston: Allyn and Bacon, Inc., 1977), 423.

83. Ibid., 426.

84. For descriptions of the theoretical rationale, developmental-educational goals, teaching strategies, adaptation to environmentally disadvantaged children, program activities, learning goals, organization and implementation, and formative and summative evaluation see the following: Biber, "A Developmental-Interaction Approach," 423–460; Barbara Biber, "Goals and Methods in a Preschool Program for Disadvantaged Children," in *Early Childhood Education,* ed. in Bernard Spodek (Englewood Cliffs, NJ: Prentice Hall, Inc., 1973), 249–262; Barbara Biber, Edna Shapiro, and David Wickens, *Promoting Cognitive Growth: A Developmental-Interaction Point of View* (Washington, DC: National Association for the Education of Young Children, 1971); Evelyn Weber, *Ideas Influencing Early Childhood Education: A Theoretical Analysis* (New York: Teachers' College Press, 1984), 185–188; and DeVries and Kohlberg, *Constructivist Early Education,* 299–370.

85. Biber, "Goals and Methods in a Preschool Program for Disadvantaged Children," 250–252.

86. Ellis D. Evans, *Contemporary Influences in Early Childhood Education,* 2d ed. (New York: Holt, Reinhart, and Winston, 1975), 73.

87. Mary Carol Day, "A Comparative Analysis of Center-Based Preschool Programs," in *The Preschool in Action: Exploring Early Childhood Programs,* 2d ed., ed. Mary Carol Day and Ronald K. Parker (Boston: Allyn and Bacon, Inc., 1977), 464–465.

88. Constance Kamii, "A Sketch of the Piaget-Derived Preschool Curriculum Developed by the Ypsilanti Early Education Program," in *Early Childhood Education,* ed. Bernard Spodek, (Englewood Cliffs, NJ: Prentice Hall, Inc., 1973), 210.

89. Ibid., 210–211.

90. For further references on the High/Scope model see: David Weikart, L. Rogers, C. Adcock, and D. McClelland, *The Cognitively Oriented Curriculum: A Framework for Preschool Teachers* (Washington, DC: National Association for the Education of Young Children, 1971); Wortham, *Childhood, 1892–1922,* 51–52; Evans, *Contemporary Influences in Early Childhood Education,* 2d ed., 225–252; Mayer, "A Comparative Analysis of Preschool Curriculum Models," 288; DeVries and Kohlberg, *Constructivist Early Education,* 53–55, 64–70, 82–83, 85–86; George S. Morrison, *Early Childhood Education Today,* 5th ed. (New York: Merrill, 1991), 121–132; and Margaret Lay-Dopyera and John Dopyera, *Becoming a Teacher of Young Children,* 5th ed. (New York: McGraw-Hill, Inc., 1993), 193–197.

91. DeVries and Kohlberg, *Constructivist Early Education,* 60.

92. Evans, *Contemporary Influences in Early Childhood Education,* 2d ed., 222.

93. DeVries and Kohlberg, *Constructivist Early Education,* 81–82.

94. Harriet Cuffaro, "A View of Materials as the Texts of the Early Childhood Curriculum," in *Issues in Early Childhood Curriculum, Yearbook in Early Childhood Education,* Vol. 2, ed. Bernard Spodek and Olivia N. Saracho (New York: Teacher's College Press, 1991). For further information regarding the Lavatelli program see: DeVries and Kohlberg, *Constructivist Early Education,* 52–53, 60–64, 81–82; Wortham, *Childhood, 1892–1992,* 52; Evans, *Contemporary Influences in Early Childhood Education,* 2d ed., 221–225; and Lavatelli, *Piaget's Theory Applied to an Early Childhood Curriculum.*

95. Evans, *Contemporary Influences in Early Childhood Education,* 2d ed., 231.

96. For a fuller discussion of these concepts see Constance Kamii and Rheta DeVries, "Piaget for Early Education," in *The Preschool in Action Exploring Early Childhood Programs,* 2d ed., ed. Mary Carol Day and Ronald K. Parker (Boston: Allyn and Bacon, Inc., 1977), 365–420.

97. Ibid., 365–420; and DeVries and Kohlberg, *Constructivist Early Education,* 71.

98. DeVries and Kohlberg, *Constructivist Early Education,* 59; Kamii and DeVries, "Piaget for Early Education," 390. For a more detailed look at the activities developed by Kamii and DeVries see: Constance Kamii, *Number in Preschool and Kindergarten: Educational Implications of Piaget's Theory* (Washington, DC: National Association for the Education of Young Children, 1982). ("This book was written to correct the errors and inadequacies in Constance Kamii and Rheta DeVries, *Piaget, Children, and Number.*") (Washington, DC. National Association for the Education of Young Children, 1976); Constance Kamii and Rheta DeVries, *Physical Knowledge in Preschool Education: Implications of Piaget's Theory* (Englewood Cliffs, NJ: Prentice Hall, Inc., 1978); Constance Kamii and Rheta DeVries, *Group Games in Early Education: Implications of Piaget's Theory* (Washington, DC: National Association for the Education of Young Children, 1980); and Ed Labinowicz, *The Piaget Primer: Thinking. Learning. Teaching.* (Menlo Park, CA: Addison-Wesley Publishing Co., 1980).

99. Evans, *Contemporary Influences in Early Childhood Education,* 2d ed., 237.

100. Mayer, "A Comparative Analysis of Preschool Curriculum Models," 308.

101. Weber, *Ideas Influencing Early Childhood Education,* 185.

102. Gregory, with the assistance of O. L. Zangwill, *The Oxford Companion to the Mind,* 623.

103. Mayer, "A Comparative Analysis of Preschool Curriculum Models," 286–314.

104. Day, "A Comparative Analysis of Center-Based Preschool Programs," 462–487.

105. Irving E. Sigel, "Developmental Theory and Preschool Education: Issues, Problems, and Implications," in *Early Childhood Education: The Seventy-First Yearbook of the National Society for the Study of Education Part II,* ed. Ira J. Gordon (Chicago, Illinois: University of Chicago Press, 1972), 16–17.

106. Ira J. Gordon, "An Instructional Theory Approach to the Analysis of Selected Early Childhood Programs," in *Early Childhood Education: The Seventy-First Yearbook of the National Society for the Study of Education Part II,* ed. Ira J. Gordon (Chicago, Illinois: University of Chicago Press, 1972), 203–228; and Robert S. Soar and Ruth M. Soar,

"An Empirical Analysis of Selected Follow Through Programs: An Example of a Process Approach to Evaluation," in *Early Childhood Education: The Seventy-First Yearbook of the National Society for the Study of Education Part II,* ed. Ira J. Gordon (Chicago, Illinois: University of Chicago Press, 1972), 229–259.

107. Murray, "Restructuring and Constructivism," 289, 295.

108. Ibid., 298.

109. Ibid., 305.

110. Ibid.

CHAPTER 6

Maria Montessori (1870–1952)

> The teacher's task is not to talk, but to prepare and
> arrange a series of motives for cultural activity in a special
> environment made for the child.
>
> —Dr. Maria Montessori[1]

BIOGRAPHICAL PORTRAIT

Maria Montessori was born at Chiaravalle, in the province of Ancoma, Italy, on August 31, 1870. She had well-educated parents. Her father, Alessandro, was a military man. Her mother, Renilde, was a pious, articulate, and highly literate woman, for whom Montessori had great affection. Standing recounts that when Montessori was in school she had a teacher who required the students to learn by heart the lives of famous women, in order to incite the students to imitate them. When asked by the teacher whether she would like to become famous, Montessori replied, "I shall never be that. I care too much for the children of the future to add yet another biography to the list."[2]

The Montessori family moved frequently during Maria's childhood, because of her father's job as a government finance official for the tobacco industry. For twelve years she attended schools in Ancoma, and at the age of thirteen she entered a technical school. She showed a proclivity for mathematics, and an interest in biology and engineering. She decided to study medicine, and enrolled in the University of Rome. Her major interests upon entering the university were mathematics, physics, and natural science.

As the first female medical student, Montessori faced great difficulties. It was not considered proper that a girl should dissect dead bodies in the presence of men students. Therefore, she had to work in the dissecting room alone, often in the evening after dark. Montessori became the first woman in Italy to receive the degree of Doctor of Medicine, in 1896. It was a tradition in the medical school at that time that after their first year, each new graduate would deliver a public lecture to the faculty. Montessori's well-received lecture was the occasion for the reconciliation with her father, Alessandro, who had been persuaded to come to the lecture against his will.[3]

Montessori became an assistant doctor at the University of Rome psychiatric clinic. Through the free clinics, she came into frequent contact with the children of the working class and the poor. These experiences convinced her that intelligence is not rare and that most newborns come into the world with a human potential that will be barely revealed. Montessori specialized in pediatrics and psychiatry. She was quite moved by the plight of "deficient children," who in those days were placed with adults in insane asylums. Montessori, who considered herself a scientist, and not a teacher (rejecting one of the few traditional professions for women), lectured to the teachers of Rome on special education. She had studied the methods of French physicians Jean-Marc-Gaspard Itard (1775–1838) and Edouard Seguin (1812–1880). Itard is most famous for his work with the "wild boy of Aveyron," and his work with deaf mutes. Seguin, his student, is remembered for the development of methods in special education for the retarded. He considered mental deficiency to be a pedagogical rather than a medical problem. Montessori took from their work a scientific approach based on observation and experimentation.[4]

In 1899, Montessori was appointed the director of the new State Orthophrenic School for Deficient Children, which was attached to the University of Rome. She directed the school until 1901. As part of a wave of reform that she initiated, Montessori insisted that the staff speak to the inmates with the highest respect. She set up a program to teach the children how to care for themselves and their environment. She realized that her patients needed stimulation, purposeful activity, and self-esteem. Montessori visited several other European countries in order to study special education techniques in use there. After two years of work, Montessori presented several of her "deficient" adolescents to take the state standard sixth-grade examinations in the Italian public schools. All of the children were able to pass tests in reading and writing. While observers considered these results "miraculous," Montessori was searching for the reason that "normal children could be equaled in such tests by her unfortunate pupils." Between 1896 and 1906, Montessori occupied the Chair of Hygiene at the Magisturo Femminile in Rome, one of the two women's colleges that existed in Italy at that time.[5]

About 1901, Montessori withdrew from her active work with the deficients at the Orthophrenic School. She reenrolled at the University of Rome, taking courses in experimental psychology and conducting research in "pedagogical anthropology" with children in elementary schools. She was appointed to teach anthropology at the University of Rome, and filled this position between 1904 and 1908. In late 1906, she was approached by the Institutio Romano dei Beni Stabili (the Roman Association for Good Building), which was rehabilitating two blocks of apartments. These buildings had been hastily and poorly constructed during a population boom and were in poor repair. The new owners wanted to reduce or prevent vandalism by young children who were left alone all day. The organization had allocated one room in a building and decided that they needed someone to look after the children. The expenses for the "child-minding" were placed under the area of general upkeep of the building, because of their goal of preventing destruction. When Montessori was approached regarding directing this group supervision project, she readily accepted, because this would permit her to continue her work with "normal" children. Montessori designed child-sized tables, chairs, armchairs, and specific didactic materials. She was not permitted to use desks, and this was very much to her liking. On the first day of the program's existence, January 6, 1907, fifty to sixty malnourished children greeted her and her first directress. Montessori had trained this young woman, the porter's daughter, in the use of the apparatus, so that it could be accurately presented to the children. When this young woman left the job, a seamstress replaced her. Young women with formal teacher education were not sought, because Montessori wished to train her own directresses. Montessori taught the older children how to help with the everyday tasks, and soon they were assisting the directress in taking care of the school. The older children assisted in the preparation and serving of the meals and in maintaining a "spotlessly" clean environment.

Montessori created "a house for children," rather than a school. The young children learned to read and write without direct instruction. She discovered that "all children are endowed with this capacity to 'absorb' culture." Then, botany, zoology, mathematics, and geography activities were added. The children were able to absorb these elements of culture "with the same ease, spontaneously and without getting tired." Montessori stated, "And so we discovered that education is not something which the teacher does, but that it is a natural process which develops spontaneously in the human being. It is not acquired by listening to words, but in virtue of experiences in which the child acts on his environment."[6]

The response to the first Casa dei Bambini (Children's House) was so positive that in 1908 a second Children's House was opened in Milan, under the direction of Anna Naccheroni.

Montessori's lectures at the University of Rome in 1906 and 1907 led to the first official training course for directresses, which was held in 1909. Shortly thereafter, Montessori's first book appeared in Italian. *The Montessori Method: Scientific Pedagogy as Applied to Child Education in the Children's Houses* was translated into English by Anne George in 1912. George, Montessori's first American student, opened the first Montessori school in the United States in 1911, in Tarrytown, New York.

Magazine articles about Montessori's work began to appear in the United States in 1909.[7] Montessori visited the United States in 1913, the year of the founding of the Montessori Educational Association of America. Mrs. Alexander Graham Bell was its first president. Dr. P. E. Claxton, the U.S. Commissioner of Education, was chosen first vice president, and Margaret Woodrow Wilson, daughter of the president of the United States, became a member of the board of trustees.[8, 9]

In 1915, Montessori returned to the United States to give a summer course at the Panama-Pacific Exposition. This "world's fair" was held to celebrate the completion of the Panama Canal. A model Montessori class was conducted by Helen Parkhurst. Montessori herself spoke at the annual meeting of the National Education Association (NEA) in Oakland, California. She discussed her system of education, education as related to the imagination of the child, the organization of intellectual work in school, and the mother and the child.

The Montessori Association of America was dissolved in 1916, and in 1918, Montessori made her last visit to the United States. In 1915, the House of Childhood (Inc.), a New York manufacturer, began to produce Montessori materials for home and school use.[10]

Between 1914 and 1935, Montessori gave numerous lectures and training courses throughout Europe. From 1919 to 1939, she gave a course in England every other year. In 1929, the Association Montessori Internationale (AMI) was founded. Maria Montessori presided over the Association until her death, at which time her son Mario, Sr., became the president.

Montessori schools were forbidden in Germany and Italy between 1935 and 1946. Montessori left Italy and went first to Spain and later to India. She remained in India between 1939 and 1946, giving training courses and assisting in the setting up of schools in a number of Indian cities and provinces.[11] In 1947, Montessori assisted in the opening of a Training Centre in London, England, by Margaret Homfray and Phoebe Child. Following a later disagreement with Montessori, these two women continued to run the center under the name of the St. Nicholas Training Centre. (This center is still in existence today.)

Montessori continued her teacher training courses in many countries up until six months before her death. In addition, she presided over the first nine international Montessori congresses, beginning with the first held at Helsinki, Finland, in 1925.[12] Dr. Maria Montessori died on May 6, 1952, at Noordwijk-on-Sea, the Netherlands, of a cerebral hemorrhage.

In 1960, the American Montessori Society (AMS) was founded, a sign of the reemergence of the Montessori method in the United States. When Montessori's methods reappeared on the American educational scene, it was discovered that her work was related to several of the progressive educators of the early 1900s. Like Colonel Francis Parker, Montessori emphasized making the child the center of the program. Montessori echoed the emphasis of her contemporary John Dewey in stressing education through activity and self-space or auto-education. Like O[mar] K[yam] Moore, she believed in auto-education with didactic equipment.

EDUCATIONAL THOUGHT AND WRITINGS

Dr. Maria Montessori exemplifies the gifted, pioneering women who initiated new and exciting early childhood education programs in the early 1900s. She devoted her life to science, children and families, child-focused observation-based education, and to working for peace. The following quote from Dr. Mario Montessori, Jr., gives us insight into the depth and breadth of Montessori's thought processes.

> I remember her peeling potatoes and looking at them with profundity, as if they could reveal some secret of great importance. She continued her task, wondering aloud how man originally discovered the value of the potato plant, outwardly a weed with insignificant little flowers and producing poisonous fruit. What made him look further? By what trick of chance did he

discover that its usefulness to him lay not in the part of it that appeared above the surface, but in the part that was hidden in the earth?[13]

Osborn states that "she believed in the universality of children and their needs. A basic cornerstone of her work was that individuals must develop all aspects of themselves." Lillard adds that ". . . though she was a careful experimenter and a keen observer, she had no expectations of reducing her contribution to irrefutable scientific theories through laboratory procedures. Her concentration on the uniqueness of man and his spontaneous development precluded any such dream."[14]

How Children Were Treated (During the First Half of the 1900s)

Historically, very young children were regarded as primitive beings. Sometimes they were treated as miniature adults, and were expected to reason, accept responsibility, and plan for their own survival. However, Montessori came of age in a time of child welfare reform and of new recognition of the needs, capacities, and rights of children. She wrote that: "The child should not be regarded as a feeble and helpless creature . . . but as a spiritual embryo, possessed of an active psychic life from the day that he is born and guided by subtle instincts enabling him to build up the human personality." Montessori confirmed her commitment to the child both by demonstrating respect and by her view that young children could learn important concepts through their own spontaneous activity. Children who were given materials appropriate to their level of development, designed so that they could get immediate feedback from their actions, learned a great deal on their own with enjoyment.[15]

Dr. Montessori's View of Children and Their Importance

Montessori maintained that she had "discovered" the child, and the extremely important function of the child in the formation of the human personality. These discoveries occurred as a result of careful, patient, and systematic scientific observations of the spontaneous behavior of children in a prepared environment adapted to their needs. Montessori's philosophical outlook permitted her to see beyond the superficial manifestations of the children's behavior she observed. Her anthropological orientation determined her conception of education as an aid to life. Her grandson, Mario Montessori, Jr., believes that this is "the most valuable aspect of the spiritual inheritance she has left us."[16]

Maria Montessori wrote that the

"normalized" child is one who has been freed in a psychically hygienic environment to function normally. Our social environment presents obstacles to man's normal development. In normalized children, many of the features we have considered characteristic of childhood disappear. A normalized child displays an "original and normal" nature, heretofore hidden. The child's first profound interest in the Montessori material marks the beginning of his "normalization." Normalization refers to "normal functioning"—a "state of health," the necessary psychological base for the New Man's achievements in his New World. The Montessori child's manifestation of psychic health is the most important outcome of the method.[17]

THE STAGES OF DEVELOPMENT OF THE CHILD ACCORDING TO MARIA MONTESSORI

"The Montessori concept is both a philosophy of child growth and a rationale for guiding such growth. Montessori believed that education begins at birth and that the first six years of life are the most important years."[18]

Physical Development

Montessori was evenhanded in her discussion of the physical, cognitive, and affective development of the child in her writings. Later authors, writing about her method, seem to have produced more material about mental development than about the other two areas of development.

She believed that from three to six years of age the child displays a special proclivity for muscular development. Bodily metamorphosis is described in this way: "This physical transformation through which the child passes before he reaches adult proportions, throws a light on certain characteristics of children; as for example their imperfect equilibrium long after they have learned to walk. (This is because their heads are too big and their feet too small.) Who has not noticed the delight with which children will walk along a line, or a plank, or a wall, like miniature tightrope walkers?" Standing credits Montessori with first realizing the significance of the child's physical development and "seconding the child's natural tendencies. Thus there came into being those 'Exercises of Balance and Rhythm' which form a regular feature of every Casa dei Bambini."[19]

Mental Development: Sensitive Periods

The discussion of "sensitive periods" forms one of the cornerstones of Montessori's developmental theory Sensitive periods can be defined as

> blocks of time in a child's life when he is absorbed with one characteristic of his environment to the exclusion of all others. They appear in the individual as "an intense interest for repeating certain actions at length, for no obvious reason, until—because of this repetition—a fresh function suddenly appears

with explosive force." The special interior vitality and joy the child exhibits during these periods results from his intense desire to make contact with his world. It is a love of his environment that compels him to this contact. This love is not an emotional reaction, but an intellectual and spiritual desire.[20]

Children pass through definite periods in which they reveal psychic aptitudes and possibilities which afterward disappear. That is why, at particular times in their life, they reveal an intense and extraordinary interest in certain objects and exercises, which one might look for in vain at a later age. During these periods, the child focuses attention on certain aspects of the environment to the exclusion of others. Montessori believed that if the child is prevented from following the burning passion of interest during any given sensitive period, the opportunity is lost forever. He loses his special sensitivity and desire in this area, with a disturbing effect on his psychic development and maturity. Therefore, the opportunity for development in his sensitive periods must not be left to chance. As soon as one appears, the child must be assisted.[21]

Mental Development: Absorbent Mind

During his development, "the 'preschool' child displays a unique capacity for absorbing sensory impressions from his environment." This is the second cornerstone of Montessori theory, the "absorbent mind." The child learns in a different way from the adult, because the mind is not yet formed. During the preconscious state of mind, the child unconsciously absorbs knowledge of the environment directly, and incorporates it into his psychic life. The unconscious activity prepares the mind, and is succeeded by a conscious process, which establishes memory, the power to understand, and the ability to reason. By the age of three, the child has moved from the unconscious to the conscious stage of mental development, and is ready to continue the development of his mental functions.[22]

From the existing literature, it is possible to get a clear picture of Montessori's conception of "mental metamorphosis" and the stages of intellectual development. The first six years of life constitute the first stage. It is a period of "transformation" divided into two subperiods. The first substage extends from birth to three years of age, the time of the "unconscious absorbent mind." It is characterized by unconscious growth and absorption of information from the child's surroundings. Infancy is the time for education of the senses, for social education, "the time when civilization is acquired." On a less positive note, the literature recounts that because experiences in infancy have permanent effects, many defects are acquired by children neglected during their formative period. During the first two years of life, the child begins to develop a love of order and consistency, based on a vital need for a precise and determined environment. In fact, by the age of three, the child has developed fundamental personality patterns. Introjection, imitation, and identification are of particular importance in the formation of behavior patterns and the acquisition of cultural attitudes during this period.

At the age of three, the child enters the stage of the "conscious absorbent mind," which lasts until the age of six. During this time period, the child slowly brings knowledge from his unconscious to the conscious level. Orem says that during his first six years, the child forms his intelligence and, more broadly, his psyche, as he works in freedom. Adults are now consciously acknowledged by the child as the source of information on social and cultural aspects of its existence. Because of its growing interest in these, the child turns spontaneously to adults with its queries. If it is not rejected, it responds with feelings of gratitude, trust, and respect for these superior beings who are willing to help it orient itself in its world.[23] These potentialities must be adapted and internalized in accordance with the developmental pattern typical of the human species. This cannot be achieved without the help of adults, help that is available only if love is the binding force in their relationship with the child.[24]

The second stage of cognitive development encompasses the sixth through the twelfth years of life. It has been called the second stage of childhood, an intermediate period, and a period of uniform growth. From age six to nine, the child builds the artistic and academic skills that will be essential for living a full life in his specific culture. From age nine to twelve, the child is "ready to open himself to knowledge of the universe itself." During this time the child is learning with the conscious mind; therefore, the mind can soar to great heights. "This is why his schooling at this time must include as complete an exposure to the world as possible, and not be broken down into isolated units of subject matter as is now customary in traditional schools."[25]

The years from twelve to eighteen form the third transformational stage. This interval is divided into two substages: "puberty," which lasts from age twelve to fifteen years, and "adolescence," from age fifteen to eighteen years. This is the time for exploring more concentrated areas of interest in depth. "The child should be choosing the pattern of endeavor he will follow for life, and so it is a period of limiting choices. This period of decision is postponed in our culture until a later age. Since it is usually not encouraged or even permitted at the natural age, unnecessary emotional and intellectual problems occur. The adolescent rebellion so taken for granted in U.S. culture is a phenomenon not seen in many other civilizations."[26] According to Montessorian theory, after about eighteen years of age there is no longer any transformation, the individual simply becomes older. Montessori believed that adults should learn to defend the child's mind as the medical profession defends the child's body.

According to Montessori, one of the first sensitive periods to arise in a child's life is the one in which the child desires to explore the environment with his tongue and hands. If the child is given the opportunity to conduct these explorations, it leads to refinement of the senses. However, if the child is surrounded by adults who require the child to refrain from touching objects in the environment, this inner need is not met. It is through exploratory sensory and motor activity that development of the neurological structures for language occurs.

Mario Montessori argues: "The acquisition by an infant of its mother tongue is the best demonstration of that special quality in the first years of life that Montessori calls the absorbent mind." Other important sensitive periods include those for walking, intense interest in tiny objects (beginning in the second year of life), and interest in the social aspects of life. "The child becomes deeply involved in understanding the civil rights of others and establishing a community with them. He attempts to learn manners and to serve others as well as himself."[27]

Montessorian literature highlights the sensitive periods for the development of concentration (attention) and obedience (the "will"). At first, the child attends to particular objects in the environment with deep interest. Bright colors and unusual forms attract her attention. As the child has more experiences, and builds a knowledge base of the "known," there is more interest in the "novel unknown." The new ability for concentration is used to consolidate and develop personality. The child adapts to the limits of a chosen task by making decisions and taking action. The child's will is gradually developed through this adaptation.

The formation of the will consists of three stages. In the first, the child engages in many repetitions of a self-selected activity; however, the child does not obey an order unless the order coincides with a "vital urge" of the child. Later, the child "makes creative use of his abilities, accepts the responsibility of his own actions, and complies with the limits of reality." Evans says that this "allows the child to absorb the wishes of another person and manifest them in behavior (conformity)." Later, "after achieving self-discipline, the child reaches a third stage of the developed will involving the power to obey. This power is a natural phenomenon. . . . [It] is perhaps the most difficult aspect of Montessori philosophy for Americans today to understand or accept. . . . When Montessori philosophy speaks of obedience, it is referring to a natural characteristic of the human being. This natural characteristic must be developed into a controlled or intelligent obedience, a cooperation with the forces of life and nature on which the survival of human life and society depends." Evans states that a child who has reached the third stage "says to a significant other in effect, I submit my will to you. I want to obey for I enjoy the feeling it gives me."[28]

Other sensitive periods involve the development of the emotional and spiritual life of the child and the development of the child's imagination and creativity. Montessori believed that environment must be beautiful, harmonious, and based on reality in order for the child to organize his perceptions of it. After the child has developed a realistic and ordered perception of the life about him, he is capable of selecting and emphasizing processes necessary for creative endeavors. In order for creativity to develop, three qualities are required: remarkable powers of attention and concentration, considerable autonomy and independence of judgment, and an openness to truth and reality. The "Montessori classroom is also free from the judgment by an outside authority that so annihilates the creative impulse."[29]

SIMILARITIES AND DIFFERENCES
BETWEEN CHILDREN AND ADULTS

Maria Montessori unequivocally stated that there are differences between children and adults. For example, she felt that the child is in a continual state of growth and metamorphosis, whereas the adult has reached the norm of the species. She believed that the modes of learning we engage in as children will determine the modes of learning we engage in as adults. Elkind agreed that the way in which people learn as children influences the way they learn as adults. Those who learn as a result of their own activities, without the use of external rewards and punishments, acquire different patterns of learning than those who learn from materials prepared by others. As adults, the first group is likely to be independent, self-starting, and spontaneous learners, while the second will learn only from information provided by others, motivated by rewards or punishments.[30]

Montessori related this phenomenon to the development of independence and cooperation. Wolf, in her adaptation of Montessori's writings on peace, states: "The child who has never learned to act alone, to direct his own actions, to govern her own will, grows into an adult who is easily led and must always lean upon others."[31]

Montessori wrote in *Peace and Education* about conflict between the adult and the child. Adults try, through "education," to autocratically change the resistant child. If the adults misinterpret and do not recognize the independent psychic life of the child, with its own characteristics and its own ends, "there arises between the strong and the weak a struggle which is fatal to mankind." However, "when the intrinsic value of the child's personality has been recognised and he has been given room to expand, . . . (where the child creates for himself an environment suited to his spiritual growth), we have had the revelation of an entirely new child, whose astonishing characteristics are the opposite of those that had hitherto been observed." Montessori concluded that "it would be possible, by the renewing of education, to produce a better type of man."[32]

WORK AND PLAY AS DEFINED BY MARIA MONTESSORI

Dr. Maria Montessori asserted that the child's work is not similar to that of the adult. She believed that all civilizations have been based upon adult values, and have not given cognizance to the child's contribution. She said that the child's contribution is his work, the construction of the adult-that-is-to-be. She contended, as do many current child development advocates, that children work for the sake of process, rather than for a product. They use the environment to assist them in improving their abilities. Montessori's "law of independence" states that "full personality development is totally dependent on progressive release from external direction and reliance."[33]

In discussing Maria Montessori's principle of indirect preparation as an essential feature of development, Mario Montessori, Jr., wrote that "work is linked with man's creativity and is a universal phenomenon characteristic of the human species." He described Montessori's discovery: "There are potentialities in the human personality that correspond to all such universal phenomena, directing the growing individual to perform specific activities. The experiences that result from these activities are needed to prepare him to perform functions that will be relevant at a later level of integration." He concludes that "it is indirect preparation that eventually enables an individual to participate as an independent adult in those activities typical of the human species."[34]

Montessori made great distinctions between work and play. She believed that play and make-believe are an escape from reality unsuitable to the child. She said that adult imagination created this play and the child is the passive recipient. In the Montessori classroom, a child is provided with the freedom to make choices and to do real work. The child has the autonomy to decide what is engaging, "to relate to it without interruption and for as long as he likes, to discover solutions and ideas and select his answer on his own, and to communicate and share his discoveries with others at will."[35]

Montessori was an adherent of the Anticipatory Theory of play developed by Groos. Only those forms of play that had an adaptive, preparatory function were acceptable. She translated the theory into a simpler formula, "play is the child's work." Elkind, writing from a Piagetian perspective, disagreed with this view. He said that play "can serve a number of different functions." He described play as "pure *assimilation,*" stating that "when children engage in play they come to realize their personal abilities in the sense that they transform the world to adapt it to their needs. Such play is valuable insofar as it helps the child realize herself or himself as an individual." He goes on to point out that "play is indeed a preparation for adult life, if adult life is seen as including self-expression and self-realization as well as social adaptation."[36]

Elkind disputes those Montessorians who say that fantasy is essentially dishonest because stories tell about, for example, witches who fly, or discuss characters that do not exist. These proponents of Montessori believe that when the children become old enough, they will be angry at the adults who deceived them. Elkind's response is that children do not distinguish between the animate and the inanimate, and children have no sense of what adults can do. He mentions *dynamism,* which he defines as "a mechanism which encourages cognitive growth" as the child discovers "previously held ideas that are no longer acceptable," which leads to intellectual maturity. Elkind also disputes the "waste of time argument." To those who say that fantasy play is a waste of time, and give examples from the "television wasteland," Elkind replies that just because the child's desire for fantasy is exploited and abused, we should not reject the desire as bad. Elkind argues that "the desire for play and for work are both healthy and important. They need to be realized in appropriate ways and in reasonable amounts."[37]

THE AIMS AND GOALS OF EDUCATION

Montessori education has been called New Education, and equated with Expansive Education. "The joy of learning, the discovery process, peace, harmony, and cooperation are basic concepts inherent in authentic Montessori programs."[38]

Montessori viewed education as a necessity in the formation of the human personality. She "wanted to help children everywhere to love learning." Montessori utilized her knowledge of the sensitive periods in a child's development, and the environment created in her school to encourage sustained, enthusiastic work. Standing says that the freedom of the Montessori school allows children to "accomplish in a few weeks, in some particular subject, what would have taken months to learn at the tempo of ordinary class teaching."[39]

No gender differences are discussed by Montessori in her writings. She consistently refers to "the child." However, she (and the English translations of her work) used the masculine form prevalent at that time, in spite of her own feminist battles.

PRINCIPLES OF LEARNING AND INSTRUCTION

Among the ideas that set Montessori schools apart from other schools of her time were her practices of heterogeneous grouping by age, self-selected and self-paced materials, auto-education (self-correcting materials), materials that progress in difficulty from simple to more complex, materials that progress from the concrete to the abstract, graduated sequence and isolation of sensory attributes in the materials, giving extraneous cues to facilitate fine discriminations, repetition and practice, and an adaptation of the "contiguity principle" (the close association of a stimulus and a response).

THE EDUCATIONAL ENVIRONMENT — THE CHILDREN'S HOUSE (CASA DEI BAMBINI)

In designing the environment of the Casa dei Bambini, Montessori was again ahead of her time. Many of the items taken for granted in the physical settings of today's early childhood education programs originated in the Children's House. Among them were use of a large open room with secluded alcoves on the side; doors, windows, and other parts of the building proportional to the physical size of children rather than adults; child size furniture; light colored furniture and equipment; lightweight furniture that is easy for children to carry; low shelves to contain the didactic materials; and easy access for the child to necessary materials. Initially, the material was kept out of the reach of the children until the directress distributed it. Gradually the children demonstrated the ability to care for the materials. At that point, Montessori added open cabinets (now indispensable to any Montessori school), and the directress permitted the children to get their own materials.[40]

Montessori's learning games and devices were called "didactic materials." Montessori began her experiment by equipping the classroom with a variety of materials and allowing the children to choose freely among them. She noted which equipment they selected and which they did not use. The ignored materials were eliminated or adapted. The didactic materials are designed to directly prepare a child for future academic learning in the areas of language, mathematics, science, social studies, and the arts. They are divided into practical life exercises, sensorial materials, and academic materials.[41]

The *Practical Life Exercises* are based on the motor movements necessary for performing tasks of daily living and personal care. They include scrubbing the table, polishing shoes and brass objects, pouring water, and the use of a variety of tools and implements.

The *Sensorial Materials* were designed to isolate one attribute of an object, for example, color, size, shape, or weight. Included in this category of materials are the pink tower, the broad (brown) stair, cylinder blocks, knobless cylinders, smelling jars, thermic bottles, bells, baric tablets, textured cloth pieces, red rods, the geometric cabinet, and color tablets.

Each of the *Academic Materials* was prepared to assist the child in developing particular academic skill. The language materials, such as sandpaper letters, metal insets, the command game, the movable alphabet, and the farm are designed as preparation for writing and reading. The red and blue rods, golden bead materials, spindle box, fraction boards, and geometric solids prepare the child for mathematical concept development. The botany cards are used for development of science concepts, while the flags, globes, land and water form pans, and puzzle maps pave the way toward social studies concept development.

STRUCTURE AND FREEDOM IN THE USE OF MATERIALS

Several authors have applauded the intrinsic value of the Montessori materials for the mental growth of young children, while questioning the ways they have come to be used. Elkind agrees that at the beginning of instruction children should be shown how to use the materials and not just allowed to mess around with them. He believes that the initial structured use of the materials should be followed by freer, more experimental usage. This would permit those who have mastered the materials to use them in new ways so as to discover new relationships. Elkind calls this "earned freedom," which "is constructive and valuable and should not be confused with unearned freedom that is not."[42] Wentworth says that "there is no reason to stick slavishly to traditional materials and methods unless they are proved to be superior to the new ones."[43]

The Method and the didactic materials that Montessori developed, first in the State Orthophrenic School for "idiots," and later in the Casa dei Bambini for "normal children," have waxed and waned in popularity in the United States. While they were the winner of the only two gold medals awarded at the Panama-Pacific Exposition of 1915 (San Francisco World's Fair held on the opening of the Panama Canal),[44] Montessori classes were, during the same time period, being disparaged by Professor William Heard Kilpatrick of Teachers' College, Columbia University, in his 1914 volume *The Montessori System Examined*. It took nearly fifty years for Children's Houses, and the Montessori Method that supports them, to reemerge in the United States. The 1958 opening of the Whitby School in Connecticut, by Nancy McCormick Rambusch, triggered a rebirth of Montessori education in this country.

THE DIRECTRESS/DIRECTOR AND THE TEACHER'S ROLE

Montessori used the term "directress" to describe the adult who prepares the environment and guides the Montessori classroom. The first directress, a young girl who worked in the Casa dei Bambini that Dr. Montessori opened in Rome in 1907, had no educational training. This was a deliberate choice on the part of Dr. Montessori, who wanted to train her in her own methods through actual work with children. Montessori felt that an untrained individual would be an asset to her experiment because she would have no preconceived ideas about the children, the materials, or the environment that was being set up.

Montessori utilized Wundt's techniques of physiological psychology to study the children and to individualize programs for them within the prepared environment, based on adult observations. In the environment, the children "were left pretty much to their own resources as they worked with the special materials"[45] Elkind states that the Montessori teacher is as self-didactic as the child, children being the teacher's learning materials.[46] Standing's description of a directress of the 1940s provides a clear picture of her role.

> . . . gone is the teacher's high desk and stool; and—most remarkable of all—it seems at first glance as if the teacher herself has vanished too. We do discover her, eventually, down on her knees at the far end of the room, explaining something to a couple of children who are working with number materials spread out on a rug. The rest of the children (except for two or three who are waiting to speak to her) are all carrying on their own business without taking any notice of the directress whatever. . . . This is obviously a kind of school in which the adult has retired into the background, whilst the children are correspondingly more active; one might almost say they have taken over the initiative.[47]

However, Standing's description of one child's interaction with the teacher at the conclusion of an exercise involving the seven times multiplication table belies the goal of independence, as he recounts: "Quietly she gets up and goes, paper in hand, to find the directress and waits patiently for a few minutes until she is disengaged, and then shows the result of her work. The teacher looks it over, nods her head, and returns it with an approving smile; and back comes our young mathematician towards her table."[48]

Today, "The Montessori classroom director fastidiously prepares and maintains the environment. She observes the children, notes readiness for new materials, and demonstrates proper use of the materials to individual children. Generally the director is careful not to create in the children a dependence upon her for either physical help or approval."[49]

Lillard stresses the idea that "the teacher is not to teach; he or she is to guide the child—to *plan* its education for it." She states that teachers should gradually introduce very young children to more and more materials, extending the range of their options from one toy or one kind of material to one toy and two materials, and so forth. This permits the children to be successful in choosing activities they are ready for, and therefore enjoy. Confidence in their ability to make their own choices increases. The process engenders trust in their teachers, who give them new experiences and present them with challenges, but avoid overwhelming them. The security of this knowledge makes them eager for new experiences.[50]

This statement is related to J. McVickar Hunt's description of the "Problem of the Match." He reminds us that it is the teacher's task to present activities and materials that are at the child's current developmental level, or slightly above that level. If the material presented is too easy, the child will become bored very quickly. If the material is quite difficult for the child to do at that particular time, the child will become frustrated. Therefore, it is important that the teacher use her knowledge of the child to help her decide what type of activity is appropriate for each individual.

Montessori teachers are "trained to help the children emerge as they are," and "derive their gratifications as teachers from the provision of possibilities for the children's development rather than from the relationship the child might develop with the teacher." The directress does, however, intervene in cases of "disorderly or destructive" children. She will keep a child who has difficulty in working independently near her as she moves around the room. "When *he* feels he is again capable of working independently, he is free to return and set about his business independently."[51]

Lillard believes that "the future success of the relationship between teachers and children in Montessori classes will depend on the teachers' ability to choose new challenges wisely. They must use their powers of observation, their knowledge of sensitive periods, and their understanding of the Montessori material. They must direct the children, but on the basis of their own observations of the children's needs. In this sense, it is the children who must direct the adults. It is not, therefore, a case of the director and the directed. The adults and the children work together to further the children's development."[52]

MONTESSORI TEACHER TRAINING

Montessori began her teacher training system with the directresses of the various Casa dei Bambini locations in Italy. These untrained young women learned to prepare the environment, observe children, to facilitate children's interactions with the environment, and to communicate with the children in their care and their parents. As the success of the Casa dei Bambini, and Montessori's writings, became known, she traveled all over the world to present teacher training courses and lectures. She began the international training courses in 1930 in Rome. The course was composed of three main elements: Montessori lectured on a variety of subjects, a systematic study of the didactic materials was supervised by her assistants, and students made a series of visits totaling no less than fifty hours of observation in recognized Montessori schools. At the end of six months, the students completed a book on the materials, and written and oral examinations. Those successfully completing all of the elements were granted a diploma, signed by Dr. Montessori, which entitled the holder to open a Montessori school. After two years of satisfactory work in a Montessori class, the diploma holder was endorsed as a Montessori directress.[53] Osborn affirms that Dr. Montessori meticulously trained adults, and "from these groups emerged those who would train other adults in her method and philosophy."[54]

During the 1960s, the International Training Course in the United States was a fifth-year internship program for college graduates. It included elements of theory and practice as laid down by Montessori, as well as the relation between these principles and those underlying American educational practice. Courses were taught by experienced Montessorians and qualified university lecturers. The day was divided between mornings of observation and practice teaching and afternoons of lectures on educational and developmental psychology, philosophical and social foundations of American education, and comparative methods. Three hundred hours of observation were required. The students compiled "Apparatus" books and completed oral and written practical and theoretical examinations given by external examiners. The AMI advised candidates that the most valuable training was to be found in the country in which they intended to teach, so those persons who wanted to teach in the United States should obtain their training here.[55]

The number of Montessori organizations in the United States has increased considerably since the late 1950s, and currently numbers between twenty and thirty organizations. Each of these endorses some of the one thousand teacher preparation centers. Some Montessori teachers in the United States take correspondence courses prepared by institutions overseas. In February 1988, the Association for the Accreditation of Montessori Teacher Education (AAMTE) was formed at a meeting in Berkeley, California. The organization was formed to establish "essential standards to ensure the quality of courses preparing Montessori teachers; the evaluation and accreditation of Montessori teacher education courses through a process of external peer review; and the encouragement of continued self-improvement of Montessori teacher education courses."[56]

In 1975, Evans had interjected a cautionary note: "With control of Montessori teacher training maintained by private societies, it remains to be seen how extensively Montessori education may be extended to young chil-

dren in America. State departments of public instruction are unlikely to nego-
tiate for tax-supported Montessori schools."[57] In the 1990s, there exist a handful of scattered public schools which state that they follow the Montessori
Method. The current Charter School movement includes a Montessori model.

The two membership organizations that currently represent Montessori
educators in the United States are the AMI and the AMS. AMI is headquartered in the Netherlands. AMS, headquartered in the United States, was built
on the foundation laid in 1912 by Mrs. Alexander Graham Bell. Both of these
organizations publish books and periodicals designed to maintain the connection between the Montessori teachers of today, their historical counterparts,
and Dr. Maria Montessori's work.

MONTESSORI PUBLICATIONS

Montessori was a prolific writer, and the majority of her publications have
been translated into English as well as a number of other languages. As stated
earlier, her first work, published in Italian as *Il Metodo della Pedogogia Scien-
tifica applicato all'educazione infantile nelle Case dei Bambine* was translated
by Anne E. George as *The Montessori Method*, appearing in 1912.

Other important works that appeared in the United States are: *Dr.
Montessori's Own Handbook, The Advanced Montessori Method, Volume I:
Spontaneous Activity in Education; The Advanced Montessori Method, Volume II: The Montessori Elementary Material; The Montessori Didactic Apparatus; The Absorbent Mind;* and *Peace and Education.*[58]

OBJECTIVE AND EVALUATIVE RESEARCH

Very little objective research and evaluation of the Montessori Method had
been done up to 1975. The majority of works were self-reports and observational studies. Evans[59] groups the handful of research investigations into three
categories: longitudinal measurement of changes in the behavior of one group
of Montessori children, group comparison studies using selected criteria, and
studies of the Montessori Method's influence on curriculum. Evans omits a
discussion of the Weikart studies done in Michigan. Further perusal of current
databases is needed to determine whether any more recent studies have been
done during the past two decades.

COMPARISONS WITH FROEBELIAN THEORY

Standing finds several similarities between the work of Froebel and Montessori. Both of them saw the child as active, and interacting with and acting on
the environment. This included freedom for the child to choose his own activities, and to engage in "autoeducation." Each of them created a series of materials (the Froebelian Gifts and the Montessori Didactic Materials) and activities
(the Froebelian Occupations and Montessori's activities). Both Froebel and

Montessori saw children as developing through stages, and said that there are sensitive periods within each stage. Both believed that the adult should be careful to avoid molding the child, but rather to allow the child to engage in spontaneous activity. Each of them stated that if a child is unable to complete the tasks of each stage as it proceeds, the person will never be able to regain what was lost. Both Froebel and Montessori conceived of the child as an explorer of the physical environment. Both theorists believed that there should be a "harmony between soul and body." The teacher is viewed as a guide in both methods of education.[60]

A major difference between Froebelian theory and that of Montessori is their view of the role of play, particularly fantasy play, in the development of the child. Montessori, as discussed elsewhere in this chapter, believed that play was a waste of time, at best, and could be harmful to the child. Froebelians included dramatic play as a normal part of their curriculum. Another distinction is that Froebelians worked with groups of children, while Montessorians worked with the individual child. "Froebel's religious philosophy was very largely pantheistic and Nordic; whereas Montessori's is Catholic and Latin."[61] The last difference cited by Standing is that Froebel believed that it is important to "make the inner outer," while Montessori also believed in the importance of "making the outer the inner."[62]

COMPARISONS WITH THE PSYCHOANALYTIC APPROACH

Mario Montessori[63] finds the following elements present in both Montessorian and psychoanalytic theory:

1. "... the relation of observer-participant and participant should be one of alliance based on mutual respect and confidence."
2. "The observer-participant should be carefully trained."
3. "[The observer-participant] should be interested in the phenomena he is observing and understand them."
4. "[The observer-participant] should allow situations to develop freely, abstaining from intervention when it is not necessary and acting appropriately when it is. His actions should be determined by the situation and its objectives, never by his own impulses or wishes, which might interfere with the process at hand. His aim should be to remove obstacles that inhibit the natural course of events, to promote insights that further it, and to help work these through. His attitude should be one of empathy, cooperation, and patience."

Mario Montessori cites the following differences between Montessorian and psychoanalytic theory:

1. The objectives of psychoanalysis and Montessori education are different.
2. The material that is studied differs.

COMPARISONS WITH PROGRESSIVE THEORY AND THE WORK OF DEWEY

Kilpatrick found several similarities between Dewey and Montessori. "Both have organized experimental schools; both have emphasized the freedom, self-activity, and self-education of the child; both have made large use of 'practical life' activities. In a word, the two are cooperative tendencies in opposing entrenched traditionalism."[64] However, as noted earlier, Kilpatrick was largely responsible for the fifty-year hiatus of the Montessori Method in the United States.

Kilpatrick's position was based, in part, on faculty psychology, which was popular in the United States during that time period. He said that Montessori had produced "a set of mechanically simple devices" to do the teaching. He believed that she concentrated on "devising more satisfactory methods of teaching reading and writing." On the other hand, Dewey "feels that early emphasis should be placed upon activities more vital to child life which should at the same time lead toward the mastery of our complex social environment."[65]

COMPARISONS WITH THE "OPEN CLASSROOM"

Both the Montessori and Open Classroom models broke with traditional "chalk and talk" primary school teaching. The majority of the classes provided for freedom within limits. The physical environment offered a variety of places in which to work, based on the child's preference. Montessori classrooms offered many individual work spaces, while the open classroom accommodated both individual and small group activities.

There is similarity in the classroom activities observed in both methods. In each, a child makes an individual study plan and revises it according to their own interests and wishes. Children "keep on learning of their own accord, systematically." There is voluntary self-discipline.[66] Unless one looks carefully at the materials children are utilizing, it may be difficult to distinguish one type of classroom from the other.

COMPARISONS WITH CONSTRUCTIVIST AND PIAGETIAN THEORY

Elkind (1967) wrote of the parallel areas and areas of divergence between the work of contemporaries Jean Piaget and Maria Montessori. Both scientists came from a biological orientation that led them to emphasize the normative aspects of child behavior and development. Both had empathy with the child. Piaget and Montessori extensively utilized the technique of observation of the child. Through their observations, both discovered hitherto unknown facets of child thought and behavior, which allowed them to derive general laws and principles.

Three areas of convergence discussed by Elkind and summarized by Evans are discussed later. The first area of convergence in these two theories is the dual character they both ascribe to the interaction between nature and nurture. "For mental capacities, nature provides the pattern and the time schedule of its unfolding while nurture provides the nourishment for the realization of this pattern. When we turn to the content of thought, however, nurture determines what will be learned while nature provides the prerequisite capacities."[67] A second area of convergence is the relationship between capacity and learning. Mental capacity determines learning. Capacity changes at its own rate and according to its own time schedule. The third area of convergence is the conceptual relationship between cognitive needs and repetitive behavior. Repetitive behavior is the external manifestation of cognitive growth and expresses the need of emerging cognitive abilities to realize themselves through action. For Piaget, the observations led to a new philosophy of knowledge. For Montessori, the observations led to a new philosophy of education.

WORK FOR PEACE

During the last two decades of her life, Montessori worked tirelessly for the cause of peace, and was nominated for the Nobel Peace Prize. She had come to believe that her vision of the "new man" could not come to fruition unless the child could grow up in a peaceful world. She convincingly argued, in an address to the International Bureau of Education of the League of Nations, published in 1932 as *Peace and Education,* that peace could be brought to the world through education. Since Montessori herself had been used by the Fascist government of Italy prior to her 1931 relocation to the Netherlands, she was sensitive to the political machinations which were taking place at that time. The pamphlet foreshadowed many of the damaging occurrences of the 1940s and 1950s, including World War II, and the development of the atomic bomb, both of whose fiftieth anniversaries were recently marked.

Montessori asserted that the adult who worked for peace was formed in the early stages of a child's development. This occurred through the education the child received from the environment created first by the parents and later by the Montessori directress/director. She argued that the observation and presentation methods, and the socialization methods, used by adults were an important influence in the child's life.

Montessori defined and discussed her views in *Peace and Education* (1932). She said that the usual (negative) definition of peace, "ceasing from war," is not the real concept of peace. She did not feel that the concept of peace had been adequately defined. She suggested that "true peace is the triumph of justice and love among men: it reveals the existence of a better world wherein harmony reigns." She was concerned that no formal study of peace had been undertaken. She suggested that "The science of peace ought to be open to human research and thought." Her statement, "Urgently needed is a scientific study not only of causes of war leading to their elimination but study of universal brotherhood and its enhancement,"[68] serves as a goal for the peace educators of today. She wrote that

> only two things are needed in order to establish peace in the world: above all a new type of man, a better humanity; then an environment that should no longer set a limit to the infinite desire of man. We must prepare men for the new world which is spontaneously building itself around us in a phenomenon of evolution; . . . At the same time we must gather together all the elements of this new world and organise them into a science of peace.[69]

Montessori believed that the young child, unchanged and unspoiled by societal influences (as conceptualized by Rousseau), could form the basis for rebuilding mankind in a peaceful image. She said that education could serve as an "Armament of Peace." She was quite specific in noting that:

> An education that is merely a blind struggle between the strong and the weak can only produce inefficient adults. To avoid this, we must substitute more nourishing conditions in our schools for the unfortunate circumstances to which young students are usually subjected. Sadly, children now receive rewards for triumphing over their schoolmates in competitions and excelling in examinations, which allow them to pass from one year to another of monotonous servitude.[70, 71]

A method that Montessori developed to help children learn about peace is the "silence games." One set of games, described in *The Montessori Method*, began as preparation for tests for auditory acuteness that were to be administered. Montessori assumed different positions, and maintained each pose "silently, without movement." She then asked specific children to replicate what she was doing. The children who participated discovered that it is difficult to be silent and tranquil. The other children watched and listened, and discovered that there are "degrees of silence" which they had never noticed before. Montessori concludes her discussion of these games with the observation that "the children, after they had made the effort necessary to maintain silence, enjoyed the sensation, took pleasure in the *silence* itself."

During a hearing test, Montessori established "perfect silence," and drew the children's attention to the ticking of the clock, and other little noises that are not commonly audible to the ear. She then called each child from the adjoining room in a low voice. The Silence Game develops control of movement and an awareness of self in relation to space and others. It also brings an awareness of sound to the child, and stimulates his powers of observation of the environment. Perhaps because it encourages an inner quiet and searching of self, it seems to promote the child's creative powers as well.[72]

Another "lesson in silence" involved bringing the swaddled four-month-old sister of a student into the classroom. Montessori pointed out to them the quietness of the baby, and challenged them to be as quiet as she was. As the children tiptoed around the room, she reminded them that the baby was making no sound.

In *Our Peaceful Classroom,* Wolf describes (using children's voices) some methods that are presently used to create a positive, cooperative and peaceful atmosphere in Montessori schools. Among them are the following:

> We try to speak nicely to each other and to be kind [18]. . . . We try not to hurt any plants or animals anywhere [28]. We want to take care of our earth because it gives us what we need for living [31]. Sometimes two of us want to use the same material at the same time. We might start to fight over it. Then our teacher tells us that hands are for helping, not for hurting. Our teacher asks us to think of a better way to decide who can use it. We decide to take turns because that is the most peaceful way [10–13]. . . . We also learn about the great peacemakers. They teach us to make friends with everyone. We hope to grow up in a peaceful world [58–60].[73]

Montessori believed that the problem of world peace can never be satisfactorily solved until we start with the child. "By taking the child into consideration we touch something common to all humanity. We cannot achieve world harmony simply by attempting to unite all these adult people who are so different: but we can achieve it if we begin with the child who is not born with national and racial prejudices."[74]

Chapter Summary

This chapter has reviewed the work of Dr. Maria Montessori. It discussed her view of children and their importance to society, and the stages of their development, including sensitive periods, and the idea of the absorbent mind. Montessori's views of the differences between children and adults, and between work and play, have been presented. The chapter summarized the aims, goals, content, and environment of Montessori education. It discussed the role and training of the Montessori teacher (directress), and some research done on the Montessori Method in practice. The chapter presented comparisons between Dr. Montessori's theory and Froebelian, psychoanalytic, progressive, and Piagetian theories. The chapter concluded with a discussion of Maria Montessori's work for peace in the world through the education of children.

Notes

1. Maria Montessori, *The Absorbent Mind,* trans. Claude A. Claremont (Adyar, Madras, India: Theosophical Publishing House, 1964), 5–6.
2. E. M. Standing, *Maria Montessori: Her Life and Work* (New York: New American Library, 1957), 21.
3. Elizabeth G. Hainstock, *The Essential Montessori, An Introduction to the Woman, the Writings, the Method, and the Movement* (New York: New American Library, 1978), 12, 13; and Standing, *Maria Montessori: Her Life and Work,* 21, 26–27.

4. R. C. Orem and George L. Stevens, *American Montessori Manual: Principles, Applications, Terms* (College Park, MD: Mafex Associates, Inc., Publisher, 1970), 5; and Tim Seldin, "Maria Montessori: An Historical Perspective," [paper on-line] (The Montessori Foundation, 1996); available from <http://www.montessori.org/mariawho.html>; Internet accessed 27 April 1997, 4.

5. Standing, *Maria Montessori: Her Life and Work,* 29–30, 33; Paula Polk Lillard, *Montessori: A Modern Approach* (New York: Schocken Books, 1972), 2; Orem and Stevens, *American Montessori Manual,* 6, 5; and Seldin, "Maria Montessori: An Historical Perspective," 3.

6. Orem and Stevens, *American Montessori Manual,* 6.

7. Jenny Merrill described Montessori's work in the December 1909 and March 1910 issues of the *Kindergarten Primary Magazine.* In May 1911, *McClure's Magazine* published the first of three articles, with accompanying photographs of the Casa dei Bambini.

8. The organization was influential in the 1914 U.S. Bureau of Education Bulletin, *The Montessori Method and the Kindergarten.*

9. The U.S. Bureau of Education is now the U.S. Office of Education. Hainstock, *The Essential Montessori,* 19; Maria Montessori, *The Montessori Method* [first translation 1912], with an introduction by J. McVickar Hunt (New York: Schocken Books, 1964), xii; and Orem and Stevens, *American Montessori Manual,* 6.

10. Today Neinhaus Montessori USA is the approved producer and disseminator of Montessori materials in the United States.

11. Montessori gave courses in Ahmedabad, Adyar, Kodaikanal, Kashmir, and in 1944 in Ceylon. After World War II, in 1948, Montessori gave more courses in India, in Poona and Adyar, as well as in Pakistan.

12. Hainstock, *The Essential Montessori,* 4, 22; and Standing, *Maria Montessori: Her Life and Work,* 71.

13. Mario M. Montessori, Jr., *Education for Human Development: Understanding Montessori,* with an introduction by Paula Polk Lillard, ed. (New York: Schocken Books, 1976), 97.

14. D. Keith Osborn, *Early Childhood Education in Historical Perspective,* 3rd ed. (Athens, GA: Education Associates, a division of Daye Press, Inc., 1991), 107; and Mario Montessori, *Education for Human Development,* xiv.

15. Mario Montessori, *Education for Human Development,* xii; and David Elkind, "Montessori Education: Abiding Contributions and Contemporary Challenges," *Young Children* 38, no. 2 (January 1983): 4.

16. Mario Montessori, *Education for Human Development,* 4–5.

17. Maria Montessori quoted in Orem and Stevens, *American Montessori Manual,* 38–39; and Standing, *Maria Montessori: Her Life and Work,* 82.

18. Osborn, *Early Childhood Education in Historical Perspective,* 108.

19. Standing, *Maria Montessori: Her Life and Work,* 107; Lillard, *Montessori: A Modern Approach;* and Orem and Stevens, *American Montessori Manual,* 33.

20. Maria Montessori, *The Absorbent Mind* (1964), 97, quoted in Lillard, *Montessori: A Modern Approach,* 32–33.

21. Standing, *Maria Montessori: Her Life and Work,* 120; and Maria Montessori, *The Secret of Childhood* (1963), 44, quoted in Lillard, *Montessori: A Modern Approach,* 32–33.

22. Orem and Stevens, *American Montessori Manual,* 33; Maria Montessori, *The Absorbent Mind* (1964), 25, quoted in Lillard, *Montessori: A Modern Approach,* 36–37; and Lillard, *Montessori: A Modern Approach,* 48.

23. Orem and Stevens, *American Montessori Manual,* 33; and Lillard, *Montessori: A Modern Approach,* 33; and Mario Montessori, *Education for Human Development,* 12–13.

24. Mario Montessori, *Education for Human Development,* 12–13.

25. Lillard, *Montessori: A Modern Approach,* 48.

26. Ibid.

27. Ibid., 34–36; and Mario Montessori, *Education for Human Development,* 12.

28. Lillard, *Montessori: A Modern Approach,* 39–43; and Ellis D. Evans, *Contemporary Influences in Early Childhood Education,* 2nd ed. (New York: Holt, Rinehart and Winston, Inc., 1975), 283.

29. Lillard, *Montessori: A Modern Approach,* 45.

30. Elkind, "Montessori Education," 4–5.

31. Aline D. Wolf, *Peaceful Children, Peaceful World: The Challenge of Maria Montessori* (Altoona, PA: Parent Child Press, 1989), 42.

32. Maria Montessori, *Peace and Education* (Geneva, Switzerland: International Bureau of Education, 1932), 12–13, 15.

33. Lillard, *Montessori: A Modern Approach,* 39.

34. Mario Montessori, *Education for Human Development,* 13–14.

35. Standing, *Maria Montessori: Her Life and Work,* 346; and Lillard, *Montessori: A Modern Approach,* 45–46.

36. Elkind, "Montessori Education," 5–7.

37. Ibid.

38. Orem and Stevens, *American Montessori Manual,* 112; and Osborn, *Early Childhood Education in Historical Perspective,* 107.

39. Aline D. Wolf, *Our Peaceful Classroom* (Altoona, PA: Parent Child Press, 1991), 41; and Standing, *Maria Montessori: Her Life and Work,* 133.

40. Phyllis Povell, "Maria Montessori," in *Encyclopedia of Early Childhood Education,* ed. Leslie R. Williams and Doris Pronin Fromberg (New York: Garland Publishing, Inc., 1992), 54; and Seldin, "Maria Montessori: An Historical Perspective," 7.

41. Povell, "Maria Montessori," 54.

42. Elkind, "Montessori Education," 7–8.

43. Roland A. Lubienski Wentworth, *Montessori for the New Millennium: Practical Guidance on the Teaching and Education of Children of All Ages, Based on a Rediscovery of the True Principles and Vision of Maria Montessori* (Mahwah, NJ: Lawrence Erlbaum Associates, Publishers, 1999), 110.

44. Orem and Stevens, *American Montessori Manual,* 7.

45. Povell, "Maria Montessori," 54.

46. Elkind, "Montessori Education," 4.

47. Standing, *Maria Montessori: Her Life and Work,* 184.

48. Ibid., 187.

49. Osborn, *Early Childhood Education in Historical Perspective,* 108.

50. Paula Polk Lillard, "A Montessori Classroom," in Mario M. Montessori, Jr., *Education for Human Development: Understanding Montessori,* Paula Polk Lillard, ed. (New York: Schocken Books, 1976), 115–116.

51. Nancy McCormick Rambusch, *Learning How to Learn: An American Approach to Montessori* (Baltimore, NM: Helicon Press, 1962), 92–94.

52. Lillard, "A Montessori Classroom," in *Education for Human Development,* 115–116.

53. Margaret Naumburg, as discussed in Chapter 10 in this volume, attended one of these international training courses prior to opening her first school.

54. Osborn, *Early Childhood Education in Historical Perspective,* 108.

55. Rambusch, *Learning How to Learn,* Appendix B, 137.

56. Osborn, *Early Childhood Education in Historical Perspective,* 109, 179.

57. Evans, *Contemporary Influences in Early Childhood Education,* 285.

58. Orem and Stevens, *American Montessori Manual,* xix–xx; and Library of Congress Experimental Search System <http://lcweb2.loc.gov/ . . . +Maria(+1870+1952.+)>. Among Montessori's lesser-known but important books are: Maria Montessori, *Education for a New World* (Adyar, Madras, India: Kalakshetra Publications, 1959) and Maria Montessori, *Peace and Education* (Adyar, Madras, India: Theosophical Publishing House, 1948).

59. Evans, *Contemporary Influences in Early Childhood Education,* 270–271.

60. Standing, *Maria Montessori: Her Life and Work,* 323–330; and Evelyn Weber, *The Kindergarten: Its Encounter with Educational Thought in America* (New York: Teachers College Press, 1969), 73.

61. Standing, 350.

62. Ibid., 351.

63. Mario Montessori, *Education for Human Development,* 7–8.

64. William Heard Kilpatrick, *The Montessori System Examined* (New York: Houghton Mifflin Company, 1914), 63–64.

65. Lillard, *Montessori: A Modern Approach,* 14–15; Robert H. Beck, "Kilpatrick's Critique of Montessori's Method and Theory," *Studies in Philosophy and Education* I (November 1961): 153–162; and Weber, *The Kindergarten,* 73–82

66. Wentworth, *Montessori for the New Millennium,* 104–105.

67. Evans, *Contemporary Influences in Early Childhood Education,* 280; and David Elkind, "Piaget and Montessori: Three Ideas They Have in Common," *Harvard Educational Review* 37, no. 4, (1967, Fall): 449, 535–545.

68. Orem and Stevens, *American Montessori Manual,* 114; and Standing, *Maria Montessori: Her Life and Work,* 369.

69. Maria Montessori, *Peace and Education,* 4–6, 19, 22.

70. Wolf, *Peaceful Children, Peaceful World,* 10, 37.

71. Orem, in the section of the *American Montessori Manual* entitled "Regeneration of Mankind," includes quotations from Montessori's writings regarding the tyranny of adults over children, the reformation required of the adult world, the "new teacher," and "a new humanity for a new world." Orem and Stevens, *American Montessori Manual,* 85–89.

72. Maria Montessori, *The Montessori Method,* 209–214; and Lillard, *Montessori: A Modern Approach,* 127.

73. Wolf, *Our Peaceful Classroom,* 10–13, 18, 22–23, 31, 58–60.

74. Standing, *Maria Montessori: Her Life and Work,* 157.

PART II

Early Education
in the United States

CHAPTER 7
European Settlement

> Behold the child, by nature's kindly law
> Pleased with a rattle, tickled with a straw.
> Some livelier plaything gives his youth delight,
> A little louder but as empty quite.
> —Alexander Pope, *Essay on Man* (1732)

Shortly after the arrival of Columbus in America, Spain, Portugal, England, and France each staked a claim to parts of the New World. For more than a century, Spain was the only European nation strong enough to exploit its claims in the Caribbean Sea and South America. By the beginning of the seventeenth century, France had established several fishing stations and fur-trading posts along the North American coast and the valley of the St. Lawrence River. Neither the Spanish nor the French settlements attracted many European settlers, and England became a major colonizing power in the New World.

The territory settled by the English was varied. It stretched from poor farming conditions in New England to the Chesapeake Bay region, where rivers opened a rich interior, to the semitropical land of the Carolinas and Georgia. The most common form of social organization was the close-knit farming village, which was predominant in New England. In the Chesapeake region, settlement was dispersed. In both settings, the family was the basic social unit and was expected to carry out several social functions, such as economic production, education, religious training, piety, welfare, and social control.[1]

Despite the differences between the geographic regions and the ways of earning a livelihood, the colonists had much in common. The reality of surviving in a harsh environment gave them a bond. Because many were farmers, the abundance of the land gave them the opportunity to improve their economic situations. Most colonists shared the belief that a man could better himself by his own efforts. This willingness to work hard made the colonists increasingly self-sufficient. By the middle of the eighteenth century, the colonists' 150 years of experience in the New World had created a "new man" independent of European authority.

Most colonists came to America to seek religious freedom or to improve their life situation; others were adventurers who wanted to explore the natural wealth of the New World. Upon their arrival, they became preoccupied with personal goals such as maintaining family and livelihood. In time, they established distinctly American customs so pervasive that they overcame regional differences and enabled those of European descent to consider themselves a new people.[2] For Blacks and Native Americans, however, the American experience did not lead to freedom and independence, at once, as is discussed in later chapters.

WHO WERE THE COLONISTS?

The Pilgrims who had fled England for Holland in 1607 and 1608 feared that the price of toleration might be their eventual assimilation into the Dutch population. They came to America as a community seeking to preserve its religious and cultural integrity, and though they were a minority of the population in Plymouth, where they settled, they set the dominant character and tone of the colony. Their children's education during the early years of the settlement was conducted by the family and the church rather than through any school.

The Puritans, also from England, settled in Massachusetts Bay Colony. They too came as a community with ties of family, friendship, and common loyalty. Like the Pilgrims, they were attempting to preserve their religious and cultural integrity. They were also seeking to demonstrate the nature and practicability of a divinely ordered Christian commonwealth. Education in that society was an agency for molding men.[3] Although only a few members of the nobility and the elite gentry, who sponsored and financed the colonization, migrated, the English settlers were basically representative of English society. The lesser gentry, the merchants, and the professions were somewhat better represented, and their influence was far greater than their numbers during the initial decades of the settlement. The greatest number of colonists were yeomen, husbandmen, artisans, and tradesmen, who acquired their own farms and shops. There were also some unskilled laborers, many of whom were indentured. The colonists' families were both nuclear and extended.[4]

THE COLONIAL PERIOD IN NEW ENGLAND (1620–1776)

The colonial period in America is from 1607 to 1776, the year when the thirteen colonies declared their independence from England and went on to become the United States of America.

Immigration to New England began with the settlement of Plymouth Colony in 1620 and increased in the 1630s after the founding of Massachusetts Bay Colony. The colonists, numbering about 20,000, formed the basis of a population that increased to nearly 100,000 by 1700. There was an extremely favorable demographic environment when compared to that of England: a balanced sex ratio among immigrants; most persons paid their own passage and were not prevented from marrying because of indentured servitude; a generally healthy climate; abundant land, good diet, and plenty of fuel supplies; relatively low rates of infant and maternal mortality; and generally long life expectancies. These conditions resulted in early marriages for women, large families, parents' provision for their children through gifts or inheritance of land, and large numbers of older people.[5]

Since colonial society was similar to its contemporary English counterpart, the family members continued to have the same responsibilities. The colonial household was an important agency of education, as it was the fundamental unit of social organization in New England. It served simultaneously as a center of human association, a producer of food and manufactured articles, and a focus of religious life. Colonial houses were, for the most part, small and almost always crowded, with little privacy for the individual within the family. The living space was the kitchen around the hearth, and, as in England, the business of making a living was in most households an extension of the activities of the kitchen.

The children in this society were a vital part of the labor force and assisted the family in obtaining economic self-sufficiency. Children were important for other reasons, too. Colonial parents were deeply concerned about their children's physical and spiritual welfare and, like contemporary parents, felt threatened when their children did not accept the prevailing religious and moral values. Most children learned their adult roles as apprentices in their own homes. Boys worked beside their fathers in the fields; women managed the barnyard, pigpen, garden, and orchard, where girls worked beside their mothers. There was no sharp division of labor, and in times of need or sickness, everyone did everything, as during the times of planting and harvesting. The world in which these children lived was structured. Everyone had a place in a social hierarchy. Children worked to earn their keep and to help the family survive. In return, parents were obliged to give their children a start in life.[6]

This agrarian society began to change during the eighteenth century. Increased trade, immigration, and an increase in population due to a decline in the death rate made life more heterogeneous and more complex in the colonies.[7]

Upon their arrival in the colonies, newcomers encountered very difficult conditions. In New England, the Pilgrims suffered a brief but devastating period of starvation, as we all learned in school. This was succeeded by relatively healthy conditions, when epidemics like smallpox occurred only in port towns like Boston. Although the New England Puritans were different from us in many cultural respects, they considered childhood to be a distinct phase of life.[8] According to Alice Earl, however, some of the Puritan child-rearing ideas and practices had negative effects on personality development.[9] Earle refers primarily to the severe discipline children encountered in the schools, where either a rod or a bunch of birch twigs were used on them.

Importance of Children

The Puritans' relationship with their children, their love and responsibility for them, began well before birth. The Puritans strongly sanctioned marriage for the purpose of procreation. They believed that infancy began in the womb, so parents were obliged to pray for their unborn child because it had been conceived in sin. The Puritans believed that an unborn child had an immortal soul. A mother had to take special care to ensure the child's safe delivery. Thus prenatal care was both spiritual and physical.[10]

Childbirth was at home, with a midwife assisted by the neighborhood women. Husbands were frequently nearby, but did not participate in the birth of their children.[11]

The bond between a mother and her newborn would develop during the hours, days, and weeks following birth. The Puritans were amazed by the very rapid recovery of Indian women after a child's delivery, for their own experience differed significantly. Following childbirth, an English mother was likely to be confined for a period of weeks, first to her bed, then to her room, and finally to her home. She might be helped by her family, servants, neighbors, or persons who were specifically brought into the home to care for the infant. However, unless she had difficulty nursing or had the means and desire to hire a wet nurse, the mother and the infant were in each other's presence much of the time.[12]

Weaning the child occurred between twelve and eighteen months.[13] Barring illness or accident, the first two years of an infant's life would have been relatively comfortable and tranquil. The babies slept in cradles, either in those that the Puritans brought with them or in the ones fashioned by the Native Americans.[14] A go-cart and/or standing stool were favorite devices for teaching a child to walk. Colonial parents looked for child-rearing advice in John Locke's *Thoughts on Education*. The book published in England in 1690 found its way into colonial homes. In it Locke discusses topics such as foods, bathing, and education.[15]

Child Naming

Colonial child naming shows how parents invested part of themselves in their children. Parents searched for names of deep significance and for names appropriate to conditions of profound influence to the child's life. Glory to God and having zealous ambition for the child's future were equally influential motives for the selection. Abigail and Hannah, old Hebrew names, were given frequently. Comfort, Deliverance, Temperance, Peace, Hope, Patience, Rejoice, and similar names indicative of a trait of character or virtue were also common. Double Christian names did not appear until after the American Revolution. Some parents named children after themselves, with the mother's name being given to a daughter as frequently as the father's name was given to a son. Naming children after parents and the four grandparents defined the linkages and boundaries of kinship. Names provided clues to the cultural values of the population. Naming children after parents was a practice that was not affected by economic status. Differences appear in the decision to name a child for a grandparent, with the wealthiest group placing more weight on the generational depth of their families. Some devout New Englanders often looked to providential events when selecting names.[16]

Infant Mortality/Infanticide

The death of a child was often a grim reality for the Puritan parents. Infant deaths resulted from lack of proper sanitation, which was unknown. Disinfecting was almost nonexistent except for sprinkling vinegar. Isolation of contagious diseases was a futile measure, for the colonists did not know what diseases were communicable. While infant and childhood mortality rates were lower in New England than in other parts of the colonies, death was an ever-present and unpredictable possibility.[17] This high possibility of child mortality created for many New England parents the fear of infant damnation and "cast its shadow over Puritan households in mourning for deceased babies." There was an immediacy to the evangelical preaching about hell and damnation. Baptism took place within a few days of birth, with infants "shrinking from the icy water, but crying not."[18] Some parents, in order to deal with their grief, reused the name of a dead child for a later one.[19]

Both infanticide and infant abandonment have occurred in America from the colonial period onward. During the eighteenth century in New England, there were several well-publicized cases, an occurrence that prompted local ministers to expound upon the necessity of a virtuous life and the miseries of "that soul Sin of Uncleanness," or fornication. Without exception, the mothers were put to death. There was also a published account by one of the convicted women, Rebekah Chamblit, *The Declaration, Dying Warning and Advice of Rebekah Chamblit* (1733). After the American Revolution, babies were still murdered or abandoned by desperate mothers. Notices about abandoned babies had also appeared, telling of perhaps a less sensational crime, but one still offensive to those holding idealistic notions of motherhood.[20]

Children and Clothing

There is no evidence that infants were swaddled. According to Earle's *Child Life in Colonial Days,* children in America dressed like children in England, in a style reflecting the Puritan influence (40–41). The baby dresses were shapeless "sacques" drawn at the neck with narrow cotton ferret or linen bobbin. Both boys and girls wore long linen gowns, which opened down the front (36–37). When the children reached five or six years of age, boys' and girls' clothing became differentiated. Boys wore breeches like their fathers did, a fashion that created the impression of a miniature adult. Girls wore dresses. This new way of dressing signaled to the child the beginning of the transition into the adult world.[21]

Play

Puritan children played with toys, and the Puritans did not object to their playing if it did not lead to mischief or disruption of the Sabbath. Toys for the younger children included rocking horses, push and squeak toys (cow, rooster, lamb, and horse), wheelbarrows, rattles, marbles, and tops. There were dolls and doll furniture, children's tea sets made by Staffordshire, and children's books. Older girls embroidered samplers.[22] Colonial children also had alphabet blocks. They were "letter-dice" that children could use to play a game like "royal oak," and through it they would learn to spell. The blocks were made of bone or wood.[23]

Older children played hop-scotch in the same way that children play it today. They also played "London Bridge Is Falling Down," "Here We Go 'round the Mulberry Bush," "tick-tack," and tag. They ice-skated, played with marbles, flew kites, bowled, and danced around the May Pole. Children also had sleighs, ice skates, and snowshoes. However, playing cards was fiercely hated by the Puritans, and their sale was prohibited in Puritan communities.[24]

Religion

Religion played an important part in colonial life. The child's initiation into the symbolic and ritual dimensions of religious life began at an early age. Born into a pious family, the children were surrounded from the moment of their birth by a religious atmosphere with daily family devotion, prayer, psalm-singing, and Bible readings, as well as the special character of Sabbath observances. They could not escape the impression of deep religious feeling. They certainly had familiarity with the Bible. Until after the Revolution, there were few American children who had read from any book other than the Bible, a primer, a catechism, or perhaps a hymn book or an almanac.

The usual method of reading through the Bible was in the regular succession of every chapter from beginning to end. This method did not engage the children's interest in the same way that a careful selection suitable for children would have.[25] Just how soon children were introduced to the public aspects of religious ceremony is not clear. Parents were to "Bring them to Church, and help them to remember something, and tell them the meaning of it, and take a little in good part, and encourage them, and that will make them delight in it."[26] This approach implies that because children's capacities were limited, parents were to see that the children understood at least something.

New England children were also instilled with a familiarity with death. Their *Primer,* had a couplet *On Life and Death,*

> *Life* and the *grave* two different lessons give;
> *Life* shows how to die, and *death* how to live.

Their presence at funerals was universal. In those days funerals had an entirely different status as a ceremony from today. It was a social function as well as a solemn one. It was a reunion of friends and relatives. Children as young as five and six years old attended funerals. Little girls were pallbearers of their friends, and young unmarried girls at those of their companions.[27]

Education

Because the labor of each child was required as early as possible, the everyday activities of the household provided a continuous general apprenticeship in the diverse arts of living. In addition to these apprenticeships, there was systematic instruction in reading, which was learned at home, both in England

and in the colonies. There is every indication that individual reading, responsive reading, and communal reading were daily practices in many colonial households and that reading was taught on a one-to-one basis by parents, other adults, siblings, or peers. In New England households, when there was no one equipped to teach reading, there was often a literate wife in the neighborhood who would teach reading on a regular basis for a small fee, in her kitchen, which became a "dame school." Young boys and girls attended these dame schools. In the first half of the seventeenth century, preaching and catechizing were the primary forms of education practiced in the colonies. As the communities achieved greater stability and self-confidence, schooling became more important because it was viewed by the colonists as the most important defense, after religion, in their struggle against the wilderness.[28]

It was less important for girls to acquire knowledge of matters other than their household duties. An arrangement was made for a girl to attend school, but it was not desirable that she should have a variety of knowledge. It was enough if a girl knew how to read and write and how to do some calculation. Many fathers taught their daughters these skills. Sometimes girls were admitted to public schools during the hours they were not used by the boys, from 6:00 to 7:30 in the morning and from 4:00 to 6:00 in the afternoon. The first all-girls school was established in 1780 by a Yale graduate in Middletown, Connecticut. In large cities, there were always small classes where girls could be taught the rudiments of education, and there were many private tutors who taught young misses.[29] The goal of education was to instill the habits of obedience, reverence, and industry, which were fundamental for a particular kind of adult Christian life—Puritan.

Materials Used

A child's introduction to print and literacy was connected to the family's and community's religious life. When teaching reading, the family might use in succession a hornbook, a primer, and the Bible. Seventeenth-century readers treasured certain texts—the Bible and books of devotion—which "gained in meaning as time went by." This was not a modern world in which readers sought new or novel ideas but rather a conservative world in which "certain formulas had endearing significance."[30] The study of reading began with the alphabet and syllables taken from the hornbook or ABC and then proceeded to a catechism, primer, or Psalter. These texts were imported from England.[31]

THE HORNBOOK

The first book from which colonial children learned their letters and how to spell was the hornbook. The hornbook was actually not a book at all in our sense of the word. It was a thin piece of wood, usually four by five inches long and two inches wide. It had a sheet of paper of slightly smaller size placed on it. The alphabet was printed on the top, first in capital letters, followed by lowercase letters. Below these were simple syllables such as *ab, ib, ob,* and so

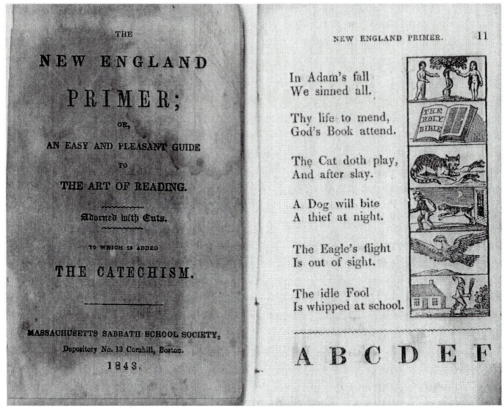

Figure 7.1 Title page and page 11 of *The New England Primer,* Massachusetts Sabbath School Society, Depository No. 13, Cornhill, Boston, 1843. *Courtesy of the Mattapoisett Historical Society.*

on; then came the Lord's Prayer. This printed page was covered with a thin sheet of yellowish horn, which was not as transparent as glass but still permitted the letters to be read through it. Both the paper and the horn were fastened around the edges to the wood by a narrow strip of metal, usually brass, which was held down by fine tacks or nails. It was a book of one page. At the lower end of the wooden back, there was usually a small handle, often pierced with a hole, so the hornbook could be carried by a string.[32]

The hornbook was succeeded by *The New England Primer; or An Easy and Pleasant Guide to the Art of Reading.* It combined into a single volume the hornbook and the catechism. The *Primer* was a book of private devotions used before and after the Reformation in England. It was the most universally studied schoolbook ever used in America. For one hundred years it was *the* schoolbook, and for another hundred years it was frequently reprinted and much used. Learning the catechism was enforced by law in New England, and the deacons and ministers visited and examined families to ensure that the law was obeyed.[33]

THE NEW ENGLAND PRIMER

Upon examination, *The New England Primer* (1843),[34] is a rather poorly printed booklet about five inches long and three inches wide with sixty-four pages. The content of the Primer is primarily religious. In addition to the items from the hornbook, it contains tables with words of one, two, three, four, and five syllables. Among the ten five-syllable words are: *a-bom-in-a-tion, ed-ifi-ca-tion, mor-ti-fi-ca-tion,* and *pu-ri-fi-ca-tion* (5–9). Following these words is the Creed. The Ten Commandments are in short and easy rhymes for children to memorize (9–10). The fashion of the day was to set everything in rhyme to facilitate memorizing. Each letter of the alphabet (11–14) is illustrated by a blurred picture of a woodcut that represents a biblical incident. It begins: "In Adam's fall, we sinned all," and ends with Z: "Zaccheus he Did climb a tree His Lord to see" (17). There is also "Duty of children to their parents" (19) and the burning of Mr. John Rogers (1554)—illustrated by a woodcut—a minister of the gospel in London, and the first Protestant martyr in Queen Mary's reign (24). Pages 33 to 54 are taken up by *The Shorter Catechism,* perhaps the most important part of the primer. It was called *Shorter* because it had 107 questions and answers instead of the 1,200 of the regular catechism as "agreed upon by the Reverend Assembly of Divines at Westminster." The questions and answers relate to the catechism. This is followed by "A dialogue Between Christ, A Youth, and the Devil" (54–61). The Primer ends with a prayer for children, in imitation of "The Lord's Prayer" (64).

When the children advanced beyond the Primer, they entered grammar school. The text for grammar school was written in Latin, not in English. The curriculum was the same as the one taught in England. It was expected to teach boys proficiency in the Latin language and provide an elementary knowledge of Greek and Hebrew in about seven years. Latin grammar was taught from Lily, a grammar text, supplemented by texts like Comenius's *Orbis Pictus.* Not all students completed the entire course. The school was open throughout the year. As a rule, the mornings were devoted to grammar and the afternoons to literature. Fridays were for review and testing of memorization, Saturdays for themes, and Sundays for catechizing and other religious exercises.[35]

Discipline

Discipline was harsh. Parents, teachers, and ministers believed that "foolishness was bound up in the heart of a child," and the only cure for that foolishness, they believed, was stern repression and sharp correction—above all, the use of the rod. They found abundant support for this belief in the Bible, their constant guide. One such disciplinarian was John Robinson (1575–1625), the Pilgrim preacher and leader who chose to stay in Holland instead of coming to America but who exerted great influence in the colonies through his writings.

He quoted from both the Old and New Testaments to encourage and support the harsh discipline afflicted on the children.[36] The following is what he said in his essay on *Children and Their Education* (1628):

> Surely there is in all children (though not alike) a stubbernes and stoutnes of minde arising from naturall pride which must in the first place be broken and beaten down that so the foundation of their education being layd in humilitie and tractablenes other virtues may in their time be built thereon.[37]

The chief purpose of discipline was to break the child's will. New England at that time was controlled both in public and in private life by the Puritan ministers who suppressed and controlled the autonomy of the children and were the accredited guardians of the schools.

A comparison between the Ancient Greek view of the child's nature and that of the Puritans will be useful and appropriate here. The Puritans beat and punished their children in an effort to drive out the inborn sin of willfulness, especially in the school situation. The Greeks, on the other hand, except for the Spartans, disciplined their children not for evildoing but rather to ensure proper growth and development.

In 1647, a law was passed in Massachusetts, which influenced the schooling for the remainder of the colonial period. It required that every town of fifty families "shall appoint one within their town to teach all children . . . to write and read . . . wages shall be paid by the parents of such children . . . or by the inhabitants in general." The law also required that any town which had one hundred families was obliged to establish a grammar school with a master to teach the youth so that they would be qualified to attend the university. If a town failed to abide, it would have to pay five hundred pounds to the next town's school until it created its own. These schools were public, but they were not free; they were supported by the parents. By 1650, schooling as an institution had been firmly transplanted to the colonies.[38]

Land was sometimes set aside to support partly the school. Such land was called the "school-meadows" and was let out for an income to pay the teacher. This compensation was a grant made on the same principle by which grants were made to physicians, tanners, and other useful persons, not to establish free education. At a later date, lotteries were a favorite method for raising money for schools. It was not until about the time of the Revolution that schooling was free. It was financed entirely by general town taxes.[39]

After 1689, there was a rapid expansion of the population, which was the result of an unusual natural increase related to social stability and economic prosperity. During the eighteenth century, the majority of the colonists continued to be English, as it had been during the seventeenth century. Other groups, however, like the Scots, Scotch-Irish, French, Germans, and Africans began to immigrate to the middle and southern colonies. The Africans were brought to America involuntarily. The impact of the new immigrants was varied from colony to colony. The least impacted was New England.[40]

Comment

Colonial portraits of children tended to differentiate them less sharply from adults in dress and stance, creating the impression of "miniature adults." These images may be the reflection of the artists' folk style rather than the reality the works portrayed.[41]

Education in the Southern Colonies

The name of Virginia was originally applied by Sir Walter Raleigh to an undefined territory along the East Coast. In 1612, it was more specifically delimited by Captain John Smith as lying between 34°N and 44°N latitudes (i.e., from the northern boundary of North Carolina to Maine). In due course, four colonies were created out of the territory, Virginia and later, six others to the south. Lord Baltimore established the colony of Maryland, and Carolina was settled by Virginians moving downstream along the Appalachian River. In 1712, the territory was formally separated into North and South Carolina. Georgia was created out of South Carolina and given to James Oglethorpe in 1732, partially to serve as a strategic buffer colony against the Spaniards of Florida and partly to function as a refuge for persecuted Protestants from England.

The Anglican Church (the Church of England) was a major force in the Southern Colonies. The church regarded education as a private concern in which each family accepted responsibility for the instruction of its members. Thus, most southerners of the time believed that education was a private matter and not a concern for the state. They pointed out that in traditional societies, a child received the most important training and instruction in the home, where he was inducted into the values of the society he is about to enter.[42]

The sons and some daughters of the plantation owners of the South had private tutors. The students began their studies as soon as it was light, completing one round of lessons before the bell rang for breakfast. After breakfast the pupils returned to school until noon. They then had a three- or four-hour recess for "diversion and dinner." Boys would ride and hunt game, and girls would play with pets or dress their dolls or help with the baking during this time period. Between 3:30 and 5:00 P.M. school was again in session. Often the children had the evenings free. The curriculum for boys included Greek and Roman classics as well as mathematics. The girls could learn French but not Latin or Greek. All children learned spelling, writing, reading, and basic arithmetic. The daughters had to learn household management skills and the social graces and domestic skills of a housewife. These included fancy needlework, dancing, and how to play musical instruments. Boys also learned to dance and enjoyed literature, music, art, and the breeding of fine horses when they became young adults.

Those who could not afford a private tutor but could afford a fee for instruction at a private school received a "more or less sound educational training according to the standard of the school." Poorer children of the South had some access to church charity schools or they were apprenticed to a trade or sent into agriculture. Very few poor children attended school.

The South was committed to agriculture, especially to the growing of tobacco. This plant exhausted the soil in about seven years; therefore, the South was characterized by larger and larger plantations because as soil was exhausted they moved onto new land. It was not until the 1830s that the benefits of farming with fertilizer were widely understood. Some southern students, including George Washington, attended "old field schools." A few neighbors got together, hired a teacher, and set him up in a shabby building on an exhausted tobacco field. They entrusted their children to his care. Washington began his education with Mr. Hobby, a teacher in an "old field school." He later rode his horse ten miles each way to study with a teacher in Fredericksburg.[43]

Thomas Jefferson's early educational experiences were directed by his father. From the age of five he had a tutor. Later, Jefferson studied at Douglas' school, which utilized a typical Latin grammar school curriculum. He also studied French.[44] Jefferson engaged in self-study both prior to attending and after graduating from the College of William and Mary. He learned several modern languages in addition to Hebrew, Latin, and Greek. He could dance, ride, and hunt. He was a musician, philosopher, inventor, archaeologist, and historian. He studied architecture and utilized the skills he gained in the construction of Monticello. His knowledge of horticulture combined with his architectural knowledge produced a beautiful and functional home. Jefferson is considered by several authors to be the exemplar of southern colonial education, and the consummate Renaissance man.

In later life, Jefferson developed his Bill for the More General Diffusion of Knowledge. This bill was presented to the Virginia State Legislature in 1779. It called for a three-tiered system of education that began with three years of free elementary-level instruction for white males and females in reading, writing, and arithmetic. Unfortunately, the bill was not funded by the Legislature and it was not until the 1870s that Virginia and most of the other southern states were willing to commit themselves to tax-supported systems of public schools.

In the Maryland colony, fines and duties on tobacco funded some public schools, but only a small percentage of the population had access to them. Slaves were not considered to have the intellectual capacity for learning; however, sometimes they were taught to read and the basic fundamentals of writing in a surreptitious manner. In most of the colonies, Dame schools were conducted by women in their own homes. The lessons were limited to the alphabet, counting, prayers, the catechism, and reading from the Bible. There were a few schools run by ministers in the Southern Colonies. There were also schools known as the Academy. This was not designed as a college preparatory school. These private schools had a curriculum that enabled young men to learn writing, bookkeeping, and related skills designed to help them in farming and business. Some Academies included girls who received training in the three R's. However, little attention was paid to young girls because they would not enter the business world.[45] The Society for the Propagation of the Gospel in Foreign Parts (SPG) was an agency of the Anglican Church, which provided money, books, teachers, and physical facilities for children who otherwise would have had no opportunity to attend school. The SPG was active in all of the thirteen original colonies in which Anglicans resided.

While slaves served the Southern Colonies, in the Middle Colonies children were brought as indentured servants. They worked on farms or as apprentices to repay their passage to the New World. Often the teachers of "old field schools" were indentured servants who had to leave Europe for one reason or another. Those indentured servants who had received a classical education were sought after as teachers, particularly in the South.

Education in the Middle Colonies

The development of the five English Middle Colonies in North America was complicated by the existence of two other European settlements. The Dutch constructed forts along various portions of the Hudson River. They purchased Manhattan Island and founded New Amsterdam as the capital of the colony of New Netherlands, which was administered by the Dutch West India Company. In 1638, the Swedes established Fort Christiana, at the site of present-day Wilmington, Delaware. By 1664, the English were in sole control of the entire eastern seaboard from Maine to South Carolina. New Amsterdam became New York in honor of James, Duke of York, upon whom was also bestowed New Jersey.[46] The charter of the Dutch West India Company, given in 1629, required colonists and wealthy landowners to support a schoolmaster, along with a minister and a comforter of the sick. The company selected the schoolmasters. The colonists were very interested in establishing elementary education. The Dutch West India Company, in accepting its obligation to provide schools, required all nine villages chartered in New Netherlands to have a publicly funded school. When the English became dominant, the Dutch schools continued to exist, but they became parochial or private institutions. The population of New York was drawn from many cultures and faiths, which were represented in the schools.

The Constitution that William Penn granted to Pennsylvanians in 1682 included requirements for a public school system that stressed religious values and a practical education in a skill or trade, but no governor, assembly, or council in the colony ever enforced the law. Schooling was left up to the various religious groups to handle as they chose. Pennsylvania became a place of great religious and ethnic diversity because Penn thought of the colony as a haven from religious persecution.[47] The Quaker schools in Pennsylvania taught reading, writing, arithmetic, religion, and some bookkeeping. They were opened to boys and girls, rich and poor alike. Quaker teachers received an apprenticeship training, which Pulliam and Van Patten called the first teacher education in America.[48] Quaker schools also provided the first education in America for blacks who were free.

Schoolhouses shaped like hexagons were a feature of education in the Middle Colonies. The Quakers built these schools for the study of the three R's, but they were wary of further education because they believed that it fostered undue pride and provoked idleness. The early country schoolhouses of New York and Pennsylvania were made of logs with dirt floors. Younger children sat on blocks or benches made of logs facing the master's desk in the center of the room. The older students sat at plank desks extending from the wall. The single master taught all the subjects in all the grades and only in the larger towns did he have the rare assistant.[49] In these colonies, the child was primarily a worker and not a student throughout the colonial period. Both girls and boys were apprenticed to masters. Girls learned to be a good wife and mother; however, the boy needed to learn a trade. Often the relationship between master and apprentice became that of father and son, but the relationship was not necessarily familial, because the apprentice was still considered the master's property. The boy could not marry, vote, or engage in trade without the master's consent.[50] Eventually the apprentice came to be treated just as any other hired hand.

Spinning schools were erected for the education of the poor. They led to the development of the clothmaking industry. As early as 1640, the magistrates of towns looked into the methods of teaching boys and girls the spinning of yarn and building a mill in which children could work at spinning cotton and wool. These spinning schools eventually led to the Industrial Revolution's importation from Europe to the United States.

The linguistic, religious, and cultural pluralism of the Middle Colonies led to colonists who placed a higher value on the power of reason than on sinfulness. Parents thus believed that love and discipline were more persuasive than the threat of Satan, or Fire and Brimstone. There were a number of separate schools for the diverse cultural and religious groups. A few private nonsectarian schools were founded in Philadelphia. Quaker schools remained under the jurisdiction of the Society of Friends. Here the students learned to read and write using the Bible and Francis Pastorius's *New Primer*, which contained many scriptural excerpts.

Pietist scholar Francis Daniel Pastorius (1651–1720) was one of the best educated men in America at the time. Pastorius was a "cultivated Frankfurt lawyer who migrated to Pennsylvania in 1683 and presided over the founding of Germantown." He taught first at the Friends' Public School (1698–1700) and later at a new subscription school in Germantown (1702–1720).[51] His primer, called *The True Reading, Spelling, and Writing of English*, was published in New York in 1697.

Benjamin Franklin exemplified the emerging merchant and entrepreneurial class in the Middle Colonies.[52] Although he had only two years of formal schooling, Franklin taught himself every subject about which he could procure a book. One of the books Franklin read was Cotton Mather's *Essays to Do Good,* which Franklin proclaimed was a cornerstone influence on his life. Franklin founded the Academy of Philadelphia. In 1749, he began a campaign to create the Academy with a publication entitled *Proposals Related to the Education of Youth in Pennsylvania.* He wrote that the youth of Pennsylvania needed an Academy in which to receive a regular education.

The school envisioned by Franklin would have one English tutor, one mathematics tutor, and one for Latin. He had to agree to Latin even though he did not think highly of classical training, in order to assure a supply of students for the Academy. Franklin wanted his students to emphasize practical learning, questioning, and inductive reasoning. They were to learn the masterful use of their native language (English), clear writing, effective speaking, and reading with understanding (in English). By a vote of the majority of the trustees, the Latin tutor became the rector, receiving twice the salary of the English master for teaching fewer students. The Latin teacher received funds to buy Latin and Greek books and supplies; however, no funds were allocated for English books or supplies for the English teacher. Mr. Dove, the original English teacher, lasted only two years. When a less able teacher replaced him, enrollment in the English course declined and the English school never regained its reputation. The number of Latin students increased and eventually the Academy became the University of Pennsylvania, the type of institution Franklin had originally rejected.[53]

Franklin's many political responsibilities in the colonies and overseas prevented him from guiding the Academy. However, in 1789, when he was eighty-three, Franklin wrote a long, scorching memorandum to the trustees, criticizing them for neglecting English studies and subverting the Academy's original design.[54]

Colonial Education in the Midwest and the Western United States

European influence spread across the continent that would later become the United States. The French settled in the Mississippi Valley; Germans, whose educational activities are described in other chapters, settled in the Midwest; and Spain colonized California. During the Age of Exploration, Spain claimed the coast of California by right of "discovery."

In the late 1700s, the Spanish became concerned over Russian encroachment into their territory. They began to colonize Alta California by building three types of institutions. The first, the *presidio,* was a fort that provided protection and housed the military. The second was the *pueblo,* a civilian town to which Spanish settlers came. The third institution of colonization was the *mission,* which became the headquarters for the Catholic Church in the New World. A string of missions, built approximately fifty miles apart, was established all along the coast of California from South to North. The purpose of these missions was to convert the indigenous people to Christianity, to teach them to work in the missions, and to make them loyal citizens of Spain. The friars held schools for the native children, teaching them the Spanish language and songs and lessons of the church. The first mission to be built was the Mission San Diego de Alcala, established on July 16, 1769. The last of the twenty-one missions to be built was Mission San Francisco de Solano, founded on July 4, 1823. The missions became the first schools in California.[55]

The first official school in the state of California was opened in San Jose in 1794, seventeen years after the founding of the pueblo. The school was housed in a public granary. Its teacher was Manuel de Vargas, a retired sergeant of the infantry. Mr. de Vargas received approximately two hundred and fifty dollars per year for his teaching duties.[56] When the Mexican regime took over rule of California from the Spanish, there was very little change in the lives of the colonists. However, education fared better under Mexico than it did under Spain. School was in session for a longer period of time and there was an improvement in the type of teacher.[57] The native Californians were interested in the education of their children. When the missions were secularized, experienced teachers were sent to the public schools that were established at each mission between 1834 and 1884. When the Americans occupied California, their first school was held in a structure that once had been a stable, located on the grounds of the Santa Clara mission. When heat was needed, a fire was made on a stone platform in the center of the room with a hole in the roof provided for the escaping smoke. The children sat on wooden boxes. They had no supplies, not even slates or paper and pencil. There were very few textbooks, and the teacher sometimes wrote difficult letters on her hand. The teacher was Olive Mann Isbell, who had emigrated from Illinois. School was in session for two months, and twenty-five children attended. In March 1847, Mrs. Isbell moved to Monterey, where she was guaranteed a salary of two hundred dollars a month by the citizens. The term consisted of three months, and all parents who were able paid a fee of six dollars per term for each child.

The first public school in California was opened in San Francisco in October 1847. The Town Council contracted for the building of a small one-room schoolhouse on the southwest corner of the plaza. A board of school trustees was elected in February 1848. The board employed Thomas Douglas as a teacher with a salary of four hundred dollars. The school was free only to indigent children. All others paid tuition. When the Gold Rush reached its peak, the number of students in the school dwindled to eight. School was closed, and in May, schoolmaster Douglas joined the others seeking his fortune in the gold mines.

The town of Monterey built a school as part of a structure that housed town meetings. The structure for the school and the Constitutional Assembly was financed by the proceeds of selling pieces of land, the labor of convicts, taxes on liquor shops, and fining of gamblers. In March 1849, the Reverend S. H. Willey opened school in the lower part of the hall.

The typical schoolroom during these times was long, narrow, and dimly lit. The children sat on wooden benches along the side of the wall, and the teacher sat on a raised platform at one end. Each child needed to approach the platform and greet the teacher upon entering the room. The master would direct the child to take his seat. After throwing his hat into the corner, each pupil was shown his reading place by an older classmate, and joined in saying the lesson as loudly as he could. The curriculum consisted mainly of learning to read, cipher, and write. The official documents of the school were copied by certain older boys who could make letter perfect copies.

In 1817 and 1818, Governor Sola informed the Viceroy that each of the four presidios and two pueblos had a primary school. The children were taught religion, reading, writing, and reckoning by settlers or "retired soldiers of good character."[58] The first school in Los Angeles under the Mexican regime was taught by Luciano Valdez. This school lasted from 1827 to 1831. Valdez was eventually dismissed by the *Ayuntamiento* (Town Council) because he attempted to control the children by means other than corporal punishment. At the time, corporal punishment was the accepted way of disciplining children.

From the time the Spanish arrived in California until the American occupation, not more than ten years of schooling was held in the pueblo of Los Angeles. The longest continuous span of instruction was between 1838 and 1844. The teacher in charge of the school during that time period, Don Ygnacio Coronel, received approximately fifteen dollars a month from city funds, which were supplemented by whatever funds he could collect from his students. Coronel had a more liberal philosophy of education than most of his predecessors. He believed that accomplishments were worthy of some kind of reward. When a reading book or a given piece of work was completed satisfactorily, the class was allowed to improvise a dance. Music on the harp was provided by Soledad Coronel, his daughter and assistant. Since creative activities such as music and dancing were not a part of the regular program, it was quite a departure that the school board allowed them at all. Soledad also had the honor of being the first woman teacher in the schools of Los Angeles.[59]

San Francisco established the first free public school in 1850. The *Ayuntamiento* passed the first public ordinance on April 4, 1850. The length of the school day was 8:30 A.M. to twelve noon and 2:00 to 5:00 P.M. from Monday through Friday. The number of pupils was limited to one hundred, and the age range from four to sixteen years. The chairman of the Committee on Education had to write an order before any child could be instructed in the school free of charge.

The School Law of 1863–1864 specified the studies to be followed in school as: arithmetic, geography, grammar, reading, writing, spelling, history of the United States, physiology, and such studies as the trustees might deem advisable. While the offerings of the school had broadened in scope, the emphasis was placed on subject matter. At this time a compulsory education law was put into place. A child could no longer be put out of school, so the curriculum began to be more student-centered.

CHAPTER SUMMARY

The colonists created a new society that was dominated by religion. The Church played an important role in society during the seventeenth century and influenced all aspects of colonial life. The children's education, manners, and morals were permeated by religion. The goal of education was to instill the habits of obedience, reverence, and industry. The methods and materials of this education, but not the content, was influenced by the European practices that the colonists had brought with them.

In the Southern and Middle Colonies, and in the Western settlements during the 1700s and early 1800s, tutorial and "old field school" methods of education were prevalent. The establishment of the missions, the later *pueblo* schools, and the first public schools in California extended primary education across the entire country.

NOTES

1. John Demos, "Families in Colonial Bristol, Rhode Island: An Exercise in Historical Demography," *William and Mary Quarterly* 25 (1968): 44–46.

2. Lawrence A. Cremin, *American Education—The Colonial Experience, 1607–1783* (New York: Harper Torchbooks, 1970), 109–112.

3. Ibid., 15.

4. Ibid., 123–125.

5. Susan Norton, "Population Growth in Colonial America: A Study of Ipswich, Massachusetts," *Population Studies* 25 (1971): 433–452; T. H. Breen and Stephen Foster, "Moving to the New World: The Character of Early Massachusetts Immigration," *William and Mary Quarterly,* 3rd ser., 30 (1973): 189–222.

6. Cremin, *American Education—The Colonial Experience,* 126–128; Alice M. Earle, *Child Life in Colonial Days* (New York: Macmillan, 1899; reprint, Williamstown, MA: Corner House Publishers, 1975), 11–12, 13 (page citations are to the reprint edition).

7. John Demos, *A Little Commonwealth: Family Life in Plymouth Colony* (New York: Oxford University Press, 1970), 124.

8. Ibid., 57–58, 139–140.

9. Earle, *Child Life in Colonial Days,* 191–211. Earle was proud of her colonial ancestry and was in close contact with the people who knew and experienced the traditions of early America. Until her time, there had been little study and less writing about life in colonial America.

10. Edmund S. Morgan, *The Puritan Family: Religion and Domestic Relations in Seventeenth-Century New England,* rev. ed. (New York: Harper & Row, Harper Torchbooks, 1966), Chapter 2 passim.

11. Laurel T. Ulrich, *Good Wives: Image and Reality in the Lives of Women in Northern New England, 1650–1750* (New York: Alfred Knopf, 1982), 126–135.

12. R. V. Schnucker, "The English Puritans and Pregnancy, Delivery and Breast Feeding," *History of Childhood Quarterly* 1 (1974): 637–658.

13. Demos, *Little Commonwealth,* 134.

14. Earle, *Child Life in Colonial Days,* 10, 14, 20–21.

15. Ibid., 23, 24–33.

16. Ibid., 13, 16–17; Daniel S. Smith, "Child-Naming Practices, Kinship Ties, and Change in Family Attitudes in Hingham, Massachusetts, 1641 to 1880," *Journal of Social History* 18 (Summer 1985): 541–565; C. John Sommerville, "English Puritans and Children," *Journal of Psychohistory* 6 (1978): 113–137.

17. Earle, *Child Life in Colonial Days,* 4–5.

18. Peter G. Slater, "From the Cradle to the Coffin: Parental Bereavement and the Shadow of Infant Damnation in Puritan Society," *Psychohistory Review* 6 (1977–1978): 5; Earle, *Child Life in Colonial Days,* 4.

19. Smith, "Child-Naming Practices," 554, 546.

20. Paul A. Gilje, "Infant Abandonment in Early Nineteenth-Century New York City: Three Cases," *Signs: Journal of Women in Culture and Society* 8 (Spring 1983): 580–590.

21. Earle, *Child Life in Colonial Days,* 34–62, describes in detail colonial children's clothing. She used portrait paintings to describe the clothing.

22. Elizabeth G. Speare, *Child Life in New England: 1790–1840* (Sturbridge, MA: Old Sturbridge Village, 1961), 1, 15, 17, 18, 20, 9. For more on toys, see Madeline and Richard Merrill, *Dolls & Toys at Essex Institute* (Salem, MA: Essex Institute, 1976); and Antonia Fraser, *A History of Toys* (New York: Delacorte Press, 1966). For children's books during the colonial and early national periods, see Monica Kiefer, *American Children through Their Books, 1700–1835* (Philadelphia: University of Pennsylvania Press, 1948).

23. Earle, *Child Life in Colonial Days,* 182.

24. Ibid., 348–355.

25. Ibid., 228.

26. John Cotton, *A Practical Commentary* (London: R. I. and E. C. for Thomas Parkhurst, 1656), 102, quoted in Ross W. Beales, Jr., "In Search of the Historical Child: Miniature Adulthood and Youth in Colonial New England," *American Quarterly* 27 (October 1975): 385.

27. *The New England Primer* (Boston: Massachusetts Sabbath School Society, Depository No. 13, Cornhill, 1843), 19; Earle, *Child Life in Colonial Days,* 242.

28. Cremin, *American Education—The Colonial Experience,* 129, 176.

29. Earle, *Child Life in Colonial Days,* 90–91, 95–96, 98–99.

30. David D. Hall, "The Uses of Literacy in New England, 1600–1850," in *Printing and Society in Early America,* ed. W. L. Joyce et al. (Worcester, MA: American Antiquarian Society, 1983), 20–26.

31. Cremin, *American Education—The Colonial Experience,* 185.

32. Earle, *Child Life in Colonial Days,* 118. Colonial children learned to read and write with the syllabic method. There is a similarity between the colonial methods and materials and those of Ancient Athens, Rome, and Comenius.

33. Cremin, *American Education—The Colonial Experience,* 394; Earle, *Child Life in Colonial Days,* 128, 132.

34. The copy of *The New England Primer* was examined at the Mattapoisett Historical Society, Mattapoisett, Massachusetts. The society also has a collection of children's books from the first half of the nineteenth century. Among them, *The Child's Book about Whales, The Amusing Alphabet,* and *The Little Sisters.*

35. Cremin, *American Education—The Colonial Experience,* 174–175, 185–186.

36. Philip J. Greven, Jr., *Child-Rearing Concepts, 1628–1861* (Itasca, IL: F. E. Peacock Publishers, 1973), 9–18.

37. John Robinson, *Children and Their Education* (n.d., n.p.), quoted in Earle, *Child Life in Colonial Days,* 191.

38. Cremin, *American Education—The Colonial Experience,* 181–182; Earle, *Child Life in Colonial Days,* 67.

39. Earle, *Child Life in Colonial Days,* 68–69.

40. Cremin, *American Education—The Colonial Experience,* 257.

41. See Mary Black and Jean Lipman, *American Folk Painting* (New York: Clarkson N. Potter, 1966), 1–15.

42. E. H. Gwynne-Thomas, *A Concise History of Education to 1900 A.D.* (Lanham, MD: University Press of America, Inc., 1981, 131–132, 139; and Karen Cheek, "Education in the Southern Colonies," in *History of American Education Web Project,* maintained by

Robert N. Barger; available from <http://sun1.iusb.edu/eduweb01/soucolon.html>; Internet accessed 26 April 1997, 1 of 2.

43. Sheldon S. Cohen, *A History of Colonial Education: 1607–1776* (New York: John Wiley & Sons, Inc., 1974), 130; Lloyd Duck, "Chapter V: Education in the Southern and Middle Colonies," in *Understanding American Education: Its Past, Practice and Promise* (Chatelaine Press, c. 1996), 2 of 30. [electronic text]; available from <http://www.chatpress.com/understanding.html#anchor165117>, <http://www.chatpress.com/uae_5.html>; Internet accessed 23 May 1998; Barbara Kaye Greenleaf, *Children through the Ages: A History of Childhood* (New York: Barnes & Noble Books, 1978), 95–96; and John D. Pulliam and James Van Patten, *History of Education in America,* 6th ed. (Englewood Cliffs, NJ: Merrill/Prentice-Hall, 1995), 26.

44. Gerald L. Gutek, *Historical and Philosophical Foundations of Education: A Biographical Introduction,* 2d ed. (Upper Saddle River, NJ: Merrill/Prentice-Hall, 1997), 165.

45. D. Keith Osborn, *Early Childhood Education in Historical Perspective,* 3d. ed. (Athens, GA: Daye Press, Inc., 1991), 25, 35.

46. Gwynne-Thomas, *A Concise History of Education to 1900 A.D.,* 132–133.

47. Duck, "Chapter V: Education in the Southern and Middle Colonies," in *Understanding American Education,* [electronic text], 20–21 of 30; and *History of American Education;* available from <http://www.digicity.com>; Internet accessed 26 April 1997, 3 of 14.

48. Pulliam and Van Patten, *History of Education in America,* 29.

49 Greenleaf, *Children through the Ages,* 94–95.

50. Ibid., 99. 1

51. Pulliam and Van Patten, *History of Education in America,* 28; and Lawrence A. Cremin, *American Education: The Colonial Experience: 1607–1783* (New York: Harper & Row, Publishers, 1970), 308–309.

52. Duck, "Chapter V: Education in the Southern and Middle Colonies," in *Understanding American Education,* [electronic text], 25 of 30.

53. Henry J. Perkinson, *Two Hundred Years of American Educational Thought* (New York: Longman, 1976), 11–13; Duck, "Chapter V: Education in the Southern and Middle Colonies," in *Understanding American Education,* [electronic text], 27 of 30; and Cremin, *American Education—The Colonial Experience,* 376.

54. Perkinson, *Two Hundred Years of American Educational Thought,* 13; and Duck, "Chapter V: Education in the Southern and Middle Colonies," in *Understanding American Education* [electronic text], 28 of 30.

55. *California Missions;* available from <http://www.mindscape.com/reference/california/mission.html>; Internet accessed 25 May 1998, 1–3 of 3.

56. Gertrude R. Martin, *The Early Days* [historical digest on-line] (Los Angeles, CA: The Los Angeles City School District, 1948); available from <http://www.lausd.kl2.ca.us/lausd/history/eyr2.html> Pioneer Schools in L.A., 3 of 31; <http://www.lausd.kl2.ca.us/lausd/history/teacher.html>; 1 of 2; Internet accessed 24 May 1998).

57. Ibid.

58. Ibid., 9 of 31.

59. Ibid., 12 of 31.

CHAPTER 8

American Educational Reformers

> And I beseech you to treasure up in your hearts these
> my parting words: *Be ashamed to die until you have
> won some victory for humanity.*
> —Horace Mann, *Commencement Address* (1859)[1]

This chapter presents short biographies and outstanding contributions of selected American educational reformers who left their mark on American education and are still pertinent today.

HORACE MANN (1796–1859)

Horace Mann gave us universal education through free public schools, introduced teacher training by creating normal schools and teachers' institutes, established public libraries for schools, and discouraged corporal punishment. These are among his many accomplishments and innovations.

Mann was born on the family farm in Franklin, Massachusetts, on May 4, 1796. He was one of five children. His father, who supported the family by cultivating a small farm, lived an upright life and had a thirst for knowledge. His mother was a woman of superior intellect and character. She imparted to him the principles by which all knowledge should be guided. Both parents, although not highly educated, taught their children habits of industry and high ideals. The father died of consumption when Mann was thirteen years old, putting the burden of running the farm on his sons Stanley and Horace. Horace inherited his father's weak lungs, which made him susceptible to illness throughout his life.

Mann's childhood was an unhappy one passed in poverty, unremitting toil, repression, and fear. He attended the district common school, which was the smallest, had the poorest schoolhouse, and employed the cheapest teachers. The schools had no comfortable seats, no blackboards, no maps or other visual aids. The studies and methods of the district school were stultifying. The masters were ignorant, and their discipline was severe and terrifying. Still more terrifying were the Sunday sermons preached by the Reverend Nathaniel Emmons in which he pictured the eternal torments of those damned.[2]

The school year was about ten weeks. Each child was supposed to have a copy of the *New England Primer*, both for learning the alphabet and for moral instruction. Long sections of the Westminster Assembly shorter catechism had to be memorized, and Reverend Emmons made regular visits to the classroom to question pupils on moral and doctrinal matters. On the last day of the school year, parents were invited for a closing "exhibition" of their children's progress during which there were questions and answers, spelling bees, arithmetic drills, and recitation of memorized poetry and orations. Once Mann had learned to read, he spent many hours in the town library reading the books that had been donated by Benjamin Franklin, a collection of 160 volumes. For six months he studied with an itinerant teacher who taught him English grammar, Greek, and Latin. This knowledge, combined with his self-education, was to qualify him for admission to Brown University as a sophomore in 1816.[3] He excelled in scientific studies, joined one of the literary groups, and graduated with honors in 1819. The theme of his graduating oration, "The Progressive Character of the Human Race," foreshadowed his life. It was at Brown that his humanitarian inclination began to blossom. This disposition toward service rather than wealth, as he noted, appeared early in his life:

> All my boyish castles in the air had reference to doing something for the benefit of mankind. The early precepts of benevolence, inculcated upon me by my parents, flowed out in this direction; and I had a conviction that knowledge was my needed instrument.[4]

After graduation, Mann went to "read law" in a lawyer's office, but after a few months he returned to Brown as a tutor of Greek and Latin at the invitation of President Messer. He accepted for two reasons: to earn some money for his legal studies and for the opportunity to improve his classical studies. In addition to teaching translation, he elucidated the text with geographical, biographical, and historical references, thus opening the minds of the students to a vast supplementary knowledge.[5]

In 1821, Mann returned to study law in Litchfield, Connecticut, and in 1823 was admitted to the bar at Dedham, Massachusetts, where he decided to settle. The principle of his professional life, never to undertake a case that he did not believe to be right, guided him throughout his life. His legal and oratorical skills earned him the respect and popularity that led to his election in 1827 to the House of Representatives of the Massachusetts Legislature. Mann's public service had begun. That same year, 1827, the legislature authorized the establishment of high schools, but none were built at that time.[6] It made compulsory, for the first time in Massachusetts, the entire support of the common schools by taxation.[7] This action, however, did not reverse the decline of the common school.

For Mann, principle was always at the forefront of his life, and his legislative career was marked by service to humanitarian ideals. In 1829, he championed a public institution for the care of the mentally ill. The result was the establishment of the State Lunatic Hospital in Worcester, the first of its kind in the United States.[8]

While Mann was at Brown, he had met President Messer's ten-year-old daughter, Charlotte. Eleven years later (1830), Charlotte became his first wife, but she died childless in 1832. Her death was one of the biggest tragedies in Mann's life and forced him to reorganize his life and perspectives.

Mann moved his law practice to Boston in 1833 and was elected to the Massachusetts Senate the same year. In Boston he became acquainted with social reformers such as Dorothea Dix (a reformer in the treatment of the insane), Charles Sumner (an abolitionist), and educational reformers like Edmund Dwight and James Carter. During his legislative career, he took an active part in the discussions about railroads, public charities, and religious liberty, but none were closer to his heart than the discussions about the education of the people.[9]

On April 20, 1837, the legislature passed an educational bill, An Act Relating to Common Schools, which provided for the establishment of a state board of education that was to employ a secretary at an annual salary of $1,000. (It was the same year that Froebel opened his institution for young children in Blankenburg, but he had not yet named it *kindergarten*.) The board was to consist of the governor and the lieutenant governor as ex-officio members and eight citizens to be appointed by the governor to serve eight-year terms without pay. This act, which created the Massachusetts Board of Education, was a major milestone in American education and affected Mann personally far more than did his pioneering work of establishing the mental institution in Worcester. The secretary's duty was to collect information, through the County Conventions established by the legislature, about the actual conditions and efficiency of the common schools, to report to the board annually, and to publicize the findings throughout the state. The board had no direct power over the schools.[10]

It was expected that the board would choose as its first secretary James G. Carter, the author of the bill, a man whose labors on behalf of education, both as a teacher and as a writer on public education, could not be surpassed. The board, however, chose Mann, who had qualities beyond those of a professional educator: prominence in public life, political power, a dedicated and unselfish personality, a lot of energy, and the ability to convert the people to believe in public education. Mann resigned from the senate, gave up his lucrative law career, and accepted the secretaryship on June 30, 1837. He wrote in his journal: "I devote myself to the supreme welfare of mankind upon earth. . . . I have faith in the improvability of the race, in the accelerated improvability."[11] Mann embarked on a twelve-year educational career that influenced not only his life but also the lives of generations of children and teachers to come.

The Massachusetts Schools before Horace Mann

In 1642, Massachusetts Bay Colony had enacted a compulsory education law. It required municipalities to educate *every child* in their jurisdictions to read the English tongue and to have knowledge of the capital laws under penalty of twenty schillings. The law further required religious instruction for all children (Indian and slave included) and training in some trade "profitable to themselves and the Commonwealth." Even though the law required compulsory education, it did not make it *free* or impose any penalty upon municipal corporations for neglecting to maintain a school. The management of schools was little more than hiring a teacher and securing a place for school to be held. It was the Law of 1647 that made school support mandatory and education universal and free. This law, the first recorded in American history, required towns with fifty or more families to appoint a teacher to instruct all children who would come to him to learn to read and write; towns with two hundred families were required to support a grammar school. Grammar school was a school where the ancient languages were taught and where youth could be "fitted for the university." The Law of 1647 laid the foundation for the free school system. The Pilgrims had conceived of a magnificent idea: common and equal opportunities of education for all.[12]

When the population began to move out of the settled communities, a single school could no longer meet the needs of the people. "Traveling schools" appeared, which continued until Horace Mann's time. He had attended one, as seen earlier, in the town of Franklin. However, areas that had been served by the traveling school began to demand permanent schools of their own, and the former central school was gradually replaced by district schools.[13]

Following the American Revolution, the Massachusetts Legislature passed the Law of 1789. It codified many of the practices that had emerged during the state's century and a half of educational practices. It authorized towns to divide themselves into districts, a practice that resulted in unbalanced school system development in the commonwealth. The richer districts made adequate provisions for their schools, while the other districts did little or nothing. The common schools began to deteriorate.[14]

As the common schools declined, private academies appeared during the second half of the eighteenth century. As they proliferated, the common schools degenerated into neglected schools for the poorer classes only. As the wealthier and better educated citizens turned away from the common schools, there were not enough educated persons left to continue them. A new phenomenon, class distinctions, appeared in Massachusetts. Free schools, the onetime glory of colonial Massachusetts, were no longer supported by the public. The effects of this attitude were evident everywhere in the short school terms, dilapidated and unsanitary schoolhouses, lack of standardized textbooks, untrained and underpaid teachers, high teacher turnover, and lack of state supervision. In addition, child labor in factories resulted in class nonattendance.[15] These were all the problems confronting Mann when he became secretary to the board of education.

Mann's View of the Purpose of Education

Mann understood the interrelationships among freedom, popular education, and the democratic process in government. He was impressed with the heterogeneity of the American population and the diversity of social, ethnic, and religious groups. He was aware, however, of the destructive possibilities of religious, political, and class discord and the institution of slavery in the

South.[16] Mann also knew that knowledge is power, but a power that could be used for good or evil. The essence of a democratic education could not only be intellectual. Moral values had to be part of it. "The whole people must be instructed in the knowledge of their duties, . . . [and] of those great truths on which alone a government like ours can be successfully conducted," he said.[17] Mann sought a common value system under which diversity might thrive. He used education—the common school—to fashion an American character. The common school would be a school common for all the people, available and equal to all, part of the birthright of every American child. Mann wanted to restore the earlier custom of having the rich and the poor educated together, where education was grounded in cultural literacy and moral character. They would mix the children of all classes, creeds, and backgrounds, and their associations would develop a spirit of harmony and respect. Through the young he could work his reforms.[18]

In 1840, the free population of the United States was 14,581,553. One fourth of this population—3,645,388—was between the ages of four and sixteen years. The number of all the children of all ages in the primary and common schools was 1,845,244, which left almost half of the children without the advantages of schooling. An average of 136,332 persons of this uneducated group would reach majority every year, becoming fathers and mothers, and electors. Mann said that "This class alone will annually furnish a number of voters far greater than the average popular majority by which our presidents have been chosen."[19] He saw this trend as a threat to democracy. As a solution he advocated that all children be in school from the ages of four to sixteen years.[20] Mann's notion of the purpose of education is stated in his *Lecture on Education:*

> Education must be universal. With us, the qualification of voters is as important as the qualification of governors. . . . The theory of our government is . . . that every man by the power of reason and the sense of duty shall become fit to be a voter. Education must prepare our citizens to become municipal officers, intelligent jurors, honest witnesses, legislators . . . to fill all the manifold relations of life.[21]

Mann's Pedagogical Method

Mann's pedagogy was influenced by Pestalozzi. The child is to be treated with tenderness and affection. Reward rather than punishment should be the motivation for instruction, with meaningful learning instead of rote memorization. Children are naturally curious, and their curiosity should be gratified. Learning and pleasure should go hand in hand. The pleasure of learning should be the stimulus and motivation to learn. A child is incapable of appreciating the ultimate value or use of knowledge. Fear has no place in learning. If a child likes his books, learning is free labor; if he revolts against them, it is slave labor.[22]

Mann saw learning as an active process in which "the effective labor must be performed by the learner himself." He emphasized the importance of motivation in learning, noting that "until a desire to learn exists with the child, some foreign force must constantly be supplied to keep him going." Mann also pointed out the important relationship between the teaching technique and learning. He suggested that the young child can be prepared for reading by being read interesting and inspiring stories, that the child's earliest words are learned as wholes, so it is inappropriate to begin with the alphabet or syllables.[23]

CORPORAL PUNISHMENT

Mann had a strong aversion to corporal punishment. "Punishment should never be inflicted, except in cases of the extreme necessity," he said. The fear of bodily pain is a degrading motive for learning. He further said: "It is a sad exchange if the blows which beat arithmetic or grammar into a boy, beat confidence and manliness out." Mann also thought that the other methods practiced at the time—imprisoning children in a dark and solitary place, bringing the whole class to a fellow pupil to ridicule and shame him—intimidated the children and "created a disgust for study" and "obstinacy of disposition."[24] One cannot train a child for freedom by using methods of slavery.

Secretary of the Board of Education (1837–1848)

Mann's task was to remedy the existing conditions as far and as soon as possible. Vested with almost no authority except to collect and disseminate information, he brought to his new duties such a degree of courage, vision, and wisdom that during the brief period of twelve years when he held office, the Massachusetts school system was almost completely transformed. His first task was to arouse and to educate public opinion about the purpose, value, and needs of public education. According to his own account, Mann used three ways to do this. First, he used the annual educational conventions in every county of the state to lecture about the conditions of the schools and the reasons and objectives of the board. He also used the conventions to learn about the schools in the county, and to collect statistics. He was authorized one annual county convention. Mann held two or more in large counties at his own expense throughout his tenure.[25] Second, he used the *Twelve Annual Reports* (1837–1848)[26] he was required to write, to present the improvement of the public schools, the cause of *education,* and its relationship to the interest of civilization and human progress. Third, he utilized the *Common School Journal* (1839–1848), which he published and edited for ten years, to give detailed and specific views about the methods and processes of instruction and training, and the management of the schools.[27]

Five months after Mann took over the secretaryship, he issued his *First Annual Report* (December 1837) to the Commonwealth of Massachusetts. It was a comprehensive survey of the condition of the schools in the state organized under four headings. First was a section on the physical condition and number of schoolhouses. His concern for the health and safety of the children led him to ask for sunlit, airy, and roomy buildings to replace the dilapidated ones that had served as schoolhouses in 1837. Second, he discussed the manner in which the school committees performed their duties. He specified their neglect in teacher selection and retention, purchasing standard school books, enforcing regular attendance, and not visiting the schools as was demanded by the law. Mann's remedies for these shortcomings were compensation for committee services, penalties for neglect of duties, and a required annual report by each town's school committee. Third was a section on apathy on the part of the community in relation to schools. He saw the apathy as being of two kinds: (1) apathy of those indifferent to all education, which, with the influx of an ignorant and degraded population, would naturally increase; (2) apathy toward the public or free schools by those who saw them as not providing the education their children needed, and who therefore sent their children in academies and private schools. In the fourth section, Mann discussed the competency of teachers. Obstacles to maintaining competent teachers included their low compensation, which prevented them from following teaching as a profession; the low standards required for teacher qualifications; and the number of individuals who went into teaching on a temporary basis.[28] Teachers' wages were extremely low when compared with what was being paid to bank cashiers, to secretaries, and to others.[29]

Teacher Training—The Normal Schools

Mann realized that there was little hope of any improvement in the common schools without improving the teaching profession. In 1838, he acquired a private gift of $10,000—from Edmund Dwight, manufacturer, philanthropist, and a member of the board, who offered it anonymously—for the establishment of state teachers' institutions, normal schools to improve the preparation of elementary teachers, on the condition that the Massachusetts Legislature match the sum.[30] It was the board's responsibility to organize the normal schools. There were no examples to follow to develop the normal schools. To make the schools most effective, they were established in different areas of the state: one in the northeast, one in the southeast, and one in the western section. Because the appropriated money was not adequate to cover the entire expense of such a plan, it was further decided to place the schools in communities where the cost of buildings, equipment, and other expenses, exclusive of instructors' salaries, would be borne by the communities where the schools would be located.

Lexington was the first town to apply and was chosen as the location for the northeastern section of the state. Shortly after, Barre, in the central region, and Bridgewater, in the southeast, were added. The school at Barre was transferred to Westfield. The Lexington school was first moved to West Newton and later to Framingham, where it remains. Bridgewater has remained in the same site since 1840. Within two years, Massachusetts had established three state normal schools, the first of their kind in the United States.[31] Today all three schools are part of the state university system.

Applicants for admission had to be sixteen years old and in good health and were required to sign a declaration of intention to teach. The entering tests were in reading, writing, orthography, English grammar, geography, and arithmetic. It soon became apparent that a major obstacle to the success of the schools was the poor preparation of students. Much time had to be devoted to correcting elementary deficiencies in the students' background. (How contemporary does this sound?)

Selection of the course of study was of crucial importance for Mann and the other board members. It was decided that the curriculum of the normal schools should be designed specifically to prepare teachers for the common schools, in order to provide a "more thorough and systematic acquaintance with the branches usually taught in common schools," along with other areas of knowledge useful to a teacher. The classical languages were omitted in favor of an introduction to geography, grammar, spelling, and arithmetic. Another feature of the program was to teach the "art of imparting instruction to the youthful mind, which will be taught in its principles, and illustrated by opportunity for practice, by means of a model school." A "school of practice" was an essential feature of teacher training institutions. From the beginning, the normal school curriculum included three elements: subject matter, methodology of teaching, and practice teaching.[32]

The professional training of teachers was therefore put on a firm basis. These state normal schools also played a part in advancing the Pestalozzian ideas and methods. Westfield was a pioneer in introducing the Pestalozzian methods into teacher training.[33]

TEACHER QUALIFICATIONS

In his *First Annual Report*, Mann said: "teaching is the most difficult of all arts, and the profoundest of sciences."[34] He outlined the following qualifications for a teacher in his *Fourth Annual Report* (1840). First was *a thorough knowledge of common school subjects*. Teachers should be well prepared in all the subjects that they are required by law to teach in the schools. The second qualification was *aptness to teach—the art of teaching*. It involves the ability both to acquire and to impart knowledge, acts that involve different talents. Aptness to teach involves the power to perceive how well the student understands the subject matter to be learned and what is the next step that should be taken. It is the power to simultaneously discover and solve the exact difficulty the learner is experiencing. Aptness to teach includes knowledge of methods and processes. The third qualification was *possessing skills in management, government, and discipline*. Although the latter are independent of the previous two qualifications, a deficiency in any one of these skills can make the others worthless and can interfere with learning. The fourth qualification was to *teach good behavior* to all youth as required by the law. The effect of either civility or discourtesy is felt directly by society. Since the teacher is likely to be a role model for the pupils, he or she should pay attention to deportment, conversation, and all personal habits that make a gentleman or a lady. The fifth qualification was possessing *morals*. Moral character is an "indispensable requisite" in the selection and appointment of teachers, the responsibility of which rests with the members of the school committees.

The *Report* ended with the need for "strict uniformity of school books." It also urged regularity and punctuality in attendance; otherwise, schooling is a waste of time and money and the loss of the best time of the young, which cannot be made up.[35]

WOMEN AS TEACHERS

Mann was a strong advocate of employing more women as teachers, especially for the earlier grades. His principal argument was that women were better suited by nature to educate and guide young children. They possess a disposition more in harmony with young children who need kindness and not force. They lay deep foundations, by training the children in the way they should go.[36] His thinking is very reminiscent of Froebel's ideas.

On May 1, 1843, Mann married his second wife, Mary Tyler Peabody (sister of Elizabeth Palmer Peabody). They sailed to Europe with two purposes: to restore his health and to discover what America might learn from European schools. He spent five months studying educational conditions in Europe. His observations and conclusions on all aspects of education were presented in his *Seventh Annual Report* (1845). His high commendation of German schools was interpreted by a considerable number of Boston schoolteachers as implying criticism of their professional preparation and practices. An acrimonious controversy ensued, from which Mann came forth victorious.[37]

In June 1846, the superintendent of the Chautauqua County Schools in New York invited Mann to visit. Mann, unable to go, sent his *Letter to School Children*[38] to its 20,000 students. He encouraged them to be industrious, temperate, clean and neat in their person and dress; gentlemanly and ladylike in their manners; kind; generous; and magnanimous. He told them to be sure to learn something every day, and that they were made to be moral and religious.[39]

Congressman (1848–1852)

Mann was elected to the United States House of Representatives to succeed ex-President John Quincy Adams, who died from a stroke in his seat on the floor of the Congress on February 23, 1848. During the first session of the Congress, Mann was also acting secretary of the Massachusetts Board of Education pending the choice of his successor. Mann devoted all of his energies to the antislavery issue. Mann's position led to open conflict with Daniel Webster, who had reversed his position on slavery and surrendered to the slave interests. Webster, who was not used to such outspoken opposition, wanted vengeance against Mann, and tried with every means to stop Mann's reelection to Congress. He almost succeeded, but the Free Soil Convention gave Mann its nomination. Mann, after a vigorous campaign was reelected for a third term.[40]

Mann gave his final speech in the House, on the legality and constitution-
ality of the Fugitive Slave Law, in February 1851. He argued that the law vio-
lated the Constitution.[41] In September 1852, he was nominated for governor
of Massachusetts by the Free Democracy of the State party. On the same day
he was offered the presidency of Antioch College, which he accepted.[42]

Antioch College

While still in Congress, Mann had been approached to become the president
of the newly established Antioch College at Yellow Springs, Ohio. The college
was founded by a new Christian denomination and was committed to coedu-
cation, nonsectarianism, and equal opportunity for Negroes. Besides serving
as the president (1853–1859), Mann taught political economy, intellectual
philosophy, moral philosophy, and natural theology. After giving the commencement address for 1859, Mann, exhausted and disappointed, retired to
his home. He died on August 2, 1859.[43]

WILLIAM TORREY HARRIS (1835–1909)

William Torrey Harris, educator and philosopher, was one of the most frequent speakers in the history of the National Education Association (NEA).
Harris was born on September 10, 1835, in North Killingly, Connecticut, and
educated in Rhode Island, Connecticut, and Massachusetts. He entered Yale
College in 1854, resigning as a "troubled junior"[44] three years later. This was
in some measure a result of his attendance at the Orphic Seer's Conversations
of Amos Bronson Alcott (1799–1888) early in 1857, which left Harris "disappointed and disillusioned by an elitist education that seemed to offer no
grander ideal for the individual and the nation."[45] Harris taught himself
shorthand, geometry, trigonometry, and German, and made a telescope. A
few months later, he turned up in St. Louis as a teacher of the then-novel Pit-
man shorthand (in a phonographic institute), and as a private tutor.[46]

Harris met Henry Conrad Brokmeyer, the initiator of the St. Louis Hegelian
movement in philosophy, literature, and education, at an informal meeting at
the St. Louis Mercantile Library in 1858. When Brokmeyer was elected to the
Missouri State Senate, Harris kept the Philosophical Society together.

At the time, St. Louis, and the nation, were going through Reconstruction,
and still bore the scars of the Civil War. Immigrants were pouring into the country in staggering numbers, and many of them headed westward. Although St.
Louis was a fluid, volatile frontier society, it had many clubs and societies, and
"circles and classes of cultivated women, who were not admitted to the Philosophical Society, but who found these less formal organizations suited to their
needs for partaking of the philosophical ferment of the city."[47] As founding editor of the *Journal of Speculative Philosophy*, Harris fought against any of the
past philosophies or philosophers being called the one true system.[48] Hegel's
dogma of thesis, antithesis, and synthesis was applied to everything. "Harris

recalled that they used the Hegelian dialectic to solve 'all problems connected with school-teaching and school-management,' and 'even the hunting of turkeys and squirrels was the occasion for the use of philosophy.' "[49]

Employment in the St. Louis School System

Harris found employment in the St. Louis public schools as an assistant teacher and teacher. His first class had 180 pupils ages ten through fifteen. With the help of the four other teachers, he established order, and put the pupils in grades.[50] It is probable that they followed the Lancastrian system of instruction. He worked his way up through the system as school principal and assistant superintendent of schools and became superintendent of the entire system in 1867, remaining in the position until 1880.[51] He endorsed Susan Blow's candidacy as the first kindergarten teacher in St. Louis, with the provision that she prepare herself for the task. Miss Blow went to New York for training in the fall of 1872, but was forced to return home at the superintendent's request, early the following spring.[52]

Superintendent Harris had several reasons for acceding to the requests of Elizabeth Peabody and Susan Blow to initiate a kindergarten in the St. Louis public school system.[53] Most children in the city attended school between the ages of seven and ten, at which time they left school to work in the factories. Children younger than seven years of age played unsupervised in the streets. Beginning the child's public education at five years of age would encourage the attendance of these children at school, and provide them with a total of five years of instruction.[54] In 1875, the state constitution, written by Brokmeyer, included a requirement that public schools would not charge tuition,[55] so there was no fee for the public kindergartens. It had been hoped that these kindergartens would attract poor children; however, "the intelligent and well-to-do were foremost in appreciating the Kindergarten and in entering their children to enjoy its benefits."[56] The school calendar was arranged around the schedule of children working on farms. In 1877, the school year was standardized at five months, which was lengthened to seven months in 1889.[57]

Harris's philosophical rationale was related to readiness. He believed that when the child began to use language, set goals, and act to realize them, the kindergarten method of instruction would prove helpful. He viewed the Mutter und Köselieder as a means of socializing children. Through participation in group activities, the child would become a member of "the social whole, . . . with special duties to perform in the life of the whole." This participation would ready the child for the methods of the primary school.[58] Harris became a staunch advocate for the kindergarten, endorsing the 1873 NEA committee report, and providing extensive oral and written testimony of his support for the movement.[59]

As superintendent of schools, Harris "employed women exclusively as educators in elementary grades. He acknowledged that women used milder forms of discipline, and that they would work for lower wages. . . . At the same time, Harris promoted education for teachers."[60]

Work in the National Education Association

From 1870 to 1909, Harris was quite active in the National Association of School Superintendents (which became the Department of Superintendence of the NEA in 1870), serving as president in 1873. He served as an NEA life director and was the 1875 national president. During his tenure as a director, he came out in favor of exhibits at the NEA annual meetings, chaired numerous committees, and gave 145 speeches,[61] on a variety of subjects, to his colleagues.

Wesley accuses the 1876 curriculum committee of outlining a "doctrinaire and pseudo-philosophical procedure of curriculum-making" for common schools, high schools, and colleges. The five "windows of the soul" and their related curriculum areas, as discussed in the report (and reiterated in Harris's book *Psychologic Foundations of Education*), included: (1) mathematics, time, space, and mechanical relations, which fall under mathematics and physics; (2) organic nature, which falls under biology, and geography; (3) literature and art, human nature as feelings, convictions, and aspirations, which fall under literature and art; (4) grammar, logic, philosophy of the intellectual structure, which fall under logic and psychology; and (5) history, the doings of the greater social self as reaction, which includes the study of sociological, political, and social institutions.[62]

The report of the Sub-Committee on the Correlation of Studies in Elementary Education of the Committee of Fifteen on Elementary Education, which he chaired, was the occasion for intense debate when it was presented to the Department of Superintendence in February 1895. The Herbartians and the advocates of child study said that the report ignored the child. Other critics said that its discussion of the logical order of topics and branches, representations of the "great divisions of human learning," psychological symmetry, correlation of the pupil course of study with the spiritual and natural environment, and the specific branches of study ignored the "prevailing definition of correlation of studies as indicating the interrelationship among the studies."[63]

Beginning in the summer of 1879, Harris taught at the Concord School of Philosophy summer sessions. Shortly thereafter, he resigned from the St. Louis Superintendency to move to Concord, Massachusetts, where the school was held. Harris was one of the few people who taught for all nine of the sessions, through 1887.[64]

United States Commissioner of Education

Harris became the United States Commissioner of Education in 1889. At the turn of the century, following Cardinal Newman's model for a liberal education, the commissioner urged that all children acquire the knowledge needed to fill the "five windows of the soul."[65] In this way, he acknowledged that all children must be educated. He believed that instruction in citizenship was a major priority of education. "Harris also recognized that, in the Industrial Age, education was needed to 'give people the power . . . to climb up to better paid and more useful industries out of lives of drudgery.' In an 1892 article for the *Atlantic Monthly*, he observed that black children had an equal need to white children: 'The Negro cannot share in the white man's freedom unless he can learn to manage machinery.' "[66] Although he served on many NEA committees appointed to secure larger appropriations for the Bureau of Education, and was commissioner until 1906, he is not on record as supporting cabinet status for the commissioner.[67]

Harris, a book lover, devised a library classification system while he was superintendent of schools in St. Louis. He maintained a close correspondence with Melvil Dewey, who probably made use of it in developing his decimal system. Under Henderson Presnell, librarian of the Department of Education from 1884 to 1907 (a term roughly corresponding to that of Harris), the Department's library was cataloged according to the Dewey Decimal System.[68] Toward the end of his life and in failing health, Harris wrote to his brother Edward about the importance of books. " 'I do not think that you quite understand what books are to me. If I were to go live in a hotel or to live in a private home of a relative or friend, I should die in a few weeks from starvation for the lack of certain mental food.' "[69] Harris died on November 5, 1909, in Providence, Rhode Island.

William Torrey Harris saw education as emanating from the family during the first five or six years of life, and schooling during the next eight to ten years, as the child became curious about the world outside the family.[70] This made him a believer in universal public education and a strong supporter of the kindergarten. He was courageous enough to support the first public school kindergarten in the United States and to disseminate knowledge about the kindergarten all over the country.

GRANVILLE STANLEY HALL (1844–1924)

G(ranville) Stanley Hall was born in Ashfield, Massachusetts, on February 1, 1844. There is contradictory information about the details, and it is impossible to determine the name he was given at birth. From the time he entered college, he used the name "G. Stanley Hall" or "Granville Stanley Hall," but he was known familiarly as Stanley throughout his boyhood and mature life.[71]

He attended a college preparatory course at Williston Academy[72] during the academic year 1862 to 1863, finishing in the middle of his class. This was sufficient for his admission to Williams College, which served the sons of middle-class homes in the Northeast and poor Congregational farmers of Massachusetts, in the fall of 1863. He ranked high in his class and graduated at twenty-three years of age, in 1867. That fall, with few other prospects, he entered Union Theological Seminary in New York City. He took advantage of much that the city had to offer, including attending lectures on reform at Cooper Union. Hall accepted financial assistance arranged by Henry Ward Beecher and traveled to Germany, where he studied philosophy at the University of Berlin. The Franco-Prussian War forced him to return to the United States, and he completed his divinity degree at Union Theological Seminary in 1871.

A friend who received a university appointment recommended Hall to replace him as tutor to the sons of banker Jesse Seligman. Hall spent two pleasant years in the liberal household, where he met Felix Adler. Adler was the director of the Workingman's School and Free Kindergarten of the Ethical Culture Society, and the developer of its curriculum. He accepted Froebel's occupations as a solution to the problems of the poor, providing children in his school with manual training or "work lessons" each week.[73] In later years, Adler and his wife formed a Society for the Study of Child Nature, which discussed such topics as the proper kinds of toys and punishments, as reported in the NEA *Proceedings* of 1894.[74] Mrs. Adler's "hints for the Scientific Observation of Children" were published in Hailmann's *The New Education*.

In 1872, Hall was offered a position at Antioch College in Yellow Springs, Ohio, teaching English literature, French and German language and literature, and philosophy. He also served as choirmaster, librarian, and occasional preacher, due to the effects of the economic depression of the 1870s.[75] During his time at Antioch he traveled to St. Louis and met with William T. Harris and other Hegelians there. Although he was disenchanted with the group's philosophy, he specifically noted the presence of "Miss Blow of kindergarten fame," at the meetings.[76] He discovered and read Wundt's *Principles of Physiological Psychology* shortly after it appeared in the United States. Although he wanted to return to Germany to study psychology, his funds took him only as far as Massachusetts. From the fall of 1876 to June 1878, he undertook a graduate research program at Harvard University, in which he worked with William James and Henry P. Bowditch. Hall's research resulted in his receipt of the first Ph.D. in psychology ever granted in the United States.[77] When his meager savings were supplemented by a gift from Mr. Seligman, he was able to leave on his second trip to Germany in June 1878.[78] He studied with Hermann von Helmholz, Wilhelm Wundt, and Carl Ludwig, at the universities in Berlin and Leipzig. Hall was Wundt's first American student.[79] In the fall of 1878, his doctoral thesis was published in *Mind*, the leading English journal of philosophy. In September 1879, he married Cornelia Fisher, whom he knew from Antioch, in Berlin.

Boston Pedagogical Lectures

When the couple returned to the United States, Hall did not have any job prospects. As he recounts in his autobiography, one Wednesday morning President Eliot of Harvard rode up to the house, rapped on the door without dismounting from his horse, and asked him to begin a course of lectures on education on Saturday of that week. There were to be twelve lectures at a fee of five dollars. On Saturday morning, the "impressive audience" included Charles Francis Adams, superintendent of schools at Quincy, an advocate of Colonel Francis Parker's new educational ideas; Mr. Philbrick, superintendent of the Boston schools; most of the school principals from Boston and the adjacent towns; Elizabeth Peabody and her disciple, Laura Pingree; and others. President Eliot's introduction stated that Harvard "had never been much impressed by pedagogy but I was a young man who had studied it abroad and this course had been instituted as an experiment." At the close of each lecture, there was an informal conference for those who desired to stay and challenge the speaker.[80]

The female teachers of Boston had both low pay and low status; therefore, they, and their male administrators, were anxious to professionalize their occupation. Froebelian kindergartens were introduced into the Boston school system during the 1870s, and the philosophies of European educators were being studied. Hall's 1881 pedagogical lectures provided both the impetus and the rationale for change, and therefore they were praised by teachers and administrators. Hall was invited to return from Baltimore for two succeeding years, and the lectures were continued by William T. Harris in the ensuing years.

Work in the National Education Association

Hall was quite active in the NEA. He was president of the Department of Higher Education, which provided a forum for college men.[81] He became a member of the elite National Council of Education of the NEA, which was organized in 1884,[82] and was named to the influential Committee on Pedagogics chaired by Harris. He took part in numerous debates, including one on health and physical education in schools. He was once again pitted against Harris, who declared that "It is a matter of history that physical education does not belong in the school." Hall's response was, "health is the criterion of everything in education."[83] Some of Hall's writings took this idea to extremes. He supported a social order "under the direction of an elite, which glorified physical vigor and juvenile idealism over intellect and mature judgment. Hall suggested a retreat from modern life to the national and racial past, with natural education leading the way."[84] These were the sentiments expressed in a later time period by the members of certain nationalist parties. Cremin states of Hall that "he injected into the mainstream of American Educational thought some of the most radical—and I happen to think virulent—doctrines of the twentieth century, and there is no understanding the present apart from his contribution."[85] Hall also defended recapitulation theory, which states that each person passes through all the stages that the human race has passed through, beginning with the primitive phase. This theory was the basis of Hall's support of the doctrine of "separate but equal" schooling for black people.

Hall participated in some of the seminars of the Concord School of Philosophy. He had a "brilliant platform method, . . . [and] preached eloquently the gospel of a wholly different psychology from that taught by Harris." Eventually the forces of James, Dewey, *et al.* overwhelmed Hegelian absolutism in American education.[86]

Hall's lectures brought him to the attention of Daniel Coit Gilman, president of Johns Hopkins University, who offered him a postdoctoral appointment in philosophy. At that time, psychology and education were still considered by many to be a part of philosophy. When Hall's pedagogical lectures proved successful in Baltimore, the president appointed him professor of psychology and pedagogy in 1884. Johns Hopkins had the only department specifically devoted to psychology in the country. Hall established the first American psychology laboratory there.[87] He was thwarted, however, in an attempt to offer a course in " 'the history of universities and learned societies' [and] . . . limited to teaching only about elementary and secondary education."[88] John Dewey did his doctoral work with Hall at Johns Hopkins, completing a dissertation on the psychology of Kant, and publishing two articles on psychology and philosophy in 1885. In October 1887, the first issue of Hall's *American Journal of Psychology* appeared. It was the first psychological journal in the United States, and was strictly limited to the "new" psychology.

Hall's 1883 study "The Contents of Children's Minds on Entering School," reprinted in the 1907 volume *Aspects of Child Life and Education by G. Stanley Hall and Some of His Pupils*, was the first of his studies using the questionnaire technique he had observed in Germany. With the permission of the school district, his lengthy "survey" (questionnaire) was administered by four kindergarten teachers to children who were just entering the first grade. The children's answers revealed an ignorance Hall found startling. However, many of the questions contained agrarian terminology or called for concepts alien to urban children, which skewed the results.[89] Hall's analysis of his data in terms of the kinds of responses given, the age, sex, ethnic background, and prior kindergarten training of his children supported such innovations as object teaching; the tendency of the child to learn first the concepts most common in his immediate environment; the need of relating new knowledge to that already firmly acquired, according to Herbart's "law of apperception"; and the effectiveness of kindergarten instruction.[90]

Hewes suggests that Hall considered himself a Froebelian, as demonstrated by passages in his book *Educational Problems*. However, he ridiculed Froebel's "Mother-Plays," and the formalization of the uses of the Gifts and Occupations,[91] suggesting that exercises, dancing, and free manipulation of the materials were more appropriate.[92] Children's art was in vogue in Europe when Hall called attention to the revealing content of children's drawings in his "Contents" study. In school curriculum, the goal of drawing was to teach children to accurately reproduce reality. Child study investigators concluded that drawing was a form of self-expression for the child.

Hall was quite influential in the formation of the child study movement, when a number of factors "came together" during the mid to late 1800s. In 1880, Charles Francis Adams foreshadowed Hall by two years by urging the superintendents of the NEA to revise their pedagogy in accord with the natural laws of assimilation and development of a child's mind, and to make education a science worthy of university study, by basing it on the study of the development of the mind.[93]

In 1881, the Boston secretary of the Education Section of the American Social Science Association (ASSA) gathered information on earlier studies of children, prepared questionnaires, and published a circular on the observation of infants, as a guide for amateur students of the child's physical and mental development. Speaking for "some educators" who were roused by recent scientific studies of animal psychology to wonder why the mind of the child did not deserve equal attention, she asked mothers or other interested observers to record such facts as the infant's first attention to stimuli, crawling, walking, and speech. The earliest child welfare workers came from the American Society for the Prevention of Cruelty to Animals (ASPCA), so the relationship between the early stages of animal and human psychology is not surprising. In 1882, the ASSA sought to become the central agency for child study, but although child psychology was discussed at its next meeting, nothing further came of the effort. Some Herbartians (American advocates of Pestalozzi) and physicians backed the movement. Individual kindergartners, new teachers of physical education who were committed to health education, and some adventurous administrators also joined. Advanced (Progressive) normal schools, such as those in Oswego, New York; Chicago; Worcester, Massachusetts; and Trenton, New Jersey, instituted a program of child study for their students. The basis for a child study movement existed. It required only a charismatic leader to find it a popular base of support and give it programmatic appeal.

In the spring of 1882, Hall issued his first call for child study in a speech to the superintendents of the NEA. His "Contents" study became a basis of the early work. His questionnaire studies were widely circulated and were emulated by professionals and lay persons, as numerous "syllabi" of questions were developed. Parents and teachers either supplied data for the researchers or used the information they gathered to aid them in working with their own children.[94] In formal studies, Hall and his colleagues provided the patterns and the plans, studied the data, and wrote conclusions, while classroom teachers made the observations and supplied the detailed information. The teachers compiled biographies of children; recorded thousands of miscellaneous facts; made measures of height, weight, and growth; collected drawings and compositions; and supplied other data. Among the normal school faculty members who assisted Hall in his work, he particularly noted the contributions of Miss Lillie Williams (later chair of the Psychology Department of the State Normal School, Trenton, New Jersey). She described the methods used in the "Contents" study and "A Study of Dolls" in *Pedagogical Seminary*, the journal Hall founded in 1891 to link psychology and pedagogy.[95]

The child study movement of the 1890s was born of the desire to find in the knowledge of the child's development at different stages the basis for a new educational system.[96] The interest Hall's work was creating led to a full committee report on "Pedagogy as a Science" at the 1884 NEA meeting. During the discussion, Harris reiterated "the 'correct' principles on which pedagogy should be based," and attempted to truncate the debate. Many other members disagreed with him, and in 1885 Harris urged educators to "join with the 'distinguished specialists' who were conducting scientific pedagogical inquiry."[97] In 1893, the NEA organized a Department of Child Study, which was formally accepted by the organization in 1894 as a clearinghouse for developments in the field.

Summer schools proliferated. The Illinois Society for the Study of Children, and the Chicago Superintendent of Schools, in collaboration with Colonel Parker's Cook County Normal School, held a four day Child Study Congress each summer beginning in 1894. This was the occasion for the meeting between Hall, Patty Smith Hill, and Anna Bryan so vividly described by Snyder.[98] The objective, scientific, disinterested observation of the child became widespread. Conclusions of varying degrees of importance and certitude were reported at NEA annual meetings. The child study movement made the child a live specimen for scientific study. Objectivity and detachment were often transformed into personal interest and resulted in greater attention to individual instruction. According to Wesley, the individual child became the center of the educational system.[99]

As interest in this type of child study waned, the NEA changed the name of the child study department (in 1911) to "Department of Mental Hygiene." By 1924, it had merged with the Department of Physical and Health Education. Child study gave parents and teachers a deeper insight into the problems of education and brought them into sympathy with such movements as the kindergarten, free drawing, nature study, and manual training. The aims and purposes were taken over by clinics and institutes of child welfare, whose findings continued to influence educational practice.[100]

Hall left Johns Hopkins to accept the presidency of the proposed new Clark University on April 5, 1888. The Worcester, Massachusetts-based graduate institution was founded with five departments: psychology, biology, chemistry, physics, and mathematics. Hall went to Europe on a recruiting and fact-finding trip. Through his network of personal acquaintances and his travels, he was able to put together a very talented faculty for the 1889 opening. Hall appointed himself professor of psychology, teaching graduate courses and holding Monday evening "seminaries" (seminars) from 7:30 P.M. to midnight. Lewis M. Terman, one of Hall's doctoral students, recalled that following the presentation of the two student research papers and the resulting discussion and debate, he found it difficult to sleep as he replayed the evening's events in his mind.[101] Hall's students received two thirds of the Ph.D.'s granted by Clark in psychology prior to 1900. Among the recipients were Henry H. Goddard, a pioneer in the study of the mentally retarded, and Arnold Gesell, whose work at Yale focused on the development of children during the first six years of life.

Fiscal problems caused by differences with Jonas Clark, and the loss of his first wife and daughter, made the early 1890s a difficult time for Hall. He delved more into developmental and educational psychology, assuming the title of professor of psychology and education around 1902. As mentioned earlier, the journal *Pedagogical Seminary: An International Record of Educational Literature, Institutions, and Progress* (renamed *The Journal of Genetic Psychology* in 1927) was founded during the 1891–1892 academic year. Hall, his faculty and students, and many other professional educators found an outlet for their work in this journal.

Hall began the Clark Summer School of Higher Pedagogy and Psychology in 1892. It attracted normal school principals and teachers, city superintendents, and a few university professors of pedagogy from all over the country. During one summer session, kindergartners Anna Bryan and Alice Putnam designed a special kindergarten "topical syllabus," which questioned whether Froebel's Gifts and Occupations had any educational value and whether they required too much "fine work," among other items.[102] Hall proposed a separate Department of Education within the university in 1891. He planned to include higher education administration, as well as elementary and secondary education. However, the financial exigencies caused him to create a subdepartment of education within the Department of Psychology in 1893 instead. Finally, in 1911, he was able to create a separate Department of Pedagogy. Hall admitted women to graduate study at Clark from the beginning, but this was not publicized until after the death in 1900 of Jonas Clark, who disapproved of the practice.[103] He reputedly offered the first course on higher education at Clark in 1893.[104]

The American Psychological Association was planned in an 1892 conference in Hall's study. It began later in the year with Hall as its first president. Hall was elected president of the APA for a second time in 1924; however, he died before the year was out, at the age of eighty.[105, 106] Hall was a genetic psychologist who was concerned with animal and human development. When he died, he left his money to Clark for founding a chair of genetic psychology—a chair now named for him.[107]

Among Hall's works related to education are the following: *Aspects of Child Life and Education by G. Stanley Hall and Some of His Pupils* edited by Theodate L. Smith, which includes his studies on "Contents," "Curiosity and Interest," "The Story of a Sandpile," "A Study of Dolls," and "Boy Life in a Country Town in Mass. 40 Years Ago," *Educational Problems*, vols. I and II; *Life and Confessions of a Psychologist*, his autobiography; and *Youth Its Education, Regimen and Hygiene. Health, Growth, and Heredity: G. Stanley Hall on Natural Education* includes excerpts from his "Child-Study and Its Relation to Education, Childhood and Adolescence, The Ideal School Based on Child Study and New Departures in Education."

WILLIAM HEARD KILPATRICK (1871–1965)

William Heard Kilpatrick was born on November 20, 1871, in White Plains, Georgia. He went to school in Georgia and received his bachelor's and master's degrees from Mercer University in Macon, Georgia, in 1891 and 1892, respectively. After receiving his master's degree, he became a teacher in the Georgia public school system, rising to principal by 1897. He then became a professor of mathematics at Mercer University, where he taught and served as acting president between 1897 and 1906. He joined the faculty of Teachers College, Columbia University in 1909 as a lecturer, and ascended through the academic ranks to become a full professor of the philosophy of education in 1918. He received his

Ph.D. degree from Columbia in 1912. He was a prominent speaker at university summer schools across the country throughout his professional life.[108]

As an ambitious young professor, Kilpatrick wrote about some of the prevailing educational theories and methods of the day. His pointed criticisms were sometimes designed to popularize his own project method through discrediting the other systems. However, Kilpatrick worked closely with Patty Smith Hill and other early childhood teacher educators at Teachers College; therefore, he had more than a passing acquaintance with the philosophy of both Froebel and Montessori. His book *Froebel's Kindergarten Principles Critically Examined* sounded the death knell for strict Froebelianism[109] in the United States, and *The Montessori System Examined* effectively halted importation of the Montessori Method into the country until the 1950s.[110]

Kilpatrick took the work of John Dewey a step further when he synthesized the project method. His pamphlet *The Project Method: The Use of the Purposeful Act in the Educative Process* suggests that such a unifying concept must "emphasize the factor of action, preferably wholehearted vigorous activity. It must at the same time provide a place for the adequate utilization of the laws of learning, and no less for the essential elements of the ethical quality of conduct."[111] He stated that the project method exemplified these three concepts. This elaboration of the method caused it to become a keystone of the progressive movement in education during the first half of the twentieth century. Many experimenters in the "new schools," as well as the progressive public schools, adopted it, and it has maintained a presence on the early education scene until today.[112]

In the forward to a 1923 book by one of his doctoral students, Ellsworth Collings, Kilpatrick penned a clear statement of the principles of the project method. He stated that

1. the pupils must purpose what they do (this is a major theme of Kilpatrick's writing, which is discussed in further detail later);
2. actual learning is never single;
3. all learning encouraged by the school is so encouraged because it is needed here and now in order to carry on better the enterprise now underway; and
4. the curriculum is a series of guided experiences so related that what is learned in one serves to elevate and enrich the subsequent stream of experience.[113]

Ward adds:

1. Students decide what the project is to be.
2. Objectives cannot be predetermined; they can only be established during a learning activity.
3. What is learned in one series of projects enriches subsequent activities.[114]

Kilpatrick stated, "As the purposeful act is thus the typical unit of the worthy life in a democratic society, so also should it be made the typical unit of school procedure."[115] In a pedagogical methods text he wrote that *purpose* is the driving or dominating factor that propels a project through to completion. One therefore purposes, makes a plan, executes it, and then judges whether the final result secures and meets the original purpose. If not, he asks, "was it plan or execution which was at fault?"[116]

As a part of his work, Kilpatrick formulated four types of projects.[117] Type I, the *Producer's Project,* produces something by embodying the idea in an external form. Examples range from the child's sand house, to painting a picture, to writing a letter or presenting a play. The purpose of the second type, the *Consumer's Project,* is to "use" and enjoy some (esthetic) experience, such as listening to a story or appreciating a sculpture. The *Problem Project,* Type III, is designed to solve a problem, or "to clear up some intellectual difficulty. Historically and individually this is probably to be thought of as an outgrowth of Type I. Almost any purpose to produce, especially if it be educative, will involve some difficulty which in turn will call for thinking. The difference between Type III and Type I is that Type III consists wholly of the problem, while Type I typically involves fashioning, with the problematic thinking only incidental."[118] The fourth type of project is designed to "obtain some item or degree of skill or knowledge." This might include such things as "the ability to manage ordinary reading matter," counting, making change, and column addition.[119]

In a series of lectures at Rutgers University in 1926, Kilpatrick elaborated upon his views of society, curriculum, and method. He said that because of an "educational decline of family and community, and in accordance with a better insight into the learning process, the school must become a place where life, real experiencing, goes on." He told his audience that in the past children in schools used the results of others' thinking; however, new psychological ideas combined with the current social crisis made it necessary for children to have experiences that promoted thinking.[120] He concluded by saying that "As teachers we must make ourselves progressively unnecessary."[121]

Insight into Kilpatrick's ideas about social change can be obtained from the fourth volume of the Kappa Delta Pi Lecture Series, in which he proposed a school program that avoided indoctrination. He said that pupils should be taught: (1) to expect social changes; (2) to wish the common good and seek it out; (3) to criticize, in the light of the common good, any existing and proposed institutions; and (4) to envision a defensible social program, with each person thinking for himself and on behalf of the whole.[122]

Kilpatrick worked for causes he believed in. A founder of Bennington College, he presided over the board of trustees from 1931 to 1938. He was also a board member of the Progressive Education Association (PEA) and fellow of both the American Association for the Advancement of Science (AAAS) and American Physical Education Association (APEA). As president of the New York Urban League between 1940 and 1951, after his retirement from Teachers College in 1938, he was able to put many of his theories to the test. He also chaired the Bureau for Intercultural Education (1946–1954), and was instrumental in the selection of the topic, *Intercultural Attitudes in the Making,* the topic of the *Ninth Yearbook of the John Dewey Society.* He died on February 13, 1965, and is buried in White Plains, Georgia.

EUDORA (1835–1904) AND WILLIAM NICHOLAS HAILMANN (1836–1920)

William Nicholas Hailmann was born on October 20, 1836, in Glarus, Switzerland, to parents who followed Pestalozzi. Shortly after he was born, they moved to Islikon in rural Thurgau, where he had access to the local shops and mills as he was growing up. He had a garden for his outdoor play, and an upstairs playroom containing blocks, tools, picture books and drawing and writing materials.[123] After learning the basics of reading and writing from his mother, he was sent to the village schoolmaster when he reached the age of six. When he laughed out loud at a friend's drawing before class began, he was summarily sent home. His next educational encounter, with a Pestalozzian teacher, was much less traumatic. The children worked in groups for the various subjects, and Hailmann took part in a French language group, in addition to his studies in the German language. At age nine, he was transferred to a structured secondary school, from which he was again dismissed. After consultation with William's former primary teacher, his parents sent him to a new private school operated by Mr. Himmel, who worked with a small group of boys using active, hands-on learning methods.

When Himmel accepted a teaching position in a nearby city high school, he took four of the boys with him to prepare them for college. Thus, at thirteen years of age, Hailmann entered the polytechnic division of the Cantonal College at Zurich.[124] Shortly before his graduation, a cousin who was visiting from the United States influenced him to come home with him. In 1852, they set sail for New York; however, a series of disagreements with the cousin prompted Hailmann to part company with him. He decided to go to Kentucky to visit a friend, the Swiss Counsel. Upon discovering that his friend had gone to Europe for a visit, Hailmann decided to remain in Louisville, and took a job working in a store.

Louisville was in the process of becoming a major commercial city because of its geographical location and features. Its large French and German population made the city quite cosmopolitan.[125] Hailmann's knowledge of modern languages enabled him to obtain a teaching position at the Henry Female College in 1853. Between 1857 and 1864, he switched to his first love, the teaching of the natural sciences. After a few years, he left the college to resume his truncated medical studies. However, a private language pupil, the Reverend John Heywood, convinced him to return to teaching at the newly organized public girls' and boys' high schools. Dismay with his students' weak academic preparation led him to investigate elementary schools in the United States and in his home country of Switzerland. On a visit to his parents in Zurich in 1860, he discovered and visited several kindergartens. Because of his Pestalozzian background, he responded favorably to the Froebelian philosophy and methods.

In 1857, Hailmann married Eudora Grover,[126] niece of the preceptress of the girls' high school. When he returned to his wife and family from Europe, the Civil War was looming. Although he joined the Union Army, his wife's illness forced him to return home and resume his high school teaching duties. In a dispute over a salary increase at the boys' high school, Hailmann resigned and was offered a position to develop Pestalozzi-Froebel methods at the German-American Academy of Louisville. Acting upon Hailmann's appeal, the school's patrons raised money for a new building, which included one of the first specially designed kindergarten rooms in the United States. His interest in promoting the incorporation of Froebelian philosophy into the upper grades was the focus of the three administrative positions he held in private German-American academies between 1865 and 1869.

Eudora Hailmann, a teacher by profession, had an interest in music and art. After the birth of her children, she volunteered as an assistant to the German-American Academy's kindergarten teacher. She began to study kindergarten methods, and made extensive tours of Swiss and German kindergartens in 1866 and 1871. Her interests were in teacher education, innovations in methods and materials, and in the establishment of schools and their supporting community organizations.[127]

In 1865, William Hailmann represented the Kentucky Teachers' Association at the Harrisburg, Pennsylvania, meeting of the National Teachers' Association, one of the forerunners of the NEA. Elizabeth Peabody organized the Froebel Institute of North America in 1877. It petitioned to become a department of the NEA in 1884. The NEA *Proceedings* of 1884 note that the Institute was authorized to organize as a department, and William Hailmann was elected its first president.[128] Eudora was elected president in 1888. Although William presided over the Elementary Department of the NEA in 1898, there are no records available that detail his reaction to the formation of the International Kindergarten Union in 1892. He and the original members of the NEA Kindergarten Department were not involved in this activity. He and his wife were active in the NEA and presented many talks at the organization's conferences. William's 1872 paper, "The Adaptation of Froebel's System of Education to American Institutions," gave rise to a study committee on the kindergarten.[129, 130] Eudora's papers on the professional training of kindergartners[131] were well received at a number of professional conferences.[132]

The principalship of the Engleman German-English Academy became available in 1874, with the death of its founder. William accepted the offer, and the Hailmann family moved to Milwaukee, Wisconsin.[133] Eudora established a transition class as a bridge between the kindergarten and first grade in the Engleman Academy. In 1875, she opened the first English-language kindergarten in Milwaukee. Kindergarten training classes in both German and English, and the establishment of a philanthropic "free kindergarten association" charity kindergarten, followed shortly thereafter. Their 1879 move to Detroit followed the same pattern, with the establishment of both German- and English-speaking kindergartens and training classes. In Detroit, William was elected as a School Inspector, his first public school position since their move to Milwaukee. Both Hailmanns taught at a summer institute they organized in 1882 on the use of Froebel's Gifts and Occupations in the primary school. Eudora devised a series of kindergarten materials during this time period.[134]

In 1883, William became the Superintendent of Schools in LaPorte, Indiana, in response to an offer to "carry out an experimental program of his own design."[135] In the eleven years of Dr. Hailmann's administration, the LaPorte school system attained a national reputation for progressive reforms. Kindergartens were established in the public schools under his direction, kindergarten principles permeated the grades, manual training was introduced in the elementary and high schools, artwork developed along rational lines never before conceived.[136] Due in large measure to his work, the Indiana State Legislature recognized the kindergarten as a tax-supported class of the Indiana public schools. This led to the incorporation of the kindergarten into the sequence of public school classes. He remained superintendent there until he was appointed federal Superintendent of Indian Schools in 1894.

During her eleven years in LaPorte, Eudora was quite busy. She established a kindergarten training school in the city, and directed the normal school kindergarten in Winona, Minnesota. (The site of the LaPorte training school is still known as a historic landmark in the city.)[137] She started transitional classes for children in the public schools who were not yet ready to begin first-grade work. In 1884, she organized the first NEA kindergarten exhibit, and she continued her exhibition work on an annual basis until 1892. Her book *Songs, Games and Rhymes for Nursery, Kindergarten and School* was published in 1887. She and her husband jointly established a summer school in LaPorte on the application of kindergarten principles to work in the grades (the common school branches),[138] to which people came from all over the country. She and their daughter Elizabeth joined William in the move to Washington, D.C. Mother and daughter set up a kindergarten and accompanying training school in the Cleveland Park section of the city.

William Hailmann's job as Superintendent of Indian Schools was to administer all schools, both on and off the reservation. In addition, he was required to select employees, prepare courses of study, select textbooks, and maintain the schools. He also carried on the responsibility of previous Superintendents as Inspector of Indian Schools.[139] He established kindergartens and kindergarten teacher training schools for Indians and visited many Indian schools during his tenure in office, which ended, due to political reasons, in 1896.[140] He then became Superintendent of Schools in Dayton, Ohio. Eudora's health, which had weakened while they were in Washington, continued to deteriorate in Ohio, and she died in 1904.

William was asked to head the Department of Psychology and History of Education at the Chicago Normal School shortly thereafter. He was able to work with small groups of students and to lecture on the subject closest to his heart.[141] While living in Chicago, Hailmann attended lectures in psychology at the University of Chicago. During the decade prior to 1914, he also taught in the normal school in Cleveland, Ohio. In 1907, he married Helena Kuhn, who moved with him to California when he accepted a teaching position at Broadoaks Kindergarten Training School in Pasadena in 1914. He was honored at the NEA annual convention in Oakland in 1915. From California, he continued his work on bridging the gap between the kindergarten and the primary grades in the elementary school. W. N. Hailmann was a prolific writer. The *Dictionary of American Biography* says that his expositions of the doctrines of Froebel are among the most lucid in educational literature. He died in Pasadena on May 13, 1920.

William and Eudora Hailmann took kindergarten and primary education and kindergarten teacher training into a new era. Their inventive, dynamic theoretical and practical work serve as an excellent model for early education professionals.

THE PROGRESSIVE MOVEMENT

During the late nineteenth century, after the Civil War, there were concerns about increased industrialization, about a political system that was ineffective, and about what was happening to American society and its children.

Before the nineteenth century, the people dealing with children were ministers, whose advice reflected the dominant attitudes of the day. However, by the end of the century, a new group of professionals had appeared—psychologists, social workers, and economists—who all wanted to reshape American society. This effort to refashion American society was called the progressive movement. Much of the effort by these reformers to improve society was focused on children and their schooling because children represent the future. The reformers sought to influence the behavior of children directly as individuals rather than as members of families, which had been the previous approach. This focus on children had begun with the creation of public schools and compulsory school attendance[142] but intensified during the late nineteenth century. Children were considered so important for the country's future that a new discipline emerged, child psychology. G. Stanley Hall was one of the leaders in this field. Progressive education was part of the larger progressive movement. According to Cremin, there is no specific definition of "progressive education" because the term meant different things to different people.[143]

JOHN DEWEY (1859–1952)

John Dewey was born in Burlington, Vermont, on October 20, 1859, the third of four sons in a middle-class family. Dewey's father came from a farmer's family, but he had moved to Burlington and gone into the grocery business. He married late in life to Lucina Rich, a woman almost twenty years his junior. The Rich family was more prosperous. Dewey's father served in the Union Army for four years during the Civil War. Dewey's mother, concerned about the long separation from her husband during his army service, moved the family to his headquarters in northern Virginia for the last winter of the war. It was a heroic move for a woman of those days. The deprivation of the devastated district made a lasting impression on the boys, even though they were young. In Virginia, Dewey and his brothers attended the local public school. He and his brother Davis were bookworms; John was bashful. Dewey experienced much moralistic pressure by the religious atmosphere that surrounded him while growing up.[144]

Dewey's boyhood surroundings played a large part in the formation of the educational theories he tried to test later on. As a boy, he participated in household activities and helped on the relatives' farms, thus being exposed to a whole range of industrial and agricultural occupations. He found school boring. He was interested in reading anything rather than his schoolbooks. By the time he reached manhood and became a teacher himself, the growth of the cities and the amount of work now done by machines rather than by people had interfered with the invaluable supplements to school education provided by the personal contacts with people in all walks of life that he had experienced during his boyhood. Dewey's realization that the most important parts of his education until he entered college were obtained outside the schoolroom played an important role in his educational work.

When he was fifteen, Dewey entered the University of Vermont, which was very small at that time. He spent the first two years studying Greek, Latin, ancient history, analytic geometry, and calculus. During his junior year, natural sciences were introduced: a course that included the theory of evolution and a course on physiology using the text written by Thomas Henry Huxley—the foremost supporter of Darwin's theory of evolution in England. From this book, Dewey derived an impressive picture of the unity of the living organism. This knowledge aroused Dewey's intellectual curiosity and established the direction of his interests.[145] Darwin's theory had supplanted the notion that human destiny is predetermined by a Supreme Power. It opened endless possibilities for human development. Like many of his contemporaries, Dewey was influenced by Darwin's theory.

After receiving his B.A. in 1879, Dewey taught at a high school in Pennsylvania. The following year he taught at a rural school in Vermont and continued reading philosophy with Professor H. A. Torrey of the University of Vermont. During this time, Dewey submitted his first piece of writing, "The Metaphysical Assumptions of Materialism," to William T. Harris, the superintendent of the St. Louis schools and the publisher of the *Journal of Speculative Philosophy,* who accepted it. Encouraged by this success, Dewey turned his mind toward teaching philosophy as a career.[146]

With $500 he had borrowed from an aunt, Dewey entered the newly founded Johns Hopkins University in the fall of 1882, from which he received his Ph.D. in 1884. Two of Dewey's teachers of philosophy at Johns Hopkins were Professor George S. Morris of the University of Michigan at Ann Arbor and Dr. G. Stanley Hall, who had just returned from Germany. When Morris returned to Michigan, he assigned Dewey to teach the undergraduate history of philosophy course at Johns Hopkins. Later, Morris offered Dewey an instructorship in philosophy at the University of Michigan. During his first winter at Michigan, Dewey met Alice Chipman, who had been teaching school for several years to earn money to complete her education. Her family background was similar to Dewey's. They were married in 1886. Dewey left the University of Michigan in 1888 to accept a professorship at the University of Minnesota. During that year, Morris died, and Dewey was invited to return to Michigan to become the chair of the Department of Philosophy. The Deweys named their third child Morris.[147]

According to Dewey, the University of Michigan was the first university in America to establish a Department of Education, which it did in the late 1870s. The department tried to make a connection between theory and practice through the actual work of teaching itself.[148] Michigan's Department of Education had strong links with the state school system. The high schools were visited by the university faculty members, who reported to the department on the preparation for college work needed for the students becoming teachers. Dewey's interest in general education was stimulated by these visits. His interest in psychology led him to study learning, attention, memory, imagination, and thinking. At this time, his observations of his three small children also gave a practical emphasis to what he had learned about the importance of proper development during the early years. Dewey had concluded that existing educational methods, especially those in the elementary schools, were not consistent with the contemporary psychological principles of normal development. Dewey was looking for an experimental school that would combine the psychological principles of learning with the principle of cooperative association that he had derived from his moral studies. At the same time, this school would release the children from the intellectual boredom he had experienced during his own school days.[149]

Dewey accepted an invitation in 1894 to join the newly established University of Chicago because pedagogy was part of the Department of Philosophy and Psychology. He published his first book, *Psychology,* in 1897 while a faculty member there.

In Chicago, Dewey found a group of parents interested in obtaining a new kind of education for their children. With their help, financial as well as moral, an elementary school was started under the auspices of the department he headed. With his wife's encouragement, Dewey established the Laboratory School at the University of Chicago in 1896. It became known as the "Dewey School," not because he was the head of it but rather "out of gratitude for [his] making the school possible by his objective and impersonal attitude of faith in the growing ability of every individual, whether child or teacher."[150] It was not a "practice" school. Rather, its relation to the department of pedagogy was the same as that which laboratories have to biology or physics, to test theories.

According to Dewey, the most important work of a university department of education "is the scientific—the contribution it makes to the progress of educational thinking,"[151] and that is why he wanted a laboratory school.

The school flourished for seven years, supported by friends and patrons. Dewey resigned in 1904 due to disagreements with the university president and joined the Philosophy Department at Columbia University, where he taught until his retirement in 1930. With Dewey's resignation and the subsequent dispersion of the faculty of the Laboratory School, this experiment in education ended.[152]

During a sabbatical (1918–1919), the Deweys visited Japan and China. Dewey was subsequently invited to lecture for a year in China. He secured a leave of absence from Columbia and returned to China for a visit that lasted for two years. After his retirement, he continued his traveling, lecturing, and writing.[153] He was widowed in 1927.

Dewey was a prolific writer. His bibliography contains more than 150 items, not all of them educational in nature. Many of his books have been translated into other languages, and many of his ideas have influenced school systems abroad. He was active in professional organizations, serving as president of the American Psychological Association (1899–1900) and the American Philosophical Society (1905–1906).[154] Dewey died on June 2, 1952.

Dewey's Pedagogic Creed (1897)

Among Dewey's many writings is *My Pedagogic Creed*, written in 1897 during the first year of the Laboratory School.[155] In it, Dewey states his pedagogy and his social philosophy, which was the antithesis of "the old education: its passivity of attitude, its mechanical massing of children, its uniformity of curriculum and method." He clearly wanted change. He thought that for too long the center of education had been the teacher and the textbook rather than the "immediate instincts and activities of the child himself."[156] Following are selected highlights. Each of the statements begins with "I believe that," omitted, to avoid redundancy.

1. What Education Is

[A]ll education proceeds by the participation of the individual in the social consciousness of the race. This process begins unconsciously almost at birth. . . . education comes through the stimulation of the child's powers by the demands of the social situation in which he finds himself. . . . The child's own instincts and powers furnish the material and give the starting point for all education. . . . [T]he individual who is to be educated is a social individual and society is an organic union of individuals. . . . Education, therefore, must begin with a psychological insight into the child's capacities, interests and habits. (77–78)

2. What the School Is

[T]he school is primarily a social institution. . . . [E]ducation, therefore, is a process of living and not preparation for future living. . . . [T]he school must represent present life . . . which he carries on in the home, in the neighborhood, or in the play-ground. . . . [T]he school life should grow gradually out of the home life. . . . Moral education centers about this conception of the schools as a mode of social life, that the best and deepest moral training is precisely that which one gets through having to enter into proper relations with others in a unity of work and thought. . . . The child should be stimulated and controlled by his work through the life of the community. . . . The discipline of the school should proceed from the life of the school as a whole and not directly from the teacher. (78)

3. The Subject Matter of Education

[T]he primary basis of education is in the child's powers at work along the same general constructive lines as those which have brought civilization into being. . . . [T]he only way to make the child conscious of his heritage is to enable him to perform those fundamental types of activity which makes civilization what it is. . . . [T]his gives the standard for the place of cooking, sewing, manual training, etc. in the school. . . . [T]here is no succession of studies in the ideal school curriculum. . . . [E]ducation must be conceived as a continuing reconstruction of experience; that the process and the goal of education are one and the same. (79)

4. The Nature of Method

[T]he question of the method is reducible to the question of the order of development of the child's powers and interests. The law of presenting and treating material is the law implicit within the child's own nature. . . . [T]he image is the greatest instrument of instruction. What a child gets out of any subject presented to him is simply the images which he himself forms with regard to it. (79–80)

5. The School and Social Progress

[E]ducation is a regulation of the process of coming to share in the social consciousness; . . . the adjustment of individual activity on the basis of this social consciousness is the only sure method of social reconstruction. . . . [I]n the ideal school we have the reconciliation of the individualistic and the institutional ideals. . . . [T]he teacher is engaged, not simply in the training of individuals, but in the formation of the proper social life. . . . [E]very teacher should realize the dignity of his calling; that he is a social servant set apart for the maintenance of proper social order and the securing of the right social growth. (80)

Dewey applied many of these points at the Laboratory School and elaborated on all of them in most of his subsequent writings.

THE DEWEY SCHOOL: THE LABORATORY SCHOOL OF THE UNIVERSITY OF CHICAGO (1896–1903)

By the time Dewey arrived at the University of Chicago, he had formulated certain philosophical and psychological ideas that he wanted to test. He wanted to reform education. The purpose of the Laboratory School, as Dewey wrote in the Introduction of the Dewey School, was "a desire to discover in administration, selection of subject matter, methods of learning, teaching, and discipline, how a school could become a cooperative community while developing in individuals their own capacities and satisfying their own needs."[157]

It was called the "Laboratory School" to emphasize its experimental character. It was specifically designed to test Dewey's idea of *education as growth,* which was new, in practice, in the actual working of the school, and in its sociological implications. He wanted to show how education in school could be made consistent with contemporary psychology. The Laboratory School opened in January 1896. By 1902, the school had grown to accommodate 140 children, 22 instructors, and 10 assistants (graduate students at the university). Initially, the children attended mixed age groups. However, with the increase in enrollment, the children were grouped according to age, and the organization of the school became more formal. These groups were not based on the ability to read or write, but on the basis of community interest, general intellectual capacity, and the ability to do certain kinds of work. The teachers were specialists in a field instead of teaching all subjects in a grade.[158] Dewey, as head of the Department of Pedagogy, was the director of the Laboratory School. Mrs. Dewey served as principal.[159]

In the Laboratory School, Dewey saw a school of demonstration, observation, and experimentation. It was founded on experimental study—study by students, and study by teachers. The students studied the pursuit of self-directed interests, which increased as they were pursued. These interests were life itself, and life knows no bounds of subject divisions. The teachers studied first because they were pioneering and second for the same reasons that the students did. There is no end to the experimenting and to the learning.

The Laboratory School, as part of the Education Department, had many resources available to the teachers for the developing curriculum, especially in the fields of science. Department heads as well as faculty were "generous with their time and facilities," and "intellectual resources were freely put at the disposal of the teachers."[160] At the time, the University of Chicago had many scientists in residence who later achieved international distinction. Many of these men, in addition to their special interests, had pedagogical interests. They communicated the excitement of their discoveries to the children.[161]

Following is what Dewey told the parents about the relationship of the school to the university: "The problem is to unify, to organize, education to bring all its various factors together, through putting it as a whole into organic union with everyday life."[162]

Unfortunately, the school continually faced financial problems. In five years, the school had outgrown three buildings, none of which had been adequately equipped. The tuition fees were kept low for the sake of the parents who otherwise may not have been able to send their children, a practice that resulted in a yearly deficit.[163]

The Curriculum

Dewey viewed the school as a social institution. He tried to relate the curriculum to real life so it would not become isolated and exist only within the school. In integrating the curriculum, he kept in mind both the nature of knowledge and the child's experience. "All studies grow out of relations in the one great common world," Dewey said.[164] When children live "in varied but concrete and active relationship to this common world," their studies will be unified naturally, and "it will no longer be a problem to correlate studies. The teacher will not have to resort to all sorts of devices to weave a little arithmetic into the history lesson, and the like."[165] Dewey was saying that if the subjects are related to real life, curriculum integration unavoidably will result. In the Laboratory School the curriculum for each subject was developed from the child's activities. The curriculum constantly addressed the changing needs and interests of the growing child. The physical and social setup of the school was carefully arranged. Appropriate subject matter was sought to further the growth of the whole child. The instructors studied and observed that the materials and methods used to present the subject matter would be suitable for the child's changing attitudes and abilities and would link what was valuable in his past experience to his present and his future. This required experimentation in classroom methods, in the use of the material in a way that control gained by the child in one situation might be transferred to the next. This ensured continuity of experience, a habit of initiative, and an increasing skill in the use of the experimental method. The plan for the life of the school, in this experiment, was a simplified and ordered continuation of the student's life at home. In this environment both new and familiar, the child, conscious of no break in his experience, could learn to become a useful member of a larger social group.[166]

Activities were the means for achieving curriculum synthesis. The curriculum evolved slowly in both subject matter and method and was the result of the combined experimental efforts of trained specialists. Emphasis was given to the use of directed experimental methods in all areas of the children's activities. This method of learning resulted in the child's increasing ability to deal with new situations. The curriculum was related to activities familiar and natural to children, and had to do with such basic and continuing needs of life as shelter, clothing, and food, areas that became the focus of a developing curriculum. The curriculum also strove to teach similarities. For example, all people past and present have lived in "houses," but the structures have varied in terms of the materials used to build them in a specific location, climate, and size. Skills in reading, writing, and numbers were developed from the needs and the results of the child's activities.[167]

The curriculum was organized around themes, and it was community oriented. The school also had an organizing core—"the idea of the schoolhouse as a home in which the activities of social or community life were carried on."

The ideal was to use and guide the child's interest in the home, his natural environment, and in himself so that he could gain social and scientifically sound notions of the functions of persons in the home; of plant and animal, including human life and their interdependence; of heat as a special form of energy used in the home, as in cooking; and of food as stored energy. The materials in the child's environment and the things that were done to and with them furnished the ideas for the initial start and choice of the activities that occupied the children in the shop, laboratory, kitchen, and studios. They furnished a thread of *continuity* because they were concerned with the fundamental requisites of living.[168]

Household Occupations

The following is an example of the theme curriculum. The theme for Groups I and II (ages four and five), the subprimary group, was Household Occupations. It was planned for the entire year, "autumn and winter, spring."[169]

The children in the subprimary group were divided into two groups, the four-year-olds, Group I, and the five-year-olds, Group II. There was nearly an equal number of boys and girls in each group. The children's parents represented many professions. The following is the daily schedule:

9:00–9:30	Handwork, cook one day a week
9:00–10:00	Songs and stories
10:00–10:30	Marching games such as "Follow the Leader" while the room was being aired and personal wants were attended to
10:40–11:15	Luncheon
11:15–11:45	Dramatic play and rhythms

The order of the daily program was not a fixed one. It varied with the work the children were doing. The aim was to have a period of relaxation follow a period of intense interest so as not to keep the children at one kind of work for too long. (There is a similarity to what we try to implement in some of today's preschool settings.) The periods of handwork included constructive work, playing with blocks, drawing, painting, modeling in clay, and working in the sand, or any other suitable medium of expression.[170] There was no distinction between work and play in the Laboratory School. Teachers used the children's play to guide them in discovering and expressing themselves. Dewey (1900), had said: "These occupations in the school shall not be mere practical devices of routine employment, but active centers of scientific insight into natural materials and processes, points of departure whence children shall be led out into a realization of the historic development of man."[171] And again in 1930, Dewey stated: "Play and industry are by no means antithetical to one another as is often assumed." "In play the activity is its own end, instead of its having an ulterior result."[172]

Because the young child is highly imitative and open to suggestion a general principle was adopted at the school that no activity should be originated by imitation. The initiative must come from the child; the model or copy may then be supplied in order to assist the child in imagining more definitely what it is that he really wants—in bringing him to consciousness. Its value is not as a model to be copied, but rather as a guide to clarity and adequacy of conception. Unless the child can get away from it to form his own imagery when it comes to expression, he remains dependent, not developed. Imitation is to reinforce and help out, not to initiate.[173]

The teacher in charge of this group was Georgia Scates. Scates was a graduate of the Free Kindergarten Association of Armour Institute. Her two assistants were students of Anna Bryan, the head of Armour Institute. Bryan and her staff had contributed suggestions for materials and objects for constructive work for the subprimary group. The teacher's role was to simplify and clarify the child's passing from the intense and narrow life of the family—where instincts and emotions have been the guides for action—into the larger and diffused activities that require intellectual control. The watchword was "continuity" to avoid breaks in the child's experience that would retard, hamper, or frustrate the spontaneous expression of his intellectual life—his thought in action. The work of the youngest children was seen as an extension of the activities of the home. Every effort was made to avoid breaks in the child's experience.[174] All of the activities laid the foundations for the beginning of study of the formal subjects.

The children also shared their home experiences. Each child's home life was used as a basis to discuss the other children's homes and families and the various persons who helped in the household: the occupations of grocer, postman, mother. The normal day in the school might consist of conversations, constructive work, stories, songs, and games, all representing attempts to begin with the familiar and steadily move toward the unfamiliar.

Midmorning luncheon was served every day. The children took charge of setting the table, serving, waiting on each other, and washing and putting away the dishes. It was discovered that the preparation for eating and the clearing activity provided continuous opportunities for self-management and initiative.[175] The many questions asked about food that required answers resulted in a visit to a farm. There the children saw orchards, the harvesting of fruit, and fields of corn. This visit was the beginning of many such activities. These varied with teacher, children, and circumstances. Part of the group played grocery store and sold fruit and sugar to those who wanted to make jelly. Some students were drivers, some were clerks, and others were mothers. The clerks were given measuring cups to measure the sugar and cranberries and paper to wrap the packages to be taken home.[176]

Along with the theme activities, specific work in languages, mathematics, the fine and industrial arts, science, music, history, and geography progressed in well-planned fashion and always with the social motive in mind. The principles governing the work of all the age groups were the same. Maintaining continuity was the guiding principle. The school was seen as an intermediary between home and the community at large.

The themes for the other groups were: Group III (age six), Social Occupations serving the Household; Group IV (age seven), Progress through Invention and Discovery; Group V (age eight), Progress through Exploration and Discovery; Group VI (age nine), Local History; Group VII (age ten), Colonial History; Group VIII (age eleven), European Background of the Colonists; and Group IX (age twelve), Experiments in Specialized Activities.

The aim of the school was to deepen and broaden the range of social contacts, of cooperative living, so that the students would be better prepared to make their future social relations worthy and fruitful.[177] According to Cremin, Dewey had rejected the child-centered emphasis of the curriculum first in *The Child and the Curriculum* (1902) and later in *Experience and Education* (1938).[178] To learn to live better, one must learn to share more abundantly in the thoughts, feelings, and interests of others. To do this with ethical regard for others is to give democracy its best definition, for, according to Dewey, "A democracy is more than a form of government; it is primarily a mode of associate living, of conjoint communicated experience."[179]

The principles of the school plan were not definite rules. They gave the general direction. Their application was in the hands of the teachers, who developed and modified them through the trial-and-error method. The teachers had great freedom in adapting the principles to the actual conditions in the classroom. The teachers were specialists in specific subjects. They were able to recognize opportunities for early learning, and their knowledge of childhood could be utilized to lead children to understanding the subject matter taught. Conference and discussion were needed to achieve unity. Unity was achieved through cooperation among the teachers and through the teachers' meetings led by Dewey.[180]

Dewey and Froebel

There is no question that the curriculum in the Laboratory School was influenced by Froebel's ideas and theories, even though Dewey did not call the younger group in his school "kindergarten" but instead labeled it "subprimary." He used many of Frobel's ideas when working with the children in the school. Dewey devoted a whole chapter, "Froebel's Educational Principles," in one of his books, *The School and Society,* to explain Froebel's educational principles.[181]

Dewey, however, took issue with Froebel's symbolism and gave the following interpretation of it. He believed that Froebel's symbolism was the result of two conditions characteristic of his time and work. First, there had been inadequate knowledge about the physiological and psychological principles of child growth with which to interpret the children's activities (play). Second, the general political and social conditions of Germany (restrictive and authoritarian) had made it impossible to achieve continuity between the cooperative life of the kindergarten and the outside world. Froebel was constrained to think of the activities "as symbolic of abstract ethical and philosophical principles."[182] Dewey justified making "kindergarten activities more natural, more direct, and more real representations of current life" because the social conditions in America differed from those of Germany during Froebel's time.[183] Dewey, like Froebel, stressed that the child's activity is the beginning of all education and that learning is part of the process of actual living. Froebel viewed education as *development*, while Dewey saw it as *growth*.

Chapter Summary

Horace Mann restored the idea of the rich and the poor educated together and introduced teacher training. The public school is one of the characteristic features of American life. There is a timeliness to Mann's idea that education needs to be grounded in cultural literacy and moral character. Mann believed that schooling would lay the foundation for the responsible exercise of citizenship in a free society.

Mann and others had come to have a new level of respect for childhood. Most of their ideas could be traced to Pestalozzi and Froebel. Harris introduced the kindergarten into the U.S. public schools. Mann and Harris were both proponents of women as elementary school teachers and of their professional development. Dewey brought increased interest in school life and work, interest in the student as a living person, and interest in current social affairs. Dewey has influenced the practices of nursery school and kindergarten as well as the practices of elementary and secondary schools and college education. Many of the innovations in his Laboratory School are common practices in today's early education programs.

Notes

1. Mary P. Mann, *Life of Horace Mann,* Centennial ed. in facsimile (Washington, DC: National Education Association, 1937), 575; *Horace Mann on the Crisis of Education,* ed. with an introduction by Louis Filler (Yellow Springs, OH: Antioch Press, 1965), 224. It is the last sentence of the last commencement address Mann gave at Antioch College in 1859.

2. Horace Mann, *"A Life and an Epoch"* in Joy Elmer Morgan, Horace Mann: His Ideas and Ideals (Washington, DC: National Home Library, 1936), 9; Henry Barnard, *Biographical Sketch of Horace Mann, LL.D.* Reprinted from Barnard's *American Journal of Education* (December 1858), 611.

3. Mann, *Life of Horace Mann,* 11–13; Barnard, *Biographical Sketch of Horace Mann,* 613–614. Mann, like Froebel, had to memorize passages from the catechism. See also Jonathan Messerli, *Horace Mann: A Biography* (New York: Alfred A. Knopf, 1972).

4. Mann, *Life of Horace Mann,* 19.

5. Barnard, *Biographical Sketch of Horace Mann,* 615.

6. Ibid., 616; Horace Mann, *The Republic and the School,* ed. Lawrence A. Cremin (New York: Columbia University, Teachers College, Bureau of Publications, 1957), 5.

7. Lawrence A. Cremin, *The American Common School* (New York: Columbia University, Teachers College, Bureau of Publications, 1951), 91, 93.

8. Mann, *Life of Horace Mann,* 56.

9. Ibid., 9, 21, 25, 29, 33, 39, 45, 47, 57.

10. Horace Mann, *Lecture on Education* (Boston: Marsh, Capen, Lyon, and Webb, 1840), 7–8. The *Lecture on Education* is the summary of defects to be remedied and of goals to be achieved in the common school system. The *Lecture* was delivered before the

County Conventions, held throughout the state, in the autumn of 1837; the members of the legislature, in 1838; and other audiences. The press regularly requested a copy. Mann decided to write it for publication in 1840. Ibid., 4. County Conventions lasted until 1842, the year the law was repealed.

11. Mann, *Life of Horace Mann*, 70, 80–81.

12. Mann, *On the Crisis of Education*, 100–103; Alice M. Earle, *Child Life in Colonial Days* (New York: Macmillan, 1899: reprint, Williamstown, MA: Corner House Publishers, 1975), 67–68 (page citations are to the reprint edition). The Boston Latin School was established in 1635; Harvard College in 1636.

13. Robert B. Downs, *Horace Mann: Champion of Public Schools* (New York: Twayne Publishers, 1974), 34.

14. Cremin, *The American Common School*, 129–131.

15. Mann, *Life of Horace Mann*, 63; Downs, *Horace Mann*, 35.

16. Horace Mann, *Go Forth and Teach: An Oration Delivered before the Authorities of the City of Boston, July 4, 1842*, centennial ed. (Washington, DC: Committee on the Horace Mann Centennial, 1937), 19, 26.

17. Ibid., 63.

18. Mann, *Life of Horace Mann*, 59–61.

19. Mann, *Go Forth and Teach*, 70–71.

20. Barnard, *Biographical Sketch of Horace Mann*, 633.

21. Mann, *Lecture on Education*, 58.

22. Ibid., 18–19, 20.

23. Mann, *The Republic and the School*, 10–11.

24. Mann, *Lecture on Education*, 45–47. For more on corporal punishment, see "School Punishments" in Mann, *Lectures and Annual Reports on Education*, 333–368. It is a lecture Mann delivered in 1839 in a course of lectures for female teachers in Boston.

25. Mann, *Life of Horace Mann*, 106. Mann contributed from his personal money to complete the Westfield and Bridgewater Normal Schools. The appropriations were not enough, and he did not want to give the schools up. After he was elected to Congress, the legislature gave him a gift of $2,000 as an acknowledgment of what he had spent for education. Ibid., 580, 584.

26. *Life and Works of Horace Mann*, 5 vols. (Boston: Lee and Shepard, 1891). Volumes two, three, and four are the *Annual Reports* Mann wrote for the Massachusetts Legislature. The *Third Annual Report* (1839) deals with the need for free public libraries as adjuncts to the public schools, for current books appropriate for children and youth, and the effect of reading on the formation and development of character. Barnard, *Biographical Sketch of Horace Mann*, 624.

27. Mann, *On the Crisis of Education*, 134–148, are some excerpts from the *Common School Journal*; Barnard, *Biographical Sketch of Horace Mann*, 622–623; Mann, *Life of Horace Mann*, 98–101. Educational journalism came of age in America with the appearance of Henry Barnard's *Connecticut Common School Journal* in 1838 and Horace Mann's *Common School Journal* in 1839.

28. Barnard, *Biographical Sketch of Horace Mann*, 623–624.

29. Downs, *Horace Mann*, 38, 44.

30. Mann, *Life of Horace Mann*, 100–101.

31. Downs, *Horace Mann*, 51.

32. Ibid., 52–53.

33. Will S. Monroe, *History of Pestalozzian Movement in the United States* (Syracuse, NY: C. W. Bardeen, 1907; reprint, New York: Arno Press and The New York Times, 1969), 135–139 (page citations are to the reprint edition).

34. Mann, *The Republic and the School*, 21.

35. Mann, *On the Crisis of Education*, 69, 71, 73, 76–77; Barnard, *Biographical Sketch of Horace Mann*, 625.

36. Mann, *Lecture on Education*, 25. See also Horace Mann, *A Few Thoughts on the Powers and Duties of Woman* (Syracuse: Hall, Mills, and Co., 1853), where he advocates for women "to enjoy the right of fair occupation and full education" (vii) and for woman "to enrobe herself in knowledge and love" (15).

37. Mann, *Life of Horace Mann,* 174–224. For a detailed account of the controversy, see Ibid., 225–257.

38. Horace Mann, "Letter to School Children," in Morgan, *Horace Mann: His Ideas and Ideals,* 105–120.

39. Ibid.) 115–120.

40. Mann, *Life of Horace Mann,* 277, 259, 265, 291–309. Mann's speeches on slavery were published separately. Horace Mann, *Slavery: Letters and Speeches* (Boston: B. B. Mussey, 1851).

41. The whole speech can be found in Horace Mann, *The Fugitive Slave Law: Speech of Horace Mann of Massachusetts* (Boston: W. S. Damrell and Co., 1851).

42. Mann, *Life of Horace Mann,* 383.

43. Ibid., 402, 553. For more details about Mann's years as president of Antioch College, see Joy Elmer Morgan, *Horace Mann at Antioch* (Washington, DC: National Education Association, 1938). Book includes the addresses and sermons Horace Mann gave while at Antioch. Mann's life with his wife, Mary P. Mann, and her contributions to his career are told in Louise H. Tharp, *Until Victory: Horace Mann and Mary Peabody* (Boston: Little, Brown, 1953). It is a romantic story directed at a mass audience. Some of Mary's contributions to education are discussed in Chapter 9 of this volume. See also Federal Writers Project, WPA, Massachusetts, *Selective and Critical Bibliography of Horace Mann* (Boston: State Department of Education, 1937).

44. Robert House, "William Torrey Harris," in *Biographical Dictionary of American Educators,* vol. 2, ed. John F. Ohles (Westport, CT: Greenwood Press, 1978), 605; and Edgar B. Wesley, *NEA: The First Hundred Years: The Building of the Teaching Profession* (New York: Harper & Brothers, 1957), 14.

45. Harlow G. Unger, "William Torrey Harris," in *Encyclopedia of American Education* (New York: Facts on File, Inc., 1996), 449.

46. Manuscript for speech dated 4/8/66. Jennie Wahlert Papers. In Box 1955–1966. Missouri Historical Society, St. Louis, 2. Jennie Wahlert was a teacher, principal, and teacher educator who lived in Missouri from 1883 to 1971. Alberta L. Meyer, "Jennie Wahlert," in *Profiles in Childhood Education, 1931–1960,* ed. ACEI Later Leaders Committee (Wheaton, NM: Association for Childhood International, 1992), 19–22; and Alberta L. Meyer, "Jennie Wahlert: Woman of Achievement," *Childhood Education* 69, no. 3 (Spring 1993): 164–166.

47. Henry A. Pochman, *New England Transcendentalism and St. Louis Hegelianism: Phases in the History of American Idealism* (Philadelphia, PA: Carl Schurz Memorial Foundation, Inc., 1948), 66.

48. Ibid., 29.

49. Ibid., 33.

50. Raymond Schuessler, "America's Forgotten Teaching Pioneer," *NRTA Journal* [magazine], September–October 1979, 16; and Manuscript for speech dated 4/8/66. Jennie Wahlert papers. In Box 1955–1966. Missouri Historical Society, St. Louis, 2.

51. Richard Field, "St. Louis Hegelians," in *The Internet Encyclopedia of Philosophy* 1996 [on-line encyclopedia]; available from <http://www.utm.edu/research/iep/h/hstlouis.html>; Internet accessed 27 May 1997, 1.

52. Susan Blow wrote to Dr. Harris: "Acting upon your suggestion that the spring would be the best time for making a 'kindergarten' experiment I have hurried somewhat in my preparation and can now state definitely that I shall be ready to commence operations by May. I beg that you will let me know whether we shall have the sympathy of the School Board." Letter of Susan E. Blow to William Torrey Harris, March 25, 1873, William Torrey Harris Papers, Box 8B-2-5 Susan Blow 1872–1880, Missouri Historical Society, St. Louis, 1–2.

53. "In 1871 Dr. Harris, as Superintendent, in examining statistics discovered the fact that most children entered school at seven, stayed only until the age of ten—He felt little hope of extending school experience for the mass of children. He recommended to the School Board that provision be made for some type of class below the primary level—A committee of three was to report whether some kind of play should be formed. The Committee visited a play school in Newark, New Jersey—reported 'such a school would train the child in perseverance, develop his personality, encourage expression of his talents and

give him ample exercise and healthful surroundings.'" Manuscript for speech dated 4/8/66. Jennie Wahlert papers. In Box 1955–1966. Missouri Historical Society, St. Louis, 2.

54. Snyder, *Dauntless Women in Childhood Education,* 61; and William T. Harris, "Report of the Superintendent, in *Seventeenth Annual Report of the Board of Directors of the St. Louis Public Schools for the Year Ending August 1871,*" in Robert H. Bremner, ed., *Children and Youth in America: A Documentary History,* 3 volumes in 5 books (Cambridge, MA: Harvard University Press, 1974), 2:1454–1455.

55. Pochman, *New England Transcendentalism and St. Louis Hegelianism,* 12.

56. *"Twenty-First Annual Report of the Board of Directors of the St. Louis Public Schools for the Year Ending August 1875,"* in Bremner, *Children and Youth in America,* 2:1455–1456.

57. Margot Ford McMillen, *Missouri's Child: Culture and Education in the Show-Me State* (Jefferson City, MO: Office of Secretary of State Rebecca McDowell Cook, 1994), 17.

58. William T. Harris, *Psychologic Foundations of Education: An Attempt to Show the Genesis of the Higher Faculties of the Mind,* International Education Series (New York: D. Appleton and Company, 1898), 315, 318. [This book was reprinted as William T. Harris, *Psychologic Foundations of Education: An Attempt to Show the Genesis of the Higher Faculties of the Mind,* in the series *American Education: Its Men, Institutions and Ideas,* ed. Lawrence A. Cremin (New York: Arno Press & The New York Times, 1969. Both editions were consulted.]

59. William T. Harris, "'Report from a Department Sub-Committee on Kindergartens,' *Journal of Social Science,* XII (1880), 8–11" in Bremner, *Children and Youth in America,* 2: 1457–1458; Wesley, *NEA: The First Hundred Years,* 158; and Harriet Niel, "William Torrey Harris," in *Pioneers of the Kindergarten in America,* ed. Caroline D. Aborn, Catharine R. Watkins, and Lucy Wheelock (New York: The Century Co., 1924), 173, 179.

60. McMillen, *Missouri's Child,* 17.

61. Wesley, *NEA: The First Hundred Years,* 45.

62. Ibid., 113; and Harris, *Psychologic Foundations of Education,* xxxi, Chapter XXXVI # 208, 321–323.

63. *Report of the Committee of Fifteen on Elementary Education with the Reports of the Sub-Committees: On the Training of Teachers; on the Correlation of Studies in Elementary Education; on the Organization of City School Systems,* by William H. Maxwell, chairman (Published for the National Education Association by New York: The American Book Company, 1895 [MDCCCXCV], 3–113, 157–197; and Wesley, *NEA: The First Hundred Years,* 186–189.

Wesley (189) says "elementary" referred to primary and grammar schools. "Psychological symmetry" referred to exercise of the faculties of the mind. Faculty psychology was later discredited.

64. Pochman, *New England Transcendentalism and St. Louis Hegelianism,* 46, 65, 81, 110; and Field, "St. Louis Hegelians," 1–2.

65. Donald Arnstine, "The Educator's Impossible Dream: Knowledge as an Educational Aim," [paper on-line] (Philosophy of Education Society); available from <http://www.ed.uiuc.edu/coe/eps/pes-yearbook/92_docs/darnstine.html>; Internet accessed 27 May 1997, 1.

66. McMillen, *Missouri's Child,* 17.

67. Wesley, *NEA: The First Hundred Years,* 245; and "The Historical Foundation of American Education," in *American Education* [database on-line] (Little Rock, AR: College of Education University of Arkansas at Little Rock ONLINE); available from <http://www.ualr.edu/~coedept/ae2300/chapters/unit1/ch4.html>; Internet accessed 27 May 1997, 6.

68. Office of Education Library, Early Years (Washington, DC: Office of Education); available from <http://inet.ed.gov/nle/early.html>; Internet accessed 27 May 1997, 1–2.

69. Schuessler, "America's Forgotten Teaching Pioneer," 16.

70. Niel, "William Torrey Harris," in *Pioneers of the Kindergarten in America,* 167; and Unger, "William Torrey Harris," 449.

71. Dorothy Ross, *G. Stanley Hall: The Psychologist as Prophet* (Chicago: University of Chicago Press, 1972), 4–6; Edwin G. Boring, *A History of Experimental Psychology* (New York: D. Appleton–Century Company Incorporated, 1929); and Edwin G. Boring, *A History of Experimental Psychology*, 2d ed. (Englewood Cliffs, NJ: Prentice-Hall, Inc., 1950), also supports the date of 1844.

72. Lester F. Goodchild, *G. Stanley Hall and the Study of Higher Education, The Review of Higher Education* 20: 1, 2 1966 [journal on-line]; available from <http://www.pressjhu.edu/cgi-bin/wwwais>; Internet accessed 7 August 1997, says Williston Seminary.

73. Dorothy W. Hewes, "W. N. Hailmann: Defender of Froebel" (Ph.D. diss., Union Graduate School, 1974), 139.

74. Robert I. Watson, "Hall, G. Stanley," in *International Encyclopedia of the Social Sciences,* vol. 18, *Bibliographical Supplement,* ed. David L. Sills (New York: Macmillan [The Free Press], 1968), 311; and Ross, *G. Stanley Hall,* 287.

75. Watson, "Hall, G. Stanley," 311.

76. G. Stanley Hall, *Life and Confessions of a Psychologist* (New York: D. Appleton and Company, 1924), 200.

77. Ross, *G. Stanley Hall,* 79; and Goodchild, *G. Stanley Hall and the Study of Higher Education,* 3.

78. Ross, *G. Stanley Hall,* 80.

79. Boring, *A History of Experimental Psychology,* 2d ed., 519.

80. Hall, *Life and Confessions of a Psychologist,* 216–218.

81. Wesley, *NEA: The First Hundred Years,* 104.

82. Ibid., 263.

83. Ibid., 120.

84. Charles E. Strickland and Charles Burgess, eds., *Health, Growth, and Heredity: G. Stanley Hall on Natural Education,* Classics in Education, no. 23, with an introduction by Lawrence Cremin (New York: Teachers College Press, 1965), 26.

85. Ibid., viii.

86. Pochman, *New England Transcendentalism and St. Louis Hegelianism,* 113–114.

87. Boring, *A History of Experimental Psychology,* 615.

88. Goodchild, *G. Stanley Hall and the Study of Higher Education,* 3.

89. Strickland and Burgess, eds., *Health, Growth, and Heredity,* 12–13; and Barbara Beatty, *Preschool Education in America: The Culture of Young Children from the Colonial Era to the Present* (New Haven, CT: Yale University Press, 1995), 76. Beatty says that "modern standards would deem many of Hall's questions culturally biased; examiners did not ask the children about objects from their everyday environment, for instance."

90. Herbart's "law of apperception" is the process of acquiring basic experiences through the senses and relating all subsequent experiences and lessons to the already acquired apperceptive mass. Wesley, *NEA: The First Hundred Years,* 188; and Ross, *G. Stanley Hall,* 127.

91. Hewes, "W. N. Hailmann: Defender of Froebel," 188, 196; and Beatty, *Preschool Education in America,* 79.

92. Ross, *G. Stanley Hall,* 298–299.

93. Ibid., 125.

94. Ibid., 126; and Strickland and Burgess, eds., *Health, Growth, and Heredity,* 11–12.

95. Hall, *Life and Confessions of a Psychologist,* 389–390; G. Stanley Hall, [edited by Theodate L. Smith], *Aspects of Child Life and Education by G. Stanley Hall and Some of His Pupils* (Boston: Ginn & Company, Publishers, 1907), 158; Ross, *G. Stanley Hall,* ftn. 291; and Lillie A. Williams, "How to Collect Data for Studies in Genetic Psychology," *Pedagogical Seminary* 3, no. 2 (1896): 419–425.

96. Nina C. Vandewalker, *The Kindergarten in American Education* (New York: Macmillan, 1923), 235. For a succinct summary of the "new" psychology and the child study movement as it related to the kindergarten, see Vandewalker. The popularization of Hall as the guiding light and mainstay of the child study movement in early childhood education literature probably is derived from the following Vandewalker statement: "For the

conception of education so reconstructed the world is indebted to Dr. G. Stanley Hall, who may appropriately be called the father of the child study movement."

97. Ross, *G. Stanley Hall,* 130.

98. Snyder, *Dauntless Women in Childhood Education,* 179.

99. Wesley, *NEA: The First Hundred Years,* 198, 199.

100. Ibid., 200; and Vandewalker, *The Kindergarten in American Education,* 237–238. See the description of the work of Lawrence Frank, Bird T. Baldwin, and Arnold Gesell in Chapter 10 in this volume for further details of this aspect.

101. Goodchild, *G. Stanley Hall and the Study of Higher Education,* 8. Terman later developed the Stanford-Binet Scales of Intelligence.

102. Beatty, *Preschool Education in America,* 77–78; Goodchild, *G. Stanley Hall and the Study of Higher Education,* 5; Ross, *G. Stanley Hall,* 281; and Ilse Forest, *Preschool Education: A Historical and Critical Study* (New York: Macmillan Company, 1927), 177–178, ftn. 178.

103. Goodchild, *G. Stanley Hall and the Study of Higher Education,* 14; and Hall, *Life and Confessions of a Psychologist,* 318.

104. C. W. Burnett, "Higher Education as Specialized Field of Study: A Review and Interpretation of the Literature." Proceedings of the first annual meeting of the Association of Professors of Higher Education. Chicago, March 5, 1972, in ed. Paul L. Dressel and Lewis B. Mayhew, *Higher Education as a Field of Study* (San Francisco, CA: Jossey-Bass Publishers, 1974), 7.

105. In 1918, at the twenty-fifth anniversary meeting, Hall, Barnes, and Burnham, three of the original members, from Clark University, were present.

106. Boring, *A History of Experimental Psychology,* 521.

107. Ibid., 522.

108. Joseph C. Bronars, Jr., "William Heard Kilpatrick," in *Biographical Dictionary of American Educators,* vol. 2, ed. John F. Ohles (Westport, CT: Greenwood Press, 1978), 746–747; and Thomas H. Johnson in consultation with Harvey Wish, "William Heard Kilpatrick," in *The Oxford Companion to American History* (New York: Oxford University Press, 1966), 198–199.

109. Hewes, "W. N. Hailmann: Defender of Froebel," 198; and Wesley, *NEA: The First Hundred Years,* 164.

110. Elizabeth Harrison and Margaret Naumburg were among the American early education innovators who visited the Casa dei Bambini in 1913, and Patty Smith Hill closely followed the activities of the group that Kilpatrick led from Teachers College. After studying or observing the Method, all of them either rejected it totally or modified its incorporation into their own educational programs. Beatty, *Preschool Education in America,* 118; Robert H. Beck, "Progressive Education and American Progressivism: Caroline Pratt," *Teachers College Record* LX (1958–1959), 200; Patty Smith Hill, "Kindergarten," in *The American Educator Encyclopedia* (Chicago: The United Educators, Inc., 1941; reprint for Fiftieth Anniversary of the Association for Childhood Education, 1942), 1957; Margaret Naumburg, "Montessori Class: Second Year," [announcement and catalog] pp. 1–13, Margaret Naumburg Papers, Education Box # 1, Department of Special Collections, Van Pelt–Dietrich Library Center, University of Pennsylvania, Philadelphia, Pennsylvania, passim; Snyder, *Dauntless Women in Childhood Education,* 268–269; and Evelyn Weber, *The Kindergarten: Its Encounter with Educational Thought in America* (New York: Teachers College Press, 1969), 72–74.

111. William Heard Kilpatrick, *The Project Method: The Use of the Purposeful Act in the Educative Process* (New York: Teachers College, Columbia University, 1918), 3.

112. See, for example: Lilian Katz and Sylvia Chard, *Engaging Children's Minds: The Project Approach.* Norwood, NJ: Ablex, 1989; Sylvia Chard, *The Project Approach Web Site* [general introduction and case study examples on-line] (Edmonton, Alberta, Canada: Faculty of Education, University of Alberta); available from <http//www.ualberta.ca/~schard//projects.html>; Internet accessed 12 February 1997; and James Ward, *History, Development and Applications of the Project Approach: An ESP Case Study* [paper on-line], 3; available from <http://www.salsem.ac.at/csacl/graphics/projectapproach.html>; Internet accessed 8 August 1997.

113. William Heard Kilpatrick, introduction to *An Experiment with a Project Curriculum,* by Ellsworth Collings (New York: Macmillan Company, 1923), xviii, xix, xx.

114. Ward, *History, Development and Applications of the Project Approach,* 3.

115. Kilpatrick, *The Project Method,* 6.

116. William Heard Kilpatrick, *Foundations of Method: Informal Talks on Teaching* in *Brief Course Series in Education,* ed. Paul Monroe (New York: Macmillan Company, 1925), 205–206.

117. William Heard Kilpatrick, *Froebel's Kindergarten Principles Critically Examined* (New York: Macmillan, 1916), 16; and William Heard Kilpatrick, *Education for a Changing Civilization: Three Lectures Delivered on the Luther Laflin Kellogg Foundation at Rutgers University, 1926* (New York: Macmillan Company, 1931), 347–348, 365–366.

118. Kilpatrick, *Education for a Changing Civilization,* 348.

119. Ibid., 366.

120. Ibid., 85, 95–96.

121. Ibid., 123.

122. William Heard Kilpatrick, *Education and the Social Crisis: A Proposed Program,* vol. 4, Kappa Delta Pi Lecture Series (New York: Liveright Publishing Corporation Publishers, 1932), 60.

123. Barbara Greenwood, "William Nicholas Hailmann," in *Pioneers of the Kindergarten in America,* 247.

124. Lewis Flint Anderson, "William Nicholas Hailmann," in Dumas Malone, ed., *Dictionary of American Biography,* vol. VIII (New York: Charles Scribner's Sons, 1932), 90; and Hewes, "W. N. Hailmann: Defender of Froebel," 19.

125. Hewes, "W. N. Hailmann: Defender of Froebel," 20.

126. Ibid., 23; Anderson., "William Nicholas Hailmann," in *Dictionary of American Biography,* 90; and Greenwood, "William Nicholas Hailmann," 254.

There is a lack of clarity in the literature about whether Mrs. Hailmann's maiden name was Grover or Lucas.

127. Hewes, "W. N. Hailmann: Defender of Froebel," 27.

128. Wesley, *NEA: The First Hundred Years,* 161.

129. Vandewalker, *The Kindergarten in American Education,* 22; Greenwood, "William Nicholas Hailmann," 254–255; and Wesley, *NEA: The First Hundred Years,* 158.

130. In addition to W. N. Hailmann, the committee included John Kraus, John Hancock, Adolph Douai, William T. Harris, George A. Baker, and J. W. Dickerson. The committee reported that

> (1) the purpose of the kindergarten was to make children happy through play; (2) that Froebel's gifts should be utilized; (3) that the child learns through his own activity; (4) that for social purposes a kindergarten requires a group of children; (5) that the teacher should be a young woman of even temper; (6) that a room, playground, and a garden should be available; (7) that liberty, not uniformity or constraint, should prevail; (8) that reading, writing and ciphering be excluded; (9) that the qualities and characteristics of the gifts should be noted and designative words therefor be learned; (10) that children learn weaving, plaiting, stringing, stitching, and lacing; (11) that kindergartens and teacher-training schools, both public and private, be established; (12) that the children tend flowers and plants; (13) that teachers study the Froebel system.

Wesley, *NEA: The First Hundred Years,* 158.

131. During that time period the term "kindergartner" referred to kindergarten teachers.

132. Vandewalker, *The Kindergarten in American Education,* 153–154.

133. Hewes, "W. N. Hailmann: Defender of Froebel," 56.

134. "It was at this time that Mrs. Hailmann devised the second gift beads. She had previously worked out the social sand-table, the doll-house, a group table, and some enlarged forms of building gifts, used under her direction for social work." Greenwood, "William Nicholas Hailmann," 256.

135. Hewes, "W. N. Hailmann: Defender of Froebel," 58.

136. Greenwood, "William Nicholas Hailmann," in *Pioneers of the Kindergarten in America*, 257; and Hewes, "W. N. Hailmann: Defender of Froebel," 59.

137. "Welcome to the LaPorte County Link LaPorte home page!"; available from <http://www.lc-link.org/lp_home.html>; Internet accessed 27 May 1997, 1.

138. The common school branches refer to subject areas such as reading, mathematics, science, and social studies taught in the elementary school curriculum. See the *Report of the Committee of Fifteen on Elementary Education with the Reports of the Sub-Committees: On the Training of Teachers; on the Correlation of Studies in Elementary Education; on the Organization of City School Systems* (1895) for further explanation of this concept.

139. Hewes, "W. N. Hailmann: Defender of Froebel," 207–208.

140. See Hewes, "W. N. Hailmann: Defender of Froebel," Section Three, Chapter III, for an extensive discussion of this period in Hailmann's life.

141. Hewes, "W. N. Hailmann: Defender of Froebel," 249. William Hailmann: Hewes lists fourteen books, along with numerous government publications and pamphlets. The most widely recognized are: *Kindergarten Culture in the Family and Kindergarten* (1873), *Twelve Lectures on the History of Pedagogy* (1974), *Early Education* (1878), *The Application of Psychology to the Art of Teaching* (1884), and a translation of Froebel's *Education of Man* with commentary (1887). He edited several periodicals during his lifetime. The most widely read were *The New Education*, which he co-edited with Eudora, and *The Kindergarten Messenger*.

142. Massachusetts passed the first statewide compulsory attendance law in 1852; Mississippi was the last of the states to pass one, in 1918. Lawrence A. Cremin, *The Transformation of the School: Progressivism in American Education, 1876–1957* (New York: Alfred A. Knopf, 1961), 126.

143. Ibid., x.

144. Jane M. Dewey, ed., "Biography of John Dewey," in *The Philosophy of Dewey*, ed. Paul A. Schilpp (Evanston and Chicago: Northwestern University, 1939), 1, 4–7. This book was written on the occasion of Dewey's eightieth birthday, October 20, 1939. The biography was written by his three daughters, Jane M. Dewey, Mrs. Granville M. Smith (Evelyn Dewey), and Mrs. W. C. Brandeur (Lucy A. Dewey), with some help from Dewey himself. Schilpp, *The Philosophy of Dewey*, xiii. For a more recent biography, see George Dykhuizen, *The Life and Mind of John Dewey* (Carbondale: Southern Illinois University Press), 1973.

145. Dewey, "Biography of John Dewey," 9–10.

146. Ibid., 13. Harris, while superintendent of the St. Louis schools, had come in contact with a group of German exiles of 1848 who were students of German thought, especially that of Schelling and Hegel.

147. Ibid., 16, 19–20, 24. The Deweys had six natural children—Frederick Archibald, born in 1887; Evelyn, born in 1890; and Morris, born in 1893. The Deweys had three more children while they lived in Chicago—Gordon Chipman, Lucy Alice, and Jane Mary. Morris and Gordon died very young. They adopted Sabino, an Italian boy, in one of their trips to Italy. He is the only one who became a teacher. He was also a designer and manufacturer of educational equipment for constructive activities. Evelyn, the oldest daughter, after visiting a number of schools, wrote *Schools for Tomorrow* with her father and *New Schools for Old*, a book dealing with rural education. For some time, she was connected with the Bureau of Educational Experiments. Later, she edited a complete report of investigations of infant development. Ibid., 35.

148. John Dewey, *The School and Society*, with introduction by Leonard Carmichael (Chicago: University of Chicago Press, 1900; reprint Phoenix Books, 1956), 92–93. The first three chapters of the book were first given as lectures by Dewey to parents and others interested in the University of Chicago Elementary School in April 1899 and appeared in the *Elementary School Record*. Ibid., 4–5. According to Jane Dewey, his biographer, the talks were given to raise money for the Laboratory School. The book was translated subsequently into many European and Oriental languages. Dewey, "Biography of John Dewey," 28.

149. Ibid., 26–27.

150. Katherine Camp Mayhew and Anna Camp Edwards, *The Dewey School: The Laboratory School of the University of Chicago, 1896–1903*, with an introduction by John

Dewey (New York: D. Appleton–Century Co., 1936), v. The book chronicles the story of the school until Dewey left it. The authors were sisters, and both were teachers at the school. Katherine, vice principal, was in charge of the developing curriculum, and head of the science department. Anna, a teacher of history during the early experimental period, later became tutor. She followed through the work of all other departments with the older children. Ibid., vii. A new book by Laurel N. Tanner, *Dewey's School, Lessons for Today* (New York: Teachers College Press, 1997), focuses on what we can learn today from Dewey as we grapple with the same problems he faced.

151. Dewey, *The School and Society,* 96.

152. Mayhew and Edwards, *The Dewey School,* 18; Dewey, "Biography of John Dewey," 28.

153. Dewey, "Biography of John Dewey," 40, 42.

154. Ibid., 44–45. For Dewey's works in translation, see Jo Ann Boydston and Robert L. Andersen, eds., *John Dewey: A Checklist of Translations, 1900–1967* (Carbondale: Southern Illinois University Press, 1969).

155. John Dewey, "My Pedagogic Creed," *The School Journal* 54 (January 16, 1897): 77–80.

156. Dewey, *The School and Society,* 34.

157. Mayhew and Edwards, *The Dewey School,* xvi.

158. Ibid., 7–8, 9, 35. This is very much like what Pestalozzi had in his school at Yverdon.

159. Dewey, "Biography of John Dewey," 29.

160. Mayhew and Edwards, *The Dewey School,* 10.

161. Ibid., 10n.

162. Dewey, *The School and Society,* 92.

163. Mayhew and Edwards, *The Dewey School,* 12.

164. Dewey, *The School and Society,* 91.

165. Ibid.

166. Mayhew and Edwards, *The Dewey School,* 20, 22.

167. Ibid., 25–26.

168. Ibid., 43.

169. Ibid., 56–66. Dewey did not call this age group "kindergarten." See also Georgia P. Scates, "The Sub-Primary (Kindergarten) Department," *Elementary School Record* 1 (June 1900): 129–142.

170. Mayhew and Edwards, *The Dewey School,* 57.

171. Dewey, *The School and Society,* 19.

172. John Dewey, *Democracy and Education* (New York: Macmillan Co., 1930), 237–238.

173. Mayhew and Edwards, *The Dewey School,* 61; Dewey, *The School and Society,* 129.

174. Mayhew and Edwards, *The Dewey School,* 58–59.

175. Scates, "The Sub-Primary," 142.

176. Mayhew and Edwards, *The Dewey School,* 64–65.

177. Ibid., 466–467.

178. Cremin, *The Transformation of the School,* 240.

179. Dewey, *Democracy and Education,* 101.

180. Mayhew and Edwards, *The Dewey School,* 42, 365–366. At the end of each quarter, each group teacher reported on the work of his or her respective group. This process allowed the teacher to evaluate the series of activities and, in light of their success or failure, to plan the succeeding program. Ibid., 69. For a complete discussion on the teachers, Ibid., 365–397. It includes "Outline of Teachers' Meeting" (368–370), prepared by Dewey, and used in the meetings. They were seminars in methods used in the school.

181. Dewey, *The School and Society,* 116–139.

182. Ibid., 121–122.

183. Ibid., 122.

CHAPTER 9

The Kindergarten Movement

[T]he system of infant culture . . . was by far the most
original, attractive, and philosophical form of infant
development the world as yet had seen.
—Henry Barnard[1]

AMERICAN BEGINNINGS

The American public learned about *kindergarten* from two articles: one by
Henry Barnard, in 1856, reporting that he had seen a *kindergarten* at the
International Exhibit of Educational Systems in London in 1854,[2] and
the other from "Kindergärten of Germany" in the November 1859 issue of
the *Christian Examiner*, the official publication of the Unitarian Church. The
second article included a summary of Froebel's ideas by the Baroness von
Marenholtz-Bülow.[3]

The kindergarten arrived in America before the Civil War during a time
when men and women, dissatisfied with American backwardness, were trying
to change American society by reforming its education to be practical, moral,
and democratic.

Kindergartens did not attract the attention and the support of the American educators of the time even though they were described in the educational
literature. Some of the reasons for this were that (1) American education was
being transformed; (2) as long as the concept of education was seen as instruction in the three R's and not as development from within of the whole child,
kindergarten theory and practice could not be universally accepted; (3) the
goals and methods of the kindergarten—self-activity and self-expression—
were too different from the existing methods to be accepted wholesale; and
(4) America was slow to recognize the value of early childhood for educational purposes, and until it did the kindergarten could have no meaning.

Primary schools, like kindergartens, were not part of the school system.
They were managed independently, and children had to be seven years of age
to enter them and had to already know how to read and write. It was about
1860 that public schools were incorporated into the grade schools.[4]

German-American Kindergartens (1855–1870)

The ill-fated 1848 Revolution in Germany, which tried to obtain more voice
and more democracy for the people, brought a large number of Germans to
the United States. They were highly educated men and women who were

familiar with and shared Froebel's ideas for a more humane education. Between 1850 and 1870, these German immigrants established private, German-American academies to educate their children and preserve their culture and language, in all the cities where they had settled: New York City; Milwakee; Detroit; Newark, New Jersey; and Louisville.[5] These schools stimulated interest in German educational practices. Horace Mann, as secretary of the board of education in Massachusetts, was one of many Americans who visited the German schools in 1843 and reported about them to the Massachusetts Legislature.

In addition to the kindergartens in these academies, there were other private, independent kindergartens. Margarethe Schurz (1833–1876) opened a small German-speaking kindergarten in her home in Watertown, Wisconsin, in 1856 (four years after Froebel's death) for the benefit of the Schurz children and those of relatives, the Jüssen clans. It was an experiment, one of the first of its kind in the United States. Her purpose was to preserve their German cultural heritage and language. She taught the children, in German, the Froebelian kindergarten songs, games, and occupations as she had studied under Froebel in 1849 in Hamburg. This kindergarten closed in 1858 when the Schurzes moved to Milwaukee.[6]

Another German-speaking kindergarten was established in Columbus, Ohio, by Miss Caroline Luise (Louisa) Frankenberg in 1836, a year before Froebel opened his institution for young children in Blankenburg and twenty years before Mrs. Schurz's kindergarten. Miss Frankenberg's trip to America was precipitated by Froebel's essay "The Renewal of Life" (1836). In it he pointed to the United States as the country best suited for his educational plans. Things did not work out for her in Columbus, and disheartened, she returned to Germany.[7] Miss Frankenberg stayed there from 1840 until 1858. While there she taught at Keilhau under Froebel's direction for six years. In 1847, she was appointed kindergarten teacher in the "Kindergarten of the Women's Charitable Institution in Dresden," and in 1852, she opened her own kindergarten in Bautzen, where she encountered opposition from the local clergy—for a total of eleven years.[8] Miss Frankenberg was a sister of Adolph Frankenberg, Froebel's friend and disciple, who had helped Froebel in Dresden during 1838–1839. She had married Professor Marquardt.[9]

For whatever reasons, Miss Frankenberg returned to Columbus in 1858, to the same house where she had lived before, and established the first practical working kindergarten in the United States there. She and the school were ahead of their time, but she had difficulty attracting many students. To the parents, the making of paper birds, boats, and caps; modeling in clay; marching; and singing were simply child's play. It was called "the play school." Children on their way to private or public schools in Columbus never failed to stop and look in the window or door and marvel at children who learned without books. As Miss Frankenberg did not speak English, she had few, if any, American pupils. To make ends meet, she added to her kindergarten lace making and other handicrafts in which she was skilled. After a fall on the ice that disabled her in her sixtieth year, Luise went to Zanesville, Ohio, and finally found a home in the Lutheran orphanage in Germantown, Pennsylvania. There she introduced the kindergarten system in 1865. Elizabeth Peabody visited Luise at the Lutheran orphanage before she went to Europe and learned from her many of Froebel's ideas, which she tried to implement in her Boston kindergarten. Luise remained in Germantown until 1882, when she died. She was buried in St. Nicholas cemetery, adjoining the orphanage.[10]

One wonders why Miss Frankenberg has been forgotten and not given credit for her work on behalf of the kindergarten in America. She was a student and disciple of Froebel at Keilhau and was an experienced kindergartner for at least twenty-five years. By contrast, Mrs. Schurz, who ran a kindergarten for the benefit of her children for only two years, is always mentioned. Is it because Mrs. Schurz was married to a prominent man?

Maria Boelte (1836–1918)

Several German-trained kindergartners migrated to America to set up kindergartens and to train kindergartners according to the Froebelian principles. One of them, Maria Boelte, was the most influential of the German kindergartners in America in the early 1870s. From her "Reminiscences of Kindergarten Work," we learn that Maria was born on November 8, 1836, in the Grand Duchy of Macklenberg-Schwerin. Her father was a lawyer, who for forty-six years was a judge and local magistrate. His oldest sister, Amély Boelte, was a popular writer who regarded the "woman's question" her special mission. Maria's mother was an accomplished pianist.[11]

Although the kindergartens were not yet in existence, Maria's early education at home included the occupations that Froebel had systematized. She practiced building with blocks, tablet-laying games, and form-laying with sticks and seeds. Beads were used for counting. She perforated forms and sewed them with colored silk (538). When Maria was eighteen years old, she received religious instruction and was confirmed. She was introduced to society, and "a happy time began." Maria spent some of her afternoons entertaining a large group of poor children on the meadow near her house. On Saturdays the children who had kept their faces and hands clean during the week received a penny. She also visited the local *Kinder-und Bewahranstalt*—Crèche (541–42).

In 1854, Maria, influenced by her aunt's ideas that she should do something useful for society, succeeded in getting her parents' permission to go to Hamburg to study the kindergarten system with Frau Froebel, Dr. Wichard Lange, Alwina Lange, his wife—a daughter of Middendorff—and others who had been trained by Froebel (542). Frau Froebel had a large private kindergarten, an intermediate class, and a training class for kindergartners and for nurses. Maria lived with Frau Froebel throughout her training. In one of their many conversations, Frau Froebel told Maria, "If we want to train in Froebel's manner, we must devote ourselves with heart and mind to the children, and live *with* them, as he did."[12]

After two years of course work, Maria went to London, where German-trained kindergartners were in demand. She joined Mme. Ronge's London kindergarten. The children were poor, neglected, and "had to be washed in the basement and clean linen aprons put over their dirty clothes."[13] While there, Maria learned English and taught kindergarten training classes. In 1862, in the London Exhibition, she exhibited kindergarten material and work prepared by her pupils. Her London experience contributed to her commitment to the kindergarten movement. In 1867, Maria left England for Hamburg, where she gave lectures in the Froebel Union (546).

While Maria was visiting her sister in Lübeck, several parents showed interest in the kindergarten. Maria opened one, even though teachers, clergymen, and physicians openly told her that they would be her opponents. She was given permission to open a kindergarten with the understanding that she would not name it. Mothers took turns visiting the kindergarten daily. Maria trained kindergartners and nurses and started an intermediate class between kindergarten and school. Maria stayed in Lübeck until 1871. Frau Froebel visited Maria (548).

After her father's death in 1871, Maria thought of coming to America. In 1872, she accepted a position in Miss Haines's school, a well-known private school for girls in New York City. Miss Haines offered Maria a year's contract to demonstrate Froebelian practices by operating a kindergarten at the school. Maria accepted the position, for she wanted to gain time and resources to open a German Froebelian kindergarten training school in America. During the second week of work, General John Eaton, the U.S. Commissioner of Education (1870–1886), made a surprise visit to her kindergarten and stayed all morning. In addition to teaching the children, Maria added a "mothers' class." Susan Blow became her pupil and joined the mothers' class, as there was not a kindergarten training class the first year. Maria also taught "kindergarten work" to two primary classes; and two evenings per week she taught a group of twenty young ladies, the rudiments of the kindergarten system.[14]

In 1873, Maria married John Kraus, a Froebel follower. Kraus had settled in San Antonio, Texas, in 1851. He wrote a series of articles in *The Army & Navy Gazette* that attracted considerable attention. Henry Barnard, in 1867, while the first United States Commissioner of Education, realizing Kraus's familiarity with the educational thought of Germany, invited him to become a member of the Bureau of Education. Kraus contributed many articles on the nature and purposes of the kindergarten, keeping the kindergarten cause before the public. In October 1873, they established a "Model Kindergarten," which was the basis for the kindergarten training school in New York.[15] In 1877, Maria Kraus-Boelte and John Kraus wrote the *Kindergarten Guide,* which was published by Ernst Steiger of New York. They felt that the existing books did not sufficiently explain the use of Froebel's materials, thus not meeting the needs of the many partially trained kindergartners. John Kraus died in 1896, and Maria continued training kindergartners alone. She retired in 1913 and died in 1918.[16]

Other German kindergartners who had migrated to America were Matilda Kriege and her daughter Alma, who had studied with the Baroness von Marenholtz-Bülow. They went to Boston in 1868, where they stayed until 1872. Madame Kriege established a kindergarten and a kindergarten training class. She trained kindergartners while her daughter taught in the kindergarten.[17]

ELIZABETH PALMER PEABODY (1804–1894)

Elizabeth Peabody was an experienced educator before she became involved with the kindergarten. Elizabeth was also involved in the political issues of the time, abolition of slavery, and the rights of American Indians. Born in Billerica, Massachusetts, May 16, 1804, to a dentist father and a teacher and administrator mother, Elizabeth was the oldest of six children, three girls and three boys. She was taught the classics—Greek and Latin—by her father, who also taught her self-control and courage, and kindness of heart. Elizabeth was an avid reader and had a great love of beauty. She was a contemporary of Thoreau, Hawthorne, Emerson, Mann, and Melville, and was a friend of Margaret Fuller. Around 1840, Elizabeth opened a store for foreign books and a library in the family home at 13 West Street in Boston. For many years it attracted scholars and students and became the center of intellectual culture. It was here that Emerson lectured and Margaret Fuller had her conversations.[18]

Elizabeth started her teaching career in Lancaster, Massachusetts, in 1820, when she was sixteen years old. The family had moved there, and her mother established a girls' school. Mary and Sophia, Elizabeth's sisters, were among her students. Elizabeth and her sisters taught school at one time or another throughout their lives. In 1834, Elizabeth collaborated with Bronson Alcott in his Temple School, a private academy in Boston. Mary had her own school for young children on West Street. Mary married Horace Mann, and Sophia married Nathaniel Hawthorne.[19]

The First American English-Speaking Kindergarten

Barnard's report on the kindergarten in his *American Journal of Education* caught Peabody's attention. Peabody met Margarethe Schurz and her daughter Agatha while they were visiting Boston in 1859. Peabody was impressed by the young girl's behavior, and Mrs. Schurz told Peabody that she had been educated at her kindergarten, which was patterned after the philosophy and methods of Froebel, and offered to send Peabody a copy of Froebel's *The Education of Man*, but Mrs. Schurz sent only the introduction. On the basis of her conversations with Margarethe and her reading, Peabody opened a kindergarten at 15 Pinkney Street on Boston's Beacon Hill in 1860. It had 30 pupils, two assistants, a French teacher, and a gym teacher. It was the first English-speaking kindergarten.[20]

Peabody began to promote the idea of the kindergarten and to explain the differences between a kindergarten and a school. The introduction of the kindergarten in America had met with some resistance because up until that point, child-rearing ideas had come from the Evangelical Protestants. The American Froebelians had to campaign for the acceptance of the kindergarten. In November 1862, Peabody wrote an article in the *Atlantic Monthly,* "The Kindergarten—What Is It?" It became the first chapter of the *Moral Culture of Infancy and Kindergarten Guide,* which was published in 1863 by Elizabeth and her sister Mary Mann—Horace Mann's widow. *The Moral Culture of Infancy and Kindergarten Guide,* has two parts—an explanation of the kindergarten, its principles, and how to conduct a kindergarten, written by Peabody; and seven letters by Mary Mann written twenty years earlier in the midst of a practical experiment she did. The school described in these letters was trying to do something similar to what Froebel was doing: "moral culture is a twin object with physical culture."[21]

By 1866, after seven years of experience with her kindergarten, Peabody became dissatisfied realizing that she had not fully grasped Froebel's ideas. She was ready to close it, although it was popular and financially successful. She became convinced that her program was too intellectual.[22] In June 1867, Peabody left for England and traveled for fifteen months in Europe "visiting kindergartens established and taught by Froebel and his carefully prepared students." She visited "authentic" kindergartens where she observed Luise Froebel in Hamburg and Madame Marquardt at Dresden. She also encouraged German Froebelians to come to America to set up kindergartens and kindergarten training schools.[23]

Upon her return to Boston in 1868, Peabody intended to create an interest in the kindergarten by giving lectures and by starting a kindergarten and a kindergarten training school. When she found the Krieges were already there, struggling with an unprepared public, Peabody put all her energies to the cause of the kindergarten.[24] She "repudiated" her 1863 *Kindergarten Guide* and replaced it with a "corrected" new edition. In the preface, she explained the errors of the first edition, and replaced fifty of its pages. The primary change in the second edition was Peabody's opposition to teaching academic subjects to young children instead of using the child's play and properly guiding it as the basis for true learning, as Froebel intended.[25]

Peabody felt bad about her premature kindergarten efforts and took personally the responsibility for the spread in the United States of "pseudokindergartens," as she called them. To spread in the United States the true kindergarten she had seen in Germany, Peabody—sixty-four years old at this time—published the *Kindergarten Messenger,* wrote and edited books and articles on the kindergarten, toured the country and gave speeches on the educational needs of the young child, lectured the kindergartners in training, corresponded with leading educators, and tried to introduce the kindergarten into the Boston public schools.[26]

In 1867, Peabody and several other interested persons, signed a petition that they presented to the Boston School Committee asking for the establishment of kindergartens in the public schools. The Committee rejected the petition. It did not consider the kindergarten sufficiently developed. In 1870, Peabody brought again the issue before the school authorities, which resulted in the establishment of an experimental kindergarten in the Boston public schools in September 1870. A pupil of Madame Kriege was the kindergartner.[27]

In 1872, Peabody was instrumental in having the U.S. Bureau of Education publish a *Circular of Information on the Kindergarten,* for free distribution. It contains a statement written by the Baroness von Marenholz-Bülow, translated by Peabody, explaining that the foundation of Froebel's system is nature.[28]

The Kindergarten Messenger (1873–1878)

In 1873, Peabody founded and published the *Kindergarten Messenger,* a monthly independent periodical twenty-four pages long for three years. The magazine filled a need. It familiarized the kindergartners with each other, afforded communication between them, and provided practical information on kindergartening. The *Kindergarten Messenger* contained theoretical and practical articles by leading kindergartners. The June 1873 issue had an essay, "The Relation of the Kindergarten to the Primary School," by Mrs. John Ogden of Ohio, a public school teacher who became a Froebel disciple. Baroness von Marenholtz-Bülow's *Education by Labor,* translated by Mary Mann, appeared in several consecutive issues during 1875. The baroness, through her writings, played an important role in the early years of the kindergarten in America. The *Kindergarten Messenger* documented the expansion of the kindergarten movement in the 1870s.

The *Messenger* also served as a forum. Several southerners had been inquiring since its beginning about how to carry Froebel's system into the South for the education of children of all colors. One corespondent proposed that a kindergarten be organized at the Hampton Institute for the benefit of the children and to train kindergartners. Peabody, an abolitionist, advanced the cause by encouraging a philanthropic young woman from the North to take up the idea of the kindergarten in the South.[29] Several years later, kindergartens were advanced by the Negro community for the benefit of their children.[30]

Unable to financially maintain the *Kindergarten Messenger,* Peabody agreed that it should become the Kindergarten Department of the weekly *New England Journal of Education.* On January 1, 1876, Peabody became the editor of the section "Kindergarten Messenger," where she continued to advance the kindergarten. Peabody discontinued the collaboration "because the editor not only advertised but recommended editorially 'a pretension of kindergarten training that is not related to Froebel's system' and did not allow her to protest in the column that she was editor."[31] In 1877, she again started the *Kindergarten Messenger,* and in 1878, she united it with the *New Education,* edited by William N. Hailmann.

Peabody edited Froebel's *Mother-Play and Nursery Songs,*[32] translated his *Education of Man,* which appeared in several issues of the *Messenger* during 1874, and published *Lectures in the Training Schools for Kindergartners.*[33]

Interest in the kindergarten created problems. Anyone could start a kindergarten, as she had done. Peabody used the *Kindergarten Messenger* to try to stop such kindergartens. She published articles criticizing "false" kindergartens.[34]

Peabody, as the editor of the "Kindergarten Messenger" section of the *New England Journal of Education,* spent several months at the Centennial Exposition. She visited and commented on the many kindergartens, and the commercial kindergarten exhibits. Her observations were reported in a series of "Letters to the Boston Meeting of Kindergartners." Peabody praised Miss Marwedel's kindergarten,[35] and described the kindergarten attended by German and American children, and General Eaton's son. It was taught in English.[36] Peabody objected to Miss Coe naming the object-teaching school of her own planning "the American Kindergarten" as "misleading and dishonest"; Miss Coe "repudiates Froebel's materials as well as the graduated processes of work for development, and begins to instruct in reading in a way of her own."[37] Kindergarten advocates were learning that popularization involved imitations.

The American Froebel Union (1877)

In an effort to establish some accountability in the expansion of kindergartens (they were part of public, private, and charity systems), Peabody and her colleagues founded the American Froebel Union in 1877. One of the objects of the Union was to raise the standards of *qualification.* The Baroness von Marenholtz-Bülow was named honorary president. The Froebelians also wanted to give their imprimatur to a "standard library" for the profession and to protect the name of the kindergarten from being confused with methods of infant training inconsistent with Froebel's ideas and system.[38]

Peabody's Involvement with Native Americans[39]

When Peabody was eighty years old, she took up the cause of the Native Americans, especially that of the Piutes or Paiutes, a tribe of three thousand. Sarah Winnemucca, one of their leaders, had come East in 1883 to get support from the reform-minded community. The Indian agents had been exploiting the Piutes, cheating them out of their treaty-guaranteed land. Peabody had studied the language and legends of the Piutes and was against the government policy that required all the Native Americans to give up their traditional ways. Peabody was also very aware of the power exerted by the Bureau of Indian Affairs. She adopted Sarah's cause and worked hard to publicize the plight of the Native Americans. Through the contributions she solicited from her friends, Peabody helped them financially. She even wrote to President Grover Cleveland's sister asking her to intercede with him on behalf of the Piutes.[40]

Elizabeth died January 3, 1894. At her funeral the casket covered with flowers was at the front of the sanctuary. After a reading of Scriptures, the kindergarten teachers sang "Lead Kindly Light." There were eulogies. Ednah Cheney recalled anecdotes from Elizabeth's childhood, and that "she was always in perfect sympathy with children." Elizabeth was buried in Sleepy Hollow Cemetery in Concord.[41]

As a memorial to Elizabeth, her friends established the "Elizabeth Peabody House" in Boston in 1895. It included a kindergarten of about thirty children.[42]

MARY TYLER PEABODY MANN (1806–1887)[43]

Mary Tyler Peabody Mann was born in Cambridge, Massachusetts, the second daughter and second of six children of Nathaniel and Elizabeth (Palmer) Peabody. She was a sister and collaborator of Elizabeth Palmer Peabody and of Sophia Peabody Hawthorne, wife of Nathaniel Hawthorne. Her father had been a schoolteacher at the time of his marriage. Her mother continued to teach or to administer schools during much of Mary's childhood. At eighteen, Mary left home to teach in Hallowell, Maine, and then she moved to Boston, where she supported herself by helping Elizabeth teach at a "dame school" for young children in Brookline. This school soon attracted a stream of tuition-paying pupils.

In 1832, Mary and Elizabeth lived in a boardinghouse in Boston. There they met Horace Mann, a fellow lodger, lawyer, and state legislator. His wife had recently died, and he appeared distraught and inconsolable. During the years 1833–1835, Mary took her semi-invalid sister Sophia to the West Indies to rebuild her health. Mary worked as a governess for a wealthy Cuban family. Following her return from Cuba, Mary had several teaching jobs, principally in Salem. After her family moved to Boston in 1839, Mary increasingly assisted Horace Mann during the early years of his educational reforms. She copied numerous letters and recorded the school statistics that formed the basis for some of his famous *Annual Reports* as the first secretary of the newly created state board of education in Massachusetts. They were married on May 1, 1843.

After a honeymoon trip to Europe, where Mann studied European schools and philanthropic institutions, Mary reared their three sons—Horace, George Combe, and Benjamin Pickman. Mann resigned his educational post to accept a seat in Congress and became embroiled in the antislavery controversy as an opponent of Daniel Webster and the Compromise of 1850. Mary gave him her constant support.

In 1853, Horace Mann became president of Antioch College, a new nonsectarian coeducational school at Yellow Springs, Ohio. Mary moved her family West with considerable optimism. The following years, however, were disappointing. Through all this, Mary fulfilled her role as the college president's wife and unofficial dean of women, coaching the girls, who came from the farms, in the social graces and proprieties familiar to the better New England families.

After her husband's death in 1859, Mary moved the family back east to Concord, Massachusetts, where she returned to running a school and became closely associated with Elizabeth's kindergarten work. She assisted at Elizabeth's Boston kindergarten and handled much of the literary side of publicizing the new movement while Elizabeth traveled and lectured. Together they published *Moral Culture of Infancy and Kindergarten Guide* (1863), on the philosophy and methods of early education. Mary's contribution was a series of seven letters, written more than twenty years earlier, in which she stressed the importance of love in teaching young children, denied the existence of original sin, insisted that children were innately good, and declared that the process of education should be one of eliciting and nurturing certain "faculties" within the child rather than of implanting facts by means of rote recitation. Mary also assisted her sister in editing the *Kindergarten Messenger,* and translated books from the German language.

Throughout her life, Mary exhibited a remarkable degree of self-denial, accepting supporting roles to her more famous husband and sister. Mary's most important literary effort was the five-volume *Life and Works of Horace Mann* (Boston: Lee and Shepard, 1891). It is the first extended biography of the educational reformer as well as the first published collection of all his writings relating to education. She also published *Christianity in the Kitchen: A Physiological Cookbook* (1857), a collection of recipes, common-sense health rules, and admonitions against intemperance. In 1883, Mary prepared for publication the memoirs of the Indian leader Sarah Winnemucca, whose cause she and Elizabeth had embraced. At eighty she wrote a novel, *Juanita: A Romance of Real Life in Cuba Fifty Years Ago* (1887). Mary died in Boston the following year of chronic bronchitis. She was buried beside Horace Mann and his first wife in the North Burial Ground in Providence, Rhode Island.

The Kindergarten in the St. Louis
Public Schools (1872–1880)

In 1870, Peabody started corresponding with William T. Harris to interest him in early childhood education and to adopt the kindergarten into the St. Louis public schools, where he was superintendent. She offered him a German-trained kindergartner.[44] Harris was interested in the kindergarten, but not on Peabody's terms.

St. Louis was a midwestern center for commerce and manufacturing, with a large German immigrant population. The German immigrants supported neighborhood kindergartens, which later provided a base of popular support for the introduction of the kindergarten in the public schools. Under the leadership of Harris, and Susan Blow's total commitment to the advancement of the kindergarten, the kindergartens entered public education and flourished. The age of school entrance was lowered and provided a longer period of education for the urban poor children. By 1876, St. Louis provided a national model for the operation and management of kindergartens, and for training kindergarten teachers.[45]

SUSAN E. BLOW (1843–1916)[46]

Susan Blow was one of the persons who along with Harris contributed to the development of the kindergartens in the St. Louis public schools. Susan was born June 7, 1843, in Carondelet—a suburb of St. Louis, Missouri—one of three daughters and two sons of Minerva and Henry Taylor Blow. Both parents were Presbyterians. Her father was a wealthy and well-educated man, a leader in St. Louis business and political circles. He served two terms in Congress (1863–1867). Her mother was a daughter of a noted St. Louis manufacturer, a very pious woman. Susan was educated by private tutors and in private schools. She was a studious, religious, introspective child. At age sixteen, she attended Miss Henrietta Haines's school for girls in New York City for two years. As a teenager, she was considered too bookish for the social scene and too young to join the Hegelian society of St. Louis. During 1869–1870, she lived in Brazil, where her father was United States Minister (ambassador), and later she traveled to Europe, where she learned about Froebel's kindergarten and bought some of the "gifts." Despite her father's objections, Susan was looking for a challenging vocation.

Harris was interested in the kindergarten as an alternative to having young children roaming the streets. For Harris, "The kindergarten is exactly adapted to the training, by mild means, of the child of great directive power into a healthful interest in his civilization."[47] He recommended to the Board of Education that some kind of classes be established for children below the age of seven.

When Susan heard of the plan she asked Harris to let her be the teacher of the kindergarten. He agreed, provided she would prepare for the job. Susan went to New York in 1872 to study the kindergarten methods with Maria Boelte. In the spring of 1873, the first public school kindergarten opened in her Carondelet home. In the fall, it moved to a new building, known as the Des Peres kindergarten. A primary teacher and two assistants were trained in kindergarten theory and practice, by Susan.[48] The Des Peres kindergarten closed in 1935.[49]

The following year Susan Blow founded a training school for kindergartners. She followed the practice established by Froebel, to place the students immediately in the classroom as assistants in the mornings, while the afternoons were for classes in theory clarifying the morning's work. For eleven years, without pay, Susan taught, organized, administered, supervised kindergartens, and trained kindergartners. She also gave an advanced training program for kindergartners on Saturdays that included studies of Greek tragedies and other great literature.

Susan's participation in the kindergarten movement was the result of her philosophical interests and her desire for service. She saw the kindergarten as devoted both to childhood and the self-culture of young women. The kindergarten expanded rapidly after its adoption by the St. Louis public schools. St. Louis was one of several kindergarten centers from which the kindergarten movement spread across the country.

After Harris left, the board of education placed the kindergartens in 1884, under elementary grade supervisors. Considering it a change for the worse, Susan and a number of her followers resigned. Many assumed leadership positions in other parts of the country. Susan's health had began to deteriorate (1883), including her eyesight. Illness and death in her immediate family further drained her strength. After she left the kindergarten, she began to travel to recover her health. She was diagnosed with Graves' disease (1888) and sought treatment in Boston. She recovered her health (1891) and moved to Cazenovia, New York, to be near her remaining sister.

Between 1894 and 1908, Susan wrote five volumes for the International Education Series edited by William T. Harris, detailing her views. Three of the books deal with Froebel's *Mother Play*,[50] one with kindergarten issues, and the fifth is a study of Dante. Susan also wrote articles for the *Kindergarten Magazine,* and traveled and lectured extensively on kindergarten, literature, and philosophy.

Susan was a lecturer at Teachers College, Columbia University (1905–1909), where she defended Froebel's point of view. She served on the advisory committee of the International Kindergarten Union (1895–1916), and the Committee of Nineteen. She supported innovations consistent with Froebel's program such as nature study and home visits, but she opposed alteration of Froebel's sequence of gifts and occupations and the neglect of his *Mother Play.* She held rigidly to her educational views in trying to maintain the kindergarten that she had tried so hard to develop. But the world was changing around her, and new ideas about education were challenging Old World traditions and standards.

Susan died on March 26, 1916.

KINDERGARTEN AND THE CENTENNIAL EXPOSITION[51]

The year 1876 was an important year for America. It celebrated the hundred years from its founding and had a lot to show off in terms of technological and industrial progress that had been accomplished. The Philadelphia Centennial of 1876 was the first American Fair of international importance after the Exhibition of 1851 in London.

Supporters of the kindergarten in America like others before them (London, 1854), seized the opportunity of the Centennial Exposition to promote the kindergarten and to familiarize the American public with its aims and methods. They believed that the kindergarten had a mission in American life and education and that the Centennial Exposition gave them the opportunity to present this message to the American public. A model kindergarten was set up in the Women's Pavilion of the Exposition grounds and remained opened for eight months until the Exposition closed. The children, three to seven years old, were orphans. Miss Ruth Rose Burritt (1832–1921), selected to be the "Centennial kindergartner," in order to make sure that the children would attend and be appropriately dressed, lived in the institution with them.[52]

The expenses for the kindergarten were covered by contributions of many friends and supporters of the kindergarten. The salary of the teacher—$1,000— had to be solicited through editorials in the *Kindergarten Messenger*.[53]

The children were taught, before large audiences, a full day of kindergarten activities using Froebel's methods and materials (gifts and occupations) produced by the Milton Bradley company and/or imported by the Steiger Company of New York. Visitors had many opportunities to observe the children at work and play, stayed for hours, and asked questions of the teacher. However, not all public reaction was favorable. Some feared that the kindergarten would interfere with the family. One parent called it "a conspiracy to rob mothers of their little ones for the benefit of the kindergartners."[54]

The Centennial Kindergarten was described in some detail in the *Philadelphia Ledger*.[55] After the Exposition, Miss Burritt was asked to stay in Philadelphia, where she organized a kindergarten and a training school, the Centennial Kindergarten Training School of Philadelphia. The idea of the kindergarten eventually spread to all parts of the United States. Four years after the Exposition, kindergartens had been organized in thirty states.[56] The Centennial Exposition gave the kindergarten additional recognition and brought it closer to general acceptance.

THE ROLE OF TOY MANUFACTURERS AND PUBLISHERS

Toy manufacturers contributed to the popularization of the kindergarten. They capitalized on the leisure time of the developing urban middle class after 1865. They also recognized that educational supplies were a profitable new aspect of their business.

The Milton Bradley Company of Springfield, Massachusetts, and the Ernst Steiger Publishing Company of New York were among the commercial companies exhibiting at the Centennial Exhibition.

Milton Bradley

Bradley became a successful businessman during the Civil War when he was asked to produce games for the Union soldiers. He had standardized crayons, colored paper, and other school supplies. Bradley was at the height of his business career when he first encountered the kindergarten. He learned about the gifts and occupations from his neighbor Edward Wiebe, a German music teacher, who said that he had learned about them from Luise Froebel in Germany

before he migrated to the United States.[57] Bradley became a strong supporter of
the kindergarten after he met Peabody in the summer of 1869.[58] In 1871, upon
Wiebe's advice, Bradley began to manufacture Froebel's materials, believing
that there would be a demand for them. He also published a manual by Wiebe,
Paradise of Childhood, to show their use. Unknown to Bradley, it was largely a
selection from Goldammer's *Kindergarten Guide,* both in terms of the content,
and the plates, including an exact translation of the Baroness von Marenholtz-Bülow's introduction to Goldammer's work, without giving her credit.
The *Guide* was presented in Chapter 4 of this volume.[59]

At the Centennial Exposition, Bradley exhibited his blocks to his new
American audience. He made strong claims that his educational materials did
not merely entertain, they also educated. He had recognized that educational
supplies were a profitable new aspect of the children's market. The kindergarten materials at the Centennial Exposition provided an inexpensive way
for American parents to sample kindergarten education.[60]

Bradley added to the kindergarten periodical literature in 1893, by purchasing the "Kindergarten News" of Buffalo, New York, and expanding it.
He used it to spread the kindergarten and its progress. In 1897, it was
renamed "Kindergarten Review."[61]

Ernst Steiger

Steiger was a New York publisher who imported Froebel's gifts and occupations. He was encouraged by Peabody to aim his publications at a larger American readership and undertook the publication of a series of "Kindergarten
Tracts" or instructive pamphlets in English that could be used to establish
home or neighborhood kindergartens. He agreed to supply these tracts at the
fairgrounds of the Centennial Exposition free of charge. Steiger advertised in
the pages of the *Kindergarten Messenger* the availability of the kindergarten
gifts with illustrations and descriptions, and of Froebelian literature like the
Kindergarten Guide and Moral Culture of the Child by Peabody and Mann.
He published Adolph Douai's *The Kindergarten: A Manual for the Introduction of Froebel's System of Primary Education* (1872), written in both English
and German. It contained the movement plays and was intended to help teachers direct kindergartens on a large scale. One of Douai's recommendations (12)
was to use two native speakers instead of one who spoke both languages to
advance bilingualism. Although Peabody had written the introduction to
Douai's book, she took issue with the author for proposing kindergartens on
a large scale, which, she pointed out, was contrary to Froebel's ideas.[62]

FREE OR CHARITY KINDERGARTENS (1873–1893)

The industrial growth and urbanization of the United States after the Civil
War had an impact on children. Increased immigration and high birthrates

among immigrants caused concern as more and more young children from different cultural backgrounds flooded city streets.

The Depression of 1873 had wiped out the existing poor-relief system. Charity workers were looking for a new system to replace the old one. Direct contact in working with the poor in the cities was one of the new aspects.[63]

Free or charity kindergartens were organized by socially concerned, American-trained Froebelian kindergartners for the children of the poor. They wanted to save the urban child and to give him a chance to rise above the disadvantages of poverty, ignorance, and neglect. These tuition-free kindergartens provided direct relief to the children through food, clothing, and education. Advocates of charity kindergartens argued that since the child learned vice, crime, intemperance, and despair before he entered school, the child could also learn habits of personal cleanliness and neatness, courtesy to others, and proper use of language in the kindergarten.[64]

Between 1880 and 1890, there were more than one hundred free-kindergarten associations in large and small cities. In the large cities, the wives of community business leaders underwrote the expenses; in smaller cities, the work of the free-kindergarten associations was supported by subscriptions.

Their goals were the same: to pay for the salaries of the kindergartners, to buy equipment, and to rent classroom space. Some free-kindergartens were supported by philanthropic individuals like Pauline Agassiz Shaw (Mrs. Quincy A. Shaw) in Boston. Many of the kindergartens Mrs. Shaw opened were located in the public school buildings, but she paid for the entire expense. As a result of her support, the kindergartens prospered and became a power in the community. By 1883, Mrs. Shaw was supporting thirty-one kindergartens in Boston, Cambridge, and Brookline. Through her support, in 1877, a kindergarten training school was established at the Boston Normal School (1852).[65]

It was Mrs. Shaw's generosity that permitted G. Stanley Hall to conduct his study in the Boston public schools. Hall wanted to find out what children knew when they entered primary school. Mrs. Shaw provided substitutes for four of her best kindergartners so that they could be freed from teaching to participate in the investigation. The results of the study, published in *The Contents of Children's Minds on Entering the Boston Public Schools* (1893),[66] supported kindergarten education for young children.

The free-kindergarten associations gradually expanded services to the community: home visits to explain the program and to help the mother with her child-rearing responsibilities, evening classes for the fathers, and afternoon classes for the mothers. The free-kindergarten associations helped in the eventual adoption of the kindergarten into the public schools.[67]

The mother classes were so successful, and the need was so great, that some free-kindergarten associations redefined their role in the urban community. Some merged with other social agencies to form social settlements, the most famous being the Hull House in Chicago.[68]

The free-kindergarten associations formed, for the first time, the basis for a highly unified kindergarten movement and helped to further familiarize the public with the principles of the kindergarten.

KATE DOUGLAS WIGGIN (1856–1923)

Kate Douglas Wiggin was born in Philadelphia. In 1873, her family moved to California. When her stepfather died, Wiggin turned to writing and teaching to earn money. Most people know her from her book *Rebecca of Sunnybrook Farm*. She was introduced to the kindergarten by Caroline Severance, at whose Los Angeles home she boarded while attending Emma Marwedel's training class. Wiggin first went to Santa Barbara to teach kindergarten and then moved to San Francisco in 1878, when Emma Marwedel asked her to become the first teacher of the Silver Street Kindergarten. The Silver Street Kindergarten was situated in the Tar Flat slum area. Silver Street enrolled children of many ethnic and cultural backgrounds.[69]

Wiggin's writings on the kindergarten were collected in the book *Children's Rights* (1892). In it she states what society's responsibilities ought to be toward the children. She stated five basic rights to which she thought all children should be entitled and provided detailed descriptions of these rights and what mothers should do to meet them.[70]

Wiggin stated that: children should have the right to be "well born" (10), and the right to a lengthy, protected, and unhurried childhood (13). Childhood was "an eternal promise which no man ever keeps" (14). Every child should have the right to a place of his own with appropriate surroundings which have some relation to his size, desires and capabilities. Children should have the right to fair discipline. They should be taught and governed by the same laws under which they would eventually live (18). Last, children should have the right to expect examples of good behavior from their parents (22). To fulfill all these rights for their children, the mothers needed to be trained.

KINDERGARTEN IN THE PUBLIC SCHOOLS (1880–1930)

The kindergarten entered the public school system in the last twenty years of the nineteenth century, and by the 1930s, it was institutionalized. The urban reformers saw the kindergarten as a way to rescue children and their parents from poverty and ignorance and to bring them into full citizenship.

The free-kindergartners who had originally called national attention to the social evils of the urban children began to have difficulties supporting, managing, and coordinating the large numbers of new teachers, children, and kindergartens that resulted from their campaign.[71] The free-kindergarten associations lacked the financial and organizational resources to sustain their educational and charitable goals. The business aspects of the kindergarten were overwhelming.[72]

In most large cities, the campaign for public-school kindergartens followed a pattern. First the press would expose the corruption and inefficiency of the public-school system. Then the free-kindergartners, along with the municipal reformers, would contrast the ideals of the free-kindergartens with the realities of public schools. The dedicated kindergartners provided needed educational and social services to the immigrant children, while the primary teachers seemed unwilling or unable to do so. This publicity often forced municipal governments to create commissions to investigate the condition of public schools, free kindergartens, and other child-saving agencies. There were hearings and testimonies by kindergartners. As the influence of the philanthropic associations broadened, the kindergartners hoped to join the wider movement for public school reform.[73]

In some instances, philanthropic kindergartens became part of the public schools, as in the case of Boston. The persistence of Elizabeth Peabody and Mrs. Shaw brought results. In 1877, Mrs. Shaw asked the Boston School Committee to investigate the value of the kindergarten. A committee was set up that recommended its adoption. In 1888, an appropriation of twenty thousand dollars was made by the city, and fourteen operating kindergartens, with all their furniture and materials, were handed by Mrs. Shaw to the city. The kindergartens were now under the principals of the school.[74]

Between 1890 and 1910, when large numbers of non-English speaking immigrants came to the American shores, the kindergarten was seen as a vehicle to "Americanize" the immigrant children. One such supporter was Richard W. Gilder, editor of *The Century,* who saw the kindergarten as the ideal place to make "good" American citizens and to help the mothers through mother classes.[75] A distinction began to develop between the needs for early education for children from the urban slums and those from other homes. Kindergartens located in the slums were to build moral, healthy, and industrious children out of unhealthy, neglected young children.[76]

The adoption of the kindergarten in public schools was greatly increased during World War I, when the socializing function of the schools was emphasized. The kindergarten had direct contact with foreign-born families. During 1918–1919, at the height of the federal government's interest in promoting Americanization, the federal government published a circular on "Americanization through the Kindergarten." Its purpose was to disseminate information about programs and techniques, especially instruction in the English language and the duties of citizenship. It was addressed to the kindergarten teacher, kindergarten teacher trainers, kindergarten supervisors, superintendents of city schools, and to presidents of kindergarten clubs. The kindergarten teacher was seen as especially fit for promoting a sympathetic and intelligent American consciousness among the women and children of different ethnic groups in her neighborhood, by teaching English, making her classroom "a small democracy," making home visits, and holding mothers' meetings.[77]

As the kindergarten became part of the public school, changes occurred and a new bureaucracy evolved. The autonomy of the kindergarten director was eliminated. The kindergarten was now supervised by the principal. The shift in supervision reflected a shift of power from women to men in the administration of the kindergarten. The most dramatic change was the double sessions. Superintendents under pressure to accommodate larger numbers of children became concerned about the kindergarten costs. In school systems with single kindergarten sessions, teachers were required to help other teachers, or work with upper-grade children. Teachers no longer did home visits or mother groups, and the contact with the urban family was eliminated. In a 1915 Bureau of Education report for the 1911–1912 school year, of 867 cities reporting, 546 had double sessions of kindergartens. Kindergarten teachers and their directors opposed the double sessions. Some districts created a new staff position of "visiting teacher," which became the school social worker.[78]

The tension between preparing children for the first grade and the Froebelian notion about the child's growth and involvement in his learning that had existed since the 1870s continued and at times accelerated. Efforts to reduce the conflict between kindergarten and first grade resulted in the merging of supervision, teacher training, and curriculum for kindergarten and elementary grades in order to align their activities and to create a connection between kindergarten and first grade that would prepare five- and six-year-olds for academic work. This influenced the elementary grades to resemble the kindergarten. Some teachers found kindergarten-trained children more ready to learn than children who had not attended kindergarten; others complained about their lack of preparation.[79]

As districts included more and more kindergartens, efforts were made to bind them to the elementary grades. Before 1910, urban school systems employed the directors from the privately funded kindergarten to be their supervisors. By 1922, half of the cities said that kindergarten supervision had been merged with that of the elementary grades.[80] The Boston public schools had a separate kindergarten department and supervisor as late as 1977.

Some school reformers had hoped that the kindergarten, with its emphasis on the development of children, would influence the rigid curriculum and instruction prevailing in the elementary schools of the late nineteenth century.

The kindergarten was seen as a solution to a number of national social issues: the advancement of black Americans, the acculturation of Native Americans, the assimilation of immigrant populations and the alleviation of inner-city social problems. Educators, reformers, and politicians were drawn to the kindergarten because of its focus on children's learning through doing, learning from each other, and learning through play-gifts, occupations, songs, art, and teamwork.

HENRY BARNARD (1811–1900)[81]

No history of early education will be complete without referring to Henry Barnard. Barnard was born in Hartford, Connecticut, on January 24, 1811. He married in September 1847 and had five children. He died on July 5, 1900, in Hartford.

Barnard was sent to the local school, which he did not like because of the teacher. (Many men became teachers at that time because they had failed in other occupations.) He preferred the outdoor life and play that helped him develop a strong body and an independent mind. He wanted to see the world and planned to run away, but he did not. His father accidentally overheard Barnard's planning with one of his friends, and realized where the problem was.

For two years, Barnard attended the Monson Academy in Massachusetts, which he enjoyed very much, graduating at fourteen years of age. While at Monson, he began to acquire a passion for books. At Yale, Barnard studied Greek and Latin literature in order to understand the development of the Greek and Roman civilizations, and, more extensively, English literature. His oratorical skills were developed at Yale.

In 1835, Barnard, having completed both his college and his law studies and having one year's experience as a teacher, went to Europe for a year of travel and study. There he became familiar with the philosophy and methods of Pestalozzi. He found European education more advanced than education in America. (Horace Mann thought similarly.) Barnard returned to Hartford in 1836 more convinced than ever that all hopes for prosperity in America should be based on universal education.

Elected as a delegate to the Connecticut General Assembly (1837–1840), he introduced the *first* bill for free education and created the Connecticut Board of Common Schools, thus bringing education under state direction and control (1837). A year later, he became the secretary of the Connecticut Board of Education, which made him virtually its superintendent of schools. He established and edited the *Connecticut Common School Journal* from 1838 to 1842, in which he published several articles on Pestalozzi. In 1839, he printed for distribution among the teachers of his state a twenty-four-page monograph on *Pestalozzi, Franklin and Oberlin*.

In 1843, he was invited by some members of the Rhode Island Assembly to help with their bill for free education. He became the state superintendent of schools in Rhode Island (1843–1849), where he implemented the bill. While there, he published and distributed among teachers more than sixteen thousand pamphlets about education and established twenty-nine libraries with more than five hundred volumes in each.

He returned to Connecticut as principal of the state normal school and superintendent of common schools (1850–1854). The governor of Connecticut commissioned Barnard as a delegate to the International Exposition of Educational Methods in London in 1854. He visited all the sections of the Exposition, and there for the first time, he saw an actual kindergarten in operation. A model kindergarten was taught by Mme. Bertha Ronge, who was putting into practice Froebel's theories, theories that Barnard had long advocated for American schools. Deeply impressed, he became a supporter and an advocate of the kindergarten. Barnard spread the idea of the kindergarten by delivering lectures about it, writing, and publishing articles in his *American Journal of Education*.

Barnard served brief terms as chancellor of the University of Wisconsin (1857–1859) and as president of St. John's College in Annapolis, Maryland (1865–1866). He was the first United States Commissioner of Education from 1867 to 1870. In a Special Report on the Organization of Public Schools in the District of Columbia submitted to the U.S. Senate in 1868, Barnard recommended

"that the lowest grade of the proposed system, the Primary School should cover the play period of the child's life," and that "the Primary School should include the institution known as the kindergarten." "As the great formative period of the human being precedes the age at which children now attend the public school, it is necessary that by some formal arrangement, public or private, the age of impression should not be lost for the best purposes, and that instruction in languages, manners, observation, and all that constitutes the early development of the human being should be begun in the proposed system; and I know of no agency so philosophical and attractive for these purposes as the Kindergarten of Froebel."[82]

Even today, the U.S. Office of Education continues to reflect the imprint of Barnard's original design: reform and promotion of education (not schools alone) through federally sponsored experimentation, research and development by scholars, and the collection and dissemination of educational statistics and information.

Barnard's American Journal of Education (1855–1882)

Barnard made his most lasting contribution to the kindergarten literature as founder and editor of the *American Journal of Education,* financing it entirely with his own resources. He published thirty-two volumes of about eight hundred pages each. Barnard drew extensively on his private library for his editorial work. The history of education and educational biography were regular features of each volume.

Through his correspondence with Elizabeth Peabody (1879), Barnard pledged to put the subject of early childhood development and training of the Froebelian kindergarten before his readers by publishing a whole volume on the subject. In 1881, he carried out his plan and issued a volume of about eight hundred pages titled *Kindergarten and Child Culture Papers: Papers on Froebel's Kindergarten, with Suggestions on Principles and Methods of Child Culture in Different Countries,* which is the most complete encyclopedia of kindergarten both in America and in Europe. The volume contains not only the literature of the kindergarten, reprinted from the *American Journal of Education* during the previous twenty-five years, but many articles especially written and translated for this volume. Peabody helped in the preparation of this volume by valuable suggestions in the range and selection of material and by her own contributions.

Barnard believed that the basic aspects of American culture were Western European in origin, and he felt obligated to transmit the best of its educational literature to his readers, thus his emphasis on the study of comparative education. He also recognized the necessity for adapting the European experience to American institutions and to the American environment.

Barnard's life spanned almost the entire nineteenth century. His contributions to the expansion, development, and improvement of education in America were manifold.

SECTION SUMMARY

Peabody and the other early Froebelians saw the kindergarten as an extension of home nurture where the child would develop into an autonomous human being through his own self-activity. The emphasis on the spiritual as well as the intellectual development of the child continued for a while in the United States. This emphasis, however, was challenged by the scientific approach that was beginning to replace the old traditions in all aspects of American life, including our approach to children. This new approach saw the schools as institutions to resocialize the child and to save society.

Wiggin was among the first advocates who articulated children's rights and parents' responsibilities toward their children, and reiterated the need for mothers to be educated.

Free or charity kindergartens were organized by socially concerned, American-trained kindergartners for the children of the poor. In their effort to save the urban child and to give him a chance to rise above the disadvantages of poverty, ignorance, and neglect, they differentiated the needs between poor and not poor children, and the kindergarten became an institution to overcome the home conditions.

One wonders if the kindergarten can be still called *kindergarten* after all the adaptations and transformations it has undergone, especially taking the spiritual development of children out of it.

KINDERGARTEN IN THE MIDWESTERN STATES

In 1938, the Association for Childhood Education (ACE) cited Illinois, Indiana, Iowa, Kentucky, Michigan, Minnesota, Missouri, Ohio, and Tennessee as comprising the midwestern states. This section provides a brief overview of the extension of the kindergarten movement to this section of the United States.

The establishment of teacher training and mothers' classes led to the expansion of the kindergarten from the East Coast to the West Coast of the United States.[83] German-born, German-trained kindergarten teacher-educators, among them Maria Kraus-Boelte and Emma Marwedel, played an important role in the expansion of kindergarten classes across the United States. They trained the first generation of indigenous American kindergarten teachers and teacher-educators. (See Figure 9.1.)

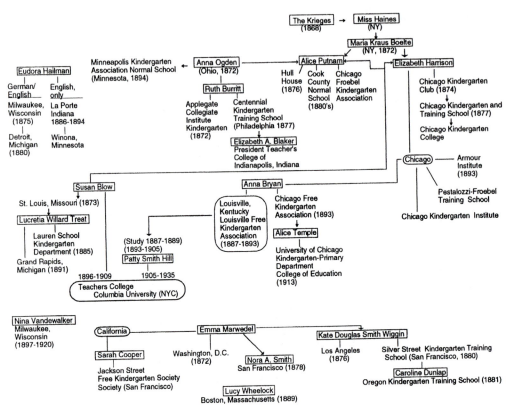

Figure 9.1 Kindergarten Teacher Education, 1850–1925.

An 1870 speech by Elizabeth Peabody on the topic of "The Genuine Kindergarten" inspired the Chicago Women's Club to sponsor a free kindergarten. This led to the 1874 founding by Alice Putnam of the first kindergarten in the city. Putnam later established the Chicago Froebel Kindergarten Association, its kindergartens, and its training school (which she conducted through the early 1900s). The Chicago Froebel Kindergarten Association training school has been called "the pioneer training school of the West." Putnam moved her training classes to the Cook County Normal School and in 1898 to the newly acquired building of Hull House. Her acceptance of Jane Addams's invitation enabled the residents to afford the cost of the new property.[84]

Elizabeth Harrison began her preparation for kindergarten work with Mrs. Putnam in 1879. In 1883, Harrison became the president of the Chicago Kindergarten Club, which met monthly to discuss educational problems and listen to cultural and educational addresses. The membership included the Froebel and Free Kindergarten Association teachers, as well as other teachers of young children.[85] Another graduate of the Free Kindergarten Association of Chicago, Anna Bryan (1887), was responsible for the development of the

Free Kindergarten Association of Louisville, Kentucky. Under Bryan's auspices, Patty Smith Hill became a kindergartner, and later a teacher-educator.

When Bryan returned to Chicago as a faculty member in 1893, Alice Temple was her student. Temple continued Bryan's work, first at the Chicago Free Kindergarten Association, and later as head of the kindergarten-primary department at the University of Chicago. There is a direct line from the German kindergarten teacher-educators to the earliest American kindergarten teacher-educators, and through them, to their students. All of the later generations of kindergarten teachers and teacher-educators in the Midwest can trace their curricula and methodology to these pioneers of kindergarten education.[86]

Kindergartens entered the Illinois public schools in a roundabout manner. In the 1880s and 1890s kindergartens sponsored by the Free Kindergarten Associations (18), the Froebel Kindergarten Association, and the Chicago Kindergarten College occupied rooms in public school buildings (19). It was not until 1892 (in Chicago) and 1907 (in Peoria) (20) that the Board of Education took over sponsorship of the kindergarten programs. In 1895, the state of Illinois passed a law permitting the establishment of kindergartens in public schools (22). Although Chicago and a handful of other cities and towns actively encouraged the establishment of public school kindergartens, smaller towns moved more slowly.[87]

The first "public Kindergarten for Colored Children" was opened in 1879. By 1938, there were "31 Kindergartens for Colored Children, successfully directed by Colored Women, graduates of the St. Louis Kindergarten Normal."[88]

Two of the earliest employer-sponsored early childhood education programs were kindergarten programs. In 1883, the San Francisco Produce Exchange Free Kindergarten was opened to "assist in rescuing children from poverty and vice." Members of the Exchange contributed seventy dollars each and other businesses donated goods and services to the free kindergartens in San Francisco. In later years, other business and professional groups pledged funds to the Exchange to support the opening of new kindergartens around the state of California. In 1892, the Colorado Fuel and Iron Company operated a kindergarten in one of their mining camps. The reason cited for the operation of the kindergarten was "to help improve and strengthen the family. Generally, owners believed that if the family was happy, workers would be more productive." Mills in Illinois, Michigan, Georgia, and South Carolina also operated free kindergartens for their employees.[89]

Milwaukee, Wisconsin, was one of the first cities in the United States to make kindergarten a part of its public school system (in 1880) (26). The Froebel Union was organized along with the public kindergartens (26). Nina Vandewalker directed the Kindergarten Department of the Milwaukee Normal School from 1897 until her appointment as the kindergarten specialist in the U.S. Bureau of Education in 1920 (26). Public school kindergartens came later (1893) to Madison, Wisconsin, home of the main State University campus (27). Wisconsin enacted "The Mandatory-on-Petition Law" (1919), which mandated the establishment of a kindergarten if parents of twenty-five children five years of age petitioned the Board of Education (24–25).[90] The states of Michigan, Minnesota, and Iowa followed a similar pattern.

In some states teacher training was a major problem. The establishment of local training schools decreased the necessity for importing teachers from the East Coast, St. Louis, or Germany. Some public school training programs later became part of a university.[91]

KINDERGARTEN IN THE WESTERN STATES

The beginnings of the kindergarten in the states of Alaska, Arizona, California, Colorado, Hawaii, Idaho, Kansas, Montana, Nebraska, Nevada, New Mexico, North and South Dakota, Oklahoma, Oregon, Texas, Utah, Washington, and Wyoming are described in a 1940 ACE publication about the western states. Selected examples of the progress of the kindergarten movement toward the Pacific Ocean are discussed below.

The first recorded California kindergarten was begun by Frau Hertha Semler (10). However, it was the influence of Elizabeth Peabody, and Felix Adler, founder of the Ethical Culture Society and School in New York City, that promoted the westward expansion of the kindergarten. Adler's lecture to prominent citizens in San Francisco hastened the organization of the Silver Street Kindergarten. Emma Marwedel organized the Froebel Educational Association of California, whose members were principals of high schools and normal schools, and city and state school superintendents (18). She joined forces with John Swett, who later became the State Superintendent of Public Instruction, to achieve passage of a law legalizing public school kindergartens in 1893 (20). Their alliance exercised the citizens' constitutional right to include in any municipal charter the educational facilities voted by the people. Marwedel also founded the California Froebel Union, which was the first early childhood professional association on the Pacific Coast, during the 1879–1880 school year (27). In later years, several "alumnae associations" of training school graduates gathered together and became the California Froebel Society. Kate Douglas Wiggin, a founder of the Society in 1883, served as its first president.[92]

Wiggin carried on the tradition of kindergarten teacher training. After consultation with Peabody, Harrison, Hailmann, and others about the course of study, she opened a training school at Silver Street during the 1880–1881 school year. She also presented her work to a broader spectrum of professionals. In an 1888 lecture to the National Conference on Charities and Correction, entitled "The Relation of the Kindergarten to Social Reform," she criticized statements about education as a panacea for reducing crime, saying it was more meaningful to speak in terms of the principles of child development. She grappled with issues that still confront us today, and foreshadowed the continuing emphasis on child development in early childhood education.

By 1897, California had passed a law providing for kindergarten departments in state normal schools, with diplomas issued for kindergarten teaching. In 1901, it strengthened the legal basis for kindergarten teaching by authorizing state and county boards of education to issue certificates to teach kindergarten classes based solely on accredited training school credentials.[93]

The influence of Susan Blow and Felix Adler was also felt in Colorado. Denver's first (private) kindergarten was begun by Eva Allen and Sally Williams, who had trained with Blow in St. Louis (29–30). The Free Kindergarten Association established philanthropic kindergartens during the 1880s. In 1893, five private kindergartens were taken over by the Board of Education, forming the beginning of the public school kindergarten program (36). The State Normal School at Greeley (1892) (31) and the Denver Normal and Preparatory School (1894) (30) offered kindergarten training.[94]

The first Oregon Kindergarten Training School was opened by Wiggin's student Caroline Dunlap. It became a branch of Wiggin's school in 1885, four years after its founding. In 1887, the first kindergarten law in Oregon made it possible for any school district with five hundred inhabitants to establish and maintain kindergartens as part of common schools. In both Oregon and Washington, a number of kindergartens were opened during the late 1890s. Western Washington and Eastern Washington Colleges of Education instituted kindergartens in their laboratory schools.[95]

Our fiftieth state had its kindergarten pioneers too. Many early kindergartens in Hawaii were sponsored by the Women's Board of Missions for the Pacific Islands. The work was supported by private subscription and donation. Frank Damon is credited with starting the first Hawaiian kindergarten in 1892. Among the original fifty-seven students were two girls with bound feet who were carried back and forth by their fathers. Alma Bixby began a kindergarten in Fairbanks, Alaska, in 1919. Two years later, public kindergartens were established in Juno.[96]

The kindergarten movement on the West Coast took a leadership role in developing programs for younger children. The Golden Gate Kindergarten Association had taken children as young as two years of age into its program since 1878. It was not until 1926 that the kindergartens were replaced with nursery schools for younger children only.[97]

The development of the kindergarten in the western half of the United States followed a pattern similar to that in the East. Private and philanthropic kindergartens were usually the first to open. They were followed immediately by teacher training courses taught by both German- and American-trained teachers. Later, kindergartens were added to the public schools; however, expansion was slowed by monetary costs and crowded conditions in schools. Laws regarding state support of kindergarten classes and specialized training and certification for the teachers were passed. The kindergarten movement, borne by kindergartners who believed in the philosophy, the program, and the ideals of Froebel, unified the education of young children during late 1800s and early 1900s.[98]

PATTY SMITH HILL (1868–1946)

Patty Smith Hill was born on March 27, 1868, and raised at Bellewood Female Seminary, the school for young women founded and headed by her father, Dr. William Wallace Hill, in Anchorage, Kentucky. Dr. Hill was an advocate of independent women, encouraging his six children, and his students, to prepare for a career. Patty's mother, Martha Jane Smith Hill, was college-educated, a most unusual status for a woman of the pre–Civil War era. Martha Jane Smith's experience of being unable to matriculate at Center College with her brother, and having to be separately tutored, must have influenced the opening of Bellewood Seminary.[99]

Mrs. Hill provided her children with indoor and outdoor play areas, including a carpentry shop, a henhouse, and a playground equipped with large boards, blocks, and empty barrels. The family lived in three different states during Patty's childhood, as her father presided over two colleges, and then passed away. The family's love of and respect for learning, and the constantly changing financial situation, left a lasting impression.

Both parents' beliefs in education for women led Patty to higher education. In fact, Dr. Hill made the statement, "It's a tragedy for women to marry for a home. Don't live with law kin! Don't even if you have to live in a hollow tree!"[100] Patty received a solid classical education at the Louisville Collegiate Institute. Immediately following her 1887 graduation, she became one of the first five students in Anna E. Bryan's newly organized training department of the Louisville Free Kindergarten Association (LFKA). The LFKA was one of the philanthropic efforts of the Holcomb Mission. Steve Holcomb, a reformed riverboat gambler, had provided money to convert the residents of urban slums to Christianity and Americanism.[101] One of the female volunteers at the mission had heard about the new kindergarten movement. She suggested that this would be an appropriate place for children too young to learn how to sew in the industrial training school of the mission.

Hill recalled that friends had contacted her to share the announcement of the training school opening. She and her mother visited Anna Bryan and tendered an invitation to dinner with the family. "Before the end of the evening, there was no question in the minds of all those who had had the opportunity of meeting Miss Bryan that it was going to be a rare opportunity to place a member of the family in her care and training."[102] Following the completion of her initial training, in February 1889, Hill was asked by Bryan to head the association's lead kindergarten.[103]

Hill continued her professional development by attending courses and workshops with her mentor and colleague, Bryan. Upon her return to Louisville following a summer of study and collaboration with G. Stanley Hall, Hill integrated her new learnings into the curriculum and methods used in her kindergarten program. The first demonstration of her innovative use of materials came as the accompaniment to Anna Bryan's 1890 address to the

National Education Association. In "The Letter Killeth," Bryan challenged the prescribed mathematical sequence used in working with Froebel's gifts. Hill presented her original activity in which the children in the Holcomb Mission demonstration kindergarten made furniture for paper dolls and other creations with the small blocks."[104]

In 1893, Patty Smith Hill became the director of the Louisville Free Kindergarten Association and began her twelve years of supervisory leadership. Hill's kindergarten philosophy was one of inclusion. The LFKA program was aimed at children from different environmental conditions; races; and physical, social, and intellectual status, especially those from "wretched and degraded homes on the other side of the tracks."[105] Sanitation and health issues were of as much concern to the kindergartners as educational issues.

Hill's curriculum development initiatives began during her days as a kindergarten teacher in Louisville, and continued during her tenure as supervisor and director of the program. According to Fowlkes, Hill claimed that reading a Dewey monograph and studying with Dewey influenced her view of creativity in children's artwork, the movement toward free play rather than the structured work of the U.S. Froebelians, and her approach to music. She

Figure 9.2 Older children in kindergarten make their own toys with tools and wood (1898). Louisville Kindergarten of Patty Smith Hill, ca. 1900, #p.7. *Courtesy of the Special Collections, Milbank Memorial Library, Teachers College, Columbia University.*

gave up many of the traditional practices, on the principle that teaching involved creative thinking. She also fostered an increasing emphasis on play in the kindergarten, beginning with her 1887 graduation address, on the theme "Deep Meaning Lies in Childish Play."[106]

At the beginning of the nineteenth century, Patty Smith Hill, under the influence of the Northern Presbyterian Church, inaugurated a kindergarten for black children in which Finnie Burton and other teachers from the demonstration kindergarten were involved. The Louisville Education Association "invited the Louisville Colored Kindergarten Association (LCKA) to become a branch of the Association."[107] The public schools in Louisville began providing classroom space for both black and white kindergartens in the same building. Mary Hill (Patty's sister) was a kindergarten teacher in the school, and Francis Ingram, who had been trained by Colonel Parker in Chicago, taught first grade. Ingram enrolled in Hill's child psychology courses, and together Ingram and the Hill sisters began to devise ways to integrate kindergarten and first grade. Temple, Dewey, and Parker were doing the same thing in Chicago.[108]

Patty Smith Hill was an early childhood teacher-educator for most of her professional life. She began her supervision of the training department of the Louisville Free Kindergarten Association with the model of apprenticeship she herself had followed. Young women were offered internship teaching positions to prepare them for assuming sole responsibility for a kindergarten classroom. Courses and workshops for in-service teachers were also provided.

The LFKA's exhibit at the 1904 St. Louis World's Fair, in Susan Blow's hometown, was critiqued by the strict Froebelians. Miss Hill, designer of the exhibit, claimed that classroom activities should be interesting to the children, have authentic value for the children, and take place in a democratic classroom setting. Children were encouraged to interact with their classmates and utilize personal initiative.[109] This was the beginning of the debate between the conservative and progressive factions in the kindergarten movement, which continued at Teachers College.

In 1905, Dean Russell of Teachers College, Columbia University in New York City invited Hill to participate in a lecture series with Susan Blow. With Hill's admission to the faculty (1905), the debate continued both in the halls of Teachers College and on the platform of the IKU. As a member of the faculty, Hill was influenced by such notables of education as Dewey, Kilpatrick, and Thorndike. She earned rapid promotions, which, according to Weber, was unusual for a woman, reaching full professor in 1922. Hill learned how to work in the male-dominated environment. She became very proficient in her own area of expertise, and turned to others for support when the foundational work had been done. In 1910, she became head of the Department of Nursery School, Kindergarten and First-Grade Education, adding a second post as director of the Institute for Child Welfare Research (later known as the Institute for Child Development) with its related nursery school, in 1921.[110] Toward the end of her tenure at Teachers College, Hill worked with the Federal Emergency Nursery Schools.

After her retirement (1935), she was involved in the first project undertaken by New College in the Manhattanville neighborhood surrounding the college. Hill arranged for the kindergarten for four-year-olds to be housed in the old Jewish Theological Seminary building. The Community Organization for Cooperative Education Incorporated (COCE) was founded to provide leadership among all the adults of Manhattanville. Hill also provided the funding for a campsite run by the COCE outside of New York City. She continued her active involvement in the profession by providing scholarships for German and Norwegian teachers to study in American universities and by participating in organizations until her death on May 26, 1946, in New York City. Her remains were buried at Cave Hill Cemetery in Louisville, Kentucky. Patty Smith Hill's papers are housed at the Filson Club (the Historical Society) in Louisville, Kentucky.[111]

The Work of Patty Smith Hill and the Publications of Patty Smith Hill

Hill's curriculum development initiatives began in the Louisville kindergartens. Reading William James's 1887 paper, "Habits," in the *Atlantic Monthly* apparently influenced her later design of a Habit Inventory based on observation of kindergarten children at play.[112] Stimulus-response psychology and Thorndike's work formed the theoretical foundation for the development of curriculum and materials. The Habit Inventory included skills, attitudes, habits, and ideas to be inculcated by teachers through classroom activity. The child's utilization of equipment in play was studied. The work in the laboratory kindergarten formed the basis for the book, *A Conduct Curriculum for the Kindergarten and First Grade* (1923), as well as two other publications by Teachers College faculty and staff.[113] The books provide numerous examples of curriculum experiences and play materials designed by Hill and her colleagues for use in the Horace Mann kindergarten supervised by the Department of Nursery, Kindergarten and First-Grade Education. The *Conduct Curriculum* emphasizes continuous development from infancy through the primary years, and continuity in curriculum, methodology, and professional education between kindergarten and first grade.

As a founding member of the two major early childhood education organizations in the United States, Hill was present at the 1892 birth of the International Kindergarten Union (IKU), and served on its Committee of Nineteen for the decade beginning in 1903. For fifty years, Hill served on numerous IKU and ACEI committees, spoke eloquently at national conferences, and wrote for the organizations' publications. She served as vice president and president of the IKU. Hill founded the National Association of Nursery Educators (NANE), by gathering a group of twenty-five nursery school and parent educators and psychologists in New York City in 1925.[114] Hill published a wide range of articles and books on topics including all areas of the early childhood education curriculum, application of philosophical principles to

Figure 9.3 Using the "Patty Smith Hill" blocks. Lincoln School, Teachers College, Columbia University, Summer Demonstration School, 1938, #TC/09, no. 13. *Courtesy of the Special Collections, Milbank Memorial Library, Teachers College, Columbia University.*

practice, experimental research in kindergarten and nursery education, the function of the kindergarten, and the education of nursery school teachers.

Patty and Mildred Hill wrote the song "Happy Birthday to You," which was published in their book *Song Stories for Children,* in 1899. When Patty won her lawsuit against the illegal use of the song in a Broadway play, she used the money received to establish nursery schools and kindergartens in New York City housing projects, where they were sorely needed. In the fall of 1996, the Hill Foundation, following Patty's instructions for future use of the money generated by the song, named ACEI the remainder beneficiary of the Hill estate.[115] This act perpetuates Patty Smith Hill's memory as a humanitarian.

The International Kindergarten Union (IKU) Committee of Nineteen (1903–1912)

Patty Smith Hill was one of the original members of the Committee of Fifteen appointed by the IKU in Pittsburgh, Pennsylvania, in April 1903. The Committee membership was expanded to nineteen, and called to order at the IKU meeting in Rochester, New York, in 1904 by chair Lucy Wheelock. The Committee met eleven times between 1904 and 1911. They considered plans of kindergarten work, methods and materials, psychology, and symbolism.[116]

Their debate, based on essential differences in the interpretation of Froebel's theory, culminated in three Committee reports.[117] The conservative report was written by Susan Blow, the liberal by Nina Vandewalker, and the conservative-liberal by Lucy Wheelock. The final report, presented at the IKU Cincinnati meeting in April 1910, contained chapters divided into sections, including: a statement of type of program, principles underlying program making, process of program making, and concrete illustrations. At the meeting, Blow presented the conservative report, Hill the liberal report, and Elizabeth Harrison the liberal-conservative report. Following review by an advisory committee, the reports were published. The 230-page conservative report (1–230), authored by Blow, is considered to be the last published report of the "Unified Program." The sixty-one-page report of the progressive subcommittee, entitled "The Principles Underlying the Selection and Organization of the Subject-Matter of the Kindergarten Program" (231–275) and "Illustrations in Practice." (276–294) was written by Hill. The short, compromise, third report was penned by Harrison (295–301).

Hill's report conceptualizes the kindergarten program as a flexible plan of action that includes the child's aims and purposes, as well as those of the teacher. It allows the teacher to select and organize "those native activities, interests, and experiences common to all children together with the subject-matter which feeds them."[118] She states that the kindergarten program is based upon the experiences of children, and that therefore they should be studied in order to discover the appropriate methods to be used. Her report expresses the liberal viewpoint that the psychological and sociological aspects of kindergarten program cannot be separated, with the sociological aspects developing social consciousness and readiness for social service in children. Hill represents the recapitulation viewpoint, in which the child is said, through education, to engage in a process by which he both "achieves and inherits the experience of the race."[119]

According to Hill, the four inalienable rights of the child are:

(a) the right to express his own ideas and experiences in order to have them rectified, interpreted or utilized for the development of himself and for the social group; (b) the right to have his own limited, narrow, and personal experience extended through those contributed by other children in the group; (c) the right to participate in the wider experience and vision of the teacher; (d) the right to come into direct contact with the experience of the race as embodied or preserved in its literature, arts, songs, games, industries, laws, and institutions.[120]

Hill's report discussed the organization of subject matter and materials into a curriculum, principles of democracy applied to the relations between teachers and children, and supervising officers and teachers. It described the teacher as a mediator between the self-activity of the child and the material of the curriculum, and as a social agent who preserves the best of the past and guides the child toward contributing his share in creating a nobler civilization in the future.

The introduction to the report volume includes a fable from Maria Kraus-Boelte describing a father and three sons whom he loved equally well. Before he died, the father gave a ring to each of the sons. When the sons approached a judge for a decision on which was the original ring, he told them that the true ring is said to have the magic power of making the owner beloved and esteemed by God and man. Since each son believed his ring to be the genuine one, each was directed to live a peaceful, charitable life, because the true ring would reveal itself only in later generations.[121] By including this fable in the introduction, Annie Laws highlights the difficulty members of the Committee, and of the IKU, had in choosing one position over the other. The controversy continued for a number of years.[122]

Patty Smith Hill's Contribution to Early Childhood Practice

Hill developed a large block set in an 1898 summer course with Dr. Luther Gulick, the father of the playground movement. Following twelve to fourteen years of experimentation, the Schoenhut Company produced these blocks, which were used in the Teachers College schools. Cuffaro states that the first Hill floor blocks were probably derived from the enlargement of Froebel's small gift blocks by Anna Bryan in Louisville. From her work with Bryan, Hill decided that larger blocks were more appropriate for children's gross motor development.[123]

The set of maple wood blocks Hill designed consisted of seven shapes based on a six-inch unit. The smallest block was $3" \times 3" \times 1"$, and the largest was $36" \times 3" \times 1.25"$. There were seven shapes in the original set, complemented by grooved corner blocks in heights of $15"$ to $27"$. The rectangular blocks would fit into the grooved corner blocks, and be stabilized through the use of pegs, copper wire rods, and girders. The deep grooves in the pillars permitted high buildings to be constructed, and the pillars would hold the blocks together at both ends. When children first started to build, they needed to be taught to fasten the blocks together with the girders at every intersection so that the blocks would not fall.[124] The size of the blocks communicated to children the scale in which they were to work, and the collaborative effort required.[125] Thus the children could build houses and stores large enough to get inside and sturdy enough so that they would not tumble down or the roofs cave in.[126] Children at the Horace Mann kindergarten produced a railroad train large enough to ride on and a wagon to substitute for the permanent large wagons often included as kindergarten equipment.[127] The first two kindergarten groups used the blocks in individual play by piling, placing them lengthwise, sliding, and making products that were named. Children in group III were self-organized into a cooperative group with a specified leader. Their constructions had a definite purpose, which was usually planned prior to starting the building. The first-grade children extended and elaborated block use in their dramatic play. The blocks were a popular choice for teacher-initiated projects related to community workers, families, and transportation.[128]

Hill's floor blocks met the criteria for play equipment that she stated in the introduction to *Permanent Play Materials for Young Children*. The first criterion was that materials must stimulate self-activity leading the child to invention, originality, ingenuity, and industry. The materials must develop the attitude of a creator and participator rather than that of a spectator. Hill's second criterion is that the materials must reach the child on his own level of maturity, be adapted to his ability to handle and manipulate them with success, to his level of interest, and to his powers of organization. Hill's third criterion was that play materials should not violate any principles of aesthetics or art, and should conform to standards of line, proportion, and color. The fourth standard stated that materials should represent good workmanship, which would allow them to stand the normal wear and tear of unskilled hands in the process of learning control. The fifth criterion stated that materials should be easily cleansed or disinfected and free from unsanitary tendencies in social play. They should be large enough to call into play the larger muscle groups and large enough to eliminate eyestrain or handstrain. The sixth criterion stated that materials must allow the child to work alone, with little or no guidance from adults, and with or without the cooperation of his playmates.[129] Published verbal descriptions, photographs, drawings, diagrams, and reprints of catalog pages prove that the Hill floor blocks demonstrate each of these six criteria.

Confirmation of Hill's influence on Caroline Pratt comes from a section in *I Learn from Children*. Pratt states,

> I have seen children playing with blocks at Teachers' College, when the gifted Patty Hill had charge of the kindergarten there. She had designed the blocks herself, for the children in her classes to use during their free periods. They were not a part of her teaching program, but I had watched what the children had done with them during those short play periods when they could do what they liked. . . . [O]f all the materials which I had seen offered to children ("thrust upon" would better fit the situation), these blocks of Patty Hill's seemed to me best suited to children's purposes. A simple geometrical shape could become any number of things to a child. It could be a truck or a boat or the car of a train. He could build buildings with it, from barns to skyscrapers. I could see the children of my as yet unborn school constructing a complete community with blocks.[130]

The design of the Hill blocks, the Hill-Hart chairs, and much of the dramatic play equipment was based on scientific observation of children at play.[131]

The skill children demonstrated in handling blocks, their ability to work cooperatively, and the understanding they demonstrated in enacting family and occupational roles became behaviors to be observed, measured, and shaped with scientific accuracy. The shift in Hill's philosophy demonstrates the influence of her Teachers College colleagues, Thorndike, Dewey, and Kilpatrick. This focus is reflected in the writing she did during her tenure on the college faculty, recounting work sponsored by the Department of Nursery-Kindergarten-Primary Education and work in the Speyer and Horace Mann Schools. Hill adopted Kilpatrick's statement that nothing has been learned until it has been made over into an actual way of behaving.[132]

In 1905, Luella A. Palmer, a graduate student at Teachers College, developed the first curriculum for her group of three- to six-year-old children at Speyer School. It formed a foundation for later experiments. According to Hill, this was one of the earliest attempts to apply the principles of democracy to school organization. The teacher in the Speyer kindergarten was considered to be a wiser, more experienced member of the social group. Her knowledge and technique were "to be at the disposal of the children, when she or they felt the need of adult direction."[133]

Hill's second experiment, ten years later, was done at the Horace Mann School with the children of the faculty, trustees, and others in the higher income brackets. The teachers, Agnes Burke, Edith Conrad, Alice Dalgliesh, Charlotte Garrison, Edna Hughes, Mary Rankin, and Alice Thorn, were trained to observe and record what the children did and their resulting achievements. The curriculum of the kindergarten and first grade was gradually transformed to apply the principles of habit formation to all the school subjects. Instead of specifying a story, song, or game, the *Conduct Curriculum* stated when the song or story should be listened to or the song sung, and told which objective, if attained, would lead to the changes in thought, feeling, and conduct.

The children were to use the available materials to carry out problems of their own design, and then they were to respond to the stimuli provided by the group of children or by the teacher. Each child was to follow Kilpatrick's suggestions of focusing, planning, carrying out, and judging the result of the problem-solving. The subject matter of the curriculum was to be supplied by both the children and the teacher. Some portions of the curriculum came from tradition, for example, holidays and activities that recur each year.

The teacher designed an environment that would bring out the desired responses in the children. She was to raise the standards of work step by step by providing help and guidance. The teacher's observations of the children's achievement fell under the following categories: "the ability to initiate purposes and plans, to persevere at a job despite difficulties, to lead and follow intelligently, to work alone or in a group, to know when one needs help and how to secure that help, and the ability to give fair criticism and to profit by it."[134]

When the *Conduct Curriculum* was introduced, Hill was already preoccupied with a new interest, the nursery school.[135] Hill's contribution to the development of the *Conduct Curriculum* was the integration of theory and practice as an interrelated whole. Her major contributions to early childhood education were: a belief in learning through play, her devotion to continuity between kindergarten and first grade, her stress on parent involvement, her emphasis on careful observation for assessment of young children, and her advocacy of a creative approach to art and music experiences. Hill adapted her curricula to variations in environment, and developmental differences in children. Hill's support of teachers was legendary. Patty Smith Hill, a pioneer in the progressive education movement, was an early childhood teacher educator of note. She is best remembered for her devotion to community service and child advocacy.

ALICE B. TEMPLE (1866–1946)

Alice Temple was born in Chicago, Illinois, on March 1, 1866. She grew up, went to school, and worked all of her life in Chicago. A letter by her niece, Mrs. William L. Chenery, states that the Chicago of 1889, when Alice graduated from high school, was a smaller and simpler city than in the 1960s.[136] Although she had grown up in relatively comfortable circumstances, she had observed the poverty of the slums and the working people in her father's factory.

At the age of eighteen, Alice Temple made the obvious choice for a woman who had a natural liking for children,[137] and entered initial teacher training at the Chicago Free Kindergarten Association. She was a student, and later a colleague of Anna Bryan. In 1904, she resigned from her teaching position to become a full-time student at the University of Chicago. Later, she taught in the Department of Kindergarten Education, and, in 1909, became the director of the department. In 1913, Temple organized the University Kindergarten-Primary Department in the College of Education. For more than ten years, Temple and Dean Samuel Chester Parker studied the kindergarten and first-grade classes in the university elementary school. This investigation led to their later publications regarding a unified kindergarten–first-grade curriculum. As a result of her studies with John Dewey and her work in the University of Chicago Laboratory School, Temple became a member of the progressive wing of the kindergarten movement.[138] The Kindergarten-Primary Department began a three- and later four-year course leading to a bachelor's degree in teaching. There was also a graduate program to prepare training teachers and supervisors. Her work at the university led to her survey of the Richmond, Indiana, kindergartens, later published by the University of Chicago Press.

Temple became a member of the IKU in 1900, and remained a member of the IKU and Association for Childhood Education (ACE) until her death. At the 1900 meeting of the IKU, Temple discussed the usefulness of the Froebelian gifts and occupations. She found the blocks, used for building, the most satisfactory, because they involved the child in repetition, imitation, making and unmaking, construction, and creation. Her approach, however, was eclectic, as exemplified by the inclusion of larger, heavier building blocks, dolls and a playhouse, toy animals and utensils, and tools in the kindergarten classroom. She praised those "occupations" that permitted children the most independence, for example, clay and sand modeling, free drawing, cutting, painting, and work with paper, scissors, and paste.[139]

Temple served on a number of IKU and ACE committees, including the Committee for Cooperation with the National Education Association (NEA), and its successor, the Council of Supervisors and Training Teachers. She was a member of the national board of the IKU, and presided over the organization between 1925 and 1927.

She served on the editorial board of *Childhood Education* from 1924 through 1943. Among the articles she contributed were those dealing with the administration and supervision of student teaching, the child's social understanding, and the history of the kindergarten in America. She chaired the Committee on Book Reviews between 1928 and 1943.

As a result of her organization work, Temple was well aware of the ferment in kindergarten and first-grade program development. The relationship between kindergarten and the primary grades was one of the most frequently discussed issues at the annual meeting of the NEA Kindergarten Department. By 1926, the Kindergarten Department of the NEA had become the Kindergarten-Primary Department.[140]

Temple pioneered both kindergarten-primary curriculum and kindergarten-primary teacher education through her curriculum work in the University of Chicago elementary school and her work with students in the School of Education. Her 1925 co-authored book, *Unified Kindergarten and First-Grade Teaching*, served as a blueprint for the initiation of kindergarten-primary curricula around the United States. Based on eleven years of practical work, the book proposed to assist kindergarten and first-grade teachers, school superintendents, and supervisors in coordinating pupil activities in the kindergarten and the first grade, demonstrating that there was no break between the two grades in either curriculum or methods. The authors discuss types of learning, detail pupil activities incorporating provision for individual differences, and describe problem-solving and project teaching.

The discussion of the extension of kindergarten activities into first grade, in the chapter on history of unification, cites three influences of the kindergarten on first grade. They are: "(1) a change in the general spirit of the work so as to make it more active and playful; (2) modification in the teaching of some of the standard first-grade subjects, such as music, which had been added to some of the old-fashioned American first grades during the nineteenth century; and (3) the introduction of new subjects, such as handwork and games."[141] Some of the influences of the first grade on the kindergarten were: the inclusion of arithmetic content in the handwork and games of the kindergarten, and the inclusion of beginning reading for those children in kindergarten who are mentally capable of making easy progress with it.[142]

The conceptions of problem-solving and project teaching articulated by Parker and Temple have remained with us to the present day. The authors caution teachers to avoid confusing project teaching and motivation. They define motivation as "well-defined pupil purposes and whole-hearted interests," and project teaching as "the contriving, devising, and planning by the pupil of some practical activity—something to be done."[143]

The work and publications of Parker, Temple, and Hill served as models for those kindergarten and first-grade teachers, and administrators and supervisors, who wished to adopt kindergarten-primary education. The principles of unified kindergarten-primary education, improvement in behavior, and working through pupils' interests are as essential for older children as they are in the lower grades. Davis states that kindergarten activities should contain the beginnings of all the elementary school activities, and that kindergarten preparation will assist children in understanding the subject matter of the primary grades. The teacher is challenged to fit the program of work to the children's interests and abilities, and to relate her work to that in other grades. In addition, the teacher is asked to build an atmosphere of growth and happiness in the classroom.[144]

By 1926, knowledge of the effective ways by which children learn and the desirable changes in their thinking and modes of behavior had become important in planning kindergarten and primary curricula. There was a shift from emphasis upon subject matter to emphasis on child development. This shift was anticipated by the record-keeping movement in kindergarten education and the experimental work carried out in some public and private schools. The kindergarten movement influenced increased interest in character education and the encouragement of children's creative expression. The integration of school subjects around "activities" influenced the physical environment of the classroom. "Units of interest" in courses of study required "units of interest" in classroom arrangement, and particular apparatus and equipment present in the classroom.[145]

First-grade teachers' response to the work of the progressive kindergartners and their criticisms of primary-grade teaching was mixed. The kindergartners maintained that "the importance of a satisfactory elementary school experience as the key to continued participation in formal education" was based upon the continuation of kindergarten methods into first grade. Although Wesley said that it would "be difficult to overstate the effect of the kindergarten upon the reconstruction of the curriculum, . . . [and that] the kindergarten method of direct experience, self-activity, self-expression, and group cooperation spread at once into the primary grades . . . ," it took many years for the integration to occur. Nor was the task of the kindergarten progressives an easy one. In a letter to Miss Clay Franks, written in October 1939, Temple stated, "We worked hard during my presidency [of the IKU] to bring about a union with the Primary Council, but the members were not yet ready for it then." It took until 1931 for the campaign to merge the IKU with the National Council of Primary Education to be successful.[146]

Alice Temple died in New Rochelle, New York, on January 6, 1946. Temple's influence upon the unified curriculum and teacher training was extensive. Supply and demand, precedent, or modern principles of education determined whether or not a teacher training institution offered curricula for kindergarten, kindergarten-primary, or primary teachers. Temple was in the forefront of the development of the kindergarten-primary teacher education curriculum. She believed that teachers of young children needed to know what educational experiences preceded and followed the work they carried on in a specific grade.

Unified Kindergarten and First Grade Teaching states that practical teacher training for a unified curriculum should include: "(1) the subject matter she is to teach; (2) certain skills; (3) the use of many devices; (4) [and] understanding and applying the general principles of teaching."[147] Thus, Temple proposed a teacher education curriculum consisting of an introduction to the scientific and psychological study of education; general methods and types of teaching; the equipping, managing, and testing of kindergartens and first grades; and construction of kindergarten-primary curricula.[148] Alice Temple made major contributions to the unification of nursery school, kindergarten, and primary education through her teaching, work with children, and writing.

THE TRAINING OF KINDERGARTEN TEACHERS

The history of kindergarten teacher training is the story of people as well as institutions. Formal kindergarten teacher training in the United States was initiated by German-trained women. The early kindergartens had attached training departments. Their graduates later became the supervisors and trainers of other "kindergartners." The popular literature of the early 1800s, and the advent of improved printing processes after 1830, led to "the publications of cheap books, newspapers, and periodicals for mass consumption, vastly expanding readership and providing new opportunities for writers. For the first time, large numbers of talented women took up publication."[149]

Thompson discusses the role of ladies' magazines and other publications for women in preparing female teachers of young children. In a thoroughly practical way, the editors of the ladies' magazines promoted teaching as a desirable employment for a young lady. The women editors reported on the National Popular Education Association, which was formed for the purpose of sending female teachers from the eastern states to the West and southwestern United States. While the training of teachers under private auspices was deemed desirable, the editors believed that teachers for the public schools should be trained at public expense. As early as 1829, Mrs. [Sarah] Hale wrote about her "'favorite project,' the desirability of young ladies preparing themselves to be teachers."[150] The value of preparation for teaching had long been appreciated.

Another aspect of the education of teachers was the training of teachers-in-service, through books and magazines for teachers and through teachers' institutes and conventions. These phases of professional education were presented in the magazines for ladies and the literary periodicals. Although these publications described and participated in the movement to secure trained teachers, and to provide in-service training for teachers, some of the writers were frank in exposing what they deemed to be the defects of contemporary education, while others showed a rare understanding of the work and the aims of teachers.[151]

The Beginnings of Kindergarten Teacher Education in the United States

After the Civil War, beginning in approximately 1868, German-trained kindergarten instructors came to the United States. Support for German kindergarten training came from within and outside of the kindergarten movement. Catherine Beecher, a domestic reformer, felt that "the rigor of German kindergarten methods and training could help restore dignity to domestic science and thus enhance women's role." She postulated a "Women's University," that would include kindergarten, primary school, preparatory school, college, and professional school. This institution would embrace "the whole course of woman's training from infancy to a self-supporting profession."[152]

In the early 1870s, most women were more content with the twenty-six-week training program initiated by Mathilda Kriege and her daughter. When the Krieges felt that six months training was too abbreviated, they returned to Berlin for additional education in 1867, and in 1868, they opened a training school and kindergarten at Miss Haines' Private School in New York City. Susan Blow convinced Maria Boelte to personally train her, in 1872. Following her marriage to Professor Kraus, Maria and her husband opened the New York Seminary for Kindergartners. They hoped to attract female academy students and recent immigrants from overseas. The program included one year of course work and one year of practice teaching. A model kindergarten was opened on the seminary premises, as was the case at many of the training institutions of the time.

Individual women, with either their own funds or the support of others, began to open kindergarten training classes around the country. The number of trained "kindergartners" multiplied, due to this series of individual efforts. As shown in Figure 9.1, there were many interrelationships among kindergarten teacher-educators and their training institutions from the earliest days. In the East, Boston, Philadelphia, and New York City were focal points. In the Midwest and the southern regions, St. Louis, Chicago, Louisville, and Milwaukee drew kindergartners-in-training. In the West, San Francisco was the hub of early training efforts.

Many of the women moved to several locations during their career, of their own volition, to seek further training or better opportunities, or because they accompanied their husbands when they made career moves. Such was the case with Anna Ogden, Eudora Hailmann, Anna Bryan, Alice Putnam, Susan Blow, Elizabeth Harrison, Alice Temple, and Emma Marwedel, whose lives exemplify the professional development of their times.[153]

The curricula of the teacher training courses had many similarities, because their authors maintained contacts through the IKU, professional publications, and personal visits and communications. However, the schism that began about 1900 led to the addition of new subjects in some training schools and colleges. All programs maintained the central core of practical experience working with children as the basis for professional learning.

Two-Year Training Courses

During the last half of the nineteenth century, many students took a two-year training course in either a private training school or a public normal school. Only a handful of institutions offered an optional third-year course. Mary J. Garland was one of the first trainers to move from requiring one, to requiring two years of training classes.[154]

An average two-year kindergarten training program included courses in child study, psychology, or educational psychology; physiology or child hygiene; sociology or social welfare; reading of literature; children's literature and storytelling; oral composition (public speaking); music; physical culture and games or physical training or folk dances; art (sometimes stipulated as color and modeling); ethics; biblical history; and homemaking. One training college required that three theses be written prior to graduation.

Figure 9.4 Washington, D.C., Kindergarten. Photograph by Frances Benjamin Johnston, ca. 1900. *Courtesy of the Library of Congress, Washington, D.C.*

Another part of the program consisted of courses in the principles and philosophy of education; school management or school organization; school law; and training and practical drill in school room management. The young "kindergartners-in-training" often studied great educators in courses bearing such titles as history of education, Froebel(ian) philosophy, or reminiscences of Froebel. These courses were placed in the second or third year of the training program.

The kindergarten-specific portion of the program included kindergarten principles and methods; kindergarten curricula; kindergarten gifts and occupations and their history; kindergarten songs and games or the practical study of Froebel's mother plays; and both kindergarten manual activities, also known as constructive occupations, and industrial or manual arts and handwork. Advanced theory in kindergarten study could have included symbolic education and Froebel's *Education of Man*.

Practical work was a very important part of the training. Students were required to study program planning, to develop a "program book," and to then study program making or program work. In the great majority of training programs, the morning was spent in practical application of theory. All schools required some form of daily practical work in a classroom with children. On the student's individual program would be found such course titles as: observation and practice in kindergarten (during the first year), practice in kindergarten (in the second year), observation and classroom management, practice teaching, or observation and student teaching.[155]

Although Susan Blow told Elizabeth Harrison that she was "heartsick about the poor quality of kindergarten training in the country," a number of state and city normal schools had initiated kindergarten teacher training during the late 1870s and early 1880s. The progressive normal schools at Oswego and Fredonia, New York, added kindergarten training in 1882 along with the normal schools of Emporia, Kansas, and those in Connecticut. In 1889, the state of Michigan followed suit. According to Vandewalker, an exact date for the establishment of the kindergarten departments in many normal schools could not be ascertained. During the time period 1880 to 1895, the city normal schools in New York City (under the direction of Thomas Hunter), Boston, and the Philadelphia Girls' Normal School (under the superintendency of James MacAlister) added a kindergarten training department. They agreed with the statement made by Commissioner William Torrey Harris in 1884, that "It is through the normal school that the adjustment of Froebel's system to our public schools must be made, if it is to be made at all." In Chicago, public pressure and the existence of six private training academies prevented the addition of a kindergarten training department to the Chicago Normal School, although the Cook County Normal School did begin one in 1883.[156]

A highly subjective article in the April 1878 issue of *Harper's New Monthly Magazine*, accompanied by vivid sketches, describes in great detail the program of an average day at the Normal College of New York City.[157] In

1874, when the model school moved to a new building, President Thomas Hunter had succeeded in providing all the elements of a Froebelian kindergarten, including a kindergartner trained by Maria Kraus, and he reported remarkable results. According to Hunter, the future teachers at the Normal College learned about child nature as they never could have from ordinary textbooks, and they were prepared to "enter upon their work with a loftier idea of their duties and responsibilities and with a broader humanity for the efforts and miseries of their fellow human beings."[158]

Students who attended the New York City Normal College during the late 1800s and early 1900s studied Latin, German, or French; ancient and modern history; mathematics (algebra and plain geometry); sciences (physics, botany, astronomy, chemistry, zoology, geology, mineralogy, and physiology); music; drawing; penmanship; English composition, rhetoric, and English language and literature. Their professional studies included a year of primary school subjects and methods, as well as intellectual philosophy and the theory of teaching. They engaged in teaching practice in the model school, which included a female grammar school, a "mixed" (male and female) primary school and a kindergarten, under experienced critic-teachers.[159]

The third-year course was designed to prepare the "kindergartner" to teach at the primary level. Academic content courses taken included: geography, literature, philosophy of literature, myth study, language, nature study, vocal music, drawing and water color, art history, decorative design, and philosophy of architecture. Among the education courses offered were: reading, child culture, primary methods, primary curricula, games, grade work, school economics, and school administration.[160]

In New York City, School Superintendent Maxwell supported kindergarten training departments. Established in the last decade of the nineteenth century, the Maxwell Training School for Teachers in Brooklyn, New York; the New York Training School for Teachers in Manhattan; and the Jamaica Training School for Teachers in Jamaica, Queens, provided teachers for New York City's burgeoning school system until February 1933, when they were closed as an economy measure. For young women who intended to teach in the New York City public schools, "the three municipal teacher-training schools were the most attractive option available. Besides offering free professional training, the schools provided direct preparation for the examination for a teacher's license. Other advantages included being able to observe experienced and proficient teaching and classroom management in model schools, as well as practice teaching under the training schools' supervision and direction, while receiving paid remuneration as student-teachers."[161]

The (two-year) course of study offered at the training schools from their inception until 1923 was a combination of theoretical and practical work. A thorough study was made of the methods of teaching employed in New York City's elementary schools. Students received a broad foundation in the principles and history of education, including the study of psychology and educational measurements. Observation of skilled teachers working with children in various grades of the city's schools began in the first semester and continued throughout the two-year course. Twenty weeks of practice in the elementary school under the supervision of critic-teachers from the training schools alternated with theory work during the second year. During the training schools' period of unrivaled popularity, the city's Board of Education replicated attempts by teacher educators throughout the nation to upgrade the teaching profession by raising standards of admission, revising the curriculum, and extending the years of schooling for teacher trainees. In 1923, the board introduced its three-year curriculum, which was maintained by the training schools until 1929.[162]

Three-Year and Longer Courses

The kindergarten training school begun by Lucy Wheelock in 1889 is now known as Wheelock College. It moved a number of times to larger quarters in order to make room for its associated Child Garden (kindergarten). In 1925, Wheelock instituted a three-year teacher preparation program. The first two years of study were conducted at Wheelock, with a third year at Boston University School of Education. From the beginning, the Wheelock School emphasized "the practice work and had under its management about fifteen different settlements and mission schools for observation and practice. Third year students are in charge of the classes and are given experience which *qualifies them for directors' positions* on graduation."[163]

New College of Columbia University

New College was headed by Thomas Alexander, who had come from Peabody College in Tennessee. Its purpose was the initial preparation of nursery, kindergarten-primary, and elementary school teachers. It was organized as a separate unit within Teachers College, with a separate faculty and staff. In the application, students were queried as to their reasons for wanting to teach young children. They entered a program tailored to their needs and pace.

A novel aspect of the New College program was the Initial Community Experiences.[164] Each entering student was required to spend his or her first summer in a period of residence and study at the New College community in North Carolina, which Patty Smith Hill helped to secure and finance. The faculty, entering students and some advanced students, lived and worked together on the farm. All the work of maintaining the farm, cultivating and harvesting the gardens, preparing meals, and operating the houses "devolved on students and staff members." In the fall, the group relocated to the New York campus at Teachers College of Columbia University. Here they began a two-year pre-program that included background studies in English, natural and social science, philosophy, the arts, physical education, and a foreign language. Some students worked in an industrial or a commercial field to gain a "realistic picture of social conditions."[165]

At this juncture, the students sat for the first of two comprehensive examinations, to apply for professional work in the field of education. They participated in the Education Seminar, as well as courses in the philosophy, sociology, psychology, economics, and history of education and comparative education. Each student participated in an eight-month period of foreign study, together with a group of their peers and a New College instructor. They were expected to study the social, economic, and cultural life of the country they visited, and to investigate a "special problem related to the provisions made for the care and education of young children."[166, 167] Upon their return to New York, the students resumed work in their major field of specialization, early childhood education, as well as a field of secondary interest.

Some of these students shared professor Hill's concern over the adjacent Manhattanville neighborhood. They decided to spend the summer of 1934 finding out what really went on in the neighborhood. They explored the stores, shops, eating places, and streets filled with children. According to Snyder, the experience was shocking to them, and they poured out their feelings in moving verse and prose, realistic sketches, and snapshots. The book they produced was presented to their seminar in the fall.[168] One of the first major projects undertaken by New College in the neighborhood was the establishment of a kindergarten for four-year-olds, which was housed in the same building as the Federal Emergency Nursery School classes for younger children.

The students then chose an internship problem upon which to base their thesis. They sat for the second comprehensive examination, by which they gained admission to internship teaching. Upon completion of the entire program, the student took the final examination for the Master of Arts degree. At this point, the student's total record was reviewed, and those students who met all of the criteria were awarded the degree of Master of Arts by Columbia University.

In later years, the Ann-Reno Institute initiated a five-year plan for the preparation of teachers of nursery schools, kindergartens, and primary grades.[169] The first three years of this program, begun in 1939, were provided by the Institute faculty. After completion of the program, the student was admitted, by special arrangement, for two years of study at Teachers College. Upon completion of the total program, the student would receive a Master of Arts degree from Columbia University Teachers College. The program included study of cultural areas (English, social studies, science, mathematics, the arts, and technical areas), professional courses (human growth and development, curriculum development, reading and children's literature, and professional seminars), and intern teaching. The program was accredited by the Teacher Education and Certification Division of the New York State Education Department.

The outline for the course in Curriculum Construction and Kindergarten Techniques parallels those of today, including the history of educators of young children for the twentieth century, early education in the seventeenth through the nineteenth centuries, Froebel's life and work, and the selection and use of kindergarten curriculum materials. Room arrangement and placement of materials; individual areas, such as housekeeping, blocks, sand, active play apparatus for indoor and outdoor use, paint, clay, wood, paper and cloth; and provisions for health and discipline were included. Hands-on work with the materials in the college served as the precursor to today's professional development courses.[170] In fact, the similarities between current and past teacher education practices are striking.

The Midwest and the West

The majority of university training for kindergarten teachers ("kindergartners") took place at Teachers College of Columbia University and earlier at the University of Chicago. John Dewey played a major role in kindergarten teacher training during the decades from 1900 to 1950. In 1897, he hosted a Kindergarten Conference, which built on the overtures made by University of Chicago President Harper, and attracted many "free-kindergarten" leaders. Dewey maintained an ongoing relationship with "the radical Froebelians of Hull House," where he remained a guest lecturer in the kindergarten training program of Alice Putnam.

Kindergartners studied Dewey's writings during their preservice and inservice years. Students and readers knew that Dewey's ideas and innovations were based on work with real children, their teachers, and parents because they read both his accounts and those of the teachers about how specific activities corresponded to the children's growth. There were also "visiting days" for observation at the Laboratory School.[171]

When Dewey moved from the University of Chicago to Teachers College of Columbia University, he took with him the lessons learned in the Laboratory School. As a Teachers College professor, Dewey influenced all of the early childhood teacher educators of his day, through his articles and books, through his personal contacts, and his interactions with faculty colleagues, such as Patty Smith Hill. She knew of Dewey's work prior to coming to the college, and incorporated it into her professional development activities in both Louisville and New York.

Lucy Gage, a well-known early childhood teacher-educator of the period was one of Dewey's students. She entered kindergarten teacher training at Epworth University, in Oklahoma City, Oklahoma, and moved to the Kalamazoo State Normal School in Michigan in 1907. Gage joined the faculty at George Peabody College for Teachers in Nashville, Tennessee, in 1920. Because she did not yet have a bachelor's degree, she was advised to complete her academic course work. She managed to achieve this objective at Teachers College, Columbia University, within one year, returning to Peabody, where she taught until 1942.[172] The early 1900s also saw the opening of the Topeka, Kansas, Church Kindergarten and Training School.[173]

Alice Temple created and developed a program for the kindergarten-primary certificate at the University of Chicago. It became one of the two major centers for those wishing a variety of teaching options during the early 1900s. The requirements in the 1915 university catalog included basic courses in the social sciences, language, mathematics, and natural sciences. Other requirements were a satisfactory command of the English language, taking physical culture and lessons on personal hygiene, and satisfactorily completing sixteen majors with thirty-six grade points, distributed among practice teaching, kindergarten-primary, and electives. Differences included the fact that those specializing in kindergarten chose between elementary educational psychology and methods of elementary education, while those in primary teaching had no educational psychology; and that the kindergarten specialization had two practice periods in kindergarten and one in primary level, while the primary reversed this order. Geography and mathematics were required of the primary teacher education candidates but not of those in the kindergarten specialization.[174]

Kindergarten teacher training schools reached the West Coast with the opening of the Broadoaks Kindergarten Training School. Between 1914 and his death in 1920, William Hailmann was on the faculty at Broadoaks.[175]

Standards and Programs

By the 1930s, teachers' colleges had added a third year of study, with some institutions requiring it and others keeping it optional. Kindergarten teaching had always required specialized training and considered it important to maintain high standards. Its excellence influenced normal schools, which began to incorporate kindergarten courses into their curriculum. Such courses introduced educational innovation to future elementary school teachers. The rigorous entrance requirements for admission to a high-quality kindergarten training school influenced the entrance standards of the normal schools. The kindergarten movement also alerted normal schools and later teachers' colleges to the significance of understanding child growth and development.[176]

The programs and courses of study set up by teacher educators fit within the context of the educational system of the time period and place. They exemplified the societal view of early childhood educators and their instructors. Teacher educators were proactive in this regard through their choices of pedagogical literature, course and program content, and practicum experiences. Training institutions were culturally influential through their admission and retention criteria, their intellectual environment, their view of the woman's role in society, and their assistance to graduates in obtaining suitable teaching positions.[177]

The major stated prerequisites for entry into kindergarten, and later kindergarten-primary, training in the United States during the time period 1850–1930 included being at least eighteen years of age and completion of a high school course or the equivalent, as demonstrated by a diploma or certificate. A few kindergarten training programs asked for a normal school diploma.

Many nursery, kindergarten, and primary school teachers never went beyond the normal school. In interviews, both published and unpublished, retired teachers in the New York City public school system spoke of the fact that one of the incentives for seeking a baccalaureate degree was that this enabled one to earn a higher salary, as well as to rise in the school system hierarchy.[178] Sometimes training colleges gave entrance credits for previous training, occasionally with a one-month probation period to allow the current training institution to assess what the candidate had retained from that learning experience. The Law Froebel Kindergarten Training School of Culture for Young Women offered its graduates the opportunity to continue their education at "Toledo Municipal University and others of the first class," thus providing "special inducements to young women desiring a vocation and a university degree."[179] The agreement with Toledo Municipal University allowed graduates of the kindergarten training school two years' credit in the elementary education course, leading to the B.Ed. degree and nineteen credits in the course leading to the B.A. degree.

Gender Issues

A frequently assumed criterion for entry into kindergarten training was that the candidate be female, because early childhood education was one of the few acceptable professions for women during this time period. Many of the prospectuses for kindergarten training institutions opened with the following quotation from Elizabeth Peabody: "To be a kindergartner is the perfect development of womanliness—a working (with God) at the very fountain of artistic and intellectual power and moral character. It is, therefore, the highest finish that can be given to a woman's education, to be educated for a kindergartner."[180]

Another assumption was that upon marriage (for which teaching young children prepared one), the young woman would leave the profession to raise her own children. In the 1880s, girls faced the choice of teaching and spinsterhood or marriage. Their parents often felt more at ease with "the prospect of kindergartening, since the stress kindergartners laid on the responsibilities and duties of motherhood contributed heavily to its general social as well as parental acceptability. It seemed to provide a woman with a vocation that purportedly would not subvert her maternal instincts."[181]

Among the few reasons a woman in the United States would return to teaching young children after marriage were that she was widowed, impoverished, or, less frequently, divorced. However, a number of married kindergarten teachers later became supervisors of kindergartens or faculty members of kindergarten normal schools, seminaries, institutes, or training colleges.

Teacher candidates were required to be moral and "of good character." The importance attached to this criterion is demonstrated by reports from archival sources stating that references for credential letters were sought from the young woman's pastor, or the principal of the last school she attended. Some training programs required a six- to eight-week probationary period in order for the faculty to assess this characteristic. Good health and fitness, refinement and "general culture," and musical ability were other important admission criteria. Native ability (as a teacher), a sympathetic attitude toward or a love for children, and mental maturity or scholarship were other traits considered essential in a teacher candidate by certain kindergarten training colleges.

According to Ross, "kindergarten training schools generally had admission procedures that were in many cases more selective than state normal schools." While a number of training schools rigorously utilized the criteria enumerated earlier, others "kept their requirements loose: a genuine love for children and interest in working and playing with them; musical ability; maturity; and a reasonably substantial educational background." By comparison, the best state and county normal schools of the 1880s did not require a high school diploma, asking that their applicants be sixteen years of age, "in good health, have a certificate attesting to their good moral fiber, and be able to pass an examination of basic subjects taught in elementary school."[182]

Influence of Licensure and Certification

Government licensing and certification standards have had a major impact on early childhood teacher training. Historical prospectuses of several kindergarten training institutions from the early 1900s, and the more recent college catalogs examined in the University of Maryland ACEI archives, include statements regarding student eligibility for certification. Some of the most recent catalogs also include information regarding the participation of a particular institution in the National Council for Accreditation of Teacher Education (NCATE), the national organization in the United States that certifies schools and colleges of education. Federal documents of the early 1900s suggested that kindergarten teachers required increased professional preparation, and that changes be made in the kindergarten training schools.[183] As kindergartners began to achieve city and state certification, they came under the purview of the city and state bureaus and departments of education, and the requirements for their training courses were increased.

A study by Jan McCarthy (1988), *State Certification of Early Childhood Teachers: Analysis of the 50 States and the District of Columbia*, noted that twenty-three states and the District of Columbia had certification identified as early childhood education. The description of teachers of children aged five through nine years included such terms as: teacher of young children, kindergarten to grade four certification, kindergarten-primary, nursery to grade six, and early childhood and kindergarten education. The nomenclature used to describe programs designed to prepare teachers of children under five includes such terms as: pre-kindergarten, nursery school, and preschool. A total of thirty-two states and the District of Columbia had some type of certification for the preparation of teachers of young children. Fourteen states had some type of endorsement to an elementary education certificate. Almost half the states offered neither certification nor endorsement for early childhood education. McCarthy reached the conclusion that there was no defined span that early childhood encompasses that was accepted nationwide, by all of the states.[184] This was reiterated by McCarthy in June and November 1998 conference presentations. However, in 1997, sixteen states had licensure requirements for teachers preparing to work with children aged zero to eight years, while an additional seventeen states and the District of Columbia had licensure for those preparing to work with years three through six. Three states defined early childhood as five through nine years. Five states had an endorsement to an elementary license, while ten states included kindergarten in their elementary license. Although state early childhood teacher education has been strengthened during the time period between the two studies, much work still remains to be done in the field of early childhood teacher licensure in the United States.[185]

Section Summary

German-trained kindergarten teacher-educators continued to wield influence as the kindergarten movement worked its way across the country. Elizabeth Peabody, John Dewey, and Felix Adler played important roles in the expansion of the kindergarten to the West Coast of the United States. Patty Smith Hill, Alice Temple, and Nina Vandewalker played a pivotal role in the development of both theory and practice through their courses, publications, and organizational work.

Kindergarten teacher education moved from private training classes to normal schools to colleges through the hard work and determination of many kindergarten advocates. The high standards set by the original "kindergartners" were maintained by their successors, as individual states began to recognize early childhood education as a distinct area of licensure and certification.

Notes

1. Henry Barnard, quoting himself in Henry Barnard, *Kindergarten and Child Culture Papers: Papers on Froebel's Kindergarten, with Suggestions on Principles and Methods of Child Culture in Different Countries,* rev. ed. (Hartford, CT: Office of Barnard's *American Journal of Education,* 1884), 1.

2. Henry Barnard, "The Educational Exhibition of London and the Recent Educational Movement in Great Britain," *American Journal of Education* 2 (1856): 8.

3. "Kindergärten of Germany," *The Christian Examiner* 67, 5th ser. (November 1859): 313–339. This feature contains three articles, two by the Baroness von Marenholtz-Bülow—"Les Jardins d' Enfants, Nouvelle Methode d'Education et d'Instruction de Frederic Froebel" and "Woman's Educational Mission"—and "A Practical Guide to the

English Kindergarten," by Johannes and Bertha Ronge. The articles were reviewed by Ednah D. Cheney and Anna Q. T. Parsons and include many excerpts. Cf. Fanny L. Macdaniel and Anna Q. T. Parsons, "The Seed-Time of Kindergarten Thought in America," *Kindergarten Review* 14 (May 1904): 545.

4. Nina Vandewalker, *The Kindergarten in American Education* (New York: Macmillan, 1923), 4. It is a good resource for the early years of the kindergarten in America.

5. Ibid., 12–14.

6. Elizabeth Jenkins, "How the Kindergarten Found Its Way to America," reprinted from *Wisconsin Magazine of History* 19, no. 1 (September 1930): 4, 7; Hans L. Trefousse, *Carl Schurz: A Biography* (Knoxville: University of Tennessee Press, 1982), 64; Jonathan Messerli, "Margarethe Meyer Schurz," in *Notable American Women, 1607–1950, Biographical Dictionary,* 3 volumes, eds. Edward T. James and Janet W. James (Cambridge: The Belknap Press at Harvard University Press, 1971), 3: 242–243.

7. Lida Rose McCabe, "Columbus: The Cradle of America's Kindergarten," *The Ohio State Journal,* 62 (31 March 1901): 1–2 (Columbus: Ohio Historical Society Microfilms). Article includes photographs of Miss Frankenberg and her school. "The Chronological Abstract" in *Autobiography of Friedrich Froebel,* trans. and ed. Emilie Michaelis and H. Keatley Moore (Syracuse, NY: C. W. Bardeen, 1908), 142, confirms that Froebel did write "The New Year 1836 Demands a Renewal of Life."

8. These events, and Froebel's interest, advice, and support to his former student, are recorded in "Seven Letters of Froebel to the Kindergarten Teacher, Mlle. Luise Frankenberg," in *Froebel's Letters on the Kindergarten,* ed. and ann. Emilie Michaelis and H. Keatley Moore (Syracuse, NY: C. W. Bardeen, 1896), 236–247. The letters were written between November 13, 1846, and January 29, 1852, from Keilhau and Marienthal.

9. Froebel to Luise, Keilhau, 13 November 1846. Ibid., 236n.

10. McCabe, "Columbus: The Cradle of America's Kindergarten," 1–2. The orphanage records chronicle Miss Peabody's visit. Ibid.

11. Maria Kraus-Boelte, "Reminiscences of Kindergarten Work," in Barnard, *Papers on Froebel's Kindergarten,* 537–550.

12. Mafia Kraus-Boelte, "Experience of a Kindergartner," *Kindergarten Messenger* 3 (January, February, and March 1875): 38.

13. Ibid., 40.

14. Ibid., 56–57; Vandewalker, *The Kindergarten in American Education,* 30.

15. For a description of the "Model Kindergarten," see Barnard, *Papers on Froebel's Kindergarten,* 551–558, and "A Day in Mrs. Kraus-Boelte's Kindergarten," *Kindergarten Messenger* 3 (August 1875): 181–189.

16. Anna K. Harvey, "Maria Kraus-Boelte," in International Kindergarten Union (IKU) Committee of Nineteen, *Pioneers of the Kindergarten in America* (New York: Century, 1924), 75–84.

17. Fanny L. Johnson, "History of the Kindergarten Movement in Boston," *Kindergarten Review* 12 (April 1902) 474–475. See also Caroline D. Aborn, "Matilda Kriege," in *Pioneers of the Kindergarten,* 91–94.

18. Ednah D. Cheney, "Elizabeth Palmer Peabody," *Kindergarten Review* 14 (May 1904): 533, 535; Anna Q. T. Parsons, "Reminiscences of Miss Peabody," *Kindergarten Review* 14 (May 1904): 539, 540. This issue has several articles on Peabody.

19. Mary J. Garland, "Elizabeth Palmer Peabody," and Lucy Wheelock, "Miss Peabody as I Knew Her," in *Pioneers of the Kindergarten,* 19–25 and 26–39. For more about Elizabeth Peabody, see Margaret Neussendorfer, *An Education by Ancestors: The Roots of Elizabeth Palmer Peabody* (Cambridge: The Mary Ingraham Bunting Institute of Radcliffe College, 1980); and Bruce Ronda, ed., *Letters of Elizabeth Palmer Peabody: American Renaissance Woman* (Middletown, CT: Wesleyan University Press, 1984).

20. Elizabeth Peabody, "Origin and Growth of the Kindergarten," *Education* 2 (May 1882): 507–527; Ruth Baylor, *Elizabeth Palmer Peabody: Kindergarten Pioneer* (Philadelphia: University of Pennsylvania Press, 1965), 30.

21. Mrs. Horace Mann and Elizabeth Peabody, *Moral Culture of Infancy and Kindergarten Guide, With Music for the Plays* (Boston: T. O. H. P. Burnham, 1863), iv.

22. Elizabeth Peabody, "Our Reason for Being," *Kindergarten Messenger* 1 (May 1873): 1.

23. Elizabeth Peabody, "Development of the Kindergarten," Barnard, *Papers on Froebel's Kindergarten,* 10.

24. Johnson, "History of the Kindergarten Movement in Boston," 474.

25. Peabody, "Our Reason for Being," 2; idem, "Development of Kindergarten," in Barnard, *Papers on Froebel's Kindergarten,* 10–11; Elizabeth Peabody and Mary P. Mann, *Moral Culture of Infancy and Kindergarten Guide* (New York: J. W. Schermerhorn, 1870), v.

26. Peabody, "Origin and Growth of the Kindergarten," 524.

27. Johnson, "The Kindergarten Movement in Boston," 475.

28. The U.S. Bureau of Education, *Circular of Information on the Kindergarten* (Washington: Government Printing Office, July 1872.) Cf. *Kindergarten Messenger* 1 (May 1873): 7.

29. *Kindergarten Messenger,* 3 (August 1875): 191–192. The names of the correspondents were not given.

30. Alice Dugget Cary, "Kindergarten for Negro Children," *Southern Workman* 29 (August 1900): 461–463. For more about kindergarten and Black children, see Chapter 15 of this volume.

31. Elizabeth Peabody, "Valedictory of the Kindergarten Messenger," *New England Journal of Education* 3 (30 December 1876): 297; "Prospectus," *Kindergarten Messenger,* n.s., 1 (January and February 1877): 1; and idem, "Development of Kindergarten," 15.

32. Macdaniel and Parsons, "The Seed-time of Kindergarten Thought in America," 546. Friedrich Froebel, *Froebel's Mother-Play and Nursery Songs,* trans. Fannie E. Dwight and Josephine Jarvis, ed. Elizabeth P. Peabody (Boston: Lothrop, Lee and Shepard Co., 1878). In 1867–1868, Peabody wrote a series of articles for the *New York Herald* and for the *Health Herald.* Vandewalker, *The Kindergarten in American Education,* 28–29.

33. Elizabeth P. Peabody, *Lectures in the Training Schools for Kindergartners* (Boston: D. C. Heath & Co., 1893). It is a series of eight lectures Peabody gave for about ten years to kindergartners in training in Boston and other cities. It discusses the use of language, how to observe children, and the education of those who want to become kindergartners. The appendix had "The Song of the Weather," and "The Lord's Prayer."

34. Elizabeth Peabody, "Genuine Kindergarten," *Kindergarten Messenger* 1 (July 1873): 5–9.

35. "Letters to the Boston Meeting of Kindergartners," *New England Journal Education* 3 (20 May 1876): 249, and (27 May 1876): 261.

36. Ibid., (May 27 1876): 261.

37. Ibid., (3 June 1876): 273. Object teaching is instruction by observation in contrast to the book learning. You look at the object and you describe it.

38. "The American Froebel Union," *Kindergarten Messenger* n.s., 1 (September–October 1877): 152–157; "Constitution," 157; and "By Laws," 158–260.

39. Peabody's interest in the American Indians began in childhood. An uncle of her mother had married an Indian woman in Michigan, and their children visited the Peabody family in Salem when Elizabeth and Sophia were children. Cheney, "Elizabeth Palmer Peabody," 537n.

40. Ronda, ed., *Letters of Elizabeth Palmer Peabody,* 396–398. For more about Native Americans and Sara Winnemucca, see Chapter 14 of this volume.

41. Ednah Cheney, "Funeral Service," *Kindergarten News* 4 (February 1894): 46. Several other articles in this issue paid tribute to Elizabeth Palmer Peabody.

42. Johnson, "History of the Kindergarten Movement in Boston," 480; "Elizabeth Peabody House: The Kindergarten Settlement of Boston," *Kindergarten Review* 12 (October 1901): 63–67.

43. The material on Mary Mann came from the following sources: Jonathan Messerli, "Mary Tyler Peabody Mann," *Notable American Women,* 2: 488–489; see also J. E. Roberts, "Horace Mann and the Peabody Sisters," *New England Quest* (June 1945), and two semihistorical biographies by Louise H. Tharp, *The Peabody Sisters of Salem* (Boston: Little Brown and Co., 1950) and *Until Victory: Horace Mann and Mary Peabody* (Boston: Little Brown and Co., 1953).

44. Elizabeth Peabody to William T. Harris, 18 May 1870 and 25 August 1870, quoted in Ronda, ed., *Letters of Elizabeth Palmer Peabody,* 358–363. William T. Harris was discussed in Chapter 8 of this volume.

45. For more about the kindergartens of St. Louis, see *Kindergarten Messenger,* n.s., 1 (July and August 1877): 118–121; and Selwyn K. Troen, *The Public Schools: Shaping the St. Louis System, 1838–1900* (Columbia: University of Missouri Press, 1976), 99–115. For Harris's view on the kindergarten in public schools, see William T. Harris, "Kindergarten in the Public School System," in Barnard, *Papers on Froebel's Kindergarten,* 625–641. Describes the problems of urban poverty and the kindergarten work in St. Louis.

46. The material on Susan E. Blow came from the following sources: Laura Fisher, "Susan E. Blow," in *Pioneers of the Kindergarten in America,* 184–203; Dorothy Ross, "Susan Elizabeth Blow," *Notable American Women,* 1: 181–183; and Agnes Snyder, *Dauntless Women in Childhood Education, 1856–1931* (Washington, DC: Association for Childhood Education International, 1972), 59–85.

47. Harriet Niel, "William T. Harris" in *Pioneers of the Kindergarten in America,* 173.

48. Fisher, "Susan E. Blow," 188.

49. The Carondelet Historical Society and the Susan E. Blow Foundation raised money to restore the school. NiNi Harris, "The Carondelet Historic Center and Susan E. Blow," *Childhood Education* 59 (May–June 1983): 336–338.

50. Susan E. Blow, *Symbolic Education, a Commentary on Froebel's Mother Play, The Mottoes and Commentaries of Friedrich Froebel's Mother Play, Songs and Music of Friedrich Froebel's Mother Play, Letters to a Mother on the Philosophy of Froebel, and Educational Issues in the Kindergarten* (New York: D. Appleton and Co., 1894, 1895, 1899, 1908). For an analysis of Blow's books on *Mother Play,* see Fisher, "Susan E. Blow," 194–200. For a bibliography about Susan Blow, see Lizzie Lee Kirk, *A Bibliography of Materials by and About Susan Elizabeth Blow* (St. Louis: Board of Education, 1961). Snyder, *Dauntless Women,* 79n.

51. For a description and importance of the Centennial, see Lawrence A. Cremin, *American Education: The National Experience, 1783–1876* (New York: Harper & Row, 1980), 332–334; and Jeanne M. Weimann, *The Fair Women* (Chicago: Academy Press, 1981).

52. Nina Vandewalker, "Ruth Burritt, The Centennial Kindergartner," in *Pioneers of the Kindergarten,* 134–146. The "Centennial Kindergarten" was strictly Froebelian.

53. "Centennial Kindergarten," *Kindergarten Messenger* 3 (June 1875): 121–122; "The Kindergarten at the Centennial," *Kindergarten Messenger* 3 (August 1875): 169–171.

54. "Letters to the Boston Meeting of Kindergartens," *New England Journal of Education* 4 (30 September 1876): 138.

55. *Philadelphia Ledger,* 1876, quoted in "Impressions Made by the Centennial Kindergarten," *Kindergarten Messenger,* n.s., 1 (January and February 1877): 6–10.

56. Vandewalker, "Ruth Burritt, The Centennial Kindergartner," in *Pioneers of the Kindergarten,* 141–142, 135.

57. Milton Bradley Company, *Milton Bradley, a Successful Man* (Springfield, MA: Milton Bradley Co., 1910), 29. Book was published to commemorate the fiftieth anniversary of the founding of the company. See also James J. Shea, *The Milton Bradley Story* (New York: The Newcomen Society in North America, 1973).

58. Milton Bradley, "A Reminiscence of Miss Peabody," *Kindergarten News* 4 (February 1894): 39–40; Milton Bradley Company, *Milton Bradley, a Successful Man,* 31; Shea, *The Milton Bradley Story,* 11.

59. Peabody, "Development of Kindergarten," 14; Hermann Goldammer, *The Kindergarten Guide to Froebel's Method of Education, Gifts, and Occupations,* with an introduction by the Baroness von Bülow, trans. William Wright, 2nd ed. (London: Williams & Norgate, 1895). In the preface of Edward Wiebe's *The Paradise of Childhood: A Practical Guide to the Kindergarten,* ed. Milton Bradley (Springfield, MA: Milton Bradley Co., 1907), Bradley confirms Peabody's comments about Wiebe's book. Ibid., 5, 7.

60. "Milton Bradley," *Kindergarten Review* 23 (September 1911): 63.

61. Milton Bradley Company, *Milton Bradley,* 67–68.

62. "Kindergarten Literature," *Kindergarten Messenger* 1 (July 1873): 13. For a contemporary look at commercial exhibits, see Dorothy W. Hewes, "Early Childhood Commercial Exhibits: 1890 and 1990." National Association for the Education of Young Children (Washington, DC, 16 November 1990) ED 330 431.

63. Robert H. Bremner, "Scientific Philanthropy, 1873–93," *Social Service Review* 30 (June 1956): 168. See also "Charity Kindergartens in the United States," in Barnard, *Papers on Froebel's Kindergarten,* 651–653.

64. Marvin Lazerson, "Social Reform and Early Childhood Education," *Urban Education 5,* no. 1 (1970): 83–102; idem, "Urban Reform and the Schools: Kindergartens in Massachusetts, 1870–1915," *History of Education Quarterly* 11 (Summer 1971): 115–142.

65. Johnson, "History of the Kindergarten Movement in Boston," 476–477; Vandewalker, *The Kindergarten in American Education,* 58.

66. Johnson, 477. For Pauline Agassiz Shaw's life, see "Pauline Agassiz Shaw," Charles W. Eliot, "Tribute," and Laura Fisher, "Mrs. Shaw's Service to the Kindergarten," in *Pioneers of the Kindergarten,* 98–99, 101–102, and 103–108.

67. Vandewalker, *The Kindergarten in American Education,* 61–63.

68. Jane Addams, *Twenty Years at Hull House, with Autobiographical Notes* (New York: Macmillan, 1910; reprint, New York: New American Library, 1960). See also Amalie Hofer, "The Social Settlement and the Kindergarten," *Kindergarten Magazine* 8 (September 1895): 47–59.

69. Lucy Wheelock, "A Tribute to Kate Douglas Wiggin," in *Pioneers of the Kindergarten,* 283–295 and 296–298; Snyder, *Dauntless Women,* 89–123.

70. Kate Douglas Wiggin, *Children's Rights: A Book of Nursery Logic* (Boston: Houghton Mifflin, 1892). Chapter 1 is "The Rights of the Child," 1–24. See also V. Celia Lascarides, "United States' Contribution to Children's Rights: An Overview of the 20th Century," *International Journal of Early Childhood* 24 (October 1992): 41–44. With her sister Nora Archibald Smith, Wiggins co-authored a three-volume book, *The Republic of Childhood* (Boston: Houghton Mifflin, 1895, 1896). Vol. I, *Froebel's Gifts* (1895); Vol. II, *Froebel's Occupations;* and Vol. III, *Kindergarten Principles and Practice* (1896).

71. Vandewalker, *The Kindergarten in American Education,* 56–58, 66.

72. Stella Wood, "The Kindergartner as a Business Woman," *Kindergarten Review* 22 (September 1911): 16–19.

73. David B. Tyack, *The One Best System: A History of American Urban Education* (Cambridge: Harvard University Press, 1974), 133–139.

74. Johnson, "History of the Kindergarten Movement in Boston," 478–479. In Massachusetts there was no restriction in the age of public school education. Age admission to school varied from state to state. Vandewalker, *The Kindergarten in American Education,* 187–189. For Boston school politics and the role the women played, see Polly W. Kaufman, *Boston Women and City School Politics, 1872–1902* (New York: Garland, 1994).

75. Richard W. Gilder, "The Kindergarten: An Uplifting Social Influence in the Home and District," *Kindergarten Review* 14 (September 1903): 1–10. Gilder delivered this address before the Kindergarten Department of the NEA, Boston, July 10, 1903. See also V. Celia Lascarides, "A Sociological Study of Urban Bilingual and Regular Kindergartens" (Ed.D. diss. Boston University, 1979).

76. William T. Harris, "The Kindergarten as a Preparation for the Highest Civilization," *Kindergarten Review* 13 (June 1903): 631–636. Address delivered before the IKU Pittsburgh, April 15, 1903.

77. U.S. Department of the Interior, Bureau of Education, Americanization Division, "Americanization through the kindergarten," *Americanization* (January 1, 1919): 1, 6, 8, 11, partially reprinted in Robert H. Bremner, ed., *Children and Youth in America: A Documentary History,* 3 volumes in 5 books (Cambridge, MA: Harvard University Press, 1970–1974), 2: 1460–1462.

78. Luella A. Palmer, *Adjustment between Kindergarten and First Grade, Including a Study of Double Sessions in the Kindergarten,* U.S. Bureau of Education Bulletin No. 24 (Washington, DC: U.S. Bureau of Education, 1915), 21, 22; Marvin Lazerson, "Urban Reform and the Schools: Kindergartens in Massachusetts, 1870–1915," 133; Almira M. Winchester, *Kindergarten Supervision in City Schools,* U.S. Bureau of Education Bulletin No. 38 (Washington, DC: U.S. Bureau of Education, 1918), 8–9, 24, 30.

79. Vandewalker, *The Kindergarten in American Education,* 191–192; Alice Temple, *A Survey of the Kindergartens in Richmond, Indiana* (Chicago: University of Chicago Press, 1917), 24. It is this author's impression that this mix of praise and criticism about

kindergarten-trained children, heard even today, seems to reflect the differences of teachers' philosophical beliefs about children's needs and their education rather than the efficacy of the kindergarten.

80. Mary Dabney Davis, *General Practice in Kindergarten Education in the U.S.* (Washington, DC: National Education Association, 1925), 160.

81. The material for this section came from the following sources: James L. Hughes, "Personal Recollections of Henry Barnard, 1811–1900," and A. E. Winship, "Henry Barnard the Educator," in *Pioneers of the Kindergarten*, 39–67 and 68–74; Robert B. Downs, *Henry Barnard* (Boston: Twayne Publishers, 1977).

82. Barnard, *Papers on Froebel's Kindergarten*, 370.

83. D. Keith Osborn, *Early Childhood Education in Historical Perspective*, 3d ed. (Athens, GA: Education Associates, 1991), 62.

84. Osborn, *Early Childhood Education in Historical Perspective*, 63; Edna Dean Baker, "The Kindergarten in Illinois," in *History of the Kindergarten Movement in the Mid-Western States and in New York*, Association for Childhood Education (Washington, DC: Author, April 1938), 19; Bertha Payne Newell, "Alice H. Putnam," *Pioneers of the Kindergarten in America* [Authorized by the International Kindergarten Union] (New York: The Century Company, 1924), 207; and Elizabeth Dale Ross, *The Kindergarten Crusade: The Establishment of Preschool Education in the United States* (Athens, OH: Ohio University Press, 1976), 46.

85. Snyder, *Dauntless Women*, 134–137 passim, 240; Ross, *The Kindergarten Crusade*, 55–57; Barbara Beatty, *Preschool Education in America: The Culture of Young Children from the Colonial Era to the Present* (New Haven, CT: Yale University Press, 1995), 86–87; Baker, "The Kindergarten in Illinois," 19; and Patty Smith Hill, "Anna E. Bryan: 1857–1901," *Pioneers of the Kindergarten in America* [Authorized by the International Kindergarten Union] (New York: The Century Company, 1924), 226.

86. Snyder, *Dauntless Women*, 190–191, 240; and. Hill, "Anna E. Bryan: 1857–1901," 226.

87. Baker, "The Kindergarten in Illinois," 18–20, 22.

88. Elizabeth Whitney and Katherine Ridgeway, "The Kindergarten Movement in Kansas City," in *History of the Kindergarten Movement in the Mid-Western States and in New York*, 40.

89. Ross, *The Kindergarten Crusade*, 25–26; and Osborn, *Early Childhood Education in Historical Perspective*, 88.

90. Caroline W. Barbour, "Kindergarten Education in Wisconsin," in *History of the Kindergarten Movement in the Mid-Western States and in New York*, 24–27.

The Froebel Union, the professional association, was later called the Milwaukee Kindergarten Association.

91. Elizabeth Webster, "Kindergarten Education in Michigan," in *History of the Kindergarten Movement in the Mid-Western States and in New York*, 34; and Lou A. Shepherd, "The Development of the Kindergarten Movement in Iowa," in *History of the Kindergarten Movement in the Mid-Western States and in New York*, 51.

92. Snyder, *Dauntless Women*, 99, 100; Nora Archibald Smith, "Kate Douglas Wiggin: 1856–1923." in *Pioneers of the Kindergarten in America*, 286, 292; Earl Barnes, "Emma Marwedel," in *Pioneers of the Kindergarten in America*, 266; Beatty, *Preschool Education in America*, 93; Anna Irene Jenkins, "California," in *History of the Kindergarten Movement in the Western States, Hawaii and Alaska*, Association for Childhood Education International (Washington, DC: Author, 1940), 10, 18, 20, 27; and Osborn, *Early Childhood Education in Historical Perspective*, 74.

93. Smith, "Kate Douglas Wiggin: 1856–1923," 291; Ross, *The Kindergarten Crusade*, 38; and Jenkins, "California," 17.

94. Helen R. Gumlick, "Colorado," in *History of the Kindergarten Movement in the Western States, Hawaii and Alaska*, Association for Childhood Education International (Washington, DC: Author, 1940), 29–31; and Osborn, *Early Childhood Education in Historical Perspective*, 74.

95. Mignonne Goddard Stanwood and Florence Wright, compilers, Mrs. George H. Root, reporter, "Oregon," in *History of the Kindergarten Movement in the Western States*,

Hawaii and Alaska, 44; and "Washington," in *History of the Kindergarten Movement in the Western States, Hawaii and Alaska,* 59.

96. "Hawaii," in *History of the Kindergarten Movement in the Western States, Hawaii and Alaska,* 63; and "Alaska," in *History of the Kindergarten Movement in the Western States, Hawaii and Alaska,* 67.

97. Rhoda Kellogg, *Nursery School Guide: Theory and Practice for Teachers and Parents* (Boston: Houghton Mifflin Company, 1941), 7; Dorothy W. Hewes, "W. N. Hailmann: Defender of Froebel" (Ph.D. diss., Union Graduate School, 1974), 268; and Abigail Adams Eliot, "Nursery Schools Fifty Years Ago," *Young Children* 27(4) (April 1972), 211.

98. National Society for the Study of Education (NSSE), *The Twenty-Eighth Yearbook of the National Society for the Study of Education,* ed. Guy Montrose Whipple (Bloomington, IL: Public School Publishing Company, 1929), 35–36.

99. Mary Anne Fowlkes, "Patty Smith Hill: Pivotal Figure in Childhood Education" (paper presented at the anniversary meeting of the Association for Childhood Education International: One Hundred Years of Kindergarten, Saratoga Springs, New York, October 1992), 3 and Appendix I "Patty Smith Hill Chronology"; and Mary Anne Fowlkes, "Patty Smith Hill of Louisville: Her Role in the Americanization of the Kindergarten" (paper presented at the annual meeting of the National Association for the Education of Young Children, Chicago, Illinois: 13 November 1987), 1.

100. Fowlkes, "Patty Smith Hill of Louisville: Her Role in the Americanization of the Kindergarten," 1.

101. Ibid., 5–6; and Fowlkes, "Patty Smith Hill: Pivotal Figure in Childhood Education," 2.

102. Hill, "Anna E. Bryan: 1857–1901," 224.

103. Ibid., 226.

104. Fowlkes, "Patty Smith Hill: Pivotal Figure in Childhood Education," 11; and Fowlkes, "Patty Smith Hill of Louisville: Her Role in the Americanization of the Kindergarten," 3–4.

105. Snyder, *Dauntless Women,* 242.

106. Fowlkes, "Patty Smith Hill of Louisville: Her Role in the Americanization of the Kindergarten," 4–5.

107. Ibid., 21.

108. Ibid., 19.

109. Ibid., 23.

110. The Rockefeller Foundation funding that Lawrence Frank distributed provided the support for this institute. Evelyn Weber, *The Kindergarten: Its Encounter with Educational Thought in America* (New York: Teachers College Press, 1969), 258, 120; and Dorothy Hewes, "Patty Smith Hill: Pioneer for Young Children," *Young Children* XXXI, no. 4 (May 1976), 302–303.

111. Fowlkes, "Patty Smith Hill: Pivotal Figure in Childhood Education," Appendix I; and Mary Anne Fowlkes, "Kentucky Kindergartens: Voices from the Past" (paper presented at the Filson Club, Louisville, Kentucky, Summer 1986) TMs, 10.

112. Fowlkes, "Patty Smith Hill: Pivotal Figure in Childhood Education," 17; and Weber, *The Kindergarten: Its Encounter with Educational Thought in America,* 102–103, 126, 131–133.

113. Charlotte G. Garrison, *Permanent Play Materials for Young Children* (New York: Charles Scribner's Sons, 1926), 26–35; and Charlotte Gano Garrison, Emma Dickson Sheehy, and Alice Daigliesh, *The Horace Mann Kindergarten for Five-Year-Old Children,* with an introduction by Patty Smith Hill (New York: Bureau of Publications, Teachers College, Columbia University, 1937), vii.

114. Dorothy Hewes and National Association for the Education of Young Children Organizational History and Archives Committee, "NAEYC's First Half Century: 1936–1976." *Young Children* XXXI, no. 6 (September 1976): 463.

115. Gerald C. Odland, "The Gift of Music," *Childhood Education* 73, no. 1 (Fall 1996), 32B–32C.

116. According to Annie Laws, the second chair of the Committee, the question of self-activity aroused a very spirited discussion. IKU, *Kindergarten: Reports of the Com-*

mitte of Nineteen on the Theory and Practice of the Kindergarten, with an introduction by Annie Laws (Boston: Houghton Mifflin Company, 1913), xi.

117. International Kindergarten Union (IKU), *The Kindergarten: Reports of the Committee of Nineteen on the Theory and Practice of the Kindergarten,* ed. Lucy Wheelock (Boston: Houghton Mifflin Company, 1913), 1–301, passim.

118. Patty Smith Hill, "Second Report," in *The Kindergarten: Reports of the Committee of Nineteen on the Theory and Practice of the Kindergarten,* ed. Lucy Wheelock [Authorized by the IKU] (Boston: Houghton Mifflin Company, 1913), 234.

119. Ibid., 236, 237.

120. Ibid., 250.

121. Ibid., xv.

122. See also: Michael Steven Shapiro, *Child's Garden: The Kindergarten Movement from Froebel to Dewey* (University Park: Pennsylvania University Press, 1983), 174–183.

123. Fowlkes, "Patty Smith Hill of Louisville: Her Role in the Americanization of the Kindergarten," 8; and Harriet K. Cuffaro, "A View of Materials as the Texts of the Early Childhood Curriculum," in *Yearbook in Early Childhood Education Volume 2: Issues in Early Childhood Curriculum,* ed. Bernard Spodek and Olivia N. Saracho (New York: Teachers College Press, 1991), 71.

124. Garrison, *Permanent Play Materials for Young Children,* 26, 29; and Eugene F. Provenzo, Jr., and Arlene Brett, *The Complete Block Book* (Syracuse, NY: Syracuse University Press, 1983), 29.

125. Cuffaro, "A View of Materials as the Texts of the Early Childhood Curriculum," 71–72.

126. Mary Anne Fowlkes, "Gifts from Childhood's Godmother—Patty Smith Hill," *Childhood Education* 61, no. 1 (1984), reprinted in James D. Quisenberry, E. Anne Eddowes, and Sandra L. Robinson, eds. *Readings from Childhood Education* (Washington, DC: Association for Childhood Education International, 1991), 13.

127. Garrison, *Permanent Play Materials for Young Children,* 29–30.

128. Agnes Burke [and teachers of kindergarten and first grade education, Horace Mann School, New York], *A Conduct Curriculum for the Kindergarten and First Grade,* with an introduction by Patty Smith Hill (New York: Charles Scribner's Sons, 1923), xv, xvii–xviii, 11–12; Snyder, *Dauntless Women,* 22–25 [adapted]; Garrison, Sheehy, and Dalgliesh, *The Horace Mann Kindergarten for Five-Year-Old Children,* 107; Cuffaro, "A View of Materials as the Texts of the Early Childhood Curriculum," 72; and Garrison, *Permanent Play Materials for Young Children,* 35.

129. Garrison, *Permanent Play Materials for Young Children,* xv–xvi.

130. Caroline Pratt [with Leila V. Scott, Ruth Goode, and Max Sellers] *I Learn from Children: An Adventure in Progressive Education* (New York: Simon & Schuster, 1948), 29.

131. Fowlkes, "Patty Smith Hill: Pivotal Figure in Childhood Education," 25.

132. Cuffaro, "A View of Materials as the Texts of the Early Childhood Curriculum," 72; and William Heard Kilpatrick, *Foundations of Method: Informal Talks on Teaching* (New York: Macmillan Company, 1925), 277.

133. Patty Smith Hill, "Introduction" in *A Conduct Curriculum for the Kindergarten and First Grade,* xi.

134. Burke, *A Conduct Curriculum for the Kindergarten and First Grade,* with an introduction by Patty Smith Hill, xv, xvii–xviii, 11–12; and Snyder, *Dauntless Women,* 262 [adapted].

135. Fowlkes, "Patty Smith Hill: Pivotal Figure in Childhood Education," 26.

136. Snyder, *Dauntless Women,* 192.

137. Ibid.

138. Shapiro, *Child's Garden,* 174, 186.

139. Snyder, *Dauntless Women,* 209.

140. Edgar B. Wesley, *NEA: The First Hundred Years: The Building of the Teaching Profession* (New York: Harper & Row Brothers, 1957), 162, 164; and Mary Dabney Davis, *Nursery-Kindergarten-Primary Education in 1924–1926* (Bulletin), 1927, no. 28 (Washington, DC: United States Government Printing Office, 1927), 45.

141. Samuel Chester Parker and Alice Temple, *Unified Kindergarten and First-Grade Teaching* (Boston: Ginn and Company, 1925), 18.

142. See also: Blythe S. F. Hinitz, "The Development of Creative Movement within Early Childhood Education, 1920 to 1970" (Ed.D. diss., Temple University, 1977), 21, 34.

143. Parker and Temple, *Unified Kindergarten and First-Grade Teaching*, 2,14, 273.

144. Davis, *Nursery-Kindergarten-Primary Education in 1924–1926*, 12.

145. Ibid., 16, 18, 19–20. Diagrammatic examples of classrooms are provided in Davis's report.

146. Marvin Lazerson, "Social Reform and Early Childhood Education: Some Historical Perspectives," in *As the Twig Is Bent: Readings in Early Childhood Education*, ed. Robert H. Anderson and Harold G. Shane (Boston: Houghton Mifflin Company, 1971), 27; Wesley, *NEA: The First Hundred Years*, 164; Snyder, *Dauntless Women*, 191, 224; and Shapiro, *Child's Garden*, 190.

147. Parker and Temple, *Unified Kindergarten and First-Grade Teaching*, 26–27.

148. Snyder, *Dauntless Women*, 198.

149. Charles E. Strickland, "Paths Not Taken: Seminal Models of Early Childhood Education in Jacksonian America," in *Handbook of Research in Early Childhood Education*, ed. Bernard Spodek (New York: The Free Press, 1982), 331.

150. E. W. Thompson, *Education for Ladies, 1830–1860*. Chapter Seven, "Normal Schools and the Training of Teachers" (Morningside Heights, NY: King's Crown Press, 1947), 93–95, in ACEI Book Collection, #294. Special Collections, University of Maryland at College Park Libraries.

151. Ibid., 104.

152. Shapiro, *Child's Garden*, 39–40.

153. Vandewalker, "Ruth Burritt, The Centennial Kindergartner: 1832–1921," 136–137, 141–143; Stella Louise Wood, "Anna Ogden: 1842–1908," in *Pioneers of the Kindergarten in America*, 231–232; Vandewalker, *The Kindergarten in American Education*, 14, 18, 20, 66–67; Shapiro, *Child's Garden*, 60–62, 155–156; Snyder, *Dauntless Women*, 77–79, 97, 104–105, 127, 134–135, 139–140; Bertha Payne Newell, "Alice H. Putnam: 1841–1919," in *Pioneers of the Kindergarten in America*, 209–216; Dorothy W. Hewes, "Historical Foundations of Early Childhood Teacher Training: The Evolution of Kindergarten Teacher Preparation," in *Early Childhood Teacher Preparation*, ed. B. Spodek and O. N. Saracho, (New York: Teachers College Press, 1990), 56, 59; Anna K. Stovall, "Sarah B. Cooper: 1834–1896," in *Pioneers of the Kindergarten in America*, 274; and Elizabeth Harrison, "The Growth of the Kindergarten in the United States," in *Pioneers of the Kindergarten in America*, 9.

154. Margaret J. Stannard, "Mary J. Garland: 1834–1901," in *Pioneers of the Kindergarten in America*, 112–117; and Clara Wheeler, "Mrs. Lucretia Willard: 1838–1904," in *Pioneers of the Kindergarten in America*, 234–238.

155. Prospectus and course outlines (1939), Ann-Reno Institute, Teachers College, Columbia University. [In ACEI Collection, Record Group IV, Box 4. Special Collections, University of Maryland at College Park Libraries]; Prospectus, *The Elizabeth E. Mathews Normal Training School*, Portland, Oregon; Prospectus, *The Fort Worth Kindergarten Training School* (1913–1914), Texas; Prospectus, *The Froebel Kindergarten Training School* (1918–1919), Kansas City, Missouri; Prospectus, *The Froebel School of Kindergarten Normal Classes* (Miss Annie Coolidge Rust), Boston, Massachusetts; Prospectus, *The Froebelian School for Women* (Miss Wright); Prospectus, *The Kindergarten Inn for Women and Children*, Philadelphia, Pennsylvania (1914); Prospectus, *The Kindergarten Collegiate Institute*, Chicago, Illinois; Prospectus, *The Chicago Free Kindergarten Association*, Illinois; Prospectus, *The Law Froebel Kindergarten Training School and School of Culture for Young Women*, Toledo, Ohio; Prospectus, *Miami Kindergarten and Primary Normal School*, Miami, Florida (1920); Prospectus, *The Richmond Training School for Kindergartners*, Virginia (1915); Prospectus, *San Antonio Kindergarten Training School*, Texas (1911–1912); Prospectus, *Sioux Falls Kindergarten College*, South Dakota (1912); and Prospectus, *The South Carolina Kindergarten Association*, Charleston, South Carolina (1909–1910). All the prospectuses are in the ACEI Collection, Record Group V, Box 7. Special Collections, University of Maryland at College Park Libraries.

156. Shapiro, *Child's Garden*, 149; Vandewalker, *The Kindergarten in American Education*, 192.

157. "The Normal College of New York City," *Harper's New Monthly Magazine,* April 1878, 673–674. In ACEI Collection, Record Group V, Box 7. Special Collections, University of Maryland at College Park Libraries.

158. Ross, *The Kindergarten Crusade,* 54.

It is of interest to note that Hunter College (renamed for its first president), a part of the City University of New York, continues to train early childhood and elementary school teachers to this day.

159. "The Normal College of New York City," *Harper's New Monthly Magazine,* April 1878, 678–679, 681–682.

160. Blythe F. Hinitz, "The Transmission of Culture through Early Childhood Teacher Education in the United States and England between 1850 and 1990: Examples from Archival and Interview Research" (Paper presented at ISCHE XVI [The Sixteenth meeting of the International Standing Committee on the History of Education], Amsterdam, The Netherlands, August 1994), 12.

161. Ruth Jacknow Markowitz, *My Daughter, The Teacher: Jewish Teachers in the New York City Schools* (New Brunswick, NJ: Rutgers University Press, 1993), 19, 21.

162. Gertrude A. (Nachitowitz) Farb, interviews by Blythe F. Hinitz, 1991, 1993.

163. Lucy Wheelock, "The Wheelock School," in *Childhood Education* III, no. 2 (October 1926): 89. In ACEI Collection, Record Group IV, Box 20. Special Collections, University of Maryland at College Park Libraries.

164. New College Bulletin (New York: Teachers College, Columbia University) 1st Series No. 1 (1937–1938), 10–11.

165. Ibid., 11–12, 14.

166. Parallels can be seen in current international study and exchange schemes under the auspices of several colleges, universities, and organizations.

167. New College Bulletin, 16–17.

168. Snyder, *Dauntless Women,* 339, 241, 273–278, passim.

169. Ibid., 275; and The Ann-Reno Institute, *A New Plan for Teacher Education* (New York: Author, 1939).

170. "Principles of Curriculum and Techniques of Teaching," TMs (photocopy) and "Social Studies," TMs (photocopy) Record Group IV, Box 4, ACEI Collection, Archives and Manuscripts, Maryland Room, University of Maryland at College Park Libraries, College Park, Maryland.

171. Shapiro, *Child's Garden,* 155; and Laurel M. Tanner, *Dewey's Laboratory School: Lessons for Today* (New York: Teachers College Press, 1997), 9.

172. Snyder, *Dauntless Women,* 334–343. See Snyder, *Dauntless Women,* pages 336–338 for descriptions of the program in kindergarten education designed by Lucy Gage in 1908 and then following her second visit to Teachers College, in 1915. In the second set of courses, one can see the shift toward the unified kindergarten primary curriculum.

173. Vandewalker, *The Kindergarten in American Education,* 71.

174. Snyder, *Dauntless Women,* 197–198.

175. Hewes "Historical Foundations of Early Childhood Teacher Training," 264.

176. Ross, *The Kindergarten Crusade,* 64.

177. Gertrude A. (Nachitowitz) Farb, interviews by Blythe F. Hinitz, 1991, 1993.

178. Ibid.; and Markowitz, *My Daughter, the Teacher,* 8, 12, 22, 32.

179. Prospectus of the Law Froebel Kindergarten Training School, Toledo, Ohio, in ACEI Collection, Record Group V, Box 7, Special Collections, University of Maryland.

180. Peabody, *Lectures in the Training Schools for Kindergartners,* 13. See Barbara Beatty, *Preschool Education in America: The Culture of Young Childen from the Colonial Era to the Present* (New Haven, CT: Yale University Press, 1995), 61–62, for a further discussion of Peabody's "efforts to promote kindergartening as a vocation for American women."

181. Ross, *The Kindergarten Crusade,* 52–53.

182. Ibid., 59–60.

183. Nina C. Vandewalker, *The Standardizing of Kindergarten Training* (Washington, DC: United States Bureau of Education Bulletin No. 6, 1914), 114–118; and Nina C. Vandewalker, "The Curriculum and Methods of the Kindergarten Training School," *Kindergarten Review* 13 (June 1903), 643; both cited in Shapiro, *Child's Garden,* 149.

184. James M. Cooper and Corinne E. Eisenhart, "The Influence of Recent Educational Reforms on Early Childhood Teacher Education Programs" in *Early Childhood Teacher Preparation,* ed. Bernard Spodek and Olivia N. Saracho (New York: Teachers College Press, 1990), 185; and Jan McCarthy, *State Certification of Early Childhood Teachers: Analysis of the 50 States and the District of Columbia* (Washington, DC: National Association for the Education of Young Children, 1988). (Originally presented January 26, 1988, at NAEYC Colloquium: Early Childhood Teacher Education: Traditions and Trends, Fountainebleau Hilton Resort, Miami, FL), 2–5. (Cooper and Eisenhart's discussion is based on Jan McCarthy's data.)

185. Jan McCarthy, "Early Childhood Teacher Licensure Revisited" (paper presented at Building Professional Partnerships, the Seventh Annual Conference of NAEYC's National Institute for Early Childhood Professional Development, Miami, Florida, 18 June 1998); and Jan McCarthy, Josué Cruz, Jr., and Nancy Ratcliff, "Early Childhood Teacher Licensure Patterns: A State by State Analysis" (paper presented at National Association for the Education of Children Annual Conference, Toronto, Canada, 20 November 1998).

CHAPTER 10
The Nursery School Movement

Educate every child as if he were your own.[1]
—Margaret McMillan

The nursery schools like the kindergartens before them came to the American shores from Europe in the early 1920s. The nursery schools came from England. They were child-saving institutions. The purpose of the English nursery schools was to provide a desirable environment from the standpoint of the child's physical, mental, and social needs. Additionally included was expert guidance for the parents of the less economically advantaged children. Nursery schools provided a clean and safe place for the children to get nutritious food, have health inspections, and planned activities for them to do.[2]

Originally the nursery schools were philanthropic, but the Fisher Educational Act of 1918 made possible the establishment of nursery schools throughout England for children over two and under five years of age. As part of the national school system, the nursery schools were subject to the regulations of the Board of Education and they were open to inspection by the Local Educational Authority. The Board of Education also defined standards for nursery schools regarding the following points: (1) the physical care of the children, including medical inspection and supervision as well as health education; (2) the mental and social education of the children; (3) the administrative details of the institution; and (4) the staffing of the institution.[3]

The introduction of the nursery school into the United States is closely associated with the history of women. The first private nursery schools were founded either by women of means or those whose husbands and friends had the wealth to support the project. In many instances, the founding philanthropists oversaw the financial aspects of the program, leaving the health, nutrition, and education aspects to the staff members. In other cases, the founders were heavily involved in the setting up and running of the school, either because they subscribed to a particular educational or religious philosophy, or because they had expertise in child development and related fields.

The American nursery school was the outcome of an interest in pre-kindergarten education, which resulted from advances in science and social needs. A scientific interest in early childhood arose from a new emphasis in the sciences of biology, physiology, psychology, and medicine. Experimental efforts in the field of mental hygiene produced new insights. Mental hygiene was especially concerned with the preschool period because of its emphasis on prevention, and the belief that the earlier the work was started, the more effective it would be. Psychologists and child development specialists at institutions of higher education had research as their main thrust when they initiated nursery schools for the dual purposes of providing subjects for their studies and guiding young children's development. Parental education became increasingly important for social improvement. The appearance of the nursery school movement, in the 1920s, lent additional credence to the idea that the education of young children outside the home might, in fact, represent a positive good rather than an unfortunate necessity.[4]

Several types of nursery schools were established in the United States. The first U.S. nursery schools were private, begun by women who wanted both to help children to achieve their full potential and to learn about child development. As nursery schools evolved, they came to include private for-profit schools, welfare-related and charity nurseries, laboratory nursery schools, and parent-cooperative nursery schools. Today's owner-operated, proprietary and private, as well as the publicly funded, nursery schools stand on the foundation laid by the founders of the nursery school movement.

One of the characteristics of the growth of the American nursery schools during 1919–1923 had been the variety of avenues that led to the establishment of nursery schools. A few examples are: departments of psychology, education and home economics in universities; individuals and groups other than universities, interested in research to increase the knowledge of preschool children; parents wanting to provide for the education of their young children; individuals and associations interested in improving the educational status of the day nursery.

As a result of the variety of agencies involved in the development of the American nursery school, the nursery schools vary widely from each other.[5] Psychological research, home economics, educational methods and curricula, preschool clinics, professional careers for married women, philanthropy, and mothers' cooperative care of children were additional reasons for nursery schools. Several of the pioneer nursery schools came into being at about the same time—the Merrill-Palmer Nursery School in Detroit and the Ruggles Street Nursery School and Training Centre in Boston. This was probably due to the fact that several Americans went to Europe to study the McMillan Nursery School in England or the Casa dei Bambini of Montessori in Rome, at about the same time. English nursery school teachers[6] came to America, as the German kindergartners had done fifty years earlier.

Shortly after their founding, a number of the nursery schools became teacher training sites, as normal schools and universities read the results of the research done by these early childhood educators. In the early years of nursery school development, teachers were trained by apprenticeship in an existing facility. Normal schools later developed nursery teacher training departments. However, these often were under the auspices of departments of home economics or child care, rather than education. It is for this reason that up until the present time, nursery school teacher education is found in departments of family science and consumer studies, child development, and human services, as well as in schools of education.

Caroline Pratt (1867–1954)

Caroline Pratt, founder of the Play School (later the City and Country School), was born on May 13, 1867, and grew up on her parents' farm in Fayetteville, New York. At sixteen years of age, she taught in the local one-room school during the summer, and by seventeen, she was teaching full time in the school. In 1892, she was offered a scholarship to study kindergarten methods at Teachers College, Columbia University. She has written that she found Froebelian kindergarten doctrines "mythical fol-de-rol,"[7] and she switched to manual training, graduating in 1894. She took a position teaching manual training at the Normal School for Girls in Philadelphia. While she was working in Philadelphia, she studied at the University of Pennsylvania and attended a summer course in *slöjd* at a manual training school in Sweden.[8] None of this work proved very satisfying to Pratt, so she was glad to meet Helen Marot, "a 32 year old Quaker who had organized a library for those interested in social and economic problems."[9] She joined Marot in an investigation of the custom tailoring trades in Philadelphia, and then moved with her to New York City, where both became active in the formation of the Women's Trade Union League (WTUL).[10] Pratt and Marot lived together until Marot's death in 1940.

Disenchanted with her three part-time manual training jobs, in 1913 she approached Miss May Matthews, the head of Hartley House, which was affiliated with the Henry Street Settlement. She was permitted to use the assembly room, with the stipulation that everything must be picked up and put away at the end of each session.[11] With the financial backing of Edna Smith, Pratt opened the Play School in Greenwich Village in 1914, with six five-year-old neighborhood children.[12] Although originally focused on providing an enriched life for young slum children, it soon became an experiment in creative education for all children, regardless of economic status.[13] The next year, Pratt, Marot, and Smith bought a house on West Thirteenth Street that housed the expanded program. During this time period, Pratt designed and made a set of "unit blocks," as well as "do-withs," which were small wooden figures to accompany the blocks. In November 1913, Lucy Sprague Mitchell was introduced to her by Harriet Johnson, whom Pratt knew from her work at Hartley House, and by 1915 Mitchell had developed a plan for moving the school to a building behind her home on Washington Square North.

Over the years, Pratt and Mitchell had major differences over administration of the school, and the publication of Mitchell's book *The Here and Now Story Book*. Mitchell discontinued teaching at the school in 1928, and in 1940 payment on the last personal loan she had made toward its mortgage was completed. Pratt retired as director in 1945 and died on June 6, 1954.[14]

Caroline Pratt produced several books and pamphlets recounting the story of the City and Country School, its philosophy, and curriculum, with the assistance of teachers at the school, and the staff of the Bureau of Educational

Experiments (BEE). Among the publications are: *Experimental Practice in the City and Country School* (1924), *Before Books* (1926), and *I Learn from Children* (1948). Pratt made a lasting contribution to nursery school education and to its teachers' professional development.

City and Country School (1916)
(The Play School [1914])

In October 1916, the Play School began in a converted stable on MacDougal Alley. "The name . . . 'The Play School,' reflects a special interest of the founder, her original inquiry into the educational possibilities of children's play and its place in school procedure." Pratt strongly believed that "the pursuit of information is never regarded as an object in itself. It is the *process of getting the information* which is important." Another goal of this child-centered school was to "radically revise the traditional sexual division of labor and promote equality between the sexes." A third goal was to "liberate the creative impulses of its students; [however], the mainspring of its pedagogy was political. Pratt . . . identified herself as a revolutionary Socialist, but in fact (according to Antler), no more complete representation of the Deweyite vision of the school as a social reform agency could be found than in the new school on MacDougal Alley."[15]

The year 1921 saw a move to new quarters in six buildings on West Twelfth and Thirteenth Streets purchased by the Mitchells to house both their home and the school. At this time the name changed from Play School to City and Country School to connote what the children considered more serious purposes. The school became City and Country School "in recognition of the summer farm program which Pratt and Lucy Mitchell had established at Hopewell Junction, New York. Nevertheless Pratt always preferred the original name."[16]

The school's philosophy was: "To study the interests and abilities of the growing child as they are manifested, to supply an environment that, step by step, shall meet the needs of his development, stimulate his activities, and orient him in his enlarging world, and that shall at the same time afford him effective experiences in social living."[17] The physical environment included individual clothes lockers and storage compartments, and was free of desks, permitting children to work independently or in small groups.[18]

Pratt was not in favor of detailed planning. In her autobiography, she expresses a preference for review of the records of previous children and teachers. Although there was no formal curriculum document, at the teachers' request, a design for curriculum organization was formulated and used. The plan was divided into four categories, which provided a framework for teacher preparation for and recording of the children's work. The categories used included: "Play Experiences, such as block building, dramatic play, art" and play with "big materials"; and Practical Experiences, into which fell shop work, cooking, sewing, clay, and care of materials. These two were the core of the curriculum. Skills or Techniques (later called Special Training) included "the experiences directed toward certain ends and the acquisition of special techniques." Sense-training, physical exercise, number work, reading, language arts, and music techniques were part of this category. Enrichment of Experience (later called Organization of Information), which included such things as science, trips, discussions, dramatizations, the use of books and stories, all the ways of seeking and pooling information, was the way in which the children reached out for new knowledge.[19]

Jobs for each group of children aged seven to thirteen supplemented the original play program for children aged two to seven. "In this program, traditional school work—history, geography, literature, etc.—was not taught as individual subjects, but stemmed from the central enterprise of a particular class—the printing of a newspaper, the buying and selling of school supplies, the selling of shop products—conducted throughout the school year." Each group's job was a necessary function of the school, and in addition to providing multiple learning experiences and projects, it alleviated the workload of the underpaid school staff.[20] Pratt justified the school's learning methods through written descriptions of staff planning discussions, incorporation of current events into the curriculum, and the novel organization and use of the school library.[21] When the school found it necessary to incorporate under the laws of the state of New York, the teachers' committee became the corporate board, with the principal as president, and the secretary and treasurer fulfilling the same functions on the incorporation papers.[22]

THE BUREAU OF EDUCATIONAL EXPERIMENTS (1916)

In 1916, Lucy Sprague Mitchell, along with Caroline Pratt and Harriet Johnson, founded the BEE. Its early aims were: "first, to conduct researches which will lead to further and fuller data concerning children's growth, and second, to bring schools and specialists dealing with various aspects of children into intimate and working contact with one another."[23] A summary written in 1917 states:

> The BEE is made up of a group of persons who are engaged in first-hand efforts for improving education of children, and who have all shared in the general movement that has brought about a more scientific study of them. They feel that the development of some more comprehensive plans for utilizing the results of the recent interest in "free education" is the next step, and that it depends essentially upon securing a closer cooperation among experimenters.
>
> Among the noticeable features of the present education situation are: a broader view of education which makes well-considered experimenting a much sought for opportunity; the emergence of a considerable number of educators who are really experimentally minded; the accumulation of a large amount of highly specialized experience; the appearance of a considerable literature

dealing with experimental procedures; and the gradual sorting out of doubt-ful experiments from those that have more permanent usefulness. To this sit-uation the Bureau hopes to contribute by affording an opportunity to increase the value of all experiments through cooperative effort, and by pre-serving and making permanent those experiments that may suitably become parts of an organized system of experimental education.

The Bureau aims to accomplish these ends by giving support to present experiments; by initiating new experiments; by collecting and making avail-able for public use information about the whole field of experiments in edu-cation; and by hastening the introduction of newly acquired methods through student teaching experiments.[24]

Barbara Biber wrote in 1936 that "although in its early years the Bureau was primarily an organization for child research, its psychological attitude toward research indicated an approach consistently educational as well as sci-entific."[25] The BEE studied growth in terms of maturity rather than age levels. It looked at the relationship between psychological and physical develop-ment, choosing experimental schools as its laboratory in order to study the child in a natural setting.[26] After working with several experimental schools in New York City, and then exclusively with City and Country School, the Bureau approved a plan for work with younger children submitted by Harriet Johnson.

HARRIET MERRILL JOHNSON (1867–1934)

Harriet Merrill Johnson was born on August 28, 1867, in Portland, Maine. She attended public schools and taught in a private school in Maine. In 1895, she entered Massachusetts Homeopathic Hospital nurses' training course and worked for several years as a nurse upon completion of her studies. In 1902, she attended Teachers College, Columbia University for further study in nurs-ing and health. She became a member of the Henry Street Settlement staff, as a district nurse at Hartley House. After study at the New School for Social Research, she organized and became head of the Public Education Associa-tion (PEA) Visiting Teachers staff in 1905. Her interest in the problems of maladjusted children in the public schools led to a meeting with Lucy Sprague Mitchell, when Mitchell worked as a visiting teacher at a downtown public school.[27]

Johnson, who was called "John" by the Mitchells, shared her life with Harriet Forbes, another nurse. Together they adopted a baby girl. Johnson, the parent of record, learned about many of the practical aspects of child development from her young daughter, Polly Forbes-Johnson. To deepen her knowledge, Johnson became a staff member of the Psychological Survey, which conducted an investigation in various public schools, and acted as advi-sor to a small parent-organized nursery school at Greenwich House. She was on the BEE research staff, and served as general secretary during the formative years. Her major research interest in the development of the whole child led her to nursery school work. "Johnson approached the problem of a nursery school with the educational viewpoint of working out an environment suited to the growth needs of two-and-three-year-olds; and from the scientific viewpoint of recording and analyzing their physiological and psychological development. She was singularly fitted by training and temperament to understand the wide gamut of these needs."[28]

Johnson was an integral part of the teaching faculty and central staff of the Cooperative School for Student Teachers (which later became Bank Street College of Education), between 1930 and 1934. This undertaking was designed to provide appropriately educated teachers for experimental schools. She co-edited the Cooperating School pamphlets from 1932 until her death on February 21, 1934.

A cogent and prolific writer, Johnson was well aware of the research and experimental undertakings of her day. Surviving works include books, pamphlets, and articles completed during her lifetime, and posthumous publications. Her books *Children in the Nursery School* and *School Begins at Two: A Book for Teachers and Parents* could easily be utilized in current nursery school methods courses. Journal articles such as "Educational Implications of the Nursery School" and "The Education of the Nursery School Child" are similarly applicable today. The descriptive bulletin *A Nursery School Experiment,* which was reprinted in *Experimental Schools Revisited,* describes the BEE Nursery School with clarity. Taken together, Johnson's publications provide a foundation of action research that inform and edify the contemporary student of the nursery school.

As a teacher-educator and staff member of the BEE, Johnson shared herself and her school with professional colleagues to the end. According to Mitchell, Johnson's interests included the socioeconomic problems of parents, experimental education, and child research. She "had a rare ability shown both in her genius for friendship and in her work. She understood the way other people thought and felt and learned even from seemingly alien minds. This, combined with a singular integrity of purpose and thinking, enriched her own deep experiences."[29] Johnson's writing guides us to this day. A multifaceted, multitalented woman, Harriet Johnson is remembered as a pioneer in nursery school education.

The Bureau of Educational Experiments Nursery School (1919)

The BEE decided that it needed to work with younger children. To study the growth of children in the first three years of life, the Bureau opened the Nursery School in 1919. The BEE designed an environment to give babies rich sense and motor experiences, scope for learning through experimentation, adventure without danger to life or limb, and contacts with others without demanding inappropriate adjustments. Enrollment was limited to one group of eight children ranging in age from fourteen or eighteen months to three years. The youngest children were given preference, regardless of the order of application. Detailed records of the children were kept both by the teachers and by recorders, such as Mary Marot, from the BEE staff. After the publication of *Children in the Nursery School* in 1928, the age range of the Bureau Nursery School was extended to cover the ages between two and six.[30]

Johnson's ideas and words from the 1920s, novel and inspirational in her own time, are widely accepted today. Her "Working Hypothesis of a Nursery School—statements of a school philosophy" included the following ideas:

> *"Children need to explore and experiment, to create and understand."*
> *"Play materials serve as tools for expression."*
> *"Dramatic play is the child's way of organizing experience."*
> *"Whenever the opportunity for a choice is offered a child it shall be genuine."*
> *"Play schemes are a vehicle for constructive social relations."*
> *"A child can comprehend readily when his experience is kept real and simple."*
> *"Trips for children need to be planned toward continuity and relevance of experience."*
> *"The teacher's role is distinct from that of the parent."*[31]

Johnson initiated procedures in the nursery school that were "like that in a family, informal and as casual as possible."[32]

"Experimental schools were then (1916) in the early stage of working out a curriculum based upon experience rather than upon content. The more consistent of them—a more accurate word than 'radical'—were attempting to make the school a laboratory where children could make strategic discoveries about things and people, a place where experience would pass over readily and naturally into expression."[33] Johnson directed the nursery school from 1919 to 1930, at which time she became codirector with Jesse Stanton until 1934. The school was renamed in her honor after her demise. Johnson's skill made possible the close integration of research and schooling at the nursery school.[34]

LITTLE RED SCHOOLHOUSE (1929)

Little Red Schoolhouse was begun by Elisabeth Irwin in 1929. This experimental program, sponsored by the PEA, was housed at Public School 41 in the Greenwich Village section of New York City. Irwin stayed with her first-grade students through the sixth grade. As at the City and Country School, academic instruction began in the second grade. The previous year consisted of block and dramatic play, trips, and creative experiences.

At P.S. 41, Irwin and her five colleagues were able to work with a kindergarten and two first-grade classes. The program staff was also responsible for training and supervising teachers in the upper grades. Included in the program was a June visit to a summer camp, at which the city children were in "culture shock." They discovered that teachers do sleep and that vegetables come from the ground, not supermarkets. Unfortunately, when the PEA discontinued its funding for the project, the Board of Education also withdrew its support. In spite of a favorable evaluation from the dean of education at City College, the Board review committee decided the program offered children "too much freedom" in school. The administrative and fiscal difficulties could not be overcome, so the public school program was closed. Irwin was able to reopen Little Red Schoolhouse as a private school during the fall of 1932. She continued to have large classes of thirty-five students, and charged a tuition equivalent to the per capita cost of a child's education to the city schools.[35]

MARGARET NAUMBURG (1890–1983)

Margaret Naumburg was twice a pioneer. She founded the Children's School, as a nursery school whose philosophy represented Freudian psychoanalytic theory. Naumburg was also the founder of art therapy in the United States. This art therapy background appears to have had an influence on the curriculum and methods implemented at the Children's School.

Margaret Naumburg was born on May 14, 1890, in New York City. She received her bachelor of arts degree from Barnard College, where she had been an enthusiastic student of Dewey and president of the Socialist Club.[36] She went to Europe just prior to World War I to study at the London School of Economics. Becoming disillusioned with socialism, she went to Rome, to the Casa dei Bambini. Although, according to Cremin, they did not get along too well, in 1913 she received her teachers' diploma for work done under the personal supervision of Dr. Maria Montessori.[37] Upon her return to New York, she managed a Montessori kindergarten at the Henry Street Settlement, but she found "the Method dull and unimaginative."[38] During 1914, Naumburg continued her studies, taking summer teachers' training courses.[39] Her study with F. Matthias Alexander in London exposed her to the ideas of psychoanalysis and psychoanalytic theory. Freud's detailed tracing of psychological development drew sharp attention to the child as an individual with his own inner life and needs. "Because this new psychology presented, for the first time, a fully dimensional picture of the child, it offered a framework within which a genuinely fresh approach to education could be devised—an approach that put education at the service of the child, and not the child at the service of education."[40] Naumburg vowed to "open a school of her own in which the emotional side of education would have parity with the intellectual. The year 1914 also marked the beginning of a three-year period of analysis under the Jungian psychiatrists Beatrice Hinkle and A. A. Bell."[41] During this time period, she "tried an experiment in the kindergarten department of the New York City schools," developing frustration over her inability to "obtain even the minimum necessities in equipment." When other public school teachers told her that she had not been there long enough, and it was necessary to conform or resign, she left the position after six months.[42]

Naumburg and her friend Claire H. Raphael founded a Montessori Class at the Leete School on East Sixtieth Street in Manhattan, which met from 1914 to 1916. This eclectic program, which utilized the variety of training that she had completed, marked for Naumburg the beginning of the Children's School.

After she retired from active direction of the Children's School, Naumburg focused her attention upon study and writing. The publication of Naumburg's *The Child and the World: Dialogues in Modern Education*, in 1928, caused quite a stir. The dialogue format provided a vehicle for clearly stating both the burning questions about Walden School philosophy and method, and her thoughtful responses. The questioners of the director included a midwestern public school superintendent, two normal school students, a sociologist, a university professor, and a modern stage producer. Other dialogues between the school psychologist and parents and between a public school teacher and a "new school" teacher represent different approaches to discussion. Naumburg distinguished between laboratory schools that "are merely liberal and those that are truly experimental," considered the relationship of the individual and the social group, discussed the limitations of behaviorist theory, presented the role of the teacher as observer, and described several new techniques (such as psychoanalysis and physical coordination) that were being used for the first time at Walden School.

By the 1930s, Naumburg had begun work at New York Psychiatric Institute, where she used artistic expression as a means of diagnosing and treating disturbed adults and children. The undated manuscript of a talk she gave at the Children's Center on art therapy notes that she used a two-pronged approach. She "held a weekly staff conference to orient them to theories and methods by which more spontaneous emotional expression in the arts can be developed in the nursery school groups." Second, she made "visits, whenever there was free time to study the activities of the children in the nursery school groups and make practical suggestions to the teachers."[43] She remained active in her roles as founder and advisory director until her death in 1983.[44]

Walden School (The Children's School) (1914)

The name the Children's School "provides the key to its effort: to provide a curriculum built on the 'apparently unlimited desire and interest of children to know and to do and to be.'"[45] The fortieth anniversary bulletin describes the prevailing harsh theories of child care in 1914, going on to state that these theories were beginning to be questioned. "Lineal descendants of Pestalozzi, Froebel and Herbart were instituting changes in small schools here and in Europe and influencing the *avant garde* thought in education. John Dewey's work had begun to have its effect on the educational world."[46] A glance at the second catalog and prospectus of Naumburg's Montessori Class shows an eclectic use of both the theory and practice of the Montessori Method.

Naumburg's insights into young children are apparent in the following paragraph from her 1915 catalog. "This concentration on one subject through the volition of the children, gets up a momentum to carry them through to real achievement. At first children flit from one thing to another, showing little concentration. But from day to day an evident change takes place in the entire group, in some more rapidly than others, until gradually the whole class becomes a self-directing community. A day in a Montessori class is based on no preconceived program. The curriculum has grown out of the needs of the children."[47]

When the number of students multiplied, Raphael departed, the school moved to rented brownstone buildings on West Sixty-Eighth Street, and changed its name. A fifth-grade Walden student, Maro Avakian, wrote after interviewing Naumburg in 1964, "Before it was called 'Walden,' Walden School was known as 'The Children's School,' until the older children protested."[48] Naumburg's rationale for the choice was: "The school is part of that main current of American democratic traditions of which the New England Transcendentalists were one expression, among these, Henry David Thoreau, after one of whose works the school is named. This is a current which asserts the right of the individual against the pressures for massive conformity, and the rights of minorities against the oppressions of majorities."[49]

Two of the 1964 students' recorded impressions included a statement that Naumburg had the first nursery school in New York City. Although Pratt probably would have taken issue with this, the Children's School certainly was among the very first nursery schools in the city, as well as one of the oldest experimental schools in the country. It followed the educational approach of John Dewey; used the implications of psychoanalysis to find new, more genuine understandings of the "whole child"; and sought by new methods to release his full potential. The analytically oriented staff and parent body were aware of the dominant role played by the emotions, were willing to try out new theories on the meaning and scope of education, and accepted the concept of "learning by doing." It was found that the capacity to learn was seriously diminished by a child's feelings of insecurity, shame, guilt, frustration, or fear. The environment of home and school needed to offer the child protection and support. It was felt that during the early years, the child's primitive drives and impulses should be understood and released, rather than merely suppressed or arbitrarily controlled. It was deemed more important for the child to express his own honest ideas and feelings than to provide the adults with the answers they expected or demanded. A personal relationship, which served as a major vehicle for the child's growth and education, was established between the students and their teachers.[50]

In a 1917 publication, Naumburg identified a use of psychoanalysis in dealing with practical classroom problems. She stated, "The usual attempt at a surface solution of a child's behavior when, for instance, he lies or shows fear, is similar to the act of cutting off the top of a weed with the roots still in the ground. . . . Education has missed the real significance of the child's behaviors, by treating surface actions as isolated conditions. Having failed to recognize the true sources of behavior, it has been unable effectively to correct and guide the impulses of human growth."[51]

In 1922, Naumburg retired from the active direction of Walden School. Margaret Pollitzer and Elizabeth Goldsmith became codirectors, while she remained as advisory director. By 1931, Pollitzer was advisory director and Goldsmith was director and psychologist. Both successors wrote about the experimental work of the school in professional publications, such as *Progressive Education* and the 1929 *National Society for the Study of Education (NSSE) Yearbook*.[52] Stating that "the first five years of a child's life are most significant, most plastic, and therefore most creative educationally,"[53] Goldsmith outlined the major tenets of the Walden Nursery School program. One basic principle was to provide "a habit clinic for both parents and children." Another was the provision of an all-day program, in order to affect habit formation and to utilize psychoanalytic methods in their "handling of sex problems." In frequent conferences with parents, they emphasized "the need of answering questions of little children about birth and their bodily structures, this to be done in a natural, simple way at the level of understanding of the child."[54] Over the years, Walden School had many directors,[55] including (in 1964) Dr. Milton Akers, who later became executive director of the National Association for the Education of Young Children (NAEYC).

The fiftieth anniversary publication succinctly summarizes Naumburg's work in this way: "She wanted to help the nursery school children with whom she worked to develop to the limit of their potentials and in accordance with their individual needs. Miss Naumburg was persuaded that the traditional methods of education could never achieve this aim."[56] The basic premise of Naumburg's pedagogy was creative teaching. The group teachers in her school were depended on to encourage and develop all the creative activities and interests, whether in the arts or in the tool subjects. Margaret Naumburg made Walden School a model of progressive education.

CREATIVE ARTS IN THE EXPERIMENTAL NURSERY SCHOOLS

Walden School and the City and Country School placed great emphasis on expressive work in the creative arts. Artist-teachers Hughes Mearns and Satis Coleman of the Lincoln School, Lucy Sprague Mitchell and Willy Levin of the City and Country School, and Florence Cane of the Walden School were employed to foster a pedagogical version of the expressionist credo. If one examines the poems, music, painting, sculpture, and theater sets that fill the pages of *Progressive Education* during the 1920s, one can sense the elation the progressives themselves must have felt. When the artist-teachers were asked the clue to their success, they answered as if in chorus: "Take the lid off youth!"[57] Mitchell made the case for maps as artistic expression. She asked:

"Is it too much to hope that the children will never make the devastating divorce of these two elements which makes most adults feel that a scientist cannot be an artist or an artist a scientist?"[58] That is a question worth pondering in our own time.

PARENT COOPERATIVE PRESCHOOLS IN THE UNITED STATES (1915, 1916)

Parent cooperative preschools are designed as educational experiences for young children *and* their parents. As such, they are "unique educational enterprises because they include as learners two diverse populations—parents and children. Few programs focus attention on these widely disparate age groups at the same time and under the same roof."[59] This statement is the undergirding principle of all parent cooperative preschools, whether they be, as most are, nursery schools, or kindergartens. Forest says that the cooperative nursery school is a distinctly American version of the nursery school plan.[60]

Katherine Whiteside Taylor, founder of one of the very first cooperatives, was well aware of the needs of the young educated mother who is suddenly isolated at home caring for her offspring. When she gave birth to her children, "she wanted very much to be involved in their education and to understand their developmental stages. To that end she initiated the formation of the Child Study section of the East Bay Branch of the American Association of University Women (A.A.U.W.)."[61] As the wife of a doctoral candidate at the University of California in Berkeley, she was able to make many contacts that aided in her study of child development. Taylor and her colleagues learned about the McMillan sisters' English nursery school and some of the first cooperative nursery schools in the United States.

According to Hewes, the Northside Cooperative Nursery School in Pasadena, California, established in 1915, was the first cooperative in the United States.[62] Faculty wives at the University of Chicago began a cooperative in 1916, "to secure social education for their children, parent education for themselves," "to widen their own experience with children," and to give themselves a little free time, perhaps for Red Cross work during World War I.[63] Forest cites a 1925 article by Althea Bass on two inherent dangers in the formation of a cooperative school, "(1) that parents will be tempted to consider the school merely a 'parking place' for their children; (2) that groups of parents will too readily undertake the organization of groups without providing for any trained leadership."[64] Taylor and her associates probably became aware of these difficulties as they set up their school.

In an interview, Taylor suggested that it was the Cambridge Nursery School in Massachusetts, organized by a group of mothers in 1923, that first demonstrated all the characteristics that define a parent cooperative. "They organized the school themselves. They sought a trained teacher, and brought one over from the McMillan Centre in London. And they, themselves, the parents, worked in the school."[65]

Another cooperative of which the Berkeley study group was probably aware was the Northampton Cooperative Nursery School of the Institute for the Coordination of Women's Interests at Smith College, which was formed "for the express purpose of providing uninterrupted periods of free time for mothers."[66] This 1926 venture was not founded by the parents themselves. It was part of a research study to determine whether an average group of mothers could cooperatively organize and institute a model program with local resources. The renamed Smith College Cooperative Nursery School was administered by the college, and therefore it did not meet all of Taylor's criteria.[67]

Although there is disagreement regarding which was the first cooperative, schools began at several sites during the 1920s, including Schenectady, New York; the University of California at Los Angeles; and Berkeley, California, where the Children's Community was founded by Taylor and her study group.[68] With the cooperation of the new Institute of Child Welfare at the University of California, and several university faculty members, the AAUW Berkeley Child Study Section founded their cooperative nursery school in 1927.[69] Helen Pennock, the original teacher-supervisor, had been trained at the Ruggles Street Nursery School. Taylor was the parent-director, with three mother-supervisors, a cook, and a janitor to round out the staff. Each mother was required to work one full day a week, assisting the director, the supervisor, and the cook in turn. The school's philosophy echoed Dewey's "learning by doing" approach, with time for free play indoors and outside. Initially, the children remained until 4:00 P.M., but in the second year of operation the hours were shortened. The curriculum "drew inspiration from Montessori, Dewey, Gesell, Freud and the progressive school movement."[70] The creative arts were an important part of the program. Art materials to foster the creative process were made available, but structure was not imposed. The name "Children's Community" was carefully chosen to signify the community that parents and children built together.[71]

In 1928, a second group of parents from the Berkeley study group set up the Berkeley Hills School.[72] The Children's Community and the Berkeley Hills School are the two oldest continually operating parent cooperatives in existence today. By the 1940s, cooperatives had opened in other cities in the United States and Canada.[73]

Taylor defined a parent cooperative as covering "all the educational groups organized by parents for their preschool children and themselves. Alternative terms are nursery schools, cooperatives, nurseries, play groups, preschools, or play centers, depending upon the particular location and setup."[74] Among the features that differentiate the parent cooperative from other types of early childhood education programs are the following:[75]

1. Cooperative nursery schools are organized by parents, not by professionals.
2. They come into being because parents themselves are trying to meet their own needs and the needs of their children.

3. The school has professional guidance. The teacher must be skilled not only in nursery education, but she must have the confidence of the parents and must work with them as well as with children.

Parents send their child to a cooperative preschool for many reasons. A primary motivation is to learn more about child nurture. The camaraderie of the cooperative becomes a positive force in the parents' (particularly the mothers') own adult mental health. Lower tuition, convenient location, and the possibility of car pools are important factors. Some parents are intrigued with the notion of a school that is run cooperatively by parents and teacher.[76]

The success of the parent cooperative nursery school "has not depended upon the continuance of the same leadership over the years, but rather upon the continual development of new leaders, often with continuing and vigorous growth when the pioneering and succeeding officers go on to other activities and new ones take their places." "For some it has become a turning point in their lives; they later become leaders in their communities. Some mothers make decisions about their careers and education which affect the pattern of the rest of their lives." "A large segment of our early childhood leadership, including university faculty, got introduced to the profession while they were parents in these schools, and in their positions of responsibility they staunchly believe in learning-by-doing."[77]

The cooperative preschool movement has spawned councils, publications, and an international organization. Beginning with the Montgomery County, Maryland, Council formed in 1944 and the East Bay [Regional] Cooperative Council in 1945, a number of state and regional groups were formed. The founding of a national organization was first discussed at meetings in 1953, and 1956, but the American Council of Parent Cooperatives was not formally chartered until August 1960 at Teachers College of Columbia University, under the sponsorship of Dr. Kenneth Wann. Between 1956 and 1960, some officials of the NANE were concerned that the formation of a new organization might split the nursery school movement; however, "there has been ample room for two organizations, and more than enough work for both to do."[78] At the 1964 annual conference, the organization's name was changed to Parent Cooperative Preschools International (PCPI), to formally indicate its worldwide membership. The Katherine Whiteside Taylor Centre in Baie D'Urfe, Quebec, Canada, which opened in 1969, became the international office of PCPI. The organization also maintains a United States office and in 1997 became a member of the National Cooperative Business Association.[79]

The parent cooperative nursery school movement made several important contributions to the development of the Head Start program. Among them are: the parent participation requirement, participation by volunteers, and the use of paraprofessionals.[80] Although the majority of parent cooperatives are run by white middle-class professional parents, they do reach out for inclusion of diverse individuals. As Taylor wrote, "years before the Head Start program was thought of, a parent cooperative took lodging in an underprivileged area to help the surrounding families as well as to give their own children contact with those of different racial, economic and cultural backgrounds. When wistful faces looked through the fence and none could be enrolled because their mothers worked full-time, a group of members . . . volunteered to give two extra days a month to maintain adequate staffing, thus making it possible for these children to come."[81]

Teacher Training

The professional teacher in a parent cooperative preschool must be equipped to work equally well with adults and children. Among the *Suggestions for a Course of Study on Parent Cooperative Nursery School* prepared by the Special Committee on Teacher Education of the California Council of Cooperative Nursery Schools are the following "Suggestions for Teacher Education for Prospective Directors and Teachers of Parent Cooperative Nursery Schools":

1. child growth and development
2. psychology of early childhood
3. group dynamics
4. parent education
5. participation and leadership experience with parent groups
6. roles in the cooperative nursery school
7. administration of a nursery school
    a. organization
    b. procedures
8. history of parent cooperatives
9. methods of teaching in cooperative nursery schools
10. family life education
11. community resources

As Taylor points out, "these recommendations cover a wider area than the usual courses required for a degree in early childhood education."[82]

The parent cooperative preschool movement has made an important contribution to the lives of children and adults over its eighty-year history. It has demonstrated the magnitude of what parents can do for themselves, their children, the profession of early childhood education, and the world community, when given appropriate professional guidance and encouragement to build and use their strengths.

BIRD T. BALDWIN (1875–1928)

Bird T. Baldwin had a distinguished career in psychology prior to assuming the first directorship of the Iowa Child Welfare Research Station (ICWRS). Baldwin, a Quaker born in Marshalton, Pennsylvania, in 1875, received his

B.S. from Swarthmore in 1900 and his Ph.D. from Harvard in 1905. According to Cravens, his dissertation study consisted of taking rigorous anthropometric measurements of children, distinguished by sex and race, and then attempting to correlate these with measures of chronological, physiological, and school age. In his work, he did not compare presumed racial types. Baldwin was interested in the relations between physical and mental growth. During his graduate program, he spent time studying abroad, at the University of Leipzig. Upon his return home, he met Robert M. Yerkes, the Harvard comparative psychologist, whose version of genetic psychology contrasted with Hall's, by including normal and subnormal, abnormal, defective children.[83]

His first professorship was in psychology at West Chester (Pennsylvania) State Normal School. In 1914, he published a general summary of his intensive research on growth in normal children. The publication described the five interrelated ages of a child.[84] Although Baldwin departed somewhat from the assumptions made in the child psychology of his time, he did not question the work of Hall, Terman, and Goddard, even if he did not endorse their premises.

Baldwin headed the ICWRS from its inception in 1917 to 1928. As director, he held a dean's rank and reported directly to the president. President Jessup guided Baldwin's political and public relations activities on the station's behalf, but he did not interfere with the implementation of Baldwin's ideas. Within the station's ranks, Baldwin was the dominant intellectual figure.[85]

Baldwin outlined his plans for the Station's research program immediately upon his arrival in Iowa City. The university administration reviewed the twenty-eight possible projects prior to his departure for a one-year leave of service as a major in the U.S. Sanitary Corps at Walter Reed Hospital, in order to peacefully fulfill his military obligation. In January 1918, the ICWRS began its contribution to President Woodrow Wilson's Children's Year by organizing a survey of the health and well-being of Iowa children in wartime. This study fulfilled the mission of the ICWRS, "scientific study of the child and . . . dissemination of that knowledge."[86]

Baldwin attempted to use the influence of his position as chair of the Committee on Child Welfare of the National Research Council, Division of Anthropology and Psychology, to obtain money for the ICWRS and the nursery school, in the spring of 1920. He was unsuccessful in obtaining funds from the Laura Spelman Rockefeller Memorial. His 1922 success freed Baldwin and the Station "from direct face-to-face politicking [sic] with its lay constituents."[87] As described later, the nursery school grew into a large research-oriented child development center.[88]

In 1923, Baldwin became a consultant to the Cleveland, Ohio, public schools. He selected 3,500 students from kindergarten through junior high school for whom he compared physical and mental data from physical, medical, dental, nutritional, mental examinations, and intelligence tests.[89] He theorized that mental development awaited physiological development and that, therefore, those who were physiologically advanced should be promoted to a grade level congruent with their development. He also thought that different racial and ethnic groups had different norms of development. The Cleveland project verified the assumption that the child's capacity for education was not limited to a few school subjects but included other phases of mental development, such as the aesthetic and emotional life and the child's capacity for physical and social growth.[90] As a result of his research, Baldwin told the school district that factors other than innate intelligence and class standing must be considered in school placement.

During his tenure as center director, Baldwin authored eighty-two publications and gave almost one hundred addresses before civic, professional, and scientific groups. His themes included physical and physiological maturation, the relationships between physiological and mental growth, and the importance of personality and social development as compared with the intelligence quotient. He argued that a child's basic nature and attributes were established by the time he entered public school, and therefore a child's proper development during the preschool years was very important. He insisted that child science had to be developed and managed by experts, meaning professionals trained in science. By the same token, the responsibilities of parenthood in today's modern, complex, technological society were such that parenthood must become a profession.[91] Weber says that the kindergarten movement could not remain immune to these discussions of individual differences and the vast range of individual performance and achievement.[92]

Baldwin and Lorle I. Stecher wrote one of the first general texts based on scientific work in a preschool laboratory, *The Psychology of the Preschool Child*.[93] Research on farm children was the first major investigation executed at the ICWRS with the Laura Spelman Rockefeller Memorial's support.[94] After criticizing the premise of the 1928 *NSSE Yearbook*, on the role of inheritance in intelligence, Baldwin's work appeared posthumously in the 1929 *Yearbook*.[95]

Baldwin wanted the field to be as professional and scientific as possible, and therefore, the research projects he chose for the ICWRS presented distinctions between child science and its antecedent and founding fields of psychology, physical growth, physiology, and pediatrics. In addition, Baldwin wanted to make science more important than child welfare and social activism on the part of the professionals.[96] The study of child personality and behavior had begun at the ICWRS before Baldwin's death from an infection on May 9, 1928. In the early years, Baldwin influenced the ICWRS's intellectual direction more than had any other single person.[97]

Iowa Child Welfare Research Station (1921)

The ICWRS preschool (psychological) laboratory was opened in October 1921.[98] The funds, originally from the Women's Christian Temperance Union (WCTU), were designated for work in "eugenics." To them it meant "socialization into proper habits of health, diet and sobriety for the young, plus a need to watch out for partners of the opposite sex who came from the wrong side of the tracks, had peculiar relatives, or otherwise did not conform to community standards of 'being nice.'" This was not the same definition utilized by the leaders of the eugenics movement, who were "ultranationalistic and racist" and believed in "sterilization of unfit races."[99] The WCTU Jubilee Fund's grant marked a watershed in the ICWRS's history, signifying that it was a national institution. The WCTU's prestige in child welfare and women's issues conferred prestige upon the ICWRS.[100] The agreement between the ICWRS and the WCTU stipulated that the station faculty was to have complete control over its own research agenda. This fact, and a Hornell Hart research project on rural and urban life, enabled the ICWRS to shift from WCTU to foundation sponsorship in later years.

The original program was designed for children from two to six years of age, who attended for half a day. Although activities were planned with the children's interests in mind, the preschool was first and foremost a research facility for graduate students and faculty members of the university. Studies in the areas of mental and social development of young children, physical and nutritional development, and parent education were completed and published. By 1929, the original preschool laboratory had been split into three divisions, organized on the basis of the children's maturity and development.[101] A fourth division, the Preschool Home laboratory had been added in 1925. Its purpose was to model the best methods of feeding, sleep, and play schedules, and training in mental development and behavior. The children in this laboratory attended from 9:00 A.M. until 4:00 P.M. Some remained all night. Baldwin was interested in learning from this experiment what factors constituted a home, as distinct from a school, environment.

The flexible program of the preschool laboratory included free play with materials; storytelling; music, singing, and rhythmic games; and group conversation. Snacks and meals, often part of a nutrition research project, were served in all preschool groups. The physical facility housed playrooms, a lavatory, a pantry, several examination and testing rooms, and an outdoor play yard. A fifth group on infant metabolism was housed in the Childrens' Hospital. The ICWRS served as the coordinating center for all the work in child development, child study, and parent education conducted by the three state educational institutions and various public school systems in Iowa.[102] In performing these functions, the ICWRS was fulfilling the dreams of both Baldwin and Lawrence Frank.

LAND-GRANT COLLEGES/HOME ECONOMICS

Long before the widespread interest in the young child, home economics departments in land-grant colleges throughout the country were engaged in programs of vocational homemaking through college curricula and extension courses. Because they had established contacts with women in the home and because they could offer materials that appeared to be immediately practical to the homemaker, home economics teachers were able to pave the way for later developments in the field of nursery education.

The land-grant colleges are United States institutions of higher learning established under the provision of the Morrill Act passed by the Congress and signed by President Lincoln in 1862. The land-grant colleges were to provide advanced education for the emerging professions in agriculture, engineering, homemaking, and the growing industry and commerce of the country. The older system of higher education inherited from Europe prepared young men for careers as ministers, lawyers, and physicians, the older professions.

The new country needed institutions to prepare young people for new careers. Originally the land-grant colleges were colleges of agriculture and mechanic arts. Their programs, however, were broadened and extended. Many developed into comprehensive institutions for higher learning. The land-grant colleges pioneered important innovations. They established higher education at low cost, research as a legitimate function of higher education, and the elevation of practical arts and sciences, like home economics, into academic status. Since World War II, the land-grant institutions have taken the lead in international cooperative programs like agriculture and the environment in the emerging nations.[103]

The Nursery School of the Iowa State College of Agriculture and Mechanic Arts at Ames (1924)

The nursery school at the Iowa State College was established (1924) to serve as an observation laboratory for the students of home economics. The focus of home economics at this college was homemaking. The senior women were required to take a four-quarter credit course in which the nursery school was used as the laboratory. Each student spent a minimum of twenty hours observing and working with children in the nursery school. This experience gave the young women an opportunity to be trained in, and become familiar with, the care and training of children, which is an important function of home life.

The emphasis of the nursery school program was to help children form correct biological habits, such as eating, sleeping, and elimination. The children had many opportunities to interact with other children under adult supervision. Each child developed an appreciation for social relationships by sharing play materials and equipment, maintaining individual rights, obeying authority, practicing self-control in waiting for a turn, and helping others. Teaching children was through the indirect method in which the teachers pointed out important learning in a particular context.[104]

The staff consisted of the director, a consulting psychologist, and two nursery school teachers. There were also a doctor in nutrition, a doctor of medicine, and the head of the Physical Educational Department at the college. The nursery school was housed in a three-story building at the edge of the campus. The first floor had the kitchen, one of the toilet rooms, the cloak room, and three offices. The playrooms were on the second floor. The third floor was used for sleeping or for play in rainy weather.

A large play space had been fenced in for outdoor activities. It contained a jungle gym, a large tent, a swing, bars, a sandbox, a garden, houses for animals, many trees (some of which the children were allowed to climb), plenty of grass, and plenty of shade. The children planted vegetable and flower gardens. They also took trips to the post office to mail a letter, to the dairy department, to the barns of the Animal Husbandry Department to see the young pigs, lambs, calves, and colts. The nursery school was open from at 8:45 A.M. to 3:30 P.M. For the program of activities, see Appendix 1.

The lunch hour afforded a learning situation. One of the playrooms was arranged for the serving of the noon meal. A student studying child care sat at each table with three children, one of whom was chosen to be the waiter. Grace was sung, after which the waiters served the meal. At the end of the meal, the children removed their own dishes. The children learned to eat a variety of foods, to eat all of the food served to them, and to observe proper table etiquette in handling the silver. The meal provided the children with an opportunity for social conversation and to serve others.

The psychologist, the doctor of medicine, and the doctor of nutrition all cooperated with the nursery school staff and parents. The psychologist held weekly conferences with the staff. The doctor of nutrition attended these conferences when needed. All children had a complete physical examination upon entrance and were examined every morning by a nurse from the hospital to see that they were not bringing into the nursery school any kind of contagion. For any illness that developed during the day, the campus physician was on call.[105]

SELECTION OF CHILDREN
The children of the nursery school came from a selected group of parents, mainly those connected with the college students, faculty, and staff. The long waiting list enabled the nursery school staff to require cooperation from the parents.

No children were admitted to the nursery school who were not healthy or who seemed to be mentally retarded. Children were selected to represent, as nearly as possible, normal healthy childhood. The average enrollment was about thirty children. The ratio of children to teacher was approximately twelve to one.

Children were encouraged to stay for two or three years. The nursery school preferred to admit only younger children, but this was not always possible because of the demands made by the parents who felt that their children should have the privilege of attending the nursery school while they were studying or teaching at the college.[106]

PARENT INVOLVEMENT
Both parents were expected to attend at least two meetings each quarter. One was a meeting for all parents to discuss topics of general interest. At the other,

both parents had a conference with the director, the psychologist, the doctor of nutrition, and the nursery school teachers about the child.

CHILDREN'S RECORDS
The nursery school kept attendance records and reasons for absence, physical growth records for height and weight, which were taken every two weeks, and records for food intake during the noonday lunch and for sleep during nap. They also kept mental growth records. The psychologist tested each child, using the following tests: the Stanford Revision Binet, the Blanton Speech, and the Kuhlmann Intelligence. Each child was tested soon after he entered the nursery school and had sufficiently adjusted to take the test. Afterward, each child was tested approximately every six months.

In addition to the tests, the nursery school teachers, director, and psychologist kept full account of problems of any kind that might arise. Teachers always had notebooks in their pockets, and anything that seemed significant was recorded immediately. This material was turned over to the psychologist for compilation and interpretation.[107]

The primary aim of the nursery school was to teach college students the best known methods of meeting the problems of child care and training as they would arise in the home situation.

In 1959, the Iowa State College of Agriculture and Mechanic Arts became the Iowa State University of Science and Technology at Ames, Iowa. The nursery school, still in operation, is now called the Child Development Lab School. It offers a program for about one hundred children ages three to six years old, including special needs children. Since 1954, it has been offering an after school program for forty children ages five to twelve years old.[108]

EDNA NOBLE WHITE (1879–1954)

Edna Noble White was a pioneer in child development, nursery school education, and parent education. She was born on June 3, 1879, in Fairmount, Illinois, the younger daughter and second of three children of Angeline (Noble) and Alexander L. White. Her father, a native of Logan, Ohio, was manager of a firm dealing in lumber, hardware, and agricultural implements and held several posts in the town government. Her mother, born in Indiana, was well educated and active in community affairs. White lived most of her adult life with her sister and acted as foster mother to her brother's two sons. She never married.

After she graduated from the Fairmount High School and received her B.A. from the University of Illinois in 1906, White taught high school in Danville, Illinois, and at the Lewis Institute in Chicago. She joined the Home Economics Department of Ohio State University in 1908. Home economics was a new profession for women that applied science to domestic issues. By 1915, she had become a full professor in charge of teacher training, supervisor of the home economics extension service, and chair of the department.

Her work with flood disasters and during World War I as director of the Ohio food conservation for the Council of National Defense earned her a reputation beyond the state.[109]

White was chosen in 1919 to be the founding director of the Merrill-Palmer Motherhood and Home Training School in Detroit, funded by the will of Lizzie Merrill Palmer, widow of Senator Thomas W. Palmer of Michigan. Mrs. Palmer left three million dollars for the founding and maintenance of a private school to train young women for motherhood and homemaking. There was no established model for the kind of school and research center White was asked to develop at the Merrill-Palmer. White went to England to study the nursery school and nursery education with Margaret McMillan, like Abigail Adams Eliot did. White found that McMillan's emphasis on children's physical health fit well with her training in home economics and nutrition.

Upon her return, in the spring of 1921, White presented to the board of the Merrill-Palmer a plan to establish an experimental nursery school. When it opened in 1922, it was the second center for child development research in this country (the first was the Iowa Child Welfare Research Station, founded in 1917). For many years, the Merrill-Palmer was the only research center not affiliated with a university. White wanted to go beyond the traditional interpretation of motherhood training as merely practical instruction in homemaking skills. She wanted to prove that the physical, mental, and emotional development of children was worthy of study at the college level. From a first class of thirty children and six students recruited from Michigan State University, Merrill-Palmer grew to attract the attention of educators throughout the world. Initially, the courses lasted six months; later a one-year residency requirement was set for the master's degree candidates.

Through White's efforts, cooperative programs were established with many colleges and universities. Undergraduates took courses for credit at Merrill-Palmer. The Merrill-Palmer laboratory nursery school was unlike the nursery schools in England—established primarily for the physical care of poor children. It was designed to guide college students and parents to learn more about child growth and development and to provide opportunities for research on child development and parent education. The growth of the school coincided with the development of the parent education movement in the United States.[110]

White gathered together specialists in pediatrics, nutrition, psychology, education, home economics, and social work. She organized the staff so as to integrate their knowledge and methods of teaching into the development of an all-round view of the developing child. She initiated one of the first interdisciplinary efforts in the new field of child development. Focusing at first on the preschool child, Merrill-Palmer soon broadened its view to include all phases of development from conception to adulthood and began some of the first longitudinal studies of children. The nursery school collected and disseminated large amounts of information about young children and their families. Another innovation was the shift from the individual child to the family as the unit of study. The fame of the Merrill-Palmer School reached distant parts of the world; the king of Siam, greeting visitors from Detroit, is said to have welcomed them "as from the home of Merrill-Palmer."[111]

White believed that the Merrill-Palmer should serve the community. She initiated programs at the city and state levels, such as the Visiting Housekeepers and the Detroit Youth Council; many of these programs were later taken over by other institutions. Above all, White believed that Merrill-Palmer must never crystallize its program or become static in what it does. If this ever happened, it could never justify its existence.[112] A similar thought had been expressed by Froebel about his program and materials some fifty years earlier in Germany.

White disseminated her ideas on child development and parent education through her writing, including: "Parent Education in the Emergency," *School and Society* (November 24, 1934); "The Nursery School—A Teacher for Parents," *Child Study* (October 1926); "The Objectives of the American Nursery School," *The Family* (April 1928); "The Role of Home Economics in Parent Education," *Bulletin American Home Economics Association* (January 1929). White was a leader in many professional organizations: president of the American Home Economics Association from 1918 to 1920, and served as chair of its advisory committee on child development and parent education. In 1923, White became an advisor to Larry Frank, who was interested in the use of nursery schools to train mothers. She served as chairman of the National Council on Parent Education from 1925 to 1937, when parent education reached its height. White was a member of the National Advisory Committee on Nursery Schools of the Works Progress Administration, organized during the 1930s depression. She represented the National Council on Parent Education and served as the chair of the advisory committee for the entire duration of the program.[113]

After White retired from Merrill-Palmer in 1947, she served with the American Mission to Greece, where she helped organize the study of child development and family life in the Greek universities. When she returned to the United States, she developed and administered a gerontology program in Detroit. She received honorary degrees from four colleges and universities. She died suddenly of a heart attack at her home in Highland Park, Michigan, in 1954. Her papers are at the Merrill-Palmer Institute Archives in Detroit.[114]

THE MERRILL-PALMER NURSERY SCHOOL (1921)

The Merrill-Palmer Nursery School was part of the Merrill-Palmer Motherhood and Hometraining School, in Detroit. It was both a research center for the development of an educational program for children under five, and a training center for preparing young women in the physical, mental, educational, and social care of young children. So when they are faced with children's problems as mothers, teachers, social workers, or nurses, they will have usable information to handle the task.[115] It was endowed by the will of Mrs. Lizzie Merrill Palmer for the training of girls for motherhood.[116]

A corporation of five men was formed in October 1918. Their first act was to select six women whose responsibility was the actual organization of the school from the point of view of the needs of girls and women. Edna Noble White, head of the Home Economics Department at Ohio State University and president of the National Home Economics Association at the time, was appointed as general director and began her work in February 1920.

White submitted the plan to establish an experimental nursery school to the board of directors in the spring of 1921. It was developed along the lines of the nursery schools in England under the Fisher Act. Its aim was to provide an adequate laboratory for the training of girls in child care, and of measuring the value of certain types of training for children of preschool age. The board wanted a prominent woman to pioneer the new field in America. Miss Emma Henton, head of an English nursery school, became the teacher. Helen T. Woolley, a psychologist from the Cincinnati public schools, became the director of the nursery school and began to organize it in the fall of 1921. The school opened in January 1922 with thirty children. Michigan Agricultural College permitted senior women students to enter the Merrill-Palmer School in groups of six, for a twelve-week term of instruction in homemaking and child care. The students in training, both graduate and undergraduate, studied all aspects of the young child's development—child health and nutrition, education and its methods, the forming of character and personality, child psychology, child management, and mental and social progress.[117] The children in the nursery school provided the students with practical experience, fulfilling the intent of Mrs. Palmer's will.

Educators, especially in the field of home economics, had been aware for some time of the need to give students some practical knowledge in addition to theoretical knowledge of the child. More knowledge of child life was needed in a setting that would be of unquestioned advantage to the child and where students would have experiences in observing and working with children.

Organization

The equipment of the nursery school was chosen with the idea of providing the children with an adequate and attractive environment. The daily program included activities connected with housekeeping, care of plants and birds, block-building, the use of Montessori apparatus, drawing, modeling, woodworking, music, storytelling, and dramatic reproduction of stories. The floors of the play rooms were heavy linoleum, easy to clean. The furniture was child sized. Low shelves lined the walls so the children can have easy access to toys, blocks, books, and other material. Outdoors were tiny teeters, slides and swings, and a big sandpile. Velocipedes, wagons, kiddie cars, sand pails and shovels, and little gardening tools were brought to the outdoors. The second year, the house next door was bought for living quarters for the students and the staff. A small house in the back was equipped as a laboratory for mental testing.[118]

The children were in the nursery school from about 8:00 A.M. until 3:30 P.M. They represented a variety of family backgrounds within the wide range of the middle class. Physical examinations, mental tests, and family and developmental histories were taken before admission. These assured the school that the child was normal physically and mentally and that the family would give a cordial cooperation that was required.[119]

The nursery school wanted to study the growth and development of normal children, and for that purpose it was desirable to have the children remain for as long a period of time as possible. Therefore, the general policy was to admit a child at as early an age as it was practical. A child could be admitted to the nursery school at eighteen months, and could remain in the school until the end of the semester following his fifth birthday. Rarely was a child admitted after his third birthday. On occasions, when the numbers between three- and four-year-olds had been reduced by the premature withdrawal of a child, another child of the same age and sex was selected to fill that place. This was done because the school desired to have its fifty-five children represent all ages between eighteen months and five years and to be fairly evenly divided between the sexes.[120]

The nursery school children were divided into two groups: one group had thirty children (the whole range of ages represented), and the other, of twenty-five children, with the oldest three years and seven months of age. The school had adopted this policy because it wished to have one group that was more or less typical of what must inevitably be found in most nursery schools of small size. That is, children of various ages from eighteen months to five years in a single unit. When all ages were represented, there was the advantage that the older children have experiences in the consideration and care of smaller children. The school also believed that there were certain advantages in having children in one group who are nearly of the same age, because there is a difference in the rate of development between the child of eighteen months and the child of five years. The choice of whether to place a child in one group or the other was made on the basis of the child's physical and social needs.

The younger group had the rooms on the first floor, and the added advantage of an outdoor shelter where they slept daily, even during the winter months—very much like in the McMillan nursery school.[121]

Each group of children had two teachers assisted by students. The teachers also had the responsibility of training the students in the actual practice of dealing with the children as situations arose. The nursery school teachers came from England, since at that time there were no women trained for nursery school work in the United States and the school continued to look to England for its teachers for a while. The English-trained woman had an all-round point of view that gave her an excellent sense of balance between the physical, mental, and social values in child care. It fitted her particularly well to work with a staff of specialists—for the staff of the school included many more professionals than the nursery school teachers.[122]

The physical care of the children was under the supervision of a physician, a nutritionist, and their assistants. Other specialists were called in from time to time as the need arose. The mental growth and development of the children was the concern of psychologists who did the mental testing and advised the teachers how to guide the children in terms of their behavior and mental stimulation. Knowledge of the children's home conditions was gathered by a female home visitor. Through these contacts with the parents, better cooperation was sought, and a program in parental education was developed with the assistance of the whole staff. Research in the physical, mental, emotional, and social development of the nursery school child was carried on.[123]

Childen's Records

Daily records were kept at school regarding the child's attendance, causes for absence, elimination at school, amount of food eaten, time taken for eating dinner (dinner was planned to meet half of the child's daily food requirement), the nap periods, and other events and behavior as they were considered important for notation. A daily report was sent home with each child to give the parents information on these aspects. Daily reports from the home were asked in order that the school may have information on home meals, the night's sleep, elimination, and water intake. The school menus for the following week were sent home once a week so that the home menus might be more intelligently planned with knowledge of what the child would eat at school. This latter practice is still in use in some preschool settings today.

The children were given a complete physical examination, twice a year, and they were weighed and measured monthly. A report was sent to the parents. Twice a year, at six-month intervals, the children were given a mental test. The record included the rating score and comments on the child's personality traits as shown by his behavior in the test situation.[124] The field of mental testing was relatively new with young children. Those testing young children recognized the difficulty of getting reliable results.

Once a year, a summary of the child's growth and development—physical, mental, and social—was made from the combined observations of the staff members who were familiar with the child. A copy of this summary was sent to the parents, with recommendations as to methods of dealing with the child at home. These records had various objects in view, and they brought together material that might add to the knowledge of child life, might be used for teaching purposes, might help in dealing more adequately with the individual child, and which would be helpful to the parents in dealing with their child.[125]

The Merrill-Palmer Institute graduated its last class in 1980 as an independent school. It officially reopened as the Merrill-Palmer Institute at the Wayne State University, Detroit, in 1982. The Merrill-Palmer Nursery School became part of the Wayne State University in 1981. It is now called the Child

Development Lab. It is in the same location as before, and it is under the Department of Psychology at Wayne State University. Wayne State University bought the physical plant of Merrill-Palmer, when they experienced financial difficulties in the late 1970s.[126]

ARNOLD LUCIUS GESELL (1880–1961)

Gesell was born in Alma, Wisconsin, on June 21, 1880, and died May 29, 1961. He was the eldest of five children of Gerhard Gesell, a photographer, and Christine Giesen, a teacher. He had two brothers and two sisters. His father had a strong interest in the education of his children, and his mother was a successful elementary school teacher. After graduating from high school in 1896, Gesell took the teacher's training course at the Stevens Point, Wisconsin, Normal School, and then, for a short time, taught at the high school in that town. In 1903, he received the B.Ph. at the University of Wisconsin. Soon afterward, he became principal of the Chippewa Falls High School in Wisconsin, where he was influenced by Joseph Jastrow, professor of psychology at the University of Wisconsin. Jastrow encouraged Gesell to enroll at Clark University in Worcester, Massachusetts, where he studied the new field of child psychology under G. Stanley Hall and obtained a Ph.D. degree in 1906.

After receiving his doctorate, Gesell was invited to the State Normal School in Los Angeles, California, where he taught for two years. There he met Beatrice Chandler, one of his fellow teachers who taught child psychology. They were married in February 1909. They had a daughter and a son. Their daughter helped with the compilation of the pictorial volume *How a Baby Grows*. Neither of Gesells' two children nor his five grandchildren were used as models or clinical subjects in the photographs.

Gesell and his wife, in the summer of 1909, spent some time at the Pennsylvania Training School for Feeble Minded Children, the country's first psychological clinic. During his second year of teaching at Los Angeles, he became very aware of his need for a better background from which to approach the problems he encountered with the "backward" children. He thought he needed to learn something about medicine and decided to attend medical school. He spent the year 1910–1911 at the University of Wisconsin studying human anatomy and histology. In 1911, he accepted an invitation to the recently established Department of Education at Yale. Gesell was able to arrange to teach his courses in the graduate school at Yale and concurrently be a medical student in the Medical Department. He was interested in studying retarded children. The dean of the medical school, supportive of Gesell's plans, gave him a room in the New Haven Dispensary and appointed him director of what was then called the Juvenile Psycho Clinic, to study retarded children. This is how a psycho-clinic for children was established in 1911, and was the beginning of the Yale Clinic for Child Development. In 1912, Gesell and his wife co-authored *The Normal Child and Primary Education*.[127]

Gesell received his M.D. degree in 1915, and was appointed professor of child hygiene at the Yale Medical School. For the next four years, he also served as school psychologist for the Connecticut State Board of Education. There he devised individual educational programs for handicapped children. Many of his writings during that time dealt with mental retardation. In 1918, he made a survey of student mental development in the elementary schools of New Haven, and wrote the report *Exceptional Children and Public School Policy*. As a result of Gesell's study, the governor of Connecticut set up a Commission on Child Welfare, which developed special classes for handicapped children in New Haven.[128]

Gesell was dissatisfied with the numerical methods of mental tests as measurements of intelligence and shifted his attention to the preschool child instituting his own normative studies to assess the mental development in childhood. Several hundred infants and young children were studied at the ages of 4, 6, 12, 18, 24, 36, 48, and 60 months to establish developmental norms for children one through five years of age. Through these studies it became increasingly evident to him that "infants show individual differences and deviations in mental health similar to those of school children." It also became obvious to Gesell that the foundation of mental health, like that of physical health, should be laid in the preschool years. He concluded that individualized child guidance was needed to meet the numerous problems of growth. If guidance was to be timely and preventive, it must start early. Parent and child guidance had to be simultaneous and could not be separated.[129]

Gesell and the Preschool Child

In 1923, Gesell published *The Pre-School Child from the Standpoint of Public Hygiene and Education*. In it he presents his views about the importance of the preschool years, the contributions the nursery schools could make in the growth and education for both the normal and the handicapped child, and describes existing models of nursery schools. He also points out the role the nursery school could play in the guidance of both parents and children.[130]

In 1924, Gesell instituted the use of cinematography in evaluating infant development. He obtained voluminous pictorial records of infant behavior from birth throughout early childhood and up to the age of ten. He and his co-workers were able to determine normal ranges of child development as well as behavioral patterns from these records.[131] Many publications resulted from this research, including *The Mental Growth of the Pre-School Child* (1925), amply illustrated with photographs. These publications were important not only to the scientific community but also to the general public because of the light they shed on the rearing of children.

In 1926, with a grant from the Laura Spelman Rockefeller Memorial, Gesell established the Guidance Nursery School, as an adjunct to the service division of the Yale Psycho-Clinic. He built a photographic lab at the clinic and continued the photographic research, which later became the two *Photographic Atlases of Infant Behavior* (1934).[132]

Gesell saw the education of the preschool child in terms of growth instead of in terms of instruction or even training.[133] His interest in the nursery school movement and in the nursery schools continued with the publication of the book *Infant and Child Culture of Today: The Guidance and Development in Home and Nursery School* (1943). In it Gesell presents age levels from four weeks old to five years of age and after. Beginning with the eighteen-month-old child, Gesell provides detailed information for: (1) the child's behavior profile; (2) what the nursery school day should be like; (3) cultural and creative activities; (4) the child's behavior in the nursery school, what may one expect of children in a particular age group in response to books, music, painting, finger-painting, clay, blocks, and so on; and (5) techniques for the nursery school teacher to use in working successfully with children.[134]

Gesell's Developmental Theory

Gesell's developmental theory is based on the biological model of development. He drew continuous parallels between physical growth and all other aspects of growth taking place within the child: mental, emotional, intellectual, social. Gesell's theory was influenced by the Darwinian theory. Gesell's teacher, G. Stanley Hall, was a strong proponent of Darwinian theory. Hall had taken the provocative position that the individual child retraces, in his personal development, the essential stages of the evolutionary development of the species. He popularized the expression, *ontogeny recapitulates phylogeny.* If evolution was to be understood, children had to be observed, with as little imposition from external controls as possible.[135] And what better place to carry out these observations but where children gathered—the nursery school.

Gesell, as a maturational theorist, believed in the influence of maturation on child development. He saw the child as a potential adult, determined by his genetic inheritance and containing with him at birth the beginnings of all he will become. Given the proper attention, the child will unfold according to some predetermined pattern of time and sequence. Things will happen when they will be ready to do so.

Through the detailed study of the development of children, from one month to five years of age, Gesell established the fact that human behavior does develop in a patterned orderly manner through successive stages that are alike in quality and sequence, even though not necessarily exact in timing from child to child. No stage is sharply marked off from the other. Each stage blends into the next; no stage is altogether independent. A stage represents the total state of the organism at a given period of time. For example, Gesell equates stage with the typical behavior pattern of an age period. At each stage, children should have acquired certain traits or abilities, such as, there is a stage of "four-year-olds."[136]

Gesell organized his research in terms of four major fields of behavior, comprising most of the observable patterns that resulted in the development of normative data known as the Gesell Developmental Schedules. The four major areas of behavior are:

Motor characteristics, which include posture, prehension, locomotion, general bodily coordination, and specific motor skills.

Adaptive behavior is concerned with perceptual, manual, orientational, and verbal adjustments. It reflects the child's capacity to initiate new experiences and to profit by past ones. This adaptation includes alertness, intelligence, and various forms of constructiveness and exploitation.

Language embraces all behavior that has to do with soliloquy, dramatic expression, communication, and comprehension.

Personal-social behavior includes the child's personal reactions to other persons and to the impacts of culture; his adjustments to domestic life, to property, to social groups, and community conventions.[137]

According to Louise Ames (1962), Gesell's work met with opposition both from behaviorists and from colleagues of a Freudian persuasion, who, in their own separate ways, believed that the organism can be studied only as it is affected by its environment.[138]

Gesell's theory is a multifaceted effort to gain concrete knowledge of human development. His method is readily accessible for duplication. He has left us collections of photographs and cinematic demonstrations. He never forgot that regardless of the separateness of the major patterns of development, the child develops in an integrated way. He was a prolific writer. His bibliography numbers about four hundred items (1905–1957), books, articles, monographs, and films.[139] Gesell's papers are at the Library of Congress, Medical Collection in Washington, D.C.

THE GUIDANCE NURSERY OF THE YALE PSYCHO-CLINIC (1926)

The Guidance Nursery was organized in 1926 by Gesell, as an adjunct to the Yale Psycho-Clinic. Its purpose was to provide facilities for the observation and guidance of young children and to develop flexible, individualized procedures for the guidance of parents. It was not a nursery school but an adaptation of the nursery school idea to the needs of a service clinic.[140]

At the beginning, only "problem children" were admitted in small groups of three to six. The nursery had no fixed enrollment. The organization and program therefore differed from that of a nursery school. The guidance work was conducted on a dispensatory basis (as in a health clinic when the need arose), and the procedure was varied to meet the needs of individual parents or children. Its activities and attendance varied from week to week and from day to day. The children attending were from eighteen months to five years of age. The duration of each child's stay depended on the extent of the problems. Some children attended one or two days a week, others every day. Only a few children attended throughout the year. The parent was expected to observe the child's behavior in the nursery from behind one-way-vision screens, and to discuss it with the guidance teacher, who in turn made home visits to observe the parents' management of the child, and to give further guidance in the home.[141]

In 1929, it was decided to start a continuous attendance group made up of children who had no special problems. Five stable, intelligent children varying in age around two years were chosen to attend school daily throughout the year. To this group were added children with problems, who attended for short periods of time and who were observed and studied intensively by the parents and the clinic staff. In 1935, the nursery school expanded so that two groups of children from two to three, and from three to five years of age, attended simultaneously. In this way, more children could be followed with a greater number of contemporaries for comparison. The service was free until 1936.

In 1939, the normal child acceptance was discontinued, since many "normal" children had difficulties comparable to those of the "problem" children. The emphasis also changed from studying problems to analyzing behavior as it related to various types of personality and different levels of development. To obtain a cross section of development at succeeding age levels, the children were divided into five groups: 18–21 months; 21–24 months; 24–30 months; 30–36 months; and 36–42 months. The children attended throughout the academic year and could stay at the nursery for two or three years. A tuition of fifty cents a morning was charged, but there was a sliding fee scale for parents who were unable to afford the fee. Occasionally, there were scholarships for children who would otherwise be unable to attend. The tuition charged was based on the actual days the child attended and not on the entire term.[142]

The Guidance Nursery provided observational and training opportunities for advanced students in the field of child development. The arrangements were made flexible to permit intensive work with significant cases and to aid in the defining of new methods of approach in child and parent guidance. It also tried to demonstrate that certain types of work in the field of preschool and parental education could be economically undertaken in connection with kindergarten and other agencies, without the more elaborate provisions of a congregate nursery school. All problems of behavior and training, whether in normal, atypical, or handicapped preschool children, required some degree of individual study and of individual adjustment. To a considerable extent, these problems involved the home situation and the parent-child relationship.[143]

Personnel and Organization

The nursery was under the supervision of a pediatrician who gave developmental examinations of the children prior to admission, and conducted repeated interviews with the parents as a way of guidance. The children were examined at six-month intervals. In selected cases, examinations were also made during infancy and continued up to the age of six.

The staff included a principal, an associate guidance teacher, two assistants, and two home externs who divided their time between the Guidance

Nursery and the homes of the children who attended the nursery. The extern lived in a home, which provided a twenty-four-hour association with the child under observation. This arrangement served to define the problems of home guidance in relation to the nursery guidance. All concerns were discussed in weekly conferences of the staff under the direction of the pediatrician. The Guidance Nursery school was housed in the Yale Clinic of Child Development, which was a subdivision of the School of Medicine of Yale University. A play court and a grassy play yard were immediately accessible. The outdoor equipment consisted of a sandbox, slides, seesaw, ladders, carts, and wheeled toys.

The Guidance Nursery was a bright, homelike nursery with a fireplace, and a small cloakroom with lavatory. Built into one corner of the nursery was a small indoor play pond. Built into an adjoining corner was an inconspicuous, but roomy, observation alcove for the use of parents and other observers.

One-Way-Vision Screen

The observation alcove was essentially a carpeted and draped room with chairs, and a screen partition that had the appearance of a solid wall when viewed from the nursery side. This screen was constructed of ordinary commercial wire netting (sixteen mesh), painted with several thin coats of white enamel paint on the nursery side surface. Viewed from the nursery side, the screen appeared to have a solid surface. From the interior, however, it was sufficiently transparent to give the observer a view of the entire nursery.[144]

Equipment and Activities

The nursery was equipped with a varied assortment of toys, including large building blocks and other constructive materials. This equipment gave the child ample chance to display his traits and abilities both in independent and in social situations. The mother of the child could take a seat in the observation alcove, which gave her a wholesomely detached point of view for following his behavior through the screen. The equipment was simple and the essentials may be readily duplicated. Even the play pond was of very simple construction. It consisted of nothing more than a shallow basin (four feet by six) made of galvanized sheet metal, painted marine green, and supplied with a central fountain. Planks served as bridges and the floating toys, the sticks to poke with, and the strings to pull provided endless opportunity for constructive play.[145]

There was no fixed program of activities. The procedure with the individual child was planned and carried out according to his needs on the basis of the problems shown. The child was introduced into the nursery situation informally. Each child was expected to do what he could do toward removing his outer clothing and hanging it up. The child was permitted, as far as possible, to follow his own interests in his activities. There were plenty of opportunities for the child to "work" at problems requiring intelligence, motor coordination, conversation, and emotional control. Under the guidance of the guidance teacher, the child learned to make adjustments. The guidance teacher did not "teach" the child in the ordinary sense but rather "guided" him. There were no set lessons. Interference and suggestions on the part of the guidance teacher or any other adult present were kept at a minimum. This aim was substantially helped by having the mother seated in the observation alcove, from where she could observe all the activities, keeping the child ignorant of her presence, and effectively restraining her tendencies to step into a situation that might cause her concern.

The parents, like the children, were, for the most part, seen individually. The guidance took the form of consultation and conference rather than formal group instruction. The problems of child management were discussed in terms of the specific child and concretely in relation to his reported behavior and his actual behavior at the clinic. Thus, the parent guidance and the child guidance were carried on conjointly in a natural context and in direct relation to a concrete situation.[146]

Children's Records

In order to understand the status of a problem at any given time, it was necessary to have records showing its history. Each history folder of the Yale Psycho-Clinic contained a face sheet on which statistical and identifying information from all sources was brought together. This face sheet contained also a brief clinical summary describing the nature of the case, the results of the developmental examination, and recommendations for handling the problem.[147]

By 1948, Gesell would be required by custom to resign his position at Yale, and a successor will follow. According to Ames (1989), the way Yale went about this was less than cordial. Instead of finding a successor to Gesell "of impressive stature . . . who respected the Gesell work," a committee was formed on child development to "decide what to do about Child Development." "What they decided to do was, to get rid of us. Dr. Milton J. F. Senn was engaged to direct this dismemberment."[148] Gesell and his colleagues were permitted two "transition years" supported by a grant from the American Optical Company, who underwrote a new interest of Gesell's—the study of the development of vision in infant and child.

By the spring of 1950, the two years were up. The staff decided to remain in New Haven for personal and professional reasons. Through the generosity of his longtime colleague, Dr. Ilg, a building was bought and the Gesell Institute was founded in Gesell's honor. Gesell joined it as research consultant, and the work continued as before. A nursery school was begun in 1951. The staff worked for two years without pay. But the work continued as before. In 1956, *Youth: The Years from Ten to Sixteen* was published, which culminated the longitudinal study of age differences.[149]

The Guidance Nursery school demonstrated that it was possible to conduct certain forms of work in preschool and parental education on a dispensatory basis. The organization and procedure were relatively simple and economical. They did not entail full-time attendance and the congregate type of school grouping. These procedures had the same individualized adaptability that characterized a child health center, a hospital, or a modern dispensary. It had been shown that for many diverse types of child-development problems, *occasional* contacts with a guidance unit were effective.

LAWRENCE KELSO FRANK (1890–1968)

Lawrence Kelso Frank is often referred to as the father of the child development and parent education movement. He was born in Cincinnati, Ohio, on December 6, 1890. He had a painful childhood and adolescence because of the separation of his parents when he was six, and the problematic economic circumstances this entailed. In 1912, he received his bachelor of arts degree from Columbia University, with a major in economics. John Dewey, one of his favorite professors, introduced him to the "blossoming New York progressive education movement, which was the left wing insofar as the national movement was concerned." Dewey also taught Frank that "human progress consisted of the application of individual intelligence upon problems of survival value." Frank was also influenced by Thorstein Veblen, from whom he learned that "human nature and institutions were related; to change the latter held out the promise of altering the former."[150]

As a student, Frank investigated population changes and mortality on the Lower West Side of New York City for the Bureau of Social Research. That was the beginning of his long interest in infant and maternal mortality of the poor. In the summer of 1911, the year before the creation of the U.S. Children's Bureau, he examined child labor in canning factories, and worked for several municipal reform organizations. At the request of Frances Perkins, Franklin Roosevelt's Secretary of Labor, he became secretary of the citizen's committee on fire prevention in 1911. Frank gave credit to Perkins for teaching him how to go about doing things for people and developing his energy and enthusiasm.[151]

During World War I, Frank became an economist for the War Industries Board. While he was working there, he met Wesley Clair Mitchell, who was famous for his studies of business cycles, and Lucy Sprague Mitchell, Wesley's wife. "The Mitchells opened Frank's eyes to the countless ways that social science, if applied to social problems, could lead to a better and brighter tomorrow. As Wesley taught Frank about economics and social reform, so Lucy introduced him to what would be his lifelong field of expertise: child study and the family."[152]

Frank became good friends with both Mitchells. He discovered progressive education, and was so pleased with his own children's years at the BEE Nursery School and the City and Country School that he agreed to serve on the BEE Working Council.[153] In 1920, the Mitchells helped Frank secure the position of business manager for the New School for Social Research. As a social reconstructionist, he published articles asserting that education was a means to that end. He drew parallels between progressive education in the public schools as an agent of democratic social change, and parent education in Deweyite methods of intelligent problem solving to be used in raising their children in the home.

Frank was appointed associate director of programs at the Laura Spelman Rockefeller Memorial by Beardsley Ruml in the spring of 1923. At his urging, the trustees decided to use available funds to support child study. Several promising universities received major grants for social scientific research.[154] During the years 1923 to 1930, when he worked at the Spelman Memorial, Frank was known to make strong suggestions to those seeking funding regarding their projects. For example, in 1925 he envisioned a statewide system in Iowa to include ICWRS, Iowa State College of Agriculture and Mechanic Arts, and Iowa State Teachers College in Cedar Falls. When Rockefeller funds were granted in the fall of 1926, the state Board of Education created the Iowa State Council on Child Study. ICWRS became the coordinating center for child study and parent education, but the roles of the three public institutions were prescribed, to prevent duplication and to ensure the highest degree of efficiency and cooperation.[155] Frank also developed a statewide plan for New York, based on the Iowa model, which began in 1930.[156]

Among the other programs sponsored by the Spelman Memorial were: parent education and child study programs at the University of Cincinnati and the University of Georgia for urban and southern whites and blacks; the National Council of Parent Education; and the creation of the National Research Council, Division of Anthropology and Psychology in 1920. In 1933 the Committee on Child Welfare became the Society for Research in Child Development (SRCD). In 1929, the Spelman Memorial was consolidated with the Rockefeller Foundation, and dissemination of funds for child study and parent education continued through the Spelman Fund. Frank negotiated massive grants to Iowa, Teachers College, Minnesota, and Yale.

In October 1931, Frank became the program officer for the General Education Board (GEB), a Rockefeller philanthropy. His function was to administer a grant program on adolescence. Neither the Federal Emergency Relief Administration (FERA) nor the Office of Education could afford to fund the administrative personnel for the FERA program in states and local school districts. FERA funds were limited to employment of teachers and other necessary personnel, chiefly construction workers, who would make the nursery school program viable. Through a complicated process that Frank masterminded, GEB made money available to states that applied for FERA program funds between 1934 and 1936, so that the states could appoint functionaries. Stoddard (director of the ICWRS) applied for funds from the emergency nursery school program and arranged for Harold H. Anderson, an Iowa staff member, to become the program's regional advisor for Iowa, Kansas, Nebraska, and Missouri. "The emergency nursery schools were intended for children from the most destitute families, not from middle-class families. Here was the social intervention that Stoddard had argued for, and the recognition of asymmetry in the supposedly smoothly functioning social system."[157]

During the Great Depression of the 1930s, when Frank was at the Spelman Fund (1930–1931) and the GEB (1931–1936), the economic emergency threatened child study and child welfare programs across the United States. Rockefeller philanthropy was supposed to be seed money, creating ventures and then withdrawing as other and more regular (usually governmental) sources of funding took over. Over time, Rockefeller philanthropy could engage in systematic social innovation, going from one set of ventures to another. Obviously, the Depression played havoc with this policy. For example, in the inevitable budget cuts following the end of Spelman Memorial funding at the host institutions, parent education programs were the most expendable components of all.[158]

Stoddard worked with Frank in the 1930s to incorporate "child development into left-liberal progressive education ideology, and to invent a science of democracy. Thanks to unforeseen events they gained an invaluable ally: Kurt Lewin." Lewin was one of a group of German Jewish scientists who were assisted by the Emergency Committee in Aid of Displaced German Scholars (ECADS) and the Rockefeller philanthropies to receive temporary two-year appointments as professors at various U.S. universities. Lewin was at Cornell University for two years, and then he was appointed at Iowa in late 1935. Frank and Stoddard negotiated a three-year grant from the GEB for Lewin and his graduate assistants. In 1940, after two intervening semesters teaching at Harvard, Lewin decided to return, in a tenured professorship, to Iowa. This had a direct impact upon the ICWRS research program. At a December 1935 conference on topological psychology at Bryn Mawr, which was supported by GEB funds, Lewin met anthropologist Margaret Mead. They found that they shared a common interest in the utilization of social science to enhance democracy, which blossomed over the next dozen years.[159]

Before he left the world of Rockefeller philanthropy in 1936, Frank had disseminated funds to a number of research-oriented nursery schools, including the BEE, the Ruggles Street Nursery School, the Merrill-Palmer School, the Preschool Laboratories at Iowa Child Welfare Research Station, and the Smith College Cooperative Nursery School.[160] When Frank became vice president of the Josiah Macy, Jr., Foundation (1936–1942), he supported Drs. J. L. Stone and M. L. Essex in their preparation of the Vassar film series on personality development in young children. The quality and popularity of these films led to a later urgent request from the creators of the fledgling Head Start program that Joseph and Jeannette Galambos Stone prepare staff development films. Frank also fostered studies on aging and the development of gerontology during this time period. He served as secretary of the Science Committee of the National Resources Planning Board during World War II (1942–1944) and then became director of the Caroline Zachry Institute of

Human Development between 1945 and 1950. He had been introduced to Zachry by Dr. Benjamin Spock, who shared their interest in analytic theory, parent-child relationships, and progressive education.

Lawrence Frank was a prolific writer, and he won several awards for his contributions to popular adult education. His style was as varied as his subject matter. After seeing a collection of children's drawings in 1934, he wrote a theoretical article on projective techniques, and Lois Murphy and Ruth Horowitz wrote the accompanying brief descriptive article. Among the most influential of his publications for early childhood education are: *Understanding Children's Play, The Fundamental Needs of the Child*, and "The Beginnings of Child Development and Family Life Education in the Twentieth Century." *The Fundamental Needs of the Child* was a speech given to the NANE 1937 national conference in Nashville, Tennessee, and published in *Mental Hygiene* magazine. It impacted on teacher preparation, and was later made into a pamphlet. Frank interpreted depth psychology as it related to early socialization, explaining that the gradual molding of behavior to conform to acceptable societal patterns inevitably holds frustrations and anxiety.[161] *Understanding Children's Play* resulted from a 1947 grant by the National Institute of Mental Health to the Caroline Zachry Institute. Frank organized and supervised the project, Hartley directed the project, and Goldenson condensed the vast amount of data collected and revised it for publication. The book dramatically underscored the general and specific values of play. A New York State Mental Health Authority grant enabled early childhood educators to discuss the findings of the study.[162]

Frank is remembered less for his prolific output than for his stimulating, critical, and widely acknowledged effect on his peers. He knew all the leaders in the education of young children, such as Abigail Eliot, Lucy and Wesley Mitchell, Edna Noble White, Lois Barclay Murphy, Milton Senn, Benjamin Spock, Lois Hayden Meek and Herbert Stolz, and James L. Hymes, Jr. He is spoken of fondly as a "generative man," and is often quoted. It is not an overstatement to say that he invented the behavioral sciences, and certainly he left his thumbprint.[163]

ABIGAIL ADAMS ELIOT (1892–1992)

Abigail Adams Eliot was born in Dorchester, Massachusetts, on October 9, 1892, and died October 29, 1992, in Concord, Massachusetts. She was the third child of the Reverend Christopher Rhodes Eliot, pastor of the First Unitarian Church, and Mary Jackson (May) Eliot. Eliot was born to a historic family involved in social causes. Her grandfather, William G. Eliot, was one of the founders of Washington University in St. Louis (1853) and was very active in the abolitionist movement. He wrote *The Story of Archer Alexander: From Slavery to Freedom* (1863).[164]

After Eliot graduated from Radcliffe College in 1914, she worked as a "visitor" (1914–1917) in the foster-home placement department of the Children's Mission to Children in Boston.[165] While working at this job, Eliot came to the conclusion that social service alone "was not making sufficient impression on the troubles of these people."[166]

Eliot went to study at Oxford University, England (1919–1920), right after the end of World War I.[167] At Oxford, she attended lectures in economics, philosophy, and English literature and did additional work in economics with her tutor, a woman economist. This course included study of social and political problems and income distribution among families.[168] While at Oxford, Eliot visited Buzy, near Verdun, France, where she saw the devastation left by World War I in the battlefields and in the nearby villages. Eliot was stunned by the human and economic loss and saw them as strong arguments against war.[169] On her return to Boston, Eliot decided to pursue education as her profession.[170]

Eliot's Professional Development

In 1921, Eliot was approached by Mrs. Elizabeth Winsor Pearson of the Women's Education Association in Boston to go to England to study the nursery school and nursery school education with Margaret McMillan at the Rachel McMillan Nursery School. Upon her return to America, Eliot was to organize a nursery school in Boston that would be supported by the Women's Education Association. Eliot loved England and agreed to go there and study under the sponsorship of the association. Margaret McMillan had organized an open-air nursery school in 1913 in Deptford, England (four miles south of London), to improve the health of the children. Later she developed her educational system when she realized the educational opportunity she had.

Eliot became a student at the Rachel McMillan Nursery School in June 1921. She was on "practical duty six hours a day, with the three-year-old children." In addition, she attended lectures by McMillan and other instructors. To keep her clothes clean, she wore an apron and a cap.[171]

The nursery school was open from 7:00 A.M. to 6:00 P.M. McMillan believed the longer the day, the better it was for the children to be out of the slums and in a place where they had good food, daily health inspections, and adequate rest.[172] In a letter to Mrs. Pearson, Eliot said that "McMillan stressed hygiene, which will come easily in Boston . . . but very little seemed to be made of the contact with the families." Eliot continued, "The possibilities of the nursery school as educational interest me and that our school will have some things different." The letter concluded that the principal was Froebelian trained, and her ideas did not always agree with those of McMillan.[173]

Eliot was upset that McMillan appeared to be jealous of Maria Montessori's work and that she would neither allow any of Montessori's apparatus to be used in the nursery school nor permit her to visit.[174] Eliot was impressed with McMillan's personality, however.

During the five weeks in the summer that the McMillan Nursery School was closed, Eliot visited nursery schools in Bradford, where McMillan had started the school clinics that led to the founding of the nursery school; she also visited nursery schools in Leeds and York. She visited Grace Owen, who was on vacation, and stayed with her.[175] Owen was a graduate of Columbia Teachers College, and her sister was married to Professor James Cattell of Teachers College. Owen was the director of a training school and five nursery schools in Manchester and was influenced by Froebel's ideas and practices. She gave a one-year course for experienced teachers and a two-year course for all others. The board of education recognized both courses offered by Owen for certification purposes, while it recognized only the one-year course at McMillan's school. Owen saw the nursery school primarily as educational, first provided for all poor children and then for all other children. Eliot enjoyed Owen's "scientific spirit" and broad-mindedness.[176]

To gain additional experience, Eliot worked for three more months (September through December) as paid staff in charge of the toddler group of thirty-two children, from 7:00 A.M. to 6:00 P.M. with three shifts of students helping her.[177] McMillan asked Eliot to replace temporarily the teacher who went to help with the opening of an extension of the nursery school. It was built to accommodate one hundred more children and was entirely financed by the board of education. "It will be permanently staffed, have better equipment, and a better chance for following educational results," Eliot wrote to Mrs. Pearson.[178] Queen Mary (1867–1953) formally opened it on November 22, 1921, and named it the Rachel McMillan Nursery School and Training Centre.[179]

Eliot had found what she was looking for, a way to educate children so they could have a better chance in life than their parents did, thus breaking the cycle of poverty.

Eliot's Professional Career: The Ruggles Street Nursery School and Training Centre (1922–1952)

Eliot's task upon returning to Boston was to apply to the Roxbury community what she had learned in Deptford. She set up the Ruggles Street Nursery School and Training Centre, even though she felt that her preparation was far too brief for such a big undertaking.[180]

The Ruggles Street Nursery School was to train teachers for nursery schools and at the same time to provide service to the neighborhood. It was among the first such institutions, if not the first, in America. It served as the field placement for the students in the training course. Eliot accepted the first student for teacher training in September 1922.

To enhance the nursery school's reputation, Eliot went to the Harvard Graduate School of Education (1923–1925), and studied with Professor George E. Johnson, who later became a member of the advisory board of the Ruggles Street Nursery School and Training Centre and Eliot's supporter. Eliot received a master's degree in education in 1926 and a doctorate in 1930.[181] Eliot dedicated her entire professional career to nursery education.

The Ruggles Street Nursery School and Training Centre offered three levels of training to prepare women for work in a nursery school, for social work with children, or for handling children at home.

1. A two-year course for high school graduates whose previous work was college preparatory. It led to the certificate. Course work included chemistry, biology, psychology, dietetics, home nursing, household management, child care, education, sociology, government, art, music, English, preschool education, nursery school procedure, storytelling, and the family. The course demanded forty hours of work (studying, conferencing, etc.) per week during the academic year. It also required ten hours a week of practice and observation during the duration of the course. Practice was mostly at the Ruggles Street Nursery School.

2. A one-year course for students with more that high school training, for college graduates, and for graduates of kindergarten training schools, normal schools, and nurses' training schools, also leading to the certificate.

3. Special work for special students, not leading to the certificate.

Students were selected for their ability to do the academic work and for having the personality to fit this type of work.[182] The latter is similar to Froebel's requirements.

Eliot was a founding member of the National Association for Nursery Education (NANE) in 1925 with Patty Smith Hill and other nursery educators. Eliot served on the National Advisory Committee on Emergency Nursery Schools, representing NANE, throughout its duration, 1933–1943, and supervised the emergency nursery schools in Massachusetts and the other New England states.

Eliot's Philosophy Regarding Teacher Preparation

Eliot's philosophy regarding teacher preparation was gleaned from studying her notebooks that were full of classroom notes, course outlines, bibliographies, quizzes, and final examinations. It was based on two assumptions: (1) teachers, like children, grow and develop and learn the art and skill of teaching "by doing"; and (2) teachers develop both professionally and personally. She did not advocate any specific theoretical orientation, even though there had been several theoretical shifts outside Ruggles during her teaching career, nor did she advocate "cookbook" solutions. Eliot constantly emphasized the connection between theoretical learning and practical experience—teaching. Consequently, every course she taught included some form of a practicum where students got firsthand experience. She practiced McMillan's belief that there has to be a relatedness between teacher training and the content of children's programs. For example, if nursery school teachers were to teach music to the children, they needed to know something about music.[183]

Because of her deep interest in her students and her belief that well-prepared teachers *do* make a difference in the child's life, the courses that Eliot taught over a thirty-year period can be divided into two categories: (1) content courses dealing with the professional development of the teachers and (2) courses dealing with the personal development of the teachers. Both types of courses were broad in scope but specific and detailed in their content, always dovetailing theory into practice. Regardless of the specific content of the course, Eliot did three things during the first class meeting: (1) introduced the history of early childhood education, (2) explained "why the early years are important" in the child's development, and (3) presented the rationale for early childhood education.

The following are some examples of the courses Eliot taught. The Home and School Relationships course included written assignments on four practical experiences: your own home and school influences—written in class; a visit and helping in a home; a discussion with a parent to guide his thinking about the child; and a plan and implementation of a parents' meeting.[184]

In the Child Training Course (1933), the final exam questions were case studies—"A two-year-old screams when he sees the doctor—What do you think might be the cause of this, and what would you do about it?" Students had to reflect on the knowledge they had accumulated in the course and apply it to answer.[185]

Eliot taught the Adult Personality course every year. In 1936, it had the subtitle, "This course is all about you. We want you to apply it to yourself." Topics included the importance of the teacher's personality, voice and diction, and making the most of your appearance.[186] It is quite apparent that for Eliot, becoming a teacher was both a process of the acquisition of specific knowledge. She encouraged students to live a balanced life between work and play through careful time management and gave this guide for healthful living: work, 10 hours; play, 1½ hours; meals, 1½ hours; toilet, 1 hour; rest, 1 hour; sleep, 9 hours.[187] There was a constant integration between theory and practice.

Through these courses, Eliot introduced her students to the latest theory, information, or policy regarding early childhood as soon as it became available to her. An example is the course Implementing the Mid-Century White House Conference, which she taught during the summer of 1951, following her attendance of that conference.[188] Eliot had high expectations for her students to make a commitment to apply what they had learned to improve the lives of children, to nurture the children, and to support parents.[189]

Eliot retired in 1952 and went to Pacific Oaks Friends School in Pasadena, California, where she set up a training school for nursery school teachers. Two years later she returned to Massachusetts, and for the next three years she affiliated with the Brooks School in Concord, Massachusetts, where she taught two-, three-, four-, and five-year-olds and first, second, and third grades. She also became the head teacher for the four-year-olds.[190]

Parent education was Eliot's special contribution to the field of early childhood education. She was an organizational member of the Boston Parents Council in May 1930, and served as its chairperson between 1934 and 1936.

The Boston Parents Council (1930–1938) was a group of professionals and volunteers who tried to bridge the gap between the scientists of child development and the parents who were asking for information regarding normal child growth and development.

THE RUGGLES STREET NURSERY SCHOOL AND TRAINING CENTRE OF BOSTON (1922–1952)

One of the earliest nursery schools in the United States, which was more like the English nursery school than most others in the United States, was the Nursery Training School of Boston. It started as the Ruggles Street Nursery School and Training Centre. It was financially supported by the Woman's Education Association of Boston (WEA). They for many years had been initiating and furthering new lines of educational work.

In 1920, the WEA took over the use of the 147 Ruggles Street Neighborhood House from another group. It was one of the neighborhood house's founded by Mrs. Pauline Agassiz Shaw. Its only activity at that time was operating the Ruggles Street Day Nursery. The WEA wanted to organize a nursery school as a philanthropy and an educational experiment and was looking for a director. They approached Abigail Adams Eliot for the position. Eliot was sent to England by the WEA for six months to study the nursery school with Margaret McMillan, in Deptford. Deptford is one of the poorer districts in London with tenement houses. The Rachel McMillan Nursery School still exists today in the same location and serves more or less the same population. The Ruggles Street Nursery School and Training Centre was opened in January 1922, upon Eliot's return to Boston.[191] The same year another nursery school, the Merrill-Palmer, opened in Detroit.[192]

Ruggles was situated in one of the poor sections of Boston, on the border of the Irish and Black districts. Parents were skilled and unskilled workers, making twenty-five to thirty-five dollars a week. Most of the fathers could provide their large families with the necessities of life. A small number of mothers worked outside the home. The purposes of the Ruggles Street were to be threefold: to give the best possible opportunity for development to children between the ages of two and four, through an appropriate environment; to train parents through observation and conferences with experienced teachers, about the value of the physical, mental, and moral of the child; and to train young women in the science and art of nursery school education.[193]

Organization

The nursery school was housed in a remodeled dwelling that provided space, light, and sunshine. In addition to the playrooms, auxiliary rooms, and offices, there was a carpentry room, an isolation room, and a students' room. The yard had trees and a garden where flowers bloomed three seasons of the year along with all the playground equipment. The staff of the nursery school consisted of an educational advisor, a psychiatric advisor, an organizing director, five teachers (one supervisor, two teachers, and two part-time teachers in training), a nutrition worker, and a secretary. The school was open five days a week from 8:30 A.M. to 4:00 P.M. all year round. It closed for single holidays and a short vacation at Christmas. Much of the time, especially in the warm weather, the children were outdoors.[194]

On her arrival at Ruggles Street, Eliot found about thirty children ranging in age from a few weeks to fourteen years, a cook, and one woman, Annie Hall, who worked with the children. Eliot replaced the cook and kept Annie Hall. The place was spotlessly clean. There was no equipment for the children to use, but she found unused Froebelian gifts and Montessori apparatus on high shelves.[195]

It took Eliot some time to find places for the older children and the babies. She kept only children of two, three, and four years old. One of the first things she did was to shorten the day.[196] For the daily schedule, see Appendix 1.

The daily schedule was well defined but sufficiently elastic to allow for any needed changes. Ruggles had a summer schedule also. It had two periods of outdoor play in the morning. The children were kept indoors during the hottest part of the day.[197]

A public health nurse from the Child Hygiene Association came every morning to examine every child upon arrival. The mother was expected to stay until after the nurse's examination. If a child had a cold or other symptoms of illness, the child would be sent home. The nurse would later visit the home, to check on the child's health and to determine what should be done. The nurse tried to teach the mothers and children health habits.[198]

The nursery school cooperated with habit clinics, church, home and school visitors, the Family Welfare Association, the Forsyth Dental Clinic, and the Children's Hospital.

Parent Education

One of the stated purposes of Ruggles Street was to educate parents. Eliot accomplished this through personal interactions with them. Her previous work with parents as a family visitor had made her very aware of the important role that the family played in the development of the children, and she became an advocate for parent education. Eliot felt that without the cooperation of parents, the best plans for the child's physical, social, educational, moral, and spiritual development could not be achieved. The parents' interest and help were vital to a nursery school's function. There were frequent informal conferences between parents and teachers at school, on the street, and by telephone. Teachers, especially the nutrition worker, made frequent visits to the homes of the children to determine appropriate nutrition for the family. Parents were encouraged to visit their children at school whenever possible and to observe them. Mothers were urged to come regularly one day a week to observe and to help in the nursery school, which they did. Ruggles had a

"Gesell Screen" behind which visitors could sit and watch what was going on in the playroom without disturbing the children. There were regularly scheduled parents' meetings. Eliot acknowledged that many of these methods were used by the kindergartens, but they were necessary in order to establish a mutual understanding and cooperation between the nursery school and the home.[199]

Children's Records

Records were kept to promote the teachers' efficiency and to enable students and parents to understand better the development of each child. The following records were kept: social, educational, and a kindergarten questionnaire for those children who had entered kindergarten. The educational record was written for each child every three months by the head teacher in each group after conference with the other teachers who had contact with the child. Because these records were largely subjective, they were initialed. They presented a concise picture of the child's development in the control of the body, speech, sensory and emotional activity, mental powers, and moral and social behavior.[200]

In September 1922, Eliot accepted the first student to study to be a nursery school teacher. In 1926, The Ruggles Street Nursery School and Training Centre was renamed the Nursery Training School of Boston. This new name made the school less local and told its story to a larger public. In 1936, the Nursery Training School Corporation bought the houses at 355–357 Marlborough Street, Boston, and separated from the Ruggles Street Nursery School, which became an entity unto itself but remained the demonstration and practice school until 1952. As Eliot was approaching retirement in 1952, she and the corporation members had to make some decisions about the training school and the nursery. Eliot tried to affiliate the training school with one of the local colleges or universities with which she had collaborated over the years. After several rejections, the Nursery Training School of Boston became affiliated with Tufts University in Medford, Massachusetts, in 1952. In 1955, it was renamed the Eliot-Pearson School in honor of Eliot and Mrs. Pearson, the original chair of the Woman's Educational Association. In 1965, the Eliot-Pearson School became the Eliot-Pearson Department of Child Study at Tufts University.[201]

In 1952, the Ruggles Street Nursery School became part of the Associated Day Care Services of Boston, which assumed financial responsibility. After several moves within the Roxbury community, the Ruggles Street Nursery School finally moved to the Mission Hill Housing Project in 1972, and was renamed the Ruggles Street–Mission Hill Day Care Center. It is still located there today and operates under that name.[202]

JAMES L. HYMES, JR. (1913–1998)

James L. Hymes, Jr., was associated with every significant early childhood education occurrence during the past sixty years. Born on August 3, 1913, he attended public schools in the Bronx and Queens, New York, through his high school years. He received his bachelor's degree from Harvard College in 1934 in the fields of international law and relations. He had an interest in peaceful relationships and world peace, and came to believe that the development of good human beings was the basis for a better society.[203]

Hymes became a child development and parent education major at Teachers College of Columbia University. His observation activities as a 1934 research assistant brought him into contact with the nursery school of the Institute of Child Welfare Research, the first he had ever seen. He received his master's degree in 1936, and accepted a position as the Assistant State Supervisor of WPA (Works Progress Administration) Nursery Schools and Parent Education in the New York State Department of Education. Dramatic scripts he wrote on family life and child rearing were produced by local radio stations throughout the state. In 1937, he began his work with the Progressive Education Association. He served in the posts of assistant executive secretary, associate director, editor of *Progressive Education,* and managing editor of *Frontiers of Democracy.*

At the outbreak of World War II, he worked as an education writer for the Civilian Pre-Induction Training Unit at the Pentagon. It was here that Lois Stolz contacted him to invite him to become the manager of the Child Service Department of the Kaiser Shipbuilding Corporation. This entailed the planning, equipping, administration, and supervision of two centers for shipyard workers.[204] Hymes said that "it is no great trick to have an excellent child care program. It only requires a lot of money with most of it spent on *trained* staff."[205]

After the war, he returned to New York City and went to work at the Caroline Zachry Institute of Human Development assisting Lawrence Frank in implementing ideas for sensitizing teachers to children's needs. He produced a pamphlet, *A Pound of Prevention: How Teachers Can Meet the Emotional Needs of Young Children,* which served as his doctoral dissertation. He received his Ph.D. from Teachers College in 1946.

Always on the lookout for stimulating new programs, he became the coordinator of early childhood education at the State Teachers College in New Paltz, New York. New Paltz was the first college in New York State to offer a teacher education major specifically designed to certify teachers of children three years old through grade three. He continued over the years to advocate for specialized preparation for teachers working with this age group.

Jimmy Hymes was intensely involved in early childhood professional organizations throughout his lifetime. He served as president of the NANE between 1945 and 1947.[206] From 1949 to 1951, he was the Association for Childhood Education International (ACEI) vice president representing nursery schools. In 1949 he was among the founding members of the Southern Association for Children Under Six (SACUS).

Hymes continued his academic career, moving to George Peabody College in Nashville, Tennessee, in 1949, and finally, in 1957, to the University of

Maryland, from which he retired in 1970. At Maryland, he worked with the staff to design a nursery-kindergarten facility, and directed it for a time. He was also instrumental in the development of a master's degree program focusing on the preschool years.[207] Between 1964 and 1965, he served on the National Planning Committee for Head Start. He insisted that Head Start stress teacher orientation and training, and worked with D. Keith Osborn to limit class size to fifteen children. James L. Hymes, Jr., died on March 6, 1998, in Cupertino, California.

Hymes's legacy is passed down to us through his through his writing. In 1947, his chapter entitled "Parents" appeared in the *Ninth Yearbook of the John Dewey Society: Intercultural Attitudes in the Making*. The chapter introduction contains a statement that "intercultural relations means relations between people. If we wish to see the contribution of family life to intercultural education, then we must look at how the home builds into the child his capacity for human relationships."[208] He asks the reader whether the life the child leads teaches him to feel good about or to doubt himself. Hymes advocates open channels of communication between home and school, reminding teachers that from good homes they can learn ways to assist the child in building up faith in himself. He concludes that by building up the child's trust in other people, intercultural education will be taught.

A prolific author, Hymes made a sterling contribution to the history of early childhood education with his living history cassette tapes and books, and a series of pamphlets, which have now been combined into the book *Early Childhood Education: Twenty Years in Review: A Look at 1971–1990.*[209] Hymes's writing has appeared in *Childhood Education, Young Children, Grade Teacher* (in which he had a column from 1958 to 1964), yearbooks, encyclopedias, slide narratives, and on the television program *Footsteps.* Among his books are: *A Child Development Point of View* (1955) and *Teaching the Child under Six* (1968).

Hymes, a psychologist-educator, entered the child development and parent education fields when they were in their infancy. His authority evolved through disciplined study, and association with virtually every leader in his own and related fields. He deliberately developed a style of writing and lecturing that speaks to people of every educational level. He applied keen intellect, reflective interpretation, and creative thinking to all of his experiences.[210] It is for these reasons that James L. Hymes, Jr., can be labeled a pioneer of nursery school education.

TRAINING OF NURSERY SCHOOL TEACHERS

The origin of the nursery school in the United States and its teacher training component occurred at approximately the same time, during the late 1910s and early 1920s. Prior to that time, there were "dame schools" held by women in their homes, what Strickland describes as "fireside education."[211]

Margaret McMillan trained the majority of the women who began nursery schools in the United States. They traveled to England to study and work in an apprenticeship program under her tutelage, as discussed in Chapter 5.

Many of the pioneers of the 1920s nursery school movement came from fields other than nursery education, for example, social work, home economics, nursing, psychology, and kindergarten-primary education. The combination of female authors and editors of ladies' books and magazines; new data and trends in psychology, home economics, sociology, economics, and politics, as well as education; and the presence of McMillan-trained nursery school teacher-educators on U.S. soil supported the opening of the first nursery schools and their accompanying training centers.

Although preparations were made during the 1910s, the first nursery schools associated with institutions of higher education or teacher preparation programs began their official operation around 1920. Most historical sources agree that Merrill-Palmer School and Ruggles Street Nursery were among the earliest nursery teacher training institutions in the United States. Training was originally done at the on-site nursery school facility, with supporting supplementary lectures and readings provided. Johnson's later (1930s) work at the BEE is also cited in this category. Professors at private institutions of higher education, such as Patty Smith Hill at Teachers College of Columbia University and Dr. Arnold Gesell of Yale University, lectured and published widely. Their work was used by teachers for self-education, as well as texts at institutions of higher education. Summer in-service education opportunities, such as the 1922 Nursery School Education course given by Grace Owen of Manchester, England, at Teachers College, provided another avenue for professional development.[212]

During the mid-1920s, nursery laboratory schools at three state universities were used as teacher training facilities. Cora Bussey Hillis's organizational work resulted in the opening of the ICWRS in 1921. Formative work was also done by Barbara Greenwood at the University of California, Los Angeles (UCLA), and faculty members of the Institute of Child Welfare of the University of Minnesota, Minneapolis. All three of these institutions were supported by foundation money dispensed by Lawrence Frank, as were the programs at Columbia and Yale. Dr. Douglas Thom and Grace Caldwell initiated their efforts at the Play School for Habit Training in the early 1920s. National Kindergarten and Elementary College (now National-Louis University), the Cleveland Kindergarten-Primary Training School of Western Reserve University (now known as Case-Western Reserve University), and normal schools at Kalamazoo, Michigan, and Milwaukee, Wisconsin (which became part of the state college and university system in their respective states) are described by the 1929 *NSSE Yearbook* as having "typical programs for the training of teachers through contact with the nursery school and the parents of nursery-school children." The *Yearbook* comments that "some of the teacher-training institutions have opened nursery schools not in order to train nursery-school teachers but in order to give students studying to be kindergarten or primary teachers an opportunity to observe and work with younger children."[213]

Educators in experimental schools were among the first to speak and write about the type of teacher needed in a nursery school and the educational experiences that could assist her in becoming a developmentally appropriate practitioner. Margaret Naumburg, in her 1928 book, and an article in *The New Republic*,[214] challenged the worth of much of the normal school and teachers college training, as well as the philosophy and the practice of the project method and Dewey's social philosophy.

Harriet Johnson noted, in the late 1920s, that "the teacher needs first of all to *see* children," and therefore "the progressive teacher requires progressive training." Johnson believed that a teacher needs to "live in an environment which opens to her opportunities to test her own powers, to pursue lines of investigation in various fields, to try out for herself some form of art expression."[215] This was the impetus for the 1930 commencement of the Cooperative School for Student Teachers. Mitchell described the objectives of this "organization that proposes to train teachers for classroom life with children" in this way:

> It is not a definite curriculum which we wish to get over to our students. Rather, it is a point of view. Our aim is to turn out teachers whose attitude toward life is scientific. To us, this means an attitude of eager, alert observation; a constant questioning of old procedure in the light of new observations; a use of the world, as well as of books, as source material; an experimental open-mindedness, and an effort to keep as reliable records as the situation permits, in order to base the future upon accurate knowledge of what has been done. Our aim is equally to turn out students whose attitude towards their work and towards life is that of the artist. To us, this means an attitude of relish, of emotional drive, a genuine participation in some creative phase of work, and a sense that joy and beauty are legitimate possessions of all human beings, young and old, if we can produce teachers with an experimental, critical, and ardent approach to their work, we are ready to leave the future of education to them.[216]

Several professional nursery school conferences of the late 1920s and early 1930s included sessions devoted to the training of nursery school teachers. At a session of a National Committee on Nursery Schools Second Conference[217] held on Friday, April 22, 1927, from 9:30 to 12:00, the training of nursery school teachers was discussed. Research showed that women were entering the nursery school field from the following ten groups: young women in junior college courses for kindergarten-primary; kindergarten, primary and high school teachers with experience; graduates from liberal arts and home economics courses; social service workers; trained nurses; mental hygiene specialists; and mothers with and without college degrees. The consensus of the speakers was that four years of college was a desirable background for a nursery school teacher, because she must deal with specialists in the fields of nutrition, psychology, psychiatry, and pediatrics, for which "a certain intellectual breadth and professional maturity are undoubtedly essential."[218] Other recommendations included a flexible teacher education curriculum to meet the students' varied background and experiences, and the necessity of practice teaching for the acquisition of nursery school techniques. Recommended for inclusion in the scientific knowledge base for nursery school teachers were courses in chemistry ("leading to dietetics"), biology ("as a background for psychology"), case study methods ("supplementing both sociology and mental hygiene"), and "educational measurements and different types of records."

In answer to the question, "On what academic level does it seem desirable to place nursery training?," the speakers "reported training courses at various collegiate levels from the Junior College group with no experience through Senior College to graduate groups both with and without experience. It was suggested that the inexperienced Junior College student of nursery school work might qualify for the position of assistant only, but that work on a graduate level represented the ideal toward which nursery school training courses in this country are moving."[219]

Among the questions posed at National Committee on Nursery Schools Third Conference of Nursery School Workers (1929)[220] were: What constitutes good training for nursery school teachers? and what provisions exist for such training? Three different discussion groups addressed these topics, one entitled Administration of Nursery Schools, chaired by Dr. George Stoddard of the Iowa Child Welfare Research Station; a second on Training of Nursery School Teachers chaired by Grace Langdon of Teachers College, Columbia University; and the third dealing with Nursery School Training of Students in Liberal Arts Colleges chaired by Lovisa Wagoner of the Department of Child Study at Vassar College. It is instructive to note that these same divisions/areas of concern exist currently.[221]

The *Twenty-Eighth NSSE Yearbook* included separate chapters on "The Professional Training of Nursery School Teachers" (Chapter XIII) and "Professional Training for Research and Instruction in Preschool Education" (Chapter XII). The author of Chapter XIII reported that the training of nursery school teachers was still in the experimental stage. Among the entrance requirements reported on a survey questionnaire, "a definite interest in young children" was number one. All of the institutions stipulated excellent health, adequate fundamental preparation, upper-level academic status (as indicated by the fact that only one institution reported admitting students directly from high school),[222] superior scholarship, good native ability, and fine character as basic requirements. Some had additional prerequisites, such as knowledge of general psychology, knowledge of general principles of nutrition, or musical knowledge. The specific professional course requirements included child psychology, child hygiene and nutrition, physical growth, mental hygiene, educational measurements, clinical study,[223] parental education, curricula for young children, special courses in technique of nursery school teaching, preparation for carrying on independent research in her own field, and practical experience. The chapter author concludes: "Not only is it in a position to set its own standards and meet its own problems in the light of scientific fact, but further, as the latest comer in the field of education, it will conceivably influence the standards and point the way to the solution of problems of every other field of education as well."[224]

Training Teachers for the Emergency Nursery Schools

As noted in Chapter 12, Emergency Nursery Schools were set up by the federal government as one of six emergency education projects begun during the Depression era.[225] A detailed summary of the responses to surveys done in 1934 and 1935 is provided. Some of the suggestions made by the 1934 survey respondents ring true in our own day as well. For example, "Students should not be required to be eligible for relief,"[226] and "The relief program should have been planned to save the kindergarten and give employment to unemployed kindergarten-primary teachers," could easily have been written about more recent government-sponsored early education measures.

During the second year of Emergency Nursery School operation, both trained and untrained teachers were employed. Some teachers trained during the first year returned, necessitating follow-up training and provision for the teachers' continued growth.[227] New teachers and other nursery school employees needed initial training experiences. Professionals from several disciplines and specialized fields cooperated in giving the courses during the training institutes.

The National Advisory Committee on Emergency Nursery Schools published a model teacher education syllabus for nursery education. It consisted of seven sections: history and administration, health care, significant facts concerning growth and development, curriculum content and guidance, the teacher and her relationships, parent education in the nursery school, and operation and management. In the words of the committee that prepared the syllabus, it was intended "to meet the growing need for a working guide to orientation in or preparation for participation in the field of nursery education." The preface emphasizes fitting the program to varying local conditions.[228]

Nursery schools became even more important as the Depression of the 1930s gave way to World War II during the 1940s. The United States Office of Education's 1943 pamphlet *Nursery Schools Vital to the War Effort* posed the question, Does the nursery school need professionally trained teachers? and answered that: Teachers with specialized training in the field of nursery school–kindergarten education or child development are essential. They should have had some practical experience in guiding young children. In addition to teaching duties, the nursery school teacher in charge will need to assume responsibilities for supervision, planning meals, household management, parent education, training volunteers, daily health inspection, and essential record-keeping.

The teacher must have the ability to share her interests in plants, animals, rocks, music, buildings, and transportation with the children.[229]

In the *Forty-Sixth NSSE Yearbook,* Millie Almy and Agnes Snyder propose the following traits as requirements for teachers of young children: physical stamina and poise, scientific spirit, respect for personality, world-mindedness, and understanding of human development. They state that many men have highly desirable contributions to make to young children. In contrast to earlier *NSSE Yearbook* statements, they said that "teacher education must concern itself with an attempt to interest high-school people in the education of young children." The suggested 1947 teacher preparation curriculum included an emphasis on democratic principles and techniques, tying teacher education to other fields concerned with human development and social progress, individualized programs, study of a variety of approaches to child development and child guidance, expressive activities, a need for better understanding of both young children and the work of the teacher, experience in working with children at older age levels, and student teaching in community schools.[230]

Reforms in the Preparation of Early Childhood Teachers

In the 1972 *NSSE Yearbook* Spodek describes the "systems" approach to teacher training, and Combs's approach to involving students in their own learning. He contends that "the range of suggested alternatives to traditional teacher education that are being proposed today may increase the range of programs for preparing staffs of early childhood education programs."[231] Twenty years later, in the 1991 *Yearbook,* Spodek describes professionalism in the early childhood profession, noting seven suggested reforms of teacher preparation, including: "(1) abolishing undergraduate teacher education degrees, (2) creating programs of teacher education that extend beyond the bachelor's degree, (3) placing a cap on the number of credit hours in education that would be allowed toward a university degree, (4) extending the field experiences in teacher education programs, (5) creating an induction period or internship for novice teachers, (6) creating alternative approaches to teacher certification, and (7) establishing more specific forms of teacher certification."[232] His descriptions of the content of early childhood teacher preparation programs accredited either by the National Council for the Accreditation of Teacher Education (NCATE) or the individual state may be favorably compared with those presented in earlier *NSSE Yearbooks.* The teacher preparation programs at the beginning of the 1990s generally consisted of four parts: general education, foundations, instructional knowledge, and practice. The instructional knowledge component of the teacher education program is related to the various professional roles of the teacher: curriculum designer, diagnostician, organizer of instruction, manager of learning, and counselor and advisor.[233]

Lilian Katz proposed developmental stages of early childhood teachers, beginning with the Survival Stage, passing through the Consolidation and

Renewal Stages to reach the stage of teacher Maturity.[234] VanderVen devised a subsequent model composed of five stages: Novice, Initial, Informed, Complex, and Influential.[235] This 1988 model embraces a lifetime in the field. More recent discussions by VanderVen and others have enlarged the model through the conceptualization of Chaos Theory, which "reflects the recent scientific findings in which variation, disorder, surprise, unpredictability . . . are viewed as the reality of the world . . . given phenomena are multiply determined, interdependent, and non-linear. They are viewed as part of larger systems, in which they effect and are effected by, those other systems."[236] The implications of chaos for these developmental stages is to recognize the complexity and varied possible pathways for personal and career development. According to VanderVen, Chaos Theory supports constructivist early childhood professional education by espousing rich, complex, challenging environments and structured ways in which to be reflective, thus decreasing the level of supervision and organizational constraints.[237] Early childhood practitioners who are in later stages, such as Maturity, should be encouraged to think about and know themselves. This in turn enables developing teachers to function in a more complex way, and to become better able to deal with the reality of the field and the wider system. The teacher thus continues to grow in ability to think about all kinds of relevant issues. In this model, the stage theories continue to have relevance. The ability to apply chaos is empowering.[238]

The answer to the question posed through the decades, *Does the nursery school need professionally trained teachers?* has always been *Yes*. The basic tenets of developmentally appropriate nursery school teacher preparation do not appear to have changed over the years; however, the philosophy and objectives have been modified in each decade.[239]

NOTES

1. Margaret McMillan, *The Nursery School* (New York: E. P. Dutton and Co., 1919), 24.

2. Nannette Whitbread, *The Evolution of Nursery-Infant School* (London: Routledge and Kegan Paul, 1972), 67; and Ilse Forest, *Preschool Education: A Historical and Critical Study* (New York: Macmillan Co., 1927), 274.

3. Ilse Forest, *Preschool Education: A Historical and Critical Study*, 290–291.

4. Charles E. Strickland, "Paths Not Taken: Seminal Models of Early Childhood Education in Jacksonian America," in *Handbook of Research in Early Childhood Education*, ed. Bernard Spodek (New York: The Free Press, 1982), 328, 330, 337.

5. National Society for the Study of Education (NSSE), *The Twenty-Eighth Yearbook of the National Society for the Study of Education: Preschool and Parental Education*, ed. Guy M. Whipple (Bloomington, IL: Public School Publishing Company, 1929), 19–26.

6. Emma Henton, a graduate of the Gypsy Hill Training College in London, was the teacher at the Merrill-Palmer School in Detroit when it opened in 1922. Grace Owen of Manchester, England, gave a course in nursery education at Teachers College in the summer of 1922. Forest, *Preschool Education*, 298, 295n.

7. Caroline Pratt [with Leila V. Scott, Ruth Goode and Max Sellers], *I Learn from Children: An Adventure in Progressive Education* (New York: Simon & Schuster, 1948), 15.

8. Lawrence A. Cremin, *The Transformation of the School: Progressivism in American Education, 1876–1957* (New York: Vintage Books [Random House], 1961), 202.

9. Joyce Antler, *Lucy Sprague Mitchell: The Making of a Modern Woman* (New Haven, CT: Yale University Press, 1995), 237.

10. Ibid.

11. Pratt, *I Learn from Children*, 28.

12. Ibid., 37.

13. Cornelia Goldsmith, *Better Day Care for the Young Child through a Merged Governmental and Nongovernmental Effort: The Story of Day Care in New York City as the Responsibility of a Department of Health 1943–1963 and Nearly a Decade Later—1972* (Washington, DC: National Association for the Education of Young Children, 1972), 87–88.

14. Antler, *Lucy Sprague Mitchell*, 245

15. Caroline Pratt and Lula E. Wright, *Experimental Practice in the City and Country School* (New York: E. P. Dutton & Company, 1924), vii; Charlotte Winsor, ed., *Experimental Schools Revisited: Bulletins of the Bureau of Educational Experiments* (New York: Agathon Press, Inc., 1973), 28; Antler, *Lucy Sprague Mitchell*, 241, 242; Cremin, *The Transformation of the School*, 202–205; and Blythe S. F. Hinitz, "The Development of Creative Movement within Early Childhood Education, 1920 to 1970" (Ed.D. diss., Temple University, 1977), 25–26, 31.

16. Antler, *Lucy Sprague Mitchell*, 241.

17. Caroline Pratt and Jesse Stanton, *Before Books* (New York: Adelphi Company Publishers, 1926), vii; and Pratt and Wright, *Experimental Practice in the City and Country School*, v.

18. Pratt, *I Learn from Children*, 170.

19. Pratt, *I Learn from Children*, 65; and Pratt and Wright, *Experimental Practice in the City and Country School*, 57–58.

20. Pratt, *I Learn from Children*, 112, also see Chapters 8 and 9.

21. Pratt and Wright, *Experimental Practice in the City and Country School*, 17–18; and Pratt, *I Learn from Children*, 64–66, 142–145.

22. Pratt, *I Learn from Children*, 184–185.

23. Winsor, ed., Experimental Schools Revisited: Bulletins of the Bureau of Educational Experiments, 9.

24. Ibid., 8–9.

25. Harriet M. Johnson, ed. Barbara Biber, *School Begins at Two: A Book for Teachers and Parents* (New York, Agathon Press, Inc., 1936 reprinted 1970), xiii.

26. Ibid., xiv.

27. Antler, *Lucy Sprague Mitchell*, 209; and Pratt, *I Learn from Children*, 55.

28. Johnson, ed. Biber, *School Begins at Two*, xvi.

29. Lucy Sprague Mitchell, "Harriet Johnson: Pioneer 1867–1934," *Progressive Education* 11 (1934): 427.

30. Winsor, ed., *Experimental Schools Revisited: Bulletins of the Bureau of Educational Experiments*, 127–128, 137; and Harriet Johnson, *Children in the Nursery School* (New York: John Day Company, Inc.), xvi–xvii.

31. Johnson, ed. Biber, *School Begins at Two*, 101–132, passim.

32. Johnson, *Children in the Nursery School*, 60.

33. Johnson, ed. Biber, *School Begins at Two*, xiv.

34. Antler, *Lucy Sprague Mitchell*, 287.

35. Ibid., 302–304; and Charlotte B. Winsor, "Early Progressive Schools II," in *Roots of Open Education in America: Reminiscences and Reflections*, ed. Ruth Dropkin and Arthur Tobier (New York: City College Workshop Center for Open Education, December 1976), 141–143.

36. Cremin, *The Transformation of the School*, 211.

37. Some information in this section is from the Margaret Naumburg Papers, Education Boxes, Department of Special Collections, Van Pelt–Dietrich Library Center, University of Pennsylvania, Philadelphia, Pennsylvania. Cremin, *The Transformation of the School*, 211; Robert H. Beck, "Progressive Education and American Progressivism: Margaret Naumburg," *Teachers College Record* LX (1958–1959), 200; Margaret Naumburg, "Montessori Class: The House of Children," Margaret Naumburg Papers, Education Box #1, 3; Margaret Naumburg, "Montessori Class: Second Year," Margaret Naumburg Papers, Education Box #1, 3.

38. Cremin, *The Transformation of the School*, 211.

39. Naumburg, "Montessori Class: The House of Children," 3; Naumburg, "Montessori Class: Second Year," 3.

40. "Walden School on its 50th Anniversary: Its Raison D'Etre: Its Educational Pioneering: Past, Present and Future" (New York, Walden School, April 1964), 2, Margaret Naumburg Papers, Education Box #1.

41. Cremin, *The Transformation of the School*, 211.

42. Margaret Naumburg, *The Child and the World: Dialogues in Modern Education* (New York: Harcourt, Brace and Company, 1928), 32.

43. Margaret Naumburg, "Summary of Work in the Use of Art Therapy at the Children's Center and in Relation to the Nursery School and Its Staff," Ms, Margaret Naumburg Papers, Education Box #1, undated, 1–2.

44. Margaret Naumburg's papers are housed in the Special Collections Department of the Van Pelt–Dietrich Library at the University of Pennsylvania in Philadelphia.

45. Naumburg, *The Child and the World*, 211.

46. "The Walden Story: *forty years of living education:* Walden School—1914–1954" (New York: privately printed, March 16, 1954), 15, 21, Margaret Naumburg Papers, Education Box #1.

47. Naumburg, "Montessori Class: Second Year," 4.

48. Maro Avakian, [student paper], TMs, [unpaged attachment to letter], Eve Rothenberg, New York, to Margaret Naumburg, New York, 20 May 1964, in the hand of Eve Rothenberg, Margaret Naumburg Papers.

49. [Margaret Naumburg], "Statement of Philosophy," TMs, 7, Margaret Naumburg Papers, Education Box #1.

50. Goldsmith, *Better Day Care for the Young Child,* 88; and "Walden School on Its 50th Anniversary: Its Raison D'Etre: Its Educational Pioneering: Past, Present and Future" (New York, Walden School, April 1964), 1–17, Margaret Naumburg Papers, Education Box #1.

51. Margaret Naumburg, "A Direct Method of Education," TMs p. 1–9, Margaret Naumburg Papers, Education Box #1 [published in *Experimental Schools* (New York: Bureau of Educational Experiment, 1917) and reprinted in Charlotte Winsor, ed., *Experimental Schools Revisited: Bulletins of the Bureau of Educational Experiments* (New York: Agathon Press, Inc., 1973), 41].

52. NSSE, *The Twenty-Eighth Yearbook of the National Society for the Study of Education: Preschool and Parental Education,* 223–228.

53. Ibid., 223.

54. Ibid., 224–225.

55. "The Walden Story: *forty years of living education:* Walden School—1914–1954" (New York: privately printed, March 16, 1954), 15, 21, Margaret Naumburg Papers, Education Box #1.

56. "Walden School on Its 50th Anniversary: Its Raison D'Etre: Its Educational Pioneering: Past, Present and Future" (New York, Walden School, April 1964), 1, Margaret Naumburg Papers, Education Box #1.

57. Cremin, *The Transformation of the School,* 207.

58. Lucy Sprague Mitchell, "Map as Art Expression," *Progressive Education: A Quarterly Review of the Newer Tendencies in Education* III, no. 2 (April–May–June 1926): 150–153.

59. Katherine Whiteside Taylor, *Parents and Children Learn Together* (New York: Teachers College Press, 1967), i.

60. Forest, *Preschool Education,* 303.

61. Libby Byers, "Origins and Early History of the Parent Cooperative Nursery School Movement in America," 1972, EDRS, ED 091063, 48.

62. Dorothy W. Hewes, *"It's the Camaraderie"—A History of Parent Participation Preschools* (Davis, CA: Center for Cooperatives, University of California, 1998), 37–39.

63. Taylor, *Parents and Children Learn Together,* 294; and Forest, *Preschool Education,* 300.

64. Forest, *Preschool Education,* 300.

65. Abigail Adams Eliot agreed with Taylor's assessment. The school hired a British teacher trained under Margaret McMillan. Hewes, *"It's the Camaraderie,"* 40–41; and

Katherine Whiteside Taylor, "Parent Cooperative Nursery Schools," in James L. Hymes, Jr., *Living History Interviews,* 3 vols. (Carmel, CA: Hacienda Press, 1978–1979), 1:28.

66. Byers, "Origins and Early History of the Parent Cooperative Nursery School Movement," 49.

67. Dorothy W. Hewes, "Do Parent Co-op Preschools Float on Kondratieff's Economic Waves?" (paper presented at the Annual Conference of the National Association for the Education of Young Children, Atlanta, GA, 2 December 1994), EDRS, ED 379094, 8; Byers, "Origins and Early Histoty of the Parent Cooperative Nursery School Movement," 49; and NSSE, *The Twenty-Eighth Yearbook of the National Society for the Study of Education: Preschool and Parental Education,* 217–218.

68. Taylor, *Parents and Children Learn Together,* 295; Hewes, "Do Parent Co-op Preschools Float on Kondratieff's Economic Waves?", 8; and Byers, "Origins and Early History of the Parent Cooperative Nursery School Movement," 49–50.

69. They received initial funding from the Institute of Child Welfare through Dr. Edna Bailey and the Scripps Foundation. Byers, "Origins and Early History of the Parent Cooperative Nursery School Movement," 51.

Herbert Stolz, the husband of Dr. Lois Hayden Meek Stolz, who was also connected with Lawrence Frank and the Rockefeller funding of the Institute at the University of California at Berkeley, was one of the advisors. Lois Stolz was the doctoral advisor to Katherine Whiteside Taylor in 1937. They had met in California in the 1920s. Hamilton Cravens, *Before Head Start: The Iowa Station and America's Children* (Chapel Hill: University of North Carolina Press, 1993), 65–67.

70. Byers, "Origins and Early History of the Parent Cooperative Nursery School Movement," 54, 56, 57.

71. Taylor, "Parent Cooperative Nursery Schools," 1:30.

72. Hewes, "Do Parent Co-op Preschools Float on Kondratieff's Economic Waves?", 8.

73. Hewes, *"It's the Camaraderie,"* 37, 43–44. For a description of the beginnings of the cooperative movement in Detroit, taken from primary sources, see: Janet Langlois, *Serving Children Then and Now: An Oral History of Early Childhood Education and Day Care in Metropolitan Detroit* (Detroit, MI: Wayne State University, 1989).

74. Taylor, *Parents and Children Learn Together,* 13.

75. Taylor, "Parent Cooperative Nursery Schools," 1:31, 32.

76. Byers, "Origins and Early History of the Parent Cooperative Nursery School Movement," 60; Taylor, "Parent Cooperative Nursery Schools," 1:43–45.

77. "I [Dorothy Hewes] am finding that the enthusiasm of participating parents not only extends far into their alumni years but that many have become leaders of early childhood education." Hewes names such ECED leaders as Lilian Katz, Leah Adams, and Lillian Weber; Byers names eight leaders, including the president of the Northem California Association for the Education of Young Children. Hewes, "Do Parent Co-op Preschools Float on Kondratieff's Economic Waves?", 12.

Byers, "Origins and Early History of the Parent Cooperative Nursery School Movement," 60–61; and Dorothy W. Hewes, "Early Childhood Education: Its Historic Past and Promising Future" (paper presented at 20th Annual Graduation Celebration of Early Childhood Education at California State University, Long Beach, Long Beach, CA, 3 May 1995), ERIC, ED 386 274, 8.

78. Taylor, "Parent Cooperative Nursery Schools," 1:47.

79. Hewes, *"It's the Camaraderie,"* 234–236, 239–243.

80. "Co-ops have shown that lay people—parents in particular but lay people generally—can make fine contributions in the classroom, under a trained teacher." Taylor, *Parents and Children Learn Together,* 303–306; and Taylor, "Parent Cooperative Nursery Schools," 1:50.

81. Taylor, *Parents and Children Learn Together,* 303–304.

82. Ibid., 243–244. The prospective administrator of any early education program would be well advised to follow these recommendations.

83. Cravens, *Before Head Start,* 35. For further biographical information about Baldwin, see *Who Was Who in America, 1896–1993* (Chicago, IL: A. M. Marquis Co., 1994), 49.

84. Baldwin's five ages were: a chronological age, signifying the span of life; a physiological age, indicating stages of physical growth and maturity; a mental age, manifesting the development of certain instincts, capacities, and mental traits; a pedagogical age, denoting school progress; and a moral age, meaning normal moral and religious judgments. Cravens, *Before Head Start*, 28–29.

85. Ibid., 74.

86. Ibid., 36

87. Ibid., 44.

88. Forest, *Preschool Education*, 295–296; and NSSE, *The Twenty-Eighth Yearbook of the National Society for the Study of Education: Preschool and Parental Education*, 405–432.

89. Cravens, *Before Head Start*, 83.

90. Ibid., 83–84.

91. Ibid., 73.

92. Evelyn Weber, *Ideas Influencing Early Childhood Education: A Theoretical Analysis* (New York: Teachers College Press, 1984), 106.

93. Bird T. Baldwin and Lorle I. Stecher, *The Psychology of the Preschool Child* (New York: D. Appleton and Co., 1924).

94. Bird T. Baldwin, Eva Abigail Fillmore, and Lora Hadley, *Farm Children: An Investigation of Rural Child Life in Selected Areas of Iowa* (New York: D. Appleton and Co., 1930).

95. Bird T. Baldwin "Preschool Laboratories at the Iowa Child Welfare Research Station," in NSSE, *The Twenty-Eighth Yearbook of the National Society for the Study of Education: Preschool and Parental Education*, 211–217.

96. Cravens, *Before Head Start*, 139.

97. Ibid., 74.

98. NSSE, *The Twenty-Eighth Yearbook of the National Society for the Study of Education: Preschool and Parental Education*, 405–432

99. Cravens, *Before Head Start*, 37.

100. Ibid., 40.

101. NSSE, *The Twenty-Eighth Yearbook of the National Society for the Study of Education: Preschool and Parental Education*, 212.

102. Ibid., 217.

103. For more information about land-grant colleges, see Lester G. Anderson, *Land-Grant Universities and Their Continuing Challenge* (East Lansing: Michigan State University Press, 1976); for more on nursery schools in home economics departments, see John E. Anderson, "Child Development: An Historical Perspective," *Child Development* 27 (June 1956), 181–196; and Lawrence K. Frank, "The Beginnings of Child Development and Family Life Education in the Twentieth Century," *Merrill-Palmer Quarterly* 8 (October 1962), 207–227.

104. National Society for the Study of Education, "The Nursery School of the Iowa State College of Agriculture and Mechanic Arts," *Twenty-Eighth Yearbook: Early Childhood and Parental Education*, ed. Guy M. Whipple (Bloomington, IL: Public School Publishing Co., 1929), 180. Home economics tries to improve society through the family, while education tries to improve society through the child. One of the authors graduated from a similar school at Ohio State University in Columbus, established in 1925.

105. Ibid., 183

106. Ibid., 182–183.

107. Ibid., 184.

108. Personal communication with Dr. Joan Herwig, director of Child Development Lab School, Iowa State University at Ames, September 3, 1997.

109. Alice Smuts, "Edna Noble White," *Notable American Women: The Modern Period* (Cambridge, MA: Belknap Press of Harvard University Press, 1980), 728–729.

110. Elizabeth Cleveland, *Training the Toddler* (Philadelphia: Lippincott, 1925), 16–19.

111. Smuts, "Edna Noble White," 728.

112. Ibid.

113. Ibid., 729; Lawrence K. Frank, "The Beginnings of Child Development and Family Life Education in the Twentieth Century," *Merrill-Palmer Quarterly* 8 (October 1962): 211; Federal Works Agency, Work Projects Administration, Division of Service Projects, Record of Program Operation and Accomplishments: The Nursery School Program, by Grace Langdon and Isabel J. Robinson (Washington, DC: Govemment Printing Office, 1943), 44.

114. Smuts, "Edna Noble White," 729.

115. Helen T. Woolley, "Pre-school and Parental Education at the Merrill-Palmer School," *Progressive Education* 2, n. 1 (1925): 35–37. Ilse Forest, *Preschool Education* (New York: Macmillan Co., 1927), 297, 302.

116. The will of Mrs. Lizzie Merrill Palmer is quoted in Elizabeth Cleveland, *Training the Toddler* (Philadelphia: Lippincott, 1925), 14–16. This book describes and discusses the child's social and emotional life with reference to his experiences in the Merrill-Palmer nursery school. The author used vignettes from the lives of both children and teachers to illustrate the education of the children.

117. Cleveland, *Training the Toddler,* 16–18; Woolley, "Pre-school and Parental Education at the Merrill-Palmer School," 35.

118. Woolley, "Pre-school and Parental Education at the Merrill-Palmer School," 36; Cleveland, *Training the Toddler,* 19–20, 22. The students in nursery school training had live-in arrangements similar to what Froebel had for those in kindergarten training.

119. Cleveland, *Training the Todder,* 20–25.

120. Ibid., 36.

121. National Society for the Study of Education, "The Merrill-Palmer Nursery School," *Twenty-Eighth Yearbook of the National Society for the Study of Education: Preschool and Parental Education,* ed. Guy M. Whipple (Bloomington, IL: Public School Publishing Co., 1929), 197–198.

122. Helen T. Woolley, "The Nursery School at the Merrill-Palmer School in Detroit," *Childhood Education* 2 (1925): 72–73; National Society for the Study of Education, "The Merrill-Palmer Nursery School," 196.

123. Cleveland, *Training the Toddler,* 37–38.

124. National Society for the Study of Education, "The Merrill-Palmer Nursery School," 199–200. Some of the test results were reported by Helen T. Woolley, in "Validity Standards of Mental Measurements in Young Children," *School and Society* 21 (April 1925): 476–482. An informal test used to measure the mental development of children at the Merrill-Palmer was Montessori's "pink tower." It consisted of ten graduated blocks that the children placed in order from the largest to the smallest. Cleveland, *Training the Toddler,* 59–60.

125. National Society for the Study of Education, "The Merrill-Palmer Nursery School," 200.

126. Personal telecommunication with administrative assistant of the Merrill-Palmer Institute, at Wayne State University, August 26, 1997.

127. Walter R. Miles, *Arnold Lucius Gesell, 1880–1961: A Biographical Memoir,* Biographical Memoirs, no. 37 (New York: Columbia University Press, 1964, published for the National Academy of Sciences), 55–62, 68.

128. Louise B. Ames, *Arnold Gesell—Themes of His Work* (New York: Human Sciences Press, Inc., 1989), 17–18.

129. Arnold Gesell, "A Guidance Nursery School," *National Education Association Journal* 18 (April 1929): 105. On page 106, a sketch shows how the nursery school was arranged.

130. Arnold Gesell, *The Pre-School Child from the Standpoint of Public Hygiene and Education* (Boston: Houghton Mifflin, 1923), 2–12; Chapters III and VI passim, 238–245; idem, "The Significance of the Nursery School" *Childhood Education* 1, no. 1 (September 1924): 11–20.

131. Ames, *Arnold Gesell,* 159–161.

132. Ibid., 291.

133. Arnold Gesell, "The Educational Status of the Preschool Child," *School and Society* 39 (April 21, 1934): 496.

134. Amold Gesell and Frances L. Ilg, *Infant and Child in ihe Culture of Today,* 21st ed. (New York: Harper & Brothers, 1943), 131–141.

135. Sheldon White, "The Learning-Maturation Controversy: Hall to Hull," *Merrill-Palmer Quarterly* 14 (July 1968): 187–196.

136. Arnold Gesell, *The First Five Years of Life* (New York: Harper & Row, 1940), 319–324.

137. Ibid., 14.

138. Louise B. Ames. "Dr. Arnold Gesell, 1880–1961," *British Journal of Education* 32 (June 1962): 101–102.

139. For Gesell's complete bibliography, see Miles, *Arnold Lucius Gesell,* 74–96.

140. Amold Gesell, "The Guidance Nursery of the Yale Psycho-Clinic," in National Society for the Study of Education, *Twenty-Eighth Yearbook of the National Society for the Study of Education: Preschool and Parental Education,* ed. Guy M. Whipple (Bloomington, IL: Public School Publishing Co., 1929), 164.

141. Gesell, Ibid., 168; Arnold Gesell and Frances Ilg, *Infant and Child in the Culture of Today,* 21st ed. (New York: Harper & Brothers Publishers, 1943), 366.

142. Gesell and Ilg, *Infant and Child in the Culture of Today,* 367.

143. Gesell, "The Guidance Nursery of the Yale Psycho-Clinic," 164.

144. Gesell and Ilg, *Infant and Child in the Culture of Today,* 368, 370. On page 369 is the arrangement of the Yale Guidance Nursery.

145. Gesell, "The Guidance Nursery of the Yale Psycho-Clinic," 166.

146. Arnold Gesell, "Guidance Nursery," *National Education Association Journal* 18 (April 1929): 105–106.

147. Gesell, "The Guidance Nursery of the Yale Psycho-Clinic," 171–172.

148. Louise B. Ames, *Arnold Gesell—Themes of His Work* (New York: Human Sciences Press Inc., 1989), 293.

149. Ibid., 296.

150. Cravens, *Before Head Start,* 46.

151. Milton J. E. Senn, "Insights on the Child Development Movement in the United States," *Monographs of the Society for Research in Child Development,* 40 no. 3–4, Serial No. 161 (August 1975), 12.

152. Cravens, *Before Head Start,* 46.

153. Antler, *Lucy Sprague Mitchell,* 406, endnote 29.

154. The universities selected by Frank were: the Iowa Child Welfare Research Station (ICWRS), which was cited as an excellent model; Teachers College, Columbia University, as a training center for teachers in preschool and parent education; the state universities of Michigan, Wisconsin, and Illinois to study rural children and families; Arnold Gesell's Psycho-Clinic at Yale; the University of California at Berkeley Institute of Child Welfare, cited for a well-rounded program of research in child growth and development and for its nursery school; the University of Minnesota Institute of Child Welfare, which combined research and diffusion; the Merrill-Palmer School in Detroit; and Mills College in Oakland, California.

155. Cravens, *Before Head Start,* 54.

156. Frank's plan for New York State included the Department of Family Life, Child Development, and Parent Education at Cornell University, which was to train professionals in the field, conduct research, offer residential courses, and do extension work; the State University of New York at Albany and Buffalo State Teachers College, which were to educate nursery school teachers; and the Board of Public Education, which was to operate an experimental nursery school in the Albany public schools.

157. Ibid., 138–139.

158. Ibid., 154.

159. Senn, "Insights on the Child Development Movement in the United States," Appendix B, 92–93.

160. Barbara Beatty, *Preschool Education in America: The Culture of Young Children from the Colonial Era to the Present* (New Haven, CT: Yale University Press, 1995), 133; and Cravens, *Before Head Start,* 62–65.

161. Lawrence Kelso Frank, *The Fundamental Needs of the Child* (New York: National Association for Mental Health, 1952); and Weber, *Ideas Influencing Early Childhood Education,* 122–123.

162. Weber, *Ideas Influencing Early Childhood Education,* 126–127. For further information see: Ruth E. Hartley, Lawrence E. Frank, and Robert M. Goldenson, *Understanding*

Children's Play (New York: Columbia University Press, 1952) and Lawrence K. Frank, "Clues to Childhood Identity," *Childhood Education,* 42, no. 5 (1996), reprinted in James D. Quisenberry, E. Anne Eddowes, and Sandra L. Robinson, *Readings from Childhood Education* (Wheaton, MD: Association for Childhood Education International, 1991), 70.

163. Thomas J. Hurwitz, "The Educational Thought of Lawrence Kelso Frank" (Ed.D. diss., Boston University, 1979).

164. The information in this section is from the Abigail Adams Eliot Papers, Series I, Personal and Family Papers, 1858–1979; Series II, Professional Papers, 1928–1976; Series III, Photographs, 1860–1971; Schlesinger Library, Radcliffe College, Cambridge, MA; and V. Celia Lascarides, "Abigail Adams Eliot: Her Relevance for Today" (paper presented at the annual meeting of the National Association for the Education of Young Children, Atlanta, Georgia, November 5, 1983). "In Memoriam, Abigail Adams Eliot." *Young Children* 48 (March 1993); 3, 52. Eliot had two siblings: Martha May Eliot, M.D., pediatrician, chief of the Children's Bureau (1951–1956), and a founding member of UNICEF and WHO; and Dr. Frederick May Eliot, who like their father became a Unitarian minister. For more information on Eliot's family history, see folder 1, Eliot Papers.

165. Eliot's calling card, folder 11, Eliot Papers.

166. Abigail A. Eliot, Talk given at the Schlesinger Library Luncheon Series, April 13, 1982, Cronkite Graduate Center, Cambridge, MA. Personal notes of this author, who attended the luncheon.

167. Additional information about Eliot's activities while studying at Oxford, in letters to her mother, August 1919 to September 1920, folders 15 and 16, Eliot Papers.

168. Eliot's Oxford certificate, folder 11, Eliot Papers.

169. Eliot to her mother, Buzy, France, 14 December 1919, folder 16, Eliot Papers.

170. Abigail Adams Eliot, *Memoirs: A Heart of Grateful Trust,* transcribed and ed. Marjorie G. Manning (n.p. [c. 1982]), 28.

171. Eliot to her mother, 16 June 1921 and 1 July 1921, folder 20, Eliot Papers.

172. For a detailed daily schedule and activities of the Rachel McMillan Nursery School, see Eliot to Mrs. Elizabeth Pearson, 21 June 1921, folder 23, Eliot Papers.

173. Eliot to Mrs. Elizabeth Pearson, 14 June 1921, folder 23, Eliot Papers. McMillan's father was a naturalized U.S. citizen; Margaret was born in America. There appears to have been a bond between Eliot and McMillan.

174. Eliot to Mrs. Elizabeth Pearson, 20 July 1921, folder 23, Eliot Papers.

175. Eliot to her mother, 25 August 1921, folder 20, Eliot Papers.

176. Eliot to Mrs. Elizabeth Pearson, 21 August 1921, folder 23, Eliot Papers. This letter also includes in some detail Eliot's description of Owen's content for training nursery school teachers.

177. Eliot to her father, 13 and 14 August 1921, folder 20, Eliot Papers.

178. Eliot to Mrs. Elizabeth Pearson, 14 June 1921 and 7 July 1921, folder 23, Eliot Papers. In the second letter, Eliot mentioned that McMillan was corresponding with persons in Detroit who were planning to open a nursery school there, but did not mention names.

179. Eliot to her mother telling of the Queen's upcoming visit, 12 November 1921, folder 20, Eliot Papers. A dated (1921) group photograph commemorates the event.

180. Eliot to her mother, 25 August 1921, folder 20, Eliot Papers.

181. The courses Eliot took at Harvard and the term papers she wrote are in folders 28 and 29, Eliot Papers. They reflect the variety of interests that Eliot had within early childhood. Some of the topics she selected came out of her experiences teaching children, such as, "Tendencies to make and destroy as found in young children."

182. Ruggles Street Nursery School and Training Centre Bulletin, 1923–1924. The training appears to have been vigorous, of college level, and concerned with the fit between the student teacher and her future work.

183. Ibid.

184. Folder 46, Eliot Papers.

185. Folder 48, Eliot Papers.

186. From a lecture in this course, we learned that the hem line that year was 19 inches. Folder 52, Eliot Papers.

187. Adult Personality course for 1938–1939, folder 52, Eliot Papers.

188. Implementing the Mid-Century White House Conference course, Summer 1951, folder 65v, Eliot Papers. It was the fifth White House Conference on Children and Youth, and it was the largest effort on behalf of children in the history of this nation.

189. One cannot help but think of Froebel and his personal commitment in training each one of the kindergartners. Perhaps this is the distinct characteristic of individuals committed to teacher training.

190. Eliot, *Memoirs: A Heart of Grateful Trust*, 44–47.

191. Abigail A. Eliot, "Two Nursery Schools: Nurseries Working for Health, Education and Family Life." *Child Health Magazine* 5 (March 1924): 97; Dorothy B. Williams, "A Study of the Establishment and Changes Thereafter in the Operation of Ruggles Street Nursery School and Training Centre" (M.A. thesis, Eliot-Pearson School, 1957), 10–13. One of the authors visited the Rachel McMillan Nursery School in July 1989, when it was celebrating its seventy-fifth anniversary.

192. Abigail A. Eliot, "America's First Nursery Schools," in James L. Hymes, Jr., *Living History Interviews*, 3 vols. (Carmel, CA: Hacienda Press, 1978–1979), 1:16; idem "Nursery Schools Fifty Years Ago," *Young Children* 27 (April 1972): 208–214.

193. Eliot, "Two Nursery Schools," 100; Arnold Gesell, *The Preschool Child from the Standpoint of Public Hygiene and Education* (Boston: Houghton Mifflin, 1923), 243–245.

194. Eliot, "Two Nursery Schools," 97–98.

195. Abigail A. Eliot, Talk given at the Schlesinger Library Luncheon Series, April 13, 1982, Cronkite Graduate Center, Cambridge, Massachusetts. Author's personal notes.

196. Eliot, *Memoirs: A Heart of Grateful Trust*, 31–32; Hymes, *Living History Interviews* 1:16–18.

197. Eliot, "Two Nursery Schools," 98; National Society for the Study of Education, "The Nursery Training School of Boston," *Twenty-Eighth Yearbook: Early Childhood and Parental Education*, 201–202

198. Gesell, *The Preschool Child from the Standpoint of Public Hygiene and Education*, 243.

199. Abigail A. Eliot, "Educating the Parent through the Nursery School," *Childhood Education*, 3 (December 1926): 182–190; Eliot, *A Heart of Grateful Trust*, 33–34; Gesell, *The Preschool Child*, 244; and Eliot, "Two Nursery Schools," 98.

200. National Society for the Study of Education, "The Nursery Training School of Boston," 203.

201. Eliot, *A Heart of Grateful Trust*, 44–47; "Abigail Adams Eliot: A Tribute," The New England Association of Nursery Education (Spring 1952), 4–8.

202. Williams, "A Study of the Establishment and Changes Thereafter in the Operation of Ruggles Street Nursery School and Training Centre," 13. One of the authors has served as a board member to both the Ruggles Street–Mission Hill Day Care Center (1983–1993) and the Associated Day Care Services (1988–1993).

203. Mildred Dickerson, "James L. Hymes, Jr.," in *Profiles in Childhood Education, 1931–1960*, ACEI Later Leaders Committee (Wheaton, MD: Association for Childhood Education International, 1992), 82.

204. Samuel J. Braun and Esther P. Edwards, *History and Theory of Early Childhood Education* (Worthington, OH: Charles A. Jones Publishing Company, 1972), 169–176; James L. Hymes, Jr., Industrial Day Care's Roots in America (from *Proceedings of the Conference on Industry and Day Care*, 1970) in *Sources: Notable Selections in Early Childhood Education*, eds. Karen Menke Paciorek and Joyce Huth Munro (Guilford, CT: Dushkin Publishing Group/Brown & Benchmark Publishers, 1996), 283–288; and Lois Hayden Meek Stolz, "The Kaiser Child Service Centers," in James L. Hymes, Jr., *Living History Interviews*, 3 vols. (Carmel, CA: Hacienda Press, 1978–1979), 2:28–56. See Chapter 12 in this volume for a description of the Kaiser Child Service Centers.

205. Dickerson, "James L. Hymes, Jr.," 84.

206. "In Memoriam," *Young Children*, 53, no. 3 (May 1998): 46–48.

207. Dickerson, "James L. Hymes, Jr.," 85.

208. James L. Hymes, Jr., "Parents," in *Ninth Yearbook of the John Dewey Society: Intercultural Attitudes in the Making*, eds. William Heard Kilpatrick and William Van Til (New York: Harper & Brothers Publishers, 1947), 17.

209. See James L. Hymes, Jr., *Early Childhood Education: Twenty Years in Review: A Look at 1971–1990* (Washington, DC: National Association for the Education of Young Children, 1991).

210. Weber. *Ideas Influencing Early Childhood Education,* 148; and Dickerson, "James L. Hymes, Jr.," 89.

211. Strickland, "Paths Not Taken," 133.

212. Forest, *Preschool Education,* 287, 291, 295 footnote 1, 302–303.

213. Eliot, "Nursery Schools Fifty Years Ago," 210, 211, 213; Hymes, *Living History Interviews,* 1:14; and NSSE, *The Twenty-Eighth Yearbook of the National Society for the Study of Education: Preschool and Parental Education,* 32–33.

214. Margaret Naumburg, "The Crux of Progressive Education," TMs. Margaret Naumburg Papers, Education Box #1 (published in *The New Republic* 63 [June 25, 1930], 1451), 1–6; and Naumburg, *The Child and the World,* 102–122.

215. Johnson, ed. Biber, *School Begins at Two,* 101–132, 142.

216. Lucy Sprague Mitchell, "A Cooperative School for Student Teaching," in Charlotte Winsor, ed., *Experimental Schools Revisited: Bulletins of the Bureau of Educational Experiments* (New York: Agathon Press, Inc., 1973), 2. This New York institution is now known as Bank Street College of Education. See also: J. N. Washburne, "Developing a Curriculum for Teacher Education," *Progressive Education* (May 1937): 356–363. [In ACEI Collection, Record Group IV, Box 24. Special Collections, University of Maryland at College Park Libraries.]

217. National Committee on Nursery Schools (April 1927). Conference on Nursery Schools: Report of the Second Conference of Those Interested in Nursery Schools. New York: Author. 4, 10–13. [In ACEI Collection, Record Group V, Box 10. Special Collections, University of Maryland at College Park Libraries.]

The session was chaired by May Hill of Cleveland Kindergarten-Primary Training School. Edna Noble White of Merrill-Palmer School (Detroit); Grace Langdon of Teachers College, Columbia University (New York City); and Edna Dean Baker of National Kindergarten and Elementary College (Chicago) were the speakers.

218. Ibid., 11.

219. Ibid., 10–13.

220. National Committee on Nursery Schools. (1929). *Third Conference of Nursery School Workers.* Chicago, IL: Author, 44, 50. [In ACEI Collection, Record Group V, Box 10. Special Collections, University of Maryland at College Park Libraries.]

221. These have been topics of discussion at the annual conferences of the National Association of Early Childhood Teacher Educators and the National Association for the Education of Young Children in recent years.

222. NSSE, *The Twenty-Eighth Yearbook of the National Society for the Study of Education: Preschool and Parental Education,* 415–417.

223. Clinical study is defined as: "A beginning is being made in the training of nursery-school teachers in the clinical approach to the study of children." Parental education is defined as: "Preparing the nursery-school teacher for active participation in the program for parental education." Curriculum for young children is defined as: "Thorough grasp of the curricular content which meets the needs of children on the nursery-school level" (in some schools, through separate courses). Ibid., 419.

224. Ibid., 432.

225. National Advisory Committee on Emergency Nursery Schools (1935). Teacher Training for Emergency Nursery Schools, 1933–1934. In *Emergency Nursery Schools during the First Year, 1933–34.* Washington, DC: Office of Emergency Nursery Schools, Works Progress Administration, 54. [In ACEI Collection, Record Group V, Box 10. Special Collections, University of Maryland at College Park Libraries], 55, 59.

226. Ibid., 60.

227. National Advisory Committee on Emergency Nursery Schools (1936). Section D-Teacher training. In *Emergency Nursery Schools during the Second Year, 1934–35.* Washington, DC: Office of Emergency Nursery Schools, Works Progress Administration, 97. [In ACEI Collection, Record Group V, Box 10. Special Collections, University of Maryland at College Park Libraries.]

228. National Advisory Committee on Emergency Nursery Schools (1936). *Suggestion for Building Courses in Nursery Education: A Syllabus.* Bulletin No. 3. Washington, DC: Teacher Training Committee of the National Association for Nursery Education and the Office of Emergency Nursery Schools, Works Progress Administration, entire syllabus. [In ACEI Collection, Record Group V, Box 10. Special Collections, University of Maryland at College Park Libraries], 2.

229. United States Office of Education, *Nursery Schools Vital to the War Effort,* School Children and the War Series (Washington, DC: Federal Security Agency, 1943). [In ACEI Collection, Record Group V, Box 10. Special Collections, University of Maryland at College Park Libraries.], 10.

230. Millie Almy and Agnes Snyder, "The Staff and Its Preparation," in National Society for the Study of Education, *The Forty-Sixth Yearbook of the National Society for the Study of Education: Part II: Early Childhood Education,* ed. Nelson B. Henry (Chicago: University of Chicago Press, 1947), 224–229, 233–242.

231. Bernard Spodek, "Staff Requirements in Early Childhood Education," in National Society for the Study of Education, *Early Childhood Education: The Seventy-First Yearbook of the National Society for the Study of Education,* ed. Ira J. Gordon (Chicago: University of Chicago Press, 1972), 358.

232. Bernard Spodek, "Early Childhood Teacher Training: Linking Theory and Practice," in National Society for the Study of Education, *The Care and Education of America's Young Children: Obstacles and Opportunities: Ninetieth Yearbook of the National Society for the Study of Educaiton: Part I,* ed. Sharon Lynn Kagan (Chicago: University of Chicago Press, 1991), 122.

233. Ibid., 117, 119–120.

234. Lilian G. Katz, *Talks with Teachers* (Washington, DC: National Association for the Education of Young Children, 1977), 7–13.

235. Karen VanderVen, "Pathways to Professional Effectiveness for Early Childhood Educators," in *Professionalism and the Early Childhood Practitioner,* ed. Bernard Spodek, Olivia Saracho, and Donald Peters (New York: Teachers College Press, 1988), 137–160.

236. Karen VanderVen and Carlos Antonio Toffe, "Toward Transformed Mediation of Violence in Schools: The Contribution of Chaos and Complexity Theory," in *Violence in Schools: Annual Yearbook of Child Development,* ed. Stephanie U. Spina (San Francisco, CA: Jossey Bass, in press).

237. Karen VanderVen, "Chaos/Complexity Theory, Constructivism, Interdisciplinarity and Early Childhood Teacher Education," *Journal of Early Childhood Teacher Education* 18, no. 3 (Fall/Winter 1997).

238. Karen VanderVen, Personal communications, 12 June 1998 and 19 June 1998.

239. For a description of materials, equipment, and schedules used in nursery schools, see Appendices 1 and 2 of this volume.

CHAPTER 11

Day Nurseries to Day Care to Child Care to Quality 2000

Several thousand years ago, there had lived a Greek philosopher named Heraclitus, called "The Obscure." He believed that nothing was permanent except change, for even opposites, when most divergent were connected. He was able to find hidden attunement between variables. Perhaps this was what was later meant in the twentieth century, by what was then called "integration." Could the efforts on behalf of children and their families be seen whole, could they be joined to assure progress from the past to the present and from the present on into the future?[1]

Day care is child care in the absence of parents that takes place away from a child's home and in the company of other children. It may be all-day care, all-night care, or simply a two-hour drop-in arrangement. It may be provided in the child's home, a family day care home, or a child care center. A primary obstacle to the improvement of child care services has been the traditional belief that young children should never be separated from their mothers. Yet circumstances throughout history led to provision for child care services. The function of the day nursery was to care for children who remained part of the family unit but who, for social or economic reasons, could not receive parental care during the day. Originally the term "day care" referred to welfare covering all types of daytime services for the group care of young children. It later came to refer exclusively to the full-day programs set up for children of working, impoverished, or handicapped mothers.[2]

Greenman and Fuqua have stated that day care has an identity problem. They feel that misconceptions about day care arise because of the similarities between day care and purely educational programs for children, other human services, and child care in the home. The similarities mask important differences that they believe are ignored by professionals trained in early childhood education, child development, or social work. One of the purposes of day care is as an early education program; however, it is also a social service program for all children, it cares for children in groups, and it is no longer limited to children from needy families or broken homes. What constitutes "day care" for any particular child is subject to considerable variation, even within the same classroom.[3] Clarke-Stewart and Gruber found that most families had evolved a conglomeration of day care "forms" or "types." Their specialized arrangements included relatives, neighbors, paid sitters, and professional educators. These care providers were used in combination, and often changed from one month to the next.[4]

HISTORICAL CONTEXT: THE 1800S

"The history of child care matters."[5] A look at the history of the day nursery, day care, and child care demonstrates ways in which the past serves as the foundation of the present, as well as the arbiter of the future. "Baby farms" crowded children into unsanitary quarters and whisked some of them away when inspectors were due to call. This description of unregulated centers at the turn of the twentieth century finds its counterpart, unfortunately, in some centers of today.[6]

The early day nurseries in the United States were modeled upon the French *crèche*. Although its purpose was the same as that in France, to take efficient care of the children of working mothers, no attempt was made to standardize the day nursery. Because of this, individual nurseries have met their goals to a greater or lesser degree, depending upon the individual situation. The earliest recorded day nurseries in the United States were the Boston Infant School (1828) and the Nursery for the Children of Poor Women in the City of New York (1852).[7,8] The term "custodial care," which has come to be synonymous with low-quality, noneducational care, was at first used to describe the fact that early child care centers took "custody" of children while their mothers were employed. The first permanent day nursery was established in Philadelphia, Pennsylvania, in 1863, to care for children of Civil War workers. The mothers were needed to manufacture clothing for soldiers and to clean in the hospitals.[9] This was replicated during the Second World War. Day states that "during two periods of national crisis concerns about the effect of group day care on children's development and the status of the family were seldom, if ever, raised. Yet in the absence of crisis, the presumed damage to children and the family is invariably used as justification for withholding support from day care."[10]

Jacob Riis and Robert Hunter exposed the problems of the urban slums, and social settlement workers began to reside among the poor they hoped to uplift. Settlement houses were opened in Boston, New York City (Henry Street), Detroit (Franklin Settlement), and Chicago (Hull House). Youcha's moving descriptions of the women who brought their young children to the day nursery at Hull House are representative of all the settlement nurseries of the time. One mother whose child was blown off the roof as she hung out the wash at 6:00 one March morning came to the nursery and sat there forlornly. When Jane Addams asked if there was anything she could do to help, the woman wanted only one thing—a day's wages, so she could miss the next day at work. "I would like to stay home all day and hold the baby. Goosie was always asking me to hold him and I never had any time." Sometimes, however, the day nursery announcements took a condescending tone. The announcement of the establishment of the Baltimore Day Nursery in 1883 stated that it was "for the children of poor *industrious* women who are kept out of their homes all day by employment."[11]

The major purpose of the day nurseries was protective, custodial, physical care. In spite of the fact that the day nursery was an economic necessity, which sometimes prevented the surrendering of children to institutionalized care, it was used by only a small percentage of working mothers in the late 1800s and early 1900s. Among the reasons families used the day nursery were: a parent was deceased or deserted the family; the parents were separated; a parent was sick; the family was in debt; the father was out of work, not supporting the family, was insane, or was in jail. The early day nurseries and infant schools were designed to keep the children out of the orphanages, which provided custodial care outside of the home.[12]

Societal support for the day nursery as a sound child care practice never existed. Until the present, the day nursery maintained the stigma of being for poor, distressed, less effective families. However, there were other objections and problems relating to use of the day nursery. One of the most frequent objections was that of distance from the mother's home. Additionally, it was necessary for mothers to wake the children quite early in order to bring them to the day nursery prior to the start of their shift at the factory, stockyard, or tailoring establishment. In some cases, the mothers felt that the day nurseries did not care for or educate their children in a way they regarded as satisfactory. Ginsberg's pithy description of custodial care was "herding children. Feeding one end and wiping the other. No program of play or fun. No trained staff. Little or no suitable equipment. A garage, a storage place for children."[13]

The industrialization and expansion of cities in the post–Civil War period, combined with immigration, were the primary factors in the rise of protective services for children. The original purpose of the child services in centers was to meet the physical, nutritional, and health needs of neglected children. Later, they addressed the emotional, social, and intellectual development of the young children in their care. The day nursery became a change agent of social reform. Its primary purpose was to serve *pathological families*. Parent education was designed to combat ill manners, poor nutrition, poor hygiene, and non-English-speaking environments. One of the purposes of the day nursery and later the day care center was to free the mother from concern for her child's safety and well-being. The story of a Louisiana factory worker who left her three children, five years old, three years old, and three months old, locked up at home illustrates the problem. When a fire engine went past the factory, the worker was relieved that it did not turn at her corner. The inspector, noting the mother's concern, asked for the key. She discovered the children in the house. Their lunch of bread and syrup was on the table, black with ants. The five-year-old told the visiting inspector that when the whistle blows they could eat, and then give the baby her bottle. This incident led to the 1909 founding of the New Orleans Day Nursery.[14] By 1919, day care had become a central part of social welfare and an integral component of social work across the country.

Day care centers were essential to children whose parents were physically or emotionally unable to care for them. Day care appeared to be a reasonable intermediate step to be taken until the parents could be assisted to overcome their problems with a temporary or permanent disability.[15]

HISTORICAL CONTEXT: 1900–1950S

Many complicating factors impacted on the development of the day nursery. Extensive immigration led to great numbers of individuals who were not knowledgeable about life in the American city. To support their families, mothers were enticed into the factories, leaving their children in substandard care. Very few states licensed day nurseries, and the small number of measures that did exist were uneven. The health standards in the day nurseries were severely criticized by both physicians and health agencies. Health issues became a major task of the day nursery board. Members were concerned about the danger of spreading infections and contagions, undernourishment, poor mouth hygiene, and the lack of proper medical inspection. Their first efforts standardized medical inspection and supervision in the day nursery, provided an adequate diet and safe housing facilities, and looked at facilities for isolation, and the cleanliness, fresh air, and sunshine provided to the children. Progressive boards of managers voluntarily raised the health standards; however, in other cases, pressure needed to be brought. In addition to the physical facility and child health and nutrition concerns, the list of seventeen essential standards in the 1929 NSSE Yearbook includes the understanding of emotional and behavior problems of children, and some form of education. The standards contained in the yearbook are still in use in 1999.[16]

In the early 1920s, some American early educators were beginning to see the advantage of cooperation between the day nursery and the nursery school. In New York City and Philadelphia, day nurseries attempted to meet the needs of the child's intellectual and social development by providing kindergarten school training during at least part of the day. In later years, this was replaced with nursery school activities. A few of the old-time day nurseries were among the first group to become nursery schools. Almost sixty years later, Clarke-Stewart and Gruber stated, "Day care centers are basically similar to nursery schools except that they offer full-time care. Often their activities and schedules overlap with the nursery school's but are extended to more than eight hours by meals, naps, and free play."[17]

Forest believed that educational progress in the day nursery field in the 1920s was largely due to the activities of the day nursery associations. The associations stimulated the day nurseries to do constructive educational work. Active members of the associations acquainted day nursery workers with the importance of mental hygiene for the early childhood years. The associations encouraged day nursery boards to experiment. This activity led to improved child and parent education. Parent education consisted of mothers' meetings where instruction in child care, sewing, and cooking was given.[18]

TYPES OF DAY NURSERIES

The 1929 NSSE Yearbook categorizes day nurseries by their type of support. The four categories presented can still be used today. The first category, titled the *independent commercial nursery*, is currently called family child care. The friendly neighbor caring for the children of others who must work outside the home eked out two inadequate incomes.[19] These successors to the dame schools were unregulated, and the individual states decided to address the issue. In the 1990s, most states have minimal standards for family child care homes. The advent of the family child care credential of the Child Development Associate program has provided a welcome addition to the training and image of family child care providers. Resource and referral agencies across the country also offer training and certification opportunities to family child care providers. The early childhood education and child development centers of the military have devised a separate credentialing and supervision system for family child care homes on military bases.

The *philanthropic nursery* had as its goal charitable relief. The category included private individuals who organized and established a day nursery as a charity, religious organizations, welfare associations, and social settlements. The philanthropic day nursery included programs for the care of infants, preschool children, and schoolchildren. The nursery opened at 7:00 A.M., with a superintendent or nurse to do the health check for the incoming family. Each child was then taken to the appropriate room, where the day was divided into periods of indoor and outdoor work and play, rest, and meals. School-aged children were escorted to and from their building and provided with meals and appropriate after-school activities. The staff consulted with parents either at the end of the day or on evening home visits. The current full-day and extended-day child care centers are following this philanthropic model, if they hold not-for-profit status.[20]

The third category suggested in 1929 is that of the *industrial nursery*. These day nurseries were designed to attract and hold women workers. Their successors may be found in the employer-sponsored child care centers of today. According to the literature, only a few large businesses have shown interest in making child care available on the premises or nearby. Many hospitals are involved in this type of care because of their need for nurses. Other employers purchase spots in proprietary or not-for-profit centers. In the late 1960s and early 1970s, as many corporate-sponsored child care centers closed as opened.

Alluding to the patchwork system of arrangements parents piece together, Galinsky finds a relationship between the number of child care arrangements and the number of times the arrangements fall apart. Most employers prefer not to provide on-site child care as the solution to their employees' problems. Instead, they give their employees information and financial resources to meet their own child care needs. For example: child care resource and referral services, flexible spending accounts (a salary reduction plan), and parent seminars at the workplace are provided by the employer. Although Boocock reported that the success of employer child care programs was difficult to evaluate, other sources have recently stated that the provision of child care for employees leads to greater retention and lower absenteeism. Companies whose purpose is related to family needs are more likely to provide child care assistance. Location and competitive pressure often influence whether an employer will provide on-site care or purchase slots in existing child care centers. The presence of child care champions within the company, the age of the work force, and the proportion of female employees influence on-site child care development.

According to Galinsky, the companies with the most outstanding child care policies have been among the most profitable. Until recently, nonunionized companies were more likely to develop family-responsive policies. That is in the process of changing, following an agreement between AT&T and its unions to bargain for a "family-care" package. Boocock reports that "while labor unions have been innovative in providing many kinds of social services to their workers, they seem to have been strangely inactive in the area of day care." Garment industry and teachers unions have become involved in the development of child care centers. Some federal agencies have recently opened centers for children of their personnel. Many state and local governments have also entered the field by contracting with child care providers to meet employee needs.[21]

The last category cited by the 1929 *NSSE Yearbook* is that of *day nurseries in a public school system*. When the compulsory school law was put into effect in 1910, public schools were faced with the problem of younger brothers and sisters who were unprotected when older children were compelled to attend school. The day nurseries, like the public school kindergartens, were designed for Americanization of foreign children and their mothers, teaching courtesy and table manners, and preventing the absence of older children from school.[22] During the 1960s, public school systems in New York City (based on the work of Cynthia and Martin Deutsch) and Philadelphia (Get Set) incorporated programs for four-year-olds into their school systems. The 1998 *Abbott vs. Burke* court decision in New Jersey requires programs or program plans for three- and four-year-olds in 121 school districts in the state by the year 1999.[23]

Beginning in the early 1930s, the Depression era, day care was considered to be a jobs program. The staffs of day care centers, based on the nursery school rather than the day nursery pattern, were required to come from relief rolls. Following the rapid expansion of day care during World War II, the demobilization of the child care centers was as rapid as that of the army. However, according to the *Forty-Sixth NSSE Yearbook,* when federal funds for emergency nursery schools were discontinued, many public school districts provided the funds for continuation. In fact, the yearbook states that public, private, and tuition funds were used.[24]

After the war, educational literature began to assert that it was "no longer possible to distinguish between a service which gives 'care' to young children and another which 'educates' them." It was suggested that the services provided by boards of education should include three- to five-year-old children.[25] During the period following World War II up through the mid-1960s, the

United States emphasized child-centeredness. The "experts" on child development and child rearing said that children needed the full-time, devoted attention of their biological mothers, otherwise they would suffer from "deprivation." The literature of the period also focused on the first five years of life as the time of the greatest cognitive growth. Parents were supposed to not only provide for their children's physical and emotional needs, but were supposed to enjoy the process. However, the children became separated from the working life of the larger society. They were not expected to make any contribution toward the working of the community.[26]

HISTORICAL CONTEXT: 1960S–1990S

In the 1960s, the National Council of Jewish Women involved women in surveying child care in the local community. The report found that, on a nationwide basis, child care services were largely inadequate. Only 1 percent of proprietary centers were found to be superior and 15 percent were good. The remainder did not adequately meet the criteria.[27] Two other surveys done in the late 1950s reinforced the need for better care. One was a national statistical survey of "child care arrangements of full-time working mothers" by the U.S. Bureau of the Census, at the request of the Children's Bureau. The other, a 1959 Child Welfare League of America (CWLA) study, covered all daytime child care arrangements other than those of mother care. Both studies found strong and rapid changes, with increasing numbers of women going into the work force and less-than-adequate child care arrangements.[28]

Day nursery and day care associations were in the forefront of the sweeping changes. In 1892, the First National Conference of Day Nurseries drew on the staffs of the ninety nurseries in existence. This meeting led to the 1898 formation of the National Federation of Day Nurseries, which became the National Association of Day Nurseries in 1938. In 1942, it joined the CWLA, an important standard-setting organization. Elinor Guggenheimer and Sadie Ginsberg formed the Inter-City Committee for the Day Care of Children at the National Conference of Social Work, which was incorporated as the National Committee for the Day Care of Children, in New York City, in June 1960. Its purposes were: "To interpret as widely as possible the needs of children for day care; to promote good standards for day care; to encourage study and research in the field of day care; to encourage cooperative effort throughout the country toward the establishment of adequate day care services for children; to stimulate the exchange of information, ideas, and experiences in the field of day care."[29] It moved its headquarters to Washington, D.C., in 1968, becoming the Day Care and Child Development Council of America (DCCDCA). The focus was changed to a citizen action organization that initiates advocacy for child care.

The Children's Bureau and the Women's Bureau of the U.S. Department of Labor cosponsored a nationwide conference on day care in Washington, D.C., in November 1960, as a follow-up to the White House Conference on

Children and Youth. The purposes of the conference were encouraging the development of day care services for children who need them, examination of the extent and variety of day care needs and resources, identification of roadblocks, and stimulating broader community responsibility for day care services. In May 1962, the American Public Health Association (APHA) set up its first day care committee. Its first steps were to assess the health needs of children in daytime care, and the extent to which those needs were met. On July 25, 1962, President John F. Kennedy signed into law the bill appropriating the first federal funds approved by Congress for day care since World War II. However, the funds were not finally allocated until over a year later, on August 7, 1963.[30]

Until the mid-1970s, there was little governmental involvement in child care at the national level and no comprehensive national child care policy. However, following the advent of Head Start and the Work Incentive Program, substantial increases in Federal spending occurred. Indirect subsidies such as income tax deductions for child care and deductions for welfare mothers were begun. The publicity surrounding child development research, which showed the impact of early learning experiences on children's later development, was one contributing factor. A huge increase in welfare rolls and the social changes precipitated by the women's movement were additional influences. As women insisted upon being productive, contributing members of society, changes occurred that liberated both men and women from traditional roles. According to Day, the debate fomented by the National Organization of Women (NOW) in the early 1970s focused attention on the field of child care.[31, 32, 33]

Beginning with the late 1960s, many Head Start programs operated as full-day child care centers. Money for child care came through Title IVa and IVb of the Social Security Act and Titles I, III, and IV of the Elementary and Secondary Education Act (ESEA). There was additional money for special groups such as migrant children, and for children in the Model Cities Program. A 1972 study mentioned sixty federal programs that funded child care services. The Small Business Administration provided low-cost long-term loans for operators of child care centers. Corporations could be funded to establish child care services.

The federal government initiated and funded the four C's concept—community coordinated child care—to coordinate the best use of federal, state, and private funds, and to avoid duplication. Revenue sharing was supposed to provide a great deal of money for child care through the state, on a matching basis. However, only about 1 percent of all of the funds going to the states was spent on child care.[34] In 1974, the Aid to Dependent Children portion of Title IVa of the Social Security Act was combined with the child welfare provisions of the original Social Security Act into Title XX. Title XX of the Social Security Act is the largest federal social service program providing funds to states to support social services, including child care. Title XX made child care services available only to parents (usually mothers) who entered work retraining programs.

GUIDELINES, REGULATIONS, STANDARDS, AND LICENSING

The money provided for support of child care services brought with it regulations setting standards. Various levels of government set standards for physical space and facilities, staff ratio, and training requirements in child care centers. According to Boocock, it is often difficult to draw a line between standards that meet real requirements of children's welfare and those that go beyond a society's ability and willingness to invest in its children.[35]

The problem of standards, regulations, licensing, and supervision has been an ongoing one. In the 1940s, the CWLA published its *Standards for Day Care Services*. The Day Care Alliance, a coalition of seventy organizations, grew out of the 1970 White House Conference on Children and Youth. It works closely with those in Congress who are interested in child care. It has had input into the development of federal child care requirements. The Federal Interagency Day Care Requirements were approved by the Department of Health, Education, and Welfare (DHEW), the Office of Economic Opportunity (OEO), and the Department of Labor, on September 23, 1968. This set of requirements was intended to coordinate and harmonize the points of view of myriad federal agencies. In 1969, an Office of Child Development (OCD) was created in DHEW. This was an attempt to end fragmentation of responsibilities at the federal level. However, this goal has not been completely accomplished to date.[36]

Gwen Morgan is well-known for her work in the field of child care licensing and regulation. She wrote that the federal government's decision against updating its *1972 Guide for Day Care Licensing* caused it to abrogate its leadership of the states. This led to state efforts to weaken standards, exempt church-run programs, reduce staff in center-based programs, and to deregulate family day care. Morgan said, "Children do not appear to be any safer in day care in the 80s than they have been in the past."[37]

In a discussion of federal guidelines for child care, Scarr[38] stated that until the mid-1980s, advocates of quality day care were frustrated in their attempts to establish standards for all federally subsidized care. In 1980, a prestigious group of child-development advisors and experts from several federal agencies agreed on a set of standards, which have yet to be adopted by Congress. The proposed requirements included a planned daily program of developmentally appropriate activities, caregivers with specialized training, adequate and nutritious meals, information to parents about health care services, opportunities for parents to observe the operations of the care setting, parent participation in policy-making, and parent access to evaluations of the setting. The Federal Interagency group worked diligently to balance the interests of caregivers and those of the children in their care. Although the standards were modest, opponents of day care effectively blocked their adoption, so there are no set standards for care that the government buys from private providers. Some substandard centers and homes are receiving tax money to support the care of children whose parents cannot afford the full cost of child care themselves.[39]

Perhaps this was the incentive for the foundation-funded *Quality 2000* initiative. The report of the three-year project, launched in 1992, includes a look at alternative approaches to regulation from other fields. In the concluding section of the book Kagan and Cohen present recommendations for providing a quality program, parent engagement, individual licensing and professional development, facility licensing and program accreditation, funding and financing, and governance. A synopsis of the report published in September 1997 adds results for children and clear expectations to the recommendations of the Quality 2000 Initiative.[40]

FEDERAL ACTIONS

The 1970s was a time of progress and challenges in the child care field. The Mondale-Brademas Comprehensive Child Development Act, which provided for the establishment of quality day care at no cost to welfare families and on a fee-paying basis for working and middle-class families, was passed by Congress in December 1971. It was vetoed by President Richard Nixon, who said that it would "commit 'the vast moral authority of the national government to the side of communal approaches to child rearing over and against the family-centered approach.'" As Greenman and Fuqua point out, "Nixon's willingness to support, even require, day care centers for low-income women and challenge day care for other families illustrated a pervasive inconsistency in American social attitudes." The Nixon veto had a devastating effect because his Family Assistance Plan had encouraged expanded child care facilities for children of welfare mothers who choose to work, and allowed the centers to devote themselves to the development of children's minds and bodies. Nixon's successor, Gerald Ford, vetoed a similar bill and "abruptly shattered the confident vision of the steady expansion of publicly supported comprehensive childcare."[41]

The administration of President Ronald Reagan, in the early 1980s, reduced government's role in the early childhood arena. It ignored the carefully crafted Federal Interagency Day Care Requirements, cut Title XX funding and standards, cut compensatory education funding for disadvantaged children, and closed a number of innovative child care programs. Those programs that were not eliminated entirely were collapsed into block grants. The Reagan administration wanted to increase the authority of the states and to stimulate the business community to respond to social problems. It succeeded in reducing the funding for child care programs for the poorest segment of the child population. Ironically, in the fall of 1993, former President Ford became the honorary chairman of the newly formed Childcare Action Campaign. He urged fathers to become more involved in the care of their children and the arrangements made for them. Ford stated, "I have come to realize, today, universal access to quality childcare is imperative in all our communities—urban and suburban, rural and industrial, middle-class and poor. We must all become part of the effort to provide this care. And this effort must start today."[42]

In spite of the lack of government and business support, child care continued to grow. The view of Evans and her colleagues was that quality day care is not a necessary evil; it can be a positive supplement to family relationships. The literature of the 1980s cites the need and growth of day care as a service to "normal families" with working parents. Scarr highlights the continuing "national disgrace" of a lack of developmentally appropriate care for many of our nation's young children. Care is often custodial, because the caregivers are overworked; however, the children are not institutionalized, as they were in past decades.[43]

Travis and Perreault saw changes in family structure and recognition of alternate forms of care as trends of the 1980s. They looked toward a broadening of philosophy, and a definition of day care that integrates the many previous roles it has played, and accommodates the roles of the future. They stated that consumer education for parents; the development of information and referral services; and expanded, clarified administrative policies would assist in the understanding of day care programs. The NAEYC publication *Developmentally Appropriate Practice in Early Childhood Programs Serving Children from Birth through Age 8* put into writing a set of guidelines developed by the professional community for use in the Academy accreditation of child care programs. As the field of early childhood education began to move toward widely accepted standards, a Federal Child Care Bill came before the Congress. In 1990, President George Bush signed Public Law 101-508, the Federal Child Care Bill. The bill provided $2.5 billion for new federal child care, block grant funds, provisions to protect children in child care, as well as monies and tax relief to help low-income working families purchase child care.[44]

FOR-PROFIT CHILD CARE

Three types of for-profit child care centers have grown up over the years. The first is an individually owned business, with either an owner-director or a small, possibly family, administrative staff. The second type of proprietorship is a franchise operation. The franchise owner purchases a name, an operations guide, expertise, and materials for an initial investment and a continuing fee of approximately 6 percent of gross sales to the parent company. Some companies maintain training and supervision programs. Many of the initial franchises of the 1960s, 1970s, and 1980s are no longer in existence. However, a few of the original franchise operations have grown very large in the 1990s. Unfortunately, some franchise owners decided to "cut corners" and provide less than adequate supplies, equipment, facilities, and staff at their centers. This practice prompted Featherstone's 1970 article "The Day Care Problem: Kentucky Fried Children." Some people "hoped that business management would find a magic formula so that children could be well taken care of," *and* the company would make a profit. Minimal qualifications for personnel, inadequate expenditures on salaries and services, lack of staff training and preparation, a large staff turnover, and the focus on standardization and profit have been problematic in the day care franchise industry. The third category of for-profit centers are the chain-operated centers. A major difference between the franchise and chain organizations is that chains are centralized operations. The chain owns and operates every center. It establishes the site, hires the director, creates policy, supervises curriculum, and oversees each site. Several of the operations that began as franchises have now become chains.[45]

Specialized child care options from the past are being recycled. They include sick-child care, twenty-four-hour care, and drop-off care. The care of sick children was a service provided by the settlement houses in the early 1900s. During World War II, some day care centers separated children who were ill from those who were well, so that their mothers could continue in their war work. In the 1990s, some hospitals and specialized centers provide care for mildly ill or recuperating children who are not allowed to attend their usual program. Some new buildings have specialized wings with separate air filtration systems to house sick children and the medical services they require. Some businesses offer emergency care options to their employees. They contract with a health-care agency that sends a caretaker into the home when the child is ill.

Round-the-clock child care is being rediscovered. As more and more women enter the work force and must attend to business in the evenings and on weekends, or are sent on out-of-town trips, this service becomes essential. The military often accommodates families in this way. Sometimes these programs are housed in group care facilities; however, the majority utilize family child care homes. "Drop-off care" is sometimes available to children who have been preregistered but are not regular attendees of a program. It is provided on an emergency basis in times of felt need or on a weekly basis, at the discretion of the parent.

TRAINING OF PERSONNEL

Many people work in licensed child care centers, and some in accredited centers. They may have direct or indirect responsibility for the children in the program. The director is in the leadership role. Only a few states require that this person be a trained early childhood or child development professional. Teachers and caregivers also find a confusing variety of standards. Most group teachers and head teachers are licensed[46] or have formal credentials. Some paraprofessionals have Child Development Associate (CDA) or other credentials.

Historical View of the Evolution from Custodial Care to Whole Child Advocacy

The "caretaker" of young children may be a relative, friend, professional nurse, teacher, other child care specialist, or a person without special training.

These people will take care of the child for pay. The setting may be in or outside the child's home, and may range from a home setting to a large child care center. Boocock says that child care is an activity that requires full-time availability but not full-time attention and action (except for emergency situations), that child care is routine in nature, and that a limited amount of time is spent in developmental or creative activities.[47] Although child care work is routine, according to this author, and can be combined with some other kinds of activities, there is a definite limit on the number of young children an adult can look after. With this interpretation of the child care provider's role, it is easy to see how inadequate care can be given. The current thinking, expressed in the revised edition of *Developmentally Appropriate Practice in Early Childhood Programs* (1997), takes an opposing point of view. The extensive list of caregiver activities belies the statements made earlier.[48]

Over the past century, many have decried the lack of qualified personnel and opportunities for appropriate professional development. As noted in previous chapters, the training of licensed and certified early education professionals is extensive, and has been such since the beginning of the twentieth century. However, the lack of qualified personnel has always presented an acute problem. Therefore, training courses were devised.[49]

The 1940s

Almy and Snyder, writing in the *Forty-Sixth NSSE Yearbook*, showcased the demand for teachers of children under the age of six years. They envisioned an immediate need for many teachers prepared to work with nursery school children. They decried the inadequate teacher-training facilities for teachers of the nursery-school years. They stated that this training is done largely in a few private teacher-training schools and in home economics departments at state colleges and universities. According to Almy and Snyder, few state teachers' colleges have directed their attention to the specific preparation of teachers for these years.[50]

The 1970s

Spodek suggests that a "child rearer might be a role more closely approximating that of a day care worker." He states that a new kind of training would be required to prepare a person for such a role. The skills and competencies needed for such a position "might be derived from early childhood education, pediatric nursing, family-life education, and 'mothering.'" One creative training possibility would make greater use of the media. Another, borrowed from the English nursery nurses training colleges, included work on the college campus, and practical training in nursery classes or residential homes on an alternating weeks basis. The students are paid for the time they are employed in practical work. A third model is an intern teaching program, as exemplified by the state of North Dakota. A fourth training model, which is in the implementation stage today, is colleges moving into the schools. The establishment of community-based teacher education centers in schools leads to cooperation in the development of jointly sponsored programs.[51]

The 1990s

There are several nonbaccalaureate teacher education possibilities available to early childhood practitioners. In addition to the already mentioned CDA credential, they include associate degree and vocational programs, and inservice professional development. In 1997, the NAEYC reissued the guidelines for associate degree-granting institutions. The intent is to establish a standard for associate degrees in early childhood education, as preparation for entry into professional work with young children. The guidelines call for both professional studies and a general education curriculum. The professional studies curriculum includes courses and field experiences that provide theoretical knowledge and practical skills. Training at a vocational-technical school is intended to prepare students to assume the role of child care assistant in early childhood settings, under the supervision of more experienced or educated staff members. All states have vocational training programs, but available funds are seriously limited. Since the high school diploma is the highest level of education held by many individuals working in the early childhood field, vocational child care training programs may be the best method of providing for formal exposure to child development principles. Courses, conferences, and meetings provide for ongoing professional development. Family child care providers are trained by resource and referral networks or utilize videos, workshops, and meetings. According to Jorde Bloom, a debate exists about what combination of formal education, specialized training, and work experience constitutes optimum qualifications for teaching.[52]

The *1977 National Day Care Study* found that caregivers with specialized education or training relevant to young children delivered better care with superior developmental effects for children. Conversely, Whitebook and her associates found that teachers' formal education (in contrast to specialized education) was the strongest predictor of appropriate caregiving. However, both studies agreed that teacher experience is not a reliable predictor of teacher behavior. Although no federal regulations govern the qualifications of child care staff, the 1980 version of the Federal Interagency Day Care Requirements is still used by many child advocates as a guideline for minimum staff qualifications. Each state determines the qualifications for child care workers that are put forth in its own regulations. Some states spell out different qualifications for several levels of staff, assuming different goals. Some of the states require ongoing training for caregivers; however, these requirements vary considerably. As the career ladders envisioned by early childhood professional organizations are developed, implemented, and accepted, a more uniform set of guidelines for child care workers will arise. The trend of the 1990s seems to be increases in the education and training requirements for child care workers. As Jorde Bloom points out, "high standards for staff qualifications are important both to protect against poor practices and to convey a strong message to the public about the importance of the teaching and administrative roles in childcare."[53]

A Look to the Future

The themes of the 1990s, the year 2000, and beyond are: increased professional standards, quality issues, and expanded professional development. As can be gathered from the foregoing discussion, these are not new themes in day nursery, day care, and child care work. The standards of state licensing requirements, and professional organizations in early childhood education and the subject fields, will impact upon child care programs in the next decade. Quality issues are being addressed by the Quality 2000 Initiative. Professional development and staff training issues are an ongoing concern in the field. The guidelines for preparation in two-year, four-year, and graduate institutions of higher education have made an impact on the field.[54] The child care staff member of the year 2000 will be able to draw on a deep tradition and a creative knowledge base to assist him or her in working with the whole child.

NOTES

1. Cornelia Goldsmith, *Better Day Care for the Young Child through a Merged Governmental and Nongovernmental Effort: The Story of Day Care in New York City as the Responsibility of a Department of Health 1943–1963 and Nearly a Decade Later—1972* (Washington, DC: National Association for the Education of Young Children, 1972), 107.

2. Michael Langenbach and Teanna West Neskora, *Day Care Curriculum Considerations* (Columbus, OH: Charles E. Merrill Pub. Co., 1977), 17, 18, 7; NSSE, *The Twenty-Eighth Yearbook of the National Society for the Study of Education: Preschool and Parental Education,* Guy Montrose Whipple, ed. (Bloomington, IL: Public School Publishing Company, 1929), 87; and Goldsmith, *Better Day Care,* 12.

3. James T. Greenman and Robert Fuqua, *Making Day Care Better: Training, Evaluation, and the Process of Change* (New York: Teachers College Press, 1984), ix and Ricardo C. Ainslie, ed., *The Child & the Day Care Setting: Qualitative Variations & Development* (New York: Praeger Publishers, 1984), vi.

4. K. Allison Clarke-Stewart and Christian P. Gruber, "Day Care Forms & Features," in *The Child & the Day Care Setting: Qualitative Variations & Development,* ed. Ricardo C. Ainslie (New York: Praeger Publishers, 1984), 36.

5. Sharon L. Kagan, Nancy E. Cohen, and Michelle J. Newman, "Introduction," in *Reinventing Early Care in Education: A Vision for a Quality System,* ed. Sharon L. Kagan and Nancy E. Cohen (San Francisco, CA: Jossey-Bass Pubs., 1996), 4.

6. Geraldine Youcha, *Minding the Children: Childcare in America from Colonial Times to the Present* (New York: Scribner, 1995), 341.

7. Alice Sterling Honig, "Historical Overview of Child Care," in *Yearbook in ECE, Vol. 3, Issues in Child Care,* ed. B. Spodeko and O. Saracho (New York: Teachers College Press, 1992), 14; Goldsmith, *Better Day Care,* 80; and Cornelia Goldsmith, "The New York City Daycare Unit," in James L. Hymes, Jr., *Early Childhood Education Living History Interviews: Book 2: Care of the Children of Working Mothers* (Carmel, CA: Hacienda Press, 1978), 2:67–68.

8. Some sources have the opening date of the New York City day nursery as 1854, for example, Ilse Forest, *Preschool Education: A Historical and Critical Study* (New York: MacMillan Company, 1927), 312; and Sadie Ginsburg "The Childcare Center Chronicle,"

in James L. Hymes, Jr., *Early Childhood Education Living History Interviews: Book 2: Care of the Childen of Working Mothers* (Carmel, CA: Hacienda Press, 1978), 2:7.

9. NSSE, *The Twenty-Eighth Yearbook of the National Society for the Study of Education: Preschool and Parental Education,* 91.

10. David Day, *Early Childhood Education: A Human Ecological Approach* (Glenview, IL: Scott Foresman and Company, 1983), 40. See also: E. Belle Evans, Beth Shub, and Marlene Weinstein, *Day Care: How to Plan, Develop, & Operate a Day Care Center* (Boston: Beacon Press, 1971), xii; and Nancy E. Travis and Joe Perreault, "Day Care as a Resource to Families," in *Current Topics in Early Childhood Education,* vol. III, ed. Lilian G. Katz (Norwood, NJ: Ablex Pub. Co., 1980), 128–129.

11. Marvin Lazerson, "The Historical Antecedents of Early Childhood Education," in *Early Childhood Education: The Seventy-First Yearbook of the National Society for the Study of Education, Part II,* ed. Ira J. Gordon (Chicago: University of Chicago Press, 1972), 38; NSSE, *The Twenty-Eighth Yearbook of the National Society for the Study of Education: Preschool and Parental Education,* 87–95; Youcha, *Minding the Children,* 144–145; Ginsburg, "The Childcare Center Chronicle," 10; and Jane Langlois, *Serving Children Then and Now: An Oral History of Early Childhood Education and Day Care in Metropolitan Detroit* (Detroit, MI: Wayne State University, 1989), 7–8

12. Day, *Early Childhood Education,* 36–37; Forest, *Preschool Education,* 326; Honig, "Historical Overview of Child Care," 13; and Ruth Highberger and Carol Schramm, *Child Development for Day Care Workers* (Boston: Houghton Mifflin, 1976), 208–209.

13. Day, *Early Childhood Education,* 37; Forest, *Preschool Education,* 313–315; and Ginsburg, "The Childcare Center Chronicle," 12.

14. Day, *Early Childhood Education,* 39; and Ginsburg, "The Childcare Center Chronicle," 8.

15. Langenbach and Neskora, *Day Care Curriculum Considerations,* 12.

16. Forest, *Preschool Education,* 312, 313; NSSE, *The Twenty-Eighth Yearbook of the National Society for the Study of Education: Preschool and Parental Education,* 93, 96, 98, 101; and Ginsburg, "The Childcare Center Chronicle," 10–11.

17. Forest, *Preschool Education,* 327, 334; Ginsburg, "The Childcare Center Chronicle," 12; and Clarke-Stewart and Gruber, "Day Care Forms & Features," 45.

18. Forest, *Preschool Education,* 323; and, NSSE, *The Twenty-Eighth Yearbook of the National Society for the Study of Education: Preschool and Parental Education,* 99.

19. NSSE, *The Twenty-Eighth Yearbook of the National Society for the Study of Education: Preschool and Parental Education,* 88.

20. Ibid., 102–103.

21. Sarane Spence Boocock, "A Crosscultural Analysis of the Child Care System," in *Current Topics in Early Childhood Education,* vol. 1, ed. Lilian G. Katz (Norwood, NJ: Ablex Pub. Co., 1977), 95, 97; Ellen Galinsky, "The Private Sector as a Partner in Early Care and Education," in *The Care and Education of America's Young Children: Obstacles & Opportunities: Ninetieth Yearbook of the NSSE, Part I,* ed. Sharon Lynn Kagan (Chicago: University of Chicago Press, 1991), 131–132; 134–136; Ginsburg, "The Childcare Center Chronicle," 14; Day, *Early Childhood Education: A Human Ecological Approach,* 48–49; and Donald J. Cohen, *Day Care 3: Serving Preschool Children* (Washington, DC: USDHEW/OHD/OCD, 1976), 131–134.

22. NSSE, *The Twenty-Eighth Yearbook of the National Society for the Study of Education: Preschool and Parental Education,* 90.

23. Excerpts on early childhood education from supreme court of New Jersey decision *Abbott vs. Burke,* May 21, 1998. TMs, 20–29, chart (undated); Association for Children of New Jersey, Children First, School Funding to Significantly Expand Early Childhood Education; Children First, A Policy and Budget Brief on Children, June 1998; Presentation, Leo Klagholz, Commissioner of Education, Abbott District Reform and Slate, 4th Grade Test. Assembly Education Committee, 6/22/98, 2.

24. Annice M. Alt, "Schooling for Four-Year-Olds," *Child Care Center* (September 1987): 54–55; and NSSE, *The Forty-Sixth Yearbook of the National Society for the Study of Education, Part II, Early Childhood Education,* ed. Nelson B. Henry (Chicago, IL: University of Chicago Press, 1947), 50.

25. Bess Goodykoontz, Mary Dabney Davis, and Hazel F. Gabbard, "Recent History and Present Status of Education for Young Children," in *The Forty-Sixth Yearbook of the National Society for the Study of Education, Part II, Early Childhood Education*, ed. Nelson B. Henry (Chicago, IL: University of Chicago Press, 1947), 54–55.

26. Boocock, "A Crosscultural Analysis of the Child Care System," 72, 73.

27. Ginsburg, "The Childcare Center Chronicle," 24; Honig, "Historical Overview of Child Care," 20; and Maty D. Keyserling, "Windows on Day Care: A Report Based on Findings of the National Council of Jewish Women on Day Care Needs and Services in Their Community (New York: National Council of Jewish Women, 1972).

28. For a description of day care centers in Detroit housing projects, schools, and churches that met the need, taken from primary sources, see: Langlois, *Serving Children Then and Now.*

29. Goldsmith, *Better Day Care*, 101.

30. Goldsmith, *Better Day Care*, 101–103; and Ginsburg, "The Childcare Center Chronicle," 21. See Forest, *Preschool Education: A Historical and Critical Study*, 319, for a description of earlier day nursery associations.

31. Day, *Early Childhood Education: A Human Ecological Approach*, 41; Langenbach and Neskora, *Day Care Curriculum Considerations*, 10; Boocock, "A Crosscultural Analysis of the Child Care System," 94.

32. In the 1960s, the women's liberation movement, the aftermath of the dormant women's suffrage movement, was reawakened. At this time, the first two women were elected to Congress from New York City—Shirley Chisholm and Bella Abzug, who were both strong advocates of public day care. Goldsmith, *Better Day Care*, 110.

33. In the late 1990s, *Child Care Access and Choice: A Survey of Work First New Jersey Participants, Center for Employment Policy and Workforce Development*, written by Edward J. Bloustein, School for Planning and Public Policy, Rutgers, the State University, was prepared for the Department of Education of the State of New Jersey, February 23, 1998, released 5/7/98. The study used a random telephone survey of one thousand welfare-to-work recipients with children aged five or younger. It found: (1) A variety of child care options were available, (2) 75 percent were satisfied with available options, (3) 90 percent of existing child care was good to excellent, (4) 65 percent chose care with a home (versus center based) setting, (5) 50 percent reported that it was difficult to find quality care, and care was not available during hours that it was needed. *Trenton Times*, 5/10/98, p. 15, Survey, "Welfare Moms Finding Child Care." Thomas Ginsberg, *Philadelphia Inquirer Online*, 5/8/98, pp. 12–13, "Parents Leaving New Jersey Welfare Promised Child Care Options." Dave Neese, *Trentonian*, 5/8/98, p. 13, "Welfare Recipients Happy with Child Care." *Asbury Park Press*, 5/8/98, p. 10, "Study Says Welfare Mothers Finding Child Care." *Bergen County Record*, 5/8/98, p. 8, "Workfare Moms Worry; Is My Child Learning?"

34. Ginsburg, "The Childcare Center Chronicle," 18–19.

35. Barbara Finkelstein, "Casting Networks of Good Influence: The Reconstruction of Childhood in the United States, 1790–1870," in *American Childhood*, ed. Joseph M. Hawes and N. Ray Hiner (Westport, CT: Greenwood Press, 1985), 264–265; Boocock, "A Crosscultural Analysis of the Child Care System," 94–95.

36. Ginsburg, "The Childcare Center Chronicle," 19; and Goldsmith, *Better Day Care*, 114–115.

37. Gwen Morgan, "Change through Regulation," in *Making Day Care Better: Training, Evaluation, and the Process of Change*, ed. James T. Greenman and Robert W. Fuqua (New York: Teachers College Press, 1984), 163.

38. Sandra Scarr is the current president of Kinder Care Incorporated.

39. Sandra Scarr, *Mother Care/Other Care* (New York: Basic Books, Inc. Pubs., 1984), 186, 187.

40. Katherine L. Scurria, "Regulation: Alternative Approaches from Other Fields," in *Reinventing Early Care in Education: A Vision for a Quality System*, ed. Sharon L. Kagan and Nancy E. Cohen, "A Vision for a Quality Care and Education System" in *Reinventing Early Care in Education: A Vision for a Quality System*, ed. Sharon L. Kagan and Nancy E. Cohen (San Francisco CA: Jossey-Bass Pubs., 1996), 309–332; and Sharon L. Kagan and Michelle J. Neuman, "Highlights of the Quality 2000 Initiative: Not by Chance," *Young Children* 52, no. 6 (September 1997): 54–61.

41 Day, *Early Childhood Education: A Human Ecological Approach,* 40; Honig, "Historical Overview of Child Care," 20; and James T. Greenman, "Perspectives on Quality Day Care," in *Making Day Care Better: Training, Evaluation, and the Process of Change,* ed. James T. Greenman and Robert W. Fuqua (New York: Teachers College Press, 1984), 6.

42. Honig, "Historical Overview of Child Care," 22; Galinsky, "The Private Sector as a Partner in Early Care and Education," 132; Gerald Ford, "Childcare Is for Everybody," *Parade Magazine* (October 23, 1983), 16; Scarr, *Mother Care/Other Care,* 257; and Greenman, "Perspectives on Quality Day Care," 7.

43. Evans, et al., *Day Care: How to Plan, Develop, & Operate a Day Care Center,* xii; and Scarr, *Mother Care/Other Care,* 208–209.

44. Travis and Perreault, "Day Care as a Resource to Families," 135; and Honig, "Historical Overview of Child Care," 20.

45. Harriet Cuffaro, "Group Day Care: Part II: For-Profit Day Care," in *Education before Five: A Handbook on Preschool Education,* ed. Betty D. Boegehold et al. (New York: Bank Street College of Educatiom 1977), 96; Joseph Featherstone, "The Day Care Problem: Kentucky Fried Children," *The New Republic* 163, nos. 10–11 (5 and 12 September 1970): 12–16; and Ginsburg, "The Childcare Center Chronicle," 15, 16.

46. *State licensure* refers to the requirements and processes of individual states for the awarding of a teaching credential. *Certification* identifies accomplished teachers who are awarded a credential by the National Board for Professional Teaching Standards (NBPTS) after demonstrating competence in meeting the board's rigorous standards. Jan McCarthy, Josué Cruz Jr., and Nancy Ratcliff, *Early Childhood Teacher Licensure Revisited,* paper presented at Building Professional Partnerships: NAEYC's National Institute for Early Childhood Professional Development 7th Annual Conference, Miami, Florida, 18 June 1998; and Jan McCarthy, Josué Cruz, Jr., and Nancy Ratcliff, *Two National Studies: State Curriculum Guidelines and State Early Childhood Teacher Licensure,* paper presented at the annual conference of the National Association for the Education of Young Children, Toronto, Ontario, Canada, 20 November 1998.

47. Boocock, "A Crosscultural Analysis of the Child Care System," 84.

48. National Association for the Education of Young Children, *Developmentally Appropriate Practice in Early Childhood Programs,* rev. ed., ed. Sue Bredekamp and Carol Copple (Washington, DC: Author, 1997).

49. Priscilla Pemberton, "Group Day Care: Part I: An Overview," in *Education before Five: A Handbook on Preschool Education,* ed. Betty D. Boegehold et al. (New York: Bank Street College of Education, 1977), 93; and Goldsmith, *Better Day Care,* 22.

50. Mllie C. Almy and Agnes Snyder, "The Staff and Its Preparation," in *The Forty-Sixth Yearbook of the NSSE, Part II, ECE,* ed. Nelson B. Henry (Chicago: University of Chicago Press), 231–232.

51. Bernard Spodek, "Staff Requirements in Early Childhood Education," in *Early Childhood Education: The Seventy-First Yearbook of the National Society for the Study of Education, Part II,* ed. Ira J. Gordon (Chicago: University of Chicago Press, 1972), 359, 361.

52. Douglas R. Powell and Loraine Dunn, "Non-Baccalaureate Teacher Education in Early Childhood Education," in *Yearbook in Early Childhood Education, Vol. I: Early, Childhood Teacher Preparation,* ed. Bernard Spodek and Olivia N. Saracho (New York: Teachers College Press, 1990), 56–57; and Paula Jorde Bloom, "Issues in Childcare Staffing," in *Yearbook in Early Childhood Education, Vol. III: Issues in Childcare,* ed. Bernard Spodek and Olivia N. Saracho (New York: Teachers College Press, 1992), 144.

53. Jorde Bloom, "Issues in Childcare Staffing," 159.

54. National Association for the Education of Young Children, *NAEYC, DEC/CEC, NBPTS Guidelines for Preparation of Early Childhood Professionals* (Washington, DC: National Association for the Education of Young Children, 1996).

CHAPTER 12

Federal Government Involvement (1900–1950)

> For every child, spiritual and moral training to help
> him to stand firm under the pressure of life.
> —The Children's Charter[1]

The progressive era was a big humanitarian effort to apply the promise of American life—the ideal of government by, of, and for the people—to the new urban-industrial civilization that came into being during the last part of the nineteenth century. The progressive era gave rise to all sorts of federal government activity. One result of this activity was the creation of the United States Children's Bureau by an act of Congress early in 1912 and signed into law by President William Howard Taft in April of that year. The establishment of the Children's Bureau was the first recognition that the national government had a responsibility to promote the welfare of all the children of the nation.[2]

The progressive ideas about children in the twentieth century began to create an interest to protect children. This concern was especially true for children of poor families. The decennial White House Conferences on children and youth began as the nation considered that the welfare of dependent children was critical enough or was in sufficient jeopardy to require national attention. Behind these concerns was the newly articulated value that children are individuals and have rights and that parents have duties toward their children. The child was seen from the scientific point of view. There was also the assumption by the government that it has a responsibility for the protection of all children but especially for those at risk. Child-development research and the White House Conferences on children and youth are a twentieth-century phenomena.

WHITE HOUSE CONFERENCES ON CHILDREN AND YOUTH (1909–1970)

The federal government, early in the twentieth century, began the White House Conferences on Children and Youth, which called attention to the problems encountered by children and their families. These conferences called the public's attention to the problems and helped shape public policy to ameliorate them.

The first White House Conference on Children and Youth in 1909, under President Theodore Roosevelt, focused on the problems of dependent children. It declared that poverty alone should not be grounds for removing children from their families. The family was recognized, and the home life of a family was seen as the highest product of civilization. The concern for the dependent child was to help the child within the family and the home-life environment. President Theodore Roosevelt, in establishing the theme of the conference, made clear that home life could be in a foster home as well as in a child's own home. The critical factor was to make sure that home life was financially feasible. While the concept of child development was not alluded to—it was still too early to articulate such a concept—the intuition that home life was important for children prevailed. The concept of child care was articulated at the conference, and a major recommendation was the creation of an unofficial national organization for the promotion of child care. The Child Welfare League, organized in 1915, became that organization.[3]

One of the results of this conference was the establishment of the U.S. Children's Bureau in 1912 by an act of Congress signed by President Taft. The federal government for the first time recognized its responsibility to protect and promote the health and welfare of the children of the entire nation. The Children's Bureau would have broad powers. It would be an advocate for all children; it would publicize facts about the interrelated economic, social, health, and legal conditions affecting the lives of children and their families; it would promote legislation; it would offer publications on child rearing and other related issues.[4] Its mission would be to investigate and report all matters pertaining to the welfare of children and child life among all classes of the people, including the questions of infant mortality, the birthrate, orphanages, juvenile courts, desertion, dangerous occupations, accidents and diseases of children, employment, and legislation affecting children in the states and territories. Congress prohibited Children's Bureau agents to enter a home without permission because of concern about the impact of the new law on families.[5]

The second White House Conference on Children and Youth was in 1919. President Woodrow Wilson designated the year 1919 as "Children's Year." It focused on child welfare standards. Home life was again stressed as important to the welfare of children, and along with it, the need to supply an adequate income to make home life possible. Minimum standards for the welfare of children resulted from this conference. Child development was still not addressed; rather, protection of children in need of special care, entering employment, and in health care were addressed. There was also a focus on the need to protect children from the effects of war. President Wilson asked for the establishment of irreducible minimum standards for the health, education, and welfare of the American child, and immediately extended the range of interest of child welfare beyond the confines of dependency and the dependent child. Specifically minimum standards were set for home care, the employment of children, and the protection of the health of mothers and children.[6]

The third White House Conference on Children and Youth, in 1930, under President Herbert Hoover, focused on child health and protection. One of the contributions to the conference was the collection of facts on physical growth and *development* of children. One of the outcomes was the adoption of the U.S. *Children's Charter.* The Charter outlined the child's right to citizenship regardless of race, color, location, or situation. It contains nineteen articles (see Appendix 3). Article number eight provides for safe schools where children could learn. Article number ten included nursery schools and kindergartens for the young children to supplement home care, and a developmental education for every child. Article number thirteen provides for special education for handicapped children. Unfortunately, the Charter is not binding, either for the states or for the federal government, and sixty plus years later, we are still discussing the same issues that have not been resolved.[7]

President Hoover reiterated the government's responsibility for all of the children of the United States. He sought consideration for the special needs of handicapped children, but gave the highest priority to the protection and stimulation of the normal child. He pointed out, too, that the problems of children—handicapped or normal—were not always the problems of children alone; our society had produced a life of unprecedented complexity for all. In this context, he asked the conferees to explore opportunities for a creative life for all children. This was the first White House Conference on Children and Youth that incorporated facts about child development. It was also the first such conference that talked about the rights of *all* children.[8]

The fourth White House Conference on Children and Youth, in 1939, focused on "Children in a Democracy." The United States was coming out of the Depression. There were concerns for all phases of child life and for the development of the child over time, including, now, the years of youth. The conference called attention to the inequalities in opportunities available to children and youth in rural areas, among the unemployed, and in low-income, migrant, and minority groups. President Franklin D. Roosevelt gave more explicit encouragement than President Hoover to studying the problems of children as part of the problems of society. The primary objective of the conference was to consider the relationship between a successful democracy and the children who form an integral part of that democracy. This conference not only incorporated ideas of child and youth development but also recognized that inequalities in opportunity affected development.[9]

The fifth or mid-century White House Conference on Children and Youth, in 1950, was the largest effort on behalf of children in the history of the nation. The participants focused attention on emotional growth and development of children and on the development of a healthy personality. The concept of development for children and youth was now translated into recommended actions for the nation. The effects of prejudice and discrimination on personality development were discussed, and recommendations to eliminate such prejudice and discrimination were offered. President Harry S. Truman, recognizing that the conference included concerns of youth, pointed out the immediate and eventual obligations of children and youth to the nation. He linked the concern for the development of children and youth to the future well-being not only of the children and youth, but of the nation. This conference also studied the effect of mobilization and war on children and youth.[10]

The sixth conference, in 1960, was the Golden Anniversary White House Conference on Children and Youth. The theme of the conference was the promotion of opportunities for children and youth to realize their full potential for a creative life in freedom and dignity. The reports provided information on the benefits of focusing on child and youth development. President Dwight Eisenhower recognized the development of the whole child and the rights of children and youth to have special and appropriate programs to meet their physical, recreational, educational, psychological, and occupational needs. He saw the relationships between those concerns and programs and the development of spiritually and intellectually aware adults.[11]

The seventh White House Conference on Children and Youth was held in two sessions. The White House Conference on Children was held in December 1970 and addressed the age group from birth to thirteen; the White House Conference on Youth was held in April 1971 and addressed the age group 14–24. President Richard Nixon stressed the importance of children and youth developing a new sense of patriotism. The conference endorsed developmental child care for children and recommended that the federal government fund comprehensive, family-centered child care programs. This subject was identified as the number one concern of those attending the Conference on Children. The Conference on Youth stressed the right of the individual to "do his/her own thing, so long as it does not interfere with the rights of others." Both sessions emphasized the need for health insurance, experimental schools, and solutions for the pressing social needs of children and youth as well as the need for child care for the twelve million children of working mothers. (To date not all of these goals have been met.)

The concept of child development was clearly recognized in 1976 but was seen as expensive to translate into public programs. Also, research findings on the benefits of public programs have not been clear enough to justify, according to some, the expenditure. Research on child development has its own history and also reflects issues and values of different times and different researchers.[12]

For the 1980 White House Conference on Families, President Ronald Reagan replaced the national conference with state conferences.

As far as it can be determined, there was no 1990 White House Conference on Children and Youth. The conferences thus far have been unable to fulfill their goal of setting up an agenda for the coming decade. Some of the difficulty stemmed from the various advocacy groups who were unwilling to give up their own special concerns and press for a common cause for children.[13]

In October 1997, President and Mrs. Clinton hosted a White House Conference on Child Care. They brought together parents, caregivers, business leaders, and child care experts.[14]

THE EMERGENCY NURSERY SCHOOLS (1933–1943)

During the twentieth century, the United States federal government has been involved in at least three national programs of early childhood education: the

Emergency Nursery Schools (1933–1943), the Lanham Act Child Care Centers (1943–1946); and the Head Start Programs (1964 to present).

Following the 1929 stock market crash, there was a tremendous increase in unemployment in America. Public schools shortened school days and reduced teachers' salaries. The Depression that followed found the United States government unprepared to meet the major relief problem. On December 1, 1930, the unemployed numbered 6,956,000, and by the spring of 1931, had reached about 8,000,000 with 30,000,000 dependents. This rise in unemployment strained the states' relief programs and they asked the federal government to step in and help.[15]

The government responded with a series of measures. One of them was the enactment of the Federal Emergency Relief Act of 1933, which created the Federal Emergency Relief Administration (FERA). This was the first act that provided for federal relief to the unemployed through the use of federal funds. The sum of $500 million was allocated to be spent cooperatively with the states for the relief of this massive unemployment caused by the Depression. The federal government provided the funds but did not administer them locally. The FERA program was designed as a cooperative federal, state, and local effort. The funding for local programs was disbursed through a FERA state agency whose administrators and state advisory board were appointed by state governors, by federal mandate. The states supervised the work of the local relief programs, while the federal government supervised the states minimally. All applications for federal funds required approval of the state administrator, the state advisory board, and the governor before they were submitted to Washington. The relief program had two categories: funds for work wages and funds for food, shelter, groceries, household supplies, and payment of light, gas, fuel, and water bills.[16]

The federal government through the Federal Emergency Relief Administration established and maintained the emergency nursery schools, between 1933 and 1935. The Works Progress Administration (WPA) took over their operation until they were closed in 1943. This national public nursery school program was the first time that the federal government promoted group education/care for preschoolers. The program has had an influence in the expansion of nursery schools in the nation, in the setting of standards for operations, and in teacher training. The federal involvement in early education was temporary. It was a response primarily to the economic crisis and its concomitant social and political results. It established, however, a mechanism for the possible continuation of the emergency nursery schools once the crisis was over as nursery schools for *all* children.

Creation of the Emergency Nursery Schools

At the beginning of FERA, most employment was in construction: schools, streets, and recreational facilities were built. There was no federal consideration of including an employment program for teachers. By July 1933, there was increased concern in the United States Office of Education that schools throughout the country were closing for lack of funds to pay teacher salaries. The consequent unemployment of teachers was recognized as a potential problem, and the U.S. Commissioner of Education, after meeting with state superintendents of education, formulated a program to include teachers under FERA.[17]

When the Educational Division of FERA was authorized, there was no mention of including nursery schools in the program to be developed. The idea to include nursery schools occurred to a number of people at about the same time. Some people saw a connection between white-collar workers' need for employment and the unfavorable effects of the Depression on young children and suggested that some sort of program for children be set up. A few people interested in nursery schools saw this as a chance to bring the benefits of nursery schools to more children and to further the nursery school movement, which by that time was about fifteen years old.[18]

At first it was thought that the kindergartens might be included, since they were closing in many places. The Commissioner of Education, however, decided that neither kindergartens nor kindergarten children could be included, since kindergarten education was recognized as a responsibility of the public schools, and the nursery schools were for children below kindergarten age.[19]

In late September or early October 1933, Mary Dabney Davis, of the U.S. Office of Education, began preparations for the announcement of the authorization of the nursery school program and the policies that would govern them. The nursery school program was to be the sixth project of the Educational Division authorized by FERA (the other five were literacy, vocational education, workers' education, adult education, and vocational rehabilitation). The nursery school program would be administered by FERA's Educational Division and would conform to the educational policies set up by the U.S. Office of Education in conjunction with local superintendents of public schools.[20]

On October 23, 1933, Harry Hopkins, the FERA administrator, authorized the Emergency Nursery School program and notified state FERA administrators and the school superintendents of all school districts that

> the educational and health programs of nursery schools can aid as nothing else in combating the physical and mental handicaps being imposed upon on these children. . . . [T]he nursery school program includes the participation of parents. . . . [T]he rules and regulations of the Federal Emergency Relief Administration may be interpreted to provide relief wages for qualified and unemployed teachers and other workers on relief who are needed to organize and conduct nursery schools under the control of the public school systems. All plans for locating, organizing, and supervising the nursery schools shall be subject to the approval of the local superintendents of public schools and the local relief administrators.[21]

Following the general announcement, a memorandum was issued by FERA on "Policies to Govern the Organization and Conduct of Emergency Nursery Schools and the Employment of Needy Teachers and Other Workers:" This memorandum was to serve as a guide for the local public school authorities who would be submitting plans for emergency nursery schools to their state superintendents or commissioners of public instruction.

The memorandum described the general policies and procedures to be followed in planning and setting up emergency nursery schools. Nursery schools were to be housed in publicly owned or leased buildings, and they were to be under the control and supervision of the public school system.[22] This principle was adhered to throughout the FERA era and part of the time under WPA. The memorandum further stated that the nursery school program was to include the participation of parents: "Parents are both relieved from the anxieties resulting from the worry of inadequate home provisions for their young children and are included in an educational program on an adult level which will raise their morale and that of the entire family and community."[23]

Names of the Program

At the time of the authorization (1933), nursery schools funded by FERA were designated as the Emergency Nursery School Program (ENS). The choice of a name for the program was a matter of considerable discussion among the professionals, and the National Advisory Committee. There was strong feeling that the name should indicate that the program would be educational and not custodial in nature. Therefore, it was important to have "school" in the title. The creation of the ENS program was not to duplicate any existing public education program. It seemed important that the title should also indicate unmistakably the age group to be served and show that the program would not encroach upon the field of kindergarten education. "Nursery school" was currently used to designate the educational program for children below kindergarten age, as distinguished from the older day nursery program m the welfare field. "Emergency" was prefixed to the title to indicate that the program was of an emergency nature and it was not intended to be established as a permanent program. This was in response to expressed fears of school superintendents who believed that they would become responsible for the permanent downward extension of the public school system.[24]

In May 1935, President Franklin Roosevelt established the Works Progress Administration (WPA), which took over the work of the FERA. By creating the WPA, direct federal control of work relief became a national policy that continued through 1943. Under the WPA, the Emergency Nursery Schools program was officially renamed the Emergency Nursery Schools and Parent Education Program to reflect the combination of two separately operating programs. When the WPA took over the emergency nursery schools, they continued to be sponsored by the state departments of education, but sponsorship at the federal level ceased. In 1937, the word "Emergency" was dropped from the title.

In February 1942, the name was changed to the WPA Child Protection Program. The nursery school program was moved out of Educational Division. This was a critical move, for it took out of the nursery school the concept of education, creating long-range implications. Day nursery service and extended school service were added to the WPA Child Protection Program on July 1, 1942, and the program began to expand to meet the war needs. The nursery schools were to serve children two to four years of age: (1) from low-income groups, with no expenses for the families served; (2) of employed mothers, and of men and women of the armed forces and industrial workers.

The WPA Child Protection Program now included nursery schools, preschool play groups, related family-life education, day nursery service, and extended school service. The emphasis of the program changed from service for children from low-income families to service for children of working mothers in war-related industries.[25]

In December 1942, a Presidential Executive Order provided for the liquidation of the Work Progress Administration and all its programs. In January 1943, states were instructed that the WPA nursery schools should cease operation in April 1943.[26]

The National Advisory Committee and Its Role

The National Association for Nursery Education (NANE) was holding its biennial meeting in Toronto, Ontario, in October 1933 when the emergency nursery schools were authorized. Davis, the chairperson of the meeting, flew to Toronto with the signed authorization and presented it to the membership and a telegram from Hopkins asking NANE to sponsor the ENS program. Many of those present saw the ENS program as a threat to all the standards that had been developed for nursery schools in America during the previous fifteen years. They argued that the program would ruin the future of nursery schools.[27] After a long and heated discussion of both the dangers and the possibilities of the proposed project, a vote was taken. NANE accepted the challenge, decided to sponsor the program, and offered its cooperation and resources toward its success. The NANE membership also decided to ask two other national organizations interested in nursery school education to participate—the Association for Childhood Education (ACE) and the National Council of Parent Education (NCPE). Two representatives from each of the three organizations formed the National Advisory Committee on Emergency Nursery Schools.[28] For NANE were its secretary-treasurer Abigail Eliot and Lois Hayden Meek. For ACE were Edna Dean Baker and George D. Stoddard. For NCPE were Edna N. White and Ralph P. Bridgman. The committee also included Mary Dabney Davis, specialist in Nursery-Kindergarten-Primary Education, United States Office of Education, ex-officio, as president of the National Association for Nursery Education. Edna N. White was named and served as chairperson for the duration of the program.[29]

When the emergency nursery schools were first organized, the federal government had made no provisions for supervision. The Committee felt strongly that supervision was absolutely necessary in order to guarantee a program of a high-standard, professional quality. A grant for supervision was secured by the Committee from a private source, the General Education Board. Through these funds a qualified supervisor was available in each state office of education for the supervision of the emergency nursery schools in that state. Committee members also acted as regional supervisors.[30] A lot of personal time and talent were contributed by the individual Committee members to the success of this program.

Following the success of the state supervisors during the first year of operation, Hopkins authorized the employment of state supervisors as a regular part of the program for the second year.[31]

The National Advisory Committee on Emergency Nursery Schools did not meet at specific times. It met whenever necessary to give advice and to guide the program. The members served without any cost to the government. The Committee had its final meeting in Washington, D.C., on April 29 and 30, 1943. April 30 was the closing date for the nursery school program; the Committee had voted to dissolve itself as of that date. The services of the National Advisory Committee "having extended from the day of authorization of the program to the date of its close, a period of nine years, six months, and one week."[32]

National Advisory Committee Publications

The role of the National Advisory Committee on Emergency Nursery Schools was to consider and to recommend policies for the educational aspect of the emergency nursery schools. It also developed and published guides, bulletins, and related materials. Nursery education was a new adventure for most public school administrators. There were the inherent complexities in nursery education due to the specialized training of the teachers and the other personnel needed to provide for children and their families. A *Guide for Local Superintendents of Schools in Planning for Emergency Schools* (1933) and *Estimated Unit Costs for Emergency Nursery Schools* (1933) were among the first publications of the Committee. The Committee also developed five bulletins (1933–1936) dealing with all aspects of nursery education and its content.[33]

One of the most important bulletins is *Suggestions for Building Courses in Nursery Education.* It established a comprehensive teacher training process. The bulletin describes in some detail the sequence of courses necessary to train partially qualified teachers to become nursery school teachers. The first course included the history of nursery schools in the United States and the nursery school movement. This preservice training had supervised observation, practice teaching, and courses in child development and nursery school curriculum. This bulletin was sent through the state superintendent's office to the institutions that had nursery laboratory schools and prepared nursery school teachers, and now offered free training for partially qualified teachers.

The work produced in these bulletins is monumental. It articulated and exemplified nursery education, codified standards for teacher training and practice, and described and recommended appropriate daily activities for the nursery school. They gave us a blueprint. The Committee wrote also annual reports for the years 1933–1934 and 1934–1935.[34] All the materials produced by the Committee were available to the public through the U.S. Office of Education.

Purpose of the Program

The emergency nursery schools were designed to serve the following purposes: (1) to provide employment for needy and qualified teachers and other workers; and (2) to assist parents to recognize and meet the nutritional, physical, educational, and social needs of their preschool children and their families, who were suffering from economic and social difficulties.[35]

These purposes governed the emergency nursery schools until FERA was dissolved in May 1935. The WPA gradually took over the operation of the nursery schools until they were closed in 1943.

Child Eligibility

The emergency nursery schools (ENS) were to serve "children of needy and unemployed families." Children admitted to the emergency nursery schools were to be between the ages of two and the local legal age for school entrance. This left flexible the upper age, which varied from state to state. It was a nursery school program, and the authorization could not be interpreted as an opportunity to restore any educational activities for young children that had been eliminated due to the economic difficulties.[36]

Numbers of Units and Children Enrolled

During the first year, October 1933 to June 1934, there was a total of 2,979 emergency nursery schools established in 37 states, the District of Columbia, and the Virgin Islands, with 64,491 children enrolled. The numbers of nursery schools in the states ranged from one each in Mississippi and Wyoming, to 535 in Ohio. The range of children enrolled per state was from 28 in Wyoming to 10,050 in Ohio. The average enrollment per unit was 23 children.[37] Following is the distribution according to age of the enrolled children:

Under 3	4.9 percent
3, but less than 4	19.2 percent
4, but less than 5	38.2 percent
5, but less than 6	34.2 percent
6, or over	3.3 percent[38]

The largest numbers of enrolled children were from four to five and five to six years old.

During the second year, October 1934 to May 1935, there was a total of 1,913 emergency nursery schools in operation in 47 of the 48 states, the District of Columbia, and Puerto Rico, with a total of 72,404 children. Delaware had no program. Questionnaires were sent to all program units. Only 1,821 units responded. The returns showed that 148 units existed for Negro[39] children in 24 states. In states with a large Negro population, an effort was made to proportion the schools for white and Negro children according to the relative populations. One unit was reported to be for Indian children only. The number of nursery schools ranged from 1 in Utah to 346 in Massachusetts. The units reported their enrollments in terms of white, Negro, and other racial groups as follows: 61,297 (84.65%) white; 7,860 (10.85%) Negro; and 3,247 (4.5%) from other groups—Indian, Spanish American, Chinese, Japanese, and Mexican.[40]

Daily Length of the Program

In most states, the emergency nursery schools had full-day sessions for the maximum possible benefit of the children, as it was intended. There were, however, some instances where this rule could not be observed and the sessions were half-day. For example, in some locations the general relief funds from which food was bought for the emergency nursery schools made it impossible to get the necessary food for a full-day program. In other instances, cots for the children to nap were not available and the children went home after lunch.[41]

Types of Emergency Nursery Schools

Emergency nursery schools could be developed as units of preschool children integrated within elementary schools; as laboratories for courses in the care and education of preschool children in high schools, normal schools, and colleges; and as units in urban and rural areas of need, such as in mining camps and hospitals for convalescent children, on subsistence homesteads, in camps of migrant crop-pickers, and on Indian reservations.[42]

Persons Employed

It was assumed in setting up the emergency nursery schools that each unit would have a head teacher, assistant teachers as needed, a nurse, and a dietitian or cook for meal planning and cooking, as well as clerical workers and janitors. An estimated 7,448 persons were employed in the emergency nursery school program in the first year in 2,979 units.[43]

During the second year, the figures are based on the responses from 1,821 units, excluding South Dakota, the District of Columbia, and Puerto Rico.

There were 6,770 workers employed: 5,101 white, 582 Negro, and 1,093 had no identification. The total number of teachers and assistant teachers was 3,775—3,360 white, 324 Negro, and 91 had no identification.[44]

The eligibility of teachers and other workers needed for the emergency nursery schools was based on their qualifications for the work and on their need for employment. In order to avoid delays in establishing the nursery schools, the professional organizations worked through local committees to determine need.

Teacher Training

One of the major difficulties in organizing the emergency nursery schools was the lack of trained teachers in nursery education. Only a small percentage (6.5 percent) of the teachers had taught in nursery schools. The rest had teaching experience that ranged from kindergarten to high school.[45] An intensive training was needed to prepared the partially qualified teachers. The training took place while the physical plant was being prepared. At the end of the first year of operation, a survey was made to determine the scope of this training. Two questionnaires were sent to the 115 institutions—colleges, universities, and normal schools—providing the training. One was for the courses given during the academic year 1933–1934, and the other for the summer of 1934. Thirty-six institutions responded; 26 gave training during the winter, and 11 during the summer. Both white and "colored" teachers attended. In the winter session, 667 were white and 54 were "colored." In the summer session, their numbers were 691 and 54, respectively. The training was six to eight hours a day, and varied from two to eight weeks. About half of the institutions had given nursery school training prior to the emergency.[46]

The courses offered during the first year fell into the following categories: (1) administration and management; (2) child development; (3) principles of nursery school education; (4) nursery school procedures; (5) health care including nutrition; and (6) parent education. The training courses covered lectures, conferences, observation, practice teaching, individual interviews, assigned reading, and other activities.[47]

The training institutions made several suggestions for future training. Among them were: instructors to be allowed to reject from training those applicants whose personality or ability "seemed to unfit them for work with young children"; "Train students with superior backgrounds"; "Provide much in-service training."[48]

Teacher training continued during the second year (1934–1935), but now the emphasis was on more knowledge of children's characteristics, interests; appropriate ways of responding to children; understanding art, music, literature; and play materials for young children; and techniques for desirable guidance of the nursery school child. It also became evident to the Committee that the teachers needed training in a wider understanding of home and family conditions, and a broader knowledge of how to work with adults. Again the

responsibility fell on the colleges and universities who had facilities and personnel to give such training. They included state universities and state colleges, state normal schools, agricultural and mechanical arts colleges, and
private training schools, for a total of 93 institutions. Planning for the training course was a collaboration between the state supervisor of the ENS and
the staff of the institution giving the training. Often the supervisor gave the
course on "teaching techniques in the nursery school."[49] For states who could
not provide training for the teachers, FERA in cooperation with the U.S.
Office of Education, provided a series of consecutive four-week training institutes held at the National Child Research Center in Washington, from
November 1934 to April 1935.[50]

Prior to the opening of the nursery schools in the fall of 1934, there were
three training institutes for the state supervisors and other state officials of
education who wanted to attend held in Washington, D.C.; Ames, Iowa; and
Berkeley, California. Every effort was made by the Committee to help states
to maintain only those nursery schools that were accepted as "being good
nursery schools."[51]

John Anderson conducted a survey in the summer of 1934, in order to get
a picture of the children served in the emergency nursery schools, during the
first year of operation. On the basis of these findings, some of the states had to
close certain units of nursery schools that did not meet the established criteria.[52] In spite of the National Advisory Committee's efforts to provide the
children with quality programs and the precautions taken by the states, there
were some emergency nursery schools that did not come close to being good
nursery schools.

In most cases, the children benefited from balanced meals, rest, medical
care, and a chance to play in an environment conducive to normal development. They were stimulated mentally by new experiences and were helped
socially through training in good habits. Many parents who were not aware
of child care and training received direct instruction in health care, feeding,
and habit training.[53] The emergency nursery schools demonstrated the possibility of bringing to a large number of needy and underprivileged children and
their parents an institution that in the past had existed for a limited number of
a more privileged group. It can be said that the emergency nursery schools
were the predecessor of the Head Start program in the 1960s.

Parent Participation and Education

Parent education was one of the purposes for which the emergency nursery
schools were established, to assist parents in meeting the nutritional, physical,
and social needs of their children. Teachers made the initial contact between
the home and the nursery school by visiting the homes to tell parents about
the nursery school and to make arrangements for the enrollment of the child.
Teachers also visited when a child was ill, or to tell the parents about the
child's progress in school.

Parents who had no knowledge about child care and training received direct instruction in health care, feeding, and habit training. Reports and letters from parents indicate that they often adopted the methods of the nursery school at home. Parents in rural areas traveled miles to bring their children to school and to attend the parent groups. The parents gave generous support to the emergency nursery schools both in terms of time and services. Mothers washed clothes, sewed curtains and doll clothes, cooked meals, washed dishes, and scrubbed and cleaned the schoolrooms. Fathers made toys, painted furniture, built and repaired equipment, and improved school grounds.[54]

Parents were encouraged to visit the school. Mothers came more frequently than fathers. Frequently, when they brought their children in the morning, they would stay to watch their children in their activities, or they would come early in the afternoon. There were regularly scheduled meetings with individual parents to discuss the child's progress and learn from the parents about the child. The teachers often provided an outline for the parents to help them understand their observations of their child in the nursery school. The outlines varied from state to state.[55]

In many nursery schools, teachers or parent education workers led group meetings or study classes for parents. It was difficult, however, to find an appropriate time when both mothers and fathers could come. Parents' meetings had a great deal of variety. Some were primarily for the parents' recreation, like a picnic or a candy pull; others were for doing work for the school, like building playground equipment or painting furniture; still others were to discuss topics of interest to the parents, such as the purpose of the nursery school, child health, homemaking, or family relationships.[56]

On the whole children benefited from the mutual understanding of their unique characteristics, by both parents and teachers, which resulted in better guidance or in better handling of some specific difficulty either in the nursery school or at home.

Community Support and Cooperation

During the first year of the emergency nursery schools, in addition to the normal schools, teachers colleges, colleges, and universities throughout the country that made available their institutions and their staffs for the training of the teachers, various other community agencies and individuals provided services and goods. For example, emergency nursery schools were housed in lodge rooms or fraternal organizations, in the fire department, in churches, in private homes, and in the post office. Workers from the Work Relief Projects repaired and remodeled publicly owned buildings and constructed equipment.

Boys in trade schools and in manual training departments of the public schools made furniture and toys. Play equipment, clothing, cribs, and supplementary supplies, as well as services of all sorts were provided by women's clubs, church societies, parent-teacher associations, clubs such as the Kiwanis, Lions, Rotary, Elks, American Legion, Masons, the Red Cross, Boy and Girl

Scouts, American Association of University Women, Junior League, nurses associations, Salvation Army, 4-H Clubs, and many other public and private organizations. Local businesses gave both services and materials, barbers gave free haircuts to children, shoe shops repaired shoes without charge. Store-keepers and manufacturers donated boxes, paint, sand, nails, and hammers.[57]

During the second year, community support and cooperation continued and increased. Now the communities had become familiar with the services provided by the nursery schools. The same organizations continued to provide professional and educational support and services. In addition, gas and electric companies gave stoves and refrigerators, respectively. Garden clubs beautified the nursery school grounds.[58]

There is no way of measuring the support given by the various communities in the country to the nursery schools through individuals and organizations. It was this support that made it possible for the needy children to receive the care and help they needed.

LANHAM ACT CHILD CARE CENTERS (1943–1946)

When World War II broke out in Europe, the economic crisis in the United States gave way to a national war emergency. The drop in unemployment ushered in by the war lessened the need for relief and the need for emergency nursery schools, as the Depression was almost over. The demands of the defense industry, however, indicated that an increased number of women, including those with small children, would be working.

The Community Facilities (or Lanham) Act

Working women in defense were not eligible for WPA nursery schools. There were not enough facilities available near the industries to meet the demand. Young children were left unattended at home, and schoolchildren roamed the streets after school.

The Lanham Act was approved October 14, 1940, and amended in 1941, 1942, and 1943. It was named for its sponsor, Representative Fritz Garland Lanham, a Democrat from Texas. The bill made federal funds available to war-impacted communities to help with housing, sewers, roads, and hospitals. It was signed into law by President Roosevelt. Though the act was first interpreted as applicable to child care early in 1942, communities did not receive any money until October. With this money, the states were able to hire staff to plan and coordinate day care, to stimulate local programs, and to help communities through the intricacies of Lanham Act application.

Child care was only one of the many "community facilities" needed in war industry areas competing for Lanham Act funds. The communities benefiting were expected to share in the expenses. In some communities, day care was so badly needed that formalities had to be overlooked in order to get the program going quickly.[59] One way to move was to transfer the former WPA nurseries to community-sponsored, Lanham-aided projects. This was made possible when the Federal Works Agency took over the staff of the WPA Community Service program "lock, stock, and barrel" in its own community-service division.

The transfer was criticized by various federal officials who thought it was inappropriate to try to keep active former WPA nurseries that had been originally planned as relief projects, not always conveniently located for the working mothers, in the war industries, than creating new ones. The Children's Bureau and the Office of Education, joined by the Office of Community War Services, complained that under the present system there was no assurance of proper supervision of day care facilities. The spending of Lanham Act funds could not be supervised by a federal or state authority; the necessary health and welfare services were deleted before programs were approved; and the federal agencies with the longest experience and best equipped to set up standards for safeguarding children had little say during this emergency.[60] This program became part of the government bureaucracy and moved away from the original commitment of the early childhood professionals to the children.

According to Christine Heinig,[61] 1943, there were 944 WPA nursery schools serving about 39,000 children. The creation of the Lanham Act Child Care Centers was not easy. All of the old problems had to be faced again: finding staff, finding facilities, and getting equipment. And now these tasks were further complicated by wartime shortages (23).

The first need was organizational help, like that provided in 1933 by the National Advisory Committee. In October 1941, the National Commission for Young Children was created. It was sponsored by NANE, the Association for Childhood Education International (ACEI), the Progressive Education Association (PEA), and the American Association of University Women (AAUW). The Commission had eleven members representing the sponsoring organizations, including Edna Noble White, a member of the National Advisory Committee on Emergency Nursery Schools. Rose Alschuler was the chairperson of the Commission.[62] The Commission served as a clearinghouse for information and administered training courses at colleges and universities. There were no regional supervisors. Alschuler compiled a book of guidelines for Children's Centers, based on Bulletins 1, 2, and 5 of the Emergency Nursery Schools. The book emphasizes standards, daily routine, staffing and training, records, and housing. It includes drawings for a floor plan for a children's center, and suggestions, drawings, and specifications for designing equipment for nursery schools.[63] Alschuler's guidelines made the children's centers sound like nursery schools.

Heinig added that the Commission, during its two years of operation, distributed a policy sheet about the Lanham program and all kinds of lists of references, and films on the needs and guidance of children and parents during wartime. It maintained a list of names and locations of institutions offering training courses. Alschuler provided guidance and publicity through correspondence and through field trips (24).

There were similarities and differences between the Lanham Act Child Care Centers and the Emergency Nursery Schools. Administratively, the Lanham Act Centers were under the Federal Works Agency and not under the U.S. Office of Education. This difference bothered some people. The centers had to be open during the hours that mothers were at their jobs in munitions plants, shipyards, aircraft factories, and textile mills. The centers were open from at least 7:00 A.M. to 6:00 P.M., and in some places on Saturdays and Sundays; a few places were on swing shift, and all were open the full year long, including summers. They were day care. Some Lanham Act Centers served school-age children because they, too, needed day care.

The federal government paid about 66 percent of the program's cost. Local contributions were a sizable amount, and parents did pay a fee. The parents of the Lanham Act Centers were parents working in war-related industries, not the unemployed of the Depression (25).

Child Care Centers and Children Enrolled

The number of child care centers receiving financial assistance from the federal government varied from month to month. The first report in August 1943 showed 49,197 children enrolled in 1,726 centers. Enrollments, attendance, and the number of units in operation continued to increase and reached their peak in July 1944 with 3,102 units in operation serving 129,357 children. About 60 percent of the children served throughout the program were preschool children.

It is difficult to establish the total number of different children cared for during the lifetime of the Lanham Act program, since there was considerable turnover. Families moved from one area to another, changed employment, or withdrew their children for various reasons. It is estimated that roughly 550,000 to 600,000 different children received care during the period that Lanham Act funds were dispensed.[64]

The programs ended when Japan surrendered on August 14, 1945. It was announced in Washington that the Lanham Act Child Care Centers would close on October 31, 1945. But, of course, many women were still working. The war had ended, but the need for day care had not. There was a slight drop in the employment of women, from 37 percent in 1945 to 30 percent in 1946. But 30 percent meant that sixteen million women were still on a job. The need for child care was still very great.

Nine national organizations concerned with children met in Washington in September 1945: NANE, ACEI, the NEA, the National Congress of Parents and Teachers, the Child Welfare League, AAUW, the American Home Economics Association, the General Federation of Women's Clubs, and the American Association for Health, Physical Education and Recreation. They petitioned President Truman to postpone ending the Lanham Act program so states and communities could make plans to take up the program; they won a reprieve of four months. The termination date for the Lanham Child Care

Centers was postponed until the end of February 1946.[65] Communities continued programs with local funds for various periods of time. State funds were made available in California, New York, Washington, and the District of Columbia, and to a limited extent in Massachusetts. The Public Housing Administration had provided facilities for nursery schools and recreation centers in many housing projects, without charge for space for agencies that would provide services.[66]

The cause of young children had been advanced a great deal throughout these emergency programs. In 1960, the War on Poverty and another program, Head Start, were created by the federal government to help another generation of children and their families in need.

THE KAISER CHILD SERVICE CENTERS

The best known and documented of the wartime children's centers were the industry-based Child Service Centers run by the Kaiser shipyards in Portland, Oregon. World War II was at its height in 1943 on two fronts, Europe and Asia. The Kaiser shipyards were producing the heavy equipment needed to keep the troops supplied. Part of the work force in the shipyards were 25,000 women, who had come to the West Coast with their children and husbands, but now the husbands had gone to war. New housing was built to accommodate the workers, but Portland was short of child care facilities and had resisted seeking Lanham Act funds for child care programs.[67]

According to Lois Meek Stolz,[68] the director of the two centers, one at Swan Island and the other at Oregonship, Edgar Kaiser, decided to open his own model programs. They were funded with $750,000 in federal funds from the U.S. Maritime Commission, who built the buildings. The centers were specifically built to accommodate large numbers of children. Each center had fifteen rooms with 25 children to a room. Each twenty-four-hour day, 1,125 children could be accommodated (32).

The centers had several unique features. They were located at the entrance to the two shipyards, convenient for mothers on their way to work. They were operated by the shipyards, not by the public schools or community agencies. The cost was paid by the Kaiser company and by the parents using them. The parents paid a fee of five dollars per child and three dollars and seventy-five cents for each additional child for a six-day week. The children's ages ranged from eighteen months to school age. The equipment and the program were like those of the prevailing nursery school program of the time (42–43).

Extra services provided by the centers included drop-in care for children when they needed it; an infirmary for children who failed the daily health inspection because of mild illness; a rental library of children's books; a store where mothers could buy items like combs, shoelaces, and other children's items; and a mending service. The most important of all was the home food service. Menus went home to all families each week. A mother could place her order two days ahead. At the end of her shift, when she picked up her child, she took home the evening meal for the family. The meals were reasonably priced (52–53). One of the program's shortcoming was its failure to reach black mothers.

Financing the Centers

The buildings were built by the Maritime Commission, and the cost of all initial equipment was borne by the Commission. The Kaiser shipyards were operating on cost-plus contracts. The company did pay the deficit over and above the income from parent fees, but this cost was passed on to the government as part of the cost of operating the shipyards. One can say the Kaiser centers were industry based, industry supported, and federally (publicly) funded through industry.

CHAPTER SUMMARY

Early childhood education had its largest growth (over 2,000 units) between 1933 and 1946, when the federal government created and financed nursery schools through a variety of federal agencies. Three years earlier, during the 1930 White House Conference on Children and Youth, "343 nursery schools reported a total enrollment of some 6,500 children."[69]

The emergency nursery schools and their subsequent programs were possible because there already existed a well-established and functioning program of nursery education before the emergency arose. There was a strong interest in the education of the child before kindergarten. The emergency program represented the first federal recognition that the education and care of young children was a responsibility warranting the appropriation of public funds. Emergency nursery schools under FERA were identified as an educational program, were located in public school buildings, and were controlled by the local public school system. One may say that they were an enrichment program for the children suffering because of the Depression. When the WPA gradually took the program over, there was a shift in the focus. The nursery schools became more of a service for working parents.

These nursery schools became widely known and demonstrated their value as beneficial to children and families. It was hoped that the program could be incorporated into the public school system for the benefit of *all* children, as had happened in England in 1918. Unfortunately, it was not. When the federal funds ended, few nursery schools were adopted by the public schools. Bess Goodykoontz suggested two reasons why the nursery schools did not become part of the public school system. First, the funding required the establishment of local sponsoring committees of representatives of public service organizations that created a separate policy-making board, apart from the public school systems. Second, the efforts to maximize employment during the emergency years had resulted in large staffs of teachers, supervisors, and custodians, which worked against eventual adoption of emergency nursery schools as functional units of the elementary school.[70]

The creation of the emergency nursery schools placed a lot of responsibility on the professionals of the time, to which they responded valiantly.

The economic depression of the 1930s created a paradox. On one hand, the budgetary cutbacks severely affected every educational level, with kindergartens hit the worst. A survey of seven hundred cities reported that the number of kindergarten teachers had been cut by 18.9 percent between 1930 and 1933, in contrast to the general teaching cutback, which had been 5 percent. The number of kindergarten classes decreased 12.2 percent, and many cities had eliminated kindergartens altogether—one in seven cities, of those reporting.[71] On the other hand, the federal government entered massively into early education through the creation of the emergency nursery school program in October 1933 and continued with the Lanham Act Centers and the Kaiser Centers.

Notes

1. Robert H. Bremner, ed., *Children and Youth in America: A Documentary History,* 3 volumes in 5 books (Cambridge: Harvard University Press, 1970–1974), 2:106–108. See Appendix 3 for the complete Charter.

2. Ibid., 2:752.

3. *200 Hundred Years of Children,* ed. Edith H. Grotherg (U.S. Department of HEW, Office of Human Development, Office of Child Development, 1976), 409; Bremner, *Children and Youth in America,* 2:759–761.

4. Martha M. Eliot, "Six Decades of Action for Children," *Children Today* 1 (1972): 2–6.

5. Joseph M. Hawes, *The Children's Rights Movement: A History of Advocacy and Protection* (Boston: Twayne Publishers, 1991), 47. For a detailed account of the Children's Bureau, see Dorothy E. Bradbury, *Four Decades of Action for Children: A Short History of the Children's Bureau* (United States Children's Bureau Publication No. 358, Washington, DC, 1956).

6. Bremner, *Children and Youth in America,* 1:411.

7. V. Celia Lascarides, "United States Contributions to Children's Rights: An Overview of the 20th Century," *International Journal of Early Childhood* 24, no. 2 (1992): 42.

8. Bremner, *Children and Youth in America,* 1:413, 2:786–787.

9. *200 Hundred Years of Children,* 410. Note that the importance of education as it relates to democracy had been a concern of both Horace Mann and John Dewey many years before the government's interest.

10. Ibid., 411; Brenmer, *Children and Youth in America,* 3:185–187. Among those who attended the Mid-Century White House Conference on Children and Youth was Abigail Adams Eliot, as discussed in Chapter 10 of this volume.

11. Bremner, *Children and Youth in America,* 3:628–629, 704.

12. *200 Hundred Years of Children,* 412; Bremner, *Children and Youth in America,* 3:715.

13. For a further discussion on the history of the White House Conferences on Children and Youth, see Rochelle Beck, "The White House Conferences on Children: An Historical Perspective," *Harvard Educational Review* 43 (November 1973): 653–668.

14. <http:/www.naeyc.org/public-affairs/policy/10-23-97.html>; Internet accessed 14 July 1998; and <http://www.whitehouse.gov/WH/NEW/Childcare/about.html>; Internet accessed 14 July 1998.

15. *Final Report on the WPA Program, 1935–43* (Washington, DC: U.S. Government Printing Office, 1943), 2.

16. Ibid., 3; A. C. Millspaugh, *Public Welfare Organization* (Washington, DC: The Brookings Institute, 1935), 321.

17. Federal Works Agency, Work Progress Administration, Division of Service Projects, *Record of Program Operation and Accomplishnient: The Nursery School Program,*

1933–1943, by Grace Langdon and Isabel J. Robinson (Washington, DC: Government Printing Office, 1943), 2.

18. Ibid., 3. See also V. Celia Lascarides, "The Role of the United States Government in Early Education during the Depression of the 1930s." International Standing Group for the History of Early Childhood Education (11th Session, Oslo, Norway, 11 August 1989) ED 315157.

19. Federal Works Agency, WPA, Langdon and Robinson, *The Nursery School Program,* 4.

20. Ibid.

21. Harry L. Hopkins, "Announcement of Emergency Nursery Schools," *Childhood Education* 10 (December 1933): 155; Federal Works Agency, WPA, Langdon and Robinson, *The Nursery School Program,* 5.

22. Mary Dabney Davis, "Emergency Nursery Schools," *Childhood Education* 10 (January 1934): 201.

23. Federal Emergency Relief Administration, *Emergency Nursery Schools during the First Year, 1933–1934* (Washington, DC: National Advisory Committee on Emergency Nursery Schools, [1935]), 9.

24. Federal Works Agency, WPA, Langdon and Robinson, *The Nursery School Program,* 12, 14.

25. Ibid., 12–13, 15–16.

26. Ibid., 10.

27. National Association for Nursery Education, *Proceedings of the Fifth Confernce of the National Association for Nursery Education* (Toronto, Ontario, October 26–28, 1933), 91.

28. Ibid., 99.

29. *Emergency Nursery Schools during the First Year,* 6; Christine Heinig, "The Emergency Nursery Schools and the Wartime Child Care Centers: 1933–1946," in *Living History Interviews,* ed. James L. Hymes, Jr., 3 vols. (Carmel, CA: Hacienda Press, 1978–1979), 3:11–13.

30. Davis, "Emergency Nursery Schools," *Childhood Education,* 429; Heinig, "Emergency Nursery Schools and the Wartime Child Care Centers," 3:13–14.

31. *Emergency Nursery Schools during the First Year,* 14.

32 Federal Works Agency, WPA, Langdon and Robinson, *The Nursery School Program,* 47–48.

33. Federal Emergency Relief Administration, *Administration and Program of Emergency Nursery Schools* (Washington, DC: National Advisory Committee on Emergency Nursery Schools, Bulletin No. 1, 1933); idem, *Housing and Equipment of Emergency Nursery Schools* (Washington, DC: National Advisory Committee on Emergency Nursery Schools and the United States Office of Education, Bulletin No. 2, 1933); idem, The Teacher Training Committee of the National Association for Nursery Education and the Office of Emergency Nursery Schools, WPA, *Suggestions for Building Courses in Nursery Education* (Washington, DC: National Advisory Committee, Bulletin No. 3, 1936); Federal Emergency Relief Administration, *Suggestions for Record Keeping in the Nursery Schools* (Washington, DC: National Advisory Committee on Emergency Nursery Schools, Bulletin No. 4, 1936); idem, *Suggestions, Drawings, and Specifications for Nursery School Equipment,* a supplement to Bulletin No. 2 (Washington, DC: National Advisory Committee on Emergency Nursery Schools, Bulletin No. 5, 1936).

34. Federal Emergency Relief Administration, *Emergency Nursery Schools during the First Year, 1933–1934* (Washington, DC: National Advisory Committee on Emergency Nursery Schools, [1935?]); idem, *Emergency Nursery Schools during the Second Year, 1934–1935* (Washington, DC: National Advisory Committee on Emergency Nursery Schools, [1936?]).

35. Federal Works Agency, WPA, Langdon and Robinson, *The Nursery School Program,* 17–18; Mary D. Davis, "Emergency Nursery Schools," *Childhood Education* 10 (January 1934): 201. It is important to remember this dual stated purpose. Sometimes people erroneously say that the emergency nursery schools were created solely to give jobs to the unemployed.

36. *Emergency Nursery Schools during the First Year,* 10; Federal Works Agency, WPA, Langdon and Robinson, *The Nursery School Program,* 25. Abigail Adams Eliot was

one of the persons perhaps instrumental in not admitting children below three years of age. She remembered her experience at McMillan Nursery School and how difficult it was to work with thirty-two toddlers even though she had several assistants. Eliot to her father, August 13 and 14, 1921, folder 20, Abigail Adams Eliot Papers, Schlesinger Library, Radcliffe College, Cambridge, MA; Abigail Adams Eliot, *A Heart of Grateful Trust,* transcribed and ed. Marjorie G. Manning (n.p.: [c. 1982]), 41.

37. *Emergency Nursery Schools during the First Year,* 14–15.

38. Ibid., 16.

39. The terms "Negro," "Indian," and "colored" used on this and the next several pages are exactly as they were found in the reviewed literature.

40. *Emergency Nursery Schools during the Second Year,* 21–23.

41. *Emergency Nursery Schools during the First Year,* 23; *Emergency Nursery Schools during the Second Year,* 47.

42. *Emergency Nursery Schools during the First Year,* 16; Davis, "Emergency Nursery Schools," 201.

43. *Emergency Nursery Schools during the First Year,* 17.

44. *Emergency Nursery Schools during the Second Year,* 32. For all the other persons employed, see Table B, ibid., 35.

45. Figure 3, "Relative Percentages of Persons Employed as Teachers in Emergency Nursery Schools," in *Emergency Nursery Schools during the Second Year,* 40.

46. "Teacher Training for Emergency Nursery Schools, 1933–34," in *Emergency Nursery Schools during the First Year,* 54–57; Federal Works Agency, WPA, Langdon and Robinson, *The Nursery School Program,* 37; Davis, "Emergency Nursery Schools," 202.

47. "Teacher Training for Emergency Nursery Schools, 1933–34," in *Emergency Nursery Schools during the First Year,* 59. For the time allotted to each one of these courses, see ibid., 60–61.

48. Ibid., 61. These suggestions are significant for the status of early childhood education when compared with today's attitudes.

49. "Teacher Training," in *Emergency Nursery Schools during the Second Year,* 97–99. For details about the length, content, and daily schedule of teacher training during the second year, see ibid., 100–104. There is also a separate bulletin about teacher training prepared by the Committee. See, Federal Ernergency Relief Administration, The Teacher Training Committee of the National Association for Nursery Education and the Office of Emergency Nursery Schools, WPA, *Suggestions for Building Courses in Nursery Education* (Washington, DC: National Advisory Committee, Bulletin No. 3, 1936).

50. *Emergency Nursery Schools during the Second Year,* 104; Grace Langdon, "The Facts About Emergency Nursery Schools," *Childhood Education* 11 (March 1935): 257.

51. Langdon, "The Facts About Emergency Nursery Schools," 256.

52. John E. Anderson, Director, Institute of Child Development, University of Minnesota, conducted the survey and reported the results of the study "Report on the Children Served during the First Year" in *Emergency Nursery Schools during the First Year,* 38–52.

53. *Emergency Nursery Schools during the First Year,* 34.

54. *Emergency Nursery Schools during the First Year,* 30, 34, 29.

55. "Parents' Day in a Nursery School: Things to Look For," was used in Oregon. It contains seventeen items. *Emergency Nursery Schools during the Second Year,* 63–64.

56. For a complete list of the topics and their grouping, see *Emergency Nursery Schools during the Second Year,* 66–68.

57. *Emergency Nursery Schools during the First Year,* 28–29.

58. *Emergency Nursery Schools during the Second Year,* 109–110.

59. Kathryn Close, "Day Care Up to Now," *Survey Midmonthly* LXXIX (July 1943): 194–197, quoted in Bremner, *Children and Youth in America,* 3:685.

60. Ibid., 3:686.

61. Heinig, "The Emergency Nursery Schools and the Wartime Child Care Centers," 3:22–27.

62. Rose H. Alschuler, ed., *Children's Centers* (New York: William Morrow, 1942), 10. The book was issued by the National Commission for Young Children.

63. Ibid., 113–145.

64. Bremner, *Children and Youth in America,* 3:691.

65. Heinig, "The Emergency Nursery School and the Wartime Child Care Centers," 3:26.

66. Bremner, *Children and Youth in America,* 3:691.

67. Lois Meek Stolz, "The Kaiser Child Service Centers," in *Living History Interviews,* ed. James L. Hymes, Jr., 3 vols. (Carmel, CA: Hacienda Press, 1978–1979), 2:27–29. Hymes contributed much of this information, for he was the managing director of the centers; for other child care facilities in war-related industries, see Close, "Day Care Up to Now," in Bremner, *Children and Youth in America,* 3:687–688.

68. Stolz, "The Kaiser Child Service Centers," 30–33, 40–56.

69. Harold H. Anderson, "Emergency Nursery Schools," *Childhood Education* 11 (October 1934): 11.

70. Bess Goodykoontz, Mary Dabney Davis, and Hazel F. Grabbard, "Recent History and Present Status of Education for Young Children," in The National Society for the Study of Education, *Forty-Sixth Yearbook of the National Society for the Study of Education: Part II, Early Childhood Education,* ed. Nelson B. Henry (Chicago: University of Chicago Press, 1947), 49–50.

71. William G. Carr, "The Status of the Kindergarten," *Childhood Education* 10 (March 1934): 283–285. This article reviews the information of a survey on kindergartens conducted by the Research Division of the National Education Association.

CHAPTER 13
Federal Government Involvement in the 1960s and Beyond

> In the 1990s we see ever more evidence that if as a society we choose *not* to permit and provide opportunities and supports for the families and their children who are in desperate need, . . . the whole society . . . suffers— through substance abuse, child abuse, crime, illiteracy, unemployability, racial warfare, class warfare, rage, and whatever is destined to come next while the rest of us enjoy our trivial pursuits.
>
> —Polly Greenberg[1]

HEAD START

All early childhood education programs result from the social, political, economic, and scientific milieu from which they arise. Such was the case with Project Head Start, which began in the Office of Economic Opportunity of President Lyndon Baines Johnson, under the direction of R. Sargent Shriver. Head Start, even at the beginning, rested on a historical foundation of child development, child study, and research on children (the child as the object of scientific research). In addition, Head Start reflects the underlying principle of community action, an integral part of both national and early childhood history.

Previous child care, nursery school, and Federally funded preschool programs furnished an early childhood education standards, methodology, and knowledge base. The work of eminent child development scholars around the country provided theoretical research approaches and models upon which to build the new Head Start structure. The maturationist theories of Gesell, behaviorist theories, Robert R. Sears's personality and social development theories, and child anthropology theories impacted the Head Start program.[2] During the early 1960s, Hunt and Bloom described how enriching early experiences might work to increase intelligence.[3] Hunt's work dealt with the fact that both environment and quality of mothering affected intellectual growth. Bloom's work focused on "critical periods of intellectual development," a term used earlier by Maria Montessori. Bloom collected and analyzed data from longitudinal research projects all over the world, concluding that the IQ (Intelligence Quotient) score of a four-year-old could predict half of the variation in that person's IQ score when fully mature. This conclusion enabled Bloom to justify direct intervention in the lives of young at-risk children, whose development might be forever impaired by external social circumstances and events.[4]

The work of Piaget and Inhelder on cognition was becoming accepted in the United States. Research projects, such as those initiated by Cynthia and Martin Deutsch of the Institute for Developmental Studies in the New York City schools, demonstrated that preschool programs for young economically disadvantaged children were beneficial.[5] Head Start was also impacted by the group dynamics theories of Lewin, and the work on the styles of democratic, autocratic, and laissez-faire leadership. The historical roots of interest in the child's well-being, from women in the early 1900s child welfare movement, was another factor in the formation of Head Start. The name Head Start itself signified the aspirations of families, communities, the Federal government, educators, and other human services professionals for the child victims of poverty and abuse.

Many people believed that the government should take a proactive, extensive role in eradicating the negative effects of poverty on children's development. It was popularly believed that the developmental course of children, including their intellectual development, could be vastly altered through timely intervention.[6] Although previous Federally funded programs such as the WPA Depression Era Nurseries and the Lanham Act Child Care efforts existed, they were relatively short-lived. They did, however, provide a precedent for Federally funded child care programs. The Iowa, California, and other child research stations funded by foundations provided another pillar

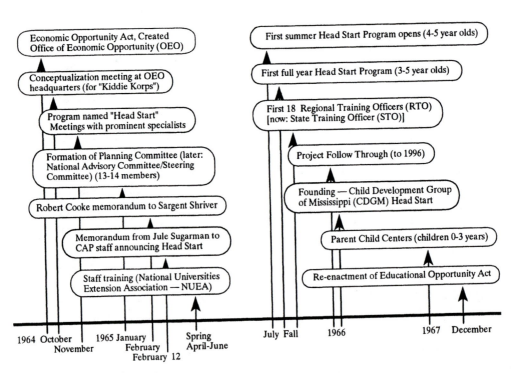

Figure 13.1 Head Start: The Beginnings.

supporting group care of young children. John B. Gardner[7] became President Johnson's Secretary of Health, Education, and Welfare in the 1960s. Gardner developed two "redistributionist projects" for the Federal government: a national program of early childhood education, and Federal assistance to established school districts for the special needs of disadvantaged at-risk children, which became Project Head Start and the Elementary and Secondary Education Act of 1965.[8]

The Johnson administration had mounting concerns about the problems of the socially, culturally, and economically disadvantaged young people of the nation. A large number of young people had truncated their formal education and were therefore prepared only for unskilled jobs. The civil rights movement had an increasing set of demands for quality, integrated education. As discussed earlier, psychologists of the 1960s had advanced new information about the influences of the environment upon the intellectual development of young children. Programs of compensatory education were starting to be developed for disadvantaged children of the 1960s. Winschel described compensatory education as the best effort of a "politico-educational complex blinded in one eye by prejudice and in the other by do-goodness—both equally detrimental to the welfare of children and society."[9] Health, malnutrition, and parental neglect headed the list of problems with adverse effects on younger children. Lack of the expectation of success and lack of appropriate experiences also impacted them.[10]

The Economic Opportunity Act (EOA) of August 1964 created the Office of Economic Opportunity in the U.S. Department of Health, Education, and Welfare. The Community Action Program (CAP) was designed to effectively help poor people improve their own lives through the availability of new resources and technical assistance. Experts in child development were flown to Washington, D.C. during November 1964 for a series of one-day meetings. Some local governments opposed the CAP's proposed placement of administrative control and resources in the hands of poor people and refused to apply for program grants. In an effort to make the CAP more palatable to local officials, while using what would have been an embarrassing budget surplus, the Head Start project was born.[11] The EOA required communities to create Community Action agencies to coordinate the programs and money for Project Head Start. The act further specified that any nonprofit organization could apply for operational money, develop a program, and operate a Head Start center. Thus, organizations such as churches, parent groups, and public schools could design a Head Start program and apply to the CAP or directly to the federal offices of Project Head Start for financing. The CAP staff placed the original Head Start programs in "America's out-of-the-way nooks and crannies," as well as in large urban centers, and outside the purview of public school systems.[12]

The rationale for Head Start was that if children from disadvantaged homes could enter school on a more even footing with middle-class children, they would have some reason to expect success from the very beginning of their schooling. They would be ready and able to learn the things the school is ready to teach them. If they experienced success, they would have the desire to continue their schooling. Upon leaving school, they would have better job opportunities than those who had dropped out; and if they took advantage of those opportunities, they would find themselves in a higher economic bracket than their parents. By virtue of their education, attitude, and financial means, they would be able to provide greater material and cultural advantages, as well as an attitude of expectation of success, for their children. Thus an upward spiral from the depths of poverty would have been created.[13]

"Beginning in 1965, the legislation for Project Head Start authorized a set of organized summer programs for children aged four and five whose socio-economic status predicted their failure or marginal success in elementary school. Action programs were accomplished through Federal grants to local community agencies whose responsibility was to guarantee that child, family, and community welfare would be maintained."[14] Head Start opened in the summer of 1965 with 561,000 children enrolled. After the first summer, it became a year-round program to assist children from poor families to become ready for school in all respects so that they could compete on a level of equality with their middle-class peers.

Definition

A Head Start agency is defined by Federal law as: Any local public or private nonprofit agency within a community, which has the power and authority to carry out the purposes of the subchapter, and to receive and administer Federal, private, and local public funds in support of a Head Start program. It is an agency capable of planning, conducting, administering, and evaluating a Head Start program. A community may be a city, county, or multicity or multicounty unit within a state, an Indian reservation, or a neighborhood or other area that provides a suitable organizational base and possesses the commonality of interest needed to operate a Head Start program.[15]

Children from families whose incomes are below the poverty line,[16] or who would potentially be eligible for public assistance, may participate in a Head Start program. Additionally, children from medically underserved areas, communities with a population of one thousand or less individuals, and those in remote locations are qualified for participation.[17]

The law stipulates that parents must directly participate in decisions affecting the character of the program. The Head Start agency must provide for regular parent participation in the implementation of the program, as well as involving them in appropriate educational services.[18] The head of each agency must coordinate with schools that will subsequently serve children in Head Start programs, the state agency responsible for administering Section 402(G) of the Social Security Act, and other programs serving the children and families served by the Head Start agency.[19]

A Head Start classroom is legally defined as a group of children supervised and taught by two paid staff members (a teacher and a teacher's aide or two teachers) and, where possible, a volunteer. Head Start family day care means Head Start services provided in a private residence other than the residence of the child receiving such services.[20]

The Conceptualization Phase

The program now known around the world as Head Start began as the subject of discussion among the new appointees of OEO, as they initiated President Johnson's War on Poverty. The "Kiddie Korps" envisioned by these divergent thinkers, social service professionals, and astute politicians was designed to help poor people improve their own lives by focusing media attention on children while simultaneously putting into place the Job Corps and other programs designed to eliminate juvenile delinquency, as well as other community action projects aimed at adults, which would not as easily find favor in the public eye.

R. Sargent Shriver of OEO had discussed the feasibility of establishing some sort of operation to widen the perspectives of deprived children with Dr. Jerome Bruner early in 1964. He was concerned "that there would be no concrete War on Poverty programs by the long, hot summer of 1965 to show to the always hovering press."[21] The (initial) plan was to involve 100,000 children who were about to enter school in 300 communities, at an estimated cost of $17 million.[22]

Authorities who attended the "test flight" meetings felt that more research and pilot programs were needed, and were not in favor of a massive summer program. The original staff idea was "a predominantly health-focused parent-involving program of lively activities appropriate for the curious minds and bodies of four-and-five-year-olds." Polly Greenberg prepared discussion papers on the next summer's program.[23] The name Head Start was selected at a brainstorming session in OEO.[24] In late November 1964, Jule Sugarman became the administrative head of the project.

Dick Boone remembered that the OEO staff planners were convinced this would be an opportunity to reach children in desperate need with multiple services, and to truly involve their families in planning programs for their own children. In addition, the parents would receive on-the-job training in a variety of human services. The center-based Head Start program for three- to five-year-olds was considered "remedial."[25] Boone's December 17, 1964, memo, entitled *Project Head Start—A Program for Disadvantaged Children Before They Enter School*, "outlines Head Start much as we know it today."[26]

Shriver appointed a National Advisory Committee headed by Dr. Robert E. Cooke (M.D.), chair of the Department of Pediatrics at the Johns Hopkins University School of Medicine, to consider the kinds of programs that might be most effective in increasing the achievement of, and opportunities for, poor children. The panel included experts from education, child development, mental health, social work, psychology, nursing, and pediatrics. The panel's recommendations, based on a "whole child" philosophy, were designed to develop children's overall social competence through the provision of comprehensive services.[27] Dr. D. Keith Osborn, who was the education consultant for Operation Head Start, suggested the concept of the child development center, which represented a coordinating agency for services for children including medical, nutritional, and social services. There was no requirement that all services were to be performed on the premises of the child care center; however, the Head Start center would serve as the umbrella coordinating agency.[28] Osborn and Dr. James L. Hymes, Jr. (Jimmy Hymes), were concerned about the adult-child ratio in the center-based program. They recommended one teacher and two other adults for every fifteen enrolled children.

The objectives detailed in the Advisory Committee's February 1965 memorandum, *Improving the Opportunities and Achievements of the Children of the Poor,* described later, continue to the present time.

Head Start has focused on improving the child's physical health and abilities and mental health from 1964 to the present. Today, Head Start is the leading health care system for the low-income children of the United States.[29] In the early years of Head Start, a principal goal was promoting the child's social competence. Parents were seen as pivotal in achieving that goal. Today, helping the emotional and social development of the child by encouraging self-confidence, spontaneity, curiosity, and self-discipline continues as a major focus of the program. A primary goal was and is increasing the sense of dignity and self-worth within the child and the family.[30] Another goal was increasing the child's capacity to relate positively to family members and others, while at the same time strengthening the family's ability to relate positively to the child and his problems. "It was always clear to the Head Start community that one of the best ways to help young children is to help their families get on their feet as well as to develop effective parenting skills."[31]

Meaningful work toward improving the child's mental processes and skills with particular attention to conceptual and verbal skills has formed a foundation for the program. These efforts have enhanced children's cognitive skills. Patterns and expectation of success have been established for the child, which create a climate of confidence for his or her future learning efforts.

The original blueprint for Head Start developed by the panel of experts in February 1965 called for unprecedented involvement of parents and other family members. Given Head Start's roots in community action and as an antipoverty program, it was natural that parent participation was emphasized.[32] The work of Urie Bronfenbrenner, who argued that intervention must focus not just on the child, but on the broader ecology of the child's environment, formed a basis for this goal. From Head Start's inception, parent involvement has taken many forms, including participating on policy councils and boards; working as classroom volunteers; and for some parents, assuming paid staff positions.[33] Today, the involvement of parents as well as communities is recognized as crucial to Head Start's success.[34] Through their involvement, the additional goal of developing in the child and his family a responsible attitude toward society and fostering constructive opportunities for society to work together with the poor in solving their problems is addressed, thus improving social responsibility.

On February 12, 1965, Sugarman sent a memo to CAP staff announcing the establishment of federal child development programs during the coming summer. The programs would involve health, social services, and educational activities for children who were about to enter school in the fall. The special staff being assembled in Washington to handle Project Head Start would be headed by Dr. Julius Richmond. Mrs. Lyndon Johnson was the Honorary Chairman of the National Committee supporting the program. Shriver was sending letters to community leaders throughout the nation that included a registration card to be returned to OEO indicating that the community was interested.[35, 36]

By early March 1965, it was clear to the planning committee that political realities dictated a nationwide program and they understood that it would be a huge undertaking. Hymes and Osborn were quite concerned that there would not be enough teachers with sufficient training to operate a program of this magnitude. "In 1965 there was only a handful of available teachers who had worked with poverty-level families, whether urban or rural. To address this problem we devised a massive orientation program for Head Start teachers, which took place all over the United States, the Virgin Islands, and Guam. Although we would have preferred a training program of longer duration, time constraints and the magnitude of the program meant that the first orientation for teachers was only six days long."[37] The National Universities Extension Association was responsible for the quick organization and preparation of more than one hundred universities throughout the country to undertake the training of these teachers. The first meeting with the universities took place on April 10, 1965, and the first training session began forty-four days later at the University of Mississippi. Approximately forty thousand teachers and an equal number of paraprofessionals attended the training sessions in 1965.[38]

EDWARD FRANK ZIGLER (1930–)

Edward Zigler was born in Kansas City, Missouri, on March 1, 1930. He completed his bachelor's degree at the University of Missouri at Kansas City in 1954 and immediately began work on his doctoral studies at the University of Texas. He received his Ph.D. in 1958, and became an assistant professor of psychology at the University of Missouri. Zigler joined the faculty at Yale University in 1959, achieving a professorship in psychology in 1967 and the Sterling Chair in 1976. He was the director of the child development program from 1961 to 1976, and headed the psychology section of the Yale Child Study Center from 1967 on. In 1977, he became the director of the Bush Centers in Child Development and Social Policy, a position that he currently retains.

Zigler's affiliation with Head Start began with his membership on the National Steering Committee from 1965 to 1970. He then became the first director of the Office of Child Development (OCD) of DHEW, taking office in 1970. During the period 1970 to 1972, he also was the Chief of the United States Children's Bureau. As noted by White, this made Zigler an archetypical member of the Head Start professional staff because he "actually went to Washington and lived there. . . . He experienced the reality of Head Start in a way that most of us did not."[39] In 1980, Zigler chaired the Fifteenth Anniversary Committee. He was a member of the National Research Council of Project Follow-Through from 1968 through 1970. In 1993, he served as a member of the Advisory Committee on Head Start Quality and Expansion.

Through his writings, Zigler has become a major historian of Project Head Start. His edited books encompass the growth and development of Head Start from the 1960s through the present. His books provide eyewitness accounts of the details of the development of this project. He has served as author, co-author, and editor of books and monographs, and articles in numerous professional journals.

In *Early Schooling: The National Debate*, Zigler posited the opinion that formal schooling for four-year-olds in public schools is inappropriate. He advocated a systems approach, with a return to the concept of the community school as a local center for all the social services required by the surrounding neighborhood. These full-service schools would provide full-day, high-quality child care for four- and even three-year-old children in their facilities. Although a developmentally appropriate educational component would be included, they would be places primarily for recreation and socialization—the real business of preschoolers. In-school day care, staffed by supervisory teachers and Child Development Associates, could easily accommodate older children after school is dismissed. For five-year-olds, Zigler proposed a half-day kindergarten followed by a half-day in-school day care program.[40] By 1996, Zigler was able to report that Schools of the 21st Century or Family Resource Centers in sixteen states had initiated "universally available child care, preschool, and family support systems open from about 7 A.M. until 6 P.M., twelve months a year," which coordinated flexibly with the work schedule of the parents, as well as traditional, formal schools. Additional Out Reach programs included parent and family day care worker education and support plans, home visitation, parent education and services, and child health screening and inoculation.[41] Senator Edward M. Kennedy cited Zigler's School of the 21st Century as exemplifying a program designed to make schools more responsive to the needs of low-income children.[42]

Zigler has been active on national committees and advisory boards.[43] He has received numerous national awards in the fields of education, child development, psychology, and special education. Most pertinent is his receipt of the National Head Start Association Award in 1990, at which time a building was dedicated as the Edward Zigler Head Start Center. Zigler has been a speaker of major importance at national and international conferences. He has been involved in the highest levels of policy determination and practice. Edward Zigler has made numerous contributions to the birth and development of Project Head Start and to the field of special education.

DONALD (KEITH) OSBORN (1927–1994)

D. Keith Osborn was born in St. Louis, Missouri, on August 10, 1927. He received his bachelor's degree from Emory University, and his master's degree in early childhood education from the State University of Iowa. In 1962, he received a doctorate in educational psychology from Wayne State University. Between 1952 and 1968, Osborn was a faculty member and division chair at Merrill-Palmer Institute in Detroit, Michigan. From 1968 on, he was a Professor of Education and Child Development at the University of Georgia in Athens.

In 1965, Osborn joined the Head Start planning committee as an education consultant and became the special consultant to the U.S. Commissioner of Education and to the Director of the OEO. He said that one of the most important recommendations of the Head Start Planning Committee Report was its insistence on a *comprehensive* program. "So many people have always seen Head Start narrowly, as simply getting kids ready for school. The Planning Committee's recommendation was much broader."[44] "There was the ferment for civil rights. . . . I think the idea of a Head Start program was seen as a special opportunity for our minority groups: our poor black children, Indian youngsters, Eskimos, Chicanos."[45]

As the assistant director of Head Start, Osborn fought for a class size of fifteen children with a teacher, an assistant, and a volunteer, or two assistants. He was also a member of the Project Follow-Through Planning Committee, which "bridged the nursery school education world and the world of elementary education."[46] As a professor of child development and education, Osborn was a member of the graduate faculty of the elementary education department at the University of Georgia. He also served on the President's Council on Early Childhood Education, and the President's Council on Television.

Osborn was actively involved in the Southern Association for Children Under Six (SACUS); the National Association for Nursery Education, which evolved into the National Association for the Education of Young Children (NAEYC); the Association for Childhood Education International (ACEI); and the U.S. National Committee of the World Organization for Preschool Education (OMEP-USNC); serving as an officer and committee chair in all of the organizations. His preferred positions were those dealing with history of early childhood education and teacher education.

Keith Osborn was a prolific author of books and articles in professional journals and magazines. He is remembered by colleagues for his unusual ability to simplify complex data and get it across in an accessible way. He viewed teachers as child developers, not as mere "instructors."[47] In his October 3, 1992, keynote address at the ACEI Centennial Celebration in Saratoga Springs, New York, he spoke of the many individuals who had influenced and connected with his own life and advised us to remember those historical and contemporary figures who inspired us.[48]

Keith Osborn's work as a professor, a historian of early childhood education, a member of professional organizations, and an originator of Head Start provides a good model for emulation by the early childhood teacher educators of the future.

THE BEGINNINGS OF HEAD START: EXAMPLES FROM THE 1960S

Variety—both in general services and levels of specificity in educational programming—was characteristic of Head Start from its inception. However, general guidelines for operation applied to all CAP local programs.[49] Urie Bronfenbrenner described the ingenious method used for the founding of the Negro Head Start in western Appalachia. Eighty-six-year-old "Mr. Peach" was a minister who had retired as the superintendent of Negro schools for the county. When he read about Head Start in a newspaper article he promptly sent to Washington for the kit of information and application materials . . . and decided that it was just what was needed in the overwhelmingly Black impoverished communities in the county. "But regulations specified that the application had to be forwarded by some 'non-profit' organization, and with a local contribution either in the form of money, staff, or facilities." When the white superintendent of schools refused a request for permission to use buildings that would be empty in the summer, "Mr. Peach" and his parishioners came up with such sites as former schoolhouses for Negro children, which were so run down they had been abandoned by the Board of Education, a refurbished rumpus room in the home of a Black physician, and the garage of an abandoned gas station. The sponsoring nonprofit agency was the "Memorial Recreation Forest." This forest had been grown from free seeds obtained from the Department of Agriculture during a reforestation project. The project was on Federal land and was used as a park. The Memorial Recreation Forest still appears on the official records of Head Start in Washington.[50]

One of the most controversial of the early Head Start programs was that run by the Child Development Group of Mississippi (CDGM). It was a twelve-thousand-child Head Start program that was run by the parents.[51] Shriver wrote that there were a lot of people who looked upon Head Start and CDGM as a means of transferring substantial sums of money directly to the black people of Mississippi for the first time, thus empowering and mobilizing them. The Federal money for organization of Head Start programs all over the state gave CDGM organizers a mandate to go into every community and organize the people politically through Head Start. As a consequence, what had been looked upon in the beginning by some in Mississippi as a harmless social program, immediately became hostile intervention by the Federal government, bent on upsetting the social structure. CDGM became a spearhead of the civil rights movement in Mississippi, and therefore bore the major brunt of the opposition of the white community in the state, and of its congressmen and senators in Washington. The political pressure forced Sargent Shriver to cut off OEO funds from this most vulnerable, most exposed new organ of Head Start in the country, during the second year of its operation.[52, 53] A new group, Mississippi Action for Progress (MAP), took over the administration of the program. Later, CDGM was reorganized and refunded, which led to disputes about which parts of the state each organization would have under its jurisdiction. Shriver contends "that if we had continued financing CDGM in its original form, not only would CDGM have been stopped but the whole War on Poverty might well have been stopped."[54]

Components of Head Start

Head Start is composed of six major parts: administration, education, social services, health services, parent involvement, and career development.[55]

HEALTH SERVICES

According to Greenberg, a person must be in good health in order to take advantage of learning and growth opportunities in school and later life. It was for this reason that a physician was selected to chair the Head Start Planning Committee, which was envisioned as a temporary outside panel of multidisciplinary experts who would give both legitimacy and expertise to this exciting new effort.[56]

The Planning Committee thought that the Head Start Child-Development Center could serve as the agency through which educational, social, psychological, nutritional, medical, and dental services might be provided in an integrated manner. Each component could draw strength from and lend support to the others. Classroom observations, for example, might detect the presence of a medical problem that after proper diagnosis might be alleviated through nutritional supplementation and the modification of activities at the Head Start center. "Abnormalities of behavior or learning, or of speech and language development, might be addressed by appropriate professionals working in close coordination with the Center staff."[57] The 1967 health services goals and guidelines included: finding all existing health defects, remedying any existing defects, ensuring a child's future health by providing preventive services, improving the health of all members of the child's family, and improving the health of the community in which the child lives. In early 1968, Head Start contracted with the American Academy of Pediatrics to provide medical services consultation to each Head Start project. Pediatricians, public health physicians, and family practitioners were trained to serve as medical consultants, visiting two or more Head Start programs at least twice a year to evaluate how well each one was achieving the goals. Thus, each Head Start project had a physician to whom it could turn for advice and for advocacy of the health-care needs of its children. The consultants served in communities other than the one in which they themselves practiced; therefore they could look objectively at the quality and efficiency of the health program.[58] Head Start continues to provide health; dental; speech, hearing, and language services; and health education for its children and families.

The Head Start nutrition program is a major part of the health component. The nutrition program has been concerned from the beginning with "the emotional, social, and cognitive aspects of snacks and mealtimes, and with the opportunities for learning presented to children, parents, and staff by food purchasing and preparation and by meal serving and cleanup."[59] In addition, the nutrition program has been a vehicle for infusing multicultural aspects into the Head Start program. This includes both the cultures of the children in the program and the foods of cultures and ethnic groups around the world.

In 1971, twenty-nine demonstration Health Start projects were funded across the country, to provide Head Start–like health services to children under the age of six who were not being screened in any other programs.[60] Unfortunately, the project was of short duration (two years), and therefore the follow-up treatment was not often provided.[61] Health Start was a forerunner of the National Early and Periodic Screening, Diagnosis, and Treatment Program (EPSDT), a part of Medicaid (Title XIX of the Social Security Act), which was legislated in 1967. EPSDT mandates that all children enrolled in Medicaid be screened on a periodic basis during early childhood, that an assessment be made of their health status, and that appropriate referrals be made. The Head Start/EPSDT Collaborative Projects of 1974 were replicable approaches to local collaboration among Head Start programs, state Medicaid agencies, and community health resources for delivery of services to young children. After the initial two-year project, the collaborative approach was integrated into all Head Start programs and a handbook showing Head Start programs how to make use of EPSDT was disseminated nationwide.[62]

SOCIAL SERVICES

Head Start has always had a social services component, to provide an organized method of assisting families to assess their needs, and to provide those services that will build upon the individual strength of families to meet their own needs. Some of the activities that the social services staff used are: community outreach, referrals, family need assessments, providing information about available community resources and how to obtain and use them, recruitment and enrollment of children, and emergency assistance and/or crisis intervention.[63] Lifesaving services have been provided to a number of families. Many of the social service workers were and are paraprofessionals who began in Head Start as parents of enrolled children.

Greenberg wrote that social services have been neglected in the Head Start budget and priorities, as they are by the nation as a whole. "From the beginning, the many dozens of gap-filling services that complete the picture for an individual—including counseling—were not given the status some of us felt they should have received."[64]

EDUCATION

The education component is an integral part of Head Start. It is designed to meet each child's individual needs, as well as those of the community served and its ethnic and cultural characteristics. If programs have a majority of bilingual children, for example, at least one teacher or aide must speak their native language. Every child receives a variety of learning experiences to foster intellectual, social, and emotional growth.[65] Prominent early childhood educators such as Jeanette Galambos Stane, Bettye Caldwell, and Blanche Persky wrote the first of the famous Rainbow Series of publications, which became the basis for the original Head Start curriculum.

PARENT INVOLVEMENT

Parents are the most important influence on a child's development. An essential part of every Head Start program is the involvement of parents in parent education, program planning, and operations activities. Many serve as members of their local program's policy councils and committees and have a voice in the administrative and managerial decisions. Parents participate in classes and workshops on child development and educational activities. Through staff visits to the home, they learn about the needs of their children and how they can participate in meeting those needs more effectively. Many parents serve as volunteers or paid staff members in their local program. They receive preference for paraprofessional positions.[66]

Evaluation

At the initial meetings of the Planning Committee, there was a controversy about whether to evaluate Head Start. Many felt that because it was a six- or eight-week program, giving some health care, but primarily a good, pleasant experience for children, there was little to evaluate. Richmond decided that no program as large as this should go unevaluated. Dr. Edmund Gordon became the first research director. Richmond commissioned Edward Zigler to put an evaluation together. He and his graduate students quickly constructed some measures and instruments. He admits that "the summer 1965 evaluation of Head Start was an absolute and total disaster," because they tried to do too much too fast. However, Zigler credits Richmond with establishing the principle that evaluation would be an integral and ongoing part of Head Start.[67]

James Hymes's retrospective assessment on his observations of the first Navajo (Pueblo) Early Childhood Education groups and the first groups of Head Start programs for Spanish-speaking children included a concern that individual programs were losing sight of the broad goals of Head Start. He also reported enthusiastic feelings and grass roots appreciation of certain values, even in programs that were not as good as they could have been. "Head

Start has brought a sense of significance and community to adults, and has opened career doors for adults."[68] Among the positive impacts of the program on education, he cited a vast increase in the number of public kindergartens and the use of aides in public school classrooms. He described a noticeable growth in the awareness of the importance of involving parents in programs for young children. On the other hand, Hymes stated that Head Start has survived but not grown nor greatly improved in quality. He believed that its "continuing failure to reach all the children who could benefit is a shame." He described a prevalent "anti-public school feeling"—a feeling that only the schools had let the poor down, not the health or legal profession, churches, or government. He decried the lack of skilled and trained teachers and top-flight educational leadership in this massive educational program. He said that "Head Start has never been financed well enough to be nearly as good as we know how to make it."[69]

Richmond divided the interpretation of Head Start research into periods of optimism and pessimism. During Phase I (1965–1969—over-optimism), Head Start was seen as successful, and claims were made from its short-term success in halting developmental attrition associated with poverty that these gains would be maintained throughout the child's education program. In Phase 2 (1969–1975—over-pessimism), the research was driven by the Westinghouse Report of 1969, "which homogenized the population in the analysis and thus missed subgroup differences, as Donald Campbell and his colleagues have shown. Findings indicated that initial positive gains from Head Start experience were 'washed out' by the third grade. Head Start gains were lost with the pervasive influence of poverty."[70]

Zigler agreed with this assessment, demonstrating that in several instances research almost led to the end of Head Start. He cited the opening sentence of Jensen's monograph, "Compensatory education has been tried and it has failed," as illustrative of the devastation caused by the Westinghouse Report. Bronfenbrenner's "fade out hypothesis" pointed out the need for more data. Ultimately, research saved Head Start and led to its expansion.[71]

During Richmond's Phase 3 (1975–1990—realistic evaluation), researchers tried to determine the effects of what works best for whom and for how long. He believes that this trend needs to be continued and expanded. *Head Start Research and Evaluation: A Blueprint for the Future* (1990) launched a plan for comprehensive and continuous effort. "The question had gradually shifted from 'Does it work?' to 'How can we make it work better?'"[72]

White (1991) recalled that in the midst of the arguments among the child welfare research stations in Iowa, California, and Minnesota, about whether IQ could be changed by preschool experience, Head Start came along. A collaboration between developmental psychology and Head Start began. However, "public discussion of Head Start got caught in the theories of developmental psychology of the day." Hunt's book restated the Wellman argument, "that preschools could modify intelligence," lending credence to the viewpoint that Head Start was about IQ modification. Others believed that the purpose of Head Start was cognitive development.[73]

In 1991, both Richmond and Zigler identified needed long-term evaluation strategies. Richmond stated that Head Start's long-term development strategies "must be examined qualitatively and quantitatively and applied to individual, family, and group and community effects."[74] Zigler formulated the "snowball hypothesis," which postulated that children who have certain experiences at age four begin kindergarten in a better position to learn. If the kindergarten teachers interact with the child in a constructive, positive way, that child goes on to the next grade even better prepared. A second hypothesis stated that, as a result of their interaction and involvement with Head Start, parents become better socializers of their children, so there would be effects among the siblings. Parents thus become "the mediators of the long-term effect of early intervention." Zigler also hypothesized that health and high-quality programs have an effect on long-term outcomes.[75] He argued against the position of the hereditarians (e.g., Jensen, Herrnstein, Eysenck), that compensatory efforts must fail since genetic factors are the overriding determinants of human behavior. Zigler believes that the nature-nurture issue is irrelevant to the issue of whether compensatory programs are of value.[76] In his address to the 1975 annual conference of NAEYC, Zigler looked at assessments of preschool compensatory education done by Bereiter, Ginsburg, Kohlberg, and White, and found them in error. "We must purge the compensatory education field, especially its bellwether—Head Start—of the theoretical excesses and fallacious views of the mid-sixties. I agree with Bettye Caldwell's (1974) assertion that at the time of the inception of Head Start we were overly optimistic concerning the amount of effort required to produce permanent changes in the quality of children's behavior and that such overoptimism had to invariably give way to the pessimism that now confronts us."[77]

Zigler asks why, when the planning committee discovered that instead of one hundred thousand children, there would be five hundred thousand children entered in the program, did they decide to greatly expand Head Start before any evaluation findings had been collected? He answers that the planning committee obtained a clear signal that the decision makers who had the clout wished to commit hundreds of millions of dollars to the Head Start program. The planners were "caught up in the environmental mystique of the mid-sixties," "were overly impressed with those preschool intervention efforts which predated the Head Start program," and "there was no evidence that such a program would have negative consequences." Decision makers took their views seriously.[78]

Twenty years later, Zigler could report that Head Start does prepare children for school. It has had "enduring effects on social competence and socio-emotional characteristics," physical health and well-being; positive impact on families; and possible benefits to the siblings of enrolled Head Start children. The financial benefit of receiving jobs and job training through Head Start, and the improvements in local communities where Head Start centers are situated, had been demonstrated.[79]

Head Start Performance Standards

The first Head Start Performance Standards were published in the Federal Register of June 30, 1975. They were implemented in 1975, ten years after the initiation of the program. The term "performance standards" refers to Head Start program function, activities, and facilities required and necessary to meet the objectives and goals of the Head Start program as they relate directly to children and their families. Grantees must develop written plans to meet or exceed these standards.[80]

During the first years of the Head Start project, administrators were reluctant to issue specific program guidelines, in order to respect local control. Policy guidelines in the area of parent participation and career development were issued in order to "force compliance by the public school delegate agencies."[81] In late 1971, Zigler formed a task force chaired by Harley Frankel and Raymond Collins. Clennie Murphy and Henlay Foster, skilled National Head Start administrators who also had experience with the program at the regional and local levels, served as staff consultants.[82] The published standards were very precise about the level of health and other comprehensive services expected, but they were not specific regarding program design or procedures. "For example, standards . . . mandate that every family receive at least two home visits by educational staff, but they do not prescribe when the visits should take place or exactly what level of staff should make them."[83] Staff-child ratios and class size were omitted from the performance standards. Zigler believes this was an unfortunate omission, because in later years staff-child ratios increased. The standards were updated in 1984 and again in the mid-1990s. The performance standards ensure that every Head Start program provides the services necessary to meet the goals of the four major components, described earlier.

The results of evaluation studies caused Federal lawmakers to write a "quality set-aside" into the Human Services Reauthorization Act of 1990. After inflation, 25 percent of expansion funds were to be used for improvements in Head Start. Half the money was allocated to increased salary and benefits and the remaining 50 percent was marked for training and technical assistance, facility improvements, and transportation. Staffing problems precipitated the inclusion of the requirement that by 1994 each center was to have at least one teacher with a CDA (Child Development Associate) credential. The most recent policy statement mandates that classroom-based staff members obtain an associate's degree by the year 2003.[84]

Professional Development and Training in Head Start

In the original Head Start program there were three training components that were developed by the Training Branch. The first of these was a forty-hour training program that took place in the week before the opening of the Head Start year. Its purpose was to prepare new and inexperienced personnel by "acquainting them with the goals and techniques of working with Head Start children."[85] The second component was a university-campus-based course called the Leadership Development Program. This eight-week program was designed to provide instruction on how to manage family, education, and work responsibilities simultaneously. Although the program sites were at universities, no credit hours were given for attendance at this program. It was quite difficult for staff members to leave their families and jobs for eight weeks. This program no longer exists.

The third type of training utilized twelve hundred outside consultants from education, health, psychology, and management who came to the program site. The National Head Start Office contracted with the consultants, who were supervised by Regional Training Officers (RTOs). Osborn proposed the concept of RTOs, trained professionals in the field of early childhood education who would go into communities to conduct training sessions and do in-service training, in 1965. They began with eighteen RTOs in the fall of 1965. Later additional personnel were added[86] and the position name was changed to State Training Officer (STO). The STO's responsibilities included conducting orientation sessions, supplying other resource people and usable materials, and arranging regional meetings on appropriate topics.

HEAD START SUPPLEMENTARY TRAINING (HSST)

In 1968, Head Start made an important transition from the idea of "staff training" to thinking in terms of the career development of its personnel. The official Head Start career-development policy appeared in September 1968. It required every Head Start agency funded after January 1969 to have a Career Development Committee, and a Director of Career Development and Training. There was to be a plan for job development that would clearly define paths or career progression within Head Start. A long-term training and education plan for both the program and each individual staff member was to be established, along with an appraisal-counseling-evaluation system.[87] The Head Start Supplementary Training Program (HSST) developed simultaneously with the career development mandate. This training program enabled Head Start staff to earn a certificate, an associate's degree, or a bachelor's degree. HSST began in 1967 and was viewed as one component of career development.

HSST was one of the most popular career development programs, because attaining college credits and a college degree were tangible steps toward upward mobility for the poor. The colleges and universities involved in the program initiated innovative educational approaches. These included dropping college entrance requirements, adjusting course content to fit the needs of Head Start staff, using alternative approaches to teaching, assisting staff in overcoming transportation problems, shifting the order of courses so that Head Start personnel could take practical courses first, and giving college credit for work experience and in-service training.[88] More than 250 colleges and universities participated in HSST.

The Child Development Associate (CDA) Credential

The Child Development Associate (CDA) credential was created in 1972 to meet the growing need for skilled child care workers to provide quality programs for young children in the United States. Zigler is credited with encouraging this new, "competency-based approach to the training of child-care personnel,"[89] by commissioning a position paper proposing the establishment of a new professional category. The eight-page document on the Child Development Associate was written by Jenni Klein, Rebekah Shuey, Barbara Biber, and NAEYC president Evangeline Omwake in late 1970. It was circulated to early education professionals with an invitation to a meeting in Washington, D.C., to share their responses, thoughts, and reactions. On January 20 and 21, 1971, thirty practitioners met at the Windsor Park Hotel and formed focus groups that produced a practical working plan for assessment and certification.[90] In the spring of 1971, Klein and Shuey assembled a task force to write draft competencies and establish guidelines for the training process. Barbara Biber played a key role in this task force. A second task force was assigned the practical issues of making the training and certification operative. A feasibility study by Marilyn Smith and Milton Akers of NAEYC recommended that a consortium of organizations concerned with young children be formed and given the responsibility for the development and awarding of the credential.[91, 92]

A Child Development Associate Consortium, a private nonprofit corporation composed of thirty-nine national associations, was formed, receiving its articles of incorporation on June 16, 1972.[93] The purpose of the Consortium was to develop assessment and credentialing. The organizations were grouped into nine interest areas with primary focus on child development, representation of ethnic-minority groups, or accreditation and certification. The Consortium had to define explicitly and objectively what competencies a person should possess when working with young children. Between 1972 and 1975, when the first twelve credentials were awarded, the Consortium defined the competencies and developed the assessment and credentialing procedures. Eleven task forces were formed, which reported about a variety of problem areas, and forty-four subcontracts for research were granted to produce relevant studies.

> There was general agreement to a "whole teacher" approach. Competency . . . was seen as an integrated pattern of skills, attitudes, and feelings that provide meaning to the discrete behaviors. "Competent teaching is not just the ability to perform skills according to a formula; it involves decisions that combine judgment and skill." . . . The CDA task force further differentiated between competence and competencies, . . . with the thrust of the CDA program on the composite development of competence. Much effort went into assuring that the competencies represented a distinct point of view about teacher-child interaction as well as specific expectations of what the optimal experience for both teacher and children in a educational setting should be.[94]

Approximately twelve hundred child development experts refined, examined, and researched the draft competencies. There was a strong sentiment that the competencies should address the diversity of children and families encompassed in preschool settings.[95]

The CDA was defined as

> an individual who has successfully completed a CDA assessment and who has been awarded the CDA Credential. A CDA is a person who is able to meet specific needs of children and who, with parents and other adults, works to nurture children's physical, social, emotional, and intellectual growth in a child development framework. The CDA conducts her/himself in an ethical manner. The CDA has demonstrated competence in the CDA competency goals through his/her work in a center-based, home visitor, or family day care program. A person who has demonstrated bilingual competence in a bilingual child care program is a CDA with a bilingual specialization.[96]

This definition is still used today.

The original set of competencies, upon which consensus was reached in 1974, were stated as child-development processes rather than IQ achievement scores. The six competency areas are:

1. Establishes and maintains a safe and healthy learning environment.
2. Advances physical and intellectual competence.
3. Builds positive self-concept and individual strength.
4. Promotes positive functioning of children and adults in a group.
5. Brings about optimal coordination of home and center child-rearing practices and expectations.
6. Carries out supplementary responsibilities related to children's programs.

These competency areas and their related thirteen functional areas (safe, healthy, environment, physical, cognitive, language, creative, self-concept, individual strength, social, group management, home center, and staff) have not changed measurably over the years, in spite of the fact that the Credential has been housed with a number of different organizations, including Bank Street College of Education, the Department of Health and Human Services, and its present home, the nonprofit Council for Early Childhood Professional Recognition.[97]

A pilot program was launched in 1974, with field tests held in spring 1974 and winter 1975. This resulted in the granting of thirty-four CDA credentials on July 24, 1975.[98] Over a twenty-year span, in excess of sixty thousand CDA credentials have been awarded, with approximately 80 percent received by employees of Head Start.

Among the distinctions between the CDA and the HSST programs is the fact that A.A. or B.A. degrees have broadly based requirements in general education, while a CDA credential is more specifically focused on competencies for working with preschool children. In addition, the CDA credential is based on actual performance with children, not completion of a prescribed number of credit hours. The CDA credential certifies that a person is competent to work with young children, while a college degree alone may not certify this. Originally, college courses were not necessary for attaining the CDA credential. This was an important distinction, because many of the Head Start employees had prior unpleasant experiences in their schooling and were reluctant to reenter the academic world. The training was organized so that academic and fieldwork became an integrated set of experiences, while being individualized according to each trainee's strengths and weaknesses. A minimum of 50 percent of the total training time was to be spent in supervised fieldwork. Whenever possible, valid academic credit was to accompany CDA training.[99]

The original credentialing model included registration with the consortium, formation of a Local Assessment Team (LAT), information collection and documentation by each of the four members of the team, a team meeting for evaluative purposes, transmittal of the documentation to the Consortium for review, and awarding of the credential. It has always been a requirement that the CDA credential be periodically renewed (currently every five years), following the initial period of credentialing.[100, 101] The CDA credentialing and assessment system was designed to "bring up the floor, not lower the ceiling."[102]

In 1990, the Council for Early Childhood Professional Recognition introduced the current Council Model for CDA, which made a number of sweeping changes. This model separated CDA assessment and training into two separate systems: one for individuals who wished to have their skills evaluated and the other for those who wished to be trained.[103] The direct assessment process requires its candidates to have completed 120 clock hours of formal child care training within a five-year period. The formal training experiences must be under the auspices of an agency or organization with expertise in early childhood teacher preparation, such as colleges and universities, vocational schools, Head Start programs, local school districts, or in-service workshops or seminars sponsored by *recognized training providers*. Educational requirements are the same for all settings, with the exception of the home visitor credential. The direct assessment system includes the candidate's preparation of a Professional Resource File; a written test, the Early Childhood Studies Review; the advisor's formal observation of the candidate's performance with children; and Parent Questionnaires submitted to the Council Rep during the verification visit. An oral interview is conducted by the Council Rep.

The CDA P3 model is a totally new design consisting of several phases. It includes self-study of the Council's *Essentials Curriculum Guide,* work with an approved advisor, an intensive training seminar, and documentation and verification of performance. The third phase is similar to that used in direct assessment.[104]

Over its greater-than-twenty-year life, the CDA credential has increasingly gained acceptance within the early education profession, among the lay public, and with the Federal legislative and administrative branches of government. Research conducted by both doctoral candidates and by the Council for Early Childhood Professional Recognition, as well as other researchers, demonstrated that the CDA credential has created a cadre of competent, skilled, educarers who provide knowledgeable care and education for young children in quality programs.[105]

CAROL BRUNSON PHILLIPS DAY (1947–)

Carol Brunson Phillips, the current Executive Director of the Council for Early Childhood Professional Recognition, was born in Chicago, Illinois, in 1947. Early in her academic career, she earned a bachelor's degree in psychology from the University of Wisconsin at Madison, a master's degree in early childhood education from the Erikson Institute, and a doctorate from the Claremont Graduate School in California. Her doctoral and postdoctoral work focused on research with African-American children. Her current work revolves around two themes, a strand that deals with racial and sociocultural context and psychology, and a second that focuses on professional and career development and credentialing.

In her chapter, "The Movement of African-American Children through Sociocultural Contexts: A Case of Conflict Resolution," Phillips describes the interaction of physical, historical, economic, and social elements to produce a sociopolitical order and an individual psychological reality. After discussing the historical reality of the child and the school, she presents a process of empowering the child that challenges teacher neutrality. In this view, "professional responsibility . . . encompasses an examination of attitudes and a continuously evolving consciousness about the sociopolitical order and the role that institutions play in perpetuating the oppression of certain segments of the population."[106] Fostering a conscious awareness of the conflicts, according to Phillips, helps children develop an appreciation for context-situated behaviors, such as the use of Ebonics and Standard English codes, and home/community versus classroom cultural experiences. This conceptualization builds on her first research publication, "Rethinking the Study of Black Behavior," in which she attempts to identify the sources of the misconceptions in the description and the behavior of Black Americans.[107] Phillips believes that "true teaching and learning involves a powerful transformation process that creates new ideas from old ones and uncovers new relations in oneself and the world. This process gives the power and responsibility to each of us to be deliberate in making value judgments about human worth."[108]

Phillips's most recent publication, *Teaching/Learning Anti-Racism: A Developmental Approach,* includes descriptions of the authors' personal experiences, and a conceptual framework and guide for implementing antiracism education with adults.[109] Her multiplicity of publications includes several journal articles on these themes. She dedicated "Nurturing Diversity for Today's Children and Tomorrow's Leaders" to Dr. Evangeline Ward, whose "distinguished work in early childhood education demonstrated for me what truly professional work must be—value-based, expert, committed and gracious."[110]

Professional Work

Phillips emulated Ward in her own professional development. She has held faculty positions at Prairie State College in Illinois and Pacific Oaks College in California. She served as a preschool teacher in a Los Angeles school, earning Life Credentials in both Early Childhood and Community College Education from the California State Department of Education. In 1979, she served on the Los Angeles Coordinating Committee for the International Year of the Child. During the 1980s, she served in executive capacities on several Pasadena task forces.[111] On September 1, 1985 she assumed the position of Executive Director of the Council for Early Childhood Professional Recognition.

Recent Publications on Credentialing

During the past decade, Phillips has concentrated on the areas of leadership and the professional development of early childhood educarers and teachers. Under her guidance, the Council developed the CDA Professional Preparation Program (CDAP$_3$). She edited the document *Essentials for Child Development Associates Working with Young Children*,[112] which is used by all CDA candidates. She contributed to several publications of NAEYC and its Institute for Early Childhood Professional Development, and to prestigious educational journals. In "At the Core: What Every Early Childhood Professional Should Know," she promulgated five themes.[113]

Writing in *Phi Delta Kappan*, Phillips described the multiple entry paths, training based on child development principles, the role of parents, responsiveness to cultural pluralism, and cooperative and differentiated leadership in the classroom, including working as members of instructional teams, which are the important themes characterizing early childhood professional education and development.[114] Following up on the fifth theme in "New Directions for Non-College/University Training,"[115] she focused on leadership as a process by which one person sets certain standards and expectations and influences the actions of others, and the ways in which the CDA Competency Standards support leadership development. Head Start Fellows and other more specifically focused leadership development programs are also discussed in this chapter.

At this time, Carol Brunson Phillips is at the "leading edge," as early childhood professional development and education move "full steam ahead" into the era of technology and interactive communication.

Head Start Training and Staff Development in the 1990s

In 1992, Head Start initiated fourteen Head Start Teaching Center Demonstration Projects in regions around the country. Most of the training centers were held in the context of an exemplary Head Start program. Effective training approaches utilized in this project include: hands-on participatory activities, individualization of training, collaborative learning processes, development of goal-setting strategies, and mentoring. Training teams that included teachers, assistant teachers, parent volunteers, supervisors, and component coordinators participated in the initial and follow-up training together. The program managers were trained in the principles of adult learning, in order to effectively continue the work at the "home site." The inclusion of administrative staff from each program in the training process assisted in extending this experience to the trainees' own centers.

The project developers faced the challenge of developing positive relationships with the "home programs," involving program directors and managers in the development of training approaches and curricula, ensuring that persons sent to the training were adequately prepared, and ensuring the transference of training to trainees' job performance. The preliminary report of the five-year study indicates that the challenge of serving a highly diversified population of programs and staff was met.[116]

Concerns About and Critiques of Professional Development and Training of Head Start Staff

Jimmy Hymes struck a discordant note in his discussion of staff training and supervision. In 1979, he was concerned that Head Start goals would be distorted in their implementation by untrained staff. He recalled that in his 1965 stay in New Mexico, he saw only one trained teacher, a graduate of Antioch, who had a Spanish-speaking aide, who obtained appropriate supplies and materials, and produced one group that "was everything that we all wanted Head Start to be."[117] In 1991, Hymes listed Head Start as his second disappointment of the time span 1971 to 1990. He stated that Head Start "did many good deeds for the parents involved, for the eleven-million-plus children it served, and especially its many handicapped preschool youngsters. . . . In terms of its potential, I think of Head Start as an under-achiever. . . . It entered the timespan and left it with too few programs reaching too few children . . . with hard-working but badly paid staff and high turnover . . . with inadequate staff training and supervision."[118] Hymes also reported that in 1971 Head Start undertook an active recruitment effort to fill at least ten percent of its spaces, nationwide, with children who required special education. This positive reaching out to young children with special needs puts new demands on Head Start teacher training.[119]

PROJECT FOLLOW-THROUGH

Operation Keep Moving, described in a speech by Shriver before the Great Cities Research Council in Milwaukee on November 18, 1966, marked the beginning of Project Follow-Through. He was concerned about reports that gains made by Head Start children were nullified when they entered the elementary school. Therefore, the alleged fade-out of Head Start effects would be countered by an intervention program for Head Start graduates from kindergarten through the third grade of elementary school. As a "programmatic mirror of Head Start, extended to children in the early grades of elementary school,"[120] Follow-Through was initially designed to include similar comprehensive delivery of health, social service, mental health, nutrition and other support services, and an emphasis on parent involvement. It was hoped that this program would make permanent Head Start children's capacity to cope more effectively with their learning programs or with the world in general. It had become blatantly apparent after Head Start was in existence for a year or so that if the gains were to be maintained, continuity had to be established between the preschool years and later schooling.[121]

Planning for Follow-Through began prior to its congressional mandate. OEO delegated Follow-Through to the U.S. Office of Education (USOE) almost immediately after it began. President Johnson urged Congress to support Follow-Through on several occasions, and in February 1967, he specifically asked for legislation for its implementation. Congress amended the Educational Opportunity Act in December 1967, establishing Project Follow-Through. USOE delegated the program to its Department of Compensatory Education. In March 1967, USOE and OEO formed the National Follow-Through Advisory Committee, and appointed Dr. Gordon Klopf as its chair. The goal was to continue the compensatory education effort by assisting children in maintaining gains in intellectual development and academic achievement through grade three, as well as building on the social gains made by children in Head Start or similar preschool programs.[122] Follow-Through continued until June 30, 1996, but at the end it had become a tiny experiment in planned curriculum variation.[123]

The pilot program of Follow-Through began in the fall of 1967 in forty school districts nationwide, with fifteen million dollars of Head Start funds. The new director, Robert Egbert, suggested an experimental design involving planned variation and sponsored models. The design called for the concurrent implementation and subsequent evaluation of differing educational approaches provided by sponsors—individuals, educational laboratories, universities, and private corporations. Sponsors bore the responsibility for model development, specification, and implementation.[124] Models implemented during this phase of Project Follow-Through included the Direct Instruction model of Carl Bereiter, Siegfried Engelmann, and Wesley Becker; the Behavior Analysis model of Donald Bushell, Jr.; the Bank Street developmental-interaction approach; the High/Scope model of David P. Weikart; the Responsive model of Glen P. Nimnicht; the Montessori method; the Tucson Early Education model; and the Florida Parent-Education model developed by Ira J. Gordon.

The USOE was unconvinced of the value of Follow-Through and mandated that 80 percent of the money fund direct services and 20 percent fund program improvement. In 1983, Follow-Through was merged with the administration of Chapter I of Title I of the ESEA of 1965. The reduction in size led to a failure to redefine the program, so what was to have been a temporary model of planned variation and sponsorship became the foundation of the program's organization throughout its life.

Although the severe cuts in funding drastically reduced the comprehensive services provided, parent involvement has always been a key element of Follow-Through. Parent Advisory Councils, consisting of at least 50 percent low-income parents, were involved in planning, decision making, and operational activities. Parent Advisory Councils have had a deciding vote in the initial selection of the sponsored model for their school, and in some program sites they maintained discretionary powers within their school district.[125]

The sponsored model approach, the distinguishing organizational component of Follow-Through, has had a major impact as an organizational strategy. "Program implementation brought together sponsors, school personnel, and parents in a way not seen in any other Federally funded early education program."[126]

The planned variation model utilized in Project Follow-Through was implemented in Head Start with the funding of the *Head Start Planned Variation Study* (HSPV) by the Office of Child Development in 1969. This was a large-scale attempt by OCD to compare the effects of eleven different curricular models within a number of different sites around the country. The developers of the various models were responsible for the training of teachers and the implementation of their programs at the various sites. About one-half of the experimental group had a Follow-Through program in the years following the Head Start experience, and one-half did not.[127, 128]

Three other studies of Head Start curriculum development looked at the extent to which the teacher or the child initiated or responded to approaches. It was found that: "Most well-developed models apparently have a general effect that is superior to the gains to be expected under conditions of no preschool. . . . With no differences among models."[129] Evans cites the following factors that impacted on successful model implementation:

1. Adequate facilities and resource materials.
2. Stable and well-organized model staffs (it was found that teacher competence and morale are the most critical aspects of any meaningful service delivery).
3. Satisfaction with the consultant services of model sponsors.
4. Belief in the value of the model content.[130]

Evaluations of the impact of the different program emphases and the extent to which the models were actually implemented in the classroom looked at the congruity between a written curriculum and the observable evidence of its execution by staff. It was found that teachers in all three model categories (pre-academic, cognitive discovery, and discovery approaches) progressed over time toward more realistic or accurate implementation of their model.[131]

Follow-Through was designed to counter the fade-out of the gains made by Head Start children; however, until the implementation of specific Transition Grant Programs, little was done to coordinate the two programs beyond mandating that 60 percent of the enrollment in Follow-Through must come from Head Start or similar programs.[132]

Bettye Caldwell has written that although Follow-Through was designed to create an educational environment that sustains gains previously made in an early childhood education program, evaluations of Follow-Through could not provide the necessary evidence. This was because not all children enrolled in a given Head Start program move ahead to the same elementary school, some of the children in a Follow-Through classroom had attended Head Start and some had not, and still other children might have participated in one of the other early childhood education programs available in a community. Therefore, the majority of evaluation studies of Follow-Through are not useful for determining whether it facilitates a smooth transition from early childhood into elementary-level programs.[133]

In 1974, when it became clear that the Follow-Through program would remain a planned variation experiment, Project Developmental Continuity (PDC) was launched to coordinate the educational and developmental approaches of Head Start and the public schools. Its objective was the development of a sequenced and continuous educational program for children from Head Start through the early primary years. Special emphasis was placed by PDC on maintaining parent involvement and on the needs of handicapped and bilingual children. Specific provision was made for Indian and Spanish-speaking children to have individualized language instruction. Input was solicited from the USOE and State Departments of Education on the site selection process. The demonstration effort was designed to develop models that could be implemented on a wide scale in nondemonstration communities. The Education Commission of the States was engaged in a related effort in some of the states where PDC models were located.[134]

Two models of PDC programs were implemented. The Preschool Linkage Model coordinated the educational and developmental approaches of Head Start and the schools. The teaching staff of both agencies agreed on an educational philosophy and approach, and provided a continuous curriculum. Parent involvement was encouraged through the Linkage Advisory Council. The second model, called the Early Childhood School, created a new institution in which Head Start was merged with an elementary school. A sequential and developmentally appropriate curriculum was planned and implemented for children ages four through eight who attended the same physical facility. Parents and staff reached mutual agreement regarding the children's curriculum.[135] "Results of the PDC effort indicated that Head Start/public school collaboration was a challenge in most of the communities, in spite of the additional resources provided by the project."[136]

The Augustus F. Hawkins Human Services Reauthorization Act of 1990 provided funding for a new Head Start transition project, which stipulated a school support team of Family Service Coordinators to help children in the early elementary years and their families access a broad range of services.[137]

The Act fostered closer links with Project Follow-Through. The Transition Project legislation sponsored by Senator Edward M. Kennedy authorized its operation between 1991 and June 30, 1997.[138] The Head Start Transition Project included as central components: coordination and joint planning for developmental continuity between the Head Start and elementary school programs; continuation of comprehensive support services during the elementary school years; and extensive parent involvement in elementary education.

The Transition Project was designed to work in the following way: When each Head Start child enters kindergarten, the child's parent, Head Start teacher, and kindergarten teacher meet to discuss the child's transition. Both Head Start and the school work with community agencies to ensure that comprehensive health and social services are available to the children and their families throughout the primary grades.[139] The Transition Project fulfilled many of the recommendations made by the Silver Ribbon Panel (May 18, 1990) to strengthen Head Start.[140]

At the Federal executive level, the formation of a joint Department of Education/Department of Health and Human Services (DOE/DHHS) Head Start/Compensatory Education Task Force stimulated work on transitions within the Office of Educational Research and Improvement (OERI) centers. ACYF encouraged Head Start grantees to form links with school systems. The Family Support Administration and ACYF fostered collaboration between Head Start and the JOBS program.[141]

PARENT AND CHILD CENTERS

Thirty-three Parent and Child Centers (PCCs) were opened in 1967 to offer supportive services and parent education to families and children from birth to age three. Twenty-two of the centers were urban and eleven were rural. The PCCs were initiated as a result of the recommendations of the 1966 DHEW Task Force on Early Childhood Development and a special White House Task Force on Early Childhood. In contrast to the center-based Head Start program, the PCC was considered to be *preventive*. The program was intended to reach children very early in life, during the gestation period. The belief that "the protection of young children from physiological trauma would lead to a reduction in developmental disturbances added to the Head Start momentum for early intervention and the Head Start concern for physical, as well as social, well-being for poor children."[142] It was felt that by the time the disadvantaged child reached the age of three, it was too late to overcome the intellectual and emotional damage inflicted by poverty, The actual design of each center was left up to the administering agency so as to ensure responsiveness to unique community needs. The essential elements required of each preventive program included comprehensive health care and activity programs for the child, social services to the entire family, parent activities, a program designed to increase the family's participation in the neighborhood and the community, and training programs for professionals and nonprofessionals.[143]

The PCC programs reached out to the geographically isolated poor in rural communities and the socially isolated in urban centers. The programs have predominantly served blacks, rural whites, Mexican-Americans, and American Indians. The overall objective of the PCC is the developmental progress of the child and prevention of developmental deficits. The intellectual stimulation of the child received the most emphasis, and the health component received very little attention.[144] Among the reasons cited for the limited health services are budgetary constraints and the fact that certain planners believed that cognitive development is more important than social-emotional or physical growth and development. The total number of Parent Child Centers had grown from 36 in 1989 to 106 in 1996. The Reauthorization Act of 1994 required that at least one PCC be established in each state to serve the needs of children under the age of three.

Extensions of the Parent Child Center Mandate

In 1973, seven PCCs were funded to provide child advocacy within their communities to promote better services for all children. According to Zigler and Styfco, the PCCs were the first program in the nation to combine elements of child advocacy, community orientation, and family support.

THE PARENT AND CHILD DEVELOPMENT CENTERS

The Parent and Child Development Centers (PCDCs), a research and demonstration project begun in 1970, were another outgrowth of the PCCs. Its function was to study infant development and the importance of the parental role in the process. A variety of models were tested, which varied with the perceived needs of the site participants. The PCDCs were "valuable laboratories for the development of sensitive service delivery systems that can be responsive to individual parents and children."[145]

EARLY HEAD START

With the advice and consultation of thirty focus groups composed of professionals in and outside of Head Start, the Reauthorization Act of 1994 developed a new initiative, entitled Early Head Start. An Advisory Committee on Services for Families with Infants and Toddlers was established by HHS Secretary Donna Shalala. The program included such services for at-risk families as prenatal care, nutrition, health care, parenting education, and family support. Early Head Start was based on research which concluded that the years from conception to age three are critical in a child's development, and that in order for children to achieve optimal growth and development, the primary entities that affect development (child development, family development, community building, and staff development) must be integrated into a collaborative and supportive network.

Three hundred Early Head Start programs began operation in 1998, based on newly revised Head Start performance standards. There are both center-based and home-based programs, with some programs incorporating elements of both. It is envisioned that staff will work with parents and children on attachment and bonding, and services will be provided to children with special needs and their families. Support services to families include job training and mental health services, as well as empowerment regarding governance of the program and making policy for the program. The foundational principles that have shaped the framework for Early Head Start include high-quality services, promotion of the healthy development and well-being of children, promotion of positive relationships and continuity, parent involvement, inclusion, support for each child's home culture and language, comprehensiveness, flexibility, collaboration with other community organizations, and smooth transition into Head Start or other preschool programs.[146]

Head Start for Children of Migrants

Beginning in 1969, Head Start set up programs for the children of migrant workers. According to Valentine, these children constitute the most educationally deprived group in the country. The migrant Head Start programs operate for very long hours, sometimes from 4:00 A.M. until midnight. Enrollment in the programs is open to infants, toddlers, and three- to five-year-olds. In 1979, Valentine wrote that Migrant Head Start was serving only 2 percent of the eligible population in twenty-one states. The Migrant Head Start programs are bilingual and bicultural, to fit the needs of the children of color and non-English speaking children who constitute their clientele. Health, education, and nutrition specialists follow the children as their parents follow the crops, setting up centers wherever families stop to work. The records of the children follow them wherever the families go. "The Migrant Head Start centers perform an important and useful function for these children and families, who are isolated from other existing programs for many reasons."[147]

The East Coast Migrant Head Start Project (ECMHSP) establishes, provides, and promotes continuity of Head Start services to migrant children and the families along the East Coast of the United States. It challenges parents to become more involved with their own child's development and in program decision making. In 1997, ECMHSP was serving 7,600 migrant infants, toddlers, and preschoolers in eighty-six centers in twelve states. The East Coast Migrant Head Start Project exemplifies the support services that Head Start provides to families who migrate to earn a living.[148]

The Office of Special Field Projects: Indian Head Start

The Office of Special Field Projects of OEO was responsible for administration of Head Start programs on sixty-five Federal Indian Reservations, in the commonwealth of Puerto Rico, on the U.S. Virgin Islands and Guam, and in the U.S. Trust Territory of the Pacific Islands.[149] According to Small, "each [of the Special Field sites] has a relationship with the United States government that might be termed 'colonial.'"[150] Several of these sites are administered by the U.S. Department of the Interior. Each site is removed from the dominant culture by distance or isolation. When Head Start began, conditions of poverty in the Special Field sites were different and more extreme than those in the rest of the United States. "Most Federal Indian Reservations, on the basis of poverty statistics, were excluded from the 10 percent nonfederal share requirement in applying for funds, a requirement in all communities applying for Head Start funds except the poorest of the poor."[151] Federal Indian Reservations vary a great deal in size, geography, culture, language, and customs. Although some reservations are places of great natural beauty, many are on the worst, most arid land in the country. Head Start's emphasis on parent participation and governance empowered the parents of Indian Head Start children. "The importance of parental involvement in the education of the young of a culture different from the dominant one is vital. If the adults of a community are trying to transmit their traditional culture from one generation to the next, they must participate in the education of their children. Head Start provided a framework and a springboard for such involvement."[152]

Local residents were often employed as assistants in Head Start classrooms. They were helpful as a bridge between the home and the Head Start classroom, as well as providing a visible model of adults in the classroom who represented the same background as the children. Through participation on the Policy Advisory Committees, parents became policy makers. In one instance, parental involvement led to the founding of the jointly funded Rough Rock Demonstration School on the Navajo Reservation. Under the auspices of both OEO and the Bureau of Indian Affairs, it included aspects of Indian and white cultures in the curriculum.[153] The inclusiveness and broad range of Head Start program standards and components encouraged Indian communities to develop curricula that reflected the needs of their population. This encouraged the preservation of cultural values in the Head Start classroom and program. In late 1965, an *Indian Teacher-Aide Handbook* was developed by Caryl and Joseph Steere and Patricia and Albert Kukulski of Arizona State University. This handbook included instructions on how to introduce Indian family relationships to non-Indian teachers.[154]

For most of the Indian Head Start programs, the grantee was the Indian Tribal Council, the elected governing body of the tribe. This was a major change from educational programs administered through the Bureau of Indian Affairs. New power and responsibility was invested in the tribal leadership because it was responsible for the quality of the programming and for meeting Federal Head Start standards. In addition, the Indians wanted teachers who were specifically trained in understanding the native culture. A series of research projects has attempted to fulfill this need over the past three decades.

Research has shown that Native American children often fall behind because they do not have the coordinated support of home and school. The major problems have been noted to be differences in communication styles and teachers' lack of knowledge of the home culture, as well as a paucity of quality materials that integrate the culture with the classroom curriculum. During 1992 and 1993, public school and Head Start teachers in Oklahoma participated in a project funded by the Eisenhower Foundation. The objectives were to train teachers, develop culturally relevant math materials, and involve families of the Seminole, Chickasaw, and Choctaw Nation Head Start programs. To facilitate family involvement, training sessions were held at the regular Head Start monthly meetings and at open houses in the elementary school. They were used to develop the concept of families as first teachers.

The activities developed during the project were drawn from traditional Native American creative arts and symbols. Examples are the "ribbon dance," the traditional clan patchwork designs, a bird claw puzzle, use of indigenous leaves, and depiction of indigenous animals in the math materials. Math materials packets were developed for home use, and the Head Start teachers decided to use them in the classroom as well. Sears and Medearis found a great deal of family involvement. Men, women, and children, both old and young, came to the meetings and participated fully in the activities. The traditional stories, finger plays, games, music and dance, and jewelry were well received. Any materials that utilized native language, and puzzles, were quite popular.

Based on suggestions of parents, some of the storybooks were translated into the native languages, and paper dolls representing tribal chiefs were developed. The researchers concluded that "by fostering the interest of families while the child is young, teachers can strengthen the bonds between school and home and help provide young children with a strong experiential background so necessary for 'school' learning most especially in mathematics."[155] According to Small, Head Start "strengthened rather than weakened communities with distinctive cultures. . . . It provided a standard and model for a comprehensive early childhood education program; it provided opportunities, both paid and voluntary, for involvement of parents and other community members in the education of the young . . . ; it provided information, communication, and technical assistance."[156] In the 1990s, several of the Native American Head Start programs designed Web sites that present their mission and program to the public. An example is the Web site of the Chickasaw Nation Head Start program.[157]

Tribal-Way-of-Knowing: Black Feet Tribe, an intergenerational research project of Dorothy Still Smoking, uses case-study design to uncover the "way-of-knowing" specific to the Black Feet tribe. Tribal elders have a tradition of transmitting the tribal language, culture, and lifestyle to the children. Using the wives of recognized tribal elders as interview mediators, the elders were asked for their perceptions of what constitutes the traditional Black Feet knowledge base, and how they believe this knowledge base should be passed on through various forms of formal and informal institutions in the community. This research will be used to help the Head Start program define its role in helping the community address issues related to the cultural threat of the loss of the traditional tribal language.[158]

Native Child develops and produces multicultural curriculum materials for preschools that have a special focus on Native American tribes. Each unit focuses on one tribe, because each culture has its own traditions and religions. On their Web site, Native Child points out that some "parts of the culture are still considered off limits for non-tribal members and fall into the category of misappropriation of traditions and rituals. To help define the line between the two, we use an icon, whenever culturally sensitive material is at hand. Showing respect for Hopi culture means refraining from making Kachina masks . . . or imitating a Kachina dance during circle time. It is culturally sensitive though, to learn songs, games, social dances, or tell tribal stories."[159]

In Alaska Project P/Pride (Parents and Partners Responsibly Involved in Development and Education) is a National Head Start/Public School Transition Demonstration Project. The University of Alaska Anchorage School of Education participates in this project with the Anchorage school district and the Head Start program. Chugiak Children's Services, and the communities of Anchorage, Chugiak, and Eagle River, collaborate in providing funding for in-kind support for the project. This project is designed to support Native American children as they make the transition from Head Start to public school.[160]

A psychologist at one of the conferences on Indian Head Start is quoted as stating that if there were only one thing he hoped the Head Start program would do for the preschool Indian child, it would be to help him feel and be able to say, "I am an Indian and I can." Small says that "this may be an impossible message for Head Start or any other program to give, and it may be an impossible and untrue message until such time as cultural differences are acknowledged and respected in the United States."[161] However, the programs cited earlier exemplify the ways in which the early childhood educators of Head Start–related programs are working with Native American families and tribes to overcome the difficulties faced by their children.

Other Head Start–Related Initiatives

The Family Support Act of 1988 (FSA) (welfare reform legislation) created the Job Opportunities and Basic Skills Training (JOBS) education and employment training program, and the Target Cities Substance Abuse program of the Office for Treatment Improvement (OTI) in the Public Health Service.[162] This legislation may have placed subtle pressure on lawmakers to increase the enrollment capacity of Head Start, because participation in the JOBS program is required for parents on welfare whose children are age three or older. Coordination of AFDC (Aid to Families with Dependent Children) child care with existing early childhood education programs was required. Collaborative planning and service delivery were essential."[163] However, statistics published in 1988 revealed that less than 20 percent of eligible three- to five-year-olds and only 6 percent of eligible migrant children were being served by the program. A number of children who could benefit from early education were instead placed in custodial day care facilities that may or may not have met their needs. For this reason, a new Head Start Family Day Care Project was implemented in 1992 to test the feasibility of delivering Head Start services in child care settings.[164]

The Basic Educational Skills Project of 1978 was founded with fifteen sites. Its goal was to assist children in mastering the preschool "work" of doing and experiencing, rather than implementing in Head Start what children do in first and second grade. This project emphasized that preschool children learn best by making use of concrete visual approaches. The initiators stressed that the project could not be a "watered-down of the elementary school curriculum."[165]

Head Start had the responsibility for administering the 1988 Comprehensive Child Development Act (P.L. 100-297). This five-year demonstration program provided intensive, comprehensive support services to children from birth to entrance into elementary school. The Act also assisted parents and other household members in locating training and employment opportunities, in securing adequate health care, nutrition assistance, and housing. Thirty-four community-based organizations conducted these demonstration projects.

Another demonstration project is the Family Service Centers. Sixty-six Head Start grantees were awarded funds to demonstrate ways that Head Start programs can work with other community agencies and organizations to effectively deal with the problems of substance abuse, illiteracy, and unemployment among Head Start families. The projects are designed to improve the literacy of both parents and other adults in Head Start families and to increase the employability of Head Start parents.[166]

Home Start

The Home Start project for children aged three to five was begun in March 1972. Sixteen demonstration projects were funded for three and a half years, to provide Head Start services to children and families in their homes. Home-based services allowed isolated families, particularly in rural areas, to receive Head Start's educational, health, and social services. The key to the operation of Home Start programs was the "home visitor," usually a community resident who had undergone some training in the principles of child development and the goals of Head Start. Home Start's guiding philosophy was that parents are the first and major educators of their children. They were encouraged to work with their children in various learning situations. The rationales for the Home Start program included the fact that, in a center-based program, there was no way to ensure that learning would be carried back into the home. In many communities throughout the country, a center-based program was not feasible because of distance or other factors. A third rationale for the Home Start program was: learning that took place in the home could be diffused to siblings of the "target child." The program guidelines for Home Start required the following components: nutrition counseling and education, health services, social and psychological services, parent and child education, and counseling regarding utilization of community resources.

The Home Start demonstration programs were dismantled in July 1975, but six Head Start Training Centers (HSTC) were established to disseminate the home-based programs to centers. Head Start centers that wanted to incorporate a "home-based option" into their ongoing activities were encouraged to incorporate home visitor programs into their comprehensive services package. In 1989, more than five hundred Head Start programs included some home-based services.[167, 168]

The Child and Family Resource Program (CFRP)

In 1973, eleven Child and Family Resource Programs were funded as part of the research and development effort of OCD. The primary goal of the CFRP was to provide and integrate the delivery of comprehensive services to families and children on an individualized basis, throughout early childhood. Families rather than children were enrolled in the CFRPs. Parents and children from birth to age eight were offered a variety of support services from which the family could choose according to their needs. A family advocate worked with each family to provide or make available prenatal care, developmental programs, pediatric care, programs to facilitate a smooth transition from preschool to elementary school, and general support services. A family needs assessment was made for each family in the program, and staff efforts were geared toward coordinating the services necessary to meet these needs. Preventive, treatment, and rehabilitative services were provided for each individual. Developmental and family support services were provided for adults and children. The CFRP reflected the 1970s understanding that no one period of life nor kind of service is critical in and of itself. All periods and developmental needs merit equal attention. The multifaceted nature and long-term commitment of the CFRPs helped to move the social sciences toward the principle of developmental continuity. Although the program was terminated by President Reagan's administration in 1983, in the 1990s the concept was partially resurrected in the form of the Comprehensive Child Development Program, serving families with children ages birth to five years.[169]

Head Start in the 1970s

In 1969, the Head Start program was transferred from OEO to OCD. President Richard M. Nixon set up OCD as a forced merger of the Children's Bureau, which had been founded in 1912, and the CAPs that had been housed at OEO. According to Zigler, "the Children's Bureau staff, a seasoned group that had changed very little since the Bureau's formation . . . and Community Action Program activists who had been in charge of Head Start at OEO were" forced to work together.[170]

The main responsibilities of OCD were: to administer social action programs for children, such as Head Start and child care, and in particular to improve the quality of Head Start; to begin coordinating the children's programs across agency lines, eliminating duplication (a goal that was popular with OMB [the Office of Management and Budget]); and to serve as an advocate for children in the Capital.[171] In 1977, OCD became the Agency for Children, Youth and Families (ACYF). With the administrative shift from HEW to the Department of Health and Human Services (DHSS), Head Start became a program within ACYF.[172]

Head Start in the 1980s and 1990s

The 1980s was a period of consolidation for Head Start. There was a slow, steady rise in enrollment. Although Head Start was included in President Reagan's 1981 "social safety net" (as one of seven programs), it was hurt by the erosion of other community services. Services in health, nutrition, and mental health on which it relied did not have budgetary or administrative support. Head Start also lost six thousand CETA (Comprehensive Employment and Training Act) workers who were dismissed when the administration ended the Act. A draft paper within ACYF recommended ending the parent and child centers to concentrate on the three- to five-year-old age range. However, Clarence Hodges, the ACYF Commissioner, backed away from most of the controversial suggested changes in the draft papers.[173] "Services failed to keep pace with the dramatic increases in the numbers of children in poverty during the 1980s."[174]

The Silver Ribbon Panel Report *Head Start: The Nation's Pride, A Nation's Challenge* was released on May 18, 1990. The major recommendations of the report included a preference for program quality over expansion. The report suggested that quality programs should be provided to all eligible three- to five-year-olds by 1994 and those less than age three by the year 2000. It stated that full-day services should be available for those needing them. It suggested that stronger linkages should be developed with other services in the early childhood community, because Head Start calls itself a child development program, which makes it more comprehensive than an educational effort.[175]

In 1993, Collins addressed the serious weakness in the staffing of the social services component, stating that some of the social services staff face the strain of caseloads of up to two hundred families.[176] Although the performance standards state that this component should identify the needs of families and work with other community agencies to develop programs to meet those needs, the majority of Head Start programs have been unable to achieve a minimal level of compliance. He points out that the model family needs assessment used by three-quarters of Head Start programs to identify social service needs does not take into account the worsening social and economic conditions, and the more severely at-risk families served in the 1990s.

Collins emphasized the development of a two-generation program strategy and research agenda for Head Start. The five key principles included: building on the existing strengths of the Head Start program; responding to child and family needs in a holistic fashion; formalizing collaboration with other federal, state, and local funding sources; developing a kit of program management tools to facilitate family support; and setting realistic goals and objectives, with accompanying systematic assessments.[177]

Contributions of Head Start and a Look Toward the Future

In 1975, Ellis Evans stated that Head Start had made several contributions, including: reintroducing strong parental involvement and family life education, fomenting scrutiny of the learning patterns and instructional problems of children who had in the past been viewed as bad risks or incapable of academic progress, and revolutionizing the design of learning materials suitable

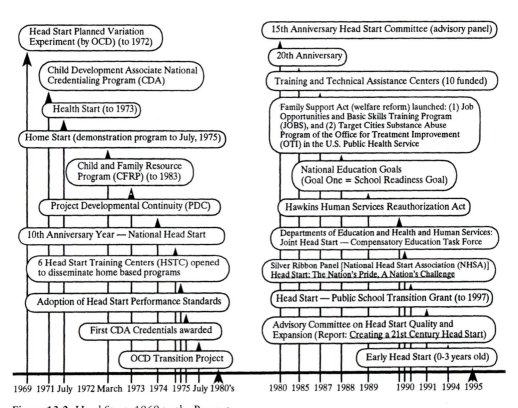

Figure 13.2 Head Start: 1969 to the Present.

for children from varied social backgrounds. Head Start facilitated the earlier identification of children whose problems or mental and physical health might otherwise have gone unnoticed or unattended. New careers for professional and paraprofessional personnel, including the economically disadvantaged, were created. The poor were given a greater involvement in decision making about institutional policies that affected them. Community institutions had therefore changed either directly or indirectly as a result of Head Start practices or the presence of the project in a given locale.[178]

Head Start has never been a program to rest on its laurels. In September 1990, the Advisory Panel presented its report, *Head Start Research and Evaluation: A Blueprint for the Future: Recommendations of the Advisory Panel for the Head Start Evaluation Design Project*. Among the report's recommendations were that "program variation must be explored while searching for explanations of differential outcomes, and that Head Start research and evaluation studies can be greatly enhanced by building on the existing strengths of programs and program staffs." The report recommended that studies be done to identify the quality ingredient in existing Head Start programs, and special subpopulations within Head Start. It also recommended that an archive of significant Head Start data be established.[179]

In June 1993, Secretary Shalala formed the Advisory Committee on Head Start Quality and Expansion to review the program and make recommendations for improvements and expansion. Its report, published in early 1994, found that, "after a period of rapid expansion, Head Start can be proud of many successes yet still needs to address existing quality problems and to be refocused to meet the challenges of a new age.[180] The crisis of a national deficit provided a strong incentive for improving the program, and unwritten requirements for accountability and cost-effectiveness. The substantial funds being granted to Head Start carry expectations that the money will be well spent.[181]

The Advisory Committee found that Head Start has been successful in improving the lives of many low-income children and their families and serving as a national laboratory for early childhood and family support. It found that most Head Start programs provide quality services; however, the quality of programs is uneven across the country. They found that there is a continuing need by a large segment of the eligible population who are not receiving Head Start services, and that in many communities and states Head Start, the public schools, and other early childhood programs and providers operate in isolation from one another. The Committee recommended that "the Head Start of the 21st century

- Ensures quality and strives to attain excellence in every local program;
- Responds flexibly to the needs of today's children and families, including those currently unserved; and
- Forges new partnerships at the community, state, and federal levels, renewing and recrafting these partnerships to fit the changes in families, communities, and state and national policy."[182]

In 1995, Head Start joined efforts throughout the Federal government to develop performance measures to promote accountability through the assessment of program quality and outcomes. The Head Start Program Performance Measures Initiative is a response to a specific legislative mandate, broader public emphasis on accountability, and the general movement toward results-oriented evaluation.

Throughout its more-than-thirty-year history, Head Start has focused on the quality of services provided and has assessed quality through "process" indicators, such as the number of teachers with early childhood education degrees or CDA credentials. These indicators have been measured primarily through compliance with the Head Start Program Performance Standards using the On-Site Program Review Instrument (OSPRI). It has also monitored programs' accomplishments with the annual collection of program-level data through the Programs Information Report (PIR) and through cost data submitted as part of the grant application process. The Head Start performance Standards define program activities, while performance measures define program results.[183, 184]

In recent years, new assessment instruments have been developed. ACYF awarded five-year grants to four Quality Research Centers. Each Center was required to team with at least one Head Start program that agreed to participate as a research partner throughout the course of the project. Performance measures were developed for each of the four domains of the Head Start program, health, education, partnerships with families, and program management and are currently being field tested.[185]

In 1996, Sherlie S. Svestka, an education advisor in the Federal Interagency Early Childhood Research Working Group of OERI, stated in the *International Journal of Early Childhood,* that "Head Start has increased national awareness of the needs of children, and has therefore helped to mobilise the nation to action on their behalf."[186]

Federal Legislation in the 1970s and Beyond

The two major Federal initiatives of the 1970s that impact present-day early childhood education are the Social Security Act of 1974 and the legislation addressing the special needs of children. Among the landmark measures were the ESEA, the Education for All Handicapped Act of 1975 (P.L. 94-142), P.L. 99-457, and IDEA (P.L. 101-476) of 1990.

TITLE XX OF THE SOCIAL SECURITY ACT OF 1974

In 1974, Congress authorized Title XX of the Social Security Act as a block grant to fund and administer what had been separate adult and child welfare programs. OMB was given the authority to create substate planning districts to coordinate all the federal human service funds that went to the states. The administration published a revised version of OMB Circular A-95, explaining the opportunity for states to assume a greater role in the planning of federally funded programs through these districts. At the beginning of the Jimmy Carter presidency, OMB wanted to place Head Start under Circular A-95. Caspar Weinberger, Secretary of HEW, became an unexpected supporter of Head Start, agreeing that the Circular did not apply to this program. He wanted to be assured that the money would go where it was intended, for Head Start rather than vocational education or some other activity.[187]

The 1974 Social Services Amendments prohibited the use Federal funds by centers that did not conform to the requirements of the Federal Panel on Early Childhood. The EOA had authorized the official responsible for Head Start and the Secretary of HEW to establish a common set of program standards and regulations and to provide mechanisms for implementing these standards at state and local levels.[188] Thus Federal funds were allocated with conditions and limitations attached to them. The Federal Panel created requirements affecting such things as adult-child ratios. The ratio for children three and four years of age was five children to one adult. For children between four and six years of age, the ratio was seven to one. The bill created an uproar because centers that did not meet the mandated ratios could not accept children of parents who used Federal funds to pay for center-based care. Furthermore, the centers could not obtain funds under the Federal Lunch Program. Because of protests and opposition, Congress suspended these adult-child ratios in 1976, and in 1978 requested an evaluation of the feasibility of the requirements.

Child care centers may receive Federal funds if they serve low-income families who are eligible for cash assistance under Title XX. The state receives support funds based on the proportion of the population that is eligible for Title XX under one of the following categories of income maintenance, Supplemental Security Income (SSI), income eligibility, and group eligibility.[189] Although Head Start made provisions for the enrollment of 10 percent nonpoor children, and some Title XX efforts use a voucher mechanism, federally subsidized services remained the province of the poor, while the middle- and upper-income children were enrolled in separate programs. Clearly federal efforts altered *who* paid but not *how* or *where* rich and poor children were served.[190]

In 1980, the Social Security Act was renamed the Social Services Block Grant (SSBG). Its level of funding has changed very little since its inception, and there are no requirements for state matching funds. Some states require local matching funds from their subdistricts.[191] SSBG provides funding to states for a broad array of services based on two fundamental principles: that state and local governments and communities are best able to determine the needs of the individuals to help them achieve self-sufficiency; and that social and economic needs are interrelated and must be met simultaneously.[192] SSBG funds granted directly to states and territories are used to prevent, reduce, or eliminate dependency and to prevent neglect, abuse, or exploitation of children and adults.

Within the specific limitations in the law, each of the states has the flexibility to determine which services will be provided, who is eligible to receive those services, and how funds will be distributed among the various services within the state. State and/or local Title XX agencies may provide the services directly or purchase them from qualified agencies and individuals. An analysis of the most recent data showed that of the top ten services offered by states under SSBG grants, number one was child day care services, which are offered by forty-seven of the fifty states.[193]

A review of the *Children's Defense Budgets* for the fiscal years 1985–1998 highlights problems with federal funding for child care. At the same time that Title XX spending effectively has been halved, the number of children living in poverty even though their parents are working has increased substantially.[194]

Low-income working parents have had to choose between moving their children to less supportive child care arrangements so that they can continue working or leaving their jobs so that someone is home to take care of the children. States are cutting back on the quality of child care provided, reducing funds for training child care workers, lowering standards for Title XX child care programs, and cutting back on the number of child care staff. Low reimbursement rates make many providers unwilling to care for Title XX–funded children, adding to already lengthy waiting lists.

The Reagan administration Block Grant of 1981 eliminated funds and added additional responsibilities to the Title XX Social Services Block Grant.[195] It ended the Work Incentive (WIN) program, which provided child care for low-income parents who are in work and training programs, and cut the child care food program.[196]

The Federal and State Action Agenda proposed by the Children's Defense Fund (CDF) in 1989 asked the Congress to pass the Act for Better Child Care (ABC), a comprehensive legislative package that would lay the foundation for a national system of safe and affordable child care by bringing the federal government into an active child care partnership with state and local governments as well as the private sector.[197] Only one in five eligible children participated in Head Start programs, while there was no major federal child care program designed explicitly to help families pay for child care. Nor was there a program to assist the states in improving the quality and expanding the supply of child care.[198] Title XX funds are also used by states to support many other child welfare and social service programs; therefore, only a portion of the total federal appropriation is actually spent on child care.

ABC was not passed. Zigler and Gilman reported that P.L. 101-508, the Child Care and Development Block Grant of 1990, was authorized at the level of $750 million for its first year and $825 million in 1992. They compare this with the initial funding of the 1971 Comprehensive Child Development Act, $2 billion. Seventy-five percent of the Block Grant was set aside for child care vouchers to assist families whose incomes are below 75 percent of the state median. The remainder of the funds was set aside for specific programs and could be used for quality improvement and staff wage subsidies. The Block Grant included an increased Earned Income Tax Credit for low-income working parents. However, the credit was nonrefundable, which meant that working-class families, with lower tax liability and fewer available funds with which to purchase child care, benefited least.[199]

While the 1992 *Children's Defense Budget* lauded major progress in child care, with the passage of the nation's first comprehensive child care legislation, there were still problems. CDF listed the following federal sources of child care funding in 1992: Head Start, the Child Care and Development Block Grant, the "At-Risk" Child Care Program, the Family Support Act Child Care programs (FSA), the Social Services Block Grant, the Dependent Care Block Grant, and the Dependent Care Tax Credit.[200]

In 1994, the Clinton administration pledged to work toward fully funding Head Start by 1999 so that all eligible children had an opportunity to participate. Congress appropriated an increase of $550 million for Head Start, and permitted programs to use funds for full-day services while continuing to develop links with the larger child care community. Child Care Block Grant money was used to improve licensing and monitoring activities that safeguard the health and safety of children in child care, to develop a resource and referral network, to invest money in training for child care providers working with children from birth to age five, and to fund new infant care programs.[201]

Persistent child care problems included: unsafe child care, the necessity for children to move frequently from one type of care arrangement to another, lengthy waiting lists for child care assistance, a shortage of affordable before- and after-school child care programs for poor and low-income families, continuing low wages for child care staff, inadequate staff training, and the fact that many children do not receive the intellectual stimulation they need to get ready for school.

States used the Social Services Block Grant funding to cover their highest priorities, such as children who are at risk for neglect or abuse, those who have special needs (disabilities), or those whose parents are working with incomes just above AFDC, including farm worker families. Only some of the states used Block Grant funds to provide services to those children of parents who are employed and receiving partial AFDC, in training and receiving AFDC, or had been on AFDC during the past year.[202] Some states shifted funds previously used for child care assistance for working families to cover the state match required for federal child care funds for families receiving AFDC.[203]

In January 1998, following the October 1997 White House Conference on Child Care, President Bill Clinton announced a new Child Care Initiative. It proposed to increase funding for the Child Care and Development Block Grant by $7.5 billion and Head Start funding by $3.4 billion over a five-year period. The proposal included assistance to child care providers for furthering their education, and meeting licensing and accreditation standards. Among other provisions, a new Early Learning Fund would provide $3 billion in formula grants to states over a five-year period. Only history will tell how much these initiatives will mean to children, after they are reviewed by Congress.[204]

SPECIAL EDUCATION

The first documented efforts to work with children who have special needs took place in the early 1800s. Jean-Marc Itard observed and recorded the progress of the "wild boy of Aveyron" and became one of the first to demonstrate attempts at understanding the child as well as developing unique teaching techniques. His student, Edouard Seguin, came to the United States and founded the American Association on Mental Deficiency. Thomas Hopkins Gallaudet began the first residential school for deaf children, the Asylum for the Education and Instruction of the Deaf and Dumb, in 1817. During the 1830s, Samuel Howe opened the New England Asylum for the Blind in Boston. These were the first schools in the United States that addressed specific handicapping conditions. In the early 1900s, Dr. Maria Montessori built upon their foundational discoveries in her work with mentally retarded children.

Alfred Binet's work in France, in the early 1900s, was designed to identify children with disabilities. Binet was commissioned to develop a test to determine which children could succeed in the public schools and which ones needed special attention. A major consideration in France at that time was the retention of special children in regular classrooms, something that American schools are dealing with currently. The French "sought to create a method of identification that would avoid the problem of prejudice. Imagine the chagrin of the French commissioners if they could witness the need for legal trials to reduce the labeling and discrimination against children with disabilities today!"[205]

In the 1920s, the United States had public and private residential schools that served separate groups of handicapped children, the blind, deaf, retarded, and epileptic, among others.[206] At that time, some local school systems began separate classes for those with a single handicap. The multiply handicapped and severely retarded continued to be sent to institutions. Bettye Caldwell has characterized the period in the United States before the 1950s as one of "forget and hide," the 1950s and 1960s as a time to "screen and segregate," and the 1970s as a time to "identify and help."[207] What the pioneers of the early 1900s had in common were general strategies that are still found highly effective today for work with students who have disabilities. Among the techniques were: individualized instruction, reinforcement, life-skills training (teaching a student skills needed to work and live independently), and sequencing of educational tasks from basic to complex.[208]

In many public schools before the 1960s, "children who were regarded as 'special' were not educated. . . . A child who was not considered 'ready' for kindergarten was sent home and allowed to wait another year to mature."[209] Before 1965, programs for the handicapped were generally designed for children who had reached the age for compulsory school attendance, six or seven years of age. However, research has shown that for some children there is a greater possibility of overcoming educational deficits if these are addressed before the kindergarten years. With the advent of Head Start, in the 1960s, the United States began to direct some attention to preschool handicapped children and their families.

Until the last half of the twentieth century, education for exceptional children was primarily a local and state concern. The federal government made few specific commitments to children with special needs, because education was under the purview of the states. It was not until 1930 that the federal government established a Section on Exceptional Children and Youth in the Office of Education of DHEW, and supported programs for exceptional children in a limited way.[210]

Litigation supporting rights for the disabled has developed from a civil rights base.[211] Beginning with *Brown versus Board of Education* (1954), which stated that children cannot be segregated in public schooling solely on the basis of race, numerous court cases had a direct impact on changing the direction of service delivery. The courts worked to "avoid overclassifying minority students as having disabilities."[212] The result of these civil rights lawsuits was a number of federal laws that affected services for individuals, particularly children with disabilities. The earliest of these laws, P.L. 85-926 (1958), provided grants to states and universities to encourage training of teachers for children with cognitive disabilities, and those with handicapping conditions.

The year 1965 was notable, with the passage of the Elementary and Secondary Education Act (ESEA) (P.L. 89-10) and the initiation of the Head Start program. The ESEA and its amendments (P.L. 89-313, P.L. 90-247, and P.L. 91-230) made available to schools large amounts of money with which to serve educationally disadvantaged and disabled children between the ages of three and twenty-one years. The ESEA created the Bureau of Education for the Handicapped, funded research and demonstration projects to improve special education, provided assistance for local education agencies in state-operated and state-supported private day and residential schools, provided regional resource centers for the improvement of education of children with handicaps, and consolidated all of the previous enactments in 1969.

P.L. 90-538, the Handicapped Children's Early Education Assistance Act of 1968, was the first federal legislation to specifically recognize the importance of early education. It provided grants for the development and implementation of experimental programs in early education for children with handicaps from birth to age six. The Handicapped Children's Early Education Program (HCEEP) was established to administer and to provide technical support for three-year demonstration programs, called First Chance projects (through the Technical Assistance and Development System [TADS]). The system, headquartered at the University of North Carolina at Chapel Hill, is now called the Early Education Program for Children with Disabilities (EEPCD), and continues to fund exemplary model programs. P.L. 90-538 and the action that resulted from it can legitimately be called the birth of early childhood special education.[213]

Head Start initiated pilot projects for mainstreaming of some children with disabilities in the late 1960s and early 1970s. In 1972, Congress mandated (in P.L. 92-424, the Economic Opportunity Amendments) that at least 10 percent of Head Start's national enrollment consist of handicapped children.[214] The pilot projects begun by Ray Collins became the nucleus of the fourteen Resource Access Projects (RAP) funded jointly by Head Start and USOE's Bureau of Education for the Handicapped. The purpose of the RAP projects was to help Head Start programs more effectively serve children with developmental disabilities by providing training and technical assistance to Head Start teachers. In collaboration with community health departments and mental health centers, speech and hearing clinics, developmental disabilities programs, colleges and universities, and private facilities, information, services, and equipment were provided. OCD staff worked with professional associations representing people with disabilities to develop manuals for use in Head Start, which became the Head Start Rainbow Series.

Teams consisting of experts, Head Start teachers, and representatives of various federal agencies combined their talents to produce the eight books. Major national, professional, and voluntary associations, as well as parents, paraprofessionals, and teachers, were asked to critique the materials at various stages of their development.[215] The first chapter in each book discussed mainstreaming, which was generally defined as "helping people with handicaps live, learn, and work in everyday settings where they will have the greatest opportunity to become as independent as possible."[216] A subdefinition for Head Start programs was: the integration of handicapped children and nonhandicapped children in the same classroom by including handicapped children in a regular preschool experience. This gives nonhandicapped children the opportunity to learn and grow by experiencing the strengths and weaknesses of their handicapped friends.[217]

Each book described a specific disability, how it affects learning in three- to five-year-olds, partnerships with parents, and the role of the teacher. A description of the Individualized Education Program (IEP) plan preparation process, inclusion of the child in the classroom, the physical facility, and informational appendices were incorporated into each volume.

The 1974 amendment and expansion of the Education of the Handicapped Act (P.L. 93-380) required states without conflicting laws to establish a plan to identify and serve all children with disabilities from birth to twenty-one years of age. This law formed the foundation for P.L. 94-142, the Education for All Handicapped Children Act of 1975, which established a national policy regarding the education of children with disabilities from ages three to twenty-one. P.L. 94-142 specifies determination of eligibility for services, the design of individual educational and behavioral programs (and development of IEPs), and ensures appropriate implementation. The major impact of this law was the provision for children six years of age and older; however, the provisions have been central in shaping the current structure of early childhood special education in the United States. The law specifies a free public education for all handicapped children between the ages of three and twenty-one. All of the rights and guarantees of the law apply to handicapped children in private as well as public schools. Each governor is required to appoint an advisory panel to advise and assist in the overall implementation of the law's requirements.[218] P.L. 94-142 also provided Preschool Incentive Grants to states that identified preschool children in need of special education services.

It took ten years before P.L. 98-199 amended the Handicapped Children's Early Education Assistance Act of 1968. The new Act provided financial incentives for states to extend service levels down to birth, and funding for the planning of statewide comprehensive services for children with handicaps. P.L. 99-457 amended the Education of the Handicapped Act of 1975 to mandate the provisions of P.L. 94-142 for children aged three to five years. It added a new grant program to assist states in establishing a comprehensive system of early intervention services for infants and toddlers with disabilities and their families. This framework acknowledges the ecological perspective of services and requires an Individualized Family Service Plan (IFSP).

As a result of Bronfenbrenner's 1997 analysis of research on young children, a substantial amount of attention became focused "on the ecologies in which children live and function and led to viewing families as systems within other systems. As a result, major changes occurred in how intervention programs interact with families, and more recently, in how early education classrooms are designed.[219]

P.L. 99-457 requires states to define "developmentally delayed," to perform comprehensive multidisciplinary evaluations, and to state a timetable for making appropriate services available to all eligible children in the state. Among the minimum components required by P.L. 99-457 are a comprehensive "child find and referral system," a public awareness program, a single line of authority in a lead agency established by the governor, a comprehensive system of personnel development, a central directory of services and research and policies and procedures for personnel standards reimbursement of funds, and procedural safeguards. P.L. 99-457 acknowledged the family to be the central focus of service, and it provided for smooth transitions as a family moves from one service or system to another.

The reauthorization of P.L. 94-142, P.L. 101-476 was called the Individuals with Disabilities Education Act (IDEA) of 1990. It reflected a change in philosophy by referring to children as individuals with disabilities instead of labeling them handicapped.[220] The IDEA continues the six key principles of P.L. 94-142: All children with disabilities must be provided a free and appropriate public education. Each student must receive a full individual examination before being placed in a special education program. The tests must be appropriate to the child's cultural and linguistic background. An IEP must be written for every student with a handicap who is receiving special education. As much as possible, handicapped children must be educated in the least restrictive environment. Due process, a set of legal procedures, ensures the fairness of educational decisions and the accountability of both professionals and parents in the making of those decisions. Part 8 of IDEA requires the states to establish eligibility criteria for children with disabilities and get them approved by the proper state source. "That approval often depended on whether the power sources in the state believed that the proposed policies would call on too many state resources."[221]

The financial implications of extending programs to cover at-risk children, and the unwillingness of state decision makers to make that level of investment in the program, caused abandonment of earlier plans. One of the clearest examples of the differences between policy development and policy application is the preparation of the IEP or IFSP, which was to be developed with parent participation, and would give the parents some say in the program for their own child. There were many difficulties in actually implementing this idea at the local level. Reviews of IEPs showed missing data; the goals and objectives appeared poorly written; and there was an unclear link between the goals, program, and assessment. The documents too often were just another set of forms to be filled out and filed. They rarely became an important part of the plan or program for the student.[222]

One of the recommendations for the IDEA reauthorization by Congress was a specification for inclusion of students with disabilities in regular classrooms. In 1994, P.L. 89-313, an amendment to the ESEA, was merged into the IDEA, and no longer exists as a separate law.[223] The Instructional Media for Handicapped Children Act of 1958 has also been merged and became Part F of the IDEA. Personnel training legislation such as P.L. 85-926 of 1958 has now become Part D of the IDEA. The 1995 IDEA revision included P.L. 94-142 of 1975. It is the permanent authorization of the Act for preschool special education students. It includes the identification, planning for, and education of children from birth to age six. Part C, dealing with special centers and projects, Part D, which deals with personnel training, Part E, about research, Part F, about media, and Part G, about technology, are discretionary components of the law. Part H of the IDEA, dealing with early intervention, requires that as of 1994 all states participating in this program provide early intervention services to all eligible infants and toddlers. The definitions of "diagnosed conditions," "developmental delays," and "at-risk status" are left to the states. This is different from Part B, which defines "children with disabilities," and gives the states little leeway.[224, 225]

In 1997, about 600,000 children with disabilities ages three through five and over 150,000 infants and toddlers were receiving early intervention services under Part H of IDEA, in such diverse settings as early intervention classrooms, family day care, their own home, as hospital in-patients, out-patient service facilities, nursery schools, and residential facilities.[226]

The child care community's ability to create inclusive programs has been limited by a lack of knowledge about the funding possibilities available under the IDEA. The Preschool Grants Program provides states with federal funding to assist local school districts in providing a free, appropriate, public education to children with disabilities ages three through five. Part H of IDEA provides funds for early intervention services for infants and toddlers who have disabilities or are at-risk of having disabilities. A child's IEP or IFSP typically covers only part of the day. Other program or funding streams need to be explored for children who require additional hours in child care, Head Start, or other preschool programs. Head Start funds, as well as those from the Child Care and Development Block Grant (CCDBG), can be used for this purpose.[227]

The history of services for young children with disabilities in Head Start is a spotty one. Large numbers of Head Start programs occupy space in older buildings or facilities that require renovation to be accessible for young children who have physical disabilities. Additional resources are needed to pay for the alterations, or to move the program to a more accessible site. The Head Start Performance Standards, which require that mental health professionals be available on a consultative basis, not that they be on the staff of the program, constrain the ability of many Head Start programs to serve children with emotional or mental limitations. The mandate that each Head Start program employ at least one teacher with a CDA does not ensure that Head Start teachers are trained to work with children who have disabilities. In 1995, the ACYF contracted for specialized training of Head Start personnel. These provisions should expand the ability of the Head Start program to carry forward an inclusion mandate.

A corollary piece of federal legislation that was enacted in 1990 was P.L. 101-336. The Americans with Disabilities Act (ADA) reaffirmed the rights of disabled individuals to equal access to facilities and opportunities. Although the Act was aimed at adults, and at attacking discrimination in the workplace, this legislation underscored the necessity for broad-based access to facilities for people with disabilities.

The federal legislation enacted over the past thirty years has provided more support for early childhood special education than at any time in past history. The Federal government has become involved in supporting young children with disabilities and their families. It has done this both through Project Head Start and through other means mandated by legislation such as IDEA. The impact of this early childhood special education legislation is now making itself felt in the elementary and secondary schools.

CHAPTER SUMMARY

This chapter has reviewed Federal government initiatives for young children and their families since 1960. It highlighted the founding, components, and development of Project Head Start. It discussed the professional development initiatives begun by Head Start, including the Child Development Associate Credential. Project Follow-Through and related programs for primary school age children, up to the current Transition Grant, were described. The history of Parent and Child Centers and their evolution into Early Head Start programs was presented. Home Start and other Head Start–related initiatives were viewed from the perspective of their relationship to other Head Start and Federal child care programs. The stories of three professionals whose lives have been connected with many of these programs were told in the chapter.

Service to special populations provided by the Migrant and Indian Head Start Programs and special education programs were discussed in the chapter. The programs for children with special needs were initially funded as a result of Federal legislation. The past three and a half decades have seen an increase in legislation supporting children and families, as described earlier.

The impact of Head Start, a program begun as a "stop gap measure" of the "War on Poverty," with sociological and political overtones, on early childhood education in the United States has been tremendous. As we look to the future of early education in the United States, the research and practical knowledge gained from the Federal programs of the past three and a half decades form a firm foundation on which to stand.

NOTES

1. Polly Greenberg, *The Devil Has Slippery Shoes: A Biased Biography of the Child Development Group of Mississippi: A Story of Maximum Feasible Poor Parent Participation* (Toronto, Ontario, Canada: Collier-Macmillan Canada Ltd., 1969; paperback reprint with new ending material, Washington, DC: Youth Policy Institute, 1990), viii (page citations are to the reprint edition).

2. Hamilton Cravens, *Before Head Start: The Iowa Station and America's Children* (Chapel Hill, NC: University of North Carolina Press, 1993), 220, 228.

3. J. McVickar Hunt, *Intelligence and Experience* (New York: Ronald Press, 1961); and Benjamin Bloom, *Stability and Change in Human Characteristics* (New York: Wiley, 1964).

4. Cravens, *Before Head Start,* 254. Gray and Klaus's research described enrichment that facilitated IQ gains through an "intervention program for young deprived children." Susan W. Gray, Rupert A. Klaus, James O. Miller, and Bettye J. Forrester, *Before First Grade: The Early Training Project for Culturally Disadvantaged Children* (New York: Teachers College Press, 1966), 1. "The overarching goal of the Early Training Project was to affect the progressive retardation often observed in children from lower economic strata as they advance through their years of schooling . . . which was a common occurrence in the 1950s." Susan W. Gray, Barbara K. Ramsey, and Rupert A. Klaus, *From 3 to 20: The Early Training Project* (Baltimore, MD: University Park Press, 1982), 14. See also: Rupert A. Klaus and Susan W. Gray, *The Early Training Project for Culturally Disadvantaged Children: A Report After Five Years* (Chicago: University of Chicago Press for the Society for Research in Child Development, 1968).

5. The theoretical bases for the programs were presented by Martin Deutsch. Martin Deutsch, "Early Social Environment: Its Influence on School Adaptation," 18–19; and idem, "Facilitating Development in the Pre-School Child: Social and Psychological Perspectives," in *Preschool Education Today: New Approaches to Teaching Three-, Four-, and Five-Year Olds,* ed. Fred M. Hechinger (Garden City, NY: Doubleday & Co., Inc., 1966), 86–87.

6. Edward Zigler, Sally J. Styfco, and Elizabeth Gilman, "The National Program for Disadvantaged Preschoolers," in *Head Start and Beyond: A National Plan for Extended*

Childhood Intervention, ed. Edward Zigler and Sally J. Styfco (New Haven, CT: Yale University Press, 1993), 1.

7. John B. Gardner received his doctorate at the Institute of Child Welfare in Berkeley, California, in the 1930s. He was employed at the Carnegie Corporation, a major educational funder, in the 1950s.

8. Cravens, *Before Head Start,* 255, 257–258.

9. James F. Winschel, "In the Dark . . . Reflections on Compensatory Education 1960–1970," in *Disadvantaged Child: Compensatory Education: A National Debate,* Vol. 3, ed. Jerome Hellmuth (New York: Brunner-Mazel, Inc., 1970), 3–4.

10. Barbara Joan Harned, "Relationships Among the Federally Sponsored Nursery Schools of the 1930's, the Federally Sponsored-Day Care Program of the 1940's, and Project Head Start" (Ph.D. diss., Rutgers, The State University, 1968), 74.

11. Edward Zigler and Sally Styfco, "Head Start and Early Childhood Intervention: The Changing Course of Social Science and Social Policy," *in Children, Families & Government: Preparing for the Twenty-First Century,* ed. Edward F. Zigler, Sharon Lynn Kagan, and Nancy W. Hall (Cambridge, England: Cambridge University Press, 1996), 42–43.

12. Polly Greenberg, "Before the Beginning: A Participant's View," *Young Children* 45, no. 6 (September 1990): 46.

13. Harned, "Relationships Among the Federally Sponsored Nursery Schools," 78.

14. Ellis Evans, *Contemporary Influences in Early Childhood Education,* 2d ed. (New York: Holt, Rinehart and Winston, Inc., 1975), 61.

15. U.S. Department of Health and Human Services: Administration for Children, Youth and Families, *Head Start Act, as Amended by P.L. 101-501.* Issuance Date 2/26/91, 10, 12.

16. The term "poverty line" means—(A) the official poverty line (as defined by the Office of Management and Budget) adjusted to reflect the percentage change in the Consumer Price Index for All Urban Consumers, issued by the Bureau of Labor Statistics, occurring in the one-year or other interval immediately preceding the date that such adjustment was made or (B) the poverty line (including any revision thereof) applicable to this subchapter for [the] fiscal year. Ibid., 3.

17. Ibid., 15.

18. Ibid., 12.

19. Ibid., 13.

20. Ibid., 3.

21. Polly Greenberg, "Before the Beginning," 42.

22. Harned, "Relationships Among the Federally Sponsored Nursery Schools," 78–79.

23. Polly Greenberg, "Before the Beginning," 44.

24. Margaret Rasmussen, "Over the Editor's Desk," *Childhood Education* XLII (September 1965): cover-3, in Harned, "Relationships Among the Federally Sponsored Nursery Schools," 79.

25. Jeanette Valentine, "Program Development in Head Start: A Multifaceted Approach to Meeting the Needs of Families and Children," in *Project Head Start: A Legacy of the War on Poverty,* 350.

26. Greenberg, "Before the Beginning," 44.

27. Harned, "Relationships Among the Federally Sponsored Nursery Schools," 79; and Zigler and Styfco, "Head Start and Early Childhood Intervention," 133–134.

28. Harned, "Relationships Among the Federally Sponsored Nursery Schools," 80–81.

29. Greenberg, "Before the Beginning," 47; and Zigler and Styfco, "Head Start and Early Childhood Intervention," 134.

30. Julius B. Richmond, Deborah J. Stipek, and Edward F. Zigler, "A Decade of Head Start," in *Project Head Start: A Legacy of the War on Poverty,* ed. Edward F. Zigler and Jeanette Valentine (New York: The Free Press, 1979), 137; Planning Committee for Project Head Start, Dr. Robert E. Cooke, *Improving the Opportunities and Achievements of the Children of the Poor,* Report of the Planning Committee, Project Head Start, February 1965, in Harned, "Relationships Among the Federally Sponsored Nursery Schools," 82;

Edith Grotberg, *Review of Research: 1965–1969* (Washington, D.C.: Project Head Start, U.S. Office of Economic Opportunity), as cited in Evans, *Contemporary Influences in Early Childhood Education,* 65; First Memorandum to Sargent Shriver (unpublished memorandum) cited in Greenberg, "Before the Beginning," 44; and Zigler and Styfco, "Head Start and Early Childhood Intervention," in *Children, Families & Government,* 134.

31. Zigler and Styfco, "Head Start and Early Childhood Intervention," 136.

32. Raymond C. Collins, "Head Start: Steps Toward a Two-Generation Program Strategy," *Young Children* 48, no. 2 (January 1993): 28.

33. Ibid., 27.

34. Zigler and Styfco, "Head Start and Early Childhood Intervention," 136.

35. Jule Sugarman, Memorandum "Project Head Start" Executive Office of the President, Washington, D.C., February 12, 1965, reference in Greenberg, "Before the Beginning," 41.

36. Judy Cauman wrote the early childhood education component of the guidelines that went out to communities which sent back the card. Later she was the first director of the Head Start national education component.

37. D. Keith Osborn, "The Early Pioneers," in *Project Head Start: A Legacy of the War on Poverty,* 106–107.

38. The author of this chapter participated in one of the first Head Start teacher preparation workshops, held at Teachers College of Columbia University in New York City in June 1965.

39. Sheldon White in "Plenary Session 1: Head Start's Future: The Challenge for Research," in *Conference Proceedings: New Directions in Child and Family Research: Shaping Head Start in the 90s (held in Arlington, Virginia 24–26 June 1991),* ed. Faith Lamb Parker (New York: National Council of Jewish Women Center for the Child, 1992), 24.

40. Edward F. Zigler, "Formal Schooling for Four-Year-Olds? No," in *Early Schooling: The National Debate,* ed. Sharon L. Kagan and Edward F. Zigler (New Haven, CT: Yale University Press, 1987), 38–39.

41. Edward F. Zigler and Elizabeth Gilman, "Not Just Any Care," in *Children, Families & Government,* 111–112.

42. Edward M. Kennedy, "The Head Start Transition Project: Head Start Goes to Elementary School," in *Head Start and Beyond: A National Plan for Extended Childhood Intervention,* ed. Edward Zigler and Sally J. Styfco (New Haven, CT: Yale University Press, 1993), 101.

43. *Who's Who in American Education, 1996–1997,* 5th ed. (New Providence, NJ: Marquis Who's Who, Inc., 1995), 964. For further information see: Edward Zigler and Mary Lang, *Child Care Choices: Balancing the Needs of Children, Families, and Society* (New York: Free Press, 1991) and Edward Zigler and Meryl Frank, *The Parental Leave Crisis: Toward a National Policy* (New Haven: Yale University Press, 1988).

44. D. Keith Osborn, "The Early Days of Project Head Start," in James L. Hymes, Jr., *Early Childhood Living History, Interviews,* Vol. 3, *Reaching Large Numbers of Children* (Carmel, CA: Hacienda Press, 1979), 34.

45. Ibid., 33.

46. "In Memoriam: D. Keith Osborn," *Young Children* 49, no. 4 (May 1994): 64.

47. Ibid., and *Who's Who in America, 1984–1985,* 43d edition (Chicago, IL: Marquis Who's Who, Inc., 1984), 2: 2484–2485. Notable works by Osborn include: D. Keith Osborn, Candice Logue, and Elaine Surbeck, *Significant Events in Early Childhood Education* (Athens, GA: University of Georgia, 1973) and D. Keith Osborn and Janie D. Osborn, *Cognition in Early Childhood* (Athens, GA: Education Associates, 1983).

48. D. Keith Osborn, "Precious Memories, How They Linger," *Childhood Education* 69, no. 2 (Winter 1992): 91. The author of this chapter, who is cited in the journal article, was present on October 3, 1992, in Saratoga Springs.

49. Evans, *Contemporary Influences in Early Childhood Education* 61; and Zigler and Styfco, "Head Start and Early Childhood Intervention," 136.

50. Urie Bronfenbrenner, "Head Start: A Retrospective View: The Founders," in *Project Head Start: A Legacy of the War on Poverty,* 83, 84.

51. Greenberg, "Before the Beginning," 47.

52. Jeanette Valentine, "The Honorable Sargent Shriver," in *Project Head Start: A Legacy of the War on Poverty,* 62.

53. Polly Greenberg was one of the three founders of CDGM, and its Director of Teacher Development and Program in 1966. For further information on CDGM see: Greenberg, *The Devil Has Slippery Shoes.*

54. Valentine, "The Honorable Sargent Shriver," 63.

55. Zigler and Styfco, "Head Start and Early Childhood Intervention," 136; and Evans, *Contemporary Influences in Early Childhood Education,* ftn. 8, 62.

56. Greenberg, "Before the Beginning," 47.

57. A. Frederick North, Jr., "Health Services in Head Start," in *Project Head Start: A Legacy of the War on Poverty,* 231.

58. Ibid., 236.

59. Ibid., 246.

60. James L. Hymes, Jr., *Early Childhood Education: Twenty Years in Review: A Look at 1971–1990* (Washington, DC: National Association for the Education of Young Children, 1991), 18.

61. Edward Zigler and Susan Muenchow, *Head Start: The Inside Story of America's Most Successful Education Experiment* (New York: Basic Books, 1992), 158–159; and Jeanette Valentine, "Program Development in Head Start: A Multifaceted Approach to Meeting the Needs of Families and Children," in *Project Head Start: A Legacy of the War on Poverty,* 356–357.

62. Valentine, "Program Development in Head Start: A Multifaceted Approach to Meeting the Needs of Families and Children," in *Project Head Start: A Legacy of the War on Poverty,* 358; and Zigler and Muenchow, *Head Start: The Inside Story of America's Most Successful Education Experiment,* 155.

63. U.S. Department of Health and Human Services (HHS), Administration for Children and Families, Administration on Children, Youth and Families (ACYF), Head Start Bureau. *Head Start: A Child Development Program, Head Start of Lane County 1995;* available from <http://www.efn.org/~hsolc/national.html>; Internet accessed 8 August 1997, 3.

64. Greenberg, "Before the Beginning," 48–49.

65. Ibid., 2.

66. Ibid., 3.

67. Edward F. Zigler, "Head Start's Future: The Challenge for Research, Plenary Session I," in *New Directions in Child and Family Research: Shaping Head Start in the 90s,* 15.

68. James L. Hymes, Jr., "Head Start, A Retrospective View: The Founders," in *Project Head Start: A Legacy of the War on Poverty,* 96.

69. Ibid., 94–197; and National Association for the Education of Young Children, "Head Start Hopes and Disappointments: An Interview with James L. Hymes, Jr.," *Young Children* 40, no. 6 (September 1985): 16.

70. Julius B. Richmond, "Head Start's Future: The Challenge for Research, Plenary Session I," in *New Directions in Child and Family Research: Shaping Head Start in the 90s,* 23.

71. Zigler, "Head Start's Future: The Challenge for Research," in *New Directions in Child and Family Research,* 15; and Edward Zigler, "Head Start: Not a Program But an Evolving Concept," in *Early Childhood Education It's an Art? It's a Science?,* ed. J. D. Andrews (Washington, DC: National Association for the Education of Young Children, 1976), 6–7.

72. Richmond, "Head Start's Future: The Challenge for Research," in *New Directions in Child and Family Research,* 23.

73. Sheldon White in "Head Start's Future: The Challenge for Research, Plenary Session I," in *New Directions in Child and Family Research,* 24.

74. Richmond, Head Start's Future: The Challenge for Research," in *New Directions in Child and Family Research,* 23.

75. Zigler, "Head Start's Future: The Challenge for Research," in *New Directions in Child and Family Research,* 15–16.

76. Zigler, "Head Start: Not a Program But an Evolving Concept," 1.

77. Ibid., 2–3.

78. Ibid., 9.

79. Edward Zigler, "What About Head Start? Policy Point of View by Edward Zigler," *Child and Poverty News & Issues* 3:3 Fall 1993 [newsletter on-line]; available from <http://cpmcnet.columbia.edu/news/childpov/newi0040.html>; Internet accessed 24 April 1997, 2; and Head Start Policy Memorandum, April 1999.

80. Valora Washington and Ura Jean Oyemade Bailey, *Project Head Start: Models and Strategies for the Twenty-First Century* (New York: Garland Publishing, Inc., 1995), 30.

81. Ibid.

82. Zigler and Muenchow, *Head Start: The Inside Story of America's Most Successful Education Experiment*, 154.

83. Ibid., 154–155.

84. Zigler, "What About Head Start? Policy Point of View," 3.

85. Penelope K. Trickett, "Career Development in Head Start," in *Project Head Start: A Legacy of the War on Poverty*, 316.

86. D. Keith Osborn, "The Early Pioneers," in *Project Head Start: A Legacy of the War on Poverty*, 108.

87. Trickett, "Career Development in Head Start," 319.

88. Ibid., 322.

89. Blythe F. Hinitz, "National Policies and Training Frameworks for Early Childhood Education in the United States: The Child Development Associate and Other Credentialing Frameworks for Paraprofessionals" (paper presented at the Second Warwick International Early Years Conference: Learning for Life, Coventry, England, 28 March 1996), 1; and Trickett, "Career Development in Head Start," 325.

90. Focus Group 1: The role of the early childhood team; Focus Group II: Definition of the role and competencies of the child development worker and characteristics of a training model; Focus Group III: Performance, evaluation, and assessment; and Focus Group IV: Certification. Roberta Wong Bouverat and Harlene Lichter Galen, *The Child Development Associate National Program: The Early Years and Pioneers* (Washington, DC: Council for Early Childhood Professional Recognition, 1994), 10–11.

91. The following ten organizations were initially recommended for membership in the consortium: American Association of Elementary Kindergarten-Nursery Educators, American Home Economics Association, Association for Childhood Education International, Black Child Development Institute, Child Welfare League of America, Day Care and Child Development Council of America, National Association for the Education of Young Children, National Committee on Education of Migrant Children, National Indian Education Advisory Council, Mexican-American Systems.

92. Milton E. Akers and Marilyn M. Smith, "Final Report: Feasibility Study for Child Development Project, September 1, 1971, submitted to the Office of Child Development," in Zigler and Muenchow, *Head Start: The Inside Story of America's Most Successful Education Experiment*, 161; and Bouverat and Galen, *The Child Development Associate National Program: The Early Years and Pioneers*, 23, 30, 36–37.

93. Bouverat and Galen, *The Child Development Associate National Program: The Early Years and Pioneers*, 46.

94. Gail Perry, "Alternate Modes of Teacher Preparation," in *Continuing Issues in Early Childhood Education*, ed. Carol Seefeldt (Columbus, OH: Merrill Publishing Co., 1990), 187.

95. Ibid.

96. Council for Early Childhood Professional Recognition, *The Child Development Associate Assessment System and Competency Standards: Preschool Care Givers in Center-Based Programs* (Washington, DC: Author, 1992), 70.

97. Hinitz, "National Policies and Training Frameworks for Early Childhood Education in the United States: The Child Development Associate," 4.

98. Bouverat and Galen, *The Child Development Associate National Program: The Early Years and Pioneers*, 100–104.

99. Trickett, "Career Development in Head Start," 328–329.

100. Hinitz, "National Policies and Training Frameworks for Early Childhood Education in the United States: The Child Development Associate," 4–5.

101. LAT included an advisor (originally called the trainer), an early childhood professional with a college degree in early childhood education or child development. The candidate was an equal voting member of the team, preparing a portfolio documenting competency in all of the functional areas. A parent/community representative had the task of collecting data from the parents or guardians of the children currently in the candidate's care and observing in the preschool setting. The fourth member of the LAT, the CDA Representative (CDA Rep) was a trained early education professional, assigned by the National Office of CDA, who conducted the team meeting and voting procedure according to strict guidelines set down by the consortium. It was the CDA Rep's responsibility to ensure that the meeting exactly followed the procedures set down by the consortium, in order that the validity and reliability of the system be maintained. CDA candidates in the system at that time were requested to take primary responsibility for the day-to-day activities of a group of children. Ibid., 5.

102. "Guest Editorial: Childcare, Then and Now: An Interview with Dr. James L. Hymes, Jr.," in *Beginnings & Beyond,* 4th ed., ed. Ann Miles Gordon and Kathryn Williams-Browne (Albany, NY: Delmar Publishers, 1995), 2.

103. Council for Early Childhood Professional Recognition, *The Council Model for CDA* (Washington, DC: Author, 1989), 1.

104. Carol Brunson Phillips, ed., *Essentials for Child Development Associates Working with Young Children* (Washington, DC: The CDA Professional Preparation Program: Council for Early Childhood Professional Recognition, 1991).

105. For further information on the development of the Child Development Associate credential, see the following references: Council for Early Childhood Professional Recognition, "CDA Gains Momentum and Status as Credit-Bearing Credential," in *Competence,* II, no. 2, (August 1994): 1, 3; Donna M. Golinick and R. C. Kunkel, "The Reform of National Accreditation," in *Phi Delta Kappan* 68, no. 4 (December 1986): 310–314; Hymes, *Early Childhood Education: Twenty Years in Review,* 142; Barbara H. Kardon, "The Child Development Associate Program and Personal Competencies as Viewed by Early Childhood Teacher Educators" (Ed.D. diss., Temple University, 1982); Jenny Klein and C. Ray Williams, "The Development of the Child Development Associate (CDA) Program," in *Young Children* 28, no. 3 (February 1973): 139–145; Carol Brunson Phillips, "The Child Developmental Associate Program: Entering a New Era," in *Young Children* 45, no. 3 (March 1990): 24–27; Carol Brunson Phillips, "Progress Update on the CDA Program," in *National Head Start Association (NHSA) Journal* 12, no. 2 (Fall 1993): 23–24; Douglas R. Powell and Loraine Dunn, "Non-Baccalaureate Teacher Education in Early Childhood Education," in Bernard Spodek and Olivia N. Saracho, eds., *Early Childhood Teacher Preparation Yearbook in Early Childhood Education,* vol. 1, 46–56; Evangeline H. Ward and CDA Staff, "The Child Development Associate Consortium's Assessment System," in *Young Children* 31, no. 4 (May 1976): 244–245; Zigler, Styfco, and Gilman, "The National Head Start Program for Disadvantaged Preschoolers," in *Head Start and Beyond: A National Plan for Extended Childhood Intervention,* 7; and Zigler and Muenchow, *Head Start: The Inside Story of America's Most Successful Education Experiment,* 159–163.

106. Carol Brunson Phillips, "The Movement of African-American Children through Sociocultural Contexts: A Case of Conflict Resolution," in *Diversity and Developmentally Appropriate Practices: Challenges for Early Childhood Education,* ed. Bruce L. Mallory and Rebecca S. New (New York: Teachers College Press, 1994), 137–154.

107. Carol Brunson Phillips, "Rethinking the Study of Black Behavior," in *Collective Monologues: Toward a Black Perspective in Education,* ed. Carol Brunson Phillips and Mary Valley (Pasadena, CA: Stage 7 Publishers, Pacific Oaks College, 1976), 11–20.

108. Bonnie Neugebauer, ed., *Alike and Different: Exploring Our Humanity with Young Children,* rev. ed., with a foreword by Carol Brunson Phillips (Washington, DC: National Association for the Education of Young Children, 1992), vi.

109. Louise Derman-Sparks and Carol Brunson Phillips, *Teaching/Learning Anti-Racism: A Developmental Approach* (New York: Teachers College Press, 1997).

110. Carol Brunson Phillips, "Nurturing Diversity for Today's Children and Tomorrow's Leaders," *Young Children* 42, no. 3 (January 1988): 42–47.

111. Bouverat and Galen, *The Child Development Associate National Program: The Early Years and Pioneers,* 73.

112. Brunson Phillips, *Essentials for Child Development Associates Working with Young Children.*

113. The five themes are: Children develop in context. Strategies for working with children are constructed each day. Effective practice requires a comprehensive set of skills. Early childhood professionals know they belong to a profession. Even skilled professionals have limitations. Carol Brunson Phillips, "At the Core: What Every Early Childhood Professional Should Know," in *The Early Childhood Career Lattice: Perspectives on Professional Development,* ed. Julienne Johnson and Janet B. McCracken (Washington, DC: National Association for the Education of Young Children, 1994), 57–59.

114. Carol Brunson Phillips, "The Challenge of Training and Credentialing Early Childhood Educators," *Phi Delta Kappan* 76, no. 3 (November 1994): 215–217.

115. Marilyn Henry and Carol Brunson Phillips, "New Directions for Non-College/University Training," in *Leadership in Early Care and Education,* ed. Sharon L. Kagan and Barbara T. Bowman (Washington, DC: National Association for the Education of Young Children, 1997), 121–128.

116. Preliminary Report on the Head Start Teaching Center Demonstration Projects: Promising Practices, Challenges Encountered, and Lessons Learned; available from <http://www.acf dhhs.gov/programs/hsb/report.html>; Internet accessed 23 July 1997, 1–9.

117. Hymes, "Head Start, A Retrospective View: The Founders," 95.

118. Hymes, *Early Childhood Education: Twenty Years in Review,* 7–8.

119. Ibid., 50.

120. Carol Doernberger and Edward Zigler, "Project Follow-Through: Intent and Reality," in *Head Start and Beyond: A National Plan for Extended Childhood Intervention,* ed. Edward Zigler and Sally J. Styfco (New Haven, CT: Yale University Press, 1993), 44–45.

121. George B. Brain and Reginald S. Lourie, "Head Start, A Retrospective View: The Founders," in *Project Head Start: A Legacy of the War on Poverty,* 76, 100.

122. Lois-ellin Datta, "Another Spring and Other Hopes: Some Findings from National Evaluations of Project Head Start," in *Project Head Start: A Legacy of the War on Poverty,* 419; and Washington and Bailey, *Project Head Start: Models and Strategies for the Twenty-First Century,* 52.

123. Zigler and Styfco, "Head Start and Early Childhood Intervention," 137.

124. Doernberger and Zigler, "Project Follow-Through: Intent and Reality," 47.

125. Ibid., 62.

126. Ibid., 65.

127. Louise B. Miller, "Development of Curriculum Models in Head Start," in *Project Head Start: A Legacy of the War on Poverty,* 200.

128. Curriculum development studies were done by: Miller and Dyer in Louisville, Kentucky, comparing the implementation of four models in fourteen Head Start classes; Karnes, comparing three models in Champaign-Urbana, Illinois; and Weikart studying three models done in Ypsilanti, Michigan.

129. Louise B. Miller, "Development of Curriculum Models in Head Start," in *Project Head Start: A Legacy of the War on Poverty,* 211.

130. Evans, *Contemporary Influences in Early Childhood Education,* 70.

131. Ibid., 69.

132. Doernberger and Zigler, "Project Follow-Through: Intent and Reality," 66

133. Bettye M. Caldwell, "Continuity in the Early Years: Transitions Between Grades and Systems," *The Care and Education of America's Young Children: Obstacles and Opportunities,* 90th Yearbook of the National Society for the Study of Education, ed. Sharon Lynn Kagan (Chicago: University of Chicago Press, 1991), 76–78.

134. Edward Zigler and Sally J. Styfco, "Strength in Unity: Consolidating Federal Education Programs for Young Children," in *Head Start and Beyond: A National Plan for Extended Childhood Intervention,* 124; Office of Child Development, Department of Health, Education and Welfare, Office of Human Development, *Project Developmental Continuity: A Head Start Demonstration Program Linking Head Start, Parents, and the Public Schools* (Washington, 1977), in *United We Stand: Collaboration for Child Care and Early Education Services,* ed. Sharon L. Kagan (New York: Teachers College Press, 1991), 51; Valentine, "Program Development in Head Start," 355; and Washington and Bailey, *Project Head Start: Models and Strategies for the Twenty-First Century,* 51.

135. Valentine, "Program Development in Head Start," 356.

136. Kagan, *United We Stand. Collaboration for Child Care and Early Education Services,* 51.

137. Collins, "Head Start: Steps Toward a Two-Generation Program Strategy," 25.

138. Kennedy, "The Head Start Transition Project: Head Start Goes to Elementary School," 99–100.

139. Zigler and Muenchow, *Head Start: The Inside Story of America's Most Successful Education Experiment,* 240; Kennedy, "The Head Start Transition Project: Head Start Goes to Elementary School," 100–101; "National Head Start–Public School Transition Study," Craig Ramey and Sharon Ramey, Civitan International Research Center, summary of the National Evaluation of this grant project for 1991–1996; available from <http://www.acf.dhhs.gov/programs/hsre/ongoing_research/hsresearch3.html>; Internet accessed 27 November 1997; and Transition: Head Start/Public School Transition Demonstration Projects; available from <http://pride.soe.uaa.alaska.edu/www/Pride/Transition sites.html>; Internet accessed November 1997, 1–2 of 2.

140. Edward Zigler and Sally J. Styfco, "Strength in Unity: Consolidating Federal Education Programs for Young Children," in *Head Start and Beyond: A National Plan for Extended Childhood Intervention,* 125; and Joan Lombardi, "Head Start: The Nation's Pride, A Nation's Challenge: Recommendations for Head Start in the 1990s: A Report on the Silver Ribbon Panel Sponsored by the National Head Start Association," *Young Children* 45, 6 (September 1990): 22–29.

141. Kagan, *United We Stand: Collaboration for Child Care and Early Education Services,* 68.

142. Donald J. Cohen, Albert J. Solnit, and Paul Wohlford, "Mental Health Services in Head Start" in *Project Head Start: A Legacy of the War on Poverty,* 265.

143. Valentine, "Program Development in Head Start," 351.

144. Ibid., 352.

145. Zigler, Styfco, and Gilman, "The National Head Start Program for Disadvantaged Preschoolers," 6, 7.

146. Zigler and Styfco, "Head Start and Early Childhood Intervention," in *Children, Families & Government,* 149; "Early Head Start: A New Era of Support and Service Begins," *Council News & Views* (December 1997): 1–2; and Statement of the Advisory Committee for Families with Infants and Toddlers, Department of Health and Human Services, September 1994, in *Council News & Views* (December 1997): 1–2.

147. Valentine, "Program Development in Head Start," 360.

148. East Coast Migrant Head Start Project; available from <http://www.ecmhsp.org/about.html>; Internet accessed 27 November 1997, 1.

149. The term "Indian" is utilized in this chapter because that is the historical reference, although members of the population prefer the term "Native American" or "American Indian." The term "Indian" will be used, in historical context throughout this chapter. The term "Native American" is used for the period 1990 and later.

150. Gloria Small, "Remote Battle Grounds: The Office of Special Field Projects," in *Project Head Start: A Legacy of the War on Poverty,* 339.

151. Ibid., 340.

152. Ibid., 343.

153. Ibid., 344.

154. Ibid., 344–348.

155. Nedra C. Sears and Linda Lee Chapman Medearis, "Educating Teachers for Family Involvement with Young Native Americans," A Natural Math Project funded by the Eisenhower Foundation for Math and Science, TMs, 1993.

156. Small, "Remote Battle Grounds," 346.

157. Chickasaw Head Start Program home page; available from <http://www.chickasaw.com/~cnation/annualreport/headstart.html>; Internet accessed 28 November 1997.

158. Dorothy Still Smoking, "Tribal-Way-of-Knowing: Blackfeet Tribe," (Montana State University, 1996–1998); available from <http://www.acf.dhhs.gov/programs/hsre/ongoing_research39.html>; Internet accessed 27 November 1997.

159. Native Child; available from <http://www.nativechild.com/curriculum.html>; Internet accessed 28 November 1997, 2.

160. Project P/Pride; available from <http://pride.soe.uaa.alaska.edu/www/pride/Transition/transition.html>; Internet accessed 28 November 1997.

161. Small, "Remote Battle Grounds," 347.

162. Collins, "Head Start: Steps Toward a Two-Generation Program Strategy," 28.

163. Kagan, *United We Stand: Collaboration for Child Care and Early Education Services,* 66.

164. Zigler, Styfco, and Gilman, "The National Head Start Program for Disadvantaged Preschoolers," 16, 28, 34; and Zigler and Styfco, "Head Start and Early Childhood Intervention," 137.

165. Hymes, *Early Childhood Education: Twenty Years in Review,* 141.

166. HHS, ACYF, Head Start Bureau, *Head Start: A Child Development Program, Head Start of Lane County, 1995,* 4.

167. Washington and Bailey, *Project Head Start: Models and Strategies for the Twenty-First Century,* 50.

168. The Home Start demonstration project was designed by Ann O'Keefe. Zigler and Muenchow, *Head Start: The Inside Story of America's Most Successful Education Experiment,* 159.

169. Zigler and Styfco, "Head Start and Early Childhood Intervention," 137; Washington and Bailey, *Project Head Start: Models and Strategies for the Twenty-First Century,* 51; and Valentine, "Program Development in Head Start," 354.

170. Zigler and Muenchow, *Head Start: The Inside Story of America's Most Successful Education Experiment,* 152.

171. Ibid., 89.

172. Washington and Bailey, *Project Head Start: Models and Strategies for the Twenty-First Century,* 27; and HHS, ACYF, Head Start Bureau, *Head Start: A Child Development Program, Head Start of Lane County 1995,* passim.

173. Hymes, *Early Childhood Education: Twenty Years in Review,* 195–196.

174. Collins, "Head Start: Steps Toward a Two-Generation Program Strategy," 27.

175. Hymes, *Early Childhood Education: Twenty Years in Review,* 401–402; and Lombardi, "Head Start: The Nation's Pride, A Nation's Challenge: Recommendations for Head Start in the 1990s," 22–29, esp. 29.

176: Collins, "Head Start: Steps Toward a Two-Generation Program Strategy," 30.

177. Ibid., 73.

178. Evans, *Contemporary Influences in Early Childhood Education,* 70–72.

179. Deborah A. Phillips and Natasha J. Kabrera, eds., *Beyond the Blueprint: Directions for Research on Head Start's Families* (Washington, DC: National Academy Press, 1996); available from <http://www.ericps.crc.uiuc.edu/nccic/research/nrc_bynd/nrc_bynd.html>; Internet accessed 12 September 1997, 9–10, 13–15.

180. Public Policy Report: Creating a 21st Century Head Start: Executive Summary of the Final Report of the Advisory Committee on Head Start Quality and Expansion, *Young Children* 49, no. 3 (March 1994): 65 (based on Advisory Committee on Head Start Quality and Expansion, *Creating a 21st Century Head Start*) (Washington, DC: U.S. Department of Health and Human Services, 1993).

181. Zigler and Styfco, "Head Start and Early Childhood Intervention," 147.

182. "Creating a Twenty-First Century Head Start: Executive Summary," 66.

183. Head Start Program Performance Measures; available from http://www.acf.dhhs.gov/programs/hsb/toc.html; Internet accessed 23 July 1997, 2, 3.

184. See pages 716–717 for a fuller discussion of the Performance Standards.

185. Head Start Program Performance Measures; available from http://www.acf.dhhs.gov/programs/hsb/toc.htm, 5.

186. Sherlie S. Svestka, "Head Start and Early Head Start Programs: What We Have Learned Over the Last 30 Years About Preschool, Families, and Communities," *International Journal of Early Childhood* 28, no. 1 (1996): 62.

187. Zigler and Muenchow, *Head Start: The Inside Story of America's Most Successful Education Experiment,* 177.

188. Robert D. Hess and Doreen J. Croft, *Teachers of Young Children,* 3d ed. (Boston: Houghton Mifflin, 1981), 383.

189. Bernard Spodek and Olivia N. Saracho, *Right from the Start: Teaching Children Ages Three to Eight* (Boston: Allyn and Bacon, 1994), 47.

190. Kagan, *United We Stand: Collaboration for Child Care and Early Education Services,* 37.

191. George S. Morrison, *Early Childhood Education Today,* 7th ed. (Upper Saddle River, NJ: Merrill, an imprint of Prentice-Hall, 1998), 449.

192. Fact sheet; available from <http://www.acf.dhhs.gov/programs/opa/facts/ ssbg.html>; Internet accessed 12 September 1997, 1.

193. Ibid., 2.

194. Children's Defense Fund, *A Children's Defense Budget: FY 1988: An Analysis of Our Nation's Investment in Children* (Washington, DC: Author, 1987), 210.

195. Children's Defense Fund, *A Children's Defense Budget: An Analysis of the President's FY 1985 Budget and Children* (Washington, DC: Author, 1984), 161–164.

196. Children's Defense Fund, *A Children's Defense Budget: An Analysis of the President's FY 1987 Budget and Children* (Washington, DC: Author, 1986), 288, 290, 294–295.

197. Children's Defense Fund, *A Vision for America's Future: An Agenda for the 1990s: A Children's Defense Budget* (Washington, DC: Author, 1989), 60, 63–65.

198. Children's Defense Fund, *S.O.S. America! A Children's Defense Budget* (Washington, DC: Author, 1990), 49–50; and Kagan, *United We Stand: Collaboration for Child Care and Early Education Services,* 67.

199. Zigler and Gilman, "Not Just Any Care," 105–106.

200. Children's Defense Fund (CDF), *The State of America's Children Yearbook 1992* (Washington, DC: Author, 1992), 18.

201. Children's Defense Fund (CDF), *The State of America's Children Yearbook 1994),* 29–31.

202. Morrison, *Early Childhood Education Today,* 449–450.

203. Ibid., 32–34; and CDF, *Yearbook 1992,* 19.

204. Katharine Q. Seelye, "Clinton Proposes $21 Billion over Five Years for Child Care," *New York Times,* 8 January 1998, A1; National Association of Child Care Resource and Referral Agencies, "President Clinton Announces Child Care Initiative," 7 January 1998 [fax]; and *The White House at Work,* "Child Care That Strengthens American Families" (Washington, DC: The White House Internet Briefing Room, 7 January 1998); available from <http://www.whitehouse.gov/WH/Work/010798.html>; Internet accessed 14 January 1998, 1–2 of 2. See also: *White House Conference on Early Childhood Development and Learning,* "Policy Announcements" (Washington, DC: The White House Internet Briefing Room, 17 April 1997); available from <http://www. whitehouse.govAWH/New/ECDC/Policy.html>; Internet accessed 14 January 1998, 1 of 2.

205. Ruth E. Cook, Annette Tessier, and M. Diane Klein, *Adapting Early Childhood Curricula for Children with Special Needs,* 3d ed. (New York: Merrill, 1992), 21.

206. Samuel J. Braun and Miriam G. Lasher, *Are You Ready to Mainstream? Helping Preschoolers with Learning and Behavior Problems* (Columbus, OH: Merrill, 1978), 4.

207. Bettye M. Caldwell, "The Importance of Beginning Early," in *Not All Little Wagons Are Red: The Exceptional Child's Early Years,* ed. J. B. Jordan and R. F. Dailey (Reston, VA: Council for Exceptional Children, 1973), 5–6.

208. Karen A. Waldron, *Introduction to a Special Education: The Inclusive Classroom* (Albany, NY; Delmar Publishers, 1995), 9–10.

209. Bernard Spodek and Olivia N. Saracho, *Dealing with Individual Differences in the Early Childhood Classroom* (White Plains, NY: Longman Publishing Group, 1994), 4; and Bernard Spodek, Olivia N. Saracho, and Richard C. Lee, *Mainstreaming Young Children* (Belmont, CA: Wadsworth Publishing Co., 1984), 3.

210. Warren Umansky and Stephen R. Hooper, *Introduction to Young Children with Special Needs,* 3d ed. (Upper Saddle River, NJ: Prentice-Hall, Inc., 1998), 2.

211. Waldron, *Introduction to a Special Education,* 14–18.

212. Ibid., 15.

213. Mark Wolery and Jan S. Wilbers, "Introduction to the Inclusion of Young Children with Special Needs in Early Childhood Programs," in *Including Children with Special*

Needs in Early Childhood Programs, ed. Mark Wolery and Jan S. Wilbers, Research Monograph of the National Association for the Education of Young Children, vol. 6 (Washington, DC: National Association for the Education of Young Children, 1994), 18; Umansky and Hooper, *Introduction to Young Children with Special Needs,* 2–7; James J. Gallagher, "Policy Development and Implementation for Children with Disabilities," in *Children, Families, & Government: Preparing for the Twenty-First Century,* 173; and Waldron, *Introduction to Special Education,* 19–23.

214. M. Zigler and Muenchow, *Head Start: The Inside Story of America's Most Successful Education Experiment,* 163.

215. Federal agencies such as the Bureau of Education for the Handicapped; the President's Committee on Mental Retardation; the Office of Developmental Disabilities; the National Institute of Mental Health; the Office of Handicapped Individuals; the National Institute of Child Health and Human Development/National Institute of Health; and the Medicaid/Early and Periodic Screening, Diagnosis, and Treatment agencies reviewed the materials during their developmental stages.

216. Lou Alonso, Colleen M. Moor, Sherry Raynor, Caren Saaz von Hippel, and Sondra Baer, *Mainstreaming Preschoolers: Children with Visual Handicaps: A Guide for Teachers, Parents, and Others Who Work With Visually Handicapped Preschoolers,* vol. G: The Rainbow Series on Mainstreaming from Project Head Start (U.S. Department of Health, Education, and Welfare, Office of Human Development Services, Administration for Children, Youth, and Families, Head Start Bureau, 1978).

Alice H. Hayden, Robert K. Smith, Caren Saaz von Hippel, and Sondra A. Baer, *Mainstreaming Preschoolers: Children with Learning Disabilities: A Guide for Teachers, Parents and Others Who Work with Learning Disabled Preschoolers,* vol. E: The Rainbow Series on Mainstreaming from Project Head Start (U.S. Department of Health, Education, and Welfare, Office of Human Development Services, Administration for Children, Youth, and Families, Head Start Bureau, 1978).

Alfred Healy, Paul McAreavey, Caren Saaz von Hippel, and Shari Harris Jones, *Mainstreaming Preschoolers: Children with Health Impairments: A Guide for Teachers, Parents, and Others Who Work with Health Impaired Preschoolers,* vol. D: The Rainbow Series on Mainstreaming from Project Head Start (U.S. Department of Health, Education, and Welfare, Office of Human Development Services, Administration for Children, Youth, and Families, Head Start Bureau, 1978).

Shari Stokes Kieran, Frances Partridge Conner, Caren Saaz von Hippel, and Sherri Harris Jones, *Mainstreaming Preschoolers: Children with Orthopedic Handicaps: A Guide for Teachers, Parents, and Others Who Work with Orthopedically Handicapped Preschoolers,* vol. B: The Rainbow Series on Mainstreaming from Project Head Start (U.S. Department of Health, Education, and Welfare, Office of Human Development Services, Administration for Children, Youth, and Families, Head Start Bureau, 1978).

Rita Ann LaPorta, Donald Ivan McGee, Audrey Simmons-Martin, Eleanor Borche, Caren Saaz von Hippel, and John Donavan, *Mainstreaming Preschoolers: Children with Hearing Impairment: A Guide for Teachers, Parents, and Others Who Work with Hearing Impaired Preschoolers,* vol. F: The Rainbow Series on Mainstreaming from Project Head Start (U.S. Department of Health, Education, and Welfare, Office of Human Development Services, Administration for Children, Youth, and Families, Head Start Bureau, 1978).

Miriam C. Lasher, Ilse Mattick, Frances J. Parkins, Caren Saaz von Hippel, and Linda Gaines Hailey, *Mainstreaming Preschoolers: Children with Emotional Disturbance: A Guide for Teachers, Parents, and Others Who Work with Emotionally Disturbed Preschoolers,* vol. C: The Rainbow Series on Mainstreaming from Project Head Start (U.S. Department of Health, Education, and Welfare, Office of Human Development Services, Administration for Children, Youth, and Families, Head Start Bureau, 1978).

Jacqueline Liebergott, Aaron Favors, Jr., Caren Saaz von Hippel, and Harriet Liftman Needleman, *Mainstreaming Preschoolers: Children with Speech and Language Impairments: A Guide for Teachers, Parents, and Others who Work with Speech and Language Impaired Preschoolers,* vol. A: The Rainbow Series on Mainstreaming from Project Head Start (U.S. Department of Health, Education, and Welfare, Office of Human Development Services, Administration for Children, Youth, and Families, Head Start Bureau, 1978).

Eleanor Whiteside Lynch, Betty Howald Simms, Caren Saaz von Hippel, and Jo Shuchat, *Mainstreaming Preschoolers: Children with Mental Retardation: A Guide for Teachers, Parents, and Others Who Work with Mentally Retarded Preschoolers,* vol. H: The Rainbow Series on Mainstreaming from Project Head Start (U.S. Department of Health, Education, and Welfare, Office of Human Development Services, Administration for Children, Youth, and Families, Head Start Bureau, 1978), 4.

217. Ibid.

218. Nancy H. Fallen with Jill E. McGovern, *Young Children with Special Needs* (Columbus, OH: Merrill, 1978), 33.

219. Wolery and Wilbers, "Introduction to the Inclusion of Young Children with Special Needs in Early Childhood Programs," 17.

220. Cook, Tessier, and Klein, *Adapting Early Childhood Curricula for Children with Special Needs,* 31.

221. Gallagher, "Policy Development and Implementation for Children with Disabilities," 174, 178.

222. Ibid., 179.

223. Frank G. Bowe, *Birth to Five: Early Childhood Special Education* (New York: Delmar Publishers, 1995), 422.

224. Ibid., 435–438.

225. For further information regarding a historical perspective on federal involvement in early childhood special education, see: Donald B. Bailey and Mark Wolery, *Teaching Infants and Preschoolers with Disabilities,* 2d ed. (New York: Merrill, 1992), 2–13; for a discussion of the history of collaboration in special education, see: Kagan, *United We Stand: Collaboration for Child Care and Early Education Services,* 52–60. In 1997, Part H of the IDEA was renamed Part C.

226. Umansky and Hooper, *Introduction to Young Children with Special Needs,* 7.

227. Sheryl Dicker and Ellen Schall, "Developing Inclusive Programs for Children with Disabilities," in *Child Care Bulletin* (July/August 1996), U.S. Department of Health and Human Services, Administration for Children and Families, Administration on Children, Youth and Families Child Care Bureau, 7.

PART III

Diverse Populations

CHAPTER 14

Native Americans[1]

> There is probably no method or device known to and
> practiced by civilized man which is not known to and
> practiced by uncivilized man in the social and moral
> training of the child.
>
> —John M. Cooper[2]

The various European words for Native Americans—*los indios, the Indians, les Indiens, die Indianer*—used in the late fifteenth and sixteenth centuries referred to a people who existed only in the European imagination. Native Americans were a heterogeneous group: nomadic hunters, farmers living in agricultural communities, or fishermen. At the time of European settlement, there were more than six hundred different languages spoken on the North American continent between the Rio Grande and the Arctic Circle.[3] Many of the original tribes have disappeared entirely, as a result of warfare, disease, or assimilation. The 1990 U.S. Census Bureau identified 136 different Native American languages. Of these, 47 were spoken in the home by fewer than 100 persons; an additional 22 were spoken by fewer than 200.[4] Even though they were native to this land, they were not citizens. Becoming citizens was a gradual process. Some Indians became citizens by specific treaties as early as 1817; others, when they received an allotment of land, and all others born within the territorial limits of the United States became citizens in 1924 by an act of Congress. The Fourteenth Amendment to the Constitution, ratified on July 9, 1868, provided that all citizens of the United States were also citizens of the "state where they reside."[5] The members of each group have retained their own identity and their own culture, never identifying themselves as belonging to a broad, generalized group characterized by the misnomer "Indians."[6]

The education of the Native American child is divided into Native American traditional child rearing and Native American education after contact with European colonists.

NATIVE AMERICAN TRADITIONAL CHILD REARING

All Native American groups required that certain skills be mastered before the young were accepted as mature members of the society. The skills fell into three areas: economic skills for survival, knowledge of the cultural heritage, and spiritual awareness. All children learned at an early age that survival depended on skills, on cooperation and sharing, and on having proper attitudes toward the earth and all life.[7]

Love and affection for their children were a high priority among the Native Americans, as were a deep concern for the physical, mental, social, moral, and religious teaching of the children. As there were no schools, the child's training was the responsibility of the immediate family, the extended family—which included the mother's brother and the father's sister—and the elders.[8] Education was a community project in which all respectable elders participated at the urging of the immediate family. The result was not only to focus community attention on the child, but also to make the child's education a constant challenge to the elders to review, analyze, and defend their cultural heritage. Their own beliefs, understanding and faith, personal integration into the culture, and collective unity were all promoted by the necessity of assuming the role of educators of their children.[9] Some Native American families were matrilineal; others were patrilineal.

Importance of Children

The major motive for having children was to gain social standing. No married person without children was considered completely adult. Having children was the normal expectation of maturity. Having children was also further evidence of one's total participation in the functioning of the social group. The group recognized parenthood as being very socially desirable by conferring prestige and practical rewards of many kinds on parents. A reasonable number of *good* children was preferable to a large number of children. From the father's point of view, an increased number of *good* children might bring greater rewards. The economic importance of children was a greater concern later in life when the parents became older. The dominant motives for childbearing and the considerations that made barrenness or sterility a tragedy were social in character, for in some tribes mothers and fathers maintained their positions of respect through their children. The mother particularly was more highly regarded if she had one well-thought-of son than if she had several less worthy ones. In some tribes, a family gained social rank by not producing too many children and by exercising self-control in spacing them two years apart. A wife who bore children shared in the public honors accorded to her warrior husband. Women were privileged to wear their hair in a special way after they had borne a child.

The sentimental attachment of mothers and fathers to their children in "primitive" societies seemed to depend on the economic situation prevailing at the time of the birth, the sex of the child, and the child's physical condition. Abortion and infanticide were quite common among the Native Americans. Infanticide was practiced—not always for economic reasons—with or without the consent of the father. Antipathy toward the responsibilities of motherhood was one of the major reasons for abortion in many southwestern tribes. Probably the long nursing period, which lasted until the child was two years old and was generally observed by "primitive" mothers, plus the taboo against having sexual relations during nursing were at least in part due to feminine concerns for keeping the family small.[10]

The training of the child began with prenatal taboos. Some tribes believed that the omniscience of the child began before birth. Therefore, an expectant mother had to be careful not to quarrel with anyone because the child understood everything and might decide not to be born into a family that quarrels. The concept of child's intimacy with the supernatural, in one form or another, was universal among the "primitive " peoples of North America.[11] In some tribes the father practiced *couvade*. On the day of the child's birth, he took to his bed, where he stayed for a few days.[12]

The Cradleboard or Portable Cradle

The infants were strapped to cradles from a few days after birth until the age of six months or one year. The cradles were made of board, bark, or wicker frames. The child spent his days bound to this frame except for necessary bathing periods. Sometimes he was taken out at night. The legs, hips, and trunk of the infant were always tightly confined. The hands and arms were likewise restrained. In the tribes, where flat heads were considered aesthetically pleasing and desirous, the natural effect of lashing a child to the cradle frame was heightened by also lashing its head down, with a board or pack of sand on top of it. With the exception of the Eskimo and a few tribes in the Southeast, which substituted hammocks, the cradleboard was used in every cultural area in North America and by every people within these areas. One cannot help but speculate on the impact this binding might have had on the child's personality and motor development during the first year of life, and for a period after the unbinding. Many observers have commented on how quiet young Native American children were and on their patience and stoicism. Observations of Hopi children regarding the effect of cradleboards on physical development appear to indicate that the cradleboard had no detectable influence on the age when children began walking.[13]

Play and Toys

A good deal of the physical training of the child came through play, ranging from roaming through the woods to highly organized team games. Native American children never quarreled at play, no matter what the provocation. Traditional tribal education was a process of culture transmission. Play was seen as training and preparation for the roles that children would assume in later life.

From the early years, the boys went with their fathers to the fields or pastures or hunting, where they would learn the practical aspects of trapping, riding, and paddling. The girls were trained in the female skills of cooking and child care by their mothers or grandmothers. This type of instruction and practice lasted for several years until puberty or adolescence.

The toys of the Native American children were actual implements in miniature made by the father, mother, or other relative. The children were supervised in their use. Pettitt,[14] citing earlier research, gives a list of forty-eight references for the use of bows and arrows and dolls in various tribes. The following are highlights of what some tribes provided for their children: *Hopi:* Every morning fathers took boys for bow and arrow practice. *Shawnee:* Bow and arrow games were encouraged by older men of the tribe. *Blackfoot:* The mother made the first bow and arrow and an imitation scalp lock of horsehair. *Crow:* The father made a son's first bow, and the grandfather placed buffalo chips for him to shoot (42). *Cheyenne:* Mothers made rag dolls representing men, women, boys, and girls. When necessary, they made babies for the play family. *Tanaino:* They gave girls carved wooden dolls and play-houses that were just like real houses in which fires could be built and cooking done. *Eskimo:* The first toy given to a boy was a sled. The children were encouraged to go hunting but only with animals that the elders said were in season. Girls were encouraged to make dolls and to dress them, with the mothers showing them how to cut out the skins (43). These examples indicate that children's play was very closely related to their later adult roles and appropriate to their environment where they lived. Childhood was considered a time for learning and testing, which required practice. Practice began with imitation. Native American children, like other children, imitated what they saw.

Childhood was not permitted to be a constant pleasure that the individual child would not want to leave. Arbitrary restrictions encouraged the child to acquire the skills and status of the mature individual. The process of moving toward adulthood included the removal of the restrictions and the granting of rewards in the form of social privileges. Girls and women were also eligible for social rewards, though the rewards were less numerous and elaborate.[15]

Discipline

Discipline was an important aspect of Native American child-rearing practices. The family was responsible for seeing that a child turned out well. Native American parents used *ridicule* to mold the child into the moral and social pattern of the tribe. They also used *praise* as an incentive. Native American parents avoided corporal punishment as a form of discipline. When they had to use corporal punishment, it was assigned to someone outside the immediate family. The family, close friends, and the whole tribe wanted to convey to the punished child that he was protected by them. Parents wanted to preserve the parent-child relationship and to maintain family unity. (What wisdom.) Another reason for not using corporal punishment was because "pain" per se could not be used as a fear-producing, coercive force in a society that placed a premium on the ability to withstand pain and suffering without flinching as part of the initiation rituals into adult society.

Childhood was closely linked with the supernatural world, a condition that also tended to inhibit corporal punishment. Infants and children, being helpless, were simultaneously susceptible to the machinations of the bad spirits and wards of the good spirits. The connection between supernatural support and parental treatment was widely used as a rationalization for the kindness and respect shown toward the child. This dual supernatural relationship tended to weaken as the child grew older.[16]

One of the persons outside the family involved with the discipline of the children was the mother's brother for the boys and the father's sister for the girls. The rationale for this choice was that the brother-sister relationship was as strong as the parent-child relationship, and a sister was expected to obey her brother. The mother's brother and the father's sister many times also acted as teachers and mentors for the children, further indicating the intense responsibilities they assumed for the father and the mother.[17]

The climax of the education for the Native American child came with the initiation rites into adulthood, which occurred near puberty or adolescence. The whole series of ceremonies were often symbolic of a new birth, and frequently a new name was given at that time.[18]

Naming of the Children

In previous chapters, we saw that other societies (ancient Greece and Rome, colonial New England) named their children shortly after their birth. The North American Indians named their children both at birth and later as part of the initiation rites into adulthood. They used ancestral names to stimulate the development of character and to promote personalities of the culturally ideal type. Their use of nicknames was related to the use of ridicule as a deterrent for unacceptable behavior and as an incentive for appropriate behavior. The unusual practice of naming a firstborn child after a parent is a further extension of the prestige-reward concept in the form of a name title.[19] One may say that the Native American naming practices were a fundamental aid in educating their children and in passing on to them certain intangible cultural values.

Comment

One cannot help but be struck by the similarities between the Native American society and those of antiquity, even though they belong to different continents and different historical times. For example, both societies practiced infanticide and held similar views of the infant's spiritual nature; both societies wanted toys to be implements for preparing the child for his adult role. The ability of boys to withstand pain as part of the rites for entering the adult society of Native Americans and the ability of the Spartan boys to withstand pain in the process of becoming warriors bring to mind Lewis Henry Morgan's comment that sociocultural systems are interconnected.[20]

EDUCATION AFTER CONTACT WITH THE EUROPEANS

The history of Native American education is long and complicated. The encounter of the Native Americans with the European cultures had an impact on both. Native Americans are a heterogeneous group with a variety of languages, cultures, and customs. The education of the Native Americans is a very complex issue because it involves Native American–United States relations and treaties, individual tribal histories, the westward expansion of the early settlers, the granting of statehood to territories, and ranching and railroads. First the colonial powers and later the United States government wanted the Native Americans to be educated in the values and goals of the white society. They completely disregarded the native cultures. Both groups believed that the purpose of education for Native Americans was acculturation and assimilation into the larger white society. They also believed that educating the Native Americans would help them become economically self-sufficient as industrialization advanced.

The Missionaries

During the early contacts between Indians and whites, the responsibility for education was borne by the missionaries, who tried to Christianize them. First came the Jesuits and the Franciscans. The majority of Jesuits, who were French, came to North America from the St. Lawrence River. Their activities lasted from 1611 to the end of the 1700s and centered on the Great Lakes and the Mississippi and its tributaries. A few Jesuits were in Florida as early as the 1500s. The Jesuits not only wanted to convert the Indians to Christianity but also wanted to "Galicize" them, for example, to educate them in the French manner. They removed the children from their families and their tribes and stressed French language, French customs, and the traditional academic subjects.

The Franciscans, who were primarily of Spanish origin, entered North America from the south and did their primary work in the Southwest. Their educational philosophy differed from that of the Jesuits. They established their missions in the Indian villages, thus keeping the families together. The mission in San Juan Capistrano, California, is such an example. They taught the Indians arts and crafts that they could use to make a living. They also showed them how to clear the land, build irrigation ditches, plow, harvest the crops, and thresh the wheat and barley. In addition, they taught the Indians carpentry, blacksmithing, masonry, spinning, weaving, and sewing, and soap and candle making. Academic subjects were less important, so there was no conscious effort to make the Indians Europeans.[21]

During the colonial times (1620–1776), the Puritans were also interested in Christianizing the Indians and introducing them to English culture. The Virginian colonists raised money in their colony and in England to organize a college for them. However, a revolt of the Indians in 1622 brought a change of attitude and almost ended all missionary efforts in Virginia for the balance of the century.

It delayed the founding of the College of William and Mary until 1691. Many Indian students were brought there to study in the succeeding years.[22]

Most of the colonies did not make an effort to educate the Indians; the New England colonies were an exception. The charter of the Massachusetts Bay Company declared that the main object of the company was to convert the natives to Christianity. In New England, the problem of proselytizing the Indians was compounded by the Congregational theology. It maintained that conversion involved not only the sacrament of baptism followed by a minimal knowledge of Christian belief and behavior, but also the experience of saving grace derived through knowledge of the Scriptures. Before 1663—when John Eliot published an Algonquian edition of the Bible—a convert either had to learn sufficient English to study the Bible and understand the subtleties of faith or had to find a clergyman with sufficient knowledge of the native language to teach him the Puritan ways. The idea of a gathered church assumed that a true Christian would live his life according to the Scriptures. Any religious conversion would have to be accompanied by a social conversion to Puritan standards of dress and deportment. There were very few converts in New England in 1640.

The situation changed when the Reverend Thomas Mayhew, Jr., of Martha's Vineyard and the Reverend John Eliot of Roxbury developed linguistic skills, preaching techniques, and organizational devices to use with native intermediaries that enabled them to convert the Indians in large numbers. Mayhew and his family carried on their missionary work for several generations. Eliot conducted his first service at Nonantum (on the Charles River, near Watertown) in 1846. He preached with such success that Indians from other villages asked him to preach to their fellow tribesmen.[23]

In 1653, the Society for the Propagation of the Gospel in New England asked the Commissioners of the United Colonies to erect an Indian College at Harvard College, which had been established in 1636. Shortly thereafter, a program was started whereby selected Indian youngsters attended preparatory studies with Elija Corlet at the Cambridge Grammar School and with Daniel Weld at Roxbury. Later, due to the efforts of John Eliot, there were schools for both youngsters and adults in the several praying towns in Massachusetts.[24] There is evidence that a John Sassamon attended Harvard for a term or two around 1853 as a protégé of John Eliot before the creation of the Indian College around 1654 or 1655. The two-story Indian College was not successful, largely because not enough Indians wanted to go to college, a matter of cultural values. It did house the press that printed the Indian Bible and other Algonquian texts translated by Eliot and his associates.[25] According to Young, there were two Indians, Joel Jacoomis and Caleb Cheesechaumuck, in the class of 1665. Jacoomis used Comenius's *Janua Linguarum* as a textbook, as is evident by his name appearing in two places in his book.[26]

John Eliot (1604–1690) was one of the most remarkable preachers/teachers of seventeenth-century New England. He came to America in 1631. He was the son of a prosperous yeoman family of East Anglia and had been highly educated in Cambridge. He was a minister and a teacher at a new congregation in Roxbury, where he held the post for forty-six years. Eliot felt that he had been called to preach to the Indians in their own language, to catechize their children, to publish books for them, and to look after their welfare. He studied their language and customs. Winning their confidence, he began to teach them habits of industry and thrift. Eliot conceived of a plan to bring the Indians together in self-governing towns where they could be taught, along with their letters, Christian ethics, and various arts and crafts. He included Greek and Latin for those he hoped would become missionaries and teachers to their own people. Eliot established fourteen towns of "praying Indians," as they were called, who were committed to the practice of Christian living as well as the profession of Christian belief.[27]

Before King Philip's War (1675), there were probably about 2,500 Christian Indians in New England, roughly representing 20 percent of the native population and concentrated mostly in the praying towns of the Massachusetts Bay Colony and the islands of Martha's Vineyard and Nantucket, where Mayhew had proselytized them. The war marked a turning point in the missionary effort. The converted Indians were among the most loyal to the colonial cause, but the hostilities dispersed them and created suspicions. The praying towns declined in number and population, and the colonies adopted a policy of restriction and supervision of Indians.[28]

Eliot's work was continued in the eighteenth century by the Reverend John Sergeant, who established in Stockbridge, Massachusetts, a day school, a boarding school, and an experimental "outing system" where Indian pupils were placed in Puritan homes during the school vacations. The Reverend Eleazar Wheelock, a minister-schoolmaster, in 1754, began tutoring selected Indian and white boys who aspired to become missionaries in his parsonage in Lebanon, Connecticut. Later, he moved his school to Hanover, New Hampshire, naming it Moor's Charity School. It eventually became Dartmouth College.[29] Wheelock and Sergeant differed from Eliot because they educated the Indian children in an environment away from their own tribes.

Education for Girls

The notion of educating Indian girls was of some concern to the New England missionaries. They had stressed the role played by Indian women in the "care of the souls of children in families for the first 7 or 8 years."[30] During Wheelock's time, when teaching Indian girls was rare, he was the first to include girls into his all-male school. Two Indian girls, a Mohegan and a Delaware, arrived at his school in 1761. Between 1761 and 1769, he enrolled sixteen Indian girls at Moor's Charity School. They came from a variety of nearby tribes. Some of the tribes had been in contact with the Europeans earlier. They were familiar with the rudiments of Christianity, knew of European goods, and spoke some English. However, they were very poor, and their material cultures had changed substantially since earlier contact with the Europeans.

Wheelock believed that the education of the Indian girls should be similar to that of the young colonial women. Therefore, girls should receive the rudiments of formal education, reading and writing, but most of the training should be for the home. Most colonial girls learned these skills in their own homes. For the Indian girls, it was different. Wheelock, wanting to keep the expenses low and lacking space in his own home, apprenticed the girls in nearby homes, to be instructed in the arts of "good House wifery." Needless to say, they were treated as servants.[31]

Other Protestant missionaries—Baptists, Quakers, Methodist, and Presbyterians—were also active in educating the Indians. The Moravians, the *Unitas Fratrum* who were persecuted in Europe (see Comenius, p. 36), had migrated to Georgia and to Pennsylvania around 1740. There they taught the Delawares and other tribes at mission sites, first in Pennsylvania and later in Ohio and Canada. Despite warfare and prejudice, the Moravians' persistence demonstrated a remarkable commitment to Christian education.[32]

Between the 1640s and the 1660s, the Indians of southern New England gradually became bilingual. The expanding colonial population needed the services of interpreters. Eliot and Mayhew also relied on the cooperation and skill of a number of Indian translators. They helped set the type for the Indian Bible in 1663 and for other religious works published in bilingual editions. These publications provided the Indians of southern New England with access to Western culture through a means not available to any other Indian group in colonial America.[33]

According to Kruse's *The Henry Rowe Schoolcraft Collection*,[34] the Bible, church catechisms, and primers were translated into many Native American languages, some of them in bilingual editions. The first and most important example is Eliot's Bible, translated into the Massachuset language, by John Eliot and Job Nesutan. Its Indian title is *Mamusee Wunneetupanatamwe Up-Biblum God Naneeswe Nukkone Testament Kah Wonk Wusku Testament* (printed by Samuel Green and Marmaduke Johnson, 1663, 2 volumes in 1 book [no. 177]). Other examples are James Evans, *The Speller and Interpreter in Indian and English for the Use of the Mission Schools, and Such as May Desire to Obtain a Knowledge of the Ojibway Tongues* (New York: D. Fanshaw, 1837 [no. 93]); Samuel Griswold Goodrich, *Abinoji Aki Tibajimouin* (text in Chippewa, taken primarily from Goodrich's *Peter Parley's Geography for Children* [Boston: Crocker and Brewster, 1840], printed for the American Board of Commissioners for Foreign Missions [no. 102]); Edwin James, *O-jib-ue Spelling Book, Designed for the Use of Native Learners* (Utica, NY: G. Tray, 1833), text in Chippewa (no. 110); Samuel W. Pond, *Dakota wiwangapi Wowapi: Catechism in the Dakota or Sioux Language* (New Haven: Hitchcock and Stafford, 1844 [no. 139]).

The Federal Years (1776–1860)

During the American Revolution, Indian education received some attention from the new government as a result of its campaign to win support from the

Indians in the fight against the British. Funds were given to ministers and teachers willing to live among the Indians and to serve as diplomatic agents. The missionaries continued to finance and to control Indian education, but the federal government became involved after it was established in 1789. The powerful tribes within America's boundaries and along its borders more or less compelled the government to assume responsibility for their education. Funds for schools and education for Indians were negotiated through the educational provisions of Indian treaties between 1788 and 1871, by executive order, and by the trade and intercourse laws enacted between 1790 and 1802.

In 1819, Congress passed an "act making provision for the civilization of the Indian tribes adjoining the frontier settlements" and authorized treaty annuities specifically for education in order to provide a constant and fixed amount of money for Indian education. The act annually appropriated

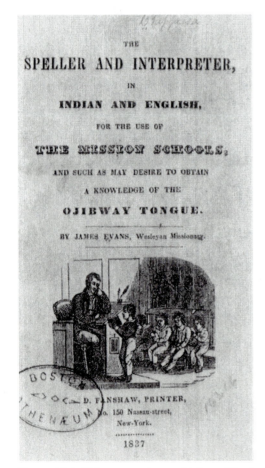

Figure 14.1 Title page and page 31 from *The Speller and Interpreter, in Indian and English, for the Use of the Mission Schools, and Such as May Desire to Obtain Knowledge of the Ojibway Tongue,* by James Evans. New York: Printed by D. Fanshaw, 1837. Rare Book PM/852/.E9. *Courtesy of the Boston Athenæum.*

$10,000 called the "civilization fund," to teach adult Indians agriculture and trades, and to teach the children reading, writing, and arithmetic.[35] Although this sum was relatively small considering the number of Indians to be educated, it encouraged the work of the missionaries and stimulated public contributions for the support of the missions. Hundreds of schools were opened in the early nineteenth century, both by missionaries and by Indian tribes. Some were boarding schools on and off reservations; others were academies. Many operated as manual labor schools, which combined academic and practical training. Others remained as day schools, either missionary or tribal. Schools for Indian children endorsed mainstream concepts of education. When public schools encouraged the teaching of good behavior, so did the Indian schools. There was neither a representative type of Indian school, nor was there a predictable Indian response to these schools.

The most widespread schooling developed among the tribes of the Southeast, especially among the Cherokee and Chocktaw. The Cherokee had established, funded, and managed bilingual schools with instruction in English and Cherokee for their children. They maintained their schools until they were forced in 1830 to leave the Southeast and resettle in the West in Indian territory (on reservations), where they reopened their schools and established additional ones. In December 1841, there was a system of eleven schools in the eight Cherokee districts, with the curricula consisting of reading, writing, arithmetic, bookkeeping, English grammar, geography, and history. By 1852, there were eleven hundred students in twenty-one schools and two academies. The Cherokee National Council, the tribal governing body, appointed a superintendent of the schools in 1853. All tribal schools had to close with the passage of the Curtis Act of 1898, which mandated the end of tribal governments in Indian territory.[36]

The Cherokee were among the most literate of the tribes. They had a written tradition. In the early nineteenth century, an elderly member of the tribe named Sequoyah came up with the Cherokee syllabary. Sequoyah figured out that all Cherokee words could be broken down into eighty-six sounds or syllables. To each he assigned a character. Many of the characters were from the English alphabet. With the help of missionaries working with the Cherokee, the Cherokee syllables were cast into type, and newspapers soon appeared in Cherokee. The Cherokee were becoming an educated people.[37] Because the Cherokee were literate, due to their own efforts, they felt entitled to hold on to their lands. However, government policy did not work that way.

As American settlers began moving westward over the Appalachian Mountains there was pressure to remove the Indians from their lands. While Presidents James Monroe (1817–1825) and John Quincy Adams (1825–1829) had used a voluntary Indian emigration policy, Andrew Jackson (1821–1837) used force. The 1830 Removal Act epitomized his Indian policy. When he wanted to move the Cherokee and they refused to leave their lands, what followed became one of the worst chapters in United States history.[38]

1860–1928 Assimilation

The Civil War dealt a blow to the school system in the Indian territories. In the decades that followed, many groups worked together to restore, improve, and expand the system. They included the Bureau of Indian Affairs (1824), missionaries, philanthropists, army officers, churches, and the Indian tribes. The reform resulted in (1) increased responsibility for education by the federal government and (2) the off-reservation boarding schools. The goal was assimilation. In 1870, Congress authorized an annual appropriation of $100,000 for the schooling of Indians. By 1893, the appropriation had reached about $2.3 million. Yet in 1880, only one out of every twelve Indian children was educated. More than half of the money went to maintain the day schools on the reservations, which were expected to provide elementary or primary education to Indian children and to prepare them to attend advanced schools.[39]

The Carlisle Indian School (1879–1918)

The off-reservation boarding school idea was advanced by Captain Richard Henry Pratt. Pratt, a Civil War veteran, was put in charge in 1875 of a group of seventy-two Indian prisoners in St. Augustine, Florida. Pratt's orders were vague as to how to treat the prisoners, and he decided to experiment with educating them. Pratt turned the prison into a school for teaching civilization to Indians, beginning with teaching them the English language. His efforts were successful for him and profitable for the Indians. In the spring of 1878, the prisoners were released. Some of them wanted to continue their education, and since neither the Indian Office nor the army had any objections, Pratt negotiated with Samuel Chapman Armstrong, the head of the Hampton Institute, and transferred twenty-two of them there.[40]

About that time, Pratt learned that Congress was looking for an army officer with "reference to Indian education." After a series of meetings with officials in Washington, including the Secretary of the Interior Carl Schurz, Pratt was authorized to recruit 125 students for the new Indian school. He was invited to inspect the unused military barracks at Carlisle, Pennsylvania, for the school's location. Pratt inspected the site and decided that, with a few changes, it would be fine. The off-reservation boarding school was meant to lower the costs of educating the young Native Americans while at the same time increasing the efficacy of their education by removing the students from their tribal environments.

Pratt recruited a small staff, including Miss Mather, who had been a teacher at St. Augustine, to oversee the Indian girls. Pratt and Miss Mather went to the Dakotas, concentrating on the Sioux at the Pine Ridge and Rosebud agencies to recruit students. The Sioux chiefs were reluctant to turn over their children, but Pratt kept telling them that the Indians' only defense against the white man was to learn his language and ways. Several chiefs agreed to hand him several children including their own, and Pratt left with sixty boys and twenty-four girls. He recruited thirty-eight more boys and fourteen girls. Pratt also arranged for eleven of the students he had sent to Hampton to come to Carlisle. On November 1, 1879, the Carlisle Indian School officially opened. It was the first and most famous off-reservation government boarding school for Indian children. Between 1879 and 1902, about twenty-five more off-reservation schools were established. Among them Haskell Institute in Lawrence, Kansas. After 1894, the boarding schools offered normal and commercial courses of study beyond the basic eight-year program. By 1900, there were 153 boarding schools with 17,708 children attending, and 154 day schools with 3,860 students.[41]

STUDENT RECRUITMENT

Most of the recruited students came voluntarily and with their parents' approval. Others who were coerced to attend were bitter. Separating from their family and community was particularly difficult for the younger children. It was easier for those who had attended day schools, for they were familiar with the ways of the whites. For the older boys, who could no longer fight to protect their homes and land, they considered it an act of bravery to attend the Carlisle School. This is how a Lakota Indian expressed it: "I thought I was going there to die; . . . I could think of white people wanting little Lakota children for no other reason than to kill them, but I thought here is my chance to prove that I can die bravely. So I went East to show my father and my people that I was brave and willing to die for them."[42]

When the parents were reluctant, resisted, or refused to send their children to boarding school, the agents either withheld the rations or used the agency police to round up the children. Sometimes the whole village refused to turn over their children. Parents slipped away for several weeks until the pressure was over, or offered orphans or children who lived on the fringe of the community. Some children ran away once in the school. Not all those attending graduated, especially in the early years.[43] Carlisle had about eight hundred students. Jim Thorpe (1886–1953) was the most famous of the Carlisle graduates. He participated in the 1912 Olympics in Stockholm and won the Decathlon.[44]

CURRICULUM

Since the children came from many tribes, it was easier to enforce the teaching and speaking of English. Once the children began to understand English, the teachers continued with the other subjects of the curriculum, including arithmetic, geography, nature study, physiology, and United States history. The purpose of these subjects was to introduce Indians to the knowledge of civilization, and to prepare them for citizenship. Of course, some aspects of the subjects taught jolted the Indians' previously held beliefs. For example, Indians believed the earth to be flat with four corners. What was most significant in teaching science to the Indians was the message conveyed. Traditionally, Indian children were taught to look on nature in ecological and spiritual terms. To know nature was to recognize one's dependency on the earth and its creatures. For the whites on the other hand, nature was to be controlled, conquered, and finally exploited.

Indian schools in addition to turning out law-abiding citizens were expected to produce citizens who were economically self-sufficient. Toward this goal, boys were also trained in trades like wagon building, harness making, tinsmithing, shoemaking, tailoring, printing, and painting. Farming was also pursued because the Indian Office insisted that the schools become as self-sufficient as possible. Products of the shop and the farm not consumed by the school were sold on the open market. The girls were instructed in cooking, canning, sewing, washing, ironing, child care, and cleaning—the standard duties of Victorian housewives. Carlisle and Haskell also offered girls training in shorthand, typing, and bookkeeping. Once the students mastered the prerequisites, they were eligible to participate in the "outing system." Pratt had initiated the outing system with the prisoners in St. Augustine, and it had been successful. Carlisle made arrangements for students to live with farm families, where they were immersed in the white culture.[45]

Pratt, although he liked the Native Americans, believed that Indian ways were in every way inferior to those of whites. He counseled all the students to forget their early years and tribal connections and to become "individualized" Americans. The education at Carlisle attempted to transform not only the material culture of the student but also cultural attitudes and values. Pratt's goal was to transform and to assimilate the Indian children by immersing them in the American culture and by teaching them the knowledge, values, mores, and habits of the Christian civilization.[46]

Pratt retired in 1904. Under his successors, Carlisle began to decline. There were problems with the dietary standards, a weakening of the school's moral atmosphere, a lack of human interest in the welfare of the student body. There was also the issue of severe corporal punishment. Students signed a petition for an official investigation of the school. In 1918, Carlisle was closed under the pretext that the facilities were needed as a hospital for the soldiers returning from World War I.[47]

One wonders if the effort to assimilate the Native Americans through education was part of the larger movement at the turn of the century to achieve national unity at a time when the nation was receiving large numbers of immigrant populations.

William N. Hailmann (1836–1920)

William N. Hailmann was appointed Superintendent of Indian Schools (1894–1898), by President Grover Cleveland. He was an outstanding educational leader, as discussed in Chapter 8. He was a Froebelian who had established a kindergarten in the German-American Academy in Milwaukee and a kindergarten training class.

Prior to becoming Superintendent of Indian Schools, Hailmann had been superintendent of the LaPorte, Indiana, public schools for the previous ten years. There he had developed a system of education based on Froebel's theory. He stressed student self-government and activity-oriented learning from kindergarten through high school. He also pointed out the importance of the family and of community participation in the schools. Hailmann accepted the position of Superintendent of Indian Schools, for he saw it as an opportunity to show the effectiveness of an education based on Froebel's ideas for all children of all ages. He believed that Froebel's ideas and methods—self-activity, cooperation, sharing of materials, and gardening—were better suited for the education of Native American children, who traditionally were more community oriented and less competitive than white children, and more attuned to their natural environment.

Hailmann was to administer all the schools on and off the reservations. He was also authorized to prepare courses of study, to select textbooks, to maintain facilities, and to select employees. He was to visit and inspect either personally or through his appointed agents, all schools for Indians and to report to the Commissioner of Indian Affairs their condition, defects, and requirements.[48]

When Hailmann became Superintendent of Indian Schools, boarding schools were a priority. He tried to introduce changes to the drudgery of the school life, to make learning more enjoyable. He introduced readers based on nature study, and began to reorganize the curriculum with a syllabus on language and another for arithmetic. They were both based on things found in the natural environment and involving hands-on activities such as counting stones. He integrated arithmetic into the school's agriculture, industrial, and domestic science programs. He encouraged storytelling of tribal legends by older students or Indian staff members, so students would have pride in their origins.

For the boarding students using the barracks for dormitories, Hailmann encouraged them to divide into smaller areas and to decorate their area. The evening hours were made social periods with staff and students playing games and providing other entertainment instead of isolated study. He stopped the practice of adults eating separately and different food. The most important change for Indian schools was in the attitude of the teachers toward the Indian students.[49] Hailmann also tried to limit the industrial work in the schools, which had become drudgery and had filtered down to the kindergarten. Estelle Brown, a Crow Creek, remembered how "small girls from the kindergarten daily darned stockings for hours on end."[50] He suggested that the Indian schools be replaced with public schools.

Hailmann introduced Froebelian kindergartens staffed by trained teachers into the reservation boarding schools. They were very successful. He stated, "The children entered into the work and games with zest and intelligence. . . . They acquired the English idiom with much ease and learned to express their ideas fully and with eagerness." By 1897, there were forty such successful kindergartens. Hailmann also introduced three normal schools and kindergarten training. At the Carlisle School and the Haskell Institute, those who had completed the teacher training course could for an additional year be trained in Froebelian kindergarten teaching.[51]

One such kindergarten is described by Lucie Calista Maley,[52] a kinder-gartner. She had worked with this group of twenty-five children for two years. They began with their home life and made teepees and moccasins and then moved to the white children's home life. She found that the Native American children had no idea of "mine and thine." They had a garden. Each child took care of his or her own plot and was responsible for the plants. The children planted seeds and through observation learned what effect sun, light, and rain had on the plants (438–439). The children were taught patriotism—they did not know that they had a share in the flag—by saluting the flag every morning. They also said their prayers and sang "love is our motto in work or in play." Courtesy to the teacher and to each other was continually taught. The kindergarten was seen as a preparation for later schooling, and to fit the children into the larger society (440–441). Erik Erikson, years later, called attention to an important feature of Sioux culture, the "give away" system of sharing that was taught to the children, which sometimes is misunderstood by the white culture. A child's property was his until he let it go. The child was expected to share, and he was shamed if he did not. The sharing of food and other property was crucial to a tribe of nomadic hunters.[53] The Sioux sharing was similar to the ideas of community encouraged in the kindergarten.

The Meriam Report

By the 1920s, it had become apparent that the federal policies of Indian education for the past fifty years had not been successful. Although 90 percent of the Indian children started school, a large proportion of them dropped out early. On some reservations, the average education level was fifth grade. Half of the children attended public schools, about a third were in schools operated by the Bureau of Indian Affairs (BIA), and about 10 percent were in private or mission schools. Those who attended BIA schools were equally enrolled in reservation and off-reservation boarding schools, with a smaller number in day schools.

Those who attended BIA boarding schools returned to their reservations and were unable to apply the training they had received. Course work in these schools was usually unrelated to the students' environment and culture. The vocational training was either not sufficient for helping students find jobs or the trades that they were taught were disappearing from the market. The concept of training for reservation life had never fulfilled the goal anticipated in 1900. The educational level of day schools was low, and the problem of the runaways became the symbol of the failure of the boarding schools.[54]

In January 1926, the Board of Indian Commissioners asked the Institute of Government Research, an independent unit of the Brookings Institution, to conduct a study of the conditions of Indian life. Lewis Meriam, one of the most knowledgeable staff members on government efficiency, was selected to lead the investigation. In January 1928, the findings were presented to the Secretary of the Interior as *The Problem of Indian Administration*, more commonly known as the *Meriam Report*.

The *Meriam Report* pointed out that the majority of Indians were very poor and had not adjusted to the economic and social system of the dominant white society. The economic development and government programs for the Indians were inadequate. A particular problem was the poor quality of Indian service personnel. Finally, the *Meriam Report* stated that the Indian problem could never be solved until the Bureau of Indian Affairs—operating since 1824–was properly funded by Congress and the BIA administration had technical expertise to modernize reservation economies. The Indian schools needed to genuinely prepare students for economic self-sufficiency and civic participation.

The *Report* also criticized the conditions in the boarding schools. Because of limited congressional appropriations, the children were denied the necessary amounts of fruits, vegetables, and milk unless the schools had their own farms and dairies. Poor nutrition combined with overcrowded dormitories and improper treatment of sick children led to epidemics.

The *Meriam Report* brought about a major shift in Indian education. Past educational efforts emphasized the removal of the child from his environment, home, and community. The current view stressed the need to connect the child's education to family and community, which was the pedagogy of progressive education, and to build on the needs and concerns of the Native Americans. Students were to be educated for as long as it was practical in day schools, where educational methods could be adapted to individual abilities, interests, and needs. The teacher was to gather material from the life of Indians so that the little children could proceed from the known to the unknown. The idea of a uniform curriculum was rejected because it ignored local conditions. It was also recommended that the upper classes of the boarding schools be brought into alignment with those of the public schools, thus encouraging students to attend college. Pre-adolescent children were to attend day schools near their homes. The new policy also opened the door for Indians' participation in decisions regarding their education. If a Native American wanted to enter mainstream white society, he should be given all the assistance and advice needed to make the necessary adjustment. But if another Native American wanted to live according to his traditional culture, he should be helped to do so.[55]

The *Meriam Report* suggested that education should be the primary function of the BIA, should be geared to all age levels, and should be tied to the community. It encouraged construction of day schools to serve as community centers, proposed extensive reform of boarding schools, and introduced Indian culture in the curriculum. It also recommended that salaries and standards be raised. Will Carlson Ryan was the first director of education of the

BIA. He was influenced by the progressive education ideas of schooling. Between 1930 and 1970, Ryan and his four successors tried to implement the recommendations of the *Meriam Report*.[56]

It was not until the mid-1930s that the BIA for the first time offered Indian children education that acknowledged the importance of their native cultures. Algebra, geometry, and ancient history were replaced with rug weaving, silver making, and tribal history. Willard W. Beatty, the second director of education (1936–1952), introduced the first bilingual texts, entitled the *Indian Life Series*. It was the first effort to meet the needs of the non-English-speaking Indian child. The chief difficulty in developing bilingual texts was the lack of written Native American languages. A large number of the languages that had survived were oral. Of equal importance for bilingual education was the preparation of Indian service teachers in the techniques of bilingual teaching. Beatty developed one of the earliest bilingual training programs in the country. He recognized that the language problem was one of the greatest problems of the Native American children.[57]

World War II and Beyond (1945–1986)

World War II touched and changed the lives of all Native Americans. Over 40,000 left their homes to participate in war-related work; 24,000 served in the U.S. Armed Forces. This meant a significant increase in income for some, but most important, it introduced new concepts and brought them a greater appreciation for the value of schooling. Between 1946 and the early 1960s, the BIA provided basic schooling for 4,300 overage Navajo students. The goal of the program was to provide in five years the same education the child would otherwise receive in ten or twelve years. The students also received vocational training to help them find jobs. Job training was primarily geared for urban living.[58]

Federal Legislation/Self-Determination

The years between 1965 and 1978 produced the most significant legislation on Indian education in American history. Under Title I of the Elementary and Secondary Education Act of 1965, Indian children in public schools qualified for special benefits as children of low-income families. It increased the amount of money available to schools already reimbursed for educating Indian children through the "federally impacted area" legislation of the 1950s and the Johnson-O'Malley Act of 1934. The legislation also provided for greater participation of Native Americans in their own schooling.[59]

Another important development in Indian education was the passage in 1968 of Title VII–Bilingual Education Act, amended in 1974 and 1978, which provided financial assistance to state and local educational agencies to meet the educational needs of children of limited English-speaking abilities. Section 706 of the 1968 Act and Section 722 of the 1974 and 1978 amendments dealt specifically with bilingual education for Native American children. Since 1968, the number of Native American Indian bilingual education programs has grown steadily. The 1978 amendment expanded the eligibility for Title VII funding to Indian students from "home environments where a language other than English has had 'significant impact' on their English proficiency."[60]

The Head Start program for Native American children was a result of the Economic Opportunity Act of 1964. Head Start is discussed in Chapter 13.

The Indian Education Act of 1972 mandated parental and community participation in the programs funded by it. It encouraged programs that stressed culturally relevant and bilingual curriculum materials, established the Office of Indian Education in the Department of Education, and created the National Advisory Council on Indian Education to review applications for grants under the Act.

The Indian Self-Determination and Education Assistance Act of 1975 implemented the "self-determination" policies stressed by Presidents Lyndon Johnson and Richard Nixon. It also introduced the incorporation of regulations drafted by Indian leaders.[61]

A federal policy statement recognizing the language rights of American Indians, Alaskan Natives, Native Hawaiians, and Pacific Islanders living in U.S. trust territories was enacted in 1990. It authorized no new programs, but it was expected to facilitate efforts to preserve indigenous languages that are unique in the United States.[62]

SARAH WINNEMUCCA (1844–1891)

Sarah Winnemucca's biography is included to give an example of the actual plight of the Native Americans. She was self-educated and spent her short life trying to improve the living conditions and the education of her people, the Puites or Pauites. Through these efforts Sarah met Elizabeth Peabody and Mary Mann during her trip to Boston in the spring of 1883. All of these persons were discussed in Chapter 9.

According to Canfield,[63] Sarah was born about 1844, into the Paiute tribe that freely roamed the plateau deserts of the Great Basin in what is today western Nevada, northeastern California, and southern Oregon. Her Indian name was "Shell-Flower." She was the second daughter and fourth of nine children of Winnemucca II, the Paiute chief. Her grandfather, Winnemucca I, better known as Captain Truckee, was impressed by the white man's ways and chose to be friends with them. In 1850, Captain Truckee took a number of his people, including his granddaughter Sarah, to work on a ranch in the San Joaquin Valley. Sarah, who had a gift for languages, learned Spanish and English. Her English improved after she had spent about a year in the home of Major William Ormsby as his daughter's companion. While there, she assumed the name Sarah and became a nominal Christian without losing her primitive beliefs, which centered on a "Spirit Father." In 1860, at her grandfather's dying request, she was sent to school at St. Mary's Convent in San

Jose, California. Her formal education ended abruptly after three weeks. Wealthy parents objected to the presence of an Indian child, forcing the nuns to send her home (3–14, 30, 31).

The influx of white settlers into western Nevada and the first clash with the Indians (the Paiute War of 1860) brought an end to the establishment of a Paiute reservation at Pyramid Lake (north of the town of Reno). There began the griefs of Sarah's people at the hands of corrupt Indian agents, who at best did nothing to help the Paiutes adjust to the white man's ways and at worst exploited them, leaving them starving and destitute. In 1865, worse trouble erupted when the Paiutes stole some white men's cattle. In retaliation, soldiers from a nearby army post marched against the Indian camp while its warriors were off on a hunt; they killed women, children, and old men; set fire to the reed huts; and were even said to have hurled small children into the flames. "I had one baby brother killed there," Sarah wrote later. Without resources, many of the Paiutes, in preference to further fighting, flocked to military posts for the rations that the army issued them. Sarah served for several years (c. 1868–1871) as post interpreter at Camp McDermit in northeastern Nevada. In 1871, Sarah married First Lieutenant Edward C. Bartlett in spite of the prohibition of marriages between Indians and whites. She left him within a year because of his intemperance. Sarah later married an Indian husband, whom she also left because he grossly abused her (24–25, 65).

In 1872, the Paiutes were sent to the Malheur Reservation in southeastern Oregon, with Samuel Parrish as the Indian agent. Sarah became Parrish's interpreter in 1875 and assisted at the agency school taught by Mrs. Parrish (94, 105).

When the Bannock War broke out in June 1878, Sarah offered her services to the army, helped to free her father and a number of his followers, and brought the troops much needed information. She then served as General Oliver O. Howard's guide, scout, and interpreter during the campaign. After the Bannock War, she lectured in San Francisco, appealing especially on behalf of the Paiutes, who had not fought but were nonetheless exiled along with the hostile Indians to the Yakima Reservation in Washington Territory (109–122).

During the winter of 1880, Sarah received an invitation to go to Washington, D.C., with her father and other tribesmen at government expense. In January 1880, she pleaded the Indians' cause with Secretary of the Interior Carl Schurz and President Rutherford B. Hayes. Secretary Schurz when meeting with Sarah gave her a letter (174) authorizing the Paiutes' return to the Malheur Reservation, where they were promised individual allotments of land. However, the Yakima Indian agent refused to release the land in his charge, fearing the Paiutes' passage would arouse the white settlers. Unfortunately, Major William V. Rinehart, the last Indian agent at Malheur, sent affidavits from white settlers that discredited Sarah to Washington.

In spite of Secretary Schurz's letter to Sarah and his promise for land, none of the Paiutes received the "land in severalty" at the Malheur Reservation, which had been allowed to revert to the public domain, seemingly for the benefit of white stock-growers. Sarah was devastated (173–175, 180–181).

Sarah next went to Vancouver (Washington) Barracks, where she taught the Bannock Indian children. While she was there, President Hayes visited the barracks. Sarah pleaded with the president to have her people gathered at one place where they could live permanently, be cared for, and be instructed. Hayes replied that he could not make any promises. There was no change in the Paiutes' life (187). Sarah was courted by Lieutenant Lewis H. Hopkins, whom she married later in 1881 (192).

Sarah and her husband arrived in Boston in the spring of 1883. Among the many sympathizers were Elizabeth Palmer Peabody and Mary Peabody Mann, whose social circle included many prominent Bostonians. They took Sarah under their wing and worked hard to advance her cause. Elizabeth proposed that Sarah give a series of lectures to inform audiences of the history and culture of the Paiutes and their present circumstances (200). Sarah decided to write about her people because she could cover only a few points in her lectures. She wrote *Life Among the Piutes: Their Wrongs and Claims,* the story of her own life, told in eight chapters (203). The book had 268 pages and a 20-page appendix, which included the letters of recommendation and affirmation in defense of her character (204). It was printed in 1883 by subscription and it cost one dollar. Mary P. Mann edited the manuscript and wrote the preface. Sarah lectured in Rhode Island, Connecticut, New York, Vermont, Massachusetts, Pennsylvania, and Maryland. After the lectures she would sign copies of the book (209). Its sale helped defray Sarah's expenses of the tour. The book was honest, free from willful misrepresentation, vivid, and full of naïve charm. Sarah secured thousands of signatures on a petition calling on the government to grant lands in severalty to the Paiutes for a reservation, to make them U.S. citizens, and to allow them to govern themselves (212). Her petition to Congress was referred to the Senate Subcommittee on Indian Affairs, where Sarah spoke at length. She pleaded for a reservation at Fort McDermit and land given to each head of a family. She asked that the annuities granted by Congress to the Paiutes be administered by the military rather than the Indian Bureau. In 1884, Congress passed such a bill, not for Fort McDermit but for another piece of land, the Pyramid Lake Reservation. It had no arable land left to be assigned to the Paiutes and the fishing was dominated by Chinese fishermen. Sarah understood that all was lost (214–215).

The Peabody Indian School

Leland Stanford, the California railroad builder, had given Sarah's brother, Natchez, 160 acres of land near Lovelock, Nevada, which Natchez tried to develop. He built a frame house there and moved with his large family and he pleaded that all of his people should receive land of their own. Sarah began holding classes for Natchez' six children. It was her intention, supported by Elizabeth Peabody, to create a school taught by and for Indians, where they would not be separated from their Indian life and languages, as they were in the government schools, which were miles away from their homes. At the same time, Peabody spent several months in Washington in the interest of her "Piute friend." Peabody was hoping that President Cleveland's Democratic government would improve the government's Indian policy (226–227).

Sarah had come to believe that she could help her people only by teaching English to the children and giving them a basic education. She also wanted to help the children to be proud of the traditional attitude of concern and caring for one another and to respect the sacredness of life around them (228). Sarah named the school the Elizabeth Peabody School in honor of her friend. She taught the children gospel hymns, which she interpreted in Paiute. She taught English by first asking each child to say something in Paiute. She then would say the words in English and would write them on the blackboard so the children could copy them in their books. She also taught them to draw and to cipher. Sarah sent examples of the children's work to Elizabeth and Mary (232). Each day after the academic subjects, Sarah taught the children to work on the ranch. The boys tended the garden and cared for the stock, and the girls cooked and sewed. Peabody called the school "a vanguard of the 'New Education' in which doing leads to thinking, and gives definite meaning to every word used."[64] Sarah's objective was to make her students teachers, to use the older ones as assistants and substitutes, and to encourage the students to undertake their own self-education as she had done.

The school and the farm interested many citizens in Nevada and on the East Coast because it was an Indian-initiated project, in contrast to the reservation farms and schools, and consequently there was great pressure on the brother and sister to succeed in light of the formidable obstacles they had faced from the beginning. Sarah at this time was sick with rheumatism and shaken with recurrent fevers.

Elizabeth and her friends sent money and goods for construction of the house that was to contain the school and a room for a white teacher whom they hoped would come from the East. The building would also serve for cooking and eating and would contain council rooms and a worship center. Sarah sent the receipts of the expenses to Elizabeth (233).

Sarah had a school building but not desks and other conveniences that government boarding schools in the area had (235). Afraid that the children would go with their families to the mountains on their annual hunt for winter food and disrupt their studies, Sarah wanted to keep them as boarders. Peabody raised $100 to keep the children as boarders during April (237).

The school interested local whites, who visited it and commented on Sarah's work. Impressed by the children's knowledge, they said that it should be assisted by the Indian Bureau. However, Sarah's school did not exist as far as the government was concerned. Unless Sarah surrendered the directorship of her school, she could not receive funds from the government (238, 239). This was during the time that schools for Indian children were run by whites, and the policy was to remove the children from their families and communities. Sarah's hopes for government support never materialized. Nevertheless, she taught for three years with remarkable success.

In 1886, Sarah's husband died of tuberculosis. Sarah, exhausted by her struggles, retired to her married sister's home in Monida, Montana, where she spent her last years in failing health, herself a victim of consumption. She died in 1891 at the age of forty-seven. *The New York Times* carried her death notice and printed a review of her zealous, adventurous life (259).

Indian Reservations

Indian reservations were originally areas of land with specific boundaries for Indian use. They were created through treaties, congressional acts, executive orders, and agreements. After the policy of tribal ownership-in-common was changed in some instances and land was allotted to individual Indians, much of the reservation land has been sold by individual Indians who preferred cash to land, and many sales have been to non-Indians.[65]

The Bureau of Indian Affairs (BIA)

The Bureau of Indian Affairs was created in 1824 by Secretary of War John C. Calhoun. Thomas L. McKenny, a former superintendent of Indian trade, became its first head. With two assistants, it was the Indian secretariat within the War Department. The secretariat granted the appropriations for annuities, approved all vouchers for expenditures, administered the funds appropriated to "civilize" the Indians, decided claims arising between Indians and whites under the trade and intercourse acts, and handled correspondence dealing with Indian affairs. In 1832, statutory authority for an Office of Indian Affairs within the War Department was obtained, and in 1849, the Office of Indian Affairs was transferred to the new Department of the Interior.[66]

In 1943, Commissioner John Collier, because of the recommendations in the *Meriam Report* and congressional pressure, transferred many of the BIA functions, such as law and order, health, and education, to tribal, state, county, or municipal governments. An example of this policy was that, in 1950, Congress authorized a joint county-Indian hospital in Albuquerque to serve both Indians and non-Indians. In 1955, the responsibility for the health of Native Americans was transferred from the BIA to the Public Health Service. From the 1940s to the 1960s, an increased number of functions were transferred to the states. The BIA was restructured and dispersed to different locations after the occupation of the BIA building in 1972 by the American Indian Movement's Trail of Broken Treaties. The BIA was removed from the jurisdiction of the Department of the Interior and placed under jurisdiction of the Secretary of Indian Affairs.

The 1975 Indian Self-Determination and Education Assistance Act implemented the "self-determination" policies. This Act has had a significant impact on the BIA and the Indian Health Service organizations, as it has encouraged tribes to operate government programs for themselves under government contracts or grants.

Education achieved some separation from the control of BIA generalists as a result of the Education Amendments Act of 1978, which established a direct line of authority from the assistant secretary to the director of education to the education personnel in the field. Indians were given preference in employment at the BIA. They currently make up the majority of the BIA's personnel.[67]

The movement was to transform the BIA from a direct operating and service agency, as it had been during the last quarter of the nineteenth and first quarter of the twentieth centuries, to a contracting or granting agency. It was a change of major magnitude.

The Bureau of Indian Affairs has been termed "a government in miniature." It combines the tremendous variety of many local and state functions with federal functions. It has the duties of a trustee that are normally found only in the private sector. It is involved in direct service operations, technical assistance, training, monitoring of work contracted outside the agency, and the surveillance of reimbursable work done by other bureaus of the Department of the Interior. The BIA also collaborates with other government services on behalf of Indian citizens. Complicating the BIA's work are racial and cultural factors, a guilt complex on the part of many citizens, and a "you owe it to us" attitude on the part of many Indians. An estimated five thousand statutes, many treaties, and thousands of court decisions on Indian policy and procedure add to this complexity.[68]

Chapter Summary

Indian tribes are no longer independent groups in the same sense that they were prior to the invasion of North America by Europeans. Indians are now citizens of the United States and of the states in which they reside. There are millions of people with some Indian blood who do not identify themselves as Indians. The Bureau of Indian Affairs serves only federally recognized Indians who are primarily located on or near federal Indian reservations. Nearly one-half of the people who identify themselves as Indians live in non-reservation situations, primarily in metropolitan areas. The states also serve large numbers of Native Americans, including many who are on federal reservations. Approximately 90 percent of all Indian children are educated in state public school systems, where their cultural identity is preserved while they are developing skills for economic self-sufficiency.

Indian education has reflected the two policies of the government: assimilation and self-determination. Today the Native Americans participate in all educational and other matters affecting their lives.

Notes

1. The terms "Native American," "Indian," or "North American Indian" are used throughout the chapter because they were found in the reviewed literature.

2. John M. Cooper, "Child Training among Primitive Peoples," *Primitive Man Quarterly Bulletin of the Catholic Anthropological Conference* 1 (1928): 12.

3. Robert Bunge, "Language: The Psyche of a People," in *Language Loyalties, A Source Book on the Official English Controversy,* ed. James Crawford (Chicago: University of Chicago Press, 1992), 377.

4. James Crawford, "Endangered Native American Languages: What Is to Be Done and Why?" *Bilingual Research Journal* 19 (Winter 1995): 19.

5. Theodore W. Taylor, *The Bureau of Indian Affairs* (Boulder, CO: Westview Press, 1984), 19. For information on the structure of Native American tribes, see Lewis Henry Morgan, *Ancient Society* (New York: Henry Holt, 1878; reprint, Tucson, AZ: University of Arizona Press, 1985), 62–234 (page citations are to the reprint edition).

6. Margaret C. Szasz, *Indian Education in the American Colonies, 1607–1783* (Albuquerque: University of New Mexico Press, 1988), 8–9.

7. Margaret C. Szasz, "Native American Children," in Joseph Hawes and N. Ray Hiner, eds., *American Childhood: A Research Guide and Historical Handbook* (Westport, CT: Greenwood Press, 1985), 314–316.

8. Cooper, "Child Training among Primitive Peoples," 10.

9. George A. Pettitt, *Primitive Education in North America* (University of California Publications in American Archaeology and Ethnology, vol. 43, 1946–1956 (Berkeley, CA, 1946; reprint, New York: Kraus Reprint Co., 1971), 3 (page citations are to the reprint edition).

10. Ibid., 7–8.

11. Ibid., 11. The idea of children being close to the supernatural was also discussed in Chapter 1 of this volume.

12. Cooper, "Child Training among Primitive Peoples," 11.

13. Wayne Dennis and Marsena G. Dennis, "Cradles and Cradling Practices of the Pueblo Indians," *American Anthropologist* 42 (January–March 1940): 107–115.

14. Pettitt, *Primitive Education,* 41–43, 46. For more about Native American toys, see Don and Debra McQuiston, *Dolls and Toys of Native America: A Journey through Childhood* (San Francisco: Chronicle Books, 1995). Plato had recommended that toys be actual implements.

15. Pettitt, *Primitive Education,* 57.

16 Ibid., 6–10, 47.

17. Ibid., 15–25.

18. Cooper, "Child Training Among Primitive Peoples," 13.

19. Pettitt, *Primitive Education,* 59–68.

20. Lewis H. Morgan (1818–1881), a cultural anthropologist, identified the various stages in cultural evolution and the factors that characterize each successive stage. He calculated that there are "seven ethnical periods" from savagery to civilization, and that all peoples could be placed somewhere on this gradation. He organized these stages according to inventions of each period. Each society goes through these stages at different times. He used the comparative method to demonstrate that societies are interconnected to the extent they go through the similar evolutionary pattern. Morgan, *Ancient Society,* 3–19.

21. Brewton Berry, *The Education of American Indians: A Survey of the Literature* (Washington, DC: United States Department of Health, Education and Welfare, Office of Economic Opportunity, 1968), 9–10. For a history of Native Americans, see Angie Debo, *A History of Indians in the United States* (Norman: University of Oklahoma Press, 1970).

22. Berry, *The Education of American Indians,* 11. For more on the churches' influence, see Francis P. Prucha, *The Churches and the Indian Schools, 1888–1912* (Lincoln: University of Nebraska Press, 1979).

23. Margaret C. Szasz, *Indian Education in the American Colonies, 1607–1783* (Albuquerque: University of New Mexico Press, 1988), 103; Lawrence A. Cremin, *American Education: The Colonial Experience, 1607–1783* (New York: Harper & Row, Harper Torchbooks, 1970), 158.

24. Cremin, *American Education,* 194.

25. Ibid., 222–223.

26. Robert F. Young, *Comenius in England* (London: Humphrey Milford, 1932; reprint, New York: Arno Press & the New York Times, 1971), 93–94.

27. Ola E. Winslow, *John Eliot: "Apostle to the Indians"* (Boston: Houghton Mifflin, 1968). It is the best biography of John Eliot.

28. Cremin, *American Education*, 160.

29. Ibid., 509; Szasz, *Indian Education*, 195, 200, 218. For a history of Dartmouth College, see Leon B. Richardson, *History of Dartmouth College* (Hanover, NH: Dartmouth College Publications, 1933).

30. Szasz, *Indian Education*, 221.

31. Ibid., 221–222.

32. Ibid., 152–154.

33. Neal E. Salisbury, "Red Puritans: The 'Praying Indians' of Massachusetts Bay and John Eliot," *William and Mary Quarterly*, 3d ser., 31 (January 1974): 27–54.

34. Robert Kruse, *The Henry Rowe Schoolcraft Collection: A Catalogue of Books in Native American Languages in the Library of the Boston Athenæum* (Boston: The Boston Athenæum, 1991). This book was part of an exhibition at the Boston Athenæum. The numbers in the parentheses in the text are the numbers referring to items in the book.

35. Margaret C. Szasz and Carmelita Ryan, "American Indian Education" in *History of Indian-White Relations*, ed. Wicomb E. Washburn, vol. 4 (Washington, DC: Smithsonian Institution, 1988), 288; Lawrence A. Cremin, *American Education: The National Experience, 1783–1876* (New York: Harper & Row, 1980), 234.

36. Szasz and Ryan, "American Indian Education," 289, 290.

37. Kruse, *The Schoolcraft Collection*, 82 (no. 208), is Sequoyah's *Cherokee Alphabet: Characters as Arranged by the Inventor*.

38. Grace S. Woodward, *The Cherokees* (Norman: University of Oklahoma Press, 1963), 195, 205, 218.

39. Szasz and Ryan, "American Indian Education," 290.

40. David W. Adams, *Education for Extinction: American Indians and the Boarding School, Experience, 1875–1928* (Lawrence: University Press of Kansas, 1995), 38–39, 44. For details about Pratt's program for the Indian prisoners, Ibid., pages 40–47. For the Indians at Hampton, see Donal F. Lindsey, *Indians at Hampton Institute, 1877–1923* (Urbana and Chicago: University of Illinois Press, 1995).

41. Adams, *Education for Extinction*, 48–49, 57–58, 62.

42. Luther Standing Bear, quoted in Adams, *Education for Extinction*, 98, 100.

43. Ibid., 211.

44. One of the authors visited the Carlisle School in July 1981.

45. Luther Standing Bear, quoted in Adams, *Education for Extinction*, 142, 144–145, 149–150, 156–163.

46. Ibid., 51–52.

47. Ibid., 323–25.

48. Dorothy W. Hewes, "Those First Good Years of Indian Education: 1894–1898," *American Indian Culture and Research Journal* 5, no. 2 (1981): 63–64. Pratt openly opposed Hailmann's authority to select the teachers for the Carlisle school. Adams, *Education for Extinction*, 322.

49. Hewes, "Those First Good Years of Indian Education," 70–71.

50. Adams, *Education for Extinction*, 151.

51. Nina Vandewalker, *The Kindergarten in American Education* (New York: Macmillan, 1923), 206–207; Hewes, "Those First Good Years of Indian Education," 71.

52. Lucie Calista Maley, "Benefit of the Kindergarten to the Indian Children," *Kindergarten Magazine* 10, no. 7 (March 1898): 438–441. There is no indication where this kindergarten was located, or if the children came from one or more tribes.

53. Erik H. Erikson, *Childhood and Society*, 2d ed., rev. and enl. (New York: Norton, 1963), 129.

54. Margaret C. Szasz, *Education and the American Indian: The Road to Self-Determination, 1928–1973* (Albuquerque: University of New Mexico Press, 1974), 2.

55. Adams, *Education for Extinction*, 331–333.

56. Szasz, *Education and the American Indian*, 3, 17.

57. Ibid., 32, 72–75.

58. Ibid., 107, 116.

59. Ibid., 181–183, 185.

60. Szasz and Ryan, "American Indian Education," 299.

61. Taylor, *The Bureau of Indian Affairs*, 144–145.

62. James Crawford, ed., *Language Loyalties* (Chicago: University of Chicago Press, 1992), 155.

63. Gae Whitney Canfield, *Sarah Winnemucca of the Northern Paiutes* (Norman: University of Oklahoma Press, 1983). "Paiutes" or "Piutes" are used interchangeably.

64. Ibid., 240. Sarah's plan of education, combining book learning with practical experience, appears to be very similar to the plan submitted by Froebel and his colleagues to the Duke of Meinengen, discussed in Chapter 4 of this volume.

65. Taylor, *The Bureau of Indian Affairs,* 79–81.

66. Ibid., 34.

67. Ibid., 39–41.

68. Ibid., 75.

CHAPTER 15
Black Americans[1]

Tisn't he who had stood and looked on that can tell
you what slavery is—'tis he who has endured.
—John Little, 1885[2]

We shall overcome, some day
—Martin Luther King

When the countries of Europe decided to develop the New World, they were primarily interested in the exploitation of its natural resources. Labor was necessary, and the cheaper the better. The Europeans looked to the Indians, who were readily available, but they were excessively inhuman in the employment of Indian slaves in the mines of Haiti, and working in the fields of the Caribbean almost wiped the Indians out. The Indians were very susceptible to the European diseases, and their background did not prepare them for the regime of the plantation system and eliminated them as workers in the economic system developed by the Europeans. The search for acceptable workers in large numbers became a major preoccupation of the English and Spanish colonists in the seventeenth century.

It was the forces let loose by the Renaissance and the Industrial Revolution that created the institution of slavery and the slave trade. The Renaissance gave man a new kind of freedom to pursue ends that would be beneficial to his soul and body. It developed to such an extent that it resulted in the destruction of long-established practices and beliefs and even in the destruction of the rights of others to pursue the same ends for their own benefit.

The last half of the fifteenth century may be considered as the years of preparation for the slave trade. The Spanish and the Portuguese were establishing orderly trade relations with the natives of Africa and were constructing forts and trading posts where they could carry on their business. It was the period when Europeans were becoming accustomed to having Negroes do their work and were finding new tasks for them. In Spain, for example, Negroes were servants. The Portuguese were the first to engage in the African slave trade. Spain had been excluded from Africa by the Papal Arbitration of 1493—which settled the conflict of colonizing the New World. What was west and south of the Azores and the Cape Verde Islands went to Spain; what was east went to Portugal. Spain was forced to grant the task of carrying slaves to her colonies to various companies and individuals from other countries.

The slave trade that developed into such big business in the seventeenth and eighteenth centuries was in the hands of Dutch, French, and English companies.[3]

Slavery became an institution used primarily for the production of goods, cotton, tobacco, and sugar cane from which wealth could be derived.

AMERICA'S PECULIAR INSTITUTION

The twenty Negroes left at Jamestown, Virginia, in 1619 were the beginning of the involuntary importation of human beings into the colonies that was not to stop until more than two centuries later. Their arrival did not solve the labor problem of the young colony. They were listed as servants in the census of 1623 and as late as 1651. Some Negroes whose period of service had expired were assigned land in much the same way that was done for white servants. The idea of having to replace the labor force, the indentured servants, every few years as their period of service expired was most unsatisfactory in a country where so much work had to be done. The answer to the problem appeared to be the perpetual servitude of Negroes, whose supply seemed inexhaustible and did not present any of the problems posed by the white servants. If they ran away, they were easy to find. If they became ungovernable, they could be treated with greater severity than the whites because they represented heathen people who would not claim the immunities accorded to Christians.[4] The slaves were treated with harshness and severity to the point of death, even though they were the foundation on which great wealth was accumulated.

THE SLAVE QUARTER

The slave quarter refers to the geographic location on the antebellum plantation that contained the living quarters of the field hands and their families.[5] The physical condition and appearance of the cabins depended on the wealth and inclination of the plantation owner. Slaves wanted their cabins out of sight and hearing of the master's house.

Each cabin was a single room of about fourteen square feet constructed of wood logs daubed with mud and sticks. It had two windows, a door, and a large, rude fireplace. There was no plastering; it had only dirt floors. Mud and stick chimneys would catch fire often.[6] Households with many children were permitted to add a second room to their cabins.

The furnishings of the cabins were generally very simple, consisting of homemade chairs, tables, and beds that could be cleaned easily and scoured with sand. In most cabins, the beds were built in a corner with one leg out and the two walls supporting the other sides. The mattresses were filled with wheat straw; each spring, they were refilled with fresh wheat straw. They had blankets and quilts filled with home-raised wool. Children slept in trundle beds that were pushed under the big bed during the day. Boxes were used for everything from bureaus and chairs to storing food. The cabins had tallow candles or lamps, a broom made of straw or corn shucks, and various cooking utensils. Gourds raised by the slaves in many sizes served many purposes.

Figure 15.1 Quarters for field slaves. *Reproduced from the Collections of the Library of Congress, Washington, D.C.*

Most slaves also possessed at least one big wooden water bucket and a large wash barrel. The most prominent feature of many cabins was the large fireplace. Many slaves did much of their cooking in a large three-legged black pot called "the spider." Both the blacks living in the cabins and the white authorities took care to ensure that the cabins were clean and sanitary.[7]

In addition to the household cabins, the slave quarter of the large plantations often contained a number of work houses: a tannery, a wash house, a smithy, a "children's house or nursery," a "sick house," and a bachelor quarters where unmarried males lived together. Many contemporary descriptions of slave quarters said that they gave the appearance of a "thriving little village." On some plantations, the slave cabins were arranged in a circle. On other plantations, the slave cabins were put up without a plan. Not all quarters were neat and orderly.[8]

The plantation was a self-sufficient community to the needs and desires of the blacks so there was no need for them to leave the plantations and have knowledge of the larger world. White ministers, doctors, and musicians were all brought to the plantation rather then letting blacks travel off the grounds.

THE BLACK FAMILY IN THE SLAVE QUARTER

The nuclear family was the family unit of the slave quarter. This family, however, was surrounded by a larger group of associations that included not only the extended family but also other persons not necessarily related by blood or marriage. This latter group might include stepparents, peer group members, community leaders, religious meeting brethren, nursery teachers, conjurers, special friends, and any other individuals who for reasons other than kinship by blood felt a responsibility to help nurture, protect, and educate any given black child.[9]

The Mother's Role

The mother was the central figure in the quarter family's education. From the time she suckled her child and rocked him in her lap, or sang him to sleep, she began to transmit values, beliefs, and feelings that later would be reinforced more deliberately. The black baby learned that comfort and security were to be found in black arms.[10] The mother, through her songs, introduced children to the religion of the quarter. As the children grew older, they learned from their mother how to care for themselves and their younger siblings.

Girls and less frequently boys learned from their mothers how to sew, spin, iron, and clean. All children were taught how to stuff mattresses; how to make candles from the fat of oxen and sheep; how to make buttons from dried gourds; how to color clothes with the dye made from the juice of wild indigo, poke berries, and walnuts; and how to make home soap.

More important than teaching her children practical skills was the role the mother played in transmitting religious beliefs, a longing for freedom, a desire to learn, a way of viewing and dealing with white people, and a sense of identification and solidarity with the other members of the quarter community.

In families where there were no grandparents, it was frequently the mother's role to transmit the stories of Africa, and the folklore and songs of the quarter community that she had learned from her own parents. These stories not only transmitted the values and attitudes from one generation to the next, but they also linked the children to their ancestors and helped cement family ties. Many times slave mothers had to teach their children to resist white abuse physically, and they had to defend their children against such abuse.

In addition to working in the fields, mothers had to cook for their families, do all their household chores, and spin, weave, and sew all at night.[11]

The Father's Role

Fathers took the responsibility to make furniture for their cabin and various other household articles, and in the process they taught their older children. Sometimes extras of these articles were sold to others, which allowed the family to buy some food or clothing that they did not receive from the master. Fathers also tended their own garden patches in the evenings and on Sundays. They went fishing and hunting and taught these skills to their sons. An important part of the father's role was to be ready to assume the double role of father and mother if and when the need arose, because of death or sale of the mother.[12]

Whatever the children's activities were during the day, nighttime was family time. Slave parents had a limited amount of time with their children—evenings and Sundays. When the parents returned from the fields, the children would return to their own cabins for the evening meal. The chores were done while supper was being prepared. The children would gather wood for the fire and bring in the water from the well. At least one of the older girls would help with the cooking while the other children worked in their own garden. Children of both sexes helped with washing, sewing, repairing furniture, and working in the garden. Often children would help their mother with spinning. Parents often took advantage of the night hours to play with and talk to their children. On other occasions, children would lie in bed and listen to their folks sing or tell stories as they sat round the fire.[13]

Child Rearing in the Slave Quarter

Children were born within their mothers' cabins. At first they were attended only by an experienced slave midwife, and it was not long before they became part of the interaction of a household that sheltered, fed, and provided for many of the human needs and wants of a number of individual slaves.

For the first few weeks, the newborn slave infant was the center of attention and concern. On most plantations, the baby's mother was allowed from two weeks to a month's "lying-in time" during which she was permitted to rest from her work in the fields and to devote her time to her new child. On many plantations, the mother and her child were attended frequently by the midwife for the first seven days. Depending on plantation rule and regulation, the child's father was allowed to visit his wife and child as soon as news of the birth reached the fields.

In addition, the overseer or the mistress of the house might visit the new baby. Occasionally, the master would come, checking out his new prospect. On most plantations, slaves were required to take their owner's surname. On some plantations they were not allowed to name their children, who were given fancy names by some member of the white family. A favored slave family would be allowed to name one child after the master. Infrequently, the slave owner named the newborn. Most often slaves were named by their parents, usually after an immediate family member. The birth of a slave child was marked by the seasons or some other important event.[14]

Importance of Children

For two slaves to have children meant that they were bound together in an affective kin group, a condition that diminished the probability of the physical separation of the mother from her family. Slave couples realized that if they had children early, their owners would have both economical and ethical reasons to allow them to stay together. Slave owners' economic calculations regularly mixed the production of wealth with the reproduction of labor.[15]

Enslavement required that the slave force reproduce itself, especially after the abolition of the overseas slave trade (1807).[16] Slave mothers welcomed their babies as a joy, loved them, and braced themselves for inevitable losses and heartaches.[17] Children born to parents owned by different owners became the property of the mother's owner.

The first few weeks of the child's life were peaceful and spent with his mother during the day. The child was well wrapped in a blanket and kept warm in a bundle before the fire or in the mother's bed, well fed from the mother's milk; and well cared for by any number of family members. The babies of the field hands sometimes accompanied their parents to work. Mothers either strapped them on their backs or left them on pallets at the end of the rows, near fences, or under trees to avoid the hot sun. They also made hammocks or swings between the trees to keep the babies off the ground.[18]

The Plantation Nursery

After the lying-in time was over, the mother had to return to full-time work in the fields. The infant was most often cared for during the day in the plantation nursery. At the nursery, the children—one to seven years old—were tended by one or two women too old to work in the fields. They were assisted by the older siblings of the infants. If an infant had no older siblings, one of the older cousins was often appointed to the job. The "nursing" of young children by the older ones did not always end well. Some children died during feeding; others were crippled.[19] On some plantations the general supervision of the nursery would be placed in the hands of some younger woman who had displayed a talent or an interest in the job. Occasionally, if an infant had a grandmother whose work days had passed, she would care for the infant at her cabin.[20]

Plantations with more than twenty slaves had nurseries located near the "big house" and supervised by the mistress of the house. The nursery ("nurse house" or "chilluns' house") was an enlarged cabin, with a sleeping room and a room for playing and eating. The mothers carried their infants in the cradles—made of boards, not more than two by three feet—in the morning and took them to their cabins at night. The cradles were arranged in rows in the nursery. Outside there was usually a fenced-in yard where the toddlers could crawl in safety. In the summer, the cradles would be placed outdoors in the shade. Summer was difficult for babies and young children. The number of children cared for at the nursery varied according to the size of the plantation's slave population. There could be about a dozen infants in the cabin.[21] The activities of the nursery depended greatly on the energy and the inclination of the women and the older children watching them.

Plantation nurseries were less than adequate. Occasionally a nursery teacher would organize games and other activities for the children. "Aunt Dinah" was such a teacher. She ran the nursery "like the kindergarten of today." Her inventiveness kept the children busy. She told children stories;

demonstrated how to make animals from potatoes, orange thorns, and feathers; and helped the children "set table" with mats made of the green leaves of the jonquils, cups and saucers of acorns, dishes of hickory hulls and any gay bit of china they could find. She had them bake mudpies in a broken stove. She helped them dress up as flowers and taught them to make decorations with chains of china blossoms and long strings of chinquapins. She even encouraged them to catch "Manny Doddles" and terrapins to keep them in the nursery as pets.[22]

One of the most important tasks of the nurse was to feed the children. Although she fed them according to instructions, later as adults they recalled the experience with distaste:

> Dere was a great long trough what went plum across de yard, and dat was where us et. For dinner us had peas or some other sort of vegetables, and corn bread. Aunt Viney crumbled up dat bread in de trough and poured de vegetables and pot likker over it. Den she blowed de horn and chillen come-a-runnin' from every which way. If us et it all up, she had to put more victuals in de trough. At nights, she crumbled de corn bread in de trough and poured buttermilk over it. Us never had nothin' but corn bread and buttermilk at night. Sometimes dat trough would be a sight, 'cause us never stopped to wash our hands, and before us had been eatin' more dan a minute or two what was in de trough would look like real mud what had come off our hands. Sometimes Aunt Viney would fuss at us and make us clean it out.[23]

Slave mothers were allowed to nurse their children three times a day—9:00 A.M., noon, and 3:00 P.M.—after they returned to work the fields. The slave women thought that five times would better for the infant and caused themselves a lot of trouble trying to maneuver the overseer to do so. Nursing conditions were inadequate. Often the nurses would bring the infants to their mother in the fields to nurse them under the hot sun.[24] Some infants would seem starved. When babies were old enough, they were fed milk, the liquor from boiled cabbage, and bread and milk together. If they had too much, they became colic.[25] Young children wore charms and greegrees on their bodies to ward off diseases.[26]

Infant mortality was high among slave women. Heavy field work could interfere with the blood supply to the placenta and jeopardize the health of the fetus. Slaveholders were aware of the relationship between heavy physical labor and low birth weight, but somehow missed the connection to the higher infant mortality rates.[27] Slave parents grieved for their dead children but were reluctant to show emotions for fear of being sold.

A small number of slave women who did not want to raise their children as slaves, especially if they had been raped by the overseer or the slave master, knew how to abort. Because childbirth deaths from natural causes were frequent, abortions could not be easily detected and never became a problem in the plantation.[28]

Clothing

Slave children, both boys and girls, were dressed in a single long shirt reaching to the ankles until they were about ten or twelve years old. The chief complaint about these shirts was their coarseness, which scratched and irritated the children's skin. Booker T. Washington remembered such a shirt and the kindness of his brother who wore it for several days until it was "broken in."[29]

Play and Games

As the children became toddlers, they came in contact with other children and began to interact with them. Through their play, they learned the values and the morals of the adult world. Two games played repeatedly by slave children were "Hide the Switch" and "No Bogeyman Tonight." In "Hide the Switch," a switch was hidden and the child who found it ran after the others in an attempt to strike them. This was one of the versions of the game that involved slave children whipping each other, as they had seen the adults whipped by the overseer. In "No Bogeyman Tonight," one slave child pretended to be an evil spirit and attempted to catch the others. Both games were the means by which slave children were able to cope with two of their greatest fears: whippings, which could result in death, and the evil spirits.[30] Another game reflected the children's slave condition: the game of playing auction. One child would be the auctioneer and pretend to sell other children to prospective buyers.[31] Peer interactions allowed the children to practice roles that they would assume more fully in later life.

Both boys and girls liked to play "grown-ups." The girls would dress up in their mothers' handkerchiefs and aprons and would make necklaces from corn beads. The boys would go hunting and fishing and practiced whittling and making baskets.[32]

The older children were also allowed to roam about the plantation in the fields, forests, and streams, an activity that provided them with hours of fun and adventure. This is not to suggest that most slave children experienced idyllic childhoods, however.

As the children reached the time when they were forced to join the plantation work force, it was with the peer group that the slave children first discovered their slave status and began to discuss it among themselves. Though their leisure time was diminished drastically, even in the fields they could talk, sing, and help each other bear the burden of slavery.[33]

Stages of Development

Most children had the run of the plantation and played with the white children without inhibitions in areas outside of the "big house," in and out of the cabins, and throughout the yards. When the children reached the work age, much of the playing was over. When they reached the social age, the interracial playing ended altogether, and the black children settled down to the existence that was the inevitable lot of the slave. These experiences were difficult for the children to comprehend and contradictory of the later behavior, such as whippings, exhibited by the white masters toward them.

The age to begin working in the fields varied from plantation to plantation and depended on the slaveholder's inclinations, and it was gradual. Most black children started working in the fields at ten years old, sometimes earlier, but others did not begin until they were older, thirteen, fourteen, and sometimes fifteen. Many planters began the "breaking" process before the slave child was strong enough to do a full-hand's work. Most quarter children between the ages of six and ten were given a variety of chores around the plantation.[34] Children, from nine to twelve years were given special tasks along with women still suckling. They picked the first balls of cotton from the lower part of the stalk, where it opened months before the rest was ready for picking.[35]

Few slave children realized the full significance of their slave status until they were forced to become an institutionalized part of the white man's work force, at which time they began to realize the ramifications of what it meant to be a slave. They faced the reality that the white world held them as slaves, but the eagerness of many boys to get behind a plow carried with it the recognition of manhood.[36]

RELIGION

Religion played an important part in the slave's life. Sundays and holidays like Christmas and Easter were strictly observed on most plantations. The promotion of religion among the slaves was the moral duty of the masters. The masters believed that although the blacks were considered inferior to the whites, they possessed souls in need of salvation. Religion also elevated the morale of the slaves and improved the quality of their services. Because the blacks on the plantation did not have the means to provide for their own religious instruction, it was left to their masters to spread the gospel among the slaves. In order to prevent improper teachings reaching the slaves, the slaveholders themselves attended to the religious training of their slaves. Many planters feared that the conversion and baptism of the slaves might be used as an argument for their emancipation.

Most plantations had chapels for the slaves. The task of the religious instructor was to impress upon the black people the supreme power and authority of the God of Christians. Obedience to his will was interpreted from carefully selected passages of the Bible. Although obedience and cheerful submission were stressed as the most important commandments, whites also taught blacks the sinfulness of stealing, lying, vandalism, harming whites, and suicide. Plantation rules were frequently imbued with religious sanctions.[37]

In large plantations, the religious instruction was left in the hands of paid missionaries of the Southern Church, hired by the planter and often observed by him. Because of the politics of their teaching position, only missionaries who were sympathetic with the South's view of slavery were sent to the plantations by church authorities. The actual instruction methods used by these missionaries and other white teachers was mainly of oral instruction and repetition. The instructor would recite certain passages, and the slave would repeat the sentences after him.[38]

Instruction in religion provided by the masters was used in an attempt to mold the black population into obedient, docile, trustworthy, and grateful servants.

The Clandestine Congregation

In addition to the church services organized and supervised by the white master in the plantations, all quarter communities organized a parallel kind of religion, their own clandestine congregation, without the approval or participation of the master or the overseers. This parallel religious congregation was an important instrument in the slave community not only to transmit and perpetuate its own religious ideals and beliefs but also for understanding secular values, and attitudes and integrating the Christian religion in what they had brought from Africa.

The leader/preacher was a religious man who had achieved a position of influence in the quarter community through his faith, his knowledge of the Bible, and his ability to read it; he had demonstrated a commitment to the welfare of the quarter community, and most important his ability to preach as his congregation wanted him to preach was respected. This preacher became the most powerful figure in the quarters.

The meetings were clandestine from one to three times a week, generally held in the woods or some other predesignated, hidden outdoor location, at night with or without moonlight. The meeting would start around 11:00 P.M. after the overseers' last round of the quarter cabins. It had three parts: a sermon by the preacher, prayers and songs, and testimonies as to faith and feeling of the Spirit by any and all members attending. The entire membership actively participated in the service with their voices as well as their bodies. They danced around in a circle holding hands accompanied by singing. The meeting was a place where slaves were free to express themselves the way they saw fit, pour out their troubles, and express their fears and joys. The meeting was the place to pass along information and where the congregation was taught to provide for the less fortunate—that it was their duty to care for, protect, and instruct other blacks—but also to regard and address each other as sisters and brothers. Children more often were left at home due to the late hour and the necessity to ensure the secrecy of the meeting.[39]

These meetings undoubtedly helped blacks to endure slavery and to survive under it, for they provided them with momentary escape.

EDUCATION

All slave states with the exception of Kentucky had laws that forbade anyone, even the master, to teach a slave to read or write. Slave owners did not want their slaves to have any access to the information gained from books, pamphlets, and newspapers. A slave who could read and write could forge passes for himself, but most important he could read information that would make him discontent with his situation and would like to be free. Slaves who disobeyed and dared either to learn or teach others to read or write were punished very severely. His finger or his hand would be cut off.[40] The discipline of slaves was very cruel, including whippings, and tied hands and feet.[41]

Generally, slave children did not have any formal education. Booker T. Washington remembered as a child carrying the books of one his young mistresses to the schoolhouse and seeing the boys and girls studying. "I had the feeling that to get into the schoolhouse and study in this way would be about the same as getting into paradise," he wrote.[42] Washington developed a deep desire for knowledge and became one of the best-known African-American educators at the turn of the twentieth century. There were, however, some slave owners who made an effort to teach both adult slaves as well as the children. Those who learned to read and write were primarily house servants. Because children often worked in the slaveholder's home before they were assigned to other jobs, they had more access to knowledge. A former slave believed that his owner taught him to read so that he might be able to use "good language around his grandchildren." Another slaveholder taught his slave to read and write so he could copy the names and addresses of patients. Louisa Cocke decided to establish a permanent school in her Virginia plantation, because she believed that the age of seven was a good age to begin teaching the slave children, and besides it took them away from the influence of the slave quarter.[43]

Following is a very brief overview of the institution of education as it relates to the African-Americans.

The Colonial Period

During the colonial period, slavery was recognized as incompatible with education because education could be a factor in destroying slavery. Christianization was the first step in a slave's American education, as it was for the Native Americans. In 1696, the Reverend Thomas Bray (a founder of the Society for the Propagation of the Gospel, 1701) was sent to Maryland by the bishop of London to encourage the conversion of adult Negroes and the education of their children.[44] Even though not very many slaves were found among the Puritans in New England, in 1674, John Eliot who had worked among the Indians, argued for the conversion of Negroes and offered to catechize them if their masters would send them to him.[45] The French and Spanish settlers were more active in educating their slaves than the English were because of their concern for Christianization. The Roman Catholics of New Orleans (1727) taught both Afro-Americans and Indians and in 1734 established a school for blacks.[46] In 1740, the Society for the Propagation of the Gospel in Foreign Parts sought to raise the level of living of all people in the South. The most conscientious efforts to improve conditions among the slaves were made by the Quakers. They protested against slave trade, worked toward abolishing slavery, and urged slaveholders to instruct their slaves.[47]

From the Revolution to the Civil War

The struggle for the rights of man, which was part of the philosophy of the American Revolution, reinforced the notion of the rights of Afro-Americans for freedom and education. Benjamin Franklin encouraged their full education. Thomas Jefferson favored industrial and agricultural education only; he did not believe in the intellectual equality of blacks.

Despite legal restrictions and the contentions of many southerners that blacks were not educable, slaves did receive limited education in parts of the South after the American Revolution—sometimes from their masters or mistresses. The case of Frederick Douglass is perhaps the best-known instance of an owner teaching the slave. His mistress taught him the A, B, C, and helped him learn to spell words of three or four letters, but when his master found out, he forbade her doing it, for it was unlawful as well as unsafe to teach a slave to read. Once Douglass learned to read and write he started teaching his "brother-slaves." After a couple of meetings the lessons were interrupted.[48]

The slaveholders were afraid that if the slaves learned to read and write, they would revolt against slavery and its conditions. Their fears were real. The Insurrection of 1800, led by the slave Gabriel Prosser, so frightened southern planters that education of blacks was later discouraged. This insurrection was followed by two other revolts, in 1822 and 1831, led by Denmark Vesey and Nat Turner, respectively, both of whom knew how to read and write. The insurrections resulted in reactionary legislation in the South that prevented the dissemination of information among Negroes by closing all the schools that they had been permitted to attend and by prohibiting them from holding meetings and religious worship. Thus, in the nineteenth century, southern blacks had to content themselves for the most part with clandestine schools and private teachers. In some isolated instances, blacks did attend mixed schools. In 1840, blacks were permitted to attend schools with white children in Wilmington, Delaware.[49]

During the post-Revolutionary period, northern blacks benefited from the trend to establish and improve schools in the new nation. For example, New Jersey began educating black children in separate schools in 1777. Quakers in Philadelphia taught black children like Anthony Benezet privately. In 1750, he opened a school for blacks in his home and kept it open for twenty years. After his death, a school for black children was built in 1787, with funds he had bequeathed.[50] The liberalism of the Revolutionary era led to the organization of Manumission Societies, first in Philadelphia and later in New York, to protect blacks from bounty hunters (manumission at that time was used interchangeably with abolition).

The New York African Free School

In 1787, the New York Manumission Society established one of the best-known schools of the period, the New York African Free School. It began with forty students of various ages, most of them born to slave parents. Cornelius Davis gave up a position teaching white children to be the school's first teacher. In 1791, a female teacher was hired to teach girls needlework, thus beginning industrial education. At first, the school encountered opposition by the whites, which resulted in inadequate means of support. About 1801, community interest in the school increased and the Negroes "became more impressed with the advantages and importance of education, and more disposed to avail themselves of the privileges offered them," and more children enrolled.[51] At this time, 130 pupils of both sexes attended, paying their instructor, a "discreet man of color," according to their ability. There was increased enrollment and improvement of the school environment with the introduction of the Lancastrian and monitorial systems of instruction. Another impetus was given to the school in 1810, when the New York State Legislature, having in mind the preparation of slaves for freedom, required masters to teach all children born of slaves to read the Scriptures. By 1820, the school had more than five hundred students.[52]

The curriculum, in addition to teaching reading, writing, arithmetic, and geography, included instruction in natural history, astronomy, navigation, advanced composition, plain sewing, knitting, marking, and moral education. It had special classes for gifted children called "Merit classes," and used the upper grade students to tutor pupils in the lower grades.[53]

Schools in Other States

In 1798, a separate school for black children was established by the blacks in Boston with a white teacher, in the home of Primus Hall, a prominent Negro. In 1880, the Negroes asked the city of Boston for a separate school, but they were refused. The Negroes established the school anyway and hired two Harvard graduates for instructors. The school was moved to the first floor of the African Meeting House on Belknap Street, where it continued to flourish. In 1812, the city of Boston noticed it and granted it $200 annually. When Abiel Smith, Esq., died in 1815 he left a legacy of $5,000, the income of which was to be appropriated "for the free instruction of colored children in reading, writing and arithmetic." The city of Boston took the school under its auspices, and a new building was erected next to the Meeting House. In February 1835, the school was named for its benefactor.[54] Today, the Abiel Smith School houses the Museum of Afro-American History in Boston.

According to Woodson, the movement for separate schools for colored children originated with the colored people, not with the whites. They felt that since the past of the blacks (slavery) was different from that of whites, they wanted "special" schools for their children. Eventually, the blacks supported a single school system that provided for democratic education. Supporting a dual school system often resulted in neglect and sometimes in the closing of the separate schools.[55]

The Civil War (1861–1865) had a greater impact on Afro-Americans than any other single event in the nation's history. Before the war, the vast majority of the black Americans were legally slaves. President Abraham Lincoln issued the Emancipation Proclamation in 1863 ending slavery in the rebellious southern states. In 1865, Congress passed the Emancipation Act, which ended slavery in *all* of the United States. America's "peculiar institution" had been stamped out, theoretically. There was a continuous strife, however, on the day-to-day living because of the Dred Scott decision of 1857 by the Supreme Court, still in effect, which said that a slave could not become free by merely living in a free state.[56] Afro-Americans could not be citizens of the United States, until constitutional amendments, legal statutes, and subsequent U.S. Supreme Court decisions all affirmed the citizenship of Afro-Americans. Freedom and citizenship were great legacies of the Civil War for Afro-Americans.

FREDERICK DOUGLASS (1817–1895)[57]

Douglass's autobiography is included here because it describes his early childhood and for his accomplishments to serve as a model and motivation to others.

Douglass was born the son of a slave mother and a white father in Maryland, and was named Frederick Augustus Washington Bailey. When he was six years old, he was taken to a nearby plantation, where he joined his older siblings and became the companion of the youngest son of the plantation owner. Later he worked as an errand boy in the shipyard of his master. He copied out letters written on lumber by carpenters and had his white playmates to show him how to write other letters. At night he practiced writing using the Bible. He experienced religious conversion and joined the Bethel African Methodist Episcopal Church in Baltimore. When his master died, the person who inherited Douglass rented him out for a year to a farmer, who was known for his brutal treatment of slaves. Douglass repeatedly got severe whippings from the farmer, and after the last one he ran away to the man who owned him, who returned Douglass to the farmer. When the farmer attacked Douglass, he resisted and he was never whipped again. He resolved to gain his freedom within a year (1836).

In 1838, Douglass became engaged to Anna Murray and entered into agreement with his owner to hire out his own labor, and to pay him three dollars a week from his wages. He moved into his own lodging, and began to study the violin. His owner suspended the arrangement, and Douglass, fearing that he would be sold, planned to escape. He was joined by Anna Murray in New York, where they got married and then went to New Bedford, Massachusetts, the whaling port. It is here that he took the name Douglass. He subscribed to *The Liberator,* the abolitionist weekly, published in Boston. He was invited to attend the Massachusetts Anti-Slavery Society convention in Nantucket, where he described his experiences as a slave.

In 1845, *Narrative of the Life of Frederick Douglass, An American Slave, Written by Himself,* was published by the Anti-Slavery Office in Boston and sold 4,500 copies. Afraid that the attention he got from his abolition activities had put his life in danger, he began an extended tour to Ireland, Scotland, and England, leaving Anna and the children behind. His English friends raised money and purchased his freedom. Douglass became legally free in December 1846, when manumission papers were filed in Baltimore. He returned to Boston in April 1847.

When the Civil War erupted in 1861, Lincoln wanted to exclude the blacks from serving in the military. Douglass argued strongly that blacks should contribute to the final destruction of slavery. He prevailed. In 1863, Douglass recruited blacks for the 54th and 55th Massachusetts Infantry Regiments, the first such regiments of black soldiers organized by a northern state. Three of his sons were in the service.[58]

After the Civil War (1865), Douglass wanted the federal government to guarantee and protect the citizenship rights of the blacks. He also pleaded for the moral responsibility of the whites to accept blacks as full members of American society.

In 1869, he was elected president of the National Convention of Colored Citizens and helped to secure the passage of resolutions supporting Republican Reconstruction policies. He attended the American Equal Rights Association meeting and urged the Association to support ratification of the Fifteenth Amendment.

Anna died in 1882 from a stroke, and he suffered from grief and depression. In 1884, he married Helen Pitts. His father-in-law, a former abolitionist, refused to admit him into his house. His interracial marriage has been criticized by both blacks and whites.

In 1889, Douglass was appointed Consul General to Haiti. All these successes caused him to have some personal difficulties in his relationship to black society.

Douglass died in 1895. He had witnessed and participated in the major events of the nineteenth century that redefined the role of blacks in American society. Douglass set an example for the generations to come by his persistence and focus on his goals.

The Reconstruction (1866–1877)

The end of the Civil War brought to the South two years of gentle Presidential Reconstruction followed by a decade of stringent "Congressional Reconstruction." One of the first objectives of the Reconstruction governments was to establish systems of public education. For their support, they levied the first universal school taxes the regions had known. Most of the Reconstruction governments made no real effort to integrate the new public schools, and while they theoretically adopted policies of equal financial support, the results of the emerging dual system were prejudicial to the Negroes. Some states followed

Figure 15.2 "Feeding the Negro Children under Charge of the Military Authorities at Hilton Head, South Carolina." Wood-engraving. *Harper's Weekly,* June 14, 1862, page 372. *Courtesy of the Boston Athenæum.*

Kentucky's lead, which levied a tax on real property for school support, plus a fifty-cent poll tax on males with children of school age, but insisted that the Negro schools should receive only the taxes paid by Negroes.

The emancipated slaves wanted schooling. Education was one of the marks of their new status, and they knew that knowledge is power. They had, however, economic problems, for they did not own any land and were trained only in agricultural skills. Negro education during the Reconstruction period came to be regarded more as a function of the federal government and of private philanthropy than a local responsibility.[59]

The Freedmen's Bureau (1865–1872)

The Civil War gave freedom to approximately four million slaves, a majority of whom were poverty stricken and uneducated. The freedmen lacked the bare necessities of life: food and clothing. The freedmen needed a lot of assistance in their transition from a life of dependency to a life of independent responsibility. Private organizations had done this work during the war. Now there was a need for a unified and comprehensive service to assume the responsibility for the well-being of needy whites and Negroes in the South. The Freedmen's Bureau was created by Congress in 1865 to provide this assistance with officials in each of the southern states. The Bureau helped refugees and freedmen with food, clothing, and medical supplies; established schools; supervised labor contracts between freedmen and their employers; managed confiscated or abandoned lands, by leasing or selling some of them to freedmen; and intervened to protect blacks from hostile white courts and legislators.[60]

The Bureau achieved its greatest success in education. It set up or supervised all kinds of schools: day, night, Sunday, and industrial schools and colleges. The Bureau cooperated closely with many religious and philanthropic organizations in the North in the founding of educational institutions in the South between 1865 and 1873. They sent funds, missionaries, and teachers to the South to further the cause of Negro education. By 1870, when the educational work of the Bureau stopped, there were 247,333 pupils in 4,329 schools, mainly for elementary education. Many of these schools were perforce segregated schools.[61]

Despite southern hostility to the Bureau and the inefficiency of many officials, it performed a vastly important task during Reconstruction.

Among the black colleges and schools that received aid from the Freedmen's Bureau were Atlanta University, in Atlanta, Fisk University in Nashville, and Howard University in Washington, D.C. They were called everything from seminaries to universities. They almost all began with teaching reading and writing and other elementary subjects necessary to educate the mostly illiterate freedmen.[62] Most influential at that time was Hampton Institute.

Hampton Normal and Agricultural Institute

The Hampton Institute was founded in 1868 at Hampton, Virginia, on an abandoned plot of land of 125 acres, to educate freedmen and women. Samuel Chapman Armstrong (1839–1893), a white teacher, an abolitionist, and a former brigadier general in the Civil War, was appointed as an agent of the Freedmen's Bureau to Hampton in 1866, to oversee the work of officers and northern missionaries as it related to the newly freed slaves. The large number of blacks who fled to Hampton drew missionaries, members of the American Missionary Association (AMA), who wanted to make Hampton their first station of ex-slaves.

Armstrong wanted a centrally located school for black students supported and operated by northern whites, where the liberal arts of the AMA schools as well as agricultural and mechanical skills would be taught. He was afraid that putting the school in the hands of former Confederates would not work. From the beginning, he sought independence from the AMA in order to advance his own plan of education and to develop all teachers and leaders of the Negro population for life in society. The Institute was organized to train young Afro-Americans, beginning at the elementary level, to teach and lead their people. In 1872, Armstrong convinced the Virginia General Assembly to allocate a third of the state's Morrill Act Land Grant Funds to Hampton, which made the school financially independent from the AMA.[63] One of its most famous graduates was Booker T. Washington, the first president of Tuskegee Institute.

Hampton also provided higher education for the Native Americans beginning in 1878, when a group of Indians came to be educated at Hampton with federal funds.

In 1922, courses leading to the bachelor of science degree were offered, and courses at the elementary and secondary level were dropped. The entire resources of the institute were then devoted to college-level education. It received its accreditation as a four-year college in 1932. Today the college has an interracial and intercultural student body and faculty.[64]

TEACHER TRAINING AT HAMPTON

Hampton's original mission was to train elementary school teachers for the South's black educational system. A condition for admission to Hampton was the "intention to remain through the whole course and become a teacher." Hampton did not offer any trade certificates until 1895. Like other normal schools of the nineteenth century, Hampton offered a curriculum of two or three years in length and did not grant a bachelor's degree. Most of Hampton's beginning students arrived with less than adequate elementary school education and successfully completed the normal school program. In general, normal school teachers tended to be older and more economically disadvantaged than college students. Normal school students sought professional education to achieve their major goal to become elementary school teachers.[65]

The teacher training program consisted of three aspects: the elementary academic program, the manual labor system, and a strict social discipline routine. The academic program in addition to preparing students to teach grade school and to pass the state teachers' certification examinations was planned mainly for the ideological training of its students. The manual labor system, organized to shape attitudes and build character through steady, hard labor, was designed to connect the theoretical and the practical lessons. The daily discipline routine served to rid the school of students at variance with the "Hampton Idea." The academic program consisted of an English course that included reading and elocution, elementary mathematics, history, literature, moral science, and political economy.[66] Hampton's education trained blacks to adjust to a life within the existing social order of that time.

In 1872, Hampton started publishing *Southern Workman,* an illustrated monthly. Helen W. Ludlow, a white woman, became the first managing editor.[67] Hampton Institute also established a folklore club, which began to collect data to document the earlier lives of the students. The use of folklore at Hampton and other schools and colleges encouraged potential donors.[68]

In the early years of the twentieth century, public education in the South received a lot of support from philanthropists. The southern states matched these private funds and by the end of World War I every state had a compulsory school law, and enough schools to implement it. This large-scale philanthropy provided buildings, endowments, scholarships, and support for teacher training and industrial education. One of the funds, the Anna T. Jeanes Fund, financed Negro supervisors to improve the quality and instruction in rural schools. Most Negro children received the *same* education as the whites, although inferior in quality and quantity.[69]

In the decades that followed Reconstruction, the Negro was stripped of his franchise and of his only means of enforcing his demand for free public education. The North abandoned its role of militant enforcer of Negro rights. Thus, a decade after the South had lost the war, the white leadership was again in power, with only abstract limitations, and was again free to define racial relationships as it saw fit.[70]

As the blacks were disenfranchised, in the 1890s, by state constitutional provisions, and their subordinate status was given legal basis in the South, their education became more segregated in the areas where mixed schools had existed before, and subsequently inequalities developed in teachers' salaries and in other provisions for education.

BOOKER T. WASHINGTON (1856–1915)[71]

Booker T. Washington was born a slave on a Virginia plantation; he was not sure of the date of his birth, or who his father was. He had no schooling as a slave. After they were freed in 1865, his mother took the children to Malden, West Virginia, to join her husband, who had a job in a salt-furnace. In 1872, Washington decided to get an education and went to Hampton Normal and Agricultural Institute, about five hundred miles from his home. After an arduous trip without money and hardly any food, he reached Hampton. He was tired, dirty from the trip, and hungry. The head teacher did not want to admit him, but he hung around. After several hours, the teacher, Miss Mary F. Mackie, told him to sweep the "recitation room." After she inspected it, she admitted Washington to the school, and offered him the job as janitor. This job helped him "work out" his expenses to the school. Washington referred to the event as "his college exam." His belief in the value of work he advocated to others and became the backbone of his educational system. Armstrong, the head of the school, became Washington's father figure. After graduating from Hampton in 1875, Washington returned to Malden to teach. He taught boys and girls as well as men and women. He "taught any one who wanted to learn anything that he could teach him."[72]

In 1878, he went to Washington, D.C., to study for a few months (he does not specify what). In 1879, he returned to Hampton, where he was appointed to teach in the newly created night school. During the 1880–1881 year, he also became supervisor of the dormitory for Native American students. In May 1881, Armstrong, who had received a letter from Tuskegee, Alabama, asking him to recommend a white man to head the new school for African-Americans, recommended Washington.

THE TUSKEGEE INSTITUTE

When Washington arrived at Tuskegee in 1881, he found no equipment to start an educational institution and a white community hostile to the idea of a school for Negroes. Washington had a twofold task: to build a school and to convince the southern whites that the students were there to learn and that the education of Negroes was in the true interest of the South. Utilizing the industrial education model of Hampton he was familiar with, and his strong belief about work, he created Tuskegee Normal and Industrial Institute. All students were required to work. The hostility toward the school began to disappear. The students were taught a trade as well as academic subjects. Washington counseled the Negroes to respect the law and to cooperate with white authorities to maintain peace. As he saw the results of this education and its effects on the South, he became convinced that this was the pattern to strengthen the Negro position throughout the area. Washington advocated a form of vocational education that was more acceptable to the southern whites. He saw this vocational education as a way to integrate fully the Negroes into the larger society. During this period, philanthropy also became an important factor in the support of black education in the South. Andrew Carnegie and John D. Rockefeller supported Tuskegee.

The publication of his *Up from Slavery: An Autobiography* (1900) enhanced Washington's status. As his prestige grew to the point where he was regarded not only as a supporter of vocational education but as the spokesman for millions of Negroes, opposition to him among his people increased. Some of it was envy. Among his opponents was W. E. B. DuBois. DuBois opposed what he thought was the narrow educational program of Washington. Others criticized him that the education he provided consigned Negroes to an inferior economic and social status in southern life. The type of education he emphasized became obsolete very soon because of the increasing industrialization of the country.[73]

In 1900, Washington organized the Negro Business League. It was one of the sponsors of the National Urban League. He also inaugurated the "Negro Health Week."[74]

The Years 1870 to 1964

Once the Negroes were disenfranchised after Reconstruction ended, laws for racial segregation began to reappear. This process began in 1870 when Tennessee enacted laws against intermarriage. Five years later, Tennessee adopted the first "Jim Crow" law, and the rest of the southern states followed. Negroes and whites were segregated on trains, in depots, and on wharves. Toward the end of the nineteenth century, after the Supreme Court in 1883 outlawed the Civil Rights Acts of 1875, they were further segregated from hotels, barber shops, restaurants, and theaters. By 1885, most southern states had laws requiring separate schools. With the adoption of new constitutions, states firmly established the color line with the most stringent segregation of the races. In 1896, the Supreme Court upheld segregation in its "separate but equal" doctrine (*dictum*) set forth in *Plessy vs. Ferguson*.[75] This segregation lasted until 1956, when the Negroes in Montgomery, Alabama, started boycotting the buses in an effort to obtain equal seating—blacks were assigned to the back of the buses—and to secure the employment of Negro bus drivers on lines serving predominantly Negro parts of the city. The leader of the boycott was the Reverend Martin Luther King.[76]

From 1896 to 1954 (when the *Brown vs. Board of Education* Supreme Court decision in Topeka, Kansas, ended segregation), the dual-system of education was developed and expanded, and the schools for the blacks increasingly deteriorated.[77] In 1957, President Dwight Eisenhower had to send federal troops to Little Rock, Arkansas, to ensure the entrance of black children into the public schools.[78] Desegregation in all aspects of life did not end until the Civil Rights Act of 1964. One of the authors remembers as a first-year student in America and member of an integrated Peace Caravan sponsored by the Friends Service Committee of Philadelphia in the summer of 1957 that blacks and whites had to line up in two different lines to buy ice cream at a Dairy Queen on the Virginia side of Washington, D.C. Asking why, she was told, "we are below the Mason-Dixon line." But it is the same country.

BLACK WOMEN'S CLUBS[79]

The end of Reconstruction brought little improvement in the economic and social status of the Negro. They needed to work out their own formulas for survival. An important agency for maintaining group cohesion was the church. As before the Civil War, the church promoted education largely by encouraging its members to become Bible readers. It also encouraged its young people to form literary societies. The church's greatest public role, however, was the increase in its function as a welfare agency.

Another manifestation of the Negroes' struggle to become socially self-sufficient was the growth of fraternal organizations and benefit associations. Some of them were local, while others had memberships in several states. They helped widows and orphans and provided opportunities for social interactions.

Although there was little extra money for philanthropic undertakings, a great effort was devoted to helping the unfortunate. One result of the social and cultural efforts was the emergence of a substantial number of Negro leaders of both sexes.

Black women began to organize local clubs in many cities to meet the urgent social needs. The absence of social welfare institutions in many southern communities and the frequent expulsion of blacks from whatever institutions existed led them to found a number of institutions.[80] The National Association of Colored Women (NACW) was organized in 1896. It united the National League of Colored Women and the National League of Afro-American Women and many other local women's organizations. Its motto was "Lifting As We Climb."[81]

It was the only national, nonsectarian body of educated Negro women organized for the definite and avowed purpose of "race elevation." The main purpose of the NACW was to relieve suffering, to preserve the independence of those helped, and to advance the cause of education. Through its local clubs in most southern states, the NACW provided kindergartens, nursery schools, or day nurseries for the working mothers; domestic science classes; orphanages; old folks' homes; free reading rooms; and girls' homes for the young women joining the work force. The NACW had a president and seven vice presidents. It was organized in departments. One of the most important departments was the kindergarten with Mrs. Haydee Campbell as its superintendent.[82]

Mary Church Terrell was the first president of the NACW. Terrell and the other women were representative of the newly emerging college-educated Negro woman.

Mary Church Terrell (1863–1954)[83]

Mary Church Terrell was born in Memphis, Tennessee, on September 23, 1863, the eldest child of Louise and Robert Church, both former slaves. Her father was the son of his master, who treated him decently but never gave him his freedom. After emancipation, he became a successful businessman and later a wealthy real estate holder. Her mother had a hair salon patronized by well-to-do white women of Memphis. The parents were divorced when she was very young. Because the Memphis schools for black children were inadequate, her parents sent her to Antioch College Model School in Yellow Springs, Ohio, when she was about six years old. Often she was the only black child in the class.

Mary attended Oberlin College—operated by abolitionists, who had opened its doors to blacks in 1835. There she pursued the "gentlemen's course"—four years of classical studies. Most women at Oberlin took the two-year ladies' curriculum. She graduated in 1884. By now her father was considered to be both a millionaire and the wealthiest black in the South. Mary had many opportunities to meet prominent blacks, among whom were Frederick Douglass and Booker T. Washington. She especially admired Douglass and started a friendship with him while she was at Oberlin, which lasted until his death.

Her accepting a job at Wilberforce College in Ohio, in 1885, angered her father who was against her working. Two years later, she went to teach in the Latin department of the Colored High School in Washington, D.C., where she met Robert T. Terrell, an 1884 Harvard College graduate. Mary received a master of arts degree from Oberlin in 1888. Her father sent her on a European tour, 1888 to 1890. She married Terrell in October 1891. Married women were barred from teaching, and Mary decided to manage her household. The lynching of her lifelong friend Tom Moss from Memphis drove her into public life.

In 1892, Mary assumed the leadership of the Colored Women's League in the District of Columbia, and in 1896 she was elected the first president of the

National Association of Colored Women. Because of her leadership in the NACW, Mary had many opportunities for service. Mary was the first Negro woman to serve on the District of Columbia Board of Education. She attended the International Congress of Women, in Berlin in 1904, and addressed the meeting successively in English, German, and French. In 1911, she was involved in organizing a birthday centenary celebration of abolitionist Harriet Beecher Stow, author of *Uncle Tom's Cabin*. In 1940, she published her autobiography, *A Colored Woman in a White World*. She died about two months after the Supreme Court's decision *Brown vs. Board of Education*, which ended segregation.

Kindergartens for Black Children

Many black women contributed in the development of kindergartens for black children. One can say that there was a parallelism between the activities of the white early kindergarten supporters and the efforts of the black women. As president of the NACW, Terrell established a kindergarten department that encouraged and supported the development of kindergartens. She also wrote an article that interpreted the work of the NACW and advanced the ideas of kindergarten in the South.[84]

The kindergarten department of the NACW was headed by Haydee Campbell, a black pioneer in early childhood education. She was native of Texas but lived in St. Louis, Missouri. Campbell had attended Oberlin College, in Ohio, and was a graduate of the St. Louis kindergarten training program. She applied and competed for the kindergarten supervisor's job. She received the highest score and became a supervisor of kindergartens for colored children in the St. Louis public schools.[85]

JOSEPHINE SILONE YATES (1859–1912)

Josephine Silone Yates, was born in 1859 on Long Island, New York, to a family well established in the community. She died suddenly on September 3, 1912. She graduated with honors from the Rhode Island State Normal School in 1877, and became the first black American certified to teach in the public schools of Rhode Island. In 1879, Yates went to teach at the Lincoln Institute in Jefferson City, Missouri, where she eventually became a full professor and department head of natural sciences. She resigned in 1889 to marry W. W. Yates, principal of the Wendell Phillips School in Kansas City, Missouri. She wrote frequently in the *Colored American Magazine,* where she described much of the early work in the kindergartens. She was president of the NACW.[86]

Yates was a great supporter of kindergartens. Reporting on a survey she had conducted about kindergartens in 1901, she found that the far South at that time had no public kindergartens for Negro children, but through the interest of private citizens and of denominational schools, private kindergartens were established. In the same article, Yates further stated that "the prime requisite for a well equipped kindergarten is a well trained teacher." "Moreover the training of kindergarten teachers for colored children must be such that it is well adapted to the special needs of the stage in race development which the Negro of the United States now exhibits." Yates also encouraged girls to become kindergarten teachers by proper training, for through the children the teachers can educate the mothers.[87]

The establishment of Froebelian kindergartens, day nurseries for the Negro children, and mother's clubs for the mothers was seen as an effort to "struggle upward," as a method of getting to the root of the problem of race elevation—"the children."[88]

Alice Dugged Cary, a teacher in an Atlanta kindergarten and a member of the NACW, advocated for kindergartens for Negro children so they can receive "proper early moral training." She thought that education without character development "will be a complete failure."[89] She stated that "if we could keep every Negro child, for three years, in a scientifically correct kindergarten, I believe the race would leap forward a century's unaided growth in one generation." She also pointed out that the Negro mother needed to be educated to work with her children.[90]

Anna J. Murray was a member of the Colored Woman's League of Washington, D.C. She established a kindergarten according to Froebelian principles for black children. Murray described her experiences in an 1900 article in the *Southern Workman*.[91] Murray persuaded the members of her organization to start a kindergarten in Washington, D.C., in October 1896 (504). Learning that an existing kindergarten was about to be abandoned for lack of funds, she asked if she could use the equipment and other materials they had. In addition, Murray was able to obtain the use of the building, heat, light, and janitor services free of charge. She operated two kindergartens: a morning kindergarten for the poor and neglected children, and an afternoon one for the more affluent ones, for a total of thirty-five children. She requested one penny a week, from the poor, and fifty cents a month from the others. The money collected from the fees was used to buy materials used in both kindergartens. Often a few dollars were left for the teachers' salary. Murray hired a white kindergartner who was paid $25 per month for eight months of the year. She had written to Boston, New York, Philadelphia, and Chicago to locate "a colored kindergartner," but found that the very few prepared were already employed. She needed to train black teachers, and within a month, she secured the services of a leading white trainer (no name is given) to train fifteen young women for the sum of $450. The fee was divided equally among the fifteen young women who wanted to be trained (505).

As soon as the training school and the model kindergarten were running smoothly, a committee was appointed to go before the municipal commissioners to ask them to make the kindergarten part of the city's public school system. A concern of one commissioner was "Where will you find teachers for your colored schools?" Once the commissioners learned that a number of young women were already being trained, they recommended the sum of

$12,000. The proposal was presented to Congress, but it was not appropriated that year.

Persistence on the part of Murray paid off, and in 1898, Congress appropriated the $12,000: $8,000 for the white kindergarten and $4,000 for the colored; this division was based on the proportion of the population. In 1899, the kindergarten received from Congress $15,000, and in 1900, $25,000, which allowed the committee to increase the number of the kindergartens (506). Murray continued to train kindergartners in Washington, D.C., to prepare them to go to the southern states, where the kindergarten program was expanding (507).

On the whole, the black women leadership was parallel to that of the white women in their efforts for woman suffrage.

As presented in Chapter 9, readers of the August 1875 *Kindergarten Messenger* were inquiring about kindergartens in the South and Elizabeth Peabody was encouraging the founding of a kindergarten at the Hampton Institute. The Hampton Institute kindergarten was part of its Whittier School. It had forty children, a colored kindergartner, and an Indian assistant. The kindergarten was a combination of practical lessons and Froebelian curriculum. After circle, some children washed and ironed dolls' clothes, while others "went to the tables for gift work." They set the tables for lunch and ate what they brought from home. After clearing the tables, it was time for paper cutting and folding or games, and gardening. Radishes and lima beans raised in the garden went home to the families. There was singing and playing in the orchestra.[92]

Peabody in a letter to Henry Barnard told us about "Training Classes for Colored Teachers," taught by Mrs. Guion Gourlay for eight months, at the Eureka Class of Kindergartners in Philadelphia, where Peabody distributed the diplomas on May 23, 1881, to nine students. Mrs. Gourlay trained colored kindergartners in the Froebelian system, "any one who was interested even if they did not have the money to pay." Peabody hoped that this would be the beginning of the Froebelian movement among the colored people for both the children and the adults.[93]

Nursery Schools

Nursery schools like the kindergartens before them began to attract the attention of and to be sponsored by black colleges and universities as an important aspect of the overall education of the African-Americans. Among the institutions that created nursery schools in the 1930s were the Hampton Institute in Virginia, the Alabama State Teachers College in Montgomery, and Spelman College in Atlanta.

SPELMAN COLLEGE NURSERY SCHOOL[94]
The Spelman College Nursery School (1930) was organized to provide: (1) an environment for the maximum development of children two to five years of age; (2) an opportunity for parents to observe practical work with young chil-

dren; and (3) training to college students for work in home economics. It admitted twenty children from a cross section of the Negro population of Atlanta. It was open from 9:00 A.M. until 3:00 P.M.

THE NURSERY SCHOOL AT ALABAMA STATE TEACHERS COLLEGE[95]

This nursery school (1930) was organized by W. McKinley Menchan, an African-American educator who pointed out, like Arnold Gesell had done a few years earlier, "that education had to go further downward in order to lay a firmer foundation, and it was incumbent upon the Negro college to take the lead in establishing this most worthy institution . . . for children of the Negro group" (338–339). Menchan started such a nursery school in the fall of 1930. The school enrolled children from twenty-two months to five years of age. They stayed at school for six hours a day, five days a week, for thirty-six weeks of the year. He pointed out that the nursery school was not a "child-parking place" for working mothers, "nor a dumping place" for mothers who wanted some free time from the care of their children. Each one of the children was busy with "educative activities" from the time he arrived at the school (339).

HAMPTON INSTITUTE'S PRESCHOOL GROUP

According to Cooper,[96] the Hampton preschool was organized during the school year 1932–1933 when a course in child development was offered for the first time. Because of financial constraints, it was not equipped as a laboratory school.

Ten children were enrolled during the year. They were between two and three years old. The mothers took turns bringing the children to school and returning them to their homes. Two mothers were in charge of the group at school. The college students observed at first and later assisted the mothers.

The children arrived at 9:00 A.M. and played until 10:00, when they washed their hands and had a glass of orange juice. Each child had his own rug on which he rested for half an hour. A period of play followed, and the children went home at 11:30 A.M. When the weather was pleasant, they stayed outside. The mothers who met regularly to discuss their concerns with a member of the home economics staff deserve much credit for the play school.

At the beginning of the 1933–1934 school year, a part-time assistant experienced in nursery school was employed. She carried on the activities started the first year, and unified them. More needed to be done about the physical examinations for children, follow-up, and nutrition. It was suggested that students should share in the further planning of the preschool group.

CHAPTER SUMMARY

This chapter described the experiences of African-Americans and their plight to secure their freedom. Their collective memory may still reflect some of their experiences during slavery. For example, being punished for wanting to learn to read may still have something to do with the attitude of some toward education. These experiences can give us some understanding and insight into the contemporary educational problems of black society.

NOTES

1. The terms "Negro," "colored," "black," "Afro-American," and "African-American" are used interchangeably throughout the text, as they have been found in the reviewed literature.

2. Norman R. Yetman, ed., *Life Under the "Peculiar Institution": Selections from the Slave Narrative Collection* (New York: Holt, Reinhart and Winston, 1970), 1. Yateman's book is based on the Federal Writers' Project, *Slave Narratives, A Folk History of Slavery in the United States from Interviews with Former Slaves* (Washington, DC, 1941).

3. John H. Franklin, *From Slavery to Freedom: A History of Negro Americans*, 3d ed. (New York: Alfred A. Knopf, 1967), 43–50. Slavery has existed since biblical times but had no racial basis.

4. Ibid., 70–71.

5. Thomas L. Webber, *Deep Like the Rivers: Education in the Slave Quarter Community, 1831–1865* (New York: Norton, 1978), x.

6. Yetman, *Life Under the "Peculiar Institution,"* 52; Louis Hughes, *Thirty Years a Slave: Autobiography of Louis Hughes* (Milwaukee: South Side Printing Co., 1897; reprint, Miami, FL: Mnemosyne Publishing, 1969), 25–26 (page citations are to the reprint edition).

7. Webber, *Deep Like the Rivers,* 6–88; Yateman, *Life Under the "Peculiar Institution,"* 72.

8. Webber, *Deep Like the Rivers,* 6–10. For photographs and drawings of the slave quarters, see John Michael Vlach, *Back of the Big House: The Architecture of Plantation Slavery* (Chapel Hill: University of North Carolina Press, 1993).

9. Herbert G. Gutman, *The Black Family in Slavery and Freedom, 1750–1925* (New York: Pantheon Books, 1976), 45–100. See also Andrew Billingsley, *Black Families in White America* (Englewood Cliffs, NJ: Prentice-Hall, 1968).

10. Yateman, *Life Under the "Peculiar Institution,"* 112.

11. Eugene Genovese, *Roll, Jordan, Roll: The World the Slaves Made* (New York: Pantheon Books, 1974), 494–499.

12. Webber, *Deep Like the Rivers,* 168–169, 172.

13. Ibid., 15–16; Yateman, *Life Under the "Peculiar Institution,"* 71–72.

14. Genovese, *Roll, Jordan, Roll,* 449–450; Gutman, *The Black Family in Slavery and Freedom,* 18

15. Gutman, *The Black Family in Slavery,* 75–76.

16. Franklin, *From Slavery to Freedom,* 153.

17. Genovese, *Roll, Jordan, Roll,* 496.

18. Webber, *Deep Like the Rivers,* 11.

19. Genovese, *Roll, Jordan, Roll,* 508–509.

20. Yateman, *Life Under the "Peculiar Institution,"* 34.

21. Estella Jones, "Georgia Narratives" XII (2) in George P. Rawick, ed., *The American Slave: A Composite Autobiography,* 19 vols. (Westport, CT: Greenwood Publishing, 1972–1977), 346. The volume number, XII, refers to the twelfth volume in the set as a whole. The number in parenthesis (2) refers to Part 2 of the narrative for Georgia, and the last figure to the appropriate page; Hughes, *Thirty Years a Slave,* 44.

22. Susan B. Eppes, *The Negro of the Old South: A Bit of Period History* (Mason, GA: J. W. Burke, 1941), quoted in Webber, *Deep Like the Rivers,* 15.

23. Yateman, *Life Under the "Peculiar Institution,"* 265.

24. Genovese, *Roll, Jordan, Roll,* 498.

25. Hughes, *Thirty Years a Slave,* 43–44.

26. Webber, *Deep Like the Rivers,* 161.

27. John Campbell, "Work, Pregnancy, and Infant Mortality among Southern Slaves," *Journal of Interdisciplinary History* 14 (Spring 1984): 792–812.

28. Genovese, *Roll, Jordan, Roll,* 486–497.

29. Booker T. Washington, *Up from Slavery* (New York: Dell, 1965), quoted in Webber, *Deep Like the Rivers,* 177.

30. David K. Wiggins, "The Play of Slave Children in the Plantation Communities of the Old South, 1820–1860," *Journal of Sport History* 7 (Summer 1980): 21–39.

31. Genovese, *Roll, Jordan, Roll,* 506.

32. Webber, *Deep Like the Rivers,* 186.

33. Ibid., 188.

34. Ibid., 21.

35. Hughes, *Thirty Years a Slave,* 31.

36. Genovese, *Roll, Jordan, Roll,* 505; Webber, *Deep Like the Rivers,* 19.

37. Webber, *Deep Like the Rivers,* 43–44, 46–47, 50–51.

38. Ibid., 52, 54.

39. Genovese, *Roll, Jordan, Roll,* 238; Webber, *Deep Like the Rivers,* 191, 196, 198, 203, 205.

40. Yateman, *Life Under the "Peculiar Institution,"* 161.

41. Hughes, *Thirty Years a Slave,* 19–21; Yateman, *Life Under the "Peculiar Institution,"* 145, 151.

42. Booker T. Washington, *Up from Slavery: An Autobiography* (n.p. 1900, 1901; reprint Williamstown, MA: Corner House Publishers, 1971), 7 (page citations are to the reprint edition).

43. Wilma King, *Stolen Childhood: Slave Youth in Nineteenth-Century America* (Bloomington & Indianapolis: Indiana University Press, 1995), 74–75.

44. Carter G. Woodson, *The Education of the Negro Prior to 1861* (New York: G. P. Putnam's Sons, 1915), 36, 33–44. Woodson conceived "Negro History Week" as a period in which the contributions of the Negro to the development of civilization would be emphasized for Negroes as well as whites. Franklin, *From Slavery to Freedom,* 565. Woodson was also the founder and editor of the *Journal of Negro History* (1916). Yateman, *Life Under the "Peculiar Institution,"* 341.

45. Lawrence A. Cremin, *American Education: The Colonial Experience, 1607–1783* (New York: Harper & Row Publishers, Harper Torchbooks, 1970), 161.

46. Theresa A. Rector, "Black Nuns as Educators," *Journal for Negro Education* 51, (Summer 1982): n238, 230–241.

47. Woodson, *The Education of the Negro,* 46.

48. Frederick Douglass, *Autobiographies: Narrative of Life of Frederick Douglass, An American Slave: My Bondage and My Freedom; and Life and Times of Frederick Douglass,* one vol. ((New York: The Library of America, 1994), 37, 526–527, 532, 541, 559–560.

49. Woodson, *The Education of the Negro,* 100–111, 157, 162–163, 165.

50. Ibid., 78, 100, 104.

51. Harry Morgan, *Historical Perspectives on the Education of Black Children* (Westport, CT: Praeger, 1995), 41–42; Woodson, *The Education of the Negro,* 97–98.

52. Woodson, *The Education of the Negro,* 97–98; Franklin, *From Slavery to Freedom,* 160.

53. Woodson, *The Education of the Negro,* 99. For more on the struggles and successes of this early venture for schools for blacks, see Charles C. Andrews, *The History of the New York African Free Schools* (New York: M. Day 1830; reprint New York: Negro Universities Press, 1969).

54. Woodson, *The Education of the Negro,* 96; *Courage and Conscience: Black and White Abolitionists in Boston,* ed. Donald M. Jacobs (Bloomington: Indiana University Press, Published for the Boston Athenæum, 1993), 209. A photograph of the Abiel Smith School is on this page.

55. Woodson, *The Education of the Negro,* 94, 149.

56. Franklin, *From Slavery to Freedom,* 267–268.

57. The highlights are taken from Frederick Douglass, *Autobiographies: Narrative of the Life of Frederick Douglass, An American Slave; My Bondage and My Freedom; and Life and Times of Frederick Douglass,* one vol. (New York: The Library of America, 1994).

58 Lewis and Charles joined the 54th Massachusetts Regiment. Frederick recruited colored troops in the Mississippi valley. Robert Gould Shaw of Boston was the commanding officer of the 54th. He was killed in the assault on Fort Wagner. Several of the men survived and received medals for their gallantry. The Robert Gould Shaw Memorial across from the State House in Boston honors the men of the 54th.

59. Harry S. Ashmore, *The Negro and the Schools* (Chapel Hill: University of North Carolina Press, 1954), 3–8.

60. Franklin, *From Slavery to Freedom*, 306–307. By 1867, there were 46 hospitals under the Bureau that treated more than 450,000 cases of illness. Ibid.

61. Ibid., 308–309. For a detailed account on the Bureau, see George R. Bentley, *A History of the Freedmen's Bureau* (Philadelphia: University of Pennsylvania Press, 1955).

62. James D. Anderson, *The Education of Blacks in the South, 1860–1935* (Chapel Hill: University of North Carolina Press, 1988), 239–240.

63. Donal F. Lindsey, *Indians at Hampton Institute, 1877–1923* (Urbana and Chicago: University of Illinois Press, 1995), 7–9.

64. Anderson, *The Education of Blacks in the South, 1860–1935*, 33–78; David W. Adams, *Education for Extinction: American Indians and the Boarding School Experience, 1875–1928* (Lawrence: University of Kansas Press, 1995), 45.

65. Anderson, *The Education of Blacks in the South, 1860–1935*, 34–35.

66. Ibid., 49.

67. For more on the role of the *Southern Workman*, see Ibid., 36–37; For Ludlow's contribution, see Lindsey, *Indians at Hampton Institute, 1877–1923*, 95, 268.

68. King, *Stolen Childhood*, 165.

69. Ashmore, *The Negro and the Schools*, 17, 19.

70. Ibid., 9–10.

71. These highlights are taken from Booker T. Washington, *Up from Slavery: An Autobiography* (n.p. 1900, 1901; reprint Williamstown, MA: Corner House Publishers, 1971).

72. Booker T. Washington, *Up from Slavery*, quoted in Robert H. Bremner, ed., *Children and Youth in America*, 3 vols., 5 books (Cambridge, MA: Harvard University Press, 1971–1974), 2:1198–1206.

73. Franklin, *From Slavery to Freedom*, 392–393.

74. Ibid., 395, 449, 565.

75. Ibid., 342. A *dictum*—a statement a court makes but is not a decision—from the case of *Plessy vs. Ferguson* (1896) became the basis for the "separate but equal" doctrine of education in the South. The U.S. Supreme Court actually went out of its way to recognize "that segregation in education was a general American practice, not a uniquely Southern one." Ashmore, *The Negro and the Schools*, 11.

76. Franklin, *From Slavery to Freedom*, 615.

77. Ashmore, *The Negro and the Schools*, 100.

78. Franklin, *From Slavery to Freedom*, 619.

79. For more details, see Booker T. Washington, *A New Negro for a New Century* (Chicago: American Publishing House, 1900; reprint, Miami, FL: Mnemosyne Publishing Inc., 1969), 379–405, 406–428 (page citations are to the reprint edition); and Charles H. Wesley, *History of the National Association of Colored Women's Clubs, Inc., A Legacy of Service* (Washington, DC: National Association of Colored Women's Clubs, 1984).

80. Franklin, *From Slavery to Freedom*, 404–407, 409.

81. Josephine S. Yates, "Kindergartens and Mothers' Clubs, as Related to the Work of the National Association of Colored Women," *The Colored American Magazine* 8 (June 1905): 311.

82. Ibid., 307. For the accomplishments of black women in many fields, see Gerda Lerner, ed., *Black Women in White America* (New York: Pantheon Books, 1972).

83. The information on Mary Church Terrell came from the following sources: "Mary Church Terrell," in *Notable Black Women*, ed. Jessie Carney Smith, 2 vols. (Detroit: Gale Research Inc., 1992), 1:1115–1119; "Mollie Church Terrell," *Noted Negro Women*, ed. M. A. Majors, M.D. (Chicago: Donahue & Henneberry, 1893; reprint, Salem, NH: Ayer Company, 1986), 321 (page citations are to the reprint edition); Elizabeth F. Chittenden "As We Climb: Mary Church Terrell," *Negro History Bulletin* 38 (February–March 1979):

351–354; and Eleanor Flexner, *Centuries of Struggle, The Woman's Rights Movement in the United States* (New York: Athenæum, 1968), 191.

84. Mary Church Terrell, "Club Work of Colored Women," *Southern Workman* 30 (August 1901): 435–438.

85. "Haydee Campbell," *Noted Negro Women*, ed. Majors, 329; Yates, "Kindergartens and Mothers' Clubs," 307.

86. "Josephine Silone Yates," in *Notable Black Women*, 1:1286–1287, and "Josephine A. Silone Yates," *Noted Negro Women*, ed. Majors, 44–50.

87. Yates, "Kindergartens and Mothers' Clubs," 309.

88. Mrs. J. Silone Yates, "Report of the National Federation of Colored Women's Clubs," *The Colored America Magazine* 8 (May 1905): 259, 261.

89. Alice Dugged Cary, "Kindergartens for Negro Children," *Southern Workman* 29 (August 1900): 462.

90. Ibid., 463. Articles like "The Successful Negro Mother," *The Colored American Magazine* 14, no. 7 (July 1908): 396, began to appear in the Negro press.

91. Anna J. Murray, "A New Key to the Situation," *Southern Workman* 29 (September 1900): 503–507.

92. "A Week in the Hampton Kindergarten," *Southern Workman* 36 (September 1907): 537–544; Mrs. Charles Bartlett Dyke, "The Beginnings of Citizenship," *Southern Workman* 29 (February 1900): 91–98. Both articles include photographs: the opening exercises of the school; children washing and ironing; taking care of babies (white dolls); singing and playing in the orchestra. E. A. Johnson, "Negro Dolls for Negro Babies," *The Colored American Magazine* 14 (November 1908): 583–584, advanced the idea that one way to teach Negro children to respect their own color is to give them colored dolls to play with.

93. "Training Classes for Colored Teachers," extracts from letter of Miss Peabody to editor of volume, Henry Barnard, *Kindergarten and Child Culture Papers: Papers on Froebel's Kindergarten, with Suggestions and Methods of Child Culture in Different Countries,* rev. ed. (Hartford, CT: Office of *Barnard's American Journal of Education,* 1884), 735–736.

94. Perlie Reed, "Spelman College Nursery School," *Spelman Messenger* 46 (1930): 12–14.

95. W. McKinley Mechan, "The Negro College Takes to the Nursery School," *School and Society* 36 (September 10, 1932): 338–340.

96. Ednora P. Cooper, "Hampton Institute's Preschool Group," *Southern Workman* 63 (July 1934): 214–215. Another example of Black initiatives for young children was the Hope Day Nursery, established in New York City (1902) and supported by a committee of Black women. Maude K. Griffin, "The Hope Day Nursery," *Colored American Magazine* 10 (June 1906): 397–400. The author of the article was recording secretary of the committee. Ibid., 400.

CHAPTER 16

Asian-Americans

> With obstacles overcome, such as inadequate equipment
> installed, nursery schools decorated, and armed with
> a better and more thorough teacher training, evacuee
> nursery school teachers are now in direct charge of
> Manzanar's youngsters ranging in age from three to five.
> —*Manzanar Free Press*
> [Manzanar Relocation Camp] (1943)[1]

Asian immigrants have come to these shores from many nations. Their stories and those of their children impact upon both the history of early childhood education and its present-day programs. Three of the major countries to which Asian-Americans trace their roots are China, Japan, and the Philippines. More recently, Southeast Asian families came to the United States. This chapter shows how the education system has both hindered and helped Asian-American children.

CHINESE

The autobiographies of Chinese-American adults, which recount their childhoods, bear testimony to the results of adult lifestyles and work, and the family living problems they created.[2] The story of Jade Snow Wong tells of a Chinese-American girl's passage through the educational and family-traditional systems that epitomize the struggles of Asian immigrants to U.S. shores. "From infancy to my sixteenth year, I was reared according to nineteenth century ideals of Chinese womanhood. I was never left alone, though it was not unusual for me to feel lonely, while surrounded by a family of seven others, and often by ten (including bachelor cousins) at meals," says Wong. Albert Yee remembers how terrified he was when he was in kindergarten in Merced, California, and the teacher punished him by putting soap and water in his mouth and keeping him after school for telling a classmate she was about to step into "shit." "I learned from that incident that the class and the teacher expected a 'Chinaboy' to be foul-mouthed and treated me as such. Sympathizing, but offering no protest to the school for such treatment, my mother told me, 'You must learn to take abuses from the whites. Try to understand and swallow your pride. Go to school and learn no matter what.'" Maxine Hong Kingston's records show that she flunked kindergarten and had a zero IQ in first grade. She spoke and read in whispers. For years she didn't speak at all, but covered her school paintings with black paint. The Chinese children were excluded from participating in the class play. Kingston wrote that "after

American school, we picked up our cigar boxes, in which we had arranged books, brushes, and an inkbox neatly, and went to Chinese school, from 5:00 to 7:30 P.M."[3]

Historical Background

The first Chinese immigrants to the United States were three boys who returned with the missionary Reverend S. R. Brown, to study at the Monson Academy in Massachusetts, in 1847.[4] Several thousand Chinese came to the United States to work as merchants and traders, despite the prohibition of the Chinese government against going abroad.[5] They paid their own way and were of a higher social class than the laborers who came later. "Historian J. O'Meara said the first Chinese to arrive on the West Coast were merchants with beautiful silks, tea and objects d'art."[6] From the 1840s to the early 1870s, after the abolition of black slavery, contract laborers brought to Hawaii and California created strong pressures for other cheap labor sources. The majority of Chinese immigrants came to work in the gold mines beginning in 1850 and on the railroads after 1865. Because of strict United States immigration laws, these men who worked the "Mountain of Gold" left their wives and families behind, forming "mutilated families."[7] On their infrequent visits to China, the "guests of the Mountain of Gold" would father more progeny for their increasingly self-sufficient wives to care for. These practices resulted in a single set of parents having a multigenerational family. In later years, when a wife and children were permitted to come to the United States, children born in California were often many years younger than their China-born siblings.[8]

What did the male laborers who came to the United States leave behind? After China's 1842 defeat in the Opium Wars, Western encroachments into China in the form of military invasion, economic colonization, and political domination began.[9] Chinese intellectuals who had studied abroad in Japan, the United States, or Europe assisted in the 1902 Qing government reform of the education system. Provisions were made for preschool education, called *mengxuetang* (school of enlightenment). After the revolution in 1911, preschools were renamed *mengyangyuan* (gardens of enlightenment and care). In 1922 they were renamed kindergartens (*youzhiyuan*).

The kindergartens in China were not the result of indigenous movements but owe their early existence to the ideas of European philosophers and educators such as Froebel and Pestalozzi. Chinese parents were comfortable with the idea of early and formal education of young children. Preschools and public and private kindergartens appeared all over China. The private kindergartens were often run by Christian missionaries. The public normal schools and junior normal schools trained child care nurses and preschool teachers.

During the pre-Western period, education in Hong Kong was closely associated with religious institutions. The Buddhist temples made a secular education, characterized by Confucian learning, available for the children of commoners.[10] From the seventeenth century on, Western influences began to be felt. This was a laissez-faire period during which missionary and philanthropic groups filled the educational void. In the late 1800s and early 1900s, minimal care and educational services were provided for young children in Hong Kong. A small number of private kindergarten and infant classes, attached to primary schools, existed. The earliest schools began around 1915. Later the colonial governments played a prominent educational role. The elitist colonial model of schooling neglected primary education for the general population. It was an educational system that was urban in both location and orientation. However, those Chinese who wanted to educate their children in the Chinese language and tradition organized village and community groups, imported teachers from a large Chinese city, or sent their children to Chinese centers of learning. The most rapid expansion of preschools and kindergartens, however, took place after World War II, during the 1950s and 1960s.[11]

The men who left either mainland China or Hong Kong in the mid- to late-1800s to seek their fortune in the United States were leaving wives who became independent and children who often received preschool education. When the Chinese first arrived in the United States, they were praised for their industriousness, lawful nature, usefulness, respect for intelligence, and creativity. However, they became the brunt of anti-immigrant feeling on the West Coast because their distinctive lifestyle and the supposed economic competition they provided to whites made them unpopular. By the 1870s, the Chinese had been denounced for "servity," deceit, and living in their own communities. They were even blamed for outbreaks of smallpox in San Francisco.[12]

California's 1879 State Constitution gave cities and towns the right to evict or segregate Chinese at will, and forbade local entities and California-chartered corporations from hiring Chinese workers. Although these provisions were found unconstitutional in a court case in 1880, it took a U.S. Supreme Court decision in 1886 (*Yick Wo vs. Hopkins*) to declare that Chinese-Americans were "persons" under the Fourteenth Amendment to the U.S. Constitution. Harsh laws were passed. In California, for example, the Chinese were forbidden, by exclusion laws passed between 1880 and 1924, to send their children to "white" schools, to wear a queue, or to own land. In 1882, the Congress passed the Chinese Exclusion Act, which was the first federal law to restrict the immigration of an entire group.[13]

The immigrant child who came to the United States at the beginning of the twentieth century had problems adjusting to the new environment. In school, as can be seen from the examples above, the children were often conspicuously different. Children gave their teachers insight into their parents' minds and introduced their parents to American customs and the English language. The children, like their mothers, gained new independence in the United States. The parents were proud of the children's achievements, although they worried that their "Americanized" children would lose respect for them and their way of life.[14] In the ethnic schools the Chinese children attended in the afternoons, evenings, and on weekends, they learned the history, literature, language, and sometimes the religion of their ancient homeland. The ethnic curriculum was less successful in homes where the Chinese language was not spoken. Ethnic education was successful, however, because the children learned that their collective past extended beyond the squalid urban tenements in which they were living. The achievements of great scholars and artists gave them hope that they could rise above their current situation. These schools also gave American-born children a better understanding of their foreign-born parents, by helping to keep the lines of communication open.[15]

Education

Anti-Chinese bias in San Francisco and other communities was particularly evident in the area of public education. Between 1871 and 1884, the San Francisco Board of School Trustees refused to acknowledge the right of children of Chinese descent to attend public schools. In response to the California Supreme Court ruling that children of all ethnic groups had the right to attend schools in the state, San Francisco initiated a "separate but equal" ordinance that forced children of Chinese ancestry to attend a segregated Chinese school.

The Family

In the traditional Chinese family, the father was the undisputed head. The obligations, responsibilities, and privileges of each family member's role were clearly delineated. Both father and mother were tendered respect and loyalty by all family members. The father usually assumed the maximum responsibility for the family's economic well-being and social status, and the mother was discouraged from working outside the home. However, when the families traveled from China to the United States, mothers were forced to work in factories or family businesses. This economic necessity led to changes in both the family and the community.[16]

In New York City, a community that had very few children previously, the most important concession to the presence of children, and of working mothers, was the establishment of a day care center.[17] In 1978, there were only three, the Chinatown Day Care Center, the Hamilton Madison House Day Care, and The Educational Alliance. Together they accommodated approximately 250 children. Sung and her staff discovered many horror stories similar to those reported by earlier factory worker mothers described in Chapter 11. Children were left alone in apartments, tied up, set in front of televisions on a daily basis, or were forced to take care of themselves.

Some of the Chinese children in New York City attended after-school centers that extended their school day from 8:30 A.M. to 6:00 P.M. The Chinatown Planning Council operated the largest program, which provided nutritious breakfasts, hot lunches, and recreational activities with snacks. Elementary school children often hurried off to garment factories right after school, to report to their mother for assignment of their daily chores before going home to an empty apartment.[18] Many of the children stayed beside their mother's sewing machine, doing their homework or helping her to get garments ready for sewing. The factory bosses did not object to the children, and accepted their daily presence after 3:00 P.M. as a normal course of events. After the children finished their homework, and if they did not have any work to do, they played with each other among the empty boxes or between the bundles of finished garments. Many children in Chinatown worked at menial tasks in the shops or factories, or had newspaper routes. These contributions to the family raised the Chinese child's sense of self-worth.[19]

Teacher Preparation

Kitano reports that "despite trends toward assimilation, traditional values and family systems persist" among Chinese-Americans.[20] West points out the difficulties a classroom teacher may experience when the values and habits of the parents differ significantly from those of the school and the teacher. She cites the example of Chinese students from a traditional background who were sent to preschool in their finest clothes, because the family considered schooling extremely important. The family also viewed teachers as the experts, and believed that they should not have parents telling them what to do. Teachers needed to consider the ideas and feelings of the caregivers of these Chinese children, when preparing curriculum activities. Paint, clay, water, mud, and other messy activities needed to have specific routines, smocks and aprons, and information to parents about the timing of exceptionally messy activities. This example points up the necessity for communication between the home and school. Teachers should become aware of the cultural and family milieu of their children, as well as presenting a variety of developmentally appropriate activities.[21]

JAPANESE

The Japanese differed from the Chinese in that they placed a priority on the development of primary education for the general population. During the Edo period, from 1603 through 1867, Japan had a feudal society. Schools to teach literary and military skills were set up for the Ruling and *Samurai* classes. In the middle of the Edo period, there were "temple schools," private schools that taught reading, writing, and arithmetic to the children of commoners. In addition, some Japanese teachers held private schools called *Shijuku* in their homes, for learning Chinese and Japanese classics, calligraphy, and the abacus.

The Meiji Restoration period, which lasted from 1867 to 1946, was a period of modernization in Japan. The Japanese Fundamental Code of Education, promulgated in 1872, created an educational system composed of elementary and middle schools and universities, as well as normal schools for the training of teachers. Shinzo Seki gathered data on the work of Friedrich Froebel during an 1872 delegation visit to Europe. He published a description of Froebel's ideas on the creative self-activity of children. On November 14,

1876, Seki became the director of the first government-sponsored kindergarten. It was connected with the Tokyo Girls' Higher Normal School. In 1878, a kindergarten training school organized by the Ministry of Education was begun at the normal school.

Early Japanese kindergartens were influenced by Froebel and the American kindergarten movement. However, the European and American influences were modified to fit the Japanese culture. The Froebel Association in Japan proposed that the Ministry of Education establish kindergarten regulations. This was done in 1899. The regulations became the foundation of the Kindergarten Act of 1926, which covered school age, hours of operation, number of children, the facilities, purposes, and curriculum. The Act and the regulations remained in effect until 1947.[22]

Japanese child care centers (*hoikuen*) and preschools (*yochien*), like their European and American counterparts, had different social origins from the kindergartens. The *hoikuen* were established to serve the children of the poor, including poor workers. The *yochien* served primarily the children of upper income families. As time went by, many *hoikuen* were founded by social reformers in response to the industrialization and urbanization of the country. Family changes and the improvement of children's health and welfare were the impetus for the spread of these centers. The pace of center openings quickened with the advent of World War II, when the conscription of women for factory work created a need for child care facilities. As in the United States, many of the child care facilities were closed at the end of World War II.[23]

Japanese first came to the U.S. mainland in 1869, shortly after the Meiji Restoration. The settlers of the California Wakamatsu Colony were young, relatively wealthy, well-educated, and seeking careers. Because of the Japanese emphasis on education, the Japanese immigrants of the 1880s were literate, unlike those from China. However, as the Japanese began to arrive on the West Coast of the United States in larger numbers, they were placed in the same inferior slots as the Chinese, whom they replaced as agricultural day laborers.[24] The Japanese came from a broad socioeconomic spectrum, so they were soon able to acquire their own farms.

Education

San Francisco passed school segregation laws against Japanese in May 1905, extending the law to "all Orientals" in October of that year. Los Angeles took the opposing position, avoiding school segregation. President Theodore Roosevelt sent his Secretary of Commerce and Labor to investigate the situation of the Japanese in America. He found that the Japanese children caused no problems in school. As a result of the investigation, the Japanese were not segregated as the Chinese had been. In return for the president's intervention, Japan limited the number of immigration visas it granted for people to come to the United States.[25] Japanese immigrants had weaker ties to family and village at home; therefore, the Japanese became assimilated into United States culture more easily.[26]

Formation of families was very important to Japanese immigrants, and thus the second and later generations of Japanese-Americans were readily acculturated. Japanese-American children entered American public schools and achieved high educational goals. Thus, the Japanese transition from "sojourner to settler" was much more rapid than that of the Chinese immigrants. The cultural assimilation of the Japanese into U.S. society, particularly in the Western states and Hawaii, made the later anti-Japanese movement and exclusionary legislation especially troubling to the Issei.[27]

The earliest recorded anti-Japanese movement, led by San Francisco newspapers, began in May 1892. It culminated in the San Francisco Board of School Trustees resolution of June 10, 1893, which relegated Japanese students to the segregated Chinese school. Intervention by the Japanese Counsel in San Francisco led to the rescinding of this resolution. The Oriental (Asiatic) Exclusion League, presided over by labor union leaders, was formed in San Francisco in May 1905. The 1907 congressional legislation and President Roosevelt's "Gentlemen's Agreement" stopped the migration of Japanese laborers to the United States. The acquisition of land by Japanese immigrants and their families was halted by the Alien Land Laws of 1913 and 1920 at 350,000 acres in California. The May 26, 1924, signing of the Japanese Exclusion Act effectively ended Japanese immigration to the United States until after World War II.[28]

The resentment against and the negative sentiments about the Japanese held by many people in the United States during the 1930s erupted into hate and suspicion following the Japanese attack on Pearl Harbor. President Franklin Delano Roosevelt signed Executive Order 9066, calling for the eviction and internment of all Japanese-Americans from the West Coast, on February 19, 1942. This order was particularly shocking to the Nisei. In spite of the hearings held by the Tolan Committee, Secretary of War Stimson declared the evacuation necessary, and used the authority granted by the president to designate military areas from which any and all persons could be excluded. Although Executive Order 9066 applied to the aliens of Germany, Italy, and other nations, it was primarily used to justify the incarceration of the Japanese. All persons of Japanese ancestry were included, thus it was not limited to suspected Japanese informants and collaborators.[29] The order was implemented by "the ineffectual and prejudiced commander of the Western Defense Command in San Francisco, Lieutenant General John De Witt."[30]

At first, assembly centers were set up at race tracks, fairgrounds, or livestock pavilions. Detainees were housed in windowless shacks or livestock stalls before being deported to relocation camps or internment camps. Little is known about the "enemy alien internment camps," which housed the prewar Issei leadership of some Japanese-American communities, as well as those deemed "disloyal" on the basis of an administered loyalty questionnaire.[31]

Descriptions of the Manzanar, Camp Harmony, and Tule Lake relocation centers are available in the literature.

Schools were omitted from the Wartime Civilian Control Administration (WCCA) plan for assembly centers and relocation camps. However, the Japanese-Americans within the camps soon saw a need for the creation of an educational structure for children and adults.[32] At Camp Harmony, in the state of Washington, classes were offered for every age group. For grades one to eight, classes were scheduled from 9:00 to 11:00 A.M. and from 2:00 to 4:00 P.M. The *Camp Harmony Newsletter* reported that 312 children of grammar school age went back to school on June 12, 1942. The program included a story hour, group singing, spelling, art and handicrafts, and outdoor recreation.[33] The instructional staff consisted of internees who had been employed as teachers prior to the evacuation, and their assistants.

At the Manzanar Relocation Camp in California, the Civilian War Relocation Authority (WRA) allocated funds for both K–12 and nursery school classes during the summer of 1942. The purpose of the nursery schools was to help preschool children overcome language difficulties and prepare for entrance into the elementary grades. Teachers were recruited from all over the country. However, one of the WRA's goals was the utilization of qualified internees in all aspects of the camps. In the case of the nursery schools in the War Relocation Centers, the availability of Nisei teachers, college students and graduates with training in child development or related fields, was a key factor in the development of high-quality preschool programs.

Trained evacuee preschool teachers worked to help "survive much of the misery, discomfort and frustration of internment life." Mary Schauland, the qualified Pre-School Supervisor, respected their work and was dedicated to quality programs. Some teachers were recruited and received training at Manzanar. About half of them were mothers of young children in the programs. Preference was given to women twenty-one to thirty-five years of age. In order to enter the thirty-day probationary period, they were required to be U.S. citizens and pass a loyalty test to the government, to speak good English, and to have at least a high school diploma.

During their probationary period the teachers-in-training worked under the direction of a regular preschool teacher, with whom they had daily conferences. The supervisor provided them with bulletins on methods and techniques, and held weekly group meetings. After successful completion of probation, they received a teaching assignment.

Professional development continued with a program of in-service reading and staff meetings covering: "aims and objectives of the program; job analysis of the teacher's work; characteristics and typical needs of young children; safety precautions and first aid; the contributions of pre-school in developing creativity; and the guidance of mental, physical, and emotional growth. Kindergarten teachers had additional work specific to older groups, including their informal experiences with the 'tool subjects' of reading, writing, spelling and arithmetic."[34]

Parents had a policy-making role, through the nursery school Parent Teacher Association (PTA). Payment of the ten cents annual dues entitled them to voting privileges at Manzanar and made them members of the national PTA. Each of the units had its own officers, which sent representatives to the Central Executive Board. They in turn were represented on the camp-wide PTA, along with the elementary school. In the preschool units, mothers served as teacher assistants, taking children to the toilets and supervising their activities. They held carnivals and bazaars to raise funds for food at social events and toys and games for the children.

In a 1988 personal communication to Dorothy Hewes, Grace Kikuchi recalled that some of her Mills College courses in child development had provided lists and measurements for equipment and furniture that were used in setting up the Topaz Relocation Camp nursery school. From the examination of items in her photographic scrapbook of Manzanar, Hewes surmises that similar basic plans were used at that camp as well.[35] The PTA took on the job of providing an appropriate environment for the early education program. Partitions, shelves, playhouse equipment, and movable screens were built with scavenged materials. The walls were calcimined in pastel shades, heavy linoleum was put down on the floors, and curtains decorated the windows. Decorative Japanese-style fences made of willow saplings enclosed the play yards. Each room had areas for imaginative and dramatic play, easel painting, clay modeling, crayons, bead stringing, and "carpentering." The activities were available on a free choice basis to all age groups. "It was assumed that individual children and those at different developmental levels would use them in ways appropriate for their innate needs, with teachers alert to situations in which adult assistance and guidance were appropriate." Rhythm instruments, pianos, and phonographs with suitable records were available. The preschools had their own circulating library, bolstered by books from the elementary school and community libraries. Science experiences included observations of classroom potted plants, goldfish, or jars of insects, and excursions to gardens and other areas within the barbed wire perimeter.

Although the program was equivalent to any other 1940s preschool, there were several problems unique to the relocation camp situation. The communal toilets, which served both living units and nursery school classrooms, were inconveniently located, so children had to be escorted for their use. They got so much usage that they could not be kept sterile, and the floors were often flooded, presenting a danger to the children. Crowding in the apartments made it difficult for children to get a good night's sleep. Therefore, six of the seven units were designated for afternoon sleep sessions. Regulations required that juice and milk stay in the communal mess halls, so they were unavailable for snacks. Children were taught to wash and cup their hands to get a drink of water.

The English language was used in all classrooms. Nisei teachers were permitted to use the Japanese language only in cases of severe emotional problems. Religious books were the only Japanese language books permitted in the camp; therefore, all storybooks were in English. The result was that all of the Manzanar children entering first grade in 1943 and 1944 had competent English abilities because of their preschool programs.[36]

In a poignant preface to her final preschool report, Genevieve Carter (1945), another supervisor, expressed appreciation for the work of the evacuee teaching staff "who shouldered full professional responsibility and entered into a wholesome work relationship with appointed staff members." She expressed hope that all would "have an opportunity to work together professionally again 'outside the barbed wire' where salaries, professional performance and recognition are on a single standard." As efforts were made to relocate internees, during 1944 and 1945, many of the teachers trained in WRA centers found employment in nursery schools and child care centers and others continued their education at colleges to acquire degrees.

Hewes indicates that "the nursery school and kindergarten programs had enthusiastic support of the camp population from the start. More than a thousand visitors attended the first open-house night." Hewes concludes that the "ability of the children to communicate in English, improved ability of the parents to take an active role in the educational institutions attended by their children, and understanding of American-style family dynamics attained through parent meetings conducted by the Pre-School Supervisor and other Caucasians could be assumed to have made a difference."[37]

The internees of Manzanar and other relocation camps gradually returned to the "outside world," after meeting "loyalty checks" under "leave clearance procedures." "On February 16, 1944, the WRA was transferred to the Department of the Interior, headed by liberal Roosevelt appointee, Secretary Harold Ickes. The war with Japan ended on VJ Day, August 15, 1945, and relocation from the camps was accelerated. The closing date set for Manzanar was December 1, 1945 and the official closing of the War Relocation Authority was June 30, 1946."[38] Hewes cites the 1972 sociological research of Maykovich, which analyzed the civil rights movements of the United States and the search for ethnic identity of young adults, as demonstrating that the Sansei "(including some who would have attended nursery schools in the camps) [were] in the forefront of the search for a new identity which rejects the role of 'Quiet Americans.' He believes that the Sansei and the Yonsei (fourth generation) will establish a new identity as a social group which transmits the true spirit of Japanese culture to a democratic multi-ethnic America."[39]

The Family

In contrast to the freedom accorded children in the camps, older Japanese-Americans returning to the community strove to restore some of the prewar family roles, such as "elderly persons were respected, younger members of the family were respectful. The father was accepted as the autocratic ruler of the household and the mother reigned over domestic affairs."[40] This was rarely accomplished in the younger generation, because internees in the camps had exercised decision-making roles and gained leadership experience, many for the first time in their lives. However, according to several authors, Japanese-American mothers of today expect their children to master emotional maturity, self-control, and social courtesy at an early age, even in the preschool years. A Japanese cultural value of knowing one's role, accepting one's place in society, and working hard to perform one's assigned task is readily visible in Japanese-American families. Members of Japanese-American families are expected to mask strong feelings that may disrupt family harmony.[41]

FILIPINOS

Filipinos entered the United States for the first time just before the turn of the twentieth century. They entered "non-quota, because the Islands were a U.S. territory until 1946. Those who came were young, male, and like the Japanese and Chinese before them, enormously unpopular. In fact, Western Congressmen advocated independence for the Philippine Islands so the population could be barred from U.S. soil. The Filipinos became agricultural laborers and domestic servants, like the Mexican-Americans."[42] According to Kitano, only a few authors have attempted to describe Filipino child-rearing patterns. The tribal, racial, cultural, and language diversity of the Filipino people prevents generalization of practices relating to early childhood.[43]

ETHNIC GROUPS COMING FROM SOUTH ASIA AFTER WORLD WAR II

Immigrants from several Southeast Asian countries came to the United States after World War II. Sikhs, Punjabis, and Gujaratis came from India, Urdu-speaking Mirpuris from Pakistan, and Bengali-speaking Sylhetis from Bangladesh. By 1980, there was a reportedly growing population of Indians in the eastern United States, particularly in New York City, New Jersey, and Pennsylvania. The majority of these people emigrated to the United States for such reasons as religious freedom, job opportunities, or education. The largest group of refugees from Southeast Asia were the Vietnamese, Cambodian, and Laotian refugees who came in five waves between 1972 and 1989, during the Vietnamese War and after the collapse of South Vietnam.

The first wave of Vietnamese people came in April 1975, after the fall of Saigon. It consisted primarily of the families of military personnel and those who were close to the South Vietnamese or American administrations in Vietnam. This was a well-educated group that was more conversant with Western culture than later waves. The Vietnamese refugees of 1975 were unique because the American government assumed the responsibility of transporting them to their new home.[44] A second wave of Vietnamese came between 1975 and 1978, and a third from 1978 to 1980. These consisted of the "boat people," families and individuals who escaped via small boats during the decade 1979 to 1989. The boat families spent a considerable amount of time in refugee camps located in Thailand, Malaysia, Indonesia, Hong Kong, or the Philippines. They represented a broad spectrum of the Vietnamese population; however, they were, by and large, urban and well educated. The women in the group usually had between five and seven years of education, and the men, seven to nine years. Some of the families had managed to store enough gold to purchase a boat or passage on a boat, although some of their escape attempts were aborted when they were detected by the Vietnamese authorities.

The fourth wave was the "Amerasians." These were families who came to the United States during the 1980s as part of the special agreement negotiated between the U.S. and Vietnamese governments. A family qualified for the program if one or more of the children had been fathered by an American serviceman during the Vietnamese War. A typical family consisted of a mother, one or two Amerasian children, children born subsequent to 1975, and sometimes the father of the additional children. The mothers and children tended to have very limited education. The fifth wave of emigration included relatives of refugees who were already in the United States who could arrange for the emigration of their spouses, children, and parents still living in Vietnam.

The final wave of Vietnamese emigrants began in 1990 and continues to the present. These are the "political prisoners." Individuals who were released from Vietnamese "reeducation" camps during the 1980s were allowed to immigrate to the United States with their families. Some of these were previous military or government personnel who were severely traumatized by exposure to abusive treatment by their captors. The Cambodians and Laotians left their countries under terrible circumstances and often had harrowing experiences on their way to the United States. Almost all of the adults suffered the trauma of losing family members, starvation, terror, and stress.[45] The majority of Cambodians came from a rural agricultural background. Most of the adult women and many men had only two or three years of elementary education. These families fled from the Khmer Rouge, who systematically destroyed traditional rural cultures and the Western-influenced urban cultures of the Cambodian people during the mid- to late-1970s. The Khmer Rouge wished to establish a pure Marxist agrarian society through destruction of those who had more than a rudimentary education. Between one million and two million Cambodians perished during the four years of the Khmer Rouge domination. The Cambodian refugees to the United States had spent up to eight years in camps in Thailand and had either trickled across the Thai border during the years of Khmer Rouge administration or in the massive exodus during the years following the Vietnamese displacement of the Khmer Rouge regime in 1979.[46]

When the Vietnamese, Cambodian, and Laotian refugees arrived, they faced poor economic conditions and racial prejudice in the United States. This led to their becoming disbursed geographically, rather than being allowed to form concentrated communities as previous Asian immigrants had done. Amerasian children and families were particularly at risk because they often lacked a family unit in a culture where the family is highly valued. However, a number of communities and religious and social service entities provided assistance to the refugees after their arrival. Large community Tet celebrations are especially important for Vietnamese refugees in the United States.[47]

From 1990 on, the Travelers and Immigrants Aid/Chicago Connections, with the support of the United Way of Chicago, initiated a family life priority grant program called the Refugee Families Program. Prior to the start of the program, a parent interview study was conducted to obtain background information for the creation of the Head Start module entitled "Enhancing Relationships between Vietnamese Refugee Families and Head Start Personnel." Dr. Daniel R. Scheinfeld of Chicago's Erikson Institute conducted the study, with translation assistance by Phuong Ngoc Chung of the Vietnamese Association of Illinois. One purpose of the study was to provide the preschool teacher serving Vietnamese refugee children with an understanding of the family and child-rearing values of their Vietnamese families. Another purpose was to design methods of parent-teacher collaboration for the introduction of important Vietnamese values and observances of family life into the classroom. The majority of the families were boat people. The others had come to the United States through the "Amerasian orderly departure program."[48] The majority of participants in the Refugee Families Program have been Cambodians, along with some Vietnamese, Sino-Vietnamese, Amerasian, Lao, Chinese, and East African families. The Cambodians had been in the United States between four and eighteen years when they entered the program.[49]

The Vietnamese Family

Many Southeast Asian groups share cultural values that influence parenting practices. Confucian principles of harmony in social relationships and in life, filial piety, ancestral unity, primogeniture, and lineage are among the core values. The principle that an individual's action will reflect positively or negatively on the entire family is passed from generation to generation. The obligation of mutual interdependence creates obligations to parents and family that are expected to outweigh personal desires or needs. Children are taught to respect their parents, older family members, and their teachers.[50]

The findings of the Scheinfeld study agree with the available literature. The results demonstrated that family harmony and happiness was a priority, along with deference to elders, morality, and adherence to parental strictures and the hierarchical order. Parents expected their children to be nurturant toward them throughout their life and to care for them in their old age. They also stated that having children strengthens the husband-wife relationship (which may be a reason why a thirty-year-old woman in one case study already had eleven children).[51]

Education

Southeast Asian parents expect and support their children's school achievement. They expect the child to be patient, independent, reflective, and quick to learn. However, they do not view themselves as facilitators of learning. In Vietnam and Cambodia, parents had been accustomed to granting the total responsibility for their children's education to educators. As reported by Scheinfeld and colleagues, several areas required "negotiation" between parents and preschool staff, including: mediating between the parents' traditional education beliefs, the staffs constructivist orientation, and the staffs expectations in preparing the children for the public school settings they would soon be entering; and the parents' reticence in taking on the role of an educational facilitator.[52]

One component of the Refugee Families Program was child-parent classes. The classes, held in people's homes, are designed to prepare the young children of refugee families for entry into public school, and to enhance the parents' capacities to nurture and support the intellectual and emotional development of their young children. Each class is composed of children and parents (mostly mothers) who meet on a regular basis with the same teacher for a nine-and-a-half-month session. The objectives for the children are (1) to foster their intellectual development by concentrating on observation skills, classification skills, and basic concepts, such as more and less, large and small, and so on; (2) to develop the specific skills that will help them make good use of the elementary school curriculum, such as some basic English vocabulary words and phrases commonly used in the classroom; and (3) to learn to use the materials normally found in preschool classes like scissors, crayons, paste, puzzles, and blocks. The children become familiar with the games and songs that are part of preschool programs, and with school routines. Language development is enhanced by reading to the children on a regular basis. The acquisition of social skills, which are expected of children entering school, is an important part of the program.[53] The preschool classes are one component of the program that also brings individual educational services for adults, health and social services, and abuse-prevention programs into the community.

CHAPTER SUMMARY

This chapter has detailed trends in the immigration and education of Asian-Americans in the United States between the 1800s and the present time. The first major migration of Chinese and Japanese men, and later women and families, occurred from 1800 to 1924. Its purpose was seeking work in order to build savings. The strong family bonds, values, and practices of the Chinese, the Japanese, and the Filipinos were not understood or they were disliked. This led to discrimination in both the work world and the educational world. Children learned to exist in the world that was created by the differing views of adults. The most discriminatory event that took place during the twentieth century was the incarceration of Japanese-Americans during World War II. However, even under these difficult circumstances, the Asian love of learning and respect for education triumphed when nursery schools, kindergartens, and primary grade classes were instituted for the children.

The children who arrived from Southeast Asia between 1972 and the present time have faced a situation that was both similar and dissimilar to that encountered by other Asians before them. The centrality of the family in their lives was often challenged. There was prejudice and discrimination, but there was also education. Community agencies, boards of education, and Head Start programs, among others, reached out to the Asian refugees with practical, innovative programs that supported both the family and educational values of those being served. Perhaps some U.S. citizens had learned the lessons of history and were determined not to repeat them.

NOTES

1. *Manzanar Free Press* (1943) in Dorothy W. Hewes, "Nisei Nursery: Preschool at Manzanar Relocation Camp 1942–1945" (discussion paper presented at the History Seminar of the Annual Conference of the National Association for the Education of Young Children, Anaheim, California, 18 November 1988), 15.

2. Maxine Seller, *To Seek America: A History: A History of Ethnic Life in the United States* (Jerome S. Ozer, Publisher, Inc., 1977), 200–201, 94; Albert H. Yee, *A Search for Meaning: Essays of a Chinese American* (San Francisco: The Chinese Historical Society, 1984), 27–28; and Toyotomi Morimoto, *Japanese Americans and Cultural Continuity: Maintaining Language and Heritage* (New York: Garland, 1997), 19.

3. Jade Snow Wong, "Puritans from the Orient: A Chinese Evolution," in Thomas C. Wheeler, ed. *The Immigrant Experience: The Anguish of Becoming American* (New York: The Dial Press, 1971), 107; Yee, *A Search for Meaning*, 6; and Maxine Hong Kingston, "A Song for a Barbarian Reed Pipe," from *The Woman-Warrior: Memoirs of a Girlhood among Ghosts*, in *Immigrant Women*, ed. Maxine Schwartz Seller, rev. 2d ed. (Albany: State University of New York Press, 1994), 312, 316, 313.

4. Betty Lee Sung, *The Story of the Chinese in America* (New York: Collier Books, 1967), 21.

5. Yee, *A Search for Meaning*, 23.

6. J. O'Meara, "The Chinese in Early Days," *Overland Monthly* 3 (1884) in Sung, *The Story of the Chinese in America*, 21.

7. Yee, *A Search for Meaning*, 23; and Sung, *The Story of the Chinese in America*, 155–156.

8. Sung, *The Story of the Chinese in America*, 157.

9. David Y. H. Wu, "Early Childhood Education in China," in *Early Childhood Education in Asia and the Pacific: A Source Book,* ed. Stephanie Feeney (New York: Garland Publishing, Inc., 1992), 2; and Harold W. Stevenson, Shinying Lee, and Theresa Graham, "Chinese and Japanese Kindergartens: Case Study in Comparative Research," in *Handbook of Research on the Education of Young Children,* ed. Bernard Spodek (New York: Macmillan Publishing Company, 1993), 519.

10. Ruth Bettelheim and Ruby Takanishi, *Early Schooling in Asia* (New York: McGraw-Hill Book Company, 1976), 13.

11. Sylvia Opper, "Early Childhood Education in Hong Kong," in *Early Childhood Education in Asia and the Pacific: A Source Book,* ed. Stephanie Feeney (New York: Garland Publishing, Inc., 1992), 29; and Bettelheim and Takanishi, *Early Schooling in Asia,* 71.

12. Law Students for Civil Rights, "San Francisco's Historical Treatment of Chinese-Americans," 1 of 2; available from <http://server.berkeley.edu/lscr/history.html>; Internet accessed 10 June 1998.

13. Elmer Clarence Sandmeyer, *The Anti-Chinese Movement in California* (Champaign: University of Illinois Press, 1991), 35–54, in Law Students for Civil Rights, "San Francisco's Historical Treatment of Chinese-Americans," 1 of 2.

14. Seller, *To Seek America,* 130–132.

15. Ibid., 162; Sung, *The Story of the Chinese in America,* 179.

16. Tommie J. Hamner and Pauline H. Turner, *Parenting in Contemporary Society,* 3d ed. (Boston: Allyn and Bacon, 1996), 178–82.

17. Betty Lee Sung, *The Adjustment Experience of Chinese Immigrant Children in New York City* (New York: Center for Migration Studies, 1987), 50.

18. Ibid., 133–134, 132–133, 127.

19. Ibid., 131.

20. Margie K. Kitano, "Early Education for Asian-American Children," in *Understanding the Multicultural Experience in Early Childhood Education,* ed. Olivia N. Saracho and Bernard Spodek (Washington, DC: National Association for the Education of Young Children, 1983), 46.

21. Betty West, "Children Are Caught—Between Home and School, Culture and School," in *Alike and Different: Exploring Our Humanity with Young Children,* ed. Bonnie Neugebauer, rev. ed. (Washington, DC: National Association for the Education of Young Children, 1992), 131–132.

22. Bettelheim and Takanishi, *Early Schooling in Asia,* 23, 26; and Catherine Lewis, "Early Childhood Education in Japan," in *Early Childhood Education in Asia and the Pacific: A Source Book,* ed. Stephanie Feeney (New York: Garland Publishing, Inc., 1992), 56.

23. Lewis, "Early Childhood Education in Japan," 57.

24. Morimoto, *Japanese Americans and Cultural Continuity,* 19.

25. Seller, *To Seek America,* 110, 202–203; and Morimoto, *Japanese Americans and Cultural Continuity,* 20–23.

26. Hamner and Turner, *Parenting in Contemporary Society,* 178.

27. The Issei were the first-generation Japanese immigrants. The Nisei were their Japanese-American children born in the United States, who held automatic U.S. citizenship. In 1941, these young adults who been "educated in American schools, and surrounded by American culture . . . were just reaching adulthood and becoming parents of the third generation, the Sansei." Hewes, "Nisei Nursery: Preschool at Manzanar Relocation Camp 1942–1945," 3. The Yonsei are the fourth generation of children.

28. "A Short Chronology of Japanese American History," adapted from ed. Brian Niiya, *Japanese American History: An A-to-Z Reference from 1868 to the Present* (New York: Facts on File, 1993), 1 of 5; available from <http://www.janet.org>; Internet accessed 17 July 1998; Hewes, "Nisei Nursery: Preschool at Manzanar Relocation Camp 1942–1945," 2; and "A Short Chronology of Japanese American History," 2 of 5.

29. "World War 2 Japanese American Internment" [paper on-line], 1–2 of 4; available from <http://www.mindscape.com/reference/california/japan.html>; Internet accessed 25 May 1998; and Hewes, "Nisei Nursery," 3–4.
The photographs of Dorothea Lange taken between 1942 and 1945 capture the poignancy of particular moments in time during the relocation period. They depict Japanese-American children and adults engaging in "normal" routines under abnormal circumstances. See, for example: Dorothea Lange, *Grandfather and Grandson* (Manzanar Relocation Camp), Photoprint, Black and White, ca. 1942 (War Relocation Authority records, The Bancroft Library, Pictorial Collection, University of California, Berkeley); [Exhibit on-line]; available from <http://sunsite.berkeley.edu/ImageFinder/Bancroft/z027.html>; Internet accessed 25 May 1998; and Dorothea Lange, *Salute of Innocence [Children of the Weill public school]* April 1942 (Prints and Photographs Division [92], Library of Congress, Washington, DC); [Exhibit on-line]; available from <http://lcweb.loc.gov/exhibits/wcf/wcf0013.html> and <http://lcweb.loc.gov/exhibits/wcf/wcf092.jpg>; Internet accessed 25 May 1998.

30. Hewes, "Nisei Nursery," 3.

31. "A Short Chronology of Japanese American History," 3–4 of 5.

32. "World War 2 Japanese American Internment," 1 of 4.

33. *Camp Harmony* [Exhibit on-line] (Japanese American Exhibit and Access Project, University of Washington Libraries, rev. 30 July 1997), 1 of 1; available from <http://weber.u.washington.edu/~mudrock/ALLEN/Exhibit/index.html>; Internet accessed 25 May 1998, and *School,* "Vacation School" (Camp Harmony Newsletter, June 12, 1942), 1 of 4, and "Class Schedule for Eight to Eleven Year Olds" Hiroyuki Ichihara Papers. Reel 2. Manuscripts and University Archives, UW Libraries), 2 of 4 [Exhibit on-line] (Japanese

American Exhibit and Access Project, University of Washington Libraries, rev. 30 July 1997); available from <http://weber.u.washington.edu/~mudrock/ALLEN/Exhibit/school.html>; Internet accessed 25 May 1998.

34. Hewes, "Nisei Nursery," 9, 10, 12–14.

35. Scrapbook of photographs depicting "Children's Work and Play Activities" at Manzanar Relocation Camp 1942–1945 (property of Dorothy W. Hewes), unpaged.

36. Hewes, "Nisei Nursery," 10–12.

37. Ibid., 18.

38. Ibid., 16–17; and "Manzanar National Historic Site," 2 of 3; available from <http://www.sierra.cc.ca.us/us395/manzanar.html>; Internet accessed 25 May 1998.

39. Hewes, "Nisei Nursery," 18.

40. Ibid., 17.

41. Kitano, "Early Education for Asian-American Children," in *Understanding the Multicultural Experience in Early Childhood Education,* 48–50; and Hamner and Turner, *Parenting in Contemporary Society,* 178, 182–183.

42. Seller, *To Seek America,* 255–257.

43. Margie K. Kitano, "Early Education for Asian American Children," in *Young Children 35,* no. 2 (January 1980): 16.

44. Janine Bempechat and Miya C. Omori, *Meeting the Educational Needs of Southeast Asian Children,* ERIC CUE Digest No. 68 (New York: ERIC Clearinghouse on Urban Education, August 1990), 1 of 4; and Seller, *To Seek America,* 265–266.

45. Daniel Scheinfeld and Lorraine B. Wallach with Trudi Langendorf, *Strengthening Refugee Families: Designing Programs for Refugee and Other Families in Need* (Chicago: Lyceum Books, Inc., 1997), 8–9; and Bempechat and Omori, *Meeting the Educational Needs of Southeast Asian Children,* 1 of 4.

46. Scheinfeld and Wallach with Langendorf, *Strengthening Refugee Families,* 7.

47. Bempechat and Omori, *Meeting the Educational Needs of Southeast Asian Children,* 2 of 4; Seller, *To Seek America,* 267; and Daniel R. Scheinfeld and Phuong Ngoc Chung, *Teacher's Manual for Tet: Introducing the Vietnamese New Year to the Pre-School Classroom* (Chicago: Erikson Institute, 1991), 7.

48. Daniel R. Scheinfeld, "Family and Child Rearing Values and Perspectives among Vietnamese Families of Head Start Children," TMs (Chicago: Erikson Institute, 1993), 1–12, passim.

49. Scheinfeld and Wallach with Langendorf, *Strengthening Refugee Families,* 4, 7.

50. Bempechat and Omori, *Meeting the Educational Needs of Southeast Asian Children,* 1 of 4; and Scheinfeld and Chung, *Teacher's Manual for Tet,* 5.

51. Scheinfeld, "Family and Child Rearing Values and Perspectives among Vietnamese Families of Head Start Children," 1–12, passim.

52. K. Kitano, "Early Education for Asian American Children," 16; Scheinfeld, "Family and Child Rearing Values and Perspectives among Vietnamese Families of Head Start Children," 9; and Scheinfeld and Wallach with Langendorf, *Strengthening Refugee Families,* 13.

53. Scheinfeld and Wallach with Langendorf, *Strengthening Refugee Families,* 25.

Chapter 17
Hispanic-Americans

Joachim

I am still here!
I have endured in the rugged mountains of our country
I have survived in the toil and slavery of the fields
I have existed
in the barrios of the city
in the suburbs of bigotry
in the minds of social snobbery
in the prisons of dejection
in the muck of exploitation
and
in the fierce heat of racial hatred
—Rodolfo "Corky" Gonzales[1]

The principal origins of Hispanic persons in the United States are the country of Mexico, the country of Cuba, and Puerto Rico. In 1990, there were twenty-two million Hispanics in the United States. They were concentrated in nine states, led by California and Texas. Eighty-five percent of Mexican-Americans lived in the Pacific, Mountain, and West South-Central regions of the country. The majority of Puerto Ricans lived in New York City and several adjacent urban areas.[2]

MEXICAN-AMERICANS

Sources cite the Mexican-American population of the United States in the 1970s as 5.5 million people, making it one of the largest cultural groups in the United States. It has been called the largest "foreign language" ethnic community in the country. "More numerous and more clearly defined as an ethnic culture than most other immigrant communities . . . Mexican-Americans are also the poorest, the least well educated, and the least socially mobile." By 1990, the Mexican-American population of the United States had reached 13.5 million people.[3]

In 1848, Mexico was defeated in the Mexican-American War. Texas and other portions of the Southwest lands were annexed. The Reclamation Act of 1902 encouraged farmers in the southern United States to overcome the labor shortage by hiring low-paid Mexican agricultural laborers.[4] When the cheap labor was needed, both legal and illegal immigration was encouraged. When jobs became scarce, all immigration was discouraged. Although the National

Origins Quota Act of 1924 limited immigration of many populations (as discussed in Chapter 16), Mexicans were excluded, as non-quota immigrants. The majority of Mexican immigrants remained in the Southwest; however, few moved to such cities as Chicago and Detroit and became acculturated. While the migrant agricultural workers maintained the unified nuclear family, when they moved to urban areas this pattern was radically altered. The parents might be employed in two different factories. Often opportunities for women to do low-paid work increased male unemployment. This disrupted family cultural patterns.[5] To counterbalance the effects of ignorance and distortion of facts, Saracho and Hancock share Mexican-American historical and recent accomplishments with their children.[6]

Economics drew the dwellers of rural areas to the city. Statistics show that in the 1950s one-half of the Mexican-American population was rural. By 1960, greater than 80 percent of this population was urban, and by 1970 the figure rose to 90 percent. One third of the total population was living in the cities of Los Angeles, California; San Antonio, Texas; San Francisco, California; and El Paso, Texas. Every city had a *barrio*. Some of these represented the original Spanish-speaking settlements around which the Anglo-Saxon city later grew.[7] The demographics show that although there were a few wealthy landowners, and a small but growing group of white-collar workers and professionals, most of the Mexican-Americans were poor.

Mexican-American culture has often been misunderstood because it has overlapping and contradictory meanings.[8] The historical, genetic, and cultural backgrounds of Mexican-Americans are quite heterogeneous. Their Spanish and Indian heritage ranges from zero to 100 percent. Further, the Spaniards who came to Mexico had a varied cultural origin including individuals of Iberian, Greek, Latin, Visigoth, Moroccan, Phoenician, Carthaginian, and other backgrounds. The native Mexicans also represented distinct groups that differed physically, socially, economically, and culturally from one another.[9] Ignorance of this heterogeneity is one of the obstacles to the development of a coherent educational policy for Mexican-Americans. Another misunderstanding is that this is a homogeneous group, characterized by low economic status and average educational achievement. The diversity of child socialization practices and their effects on the individual are also often not addressed. However, one of the stereotypes is borne out by the statistics. Mexican-American families have the highest fertility rate of any major ethnic/racial group in the United States. Evidence in the literature suggests that the influence of the Catholic church in this regard is less than might be expected.[10]

The Family

La familia is a warm, nurturing family. They usually value their relationships of cooperation rather than competition. In recent years, *machismo* has been redefined to mean family pride, respect, and honor rather than male dominance. In this new role, the father uses his authority within the family in a fair and just manner. Deference and respect is accorded to the father in this stable structure, "in which one's place is firmly established."[11] This hierarchical structure is similar to that of the Southeast Asian families described in Chapter 16. Many Mexican-American families believe that sensitivity to others' feelings is important. Shared Spanish-language background and achievement aspirations may vary as a function of generational status. Unfortunately, some parents have high aspirations but lack knowledge of Anglo society that would enable them to translate these aspirations into reality.[12]

There is often a large extended family network. Rituals associated with religious and national holidays celebrated in Mexico are retained and become part of valued family activities, along with leisure time activities engaged in as a group. Child rearing has become a joint parental obligation. In recent years, more egalitarian relationships have been established particularly with the increasing number of women working in professional capacities. Studies of Mexican-American child rearing have shown that some families are permissive; however, traditional values and authoritarian practices are more prevalent. The relationships within patriarchal, authoritarian family structures are often nurturing and affectionate, with unusual respect shown to males and the elderly. *Amor de madre* (motherly love) is believed to be a greater force than wifely love. This means that the parent-child relationship is often more important than spousal relationships.

When the child is young, most homes are child centered. Protection is provided to young children. There is an emphasis on good behavior; however, it is accompanied by a basic acceptance of the child's individuality. There is a relaxed attitude toward the child's achievement of developmental milestones. As the child becomes older, more responsible behavior is expected. Beginning at approximately five years of age and lasting through puberty, the child is assigned increasingly complex tasks and broader responsibilities, in accordance with his or her age and ability.

Education

Cultural differences, the prejudice of Anglos, and lack of education have caused problems for Mexican-Americans. First- and second-generation children have been found to perform better in school than their third-generation counterparts. In the Southwest, Mexican-American children averaged seven years of schooling in the 1970s, as compared with nine years for Black children and more than twelve years for Anglo children. It was found that four out of five children fell as much as two grades behind their Anglo peers by fifth grade. Mexican-American children were classified as retarded two and one-half times as often as other children in a primary level class.[13] The children's problems and frustrations caused the Mexican-American population to have a high school dropout rate.

Several other factors impact the education of Mexican-American children. The lack of assimilation and acculturation of this population is a major factor. The kinds and quality of formal education available are important. The nature of local and regional social systems, with more or less acceptance of the population, and the equal or unequal opportunities afforded to this minority group, have a great impact upon the children's education. The Mexican-American child must learn to function effectively in the mainstream culture, while continuing to function in and contribute to Mexican-American culture. The child's self-image is based in their culture, which has, in addition to language and heritage, a set of cultural values, and a predominant teaching style unique to the cultural system.[14] Therefore, teachers of Mexican-American children should accept and use the student's cultural and linguistic experiences in establishing educational goals. Unless a teacher recognizes and respects differences in cultural characteristics, value orientations, traditions, and lifestyles, the teacher's expectations and evaluations of classroom behavior may possibly damage the child's chance for success, or be destructive of the child's self-concept and achievement.[15] Because Castillo and Cruz view the Chicano child as "field sensitive," they believe the child will perform better when an authority figure expresses confidence in the child's ability. A child may become depressed and perform poorly when doubt is expressed about performance or ability. Research has shown that the "field sensitive" child responds better when educational material contains human content, humor, fantasy, or cooperation. The "field-independent" child demonstrates the opposite characteristics, because that child is not significantly affected by the opinions of authority figures.[16] The factors of differentiated learning styles, different responses to various types of motivation, cultural orientation, values, and the degree to which an instructional program is compatible with the student's cultural characteristics impact upon learning.[17]

Teaching strategies that indicate acceptance of child and family beliefs, such as folk medicine; cooking and nutrition experiences that reflect the Mexican-American diet; stories, fables, myths, and proverbs that teach rules and values familiar to the children; and traditional and contemporary music and dances of the Mexican culture are preferable. Castillo and Cruz developed a set of competencies for teachers of Chicano children that they believe should be demonstrated in addition to those competencies needed for work with Anglo children. The competencies include verbal and interactional behaviors that enhance the child's self-image through the use of both English and Spanish. The teacher is encouraged to foster parent involvement and to develop liaisons among the parents, the school, and the child.[18] In the three decades between the newer immigration laws of 1965 and 1995, child care centers, Head Start programs, and schools and school districts with large Mexican-American populations have begun to address the needs of children through curriculum development, family-school communication, and in-service professional development of staff.

Puerto Ricans

The Puerto Rican migration to the United States mainland has a very different history from that of the Mexican-Americans. The pre-Columbian Taino (Puerto Rican Indian) family was characterized by a simple structure and lived in agricultural villages. The men provided food and housing in the village, taught the boys, and protected the island. The women cared for the house, did the chores, and cared for the children. Adolescent girls were protected, from boys, other villages, and from the Caribs who occasionally attacked and stole the women.[19] The indigenous Tainos (particularly the males) were decimated by the Spanish colonizers who arrived in 1492. Liaisons between the Spanish men and the Taino women produced *Los Mestizos,* who had a combination of Spanish and native ancestry. European ways, which dominated the island, included the Catholic religion and the Spanish language.[20] African slaves were imported to work in the fields and houses. The buying and selling of slaves destroyed their family unity and the last name of the man in the family was lost. Female slaves bore their master's children and were required to breast-feed the master's other children. This led to a group of children called *El Mulato.*[21] Because of this history, Puerto Ricans developed many shades of skin tones, even within one family. The darkest or youngest child in a family is often called *El Negro.*

When Spain lost the Spanish-American War in 1898, it deeded Puerto Rico to the United States. In 1917, Puerto Ricans received U.S. citizenship and free education for the poor, so every family could educate its children. The University of Puerto Rico was founded, and women began to enter higher education. A new philosophy of raising children developed, viewing children as people with rights. Corporal punishment in schools was abolished, and improvement in health education and technology cut the infant death rate.[22]

The first migrants from Puerto Rico, during the nineteenth century, were political refugees from Spanish rule. The political exiles of the late 1800s were joined by those who wanted to escape poverty, or get a university education. A few Puerto Rican migrants joined revolutionary Puerto Rican groups in New York City. The first substantial migration to the mainland occurred in the time period from World War I through the 1920s. The Puerto Rican cash-based economy, which was heavily dependent on sugar before the 1940s, could not support the people. Agricultural workers began to migrate, first to Puerto Rican cities, and later to the mainland, to work.

The number of migrants from Puerto Rico waxed and waned over the decades of the twentieth century. In the 1940s, after World War II, there was a contract farm labor program. When employment and economic conditions in New York were good, people came from the island to the mainland, and when economic conditions were bad, return migration due to economic factors increased. The migrants were usually young adults seeking better conditions for their family; however, racism caused conflict and stress.[23] Among the reasons that the largest immigration took place after 1945 were: poverty on the island, control of resources by absentee owners from the mainland, overpopulation, and poor education. The government vacillated on whether instruction in Puerto Rican schools should be delivered in English or Spanish. This resulted in poor education in both languages.[24]

The Puerto Rican migration differed from that of other Hispanic populations. One-third of the Puerto Rican population has participated in migration at some time in their lives. Since they are U.S. citizens, they are accustomed to many aspects of mainland society. Geographically, Puerto Rico is close to the mainland, encouraging visits and permanent return to the island. However, some Puerto Ricans find it difficult to adjust to winter in the northeastern U.S. climate. Socially, Puerto Ricans have a dual identity. Their special status can lead to discrimination and social difficulty. Economically, the Puerto Ricans are familiar with U.S. products and have a similar school system. These factors combine to encourage migration from the island of Puerto Rico to the mainland.[25]

In 1990, Puerto Ricans were the second largest Hispanic group residing in the continental United States. There were 2.3 million Puerto Ricans, 95 percent of whom resided in urban areas. Although Mexican-Americans appeared to be the youngest of all Hispanic groups in the United States, the median age for Puerto Ricans in 1988 also revealed them to be quite young. They had a median age of 24.9 years, with 40 percent of the population under the age of 19. This may be compared to a median age for all Hispanics of 25.5 years and in the total U.S. population of 32.3 years.[26] The household composition of Puerto Rican families differs from that of other groups in both size and type. There appear to be more females, at 53.3 percent, than males at 46.7 percent of the population. This may be compared with 50.2 percent males and 49.8 percent females for Hispanics in general, and a United States population with 48.6 percent males and 51.4 percent females.

The Family

The statistics present one aspect of Puerto Rican family life, while the sociological and child development literature present a broader picture. The family size of 3.39 people more resembles the general U.S. average of 3.17 than the Hispanic average of 3.79 people. There are fewer married Puerto Rican couples than in other Hispanic populations. More female-headed households means extreme poverty, because of its association with extreme poverty in the population as a whole. In fact, it was found that one of two Puerto Rican children younger than eighteen years of age lived in poverty.

Family life is very important, and both the mother's and father's names are components of a Puerto Rican child's name. Family building is considered an important cultural goal. Children are expected to show *respeto* (respect) to their parents and other adults. Socialization takes place within the nuclear and extended family. The nuclear family consists of parents and children living together, and the extended family corresponds with natural or ritual kin who may live in the household or neighborhood. Sometimes there is an extended nuclear family, consisting of the mother, father, their children, and one mate's previous union (for example: a brother on the mother's side). The mother-based single-parent family, which consists of a mother and the children of one or more men, often reside in a home without a permanent husband or *compañero*. This leads to discipline problems because Puerto Rican women are socialized not to punish children. That is a man's job. The parenting system leads children to be loved and cherished. However, the methods of caring for children often lead to overprotection. This can become problematic when independence is curtailed and adherence to parental and family demands is encouraged.[27]

Children are at the lowest level in the family hierarchy. They have no voice in home affairs, and are not made a part of adult conversation. They are subject to parental authority and corporal punishment. Puerto Rican parents believe that children were sent by God, and in previous decades children were believed to be a man's wealth.[28] Differential treatment of children was based on sex, with boys being taught *machismo* ideals, and girls learning *marianismo* ideals. This meant that boys were supposed to demonstrate bravery, exuberance, and dominance over women, while women were to be submissive, passive, selfless, and home-centered.[29] The mother was idealized by her family. The protective system of child rearing was a problem for families when they reached the mainland, as was the large size of the family. Economic problems were created. Children of consensual unions who were viewed as part of the family on the island were stigmatized by others on the mainland as illegitimate. The sixth-grade education of the parents, while a higher level than those who stayed on the island, did not prepare the adults for the New York City job market.[30]

The Puerto Rican population both on the island and on the mainland has been the subject of a number of research studies. They depict the Puerto Rican population as "disadvantaged" or "culturally deprived," or as a political group. These studies focus on deficits and weaknesses that are often identified through biased or culturally inappropriate instruments. Some of the investigations have heavy social emphasis, including a search for programmatic relevance. This creates problems with the methodology. A "culturally syntonic" approach attempts to strike a balance between the methodological requirements and programmatic usefulness. Many of the studies reported by Ambert and Alvarez utilize a "culturally sensitive" approach.[31] Most of the studies cited in the literature deal with older children; however, they can be generalized to provide some insight into the education of young Puerto Rican children on the mainland.

Education

The education of migrant Puerto Rican children includes more than the island standards, however; it often falls below mainland standards. The literature states that in the 1960s and 1970s, Puerto Rican children who entered school for the first time knew little English. They found school frustrating and became early dropouts.[32] In New York City two-thirds of all Puerto Rican children in the public schools in the 1970s were more than two years behind in reading. Although they formed 25 percent of the school population, only 5 percent received academic high school diplomas. Some students who knew a little English hesitated to use it because they spoke badly, and this would mean loss of dignity. The high dropout rate made the Puerto Rican population less educated than other Hispanic groups, and they were therefore underrepresented in schools and colleges. Alvarez found that in 1990 Hispanics constituted 10 percent of school enrollment and that in grades one to four they actually had 11.8 percent enrollment. However, by grades eleven and twelve, there was only a 7.4 percent enrollment. In addition, the school suspension rates were high for all Hispanic teenagers, especially for Mexican-American teens.[33]

Puerto Rican parents who had left the responsibility for education to the teachers, whom they considered to be experts, did not understand school expectations for parents' participation in education programs. The mothers participated more than the fathers in the education of their children. However, they were not used to this participation. Because of her prominent role in the daily function of the family, the mother therefore became the link between the family and the school.[34] The addition of bilingual personnel in the New York City schools in the 1960s, for example, made a difference in the ensuing decades. Bilingual staff and educational materials have made the entry and transition of Puerto Rican pupils go much more smoothly in the 1990s. In schools and centers, families and children have learned both content and context that have enabled them to adapt to life on the United States mainland.

In the 1960s, federal money was provided for early childhood education programs aimed at young Hispanic children. The programs were designed to meet criteria of linguistic and cultural relevance. They addressed the relationships among self-concept, culture, and achievement as part of the child's psychological and social development.[35] In 1965, Katz and Kriegsfeld studied the use of "family schools" with young immigrant families. They concluded that it was beneficial to mix immigrant children with their English-speaking contemporaries on a fifty-fifty basis, in groups of no more than twenty. This approach assisted the children with learning English, elementary school readiness, and overcoming problems of acculturation.[36] Divine developed a bilingual publication containing learning activities and educational games that parents could use to help their preschool children develop readiness skills. Thus the federal government encouraged both center-based group programs and parents working with their children at home.[37] These examples demonstrate that the federal government has supported early childhood education and intervention programs for young Hispanic children over the past four decades.

TEACHER EDUCATION

Teachers prepared in multicultural education must also have the same knowledge, skills, and attitudes expected of all teachers of young children. The professional education literature suggests that teachers should value cultural diversity and develop respect for the child and the worth of the child's culture.[38] Foundations courses dealing with history, philosophy, sociology, economics, psychology, politics, and anthropology present the world differently from its practical reality. Through these courses, prospective teachers are helped to restructure their views of children, school, and subjects, and they become more sensitive to how children from different cultural backgrounds have been treated in school. They develop a basic understanding of how culture is reflected in thinking styles, learning styles, and language development.[39]

Teacher candidates should be aware of how the various roles of the teacher impact on children and their cultural milieu. In the role of decision maker, the teacher must make sure decisions avoid conflict with the children's cultures. As a designer of curriculum, the teacher must consider both the child's capabilities and what is considered important by the community. As a diagnostician, the educator must develop awareness of the possible cultural biases of assessments. The teacher must maintain consistent interactions with parents and community members in order that the school reinforces what is taught in the home and the home reinforces what is learned in the school.

Both preservice and in-service teachers should have hands-on experiences with appropriate practices. Concrete examples of imaginative activities that have a constructivist and multicultural basis should be provided. In their classrooms, teachers should incorporate culturally responsive experiences for all children. "Valuing each child's home culture and incorporating meaningful/active participation will enhance [the child's] interpersonal skills and contribute to academic and social success."[40]

CHAPTER SUMMARY

The history of Spanish-speaking peoples in North America dates back to the 1500s. Their history in U.S. schools and child care programs began to appear in the professional literature in the 1900s. In the decades from 1960 to the present, more attention has been focused on children representing language and cultural diversity. Federal, state, and local initiatives have provided programs (such as bilingual Head Start) and resources for the education of young children of Spanish-speaking backgrounds. As national early childhood education organizations focus on *developmentally appropriate practices* representing cultural diversity, more families and children with a Hispanic heritage will find themselves as comfortable participants and stakeholders in relevant early childhood education programs.

NOTES

1. Maxine Seller, *To Seek America: A History of Ethnic Life in the United States* (Jerome S. Ozer, Publisher, Inc., 1977), 245.

2. Tommie J. Hamner and Pauline H. Turner, *Parenting in Contemporary Society,* 3d ed. (Boston: Allyn and Bacon, 1996), 167.

3. Seller, *To Seek America,* 245; and Hamner and Turner, *Parenting in Contemporary Society,* 167.

4. Seller, *To Seek America,* 246.

5. Ibid., 252.

6. Olivia N. Saracho and Frances Martinez Hancock, "Mexican-American Culture," in *Understanding the Multicultural Experience in Early Childhood Education,* ed. Olivia N. Saracho and Bernard Spodek (Washington, DC: National Association for the Education of Young Children, 1983), 3.

7. Seller, *To Seek America,* 248. See Chapter 7 of this volume for a brief description of Spanish-speaking settlements: pueblos, presidios, and missions.

8. Saracho and Hancock, "Mexican-American Culture," 4.

9. Ibid., 4–5.
The terms used to denote the members of the Mexican-American population in the United States vary from one region of the country to another. Those in northern New Mexico and southern Colorado call themselves Spanish-Americans, while others use the terms Latin-Americans, Chicanos, Hispanos, Spanish-speaking La Raza, and Americans of Mexican decent.

10. Hamner and Turner, *Parenting in Contemporary Society,* 167.

11. Ibid., 169; and Saracho and Hancock, "Mexican-American Culture," in *Understanding the Multicultural Experience in Early Childhood Education,* 5.

12. Hamner and Turner, *Parenting in Contemporary Society,* 170–171; and Seller, *To Seek America,* 251.

13. Seller, *To Seek America,* 250.

14. Saracho and Hancock, "Mexican-American Culture," in *Understanding the Multicultural Experience in Early Childhood Education,* 7.

15. Max S. Castillo and Josué Cruz, Jr., "Special Competencies for Teachers of Preschool Chicano Children: Rationale, Content, and Assessment Process," *Young Children* XXIX, no. 6 (September 1974): 341–342.

16. Ibid., 342.

17. Ibid., 343, 347.

18. Ibid., 343–345.

19. Kenneth Arán, Herman Arthur, Ramón Colón, and Harvey Goldenberg, *Puerto Rican History and Culture: A Study Guide and Curriculum Outline* (New York: United Federation of Teachers, 1973), 87, 52.

20. Ibid., 87; and Alba N. Ambert and Clare S. Figler, "Historical and Cultural Perspectives," in *Puerto Rican Children on the Mainland,* ed. Alba N. Ambert and María D. Alvarez (New York: Garland, 1992), 18.

21. Arán et al., *Puerto Rican History and Culture,* 88–89.

22. Ibid., 89.

23. Ibid., 37; and Ambert and Figler, "Historical and Cultural Perspectives," 32, 27, 29.

24. Seller, *To Seek America,* 257.

25. Arán et al., *Puerto Rican History and Culture,* 23, 26–27.

26. María D. Alvarez, "Puerto Rican Children on the Mainland: Current Perspectives," in *Puerto Rican Children on the Mainland,* ed. Alba N. Ambert and María D. Alvarez (New York: Garland, 1992), 4.

27. Ambert and Figler, "Historical and Cultural Perspectives," 25.

28. Arán et al., *Puerto Rican History and Culture,* 88.

29. Ambert and Figler, "Historical and Cultural Perspectives," 24.

30. Seller, *To Seek America,* 261; and Alvarez, "Puerto Rican Children on the Mainland: Current Perspectives," 5.

31. Alvarez, "Puerto Rican Children on the Mainland: Current Perspectives," 10–11.

32. Seller, *To Seek America,* 260–261.

33. Ibid., 261; María D. Alvarez, "Puerto Rican Children on the Mainland: Current Perspectives," 6–8; and Arán et al., *Puerto Rican History and Culture,* 41.

34. Arán et al., *Puerto Rican History and Culture,* 93.

35. Cecilia Cota Robles Suarez, *Testimony to California Governor's Council on Child Development* (Los Angeles, California: February 14, 1981), EDRS, ED198952, micro-

fiche; and Theresa Herrera Escobedo, "Culturally Responsive Early Childhood Education Programs for Non-English Speaking Children" (Los Angeles: Cal State Los Angeles National Dissemination and Assessment Center, 1978) [QE (DHEW), Washington, DC] EDRS, ED161277.

36. Lilian Katz and Irvin Kriegsfeld, *Curriculum and Teaching Strategies for Non-English Speaking Nursery School Children in a Family School* (San Francisco: Mission Neighborhood Center, Inc., and National Council of Jewish Women, 1965), EDRS, ED053840, microfiche.

37. Jan Devine, *Home Task Book for Parents and Kids* [Pima County Schools, Tucson, Arizona] (Washington, DC: Office of Bilingual Education and Minority Language Affairs, Office of Education Right to Read Program, Department of Health, Education and Welfare, 1978), EDRS, ED 192990, microfiche.

38. Olivia N. Saracho and Bernard Spodek, "Preparing Teachers for Bilingual/Multicultural Classrooms," in *Understanding the Multicultural Experience in Early Childhood Education,* ed. Olivia N. Saracho and Bernard Spodek (Washington, DC: National Association for the Education of Young Children, 1983), 125–126.

39. Ibid., 131.

40. Ibid., 133, 139; Helen Nissani, "Early Childhood Programs for Language Minority Children," in *NCBE Focus: Occasional Papers in Bilingual Education* no. 2, (Summer 1990), 7–8 of 12; and Lourdes Diaz Soto, "Understanding Bilingual/Bicultural Young Children," in *Young Children* 46, no. 2 (January 1991): 35.

CHAPTER 18
Bilingualism

> Now the question no longer is: how shall we learn English so that
> we may take part in the social life of America and partake of her
> benefits; the big question is: how can we preserve the language of
> our ancestors here, in a strange environment, and pass on to our
> descendants the treasures which it contains?
> —Thrond Bothne (1835–1907)
> (Professor at Luther College, 1898)

Among the many innovations introduced in the public schools in the United
States since the 1960s, and one of the most controversial, is the establishment
of bilingual classes for pupils whose dominant or mother language is not English. Beginning usually at kindergarten or first-grade level and continuing in
succeeding grades, the children are taught basic concepts, reading, writing,
and some subject matter in the language they speak at home while simultaneously learning English.

Bilingual education came about as a result of the following forces: the
increased migration of Spanish speakers from Puerto Rico, Cuba, and other
Latin American countries; the awakening of ethnic identity among various
minority groups such as Native Americans and Asians who as a result of the
civil rights movement of the 1960s, sought political and economic equality for
minority groups;[1] the increased interest in the Mexican-American child after
the 1960 census;[2] and the public's awareness.[3] One study, *Equality of Educational Opportunity* (1966), showed that racial and ethnic groups were segregated from one another and that the schools did not offer equal educational
opportunities in terms of the criteria regarded as indicators of good educational quality: textbooks, libraries, curriculum offered, teacher experiences,
and education.[4] The United States Commission on Civil Rights (1975) also
called attention to the poor education of the Mexican-American child. As a
result of these concerns and activities, the "melting pot" theory of the function of the public school began to be questioned and scrutinized, and new
forms of education were devised to meet the needs of the current population.

THE RENAISSANCE OF BILINGUAL EDUCATION

A persistent theme of the literature dealing with the education of the minority
child was the *absolute necessity* for the school to build on the cultural
strengths and language that the child brought into the classroom. The curriculum should reflect the child's heritage as well as American traditions.[5] The
politicians also thought that to meet the needs of the non-English-speaking

child, the school should cultivate and reinforce the language that the child spoke at home through bilingual education. Bilingual education was seen as a means of providing a viable schooling for non-English-speaking children. In January 1967, Senator Ralph Yarborough (Democrat-Texas) introduced a bill to provide assistance to local educational agencies to establish bilingual schools for Mexican-American and Puerto Rican children. It was later reworded to include all Spanish-speaking children. His purpose was not to create pockets of different languages or to stamp out mother tongues, but to try to make the children fully literate in English.[6]

Senator Yarborough left open or ambiguous the policy question of whether the purpose of the program was to perpetuate the languages of the minority groups or to speed up their learning of English and their integration into the host country's language and culture. For the federal authorities, the Bilingual Education Act was primarily a socioeconomic measure to aid any underprivileged group, regardless of its being English-speaking poor whites, Native Americans, Blacks, or Spanish-speaking.[7] For the most part, the program has retained the cultural aspect, and the danger of nationalism has been avoided for the time being, as has happened in Quebec, Canada, and other geographic locations throughout the world.

LANGUAGES OF THE UNITED STATES

The concept of teaching in two languages is not a new idea in the history of education either in the United States or in other parts of the world, as it was seen in Chapters 1 and 2.[8] While English is the national language of the United States today, it is not a native language of the country. It was one of the group of languages brought here by the colonial powers, together with French, Spanish, and Dutch.

The non-English languages of the continental United States are commonly classified into three groups: indigenous or native languages, colonial languages, and immigrant languages.

Indigenous Languages

The indigenous languages are those formerly or currently spoken by various Indian tribes. At the time of the European settlement, there were about six hundred languages. Many of the original tribes have disappeared entirely as a result of warfare, disease, or assimilation. Since the second half of the nineteenth century, the federal government has vacillated between policies oriented toward forced de-tribalization and tribal autonomy. This on-again, off-again treatment has produced dismal results for the Indian tribes. Almost all Native Americans now speak English; a substantial number are still bilingual; and only a fraction, primarily persons of advanced age, are monolingual in one of the Native American languages. The 1990 U.S. Census Bureau identified 136 different Native American languages. Of these, 47 are spoken in the home by fewer than 100 persons; 22 are spoken by fewer than 200. The census may not be accurate, for it has no way of knowing how well or how often these people actually use the language.[9]

Colonial and Immigrant Languages

The colonial languages are those that were initially spoken by sixteenth-, seventeenth-, and eighteenth-century European colonizers of the territories that later became the continental United States. The colonial languages were English, Spanish, French, German, Russian, Swedish, and Dutch. The last three did not survive as colonial languages except in a few isolated pockets for any length of time after the mother countries involved lost control of their colonial holdings in the United States. Of the four colonial languages that have maintained continuity on American soil, English has become the recognized language of the nation and of its public and governmental institutions. The most dominant of the colonial languages is English.

Spanish, also a colonial language, today continues to have the greatest number of speakers due to recent migrations from Puerto Rico and the Latin American countries. Spanish-speaking persons are still concentrated largely in the southwestern states of Texas, New Mexico, Colorado, Utah, Arizona, Nevada, and California, but they can also be found in other states, like New York, and Florida, and major urban centers. The majority of Spanish speakers are not themselves of European-Spanish ancestry. Centuries of Spanish rule resulted in Spanish becoming the language of large indigenous populations, just as Catholicism became their religion.[10] The more recent migrants from Puerto Rico and the other Latin American countries came to the United States in search of economic advancement. They left an environment in which Spanish is culturally and legally protected for an environment where their own status and that of their language are precarious.

The situation of French as a colonial language resembles that of Spanish, since both have a continuous history spanning centuries. Two huge language islands exist, one in Quebec, Canada, and the other in the United States: a large one in New England, a smaller one in Louisiana. The greater proportion of Franco-Americans may be considered immigrant stock, inasmuch as their forebears entered the United States in the postcolonial days.[11]

German, on the other hand, although introduced on a large scale during the colonial days, was not the language of a colonial power on the American continent. The vast majority of German speakers who left their imprint on nineteenth- and twentieth-century American history have been of postcolonial immigrant origin.[12]

The Spanish, French, and German languages have long been among the most important and the most prestigious in the Western world. Even though these languages, their speakers, and the cultures that they represent have existed in the midst of the larger American culture for over two centuries, public awareness of their existence has been limited.

As the immigrants settled in the United States, they wanted schools to educate their children, and they wanted to preserve their native language and culture.[13] An example was the Germans who had settled in Pennsylvania. Long before the War of Independence, they had built a good private elementary school system on the basis of their church organization. The most comprehensive school system was that of the Lutheran and the Reformed churches. After the War of Independence, as migration continued, the parochial school was often replaced by the neighborhood school. A systematic attempt to introduce the English school into the German-speaking areas was made by the London-based Society for the Propagation of Christian Knowledge, which (1754–1763) maintained a number of bilingual schools among the Germans. When the school law (1834) established the "free school" in the state of Pennsylvania, it contained no language provision. A law of 1838 made it possible to transform the schools that had been maintained by religious groups into public schools with the greatest possible preservation of their special character.[14] Bilingual German-American Academies were organized and supported by the German intellectuals in several states and cities during the 1850s and 1860s, to educate their children. There were also German-speaking kindergartens, one, in Columbus, Ohio (1836), and another in Watertown, Wisconsin (1856) as discussed in Chapter 9 of this volume.[15]

Other historical examples of bilingual schooling are the use of the Spanish language as a medium of instruction in New Mexico since 1848, the French schools in New England, several Scandinavian and some Dutch schools in the Midwest,[16] and the use of the French language as a medium of instruction in Louisiana since 1805.[17]

To accommodate the many German speakers during the War of Independence, the Continental Congress printed German translations of many of its proclamations. The first one was in 1774. The most important German publication of the Continental Congress was the German edition of the *Articles of the Confederation*. The official recognition of the German language in the publications of the Continental Congress resulted in the strong and enthusiastic participation of most of the German minority in the War of Independence. When the Congress decided to form German troop units, there were four companies in Pennsylvania and four in Maryland, of American-born Germans.[18]

When the Civil War broke out in 1861, again many German-speaking American citizens joined in the fighting. Among them was Carl Schurz, who first served as a brigadier general in the Virginia campaign (1862) and later in the Battle of Gettysburg (1863) as a major general.[19]

There is one group of immigrants who came involuntarily to the New World: the Negro slaves. Their linguistic situation was as desperate as their plight in other aspects of their lives. Along with their loss of freedom, they were also deprived of their language. Their condition of slavery did not permit them to form natural language groups like the other immigrants did; they were deliberately separated from their pre-enslavement kin and neighbors. According to Haugen, since they spoke mutually incomprehensible languages, they were forced to adopt as much as they could of the white man's language almost immediately. They developed a *creolized* language in response to certain extraordinary situations of social contact. Grouped together on large plantations, they were able to catch scraps of language, which they fitted into certain structures that were common both to the masters' language and their original languages—from which they brought intonation, phonetics, and syntax. Negroes who were trusted servants had greater opportunities to learn English.[20]

THE TWENTIETH CENTURY

The communication between the federal government and the non-English-speaking citizens continued in the twentieth century. In 1918, the federal government established a press service that provided information to 745 newspapers in 14 languages. The press service received its materials from the various federal agencies. In 1921, it ceased to be a government agency and became an independent private agency.

The first Americanization Conference met in 1919, one year after the end of World War I. It was sponsored by the Department of the Interior in Washington. That marked the beginning of sharp suppression of almost all foreign languages.

In the 1930s, President Franklin D. Roosevelt's administration made use of the non-English press of the country to broadcast its social and economic policy. In 1937, four lengthy articles dealing with the Social Security Act of 1935 were translated by the government into twenty languages and distributed to about one thousand non-English newspapers. The Public Relations Division of the Public Housing Administration at that time distributed its press service to, among others, 682 non-English newspapers. During the 1930s, the Federal Theater Project of the Works Progress Administration (WPA) subsidized theaters conducted in minority languages.[21]

Immigrant Languages

Any consideration of languages in the United States and of bilingual education must include the immigrants' languages, for these are the most numerous, and their speakers and adherents have been exposed to the assimilative currents of American life for the shortest periods of time. Approximately between 1880 and 1920, millions of speakers of scores of languages arrived in the United States, primarily from Southern and Eastern Europe, adding to the population many linguistic and cultural ingredients. These immigrants varied greatly among themselves. While this internal diversity may not have been any greater than that of earlier immigrant groups, the recency and the size of the groups made them striking. These immigrants settled in ways that differed from those of their predecessors. They tended to remain in the cities, congregating in self-contained slum neighborhoods that perpetuated the life and customs of the Old World. They were viewed as being different from the immigrants who had preceded them. "Illiterate, docile, lacking in self-reliance and initiative, and not possessing the Anglo-Teutonic conceptions of law, order, and government, their coming has served to dilute our national stock, and to corrupt our civic life."[22]

It appears that nearly all the languages of the Old World were at some time or other brought to the New World by individuals or groups of immigrants. They differed from colonials only insofar as they settled in a country already dominated by speakers of other languages. Where conditions permitted it, immigrant speakers tended to seek out co-linguals and form distinct communities. The first generation of adult immigrants naturally found it difficult to acquire a new language, and instead tended to preserve the old language, handing it down to the next generation. The American-born generation of the immigrants learned the national language of their adopted country out of self-interest. For those who did not know which way to go regarding the language, the government took measures to more or less compel them to learn English.

One such measure was the establishment of a universal school system during the nineteenth century. It was seen as the chief instrument of national unification. Most school reformers believed that the influx of non-English immigrants during the two decades prior to the Civil War posed a threat to the national unity they sought. Beginning in this period, the schools were seen to have an Americanization mission with the immigrants.[23] Horace Mann, who was impressed with the diversity of the American people, feared that conflicts of values might rip them apart and render them powerless. Dreading the destructive possibilities of political, religious, and class differences, he sought a common value system within which diversity might flourish. This instrument would be the "common school," a school common to all people.[24]

Ethnic benefit and cultural societies, such as the Scandinavian *turners,* the Bohemian *sokol,* and the Polish *falcons,* to name a few, as well as the various ethnic churches and temples, were also involved in the Americanization process. They provided after-school classes for language learning, for example, Chinese, Hebrew, or Greek, so that the children who learned English in the public schools could maintain their mother language.[25]

The education of the child with limited English-speaking ability was not the concern of only the immigrant group to which the child belonged. In cases where the immigrant group could not provide adequately for the children, benevolent agencies were concerned and involved in their education. One such agency was the New York Children's Aid Society, which in its Third Annual Report (1856), said that in order to meet the needs of immigrant children, it had established a series of industrial schools for foreign groups.[26]

Until World War I, there was little organized pressure to impose English as the sole language in communities settled by non-English-speaking persons belonging to any of the colonial powers or any of the subsequent immigrant populations. An acute conflict between the culture of the immigrant and the culture of the United States, the host nation, arose during and after World War I when the United States and European allies were at war with the German Empire. After World War I, there was the legislative prohibition of foreign language instruction in public elementary schools in many states.[27] Interest groups such as the American Legion endorsed compulsory instruction in English as one method of Americanization.[28] The Immigration Act of 1924 put an end to the mass influx of immigrants. It created quotas that remained in effect until 1965.[29]

After the end of the war in Vietnam, the United States received large numbers of Vietnamese, Cambodians, Laotians, and other Southeast Asians. They settled in "immigrant cities" like Lowell, Massachusetts—the textile manufacturing center—which previously had received successive waves of European immigrants. All these persons needed bilingual education, and new programs were created to meet their needs.[30]

ENACTMENT OF FEDERAL LEGISLATION MANDATING BILINGUAL EDUCATION

The Civil Rights Act of 1964 gave impetus to minority groups who sought educational, political, and economic equality. In 1968, President Lyndon Johnson signed into law the Bilingual Education Act, which is Title VII of the Elementary and Secondary Education Act of 1965.

The Bilingual Education Act was conceived to rectify certain obvious educational defects of the past, to conserve the language resources of the United States, and to advance the learning of the child, irrespective of his language. It provided financial assistance to state and local educational agencies to meet the needs of children of limited English-speaking abilities. It might be said that the Bilingual Education Act was another aspect of the War on Poverty. It aimed to equalize the educational opportunity of all children, whether from English-speaking or from non-English-speaking homes. It was intended to establish bilingual instruction for all children who did not speak English and to improve learning in the classroom by using the mother languages in addition to English.

The psychological impact of the federal Bilingual Education Act cannot be overestimated. It reversed a fifty-year-old "one language" policy and committed the nation to meet the educational needs of large numbers of children of limited English-speaking ability in the United States. The Act provided financial assistance to local educational agencies for (1) bilingual education programs, (2) programs designed to impart to students a knowledge of the history and culture associated with their language, and (3) efforts to establish closer cooperation between the school and the home.

To implement bilingual education, the federal government created the Office for Bilingual Education and Minority Language Affairs (OBEMLA) and the National Clearing House for Bilingual Education. The federal legislation was followed by legislation enacted in many states. Massachusetts was the first state to mandate a Transitional Bilingual Education Law, passed in November 1971, and enacted in February 1972.[31]

DEFINITIONS OF BILINGUALISM

Many attempts have been made to produce an exact definition of bilingualism, but the only agreement among its various users is that it refers to the knowledge and use of two languages by the same person. Some writers emphasize the *use* of languages, as in "the practice of alternately using two languages."[32] Others define bilingualism as the habitual use of two languages by the same person and emphasize the fact that in its purest form, the two languages are quite separate.[33] Since it is quite possible to be bilingual without frequently using one of the two languages one knows, others have emphasized the *knowledge* or competence of the speakers. According to this definition, a bilingual is "one who knows two languages." Some scholars extend the use of the term to include the mastery of more than two languages, acknowledging that the phenomena involved are essentially similar; the latter is referred to as *multilingualism* or *polyglossy*. The ability of a speaker to "produce complete meaningful utterances in the other language" should be the lower limit of bilingualism.[34] Most students of bilingualism, however, prefer a wider definition, one which includes sociocultural knowledge.

Within this framework, the major problem is that bilinguals differ widely both in their knowledge and in their use of the two languages they have mastered. Knowledge may extend from remembering a few words of a language to the mastery possessed by a highly educated native speaker and writer.

Bilinguals may be classified according to their skill in their two languages along a more or less infinite scale. Broadly considered, some bilinguals possess one dominant and one secondary language. Others have both languages reasonably balanced. There are some bilinguals who easily switch from one language to another, and some who find it extremely difficult to do so. It is very common to find bilinguals who have specialized the use of their languages so that they can speak about some topics in one language and about other topics in the other language. The primary linguistic concern is to keep the two languages apart while speaking.

The difficulty is not only with the definition or description of bilingualism. There is lack of an adequate unified process to measure bilingualism at both the time of entry and time of exit of the students in the program. Some difficulties include the levels of proficiency, the similarity and differences between the languages, the effects through bilingualism of one language on the other, competency, and the social function of each language.[35]

One must not forget that for millions of people throughout world, bilingualism is a fact of life, if not a matter of survival. In many countries, especially the small ones, bilingualism is a way of life, a necessity that one speaks and writes in more than one language. Bilingualism becomes a problem only when a population, through emigration or conquest, becomes a part of a community where another language is spoken and this language is imposed on them through the school system or by other means.

TYPES OF BILINGUAL EDUCATION PROGRAMS

The following types of bilingual education programs reflect four different kinds of community and school objectives.

Type I: Transitional Bilingualism. It is used in the early grades to the extent necessary to allow pupils to "adjust to school" and/or to "master subject matter" until their skill in English is developed to the point that it alone can be used as the medium of instruction. These programs do not strive toward goals of fluency and literacy in both languages with opportunities throughout the curriculum for the continuing improvement toward mastery of each language. This program's objective is language shift, and it does not consider the development and support of the mother tongue.

Type II: Monoliterate Bilingualism. Programs of this type indicate goals of development in both languages for aural-oral skills but do not concern themselves with literacy skills in the non-English mother tongue. Thus, such programs emphasize developing fluency in Spanish as a link between home and school, with the school providing recognition and support for the language in the domains of home and neighborhood. They are not concerned with the development of literacy skills in the non-English mother tongue that would facilitate the child's use of the language in conjunction with work, government, religion, or book culture more generally. This type of program is intermediate in orientation between language shift and language maintenance.

Type III: Biliterate Bilingualism, Partial. This program seeks fluency and literacy in both languages, but literacy in the mother tongue is restricted to certain subject matter, usually related to the ethnic group and its cultural heritage. In such a program, reading and writing skills in the mother tongue are commonly developed in relation to the social sciences, literature, and the arts, but not to sciences and mathematics. This kind of program is clearly one of language maintenance, with a certain effort at cultural maintenance.

Type IV: Biliterate Bilingualism, Full. In this program, students are to develop all skills in both languages in all domains. Typically, both languages are used as media of instruction for all subjects (except in teaching the languages themselves). Clearly, this program is directed at language maintenance and development of the minority language. From the linguistic and psychological viewpoint, this is the ideal type of program, since it results in balanced coordinate bilinguals—children capable of thinking and expressing themselves in either of two languages independently.[36]

THE RATIONALE FOR BILINGUAL INSTRUCTION IN EARLY CHILDHOOD

With the introduction of compulsory education, kindergarten is the first stage of a child's formal education. Much of the educational concern is with "the use of language for learning and communicating."[37] Much of the child's language development is completed before he enters school. Most of the teaching in the kindergarten, and in the other grades, takes place through language, and most of the learning depends on a pupil's ability to understand what the teacher says and what is in his books. Learning depends on the interaction of the pupils with the teachers, the books, and their peers, and all these are mediated by language. Language is a critical factor in cognitive development.

Empirical evidence supports the view that reading and writing in the mother language should precede literacy in a second language. Nancy Modiano, from her research with three Indian tribes in the highlands of Mexico, reported that the children who had read first in their native language showed greater proficiency in reading Spanish (the national language) than did their controlled peers who had been instructed in their weaker language.[38] In a study in Canada, Peal and Lambert found that bilinguals who have an opportunity to develop two languages fully often demonstrate cognitive skills superior to those of their monolingual peers.[39] Primary education is vernacular education, and the children must first settle down in one linguistic and cultural milieu, their own, before they learn another language.[40] Comenius, as discussed earlier, advocated the same idea, for the values of the family and the culture are conveyed best in one's mother language.

Educators need to remember that children born into different ethnic/linguistic groups enter the larger society with a different perspective, one that is organized and presented through the grid of a particular language that they hear and learn. There is an intimate relationship among the child, his family, and their community with their language and their view of the world.

Bilingual Study Results

Although the bilingual programs were established primarily for Hispanic children, many other linguistic minorities participate in bilingual programs. A field study was conducted by one of the authors in five bilingual classrooms in the Boston public schools during 1975–1976. It was the first year of implementation of the bilingual education program at the kindergarten level, even though the Bilingual Education Law had been enacted since 1972 in Massachusetts. Boston has had some bilingual education programs for other grades since 1962. The five kindergarten classrooms studied were one Chinese and four Hispanic. Each classroom had a team of teachers: an Anglo and a bilingual teacher. The study found that the amount of English spoken and the use of the mother tongue varied greatly between and within these bilingual classrooms. The Chinese bilingual classroom used the mother tongue 48 percent of the time, which was the highest among the classrooms. The use of the mother tongue in the Hispanic classrooms ranged from 20 percent to 4 percent of the time.

The Chinese classroom had a native-speaking teacher and had formal instruction in the mother tongue three times a week The children, all Chinese with the exception of one Anglo child, were divided into four groups, including the Anglo child, and met with the teacher for 30 to 40 minutes for instruction in Chinese, which included the learning of the Chinese characters. Because of the difficulty and complexity of the Chinese characters, the children have to learn them by rote and by tracing them over and over until they reach sufficient accuracy and perfection. This classroom had separate instruction in the two languages. It appeared to be an effort to maintain the mother tongue.

The Hispanic bilingual classrooms were a mix of Hispanic—primarily Puerto Rican, black, and Anglo children representative of the communities in which they were located. None of the Spanish-speaking bilingual teachers were native speakers. They spoke a version or dialect of the language they taught that they had learned in environments different from their pupils. One of the bilingual teachers was Mexican-American from Texas; two were Anglos who had learned Spanish as a foreign language and had lived in Mexico; and the fourth was Anglo, who spoke European Spanish due to her parentage.

One of the Hispanic bilingual classrooms used the mother tongue the least amount of time—only 4 percent of the time. The mother tongue was used only when the Anglo teacher could not communicate with the children in English and would ask the bilingual teacher to translate the message for her. This was an example of an immersion program.

Two of the bilingual Hispanic classrooms used the mother tongue 16 percent and 11 percent of the time, respectively. The mother tongue was used to repeat the daily calendar in Spanish after it was done in English, to recite the colors in both languages, and to sing some Spanish songs. In these two classrooms, a limited effort was made to connect the mother tongue with the English language.

The fourth Hispanic bilingual classroom used the mother tongue 20 percent of the time, a rate that was the highest among the Hispanic classrooms. The bilingual teacher in this classroom had daily instruction in the mother tongue for about 15 minutes, while the Anglo teacher was working with the Anglo children. Instruction was concurrent but not identical. There was no effort to transfer knowledge from one language to the other. This teacher included the non-Hispanic children in some of her instruction of numbers in both languages, which was rather irregular. This classroom was like the Chinese classroom in that an effort was made at maintaining the mother tongue.

None, of the observed classrooms used the mother tongue as a transition language as required by the law. None of the observed classrooms had a bilingual curriculum that the teachers could follow. The bilingual children were taught the same kindergarten content as were the Anglo children, who had come to the kindergarten with five years of experience in listening to and speaking English at home. It appeared that the teachers implemented the bilingual program in these classrooms based on their interpretation of it.

The mother language was most frequently used, in descending order, for singing and reading, information giving, questioning children, giving commands to children, praising them; but seldom for criticizing. It was stunning to see how little the mother language was used in the daily experiences of the children. The question arose: If bilingual education is to teach the child in his mother language while the child is learning English, why was it so little observed in the five bilingual kindergarten classrooms?

The bilingual children were not assessed prior to entering the kindergarten to establish how much English they knew. They were assigned to the bilingual kindergarten primarily on the basis of their surnames, or if their parents had asked through an interpreter that their children be placed in the bilingual kindergartens. The children were not assessed at the end of the school year either. So there was no way to find out how effective was the bilingual program.[41] This lack of comprehensive testing upon entering and exiting bilingual programs still plagues bilingual education.

Current Status of Bilingual Education

Bilingual education programs are increasingly justified not so much for linguistic reasons as on the psycho-political basis that some years (five to seven are commonly suggested) of instruction primarily through the mother language are essential to the self-esteem and subsequent educational success of language-minority children.

Bilingual education has gradually lost its role as a transitional way of teaching English and now mandates a bicultural component. This mandate has been primarily shaped by the federal government at the insistence of special interest groups and their leaders. This type of program segregates the students from the mainstream.[42] Self-esteem as a raison d'être for the length of bilingual education programs has been overemphasized. There is no solid evidence that members of linguistic minorities have low self-esteem. Beatriz Arias pointed out, in reviewing the research on Mexican-Americans, that there is no reason to believe that an emphasis on the home language and culture is a paramount remedy to whatever problems of self-esteem may exist.[43]

Also, a three-year study in Dade County (Miami) compared two groups of limited-English-proficient (LEP) students who were matched for age and social class and randomly assigned to schools using Spanish and schools using English (in a curriculum designed for LEP pupils) as the primary language for instruction. The students who were being taught in English from the first day of school were apparently not suffering emotional distress, and those who were taught in Spanish did not have a noticeably higher level of self-pride.[44]

Program administrators and other professionals who benefit from employment in bilingual programs insist that children need to stay between five and seven years in bilingual programs.[45] Extending the period of bilingual education extends the period of separation of the language minority student from his peers, which is against the school desegregation efforts, and the laws.

It appears that segregation based on language is as harmful as segregation based on ethnicity. This was not at all the intention of the 1970 government guidelines on the basis of which bilingual programs were set up to benefit language minority students.[46] English-speaking Hispanics are heavily represented in the bilingual transitional programs because transfer out is rare in many of these programs, a situation that creates Hispanic tracks within the school.[47]

Lisa Delpit, a black educator, argues that to give minority children an effective command of the language and style of the dominant majority is not to disrespect their own forms of speech, but is precisely to respect *them* and their potential to be successful in the mainstream.

The well-intended introduction into public schools serving poor black children of "dialect readers" was seen by many black educators as "dooming black children to a permanent outsider caste."[48]

In the fall of 1997, the news media began reporting on a movement in the state of California by parents and teachers to repeal the mandatory bilingual education, for they believed that the children, primarily Hispanics, were shunted into a slow academic track. In June 1998, it was reported that the voters voted against the existing bilingual education program.

CHAPTER SUMMARY

Bilingualism existed in the United States since colonial times. Bilingual education took place outside the public schools by the various linguistic minorities who wanted to maintain their language and culture.

In the 1960s, bilingual education was brought into the public schools. It has been a controversial issue.

NOTES

1. Title IV (desegregation of public education) and Title VI (nondiscrimination in federally assisted programs) of the Civil Rights Act of 1964. Robert Bremner et al., *Children and Youth in America: A Documentary History*, 3 volumes in 5 (Cambridge, MA: Harvard University Press, 1970–1974), 3:1848–1851.

2. Heinz Kloss, *The American Bilingual Tradition* (Rowley, MA: Newbury House Publishers, 1977), 36. The 1960 census revealed that in the five southwestern states (Texas, New Mexico, Colorado, Arizona, and California), the population with Spanish surnames had completed an average of only 4.7 years in school compared to 8.1 years for the non-white and 12.1 years for the "Anglo" children age fourteen years or older.

3. *The New York Times* (June 18, 1967) called to the public's attention that in Texas, New Mexico, Colorado, Arizona, and California, there were 1.75 million schoolchildren with Spanish surnames whose linguistic, cultural, and psychological handicaps caused them to experience academic failure in our schools; J. W. Kobrick, in his article, "The Compelling Case for Bilingual Education," *Saturday Review* 55 (1972): 54–57, reported that of the 350 Spanish-speaking school-age children (Puerto Rican) in one of the Greater Boston area neighborhoods, 65 percent had never registered in school, many rarely attended, and others had dropped out.

4. James S. Coleman et al., *Equality of Educational Opportunity* (Washington, DC: Government Printing Office, 1966).

5. Fransesco Cordasco, *Bilingual Schooling in the United States* (New York: McGraw-Hill, 1976), discusses this issue extensively.

6. Kloss, *The American Bilingual Tradition*, 37.

7. Ibid., 39. It has always been the belief of this author, a bilingual, that bilingual education has the potential for harmonizing the ethnic values and cultural patterns of the child

with the prevailing American values and cultural patterns, and can equalize the child's opportunities to succeed in school and society.

8. See also E. Glyn Lewis, "Bilingualism and Bilingual Education: The Ancient World to the Renaissance," in Joshua Fishman, *Bilingual Education* (Rowley, MA: Newbury House Publishers, 1976), 150–200.

9. James Crawford, "Endangered Native American Languages. What Is to Be Done and Why?," *Bilingual Research Journal* (1995): 18–19.

10. Fishman, *Language Loyalty in the United States* (The Hague: Moulton and Co., 1966), 23; see also J. Burma, *Spanish-Speaking Groups in the United States* (Durham, NC: Duke University Press, 1954).

11. Kloss, *The American Bilingual Tradition*, 16.

12. Ibid., 17.

13. Fishman, *Language Loyalty*, 30. Immigrant minorities were never forbidden to organize and maintain their own communities, organizations, schools, and publications.

14. Kloss, *The American Bilingual Tradition*, 147, 149.

15. Nina Vandewalker, *The Kindergarten in American Education* (New York: Macmillan Co., 1923), 12–13, 17, 21–23, 30–33; Lida R. McCabe, "Columbus: The Cradle of America's Kindergarten," *The Ohio State Journal* 62 (31 March 1901): 1–2 (Columbus: Ohio Historical Society Microfilms); and Elizabeth Jenkins, "How the Kindergarten Found Its Way to America," *Wisconsin Journal of History* 19 (September 1930): 48–62.

16. Theodore Andersson and Mildred Boyer, *Bilingual Schooling in the United States,* 2 volumes (Washington, DC: Government Printing Office, 1970), 1:17.

17. Kloss, *The American Bilingual Tradition*, 120.

18. Ibid., 26–27, 31.

19. *Carl Schurz, Revolutionary and Statesman,* ed. Rüdiger Wersich (München: Heinz Moos Verlag, 1979), 164. Schurz was a young liberal who participated in the ill-fated German revolution of 1848. Along with many others, he fled to America, where he distinguished himself. They were educated men of substance and social standing, who contributed to American society. John F. Kennedy, *A Nation of Immigrants* (New York: Harper & Row, 1964), 52.

20. Einar Haugen, *Bilingualism in the Americas: A Bibliography and Research Guide* (Tuscaloosa: University of Alabama Press, American Dialect Society, 1956), 11, 32–33.

21. Kloss, *The American Bilingual Tradition*, 33–34. *Infant Care* published by the Children's Bureau, since 1914, had some of its editions published also in French, Slovak, Spanish, and Portuguese.

22. Ellwood P. Cubberly, *Changing Conceptions of Education* (Boston, 1909), quoted in Lawrence A. Cremin, *The Transformation of the School* (New York: Alfred Knopf, 1961), 64–75.

23. Bremner, *Children and Youth,* 1:457.

24. Horace Mann, *Lecture on Education* (Boston: Marsh, Capen Lyon and Webb, 1840), 54, 58.

25. For more about ethnic group schools and mother language maintenance, see Fishman, *Language Loyalty,* 92–126.

26. New York Children's Aid Society, *Third Annual Report,* 1856, quoted in Bremner, *Children and Youth,* 1:425.

27. The restriction of teaching in languages other than English that came about after World War I was for political rather for pedagogical reasons. Americanization meant to divest the immigrants of their ethnic character and inculcate in them the dominant Anglo-Saxon ways. Bremner, *Children and Youth in America,* 2:1326.

28. Ibid., 2:1329–1330.

29. Fishman, *Language Loyalty,* 324; James Crawford, ed., *Language Loyalties, A Source Book on the Official English Controversy* (Chicago: University of Chicago Press, 1992), 11.

30. Crawford, *Language Loyalties,* 195, 198.

31. For more on the history of U.S. language policy, see "Historical Roots of U.S. Language Policy," Ibid., 9–86. Chapter 71A of the Acts of 1971, Commonwealth of Massachusetts.

32. Max Weinreich, "The Russification of Soviet Minority Languages," *Problems of Communism* 2, no. 6 (1953): 46–57.

33. N. H. Brooks, "The Meaning of Bilingualism Today," *Foreign Language Annals* 2, no. 3 (1969): 304–309; William F. Mackey, "The Description of Bilingualism," *Canadian Journal of Linguistics* 6, no. 2 (1962): 51–58.

34. Haugen, *Bilingualism in the Americas: A Bibliography and Research Guide,* 9.

35. Mackey, "The Description of Bilingualism," 51–85; idem, "Towards a Redefinition of Bilingualism," *Journal of the Canadian Linguistic Association* 2, no. 1 (1956): 4–11.

36. Fishman, *Bilingual Education,* 24–26. Some children today may have also attended a bilingual preschool setting.

37. Courtney Cazden, "Some Implications of Research on Language Development," in *Early Education,* ed. Robert D. Hess and Roberta M. Bear (Chicago: Aldine Press, 1966), 136.

38. Nancy Modiano, "National or Mother Language in Beginning Reading: A Comparative Study," *Research in Teaching English* 1 (1968): 32–34.

39. E Peal and Wallace E. Lambert, *The Relation of Bilingualism to Intelligence* (Washington, DC: American Psychological Association, 1962).

40. Theodore Andersson, "Bilingual Education and Early Childhood," *Hispania* 57, no. 1 (1974): 77–78; UNESCO, *The Use of Vernacular Languages in Education,* Monographs on Fundamental Education, VIII (Paris: UNESCO, 1953), 11. See also H. H. Stern, *Languages and the Young School Child* (London: Oxford University Press, 1969).

41. V. Celia Lascarides, "A Sociological Study of Bilingual and Regular Kindergartens," (Ed.D. diss., Boston University, 1979), 227–238.

42. Senator Walter Huddleston, "The Misdirected Policy of Bilinguals," in *Language Loyalties, A Source Book on the Official English Controversy,* ed. James Crawford, 115–117.

43. M. Beatriz Arias, "When Hispanics Become the Majority: The Multicultural Challenge to Educational Equity," *Metas* 2 (1982): 39–40.

44. Rosalie P. Porter, *Forked Tongue: The Politics of Bilingual Education* (New York: Basic Books, 1990), 72–73.

45. Kenji Hakuta, *Mirror of Language: The Debate on Bilingualism* (New York: Basic Books, 1986), 227.

46. R. Donato, M. Menchaca, and R. R. Valencia, "Segregation, Desegregation and Integration of Chicano Students: Problems and Prospects," *Chicano Schools Failure and Success,* ed. R. R. Valencia (London: Falmer Press, 1991), 44.

47. Janet Eyler, Valerie J. Cook, and Leslie E. Ward, "Resegregation: Segregation within Desegregated Schools," *The Consequences of School Desegregation,* ed. Christine H. Rossell and Willis D. Hawley (Philadelphia: Temple University Press, 1983), 139–140.

48. Lisa Delpit, *Other People's Children: Cultural Conflict in the Classroom* (New York: New Press, 1995), 29.

CHAPTER 19

Recent Influences from Overseas (Twentieth Century)

> It is important to note that the Kibbutz and its educational
> system, which relate to the totality of human lives,
> constitute an optimal "social laboratory" for educational
> experiments, especially those which are dependent on
> communal efforts.
>
> —Ben-Peretz, Giladi, and Dror[1]

Many methods and models from overseas have impacted programs for young children in the United States. Two of the major influences during the twentieth century have come from Israel and England. The kibbutz children's houses in Israel and the open education model in England were studied intensely by professionals from the United States, who wrote about them in the literature and developed their own versions of the programs. This chapter will examine the two examples of overseas influences on early childhood education through a historical overview of each country, followed by a description of the educational program. Each section concludes with a discussion of the impact of the system on early education in the United States.

ISRAEL

Antiquity

There was a concept of childhood, among the Jews of antiquity, according to the sources. Bar-Ilan says that the number of rules in a society may be viewed as a reflection of the status of "childhood." His demonstration of the argument that the greater the number of rules, the more significant the concept of childhood, is the fact that in the biblical period rules were not in evidence; however, during the time of the Mishna and the Talmud there were many rules.[2] Child sacrifice was allowed, but rarely practiced, from the time of the Patriarchs to the reign of Josiah, and then it was banned altogether.[3] Debt-bondage, in which peasants sold themselves and their children into slavery in times of famine and bad harvests, existed. Every seventh year, the debts were canceled and slaves were freed.[4] Under the monarchy, most parents in Israel educated their children in their own homes. A marked increase in Hebrew inscriptions from the eighth century Before the Common Era (B.C.E.)[5] on, led to the conclusion that there must have been systematic teaching and schools at least in the royal fortresses and in certain villages.[6] Before the exile, young children of both sexes were under their mother's care. Later the boys accompanied their father to the field or workshop, while girls remained at home with their mothers. The children were given religious and ethical instruction by their parents and family. They learned the history of their own people and G-d's[7] dealing with them, and the Pentateuch, Psalms, and Proverbs.[8] It is surmised that whatever schools existed were held in a room in the teacher's house or the corner of a public place; however, they left no clear archaeological trace.

Bar-Ilan analyzes the violent nature of childhood in antiquity, specifically violence directed against Jewish children. He gives examples of beating and battering in the Bible and the Talmudic literature. The law of the rebellious son in Deuteronomy 21:18–21, which provides justification for parents beating their children after verbal means of persuasion fail to improve the child's conduct, is cited. According to Bar-Ilan, adults beating children was an integral part of the everyday life of Jews and non-Jews alike. Young children were subject to violent treatment by both parents and teachers, purportedly for educational reasons.[9]

The Jewish culture of antiquity showed a significant preoccupation with education. There is evidence of fairly universal literacy among the population, which derived its sanction from the Bible.[10] It is unlikely that there was a widespread school system among Jews prior to the Hellenistic Era.[11] The Bible placed responsibility for religious education upon the male head of the family.[12] According to Graves, the chief aim of education in the biblical period was religious and moral.[13]

Judaism was against infanticide and abortion. It was clearly stated that Jews had a religious duty to rear all of their children (in the first century B.C.E.).[14] There were warm emotional ties between parents and children. Although childhood in general received many warm words in Talmudic literature, the sages of the Mishnaic Period, who believed children were free from sin, said that childhood was a state of imperfection. Children often died at the tender age of four or five years.[15] Both the Mishnah and the Talmud refer to toys. Boys used wagons, girls played "five stones," and both played with balls.[16]

The Jewish school prepared children for the concrete duties of life, as well as religion and ceremonies.[17] Children were taught to live by the ideals of *Torah u'Mitzvot u'Ma'asim Tovim* (Torah and Commandments and good deeds). Instruction was given in both the holy laws and the unwritten customs. During the Talmudic age, schoolchildren had enormous prestige, because the survival of the Jewish people was contingent upon their following a Torah-centered way of life. By the second century C.E., there was a fairly extensive, if incomplete, network of schools operating in Palestine, which was designed to counter the onslaughts of Greco-Roman civilization.[18] From early times, children attended religious services. The service consisted of reading the Torah, and Homiletic discourses. These popular lectures on parts of the Scriptures were a central feature of the service.

During the Babylonian exile, schools were held in the courtyard of teachers' homes, which sometimes led to arguments with the neighbors over the noisy study habits. Simeon ben Shetah founded the elementary school system by establishing charity schools throughout Judea between 70 and 67 B.C.E. Just before the destruction of the Temple, Joshua ben Gamala set up a system of compulsory education including an elementary school and a rudimentary form of high school.[19] After 70 C.E., Greek-style schools spread slowly in both Palestine and Babylonia. Jewish elementary education became universal for boys, and any boy who had not studied Torah was called an *am ha-aretz*.

Children studied in community elementary schools (the *bet sefer*) for ten to twelve hours a day from Monday through Thursday. Special sessions were sometimes held on the Sabbath and on holidays, so that parents could visit the schools and hear the children recite.[20] Teachers wrote letters on a wax board with a stylus, and the pupils recited them. The sounds of the individual letters were said first, and then they were joined together. After children mastered elementary texts, they graduated to the Torah. They were taught to read and translate by listening to the teacher and then chanting an exact repetition of the text. A system of cantillation (*trop*) was devised to facilitate the pupil's task of memorization. The culture had no printed books. Torah and other scrolls were hand written by the scribes. Children were prohibited from writing, since all writing of scrolls was done by the community scribes, and the art was handed down in guild fashion.

From the first to the third century C.E., children learned prayers at home. In later decades, prayers were taught at school. The child learned to perform various *Mitzvot* (commandments) as soon as he could carry them out. The holidays, particularly the holiday of Passover, became a time for study. The child would begin his schooling at anywhere from three to six years of age. After the child completed the subject matter of the preceding level, he would move on to the next level.

Any individual was eligible to set up a school for children, but only one school was allowed in any locality. Parents paid the teacher a fee, which technically was for care of the children while they were at school, since no one was allowed to solicit students or profit from their learning. The teaching of children was a strict religious obligation, and theoretically nothing was allowed to interfere with it.[21]

Respect for the teacher was a keynote of the Talmudic educational system. The elementary school teacher had lower status, although he was a married man of at least forty years of age. Women were not eligible to serve as teachers of Scripture. The rod of the Bible was replaced by the strap during the Talmudic age, so corporal punishment continued in the schools.[22] According to Graves, the Jews had sufficient practical knowledge of psychology to realize that different types of mind must be approached by different methods. They therefore used pronunciation of the words of the Bible, auditory stimulation, and singing of the musical cantillation in order to assist children in learning.[23]

The objective of elementary school training was to transmit the whole Bible without any attempt to understand it; therefore, mechanical associations and arbitrary learning aids were used. In instances where understanding was important, learning took place through observation and participation. This was the case with the rules pertaining to holiday observances and the Sabbath, which were learned by actual participation in the synagogue service and observation of the rituals of the home and synagogue. Girls were excluded from the schools, although some of their fathers may have taught them at home. Just as the Mishnah forbade women from being teachers of children, they were also banned from reading Torah in the synagogue, and were not obligated to perform the time-bound positive commandments.[24]

The Middle Ages

The bulk of the Jewish population shifted from the Mediterranean coast to Central and Eastern Europe during this time period. Family size in Europe and medieval Egypt of the eleventh to the sixteenth centuries was small. Wet-nursing and swaddling were practiced. Girls were trained from an early age to carry out household tasks. Boys were allowed to roam the streets and play boisterous games. All children played ball games, tennis, and blindman's bluff, as well as quiet games with apples and nuts.

From the Middle Ages on, boys attended the *Heder* (room), in which one teacher, sometimes with an assistant, would take in twenty to thirty boys from the ages of four to thirteen. The syllabus was limited to religious instruction in the Bible, Talmud, and commentaries thereon. The language of instruction among Ashkenazi Jews (those of German or Eastern European origin) was Yiddish, while among Sephardi Jews (of Spanish or Oriental origin) it was either Ladino (a Spanish dialect) or Arabic. Hebrew was taught as a dead language. Secular subjects were not taught. During this time period girls received no formal education.[25]

Beginning in the eleventh century C.E., a spring holiday ceremony was held for five- and six-year-old boys who were about to enter *Heder*.[26] The child was placed under the coat of an important person or scholar, along with honey cakes, eggs, fruits, and nuts. The cakes or eggs were inscribed with Bible verses. A slate containing honey-covered letters was read to child, and the alphabet was recited forward and backward. Sometimes the pupil was taken to a river or pool stocked with fish. After this ceremony, the child was taken home, where the parents had a party for him. Food and drink were used as instruments to impart knowledge and as memory aids. In the early seventeenth century C.E., a father would give the boy a wafer dipped in honey. Late nineteenth-century *Heder* memoirs refer to alphabet biscuits, almonds engraved with Hebrew letters, and boys being showered with sweets and/or coins. After World War I, the *Heder* system in Europe was abandoned by most of the Ashkenazim; however, the Chasidim preserved some of the traditions.

During the Middle Ages, there were communal Jewish schools in other areas of the world, such as those in Spain. In Northern Europe, contracts were arranged between parents and teachers (for middle income children) and the wealthy hired teachers for their children. In the Islamic countries, there were special schools for children of the poor and orphans. Later the community paid tuition for their attendance at ordinary schools. Documents from the Cairo Genizah describe the medieval primary schools. Child exercise books were enlivened by pictorial illustrations, and children colored enlarged letters drawn by the teachers. The children practiced Hebrew letters on wooden boards, only until they could write their signature. There was a shortage of books. The curriculum in Spain consisted of Bible study, Hebrew grammar, and codes of law. The schools for the educated Jewish elite of Europe included Mishnah and Talmud, scientific and philosophical subjects. Learning to write was reserved for those wanting to become merchants, rabbis, doctors, or government officials.[27]

The Bar Mitzvah ceremony evolved in medieval Germany in order to counter church confirmation rites. The boy's father recited a blessing relieving himself of responsibility for his son and the son's education. The boy could now take on and consent to religious obligations. He had learned the daily prayers and how to put on *tallit* and *tefilin*.[28]

Early Modern Period

In the early modern period, the family was loving, strongly moral, and closely bonded.[29] Before 1740, there were hardly any books for children. By the end of the eighteenth century, there were hundreds of different titles. Locke was an influence on Moses Mendelssohn, the father of the *Haskalah* (enlightenment). Children were treated better than before, even indulged.[30] The Enlightenment Movement began in Germany, where, by the second half of the eighteenth century, the more opulent Jewish households had a tutor for both Jewish and secular subjects.[31]

In early nineteenth-century Europe the mother cared for and educated the child up to the age of three, four, or five. Between the ages of three and five years, he was enrolled in the beginner's *heder,* which he attended from 8:00 A.M. to 6:00 P.M., Sunday through Thursday and for a half-day on Friday. Hebrew letters were compared by the teachers to familiar objects or limbs of the body. Nonsense sentences were recited to traditional rhythmic chants. Later the boy went on to the *Chumash heder,* in which he was taught the Pentateuch (sections of the Torah reading and Rashi's commentaries). Girls either had a private tutor or learned in a girls *heder.* Subjects included the prayer book, women's prayers in Yiddish, and *Nachlas Tsvi* (a Yiddish ethical and mystical tract). Girls studied for a shorter period than boys did, for approximately four years.[32]

Kibbutz Children's Houses in Israel

The modern history of Israeli early childhood education began with the first school set up in Palestine by outside philanthropies. The Laemmel School, which opened in Jerusalem in 1856, taught its students in German. In the

Evalina de Rothschild School for girls, opened in 1864, students used French, and later English. Four European Jewish philanthropies set up kindergartens and schools in Israel. They were the Alliance Israélite Universelle of Paris, France; the Anglo-Jewish Association of London, England; Hilfsverein der Deutschen Juden (Ezra Society) of Berlin, Germany; and Hoveve Zion of Russia. In the *asile d'enfants* (the French schools), kindergartens were opened alongside of the elementary schools. Children of ages three to six learned to play and sing in French, so they were better prepared for the formal learning of reading and writing in the elementary classes.[33]

The Hebrew teachers in the colonies also felt the need for an informal preparatory stage, and the first Hebrew kindergarten was opened in Rishon-le-Zion in 1898. The kindergarten mistress had been trained at the Evalina Girls' School. In 1904, the Ezra Society opened a training college for elementary school and kindergarten teachers, in order to staff their own educational network. Their schools introduced such German pedagogical ideas as instruction in *Heimatkunde* (study of the environment), *Anschauungsunterricht* (object lessons), Georg Kerschensteiner's *Arbeitsschule* (activity method), and Froebel's "gifts" and "occupations."[34] By the time the first kibbutz, Degania, was founded in 1909, there was already an early childhood education presence in Palestine.

The first kibbutzim were founded by the members of Eastern European Jewish youth movements. The kibbutz has been described as a voluntary cooperative society that values work, economic cooperation, and political participation within the original Zionist pioneering context of the early founders. In later years, that came to include perpetuating the Zionist ideology of the particular federation, and national service.[35] Each kibbutz has a few elected officers; however, the primary decision-making body is the General Assembly. All decisions must be approved by this body, and every adult kibbutz member is entitled to a vote. Today, the de facto power in the kibbutz lies in the committees and the secretary.[36]

According to Hazan, collective education embodies the basic sociocultural, moral, and ideational values of the kibbutz movement, and reflects its way of life. Its methods and means, the relationship between the learning process and education, the organizational structure and social context have grown out of this social milieu.[37]

Communal child care and education grew out of necessity. A 1916 statement by Joseph Bussel laid the ideological foundation for communal child care and education in the kibbutz. He said:

> Childcare is not only the responsibility of the mother, but of all women. The essential thing is to preserve the principle of co-operation in everything, there should be no personal possessions, for private property hinders co-operative work. As for payment for child care, this must certainly be made from the general fund, since in communal life all expenses should be paid communally,

and nobody can be exempted simply because he has no children. In fact, all the expenses for child care should be paid for by the community.[38]

Miriam Baratz, one of the founders of Degania, took her child to work with her in the early months. Her husband, Josef, described the other difficult issues that the problem of child raising brought to the fore. "How were the women both to work and look after the children? Should each mother look after her own family and do nothing else?" The women wanted equal participation in communal work and life. One of them was chosen to look after the children during the day, in a house set aside for that purpose. This system was later adopted in all the *kvutzot*. A new mother's ability to leave her first baby in the *creche* and trust other women to look after it became one of the decisive tests of a woman's "call to the *kvutza*."[39] Gradually, the functions and position of the care giver were institutionalized, and child care became part of the regular work roster of the *kvutza*. The concept of the *metapelet* (child-care worker) and the "educational group" were born. The emergence of a structure for child care put the seal on the *kvutza* as a permanent community rather than a group in a transitory phase.[40]

Yitzhak Tabenkin, one of the early leaders of the kibbutz movement, joined Kibbutz Ein Harod with his wife and child in 1921. Tabenkin "maintained forcefully that the family was an essential component of kibbutz society. In historical perspective, therefore, it seems that, despite the tensions which it caused in certain periods, the acceptance of the nuclear family was a means of stabilizing and expanding the kibbutz."[41]

Although the children in the earliest kibbutzim were in group care during the day, they returned to their parents' quarters in the evening. The more "left wing" kibbutzim introduced group child care partially on ideological grounds—"to curtail the 'home' as a nucleus of selfish and 'bourgeois' interests; to 'free' the woman, and enable her to take an equal part with men in the work of the farm."[42] Thus the ideal was to create an egalitarian society that would free women from their economic and social dependence upon their husbands, allowing them to become the equal of men in all aspects of kibbutz life. Although the principle of communal child care was one of the cornerstones of kibbutz society, it was put into practice by the women alone. This fact is still expressed semantically in the word *metapelet*, which is used almost exclusively in the feminine gender.[43]

Communal (child) sleeping arrangements were first practiced by the members of kibbutz Kfar Gil'adi, in 1919, as a result of the Tel Hai incident, which forced them from their home and led to improvised sleeping arrangements at Kibbutz Rosh Pina. When they returned to Kfar Gil'adi itself, the communal sleeping arrangement was made permanent at the insistence of its young, ideologically extreme members, who saw it as an expression of the principle that children belong to the whole community.[44] The construction of children's houses was done for both safety and sanitary reasons originally. In the early days of the kibbutz, when it had to defend itself from outside attack, the first permanent building erected after the watchtower for defense, was the children's house, which was solidly built.[45] Until the early 1960s, the majority of kibbutzim had communal sleeping arrangements. Some of the older, more prosperous kibbutzim permitted children to spend the night with their parents.[46]

During the formative period of kibbutz education, child care was the responsibility of a known and trusted member of the community who worked with the children on a regular basis, gaining their trust and confidence. From the 1930s on, however, child care was subject to the strains of the labor shortage in the kibbutzim. Often the child care task was given to young and inexperienced women who had to gain the requisite skills in the course of their work, and sometimes at the cost of the children. In some kibbutzim, children were compelled to eat according to the dictates of the *metapelet*, and the inexperienced workers found it difficult to deal with the children's fears that were engendered by nights in the dark children's house.[47]

The kibbutz educational system now provides care and education from birth through high school and army entrance. The various kibbutz federations have impacted the child care and educational system.[48] From the 1930s through the 1950s, an infant entered the kibbutz educational system upon returning with his or her mother from the hospital, at the age of four or five days. The baby was brought to the sterile infants' house, where the nurse (*metapelet*) took over responsibility. The mother came to breast-feed daily, in the company of the other mothers. Each group of four to six babies had its own *metaplot*, who remained with them until the children reached the age of one year. This was the beginning of the formation of two emotional centers for the kibbutz infant, one consisting of the mother and the family, and the other of the *metaplot* and the group. The earliest kibbutzim felt that this maintenance of two emotional centers was the best means of moderating eminent tension in parent-child relationships.[49]

Weaning of children by the mother took place from the fourth to the eighth month so that by the end of the first year, the *metapelet* had taken over more and more activities from the mother. Habit training was begun by the *metapelet* during the second year of life and coincided with the end of weaning. Because habit training was not carried out by the mother, a more conflict-free relationship existed between her and her child, according to Lewin.[50]

At the age of one year, the child moved from the infant nursery to the toddlers' house (*bet peutot*), and two small groups were combined into one. When the children became two or three, one of the nurses was replaced by a nursery teacher.[51] Four-year-olds were transferred to the kindergarten (*gan*). The group was enlarged by the merger of two nursery groups, with one kindergarten teacher (*ganenet*) and one *metapelet*. This *kvutza* remained together as a unit until the members reached maturity, spending a portion of each day with their parents.

HaShomer HaZair pioneered the kibbutz kindergarten. Although kindergarten pedagogy was a known quantity in Israel, the kibbutz kindergarten was created in temporary conditions by the first "conquest" group at Tel Adashim and later at Kfar Gil'adi. Kindergartens rapidly became accepted as part of the educational setup, a natural extension of *pe'uton*. The curriculum was designed in widening circles centered around social studies, natural science, the children's farm, the celebration of festivals with the kibbutz community, organized games, dancing, singing, and other cultural activities. In the beginning, kindergarten and schoolteachers from outside the kibbutz were employed by the *Histadrut*.[52] Although these teachers were highly devoted men and women, believers in various forms of progressive education, they met very difficult tasks of teaching a group of children in isolated settlements who had no inherited educational tradition. The mixture of formal and informal education emphasized the values of "community, mutual aid, labour, and self-defence."[53]

The curriculum integrated the children's activities at school, at work, and at leisure into the cultural and economic activities of the kibbutz. During the eight-hour day, activities might include a lesson in shared responsibility through cleaning the rooms in the children's house as well as more typical kindergarten subjects. Community norms were taught in a series of different situations, for example: "A kibbutz teacher reads a story about economic cooperation and the child will see it in everyday life, the parent rewards the child for sharing toys, and cooperative behavior of the children's play-group is rewarded by the teacher-member."[54] The child knows that each Saturday night the parents go to the kibbutz General Assembly and the *metapelet* emphasizes consulting with the group before making a decision in the children's house.

The kibbutz kindergarten includes the first grade. Six-year-olds begin learning the "three R's" of reading, writing, and arithmetic. According to Roth, the learning is not conducted in a formal manner, but rather by including reading and arithmetic corners in the kindergarten house. There, children may find materials reflecting their present level of interest, written by the kindergarten teacher, and instruments and materials for exercises, both individual and guided. Reading and writing is centered around projects from the immediate environment. No textbooks are used. Creativity and play are encouraged, as is dramatization and games that enable the children to reenact rules of behavior and to apply cultural patterns they have already absorbed.[55] Children grow up knowing the value and importance of work, and that everyone must do their share. From kindergarten on, the educational system emphasizes cooperation in daily life and, from the early school grades, youngsters are assigned duties and make decisions with regard to their peer group.[56]

The kibbutz was expected to replace the conventional family, but unexpectedly it became a "greenhouse for that venerable institution. Children living on a kibbutz go home from the children's houses to the sort of cookie-baking, walk-taking, play-on-the-floor parents that have almost disappeared from other parts of the modern world."[57] The time from 4:00 P.M. until bedtime is reserved exclusively for the children. They are with their parents from the time the parents have finished work until supper or bedtime. By 1990, more than 60 percent of all the kibbutzim in Israel had changed to family sleeping arrangements.[58]

Much has been written about the advantages of communal versus family sleeping arrangements. In the communal arrangement, the *metapelet* wields greater influence, and there is more adherence to norms, and less discrepancy between principle and practice. In the family sleeping arrangement, there is a greater tendency to consider the child's will and postpone making educational demands of the child, for example, weaning or introducing a spoon and a cup.[59] Family-based sleeping arrangements abolish the most unique aspect of kibbutz child rearing—multiple mothering at an early age.[60] With family-based sleeping arrangements, the parents have to discipline the children, peer group influence is reduced, and changes occur in the relationships between siblings.

Fundamental social and psychological developments, successful industrialization, and economic progress that provided decent housing for every couple motivated the transition to family sleeping.[61] Several sources state that due to a shift in the attitudes of the second and third generation of *kibbutzniks*, which have strengthened individual and family ambitions and desires, kibbutz-born and -bred mothers prefer family sleeping arrangements.[62]

In the 1930s through the 1950s, some mothers resented the *metapelet* and the rigidity of the infant scheduling. Between the 1940s and the 1960s, there were some modifications. One of these was an "hour of love" instituted to allow the mother to be with the infant in the children's house during the morning, and permitting both parents and the siblings greater freedom in meeting with infants and toddlers. By the 1980s, scheduled versus feeding on demand was not an issue.[63] Due to improvement in the parents' standard of living, and medical progress on infectious diseases, parents were able to spend a great deal more time with their young children. Although the kibbutz remained and remains an "extended family," the nuclear family has come to prominence in the 1980s and 1990s.[64] It has taken over more and more daily functions that had long been considered an integral part of collective life.

Each child still remains a member of the children's society (*chevrat yeladim*), spending many of their waking hours with their peers. Family sleeping arrangements for children, greater involvement of parents in communal child rearing, and provision of more *metaplot* for infants' houses are part of the kibbutz system's increased "privatism and familism." The maturation and aging of individual kibbutz members led to the development of the family subsystem.[65] Some members of kibbutzim and some professionals fear that "the resurgence of the family may be the most serious threat the kibbutz has ever faced."[66] Others are concerned about whether the communal values and ideology of the particular kibbutz and its movement will be perpetuated by kibbutz children.[67]

Collective education is not a pedagogical experiment carried out under ideal laboratory conditions, but rather is part of the real life of a social movement. Social and economic conditions, and psychological and educational theories have always impacted on and continue to impact it. Today, the Kibbutz Education Committee must not only work out budgets, plan children's trips, and make sure that new baby houses are constructed, but they must plan ahead for adequate new staff (who must complete courses that take several years), and they must make the schedule for the staff of nurses and teachers who are currently employed by the kibbutz and its school.[68]

TRAINING OF TEACHERS

The kibbutz movement has had its own teacher training facility since the founding of the Teachers' Seminar of the Kibbutz Me'uhad by Mordechai Segal in 1939. The first permanent kibbutz Teachers' Seminar was founded in 1940 in Tel Aviv. "Created and run by leading educationalists from all three movements, it aimed to provide a cadre of teachers and *metaplot* at all levels who would combine academic training with understanding of the special nature of kibbutz society and education."[69]

The *metapelet* has played a major role in kibbutz education since the 1900s; however, there have been major changes in the role of *metaplot* since 1970. A study of positive and negative behavior demonstrated that 78.68 percent of *metapelet* behaviors were positive. Negative behavior modes constituted 21.32 percent; however, only 1.88 percent of the behaviors fell into the most negative categories (deprivation of affection, physical punishment, or frustration of the child's activities). The most frequently observed and reported behaviors were "offering information and orientation in the environment, encouraging the child's activities," and "restriction of the child's activity accompanied by explanation or a suggested alternative." This is explained as an attempt to instill courage and self-confidence in the young child, which is a primary policy in kibbutz education.

The researchers concluded that the positive attitude of the *metapelet* springs from the fact that she cares for the children of her own kibbutz, and that she is aware of and accepts the educational demands of the kibbutz. Another aspect is her "awareness that the opinion of the group's parents is an important factor determining her social standing in the kibbutz, where she lives as well as works—this being a situation specific to the kibbutz."[70] In recent decades, the *metapelet* has received more guidance and training from her own kibbutz and from the Teachers' Seminars of the kibbutz movement, in addition to cooperation from her colleagues. However, the weakening in status of children's houses and *metaplot* caused by the discontinuance of the children's communal sleeping could convert the children's house more into a child care center than a home.[71]

Impact of the Kibbutz Education System on Early Education in the United States

Over the years, a number of American sociologists, psychologists, and educators have visited and written about the kibbutz. The most widely quoted study is Bettelheim's *The Children of the Dream*, which is based on seven weeks of living in a kibbutz in the 1960s. While this book did introduce kibbutz education to the public, it may have done more harm than good. None of the empirical psychological and psychiatric research done by clinicians inside or outside of Israel supports Bettelheim's conclusions.[72] Unfortunately, many of the popular and professional conclusions about kibbutz education have been influenced by his unsubstantiated claims and critiques, including Grotberg's section in the 1972 *NSSE Yearbook*. She utilizes Bettelheim as a primary source for the kibbutz model, which she then criticizes. Grotberg states that "the kibbutz model discourages individualism in favor of group identity. It discourages close friendships in favor of the collective. It discourages attachments to parents or even care takers in favor of attachment to the group. . . . [It] is not concerned with the total child. . . . Nor do the parents contribute to the education of their children. Decisions about programs for children are made by kibbutz leaders. Parents may be involved, but only if they happen to be leaders."[73] As described earlier, these statements are erroneous. Bettelheim's book is also used by Charles Siegel in an article that castigates group child care outside of the home.[74] However, the earlier unsystematic observations were refuted by research proving that there were few or no differences between kibbutz-raised children and samples of American children. Research done in the 1980s "confirms the age-appropriate development of kibbutz children at kindergarten and early school age."[75]

The kibbutz child care and education system differs from that in the United States because the child knows the *metaplot,* who are members of the kibbutz. The child is in familiar surroundings, so that on walks and work excursions, he will see parents, friends, and neighbors. Even if the child is sleeping in the parents' apartment, he spends the entire day with the *kvutza.* Since the child has been with many of these individuals since the age of one or two years, the child gets to know the other children of the kibbutz within the same age range intimately. One of the similarities between the two systems is their basis in the progressive teacher training work of John Dewey. Near reports that Mordechai Segal was influenced by the theories of Dewey during his studies in 1931 and 1932, and prior to his arrival in Palestine.[76] Thus, there are parallels between the Israeli kibbutz educational theories and those in the United States. The kibbutz model offers examples of how child care can be used to free the working woman to use her talents. Scarr states that "there is no evidence that communal rearing with stimulating, caring adults is either the ruination or the salvation of children."[77] The *kibbutz* early education system, built on the ideas of Dewey and of communal child rearing, continues to provide for the needs of children and families today. It serves as a model of the ways in which an early education system founded out of necessity can alter its structure to accommodate changing philosophical and psychological theories and practical realities.

ENGLAND (OPEN EDUCATION)

The British Infant School–Open Education Movement rested on the philosophical foundations of Plato, Socrates, and St. Augustine. Educators wondered, as did Rousseau in an earlier age, whether schools had more negative than positive effects upon children. Were we preventing them from learning what they could learn much better by themselves, while we neglected what we alone can teach them?[78] Montessori's techniques and methods of individual work, permitting the children to proceed at their own pace, freedom within a prepared environment, and use of concrete materials were praised as models for the development of open education practices. The concept of natural child development, common to Owen, McMillan, and Froebel, was adopted.[79] Montessori and Froebel's emphasis on handiwork and the use of objects in classrooms led British teachers of the early twentieth century to introduce free movement between the classroom and the corridor or hall, which became known as the concept of in-and-out-ness in informal education.[80]

John Dewey and the progressive movement[81] in the United States have been described by Americans as a major foundation of the Open Education Movement in Great Britain, although British educators disagree, crediting instead the work of Susan Isaacs and the McMillan sisters, along with George Counts and Harold Rugg.[82] Bertrand Russell, Herbert Kohl, and John Holt have all been cited as contributors to the formation of the Open Education Movement in England and in the United States.

Piaget's work, especially as interpreted by Susan and Nathan Isaacs, forms another cornerstone of the theoretical framework. Susan Isaacs's careful observational studies of children, developmental descriptions, and notes on actual school practice were expanded upon by her husband. Nathan Isaacs broadened the implications in his wife's work and compared them with Piaget's analysis of the development of the mental structures in a child. He accepted Piaget's descriptions of the processes of assimilation, accommodation, and re-accommodation before the formation of logical relationships. Thus, Isaacs reconciled his wife's broad descriptive view of the stages of development with Piaget's stages.[83]

A major factor in the development of the Open Education Movement in England was the publication during the 1966–1967 academic year of a report from the committee chaired by Lady Bridget Plowden, entitled *Children and Their Primary Schools: A Report of the Central Advisory Council for Education*.[84, 85] Barth calls the Plowden Report "the most comprehensive and politically significant discussion to date of the rationale as well as the practices of modern British primary schools."[86]

By the 1970s, up to 15 percent of primary schools (infant plus junior schools) were Plowden-oriented. A greater percentage of nursery schools, for three- and four-year-olds, were also Plowden-oriented. Thus, although legions of early childhood and elementary educators and teacher educators from the United States traveled to England to learn about open, informal British infant and nursery schools during the late 1960s and early 1970s, the majority of the primary schools did not demonstrate that approach to learning.

Professional Development

Institutions such as Goldsmith's College, the Froebel Institute, the Rachel McMillan College, and the Mather Training College in Manchester are mentioned as early leaders in training professionals for informal education. Institutes of education attached to twenty universities were delegated by the Department of Education and Science of the Ministry of Education as coordinating facilities. Teachers who were released by their Local Education Authorities (LEA) took advanced courses at the institutes of education. The majority of professors from the United States studied or worked at the Institute of Education of the University of London, a major force to this day in early education research and scholarly activity. National curriculum projects, such as those implemented by the Nuffield Foundation and the work of Z. P. Dienes, a lecturer in mathematics at the University of Leicester, undergirded curriculum development. William P. Hull traveled to England to observe the work of Dienes in 1961. Weber and Eisner cite their work with the Nuffield Junior Science Project and the Nuffield Math Project, respectively.[87]

The Nursery School Association of Great Britain and Northern Ireland made a major contribution to the development of open and informal education through its pamphlet series and other publications. Teachers and heads of both nursery and infant schools belonged to this organization.[88]

The existence of the NNEB, a category of educator unknown in the United States, also impacted upon the development of the Open Education model. NNEBs are persons qualified by the National Nursery Examination Board. They began their two-year training at the end of the fifth form in secondary school, at approximately age fifteen or sixteen. The technological college courses focused on the physical, socioemotional, and mental development of children, and health and education theory and methods. Some of the courses were liberal arts content courses. NNEB students had practical experiences in nursery schools, residential homes, or nursery day centers throughout their two-year training program. The NNEB training "represents a professionalization of the assistant by providing a qualification that is nationally recognized, interchangeable from job to job, and kept up to the standard of the National Nursery Examination Board."[89] Some NNEB continued their higher education by entering teacher training colleges to become nursery or infant school teachers. Following the implementation of the Plowden Report, in addition to assisting with the physical needs of the child, welcoming and conversing with the children, NNEBs were given further responsibilities in regard to implementing the curriculum and interacting with the family.

Definitions and Attributes of Open Education

Open education is a way of thinking about children, about learning, and about knowledge. It may be defined in terms of surface structure (observable classroom practice) and deep structure, which requires a study of educational ideologies. One of the values of studying open education is the fact that it evolved from practice rather than from theory.[90] The following eight themes were identified and used by Thomas and Walberg to analytically review "open education" literature from Plato through the 1970s: INSTRUCTION (guidance and extension of learning), PROVISIONING (the classroom for learning), DIAGNOSIS of learning events, EVALUATION of diagnostic information, HUMANENESS (respect, openness, and warmth), SEEKING opportunities to promote growth, SELF-PERCEPTION of the teacher, and ASSUMPTIONS (ideas about children and the process of learning.)[91] They provide a framework within which to examine past practice and current usage.

The aspects of space and time are important components of open education. Some programs take place in schools without walls, and walled schools keep doors ajar. The classroom space is fluid, with open furniture arrangements forming a variety of spaces for a variety of materials. Children move from place to place at will. They freely bring objects, materials, and books into the classroom and take them out. Schedules include large blocks of time, which allow for idea development and more serious observation and study.

Spodek stated that open education is neither an organizational arrangement for schools nor an architectural form. He noted that open area, open architecture, or open space school buildings, which eliminated physical barriers, were built by many school districts in the United States. The boards of education thought that this type of building would lead to greater flexibility in school programs, that children could be organized more easily into different sized groups for different purposes, and that varied staffing patterns would occur. Problems were created because team teaching led to departmentalization and increasing teacher specialization. The lack of acoustical separation caused noise problems when classes were doing noisy and quiet activities at the same time. Large carpeted areas were less soil resistant, and thus teachers began to limit messy activities to avoid confrontations with maintenance personnel. Spodek concluded that open education can occur in both open-area schools and traditional buildings, *when teachers collaborate.*

To many, open education means an open system of communication among all persons involved in the educational enterprise. The structure of the curriculum emerges from the learning children experience instead of being dictated in advance. It is open to choices by both children and adults. Children learn by exploring the real world in all its richness and variety. They "mess around" with all kinds of learning materials to develop a "playful attitude of self expression." They explore the realm of living things. Teachers are open to the possibilities inherent in children; children are open to the possibilities inherent in other children, in materials, and in themselves. This "openness of self" helps everyone to be sensitive to and supportive of others. The teacher stimulates and guides the learning, avoiding coercion or domination. Children are respected and trusted. Thus open education becomes a form of education organized to facilitate transactions characterized by freedom of choice, joint decision-making, and highly individualized activity.[92]

Macdonald "proposed that three major liberating thrusts . . . have existed historically and have reemerged in new colors in today's world. These thrusts are for the freeing of the intellect, the connection of education with broader social concerns, for liberating structures and processes, and the moral agency and self-development of each person."[93] All of these themes have been explored by educators from the United States seeking to incorporate "open education" philosophy and practice based on the British model.

Characteristics of Open Model Nursery and Infant Schools

Many of the British open plan nursery schools of the 1960s and early 1970s were designed to serve the poor working class, and to a limited extent the immigrant child. These types of schools were often found in the cities or in rural areas hit by the impoverishment of poor crops or lessened availability of factory jobs. Class size within the nursery and infant schools was thirty to forty children. In nursery classrooms, the presence of NNEBs lowered the adult-child ratio. Many infant schools included reception classes, which were used as "a short-period sorting-out class, funneling children into family grouping."[94] The teacher of the reception class was supposed to focus on readiness for curriculum subjects such as reading, writing, and math. Play was encouraged, and in the majority of cases the reception class provided the extra support needed by five-year-old children.

The Plowden-oriented nursery and infant schools utilized family (vertical or mixed age) grouping. This form of heterogeneous school organization allowed new and younger children to learn from children who had already spent a period of time in the school. It provided new responsibilities and relationships for the chronologically older children in the class. This made it possible for a cross section of the entire school population to be represented in each classroom. The practice allowed teachers to become well acquainted with new students and to grow increasingly aware of pupil needs and learning styles over a two- or three-year period in which they interacted with the same children and their parents.[95] The teacher planned cooperative work on small-group projects in response to the great variations in children, and their special interests and needs.[96, 97]

The integrated day and the integrated curriculum are major features of open/informal education. The integrated (or free or undifferentiated) day had no separation of activities or skills and the separate scheduling of only four fixed periods: Morning Service, physical education, music and movement, and lunch.

These fixed points were designated for all children in the infant school. As a result of the undifferentiated scheduling, one could see all aspects of the curriculum and environment in use at all times. The teacher's work with an individual or a group of children for stimulus or special help could occur at any time. Classrooms were organized into a variety of learning centers, including those for science and mathematics, reading and language arts, visual arts, acting, or music.

The Froebel Institute focused on a child's free choice of activity rather than on the free day, recognizing that some teachers might want to define a broad theme or begin a thematic curriculum study. The nuclear experience, problem, or theme thus served as the basis for a variety of learning opportunities in many fields and disciplines. This approach to curriculum planning had the consequence of "ameliorating the boundary or frame around individual fields of study." Curriculum integration allows for a wide scope of acceptable modes of response from students, and thus there are a wider array of legitimate options for expression. Curriculum integration eliminates the dominance of the verbal domain, the didactic use of the spoken and written word.[98]

The Teacher

In the open education classroom, the teacher was recognized as a planner, stimulator, facilitator, counselor, and guide. As a result of observation of the child's solution of problems and use of materials, the teacher planned the setting differentially for each child. This permitted each child's education to be individualized. It necessitated that the teacher have a deep understanding of content and methodology. Curriculum and environment were designed to implement the child's purposes rather than those of the teacher. The teacher provided starting experiences, raised questions, invited children's questions and discussion, suggested possible activity lines, and introduced provocative stimuli. The teacher was required to be widely read, and utilized direct instruction when appropriate. (For example, instructing in how to use a microscope or camera.) The teacher was also a manager and evaluator who kept detailed observational records. Although Eisner states that in the early 1970s, teachers were free to select segments of curricula that seemed appropriate and to neglect the rest, today infant school teachers must adhere to the British national curriculum.[99]

Many authors have highlighted the fact that the open education curriculum focuses on the process of inquiry rather than content. Eisner stated that too little attention was paid to the selection of important concepts and generalizations. He felt that the identification of powerful concepts and generalizations does not mitigate against spontaneity in educational practice, and cautioned against the "formal" and "content" fallacies. These fallacies emphasize either how the student learns content, or the content itself, as being central to the student's learning process. Eisner states that how students inquire *and* what they inquire about is of equal significance.[100]

Impact of the British Infant Schools on Open Education in the United States

During the mid-1960s through the early 1970s, a number of early childhood and elementary educators and teacher educators traveled to England to survey the open education model nursery and infant schools. What they found was closer to Dewey's version of progressive education than what the progressive educators in the United States had demonstrated. The educators who flocked to the Reggio Emilio schools in Italy during the 1990s followed in a tradition of Americans seeking knowledge about open, creative, progressive education outside their own country.

There was a strong progressive education tradition in the United States. As pointed out by Roma Gans, James Macdonald, and Joseph Featherstone in the early 1970s, the work of Dewey, Kilpatrick, and the Progressive Education Association was a firm foundation upon which to build. Featherstone warned against our becoming "the United States of Amnesia."[101] Macdonald listed seven ideas from "our historical antecedents" that formed the legacy of the progressive education movement in the United States. They are: "(1) the school as a community, (2) the school in the community, (3) the person and his moral right to freedom and choice, (4) concern for individual differences, (5) the method of intelligence (problem solving), (6) building a curriculum through and with the students, and (7) seeing the disciplines as potential end points rather than starting points for pedagogy."[102]

Of the numerous books published in the early to mid-1970s, *The Open Classroom Reader* edited by Charles E. Silberman is one of the most comprehensive, with works from British and American sources. Sir Alec Clegg discussed the revolution that took place in the British primary schools following World War II. Cazden's interview with Susan M. Williams, headmistress of Gordonbrock Infant School in London, provides a clear picture of life in a Plowden-oriented infant school. Williams stated that the teacher goes to school prepared for anything because the school fosters child-directed learning. Teachers do plan and prepare stories and activities; however, the children select what they want to do. The teacher can see when a child is ready for further experiences or when difficulties occur. Groups of four to ten children are gathered for formal lessons. The teacher keeps records of her observations so that she knows the children and exactly where they are. Sometimes the teacher will say, "I want to work with child A and child B first thing this morning." A child is asked to demonstrate something about what she or he has done with materials before moving on to something else. The necessity to showcase a product or a process means that the child cannot flit from one thing to another. The process described by Williams formed the foundation for current work by Wasserman (play-debrief-replay) and by Katz and Chard on the project method. Silberman's exhortation to make educational changes slowly was heeded by some educators of the 1970s.[103]

The "open classroom" in U.S. schools is a carefully planned, child-centered environment, which provides varied and challenging materials. The classroom and the curriculum promote the affective, physical, and cognitive development of each child. Open education preschool and primary classrooms support individuality, promote independence, and encourage freedom. The teachers demonstrate respect for their students and encourage children to assume responsibility for their own learning. Open education is an environment in which children are free from authoritarian adults and arbitrary rules. An open program may be conducted in any physical, social, or financial setting of the school or community.[104]

A number of open education initiatives were implemented in the United States during the late 1960s and 1970s. For example, EDC began a Follow-Through model, the National Association of Independent Schools held teacher workshops in support of private school programs, and Lillian Weber developed the Open Corridor program in New York City. The goals of the open corridor project included "to better support children's learning than has been the case in compulsory education in the past. And to produce a better match between school structure and what we know of how a child learns."[105] Weber worked with five classes (one per grade level) in a single corridor in a New York City public school. Minimal changes were made in the formal classroom because the teachers were still utilizing the city-prescribed syllabi. She opened the hallway for work with children. Weber found that an external person (the advisor) was needed to support change in the new setting. The advisor "defined minimal initial conditions for change and, with the teachers, (analyzed) . . . the work for possible future developments, and for cues to further organizational changes." The advisor was necessary to support the "continuing development of the teacher's understanding and resources."[106]

Weber stated that there was only partial implementation of the Open Corridor program. She also noted that the totally open environment in a portion of the school was not only for the teachers of that corridor, but was accessible to the rest of the school. The administration, the community, and the parents were invited, monthly, to an all-school open house, and all teachers were invited weekly to open classroom workshops. Some parents were active participants; however, some of the teachers did not view the school community as including parents, so the definition of community needed to be enlarged.[107]

Weber and Spodek reported in the literature that they could get some teachers to change their ways of working as they learned that they could trust children. There was an increase in the number of alternative activities available, and teachers allowed children greater degrees of autonomy. Both Weber and Spodek held workshops on classroom organization and assisted the in-service teachers in learning alternative methods of planning and recording they needed to support children's work.[108]

Spodek initiated the University of Illinois Fellowship Program for Teacher Trainers in Early Childhood Education, which was supported by the USOE under the Education Professions Development Act. This program was designed to prepare teacher educators in early childhood education within an open education framework. The second goal was to support some Illinois teachers in their learning about open education through in-class teacher training, workshops, short courses, conferences, extension courses, and seminars.

Spodek and Manolakes's characterization of the open classroom (listed below) can easily be linked to the developmentally appropriate classroom of the 1990s. They stated: (1) school activities are goal-oriented rather than ritual-oriented; (2) school activities presented are developmentally appropriate for the children in the group; (3) children in the classroom are involved in the decision-making process of the group. Respect for children underlies the decision-making process as well as all teacher-child interactions; (4) learning is viewed as taking place as a result of the child's acting on the environment, abstracting information, and operating on this information in some intellectual manner; and (5) learning is viewed as taking place as a result of dialog.[109]

Many of the open education practices that were revived/devised during the 1970s are again in the educational limelight in the 1990s. Emphasis on child-centered learning and teaching, cooperative learning, a project approach to learning, thematic learning, developmentally appropriate practices and curricula, multi-age grouping, integrated curriculum, and parent and family involvement have all returned to both the professional literature and professional practice of early childhood educators in the United States.

CHAPTER SUMMARY

This chapter has described two sets of overseas influences that have impacted early childhood education in the United States over several decades. The *kibbutz* children's houses and *kvutzot* in Israel and the British open classroom philosophy and methods have become a part of theory and practice for those who live and work with young children in the United States.

NOTES

N.B.: According to Graves, the descendants of Jacob were called Israelites up to 536 B.C., and thereafter they were known as Jews. Frank Pierrepont Graves, *A History of Education before the Middle Ages* (New York: Macmillan Company, 1914), 114–115.

1. Miriam Ben-Peretz, Moshe Giladi, and Yuval Dror, "The Anne Frank Haven: A Case of an Alternative Educational Program in an Integrative Kibbutz Setting," *International Review of Education—Internationale Zettschrift fur Erziehungswissenschaft—Revue Internationale de Pédagogie* 38, no. 1 (1992): 48.

2. Meir Bar-Ilan, *The Emergence of Childhood: A Criteria from Antiquity;* available from <http://www.biu.ac.il/~barilm/absyaldu.html>; Internet accessed 27 April 1997. (This is an English abstract of a Hebrew document.)

3. John Cooper, *The Child in Jewish History* (Northvale, NJ: Jason Aronson, Inc., 1996), 26.

4. Ibid., 30.

5. B.C.E. stands for Before the Common Era, which corresponds to the more popular "B.C." and C.E. stands for Common Era, which corresponds to "A.D."

6. Cooper, *The Child in Jewish History,* 21.

7. G-d stands for the name of the Deity.

8. Graves, *A History of Education before the Middle Ages,* 122.

9. Meir Bar-Ilan, *The Battered Jewish Child in Antiquity;* available from <http://www.biu.ac.il/~barilm/battered.html>; Internet accessed 27 April 1997, 2, 3–4, 7.

10. Gerald Marvin Phillips, "The Theory and Practice of Rhetoric at the Babylonian Talmudic Academies from 70 C.E. to 500 C.E. as Evidenced in the Babylonian Talmud" (Ph.D. diss., Department of Speech, Western Reserve University, September 1956), 3; available from <http://www.uark.edu/depts/comminfo/sage/talmud.html/abs>; Internet accessed 13 January 1998; and John Cooper, *The Child in Jewish History* (Northvale, NJ: Jason Aronson, Inc., 1996), 21.

11. Cooper, *The Child in Jewish History,* 21; and Phillips, "The Theory and Practice of Rhetoric at the Babylonian Talmudic Academies from 70 C.E. to 500 C.E.," 17.

12. Deuteronomy VI:7. *V'she nan tam levanehcha v'debarta bam b'shevt'cha b'veytecha uv'lecht'cha vaderech uv'shachb'cha uv'kumecha.* ". . . and thou shalt teach them diligently unto thy children, and shalt talk of them when thou sittest in thy house, and when thou walkest by the way, and when thou liest down, and when thou risest up." In this passage, G-d, through Moses, commands the Jewish people to teach the Commandments and the *Shema* on a daily basis. The Commandments are to be considered as something new and fresh every day, and are to be a theme through the entire day, early and late, both at home and outside of the home. Dr. J. H. Hertz, *The Pentateuch and Haftorahs: Hebrew Text English Translation and Commentary,* 2d ed. (London: Soncino Press, 5724 [1964]), 771.

13. Graves, *A History of Education before the Middle Ages,* 122.

14. Cooper, *Child in Jewish History,* 39, 35.

15. Ibid., 73.

16. Ibid., 79.

17. Graves, *A History of Education before the Middle Ages,* 122.

18. Cooper, *The Child in Jewish History,* 85.

19. Phillips, "The Theory and Practice of Rhetoric at the Babylonian Talmudic Academies from 70 C.E. to 500 C.E.," 17.

20. Ibid., 19.

21. The Talmud says that five years old is the age for beginning this religious obligation, the study of Scripture.

22. Phillips, "The Theory and Practice of Rhetoric at the Babylonian Talmudic Academies from 70 C.E. to 500 C.E.," 18; and Cooper, *The Child in Jewish History,* 91.

23. Graves, *A History of Education before the Middle Ages,* 129–130.

24. Cooper, *The Child in Jewish History,* 94.

25. Joseph S. Bentwich, *Education in Israel* (Philadelphia: The Jewish Publication Society of America, 1965), 6.

26. Selwyn Troen and Walter Ackerman, "Israel," in *Children in Historical and Comparative Perspective: An International Handbook and Research Guide,* ed. Joseph M. Hawes and N. Ray Hiner (New York: Greenwood Press, 1991), 335.

27. Cooper, *The Child in Jewish History,* 177–181.

28. Ibid., 183.

29. Ibid., 222.

30. Locke was opposed to swaddling, wet-nursing, and the flogging of children. His theory that the child's mind was like a blank piece of paper gained wide currency during this period. Ibid., 233.

31. Cooper, *The Child in Jewish History,* 236.

32. Ibid., 271.

33. Bentwich, *Education in Israel,* 11.

34. In this passage, Kleinberger refers to the doctoral dissertation of M. Rinott on the educational activities of the Hilfsverein in Palestine. Aharon Fritz Kleinberger, *Society, Schools, and Progress in Israel* (Oxford, England: Pergamon Press, 1969), 3 1; and Bentwich, *Education in Israel,* 14.

35. Joseph Blasi, *The Communal Experience of the Kibbutz* (New Brunswick, NJ: Transaction Books, 1986), 116; and Elaine M. Solowey, "The Kibbutz in One Easy Lesson,"

Distant Star: The Electronic Magazine of the First Millennial Foundation, November 1996 [journal on-line]; available from <http://www.distant-star.com/issue1/dsfeat3.html>; Internet accessed 2 January 1998, 1.

36. Solowey, "The Kibbutz in One Easy Lesson," 1; Audrey Beth Stein, *Sexual Equality on the Israeli Kibbutz: Ideology, Reality, and the Future,* unpublished paper (December 1996); available from <http://www.stwing.upenn.edu~abstein/kibbutz/introduction.html>; Internet accessed 2 January 1998, 3; and Henry Near, *The Kibbutz Movement: A History,* vol. I: *Origins and Growth, 1909–1939* (Oxford, England: Published for the Littman Library by Oxford University Press, 1992), 81.

37. Bertha Hazan, "Introduction," in *Collective Education in the Kibbutz from Infancy to Maturity,* ed. A. I. Rabin and Bertha Hazan (New York: Springer Publishing Company, Inc., 1973), 4.

38. B. Katznelson, ed., quoting Joseph Bussel, *The Kvutza* (Heb.) (Tel Aviv, 1924), in Near, *The Kibbutz Movement: A History: Origins and Growth,* ftn. 88, 50.

39. Boris Stern, *The Kibbutz That Was* (Washington, DC: Public Affairs Press, 1965), 118; and Near, *The Kibbutz Movement: Origins and Growth,* 51.

40. Near, *The Kibbutz Movement: Origins and Growth,* 51.

41. Ibid., 91.

42. Bentwich, *Education in Israel,* 113.

43. Melford E. Spiro, with the assistance of Audrey G. Spiro, *Children of the Kibbutz* (New York: Schocken Books, 1965), 16; Near, *The Kibbutz Movement: and Growth,* 367; and Stein, *Sexual Equality on the Israeli Kibbutz,* 1.

44. Near, *The Kibbutz Movement: Origins and Growth,* 237.

45. Bruno Bettelheim, *The Children of the Dream* (New York: Macmillan, 1969), 131; and Bentwich, *Education in Israel,* 113.

46. Examples given by Stern include Degania Alef and Bet, Gesher Aziv, Ein Herod, Netzer Cyrani, Kfar Blum, and Ashdot Yakov.

47. Near, *The Kibbutz Movement: Origins and Growth,* 378.

48. In the beginning there were three major kibbutz federations: HaShomer HaZair Kibbutz Federation (Kibbutz Artzi), HaKibbutz HaMeuchad, and Ichud HaKvutzot vehaKibbutzim. The United Kibbutz Movement (Takam) was formed by Ichud and Meuchad. In 1997, 60 percent of the total kibbutz population belonged to Takam, 32 percent to Kibbutz Artzi, 6 percent to HaKibbutz HaDati (a religious Orthodox kibbutz federation), and 2 percent to a variety of other federations including Poalei Agudat Israel (religious), one communist kibbutz, United Synagogue (Kibbutz Hanaton) (Conservative), and a Reform kibbutz. International Communal Studies Association, Yad Tabenkin: Research and Documentation Center of the United Kibbutz Movement; available from <http://www.ic.org/icsa/#kibbutz.html>; Internet accessed 7 January 1998, 7.

49. Zvi Lavi, ed., *Kibbutz Members Study Kibbutz Children* (New York: Greenwood Press, 1990), 51; and Peter B. Newbauer, ed., *Children in Collectives: Child-Rearing Aims and Practices in the Kibbutz* (Springfield, IL: Charles C. Thomas Publisher, 1965), 71.

50. Gideon Lewin, "Early Childhood and Latency: Problems of Early Childhood: Infancy in Collective Education," in *Children in Collectives,* 72.

51. Near, *The Kibbutz Movement: Origins and Growth,* 237; Frieda Katz and Gideon Lewin, "Early Childhood Education," in *Collective Education in the Kibbutz from Infancy to Maturity,* ed. A. I. Rabin and Bertha Hazan (New York: Springer Publishing Company, Inc., 1973), 21–22; and Spiro, *Children of the Kibbutz,* 9.

52. The *Histadrut* is the federation of all the *kibbutzim* in Israel. It employed the teachers and sent them to the individual *kibbutz.*

53. Near, *The Kibbutz Movement: Origins and Growth,* 239.

54. Blasi, *The Communal Experience of the Kibbutz,* 122.

55. Miriam Roth, "The Kindergarten," in *Collective Education in the Kibbutz from Infancy to Maturity,* 44–45; and Avima Lombard, "Early Schooling in Israel," in *Early Schooling in England and Israel,* ed. Norma D. Feshbach, John I. Goodlad, and Avima Lombard (New York: McGraw-Hill Book Company -I/D/E/A/-A Charles F. Kettering Foundation Program, 1973), 78.

56. *Children Grow Up with Their Peer Group;* available from <http://www.israel-mfa.gov.il/facts/soc/kibbutz.html>; Internet accessed 2 January 1998.

57. Solowey, "The Kibbutz in One Easy Lesson," 2; and Bentwich, *Education in Israel,* 113.

58. Lavi, *Kibbutz Members Study Kibbutz Children,* 53; and *Children Grow Up with Their Peer Group,* 5.

59. Mordecai Kaffman, Esther Elizur, and Margalit Rabinowitz, "Early Childhood in the Kibbutz: The 1980s," in *Kibbutz Members Study Kibbutz Children,* 32–33.

60. A. I. Rabin and Benjamin Beit-Hallahmi, *Twenty Years Later: Kibbutz Children Grown Up* (New York: Springer Publishing Company, Inc., 1982), 195.

61. Lavi, *Kibbutz Members Study Kibbutz Children,* 52–53.

62. Newbauer, *Children in Collectives,* 81; Yair Palgi and Amiram Raviv, "The Perception of Family-Environmental Characteristics in Kibbutzim: A Comparison between the Two Sleeping Arrangements," in *Kibbutz Members Study Kibbutz Children,* 64–71; Yehoshua Gilad, "Development of the Educational System in One Kibbutz [Five Years after the Introduction of Conventional Sleeping Arrangements for Children]" in *Kibbutz Members Study Kibbutz Children,* 61; and Solowey, "The Kibbutz in One Easy Lesson," 3.

63. Kaffman, Elizur, and Rabinowitz, "Early Childhood in the Kibbutz: The 1980s," 17.

64. Melford E. Spiro, *Kibbutz: Venture in Utopia* (New York: Schocken Books, 1970), 124.

65. S. N. Eisenstadt, D. Weintraub, and N. Toren, "Analysis of Processes of Role Change," in *Twenty Years Later: Kibbutz Children Grown Up,* ed. A. I. Rabin and Benjamin Beit-Hallahmi (New York: Springer Publishing Company, Inc., 1982), 205.

66. Rabin and Beit-Hallahmi, *Twenty Years Later: Kibbutz Children Grown Up,* 211.

67. Spiro, *Children of the Kibbutz,* 17.

68. Blasi, *The Communal Experience of the Kibbutz,* 130.

69. Near, *The Kibbutz Movement: Origins and Growth,* 381.

70. Menachem Gerson and Alisa Schnabl-Brandes, "The Educational Approach of the Metapelet of Young Children in the Kibbutz," in *Kibbutz Members Study Kibbutz Children,* ed. Zvi Lavi (New York: Greenwood Press, 1990), 47, 49.

71. Lavi, *Kibbutz Members Study Kibbutz Children,* 53.

72. Blasi, *The Communal Experience of the Kibbutz,* 127.

73. Edith H. Grotberg, "Institutional Responsibilities for Early Childhood Education," in *Early Childhood Education 71st Yearbook of the National Society for the Study of Education, Part II,* ed. Ira J. Gordon (Chicago: University of Chicago Press, 1972), 326–327.

74. Charles Siegel, "The Brave New World of Child Care," originally published in *New Perspectives Quarterly;* available from <http://www.preservenet.com/BraveNew.html>; Internet accessed 2 January 1998, 4, 5, 8, 9.

75. Sandra Scarr, *Mother Care/Other Care* (New York: Basic Books, 1984), 218.

76. R. Porat, *The History of the Kibbutz: Communal Education 1904–1939* (Norwood, PA: Ablex, 1985), 132–133; Verbal Remarks by Professor Moshe Kerem, in *The Kibbutz Movement: Origins and Growth,* ftn. 5, 240; and Troen and Ackerman, "Israel," 344.

77. Scarr, *Mother Care/Other Care,* 219.

78. Roland S. Barth, *Open Education and the American School* (New York: Agathon Press, Inc. [Schocken Books], 1972), 59, Jean Jacques Rousseau, "Emile," in *Open Education and the American School,* 62; James B. Macdonald, "Perspective on Open Education: A Speculative Essay," in *Studies in Open Education,* ed. Bernard Spodek and Herbert J. Walberg (New York: Agathon Press [Schocken Books], 1975), 49; Susan Christie Thomas and Herbert J. Walberg, "An Analytic Review of the Literature," in *Studies in Open Education,* 27; George S. Morrison, *Early Childhood Education Today,* 7th ed. (Upper Saddle River, NJ: Merrill (an imprint of Prentice-Hall), 1998), 86; and Lillian Weber, *The English Infant School and Informal Education* (Englewood Cliffs, NJ: Prentice-Hall, 1971), 70.

79. Weber, *The English Infant School and Informal Education,* 161.

80. Institute for the Development of Educational Activities [/I/D/E/A/], *The British Infant School: Report of an International Seminar. /I/D/E/A/'s Early Childhood Series,* vol.

one (Dayton, OH: Author, 1969), 5; Bernard Spodek, "Open Education: Romance or Liberation?," in *Studies in Open Education*, 7; Macdonald, "Perspective on Open Education: A Speculative Essay," 48–52; Morrison, *Early Childhood Education Today*, 7th ed., 86; and Weber, *The English Infant School and Informal Education*, 170.

81. Charlotte Winsor provides a descriptive, firsthand account of Dewey's work at Columbia University, as well as the beginnings of several progressive schools. She touches on such institutions as the Horace Mann, Lincoln, Dalton, City and County, and Walden Schools. Also described are the Little Red Schoolhouse and the Bank Street School for Children. Charlotte B. Winsor, "Early Progressive Schools—II," in *Roots of Open Education in America*, ed. Ruth Dropkin and Arthur Tobier (New York: The City College Workshop Center for Open Education, December 1976), 135–147.

82. Eliot W. Eisner, *English Primary Schools: Some Observations and Assessments* (Washington, DC: National Association for the Education of Young Children, 1974), 78, 81–83; D. Keith Osborn, *Early Childhood Education in Historical Perspective*, 3d ed., (Athens, GA: Education Associates: A Division of the Daye Press, Inc., 1991), 158; Morrison, *Early Childhood Education Today*, 7th ed., 86; Bernard Spodek, "Extending Open Education in the United States," in *Open Education: The Legacy of the Progressive Movement: Proceedings of a Conference Sponsored by the National Association for the Education of Young Children* [Developed and Chaired by Bernard Spodek], ed. Georgianna Engstrom (Washington, DC: National Association for the Education of Young Children, 1970), 7; and Barbara Day, *Open Learning in Early Childhood* (New York: Macmillan Publishing Company, Inc., 1975), 6.

83. Weber, *The English Infant School and Informal Education*, 171.

84. The Plowden Report contained a number of specific recommendations about schooling for young children. The primary recommendation was for the immediate expansion of nursery schools, in order to make this schooling available to all children from the age of three until the age of compulsory schooling, by the late 1970s. The report recommended that all state-supported facilities for children aged three to five should include an educational component in their program and come under the jurisdiction of the Department of Education and the Local Education Authorities. This meant that the local health authority nurseries would eventually come under the jurisdiction of the Department of Education and that the ministries of Health and Education would work together in joint planning of all services for young children, including nursery schooling. The report advised that all nursery groups have one qualified teacher for every sixty children and one trained nursery assistant for every ten children. Nursery classes attached to infant schools were to be considered a regular part of those schools. The report also discussed early compensatory training for children from economically deprived backgrounds, and those with language difficulties and with potential learning difficulties. Norma D. Feshbach, John I. Goodlad, and Avima Lombard, *Early Schooling in England and Israel* (New York: McGraw-Hill Book Company [/I/D/E/A/-A] Charles F. Kettering Foundation Program, 1973), 48–49.

85. Volume I of the report dealt with the committee's general observations and recommendations. The second volume, entitled *Research and Surveys*, included statistical tables, and appendices. Lady Bridget Plowden, *Children and Their Primary Schools: A Report of the Central Advisory Council for Education*, Volume I Report, Volume II Research and Surveys (London: Her Majesty's Stationery Office, 1966–1967), passim.

86. Barth, *Open Education and the American School*, 252–253.

87. Ibid., 9; Weber, *The English Infant School and Informal Education*, 122–125; and Eisner, *English Primary Schools: Some Observations and Assessments*, 42.

88. Children in nursery schools range from three to four years of age. Children in infant schools are five to seven years of age. The infant school combined with the junior school is called the primary school. Students in junior schools range from seven to eleven years of age. Weber, *The English Infant School and Informal Education*, 47.

89. Weber, *The English Infant School and Informal Education*, 47.

90. Bernard Spodek, "Open Education: Romance or Liberation?," 5.

91. Thomas and Walberg, "An Analytic Review of the Literature," 16–19.

92. Barth, *Open Education and the American School*, 55–56; and Ellis D. Evans, *Contemporary Influences in Early Childhood Education*, 2d ed. (New York: Holt, Rinehart, and Winston, Inc., 1975), 291–292.

93. James B. Macdonald, "Perspective on Open Education," 57.

94. Weber, *The English Infant School and Informal Education,* 70, 77.

95. Ibid., 33–34, 80–81; Evans, *Contemporary Influences in Early Childhood Education,* 2d ed., 296–297; Eisner, *English Primary Schools,* 36; and [/I/D/E/A/], *The British Infant School: Report of an International Seminar,* 4.

96. Weber, *The English Infant School and Informal Education,* 37; and Eisner, *English Primary Schools,* 38.

97. The practice of cooperative projects in the United States is described by Kilpatrick in one of his books. William Heard Kilpatrick, *The Project Method: The Use of the Purposeful Act in the Educational Process* (New York: Teachers College Press, 1925). See Chapter 8 of this volume for a fuller discussion of Kilpatrick's work.

98. Eisner, *English Primary Schools,* 48–49, 52, 73; Weber, *The English Infant School and Informal Education,* 90–94; Evans, *Contemporary Influences in Early Childhood Education,* 2d ed., 293–294; and [/I/D/E/A/], *The British Infant School: Report of an International Seminar. /I/D/E/A/'s Early Childhood Series Volume One,* 5.

99. Eisner, *English Primary Schools,* 24–25, 42; Weber, *The English Infant School and Informal Education,* 104–113; and Barth, *Open Education and the American School,* 64–107.

100. Eisner, *English Primary Schools,* 78, 83.

101. Joseph Featherstone, "Dewey's Synthesis: Science and Feeling," in *Roots of Education in America,* ed. Ruth Dropkin and Arthur Tobier (New York: The City College Workshop Center for Open Education, December 1976), 124–125.

102. Macdonald, "Perspective on Open Education," 52.

103. Courtney B. Cazden, *Infant School* (Newton, MA: Education Development Center, 1969), quoted in Douglas N. Hubbard, John Salt, and Courtney B. Cazden, "The Teacher as Senior Partner," in *The Open Classroom Reader,* ed. Charles E. Silberman (New York: Random House, 1973), 252–263, passim. See: Selma Wasserman and J. W. George Ivany, *The New Teaching Elementary Science: Who's Afraid Spiders?,* 2d ed. (New York: Teachers College Press, 1996); Selma Wasserman, *Serious Players in the Primary Classroom: Empowering Children through Active Learning Experiences* (New York: Teachers College Press, 1990); Lilian G. Katz and Sylvia C. Chard, *Engaging Children's Minds: The Project Approach* (Norwood, NJ: Ablex, 1989). It is interesting to note that although these three books were published in the United States, their authors were born in British Commonwealth Countries.

104. Day, *Open Learning in Early Childhood,* 1–2; and Morrison, *Early Childhood Education Today,* 7th ed., 87.

105. Lillian Weber, "Development in Open Corridor Organization: Intent and Reality," *The National Elementary Principal* LII, no. 3 (November 1972): 58–67, in *The Open Classroom Reader,* 469–470.

106. Ibid., 473.

107. Weber, "Development in Open Corridor Organization," 479–480.

108. Ibid., 474; and Spodek, "Extending Open Education in the United States," 74.

109. Bernard Spodek and Theodore Manolakes, "In-Class Teacher Training in Open Education," in *Studies in Open Education,* 194–195.

PART IV

Professional Organizations and Conclusions

CHAPTER 20

Professional Organizations and Their Programs

> We early educators must assume the responsibility
> for planting the seeds for peace and peacefulness.
> —Evangeline H. Ward[1]

ASSOCIATION FOR CHILDHOOD EDUCATION INTERNATIONAL (ACEI)

On July 15, 1892, at Saratoga Springs, New York, the Association for Childhood Education International was born as the International Kindergarten Union (IKU). The proposal of Sarah A. Stewart of Philadelphia to make some formal organization of the kindergarten interests throughout the country was deemed "desirable." A committee was formed at the morning meeting which recommended "the organization of a National Kindergarten Union, which would in no way antagonize the Kindergarten Department of the National Education Association, but would act in sympathy and harmony with it, only extending the field of work more widely than the department had as yet been able to do." After discussion, it was decided that the International Kindergarten Union would have as its aims: gathering and disseminating knowledge of the kindergarten movement throughout the world; bringing all kindergarten interests into active cooperation; promoting the establishment of kindergartens; and elevating the standard of professional training of the kindergartners.

The *First Circular Letter* of the IKU, published in 1892, reiterated its function of "uniting in one stream" the already existing kindergarten activities. The organizers vowed to establish a high standard of training, which would direct training schools in the future preparation of teachers. They believed that the time was past when "anybody can teach little children." They felt that the kindergartner must take her place with other trained professional teachers. She must be able to see that "principles are more than method, spirit more than form, and organic relations to other departments of education of vital importance to success in her own." The work of the International Kindergarten Union would be: "to prepare an outline of study, to advise its adoption, and to give aid and counsel, whenever they are sought."[2]

The first president of the new organization, which broke from the NEA after eight years as a separate department, was Sarah Cooper of California. The Executive Committee members were charged with arranging for a fitting representation of kindergarten ideas and work at the Columbian Exposition of 1893, and taking the necessary steps to fully complete the organization of the IKU. The thirty charter members were joined by thirty-nine additional dues paying members and nine groups of kindergarten teachers that affiliated as branches during the ensuing year.[3]

An 1898 report of the Committee on Training Classes found the IKU developing into a common meeting ground for exchange of views and threshing out problems by "conservative" and "liberal" groups within the organization. At the 1900 IKU meeting in Brooklyn, New York, a committee resolution recognized the "service the IKU has rendered to the kindergarten cause in making it possible to have free and impersonal discussions of vital questions, believing that through candid presentation of different phases of work from many standpoints must come clearer insight, truer progress, and ultimately a general acceptance of the kindergarten idea."[4] As discussed in Chapter 9, the dichotomy led to the formation of the Committee of Nineteen, which explored the entire field of ideas about kindergarten training and operation methods in order to formulate a clear statement about contemporary kindergarten thought. A realistic look at the practices under discussion revealed beliefs too much at variance to permit reconciliation.[5] Thus, both

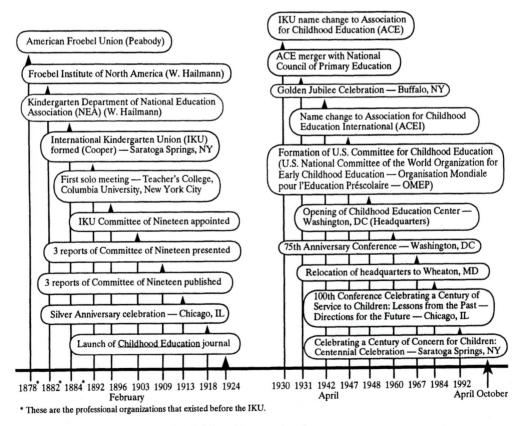

Figure 20.1 Association for Early Childhood International.

the 1909 committee reports and the related 1913 publication stated three separate viewpoints.

The ensuing years saw discussions and debates about child study and a variety of other controversial topics at the conferences and in the publications of the IKU. The establishment of a Washington, D.C., headquarters, and the launching of the organization's journal, *Childhood Education,* in 1924, provided for better communication among the membership and between the IKU and other governmental and nongovernmental entities. In adopting a new constitution in 1930, the organization changed its name to Association for Childhood Education (Nursery—Kindergarten—Primary), to better depict its membership. The following year, the National Council of Primary Education merged with the ACE. In 1947, the organization underwent another name change, to become in name what it had been in fact from the beginning, the Association for Childhood Education International.[6]

ACE participated in the formation of two other early childhood education organizations in the United States during the time period 1925 to 1950. At its 1927 meeting in New Haven, Connecticut, it heard the reports of the IKU Committees on Nursery Education (chaired by Lois Hayden Meek), Nursery Curriculum (chaired by Ada Hart Arlitt), and the "Report of Conference on Nursery Schools" (given by Patty Smith Hill). Although the Advisory Committee formed in 1926 reported that "in the interest of the movement for improved childhood education, there should be no nursery school organization at the present time,"[7] the National Association for Nursery Education was formed shortly thereafter. In 1948, the ACEI supported the formation of the U.S. Committee for Childhood Education, which became the United States National Committee of the World Organization for Early Childhood Education (Organisation Mondiale pour l'Education Préscolaire—OMEP). ACE participated fully in the mobilization for service to children during both world wars.

In 1950, attendees at the ACEI Annual Study conference in Asheville, North Carolina, participated in a demonstration of equal opportunity for participants, of all races, creeds and national origins in hotels, dining rooms, transportation facilities, and other venues. Assurance of similar provision was required of all groups inviting future ACEI conferences.[8] Wortham notes that black members' concerns about discriminatory practices at annual conferences first appeared in 1931 Executive Board minutes. The Executive Board of 1931 "did not feel it could take action to put pressure on local agencies regarding discrimination"; however they did pass a motion asking the chair of the local arrangements committee for a Washington, D.C., conference to "interview the manager of the Willard Hotel and ask him to see that all delegates receive courteous treatment." In 1933, the ACEI held a dinner at "the Negro Normal" in Nashville, Tennessee. However, the Executive Board minutes recount that "the treatment of the Negro at conventions depended on the town in which the convention was held and how all Negroes were treated in that town."[9]

At the ACEI's 1949 Executive Board meeting in Salt Lake City, Utah, the board denied the appeal of three states for a segregated ACEI State Association and addressed the request from "a Negro Branch in Washington, D.C., to the effect that a resolution be passed requiring that ACEI annual conferences be held only in cities where all registrants can enjoy the same rights and privileges as American citizens." When the association met in Asheville, the city was prepared by ACEI members, who stressed "the international character of the Association and the likelihood of having representatives of many cultures from abroad as well as America's own Negroes in attendance."[10] Bain concludes that "ACEI was well in advance of the Supreme Court decision that racial segregation in schools is unconstitutional and all the subsequent protests and test cases leading at long last to passage by congress of the Civil Rights Bill in 1964."[11]

The new headquarters building in Washington, D.C., opened to great fanfare on February 22, 1960. The Childhood Education Center had been eight years in the planning and building. It became a "laboratory for the ACEI program of action for adults who work with children,"[12] as well as the repository of the organization's archives, a demonstration center for educational equipment and materials, and home of the publications and other ACEI offices. In the mid-1960s, it housed a Resource Room designed to educate Head Start staff about appropriate early education materials. Many committee meetings, programs, and working sessions took place in the building during ACEI's twenty-five-year occupancy. As a result of declining economic and membership totals, the association sold the building and moved to Wheaton, Maryland, in 1984. The ACEI celebrated its centennial with a return to Saratoga Springs, New York. At the Centennial Celebration, leaders of past and present shared their ACEI memories with the participants. The exhibits highlighted the fact that over the past decade, ACEI journals and publications have played an important role in childhood education. As Edmund Wehrle wrote, "Throughout its one hundred year journey the ACEI has maintained its essential commitment to children's education. . . . Having largely accomplished its founding goal of spreading kindergartens across North America, new problems and challenges have taken the forefront. But the progressive spirit and dedication to education as a force for betterment has remained constant."[13]

NATIONAL ASSOCIATION FOR THE EDUCATION OF YOUNG CHILDREN (NAEYC)

The increased number of nursery schools organized between 1920 and 1925 brought about an interest among the practitioners to meet and exchange experiences and ideas, and to develop standards for programs.

Early Beginnings (1925–1945)

According to Mary Dabney Davis,[14] Professor Patty Smith Hill, of Teachers College, Columbia University, held three informal meetings during 1925 to discuss common concerns. At the last of these meetings, it was decided to hold a conference in Washington, D.C., in February 1926, for all those interested (106).

The discussions at the first meeting were about "the functions of nursery schools, their part in the total educational program, their service to parent education, and their programs for health and welfare" (107). (These concerns are still discussed today among the practitioners but are stated differently.) There were reports of existing programs. At the conclusion of the conference, an Advisory Committee on Nursery Education was appointed and charged with responsibility to study the situation.

A second conference was held in the spring of 1927, in New York City, attended by 225 people from 24 states, the District of Columbia, Hawaii, and England. They represented teachers and directors of nursery schools, college staff, kindergarten teachers, parent educators, social workers, and directors of day nurseries and play groups. A subcommittee was appointed to prepare a statement of "Minimum Essentials for Nursery Education" to be used as a guide for workers (107).

In the third meeting in Chicago in 1929, there was a "brisk" debate among those attending about whether to join an existing organization—the International Kindergarten Union—or to form a separate organization specifically for nursery school professionals. It was decided to form an independent

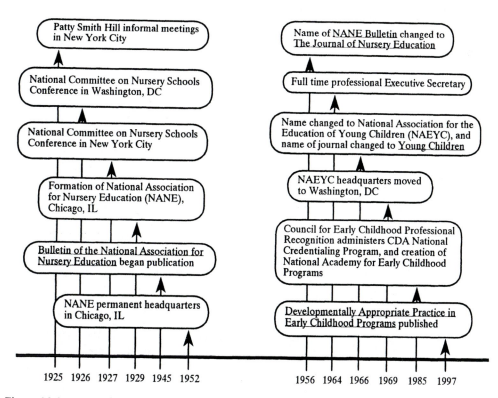

Figure 20.2 National Association for the Education of Young Children.

organization, the National Association for Nursery Education (NANE). The National Committee on Nursery Schools was assigned to draw up a constitution and bylaws for the new organization. The biennial meetings continued. Immediately, the new organization issued "Minimum Essentials for Nursery Education" (1929). It was followed in 1935 by a comprehensive bibliography (108).

NANE cooperated with the Association for Childhood Education (ACE) to prepare and conduct meetings held during annual conferences of the school administrators. For several years, NANE prepared a section on nursery education for the ACE journal *Childhood Education* (108). At times the two organizations competed, as often happens between similar organizations to the present time.

During the 1930s and up until the mid-1940s, as was discussed in Chapter 12, NANE joined with the Association for Childhood Education and the National Council of Parent Education and formed the National Advisory Committee of Emergency Nursery Schools. It helped with the organization of the Emergency Nursery Schools, a federal government–sponsored program.

Middle Years

According to Hewes,[15] in the 1950s, membership had dwindled and NANE realized the need to be updated if it was going to survive. It could no longer rely on volunteers to run the office. A permanent office was needed with a professional staff. In 1953, NANE acquired an office in Chicago with a half-time secretary. A lawyer volunteered his services to straighten out the legal matters and to incorporate NANE as a "not-for-profit corporation" in Illinois, a status held to this day (471).

Between 1956 and 1966, the membership jumped from less than one thousand to more than six thousand. In 1964, for the first time, there was a full-time professional executive secretary, Milton Akers. Grant money from the Grant Foundation, the Sears Roebuck Foundation, and other sources provided much needed assistance. The NANE office was relocated to New York City. As Head Start focused the nation's attention to the preschool child, it was decided to move to Washington, D.C. The headquarters on 1834 Connecticut Avenue was purchased in 1969 (472). Today, the NAEYC is located at 1509 16th Street, NW, Washington, D.C. The present membership is over 100,000 in 435 affiliate groups and growing.

Name Change

According to Hewes, the name change in 1964 from National Association for Nursery Education to National Association for the Education of Young Children (NAEYC) signaled several things: the commitment of the association to invest in a paid staff to provide services with the continued support of volunteers; increased attention to promotion and services through a journal and other publications; implementation of a nationwide Affiliate Group structure to implement growth through group involvement; and a name that better reflected the interests of membership.[16]

Publications

One of the strengths of NAEYC has been its publications, beginning in 1929 and continuing to date with books, pamphlets, posters, and videos. In 1945, NANE established the *NANE Bulletin,* a professional publication for early childhood educators. The early issues of the *Bulletin* were mimeographed, stapled together, and mailed to the membership four times a year. In 1956, the name of the publication was changed to *Journal of Nursery Education,* with Docia Zavitkovsky as the editor for the next ten years. The volunteers who published the *Journal* were gradually replaced by paid professionals.

In 1964, the name of the *Journal* was changed again to *Young Children,* and the first issue made its debut at the 1964 annual conference. Following this reorganization, NAEYC has experienced a tremendous growth.

In 1985, NAEYC created the National Academy of Early Childhood Programs, and the Council for Early Childhood Professional Recognition to administer the CDA National Credentialing program.

Today, NAEYC is staffed by professionals and volunteers, has several programs for professional development, and has a strong voice on behalf of children in advocacy and policy-making.

Developmentally Appropriate Practice

The publication of *Developmentally Appropriate Practice in Early Childhood Programs Serving Children from Birth through Age 8 (DAP)* in 1986 heralded a new focus in early childhood education. The original publication, with its list of appropriate and inappropriate practices, caused much ferment both in the research institutions and in classrooms for young children. As a result of many committee and individual interactions, the revised edition appeared in 1997.[17] NAEYC defined developmentally appropriate programs as those that contribute to child development. The NAEYC position statement says that developmentally appropriate practices result from the process of professionals making decisions about the well-being and education of children based on: what is known about child development and learning; what is known about the strengths, interests, and needs of each individual child in the group; and knowledge of the social and cultural contexts in which children live.[18] The guidelines include: creation of a caring community of learners, teaching to enhance development and learning, construction of appropriate curriculum, assessing children's learning and development, and establishing reciprocal relationships with families. The themes of building upon what a child knows and is able to do and establishing collaborative relationships appear throughout.[19]

The most recent *DAP* volume highlights the polarization that sometimes appears in the field. It attempts to move from "either/or" thinking to "both/and" thinking, and provides numerous examples. One is "children construct their own understanding of concepts *and* they benefit from instruction by more competent peers and adults."[20]

Questions from professionals in the field have encouraged a reconceptualization of the constructs of developmentally appropriate practices. The new *DAP* volume addresses concerns about the "push-down curriculum" of formalized instruction for young children, and skill-based instruction that is out of step with young children's development needs. The *DAP* document attempts to move early childhood education away from such inappropriate strategies as lecture, a preponderance of whole-group activities, direct instruction, drill and practice, workbooks and worksheets, and seat work. Instead it emphasizes the whole child and takes into account factors that require varied applications of curriculum. The developmentally appropriate curriculum is an interactive process in which the motivation for learning is derived from a child's natural curiosity.

Some have argued in the past that *DAP* did not meet the needs of culturally and otherwise diverse populations, perpetuating social inequity.[21] The 1997 revision attempts to address these concerns. NAEYC has revised the guidelines to reflect not only new knowledge but new political trends as well. The expanded definition of "developmentally appropriate" more clearly portrays the relationship among age, culture, and individual determinants of development.[22] The NAEYC Leading Edge Teleconference held in the spring of 1998 focused on cultural context and its relationship to *DAP*.

In addition to its focus on developmentally appropriate children's programs, the revised *DAP* document addresses professional issues. Among these is the necessity for a comprehensive professional preparation program that allows early childhood professionals to acquire the knowledge base and skills necessary for work in a developmentally appropriate classroom.[23] *DAP* addresses the continuum of possibilities for infants, toddlers, preschool children, and primary school children. The children and their adult caregivers are provided with a framework within which to formulate a program that meets individual and community needs.

Professional Programs of NAEYC

NAEYC has two affiliated professional organizations, the National Academy of Early Childhood Programs and the Council for Early Childhood Professional Recognition. Although each is headquartered in the NAEYC's Washington, D.C., building, they operate independently of the parent organization.

The National Academy of Early Childhood Programs

The National Academy of Early Childhood Programs grew out of a 1980 decision by the governing board of the NAEYC based on its concerns about the quality of early childhood programs across the country, the lack of uniform national standards, and the lack of a consensual definition of quality.

The idea of standards established and overseen by a professional organization was not new. In fact, ACEI publications have discussed quality kindergartens for over one hundred years, and NANE (forerunner of NAEYC) produced its first standards publication in 1929.[24] The ensuing publications outlined the minimal essentials for quality programs during the first fifty years of NANE and NAEYC's existence.[25] Over those first fifty years, the NAEYC publications addressed practitioners and parents together. Separate documents first appeared in the early 1980s. *How to Choose a Good Early Childhood Program* (1983) was designed to assist parents. The *Accreditation Criteria and Procedures of the National Academy of Early Childhood Programs* (1984) was aimed at professionals in the field of early childhood education. The accreditation publication placed NAEYC in a more proactive stance, because in addition to defining good practice, tools for evaluation were provided. Another difference between the publications of the 1980s and those of earlier decades was the emphasis upon staff qualifications. In both the *How to Choose* and *Accreditation Criteria and Procedures* publications, staff qualifications constituted the number one criterion, while in all previous brochures, child health and safety appeared first.[26]

A Steering Committee was formed in 1980 to explore the feasibility of a center-endorsement project.[27] Marilyn Smith, J. D. Andrews, and Sue Bredekamp, NAEYC staff members, worked with the project. Andrews proposed that NAEYC endorse child care centers, rather than certify adults or endorse colleges.[28]

Following the initial announcement at the NAEYC business meeting in 1980, the Steering Committee reviewed the literature on the effects of various program components on outcomes for children, existing systems, and organizational change. Meetings were held throughout the country during 1981 and 1982, and open hearings were held at the NAEYC Annual Conferences in 1982 and 1983, in order to receive comments about the accreditation system. In 1983 the name of the project was changed to the Center Accreditation Project (CAP).[29]

The concept of Center accreditation was embraced by many frontline teachers and directors who actively sought a way of demonstrating that their programs were of better quality than licensing required.[30] NAEYC made a serious financial as well as reputational commitment to the project. The first complete draft of the criteria appeared in *Young Children* in 1983 for membership review and comment, and the process was field tested.[31] From the first field test, it became clear that accreditation went beyond child care centers, and thus, CAP became the National Academy of Early Childhood Programs (NAECP). The system developed a separate identity from NAEYC. In 1984, the first edition of *Accreditation Criteria and Procedures of the National Academy of Early Childhood Programs* was published. It was based on the work of the Steering Committee, input from NAEYC organizational membership and members of the profession, and field testing in four areas of the United States. The criteria were officially adopted by NAEYC's Governing Board in July 1984.

The system began its official operation in 1985 with the publication of the *Guide to Accreditation by the National Academy of Early Childhood Programs,* and the availability of self-study materials. In September 1985, the month in which the first validation visit took place, NAEYC's journal *Young Children* published a synopsis of the system. The one-page summary included examples of how the accreditation system was being used across the country by child care centers, local task forces, and businesses, and provided an overview of the steps in the process.[32] From its beginnings up to the present date, the goals of the accreditation system were and are:

1. to help early childhood program personnel become involved in a process that will facilitate real and lasting improvement in the quality of the program serving young children, and
2. to evaluate the quality of the program for the purpose of accrediting those programs that substantially comply with the criteria for high-quality programs.[33]

The accreditation process includes three steps: a self-study conducted by program personnel; validators, early childhood professionals who verify the accuracy of the Program Description through an on-site visit; and a three-person Commission, which considers the validated Program Description and makes the accreditation decision.[34]

The first Commission decisions, in April 1986, accredited nineteen early childhood programs in thirteen states. They included "church-related and church-housed, Montessori, university-affiliated, corporate employer-sponsored, hospital-affiliated, parent cooperative, Title XX funded, private for-profit, [and] Piagetian," programs, "and a school for deaf children."[35] A thorough review was conducted during the first five years of the system's existence, generating several articles in *Young Children*.[36] They emphasized that the accreditation system is voluntary; therefore, center directors could set their own timelines. The self-study is self-paced, and therefore, centers could use it to make changes and improvements based on the center's goals and needs. In 1989, the Academy reviewed the accreditation criteria and proposed revisions and additions.[37] The revised criteria became available for use in July 1991.

The Academy initiated a multipronged approach to getting the system up and running. It trained validators, publicized the accreditation system, put organizational personnel and resources behind the tasks, and supported research relating to the development of the accreditation system.[38] It recognized the importance of all of the participant stakeholders in the process, including the Directors, Education Program Coordinators, and staff members of programs; Boards of Directors and sponsoring agencies; parents; and children. A 1993 survey of Directors' perceptions of the benefits of accreditation found that both the self-study and on-site validation visit were perceived to be beneficial; however, the self-study was rated as more beneficial.[39]

In their 1986 study, Bredekamp and Apple looked at the first ninety-five programs to be accredited. The components most frequently rated unacceptable in accredited programs were staff qualifications and development, health and safety, and developmentally appropriate activities that foster respect for cultural diversity and provision of multiracial and nonsexist materials. The components most frequently listed as unacceptable in deferred programs (those programs that had a validation visit but did not achieve accreditation) included curriculum, staffing, health and safety, and staff qualifications. They concluded that staff need immediate additional training in child development and early childhood education, specifically in the areas of fostering respect for diversity, systematic hand-washing procedures, fostering children's language development, and balancing teacher-directed and child-initiated activities.[40]

Some programs do not reach the stage of the validation visit, because they do not complete the self-study. Lack of time and staff turnover or program instability were the major reasons reported. Some indicated that the process of the self-study was overwhelming or that it was not a top priority within the program. The issue of lack of time, both perceived and real time constraints, might be addressed through local affiliate networking contacts, workshops, and journal articles. The area of professionalism could be addressed by promoting career ladders and training opportunities for individuals, offering updated grant information to support training, encouraging mentor-teacher initiatives, and striving for public awareness of the professional nature of services.[41]

The year 1989 marked the three-year anniversary of the system's operation. Some of the initially accredited programs required reaccreditation, in the spring of 1989, because it was necessary for reaccreditation to be completed before the current accreditation expired. In January 1990, the Academy looked at the reaccreditation process. *Young Children* reported that of the eighty-eight programs which were accredited by June 1986, 92 percent were participating actively in the accreditation system in 1989. Sixty-six percent of those programs had been reaccredited by the end of 1989. Among the conclusions reached by a limited survey of reaccredited programs were: that reaccreditation after three years is appropriate and that the process of self-study and validation is essential to both achieving high quality and maintaining it.[42]

It is important to look at the Academy accreditation process from the broader perspective of approaches to achieving quality in early childhood programs through nonregulatory and regulatory means.[43] Among the possible nonregulatory methods are: public education; training of caregivers and administrators; association memberships; newsletters, journals, and books; consultation with other professionals; and the development of resource-and-referral centers. The basic regulatory methods of achieving standards include: licensing or regulation, environmental and health codes, zoning approval, and building and fire safety rules. In most states, these constitute the baseline for licensing of early education programs. Higher levels of regulatory approval include: approval of publicly operated programs, fiscal regulation, credentialing, and accreditation. Although Morgan cites accreditation as the highest level of standard setting, Daniel cautions that it cannot be perceived as a panacea. The 1995 NAEYC president stated that, because NAEYC accreditation designation does not carry the legislated judicial authority, accreditation cannot stand in lieu of licensing.[44]

In September 1995, NAEYC held an invitational conference on accreditation in Wheaton, Illinois. Its purpose was to reflect on the past decade and apply the lessons learned to future goals and directions. The volume *NAEYC Accreditation: A Decade of Learning and the Years Ahead* was the result of the deliberations on the three conference themes: "(1) The effects of NAEYC accreditation on program quality and outcomes for children; (2) The lessons learned from accreditation, especially for supporting programs seeking accreditation and for ensuring that the system fully meets the needs of the diversity of children and families within our nation; and (3) The relationships between NAEYC accreditation and public policy."[45] The discussions and publications of the years 1995 through 1997 can be expected to impact upon the revisions to and future development of the accreditation criteria and procedures of the National Academy of Early Childhood Programs.

The National Institute for Early Childhood Professional Development

The National Institute for Early Childhood Professional Development was designed to address the need for high-quality staff in programs for children's care and education. As early as the 1970s, publications reflected research findings linking program quality with quality of the staff.[46] A two-year grant from the Carnegie Corporation of New York enabled NAEYC to initiate the Institute. Its primary purpose is to "improve the quality of early childhood services by improving the quality of professional preparation and training provided for individuals who care for and educate young children from birth through age eight. The overarching goal is to assist in the development and implementation of an effective, coordinated delivery system of early childhood professional preparation."[47] In announcing the launch of the Institute, NAEYC stated that a coordinated delivery system is an essential prerequisite to achieving viable career development for early childhood educators.

A preliminary professional development conference had been held in Miami, Florida, in January 1988. At that time, a revision of the guidelines for early childhood professional preparation programs at the higher education level was undertaken. One objective of this revision of the NCATE guidelines was to address the insufficient number of teachers with specialized early childhood preparation available to fill current positions in early childhood programs. Baccalaureate degree programs are dictated by state certification standards. There was (and is) considerable diversity among these programs. Leaders of the profession are prepared in baccalaureate and graduate degree granting institutions, and therefore the Institute stated that these institutions "play a vital role in ensuring the future of the early childhood profession."[48]

Another objective of the Institute was addressing the system for preparing nondegreed paraprofessional staff working in child care settings. A third objective was to establish guidelines for associate-degree granting institutions. The Institute pledged to address all of these barriers to providing a fully qualified work force for early childhood programs. The activities of the Institute were projected as:

- Improve quality of preservice and in-service preparation at all levels by developing standards and exploring the feasibility of developing a review system for professional preparation programs and trainers;
- Improve local capacity to advocate for and deliver effective training by developing leadership in communities;
- Develop and disseminate information and resources on effective models of professional preparation and training delivery systems;
- Coordinate professional development activity between NAEYC and the many other organizations working toward the same or similar goals;
- Advocate for federal and state policies in support of an accessible, coordinated delivery system of early childhood professional preparation and the necessary financial incentives to obtain preparation.[49]

The Institute was dedicated to standard setting, program review, leadership development, and information sharing through conferences and publications. The first Institute conference was held in Los Angeles, California, in June 1992. To date, there have been eight Institute leadership conferences.

The work on professional preparation guidelines begun in 1985 culminated in the 1996 publication of NAEYC's *Guidelines for Preparation of Early Childhood Professionals,*[50] containing three sets of collaboratively set standards: the NAEYC/Association of Teacher Educators (ATE), position statement on early childhood teacher certification (1991);[51] the ATE/Division for Early Childhood of the Council for Exceptional Children (DEC of CEC)/NAEYC guidelines for the preparation of Early Childhood Special Education professionals (1994); and the Draft Standards for National Board Certification for Early Childhood/Generalists. The National Board for Professional Teaching Standards (NBPTS) Early Childhood/Generalists Standards Committee disseminated the draft document in May 1994, resulting in its adoption in 1995.[52]

The Institute spent its first year conceptualizing a professional development system. It chose as its logo a lattice, which symbolized the career lattice of the early childhood professional. The lattice "communicates upward mobility with enhanced qualifications and improved compensation while also conveying horizontal movement across the various sectors" of the field.[53] Four major barriers to the achievement of an articulated professional development system were discussed. They included: regulatory barriers (child care licensing and teacher licensure and certification);[54] and institutional barriers among preparation programs. This barrier was addressed under the auspices of the Institute, beginning with the historic first joint meeting of the National Association of Early

Childhood Teacher Educators (NAECTE) and the American Associate Degree Early Childhood Educators (ACCESS) at the Institute's 1992 National Conference.[55] Work on lowering this barrier continues at the local, state, and national levels. Economic barriers, such as staff compensation, have been addressed by the Worthy Wage Campaign coordinated by the Child Care Employee Project and NAEYC's Full Cost of Quality Campaign.[56] The attitudinal barriers are perhaps the most difficult to circumvent. Lack of a shared nomenclature leads to communication problems. The previous lack of articulation of the shared core content knowledge base led to lack of definition. These issues were addressed during the first and second Institute conferences.[57]

Through its activities and annual leadership conference, the Institute has become a consensus-building force and a catalyst for change. Over the past eight years, it has begun to address the challenges posed by Bredekamp in her 1992 article, and it has made steady progress toward its initial goals. Standards setting, a priority of the Institute's first year, led to *Guidelines for Preparation of Early Childhood Professionals.*[58] Program review and approval became the priority of the second year, along with information sharing and dissemination.

Leadership development was the subject of the third annual Institute conference. The readings included the report of a National Black Child Development Institute (NBCDI) study, which found that although African-Americans are well represented as members of early childhood program staff and clientele, they are underrepresented at the leadership level. They have more professional experience, but less access to education and training than some other groups, which limits their upward mobility.[59] Leadership development has become a major effort of the Institute.[60]

By 1997, the Institute was ready to transform ideas into action, and made this the theme of the sixth annual conference.[61] States that had pioneered in developing coordinated training systems, developing professional registries, or statewide early childhood professional credentialing systems shared their expertise. The initial director credentialing initiatives of ten states, one religious group, and one national organization were highlighted. The implementation of these model programs and preliminary efforts have set the stage for the next phase of professional development in early childhood education in the United States.

The highlights of the *Quality 2000* initiative, reported in the September 1997 issue of *Young Children,* represent the wave of the future. Kagan and Neuman imagine a time when: quality in all family child care at center-based programs is expected and supported; staff can be flexible in using state-of-the-art strategies, technologies, and resources creatively and cost effectively;[62] all individuals working with children in early education programs have (or are actively in the process of obtaining) credentials related to their position; all staff are encouraged to pursue ongoing training and education; all training for early childhood positions is child and family focused, respecting cultural and linguistic diversity; all approved training bears credit, leads to increased credentials and compensation, and equips individuals for diverse and advanced roles.[63]

The *Quality 2000* report recommends four types of licensing standards and requirements: an administrator license, an educator license, an associate educator license, and an entry-level position requirement for all others working with young children.[64] Federal and state government initiatives announced in January 1998 dovetail the work of the Institute. Government, foundation, corporate, and other funding sources support the ongoing work. In many ways, the National Institute for Early Childhood Professional Development is rising to meet the challenges posed by Whitebook and Almy in 1986.

EVANGELINE HOWLETT WARD (1920–1985)

Evangeline Ward was born on April 12, 1920, in Portsmouth, Virginia. She attended all-black elementary and high schools that were located one block from her house.[65] She was one of the four students of the first kindergarten in the town, where she learned to read and write. These skills placed her in the second grade upon entering school. She completed elementary school at the age of eleven and high school at fifteen. After studying for a year at Shaw University, she entered Hampton Institute, where she majored in early childhood education and encountered Ida Jones Curry as an instructor. Curry had a bachelor's degree from Spelman College and a master's degree from Columbia College. She had studied with the McMillans in England, and was in charge of the Hampton nursery school. From her, Evangeline (Somerville) Jones "learned that there was such a thing as actual education of children below the age of six."[66] This realization led to Evangeline's senior project, which detailed the setting up of a nursery school. The project garnered her a graduate school scholarship for the master's program at Atlanta University in Georgia. She worked with the Spelman College Nursery School, and graduated at the age of twenty-one.

Ward dated the start of her career in early childhood education from 1941.[67] She was a public school teacher from 1941 to 1945. While she continued her education at Cornell University during the summers of 1948 and 1950, she taught first at Barber-Scotia College in North Carolina, and then at her alma mater (Hampton), where she became chair of the Department of Early Childhood Education. She remained at Hampton until 1953, when she became a doctoral student of Kenneth Wann at Teachers College of Columbia University. She received her Ed.D. in 1955, and later did postdoctoral work at Oxford University in England (1966) and at the University of St. Andrews in Scotland (1968).

Between 1955 and 1963, she was the executive director of the Nursery Foundation of St. Louis Day Care Service Agency. She married for the second time and gave birth to one son, David Nathaniel. In 1963, after her second divorce, she joined the faculty at Temple University, where she became a Full

Professor of Early Childhood Education.[68] She directed the Institute for Teachers of Young Disadvantaged Children at Temple, and led an early childhood study tour abroad in 1968. She remained on the faculty until her retirement in 1985.

Ward became involved in Head Start training in Philadelphia in conjunction with the Office of Economic Opportunity and the Model Head Start Training Center of the Philadelphia School District. During the 1960s, she recounted in an interview, she "did consulting all over the country in predominantly black communities . . . when Headstart Programs were opening. In these programs, I stressed the value of parents to many black professionals. Some of them did not understand parent's [sic] value and a lot of them still don't. Once some blacks get a few pennies and get above the poverty line, they get very strange ideas about dealing with folks at any other level. I felt that Head Start was a marvelous opportunity for some of us to get in there and promote participation with parents."[69] In a speech at a Follow Through Parent Involvement Workshop at College Station, Arkansas, in 1968, she said, "I frequently use the example of teaching as half of a process and parents and family are the most permanent and continuous teachers there are. Teaching is the part of the process that starts and cooperates with learning. It is nothing by itself. . . . If you are really teaching, the teaching is hung on the other person who is learning."[70]

In June 1975, Ward took a leave from her professional duties at Temple, to become the second executive director of the CDA Consortium. Shortly after she took office, the first credentials were awarded in a formal ceremony. She told the new Child Development Associates that "the ceremony and issuance of the first CDA Credentials represents a significant development in a profession which has begun to take charge of its own professionalism."[71]

Professional Commitments

Evangeline Ward was committed to service to her profession. She demonstrated this through her organizational involvement and professional publications.

The National Association for the Education of Young Children (NAEYC)

Ward stated that she gave twelve years of her life to NAEYC, serving on the local, state, and national levels, and as the national president from 1970 to 1974. She served on NAEYC's Governing Board longer than anyone else up to that time (from 1964 to 1976). She said: "I care about everything they do. I am not spending as much time with them as I used to because I have the notion that you must bring other people up through the system or it dies. There are too many old heads in there who have been in there forever. Young people would come in but they are not being given a fair chance. If people had not admitted us when we were young and green into the organization we would not have been able to do the things that we have done. So I feel very strongly about wanting to provide opportunities for new people to come into the organization."[72] Although she was not formally involved as an officer, Ward maintained an active presence at all local (Delaware Valley Association for the Education of Young Children [DVAEYC]) and national conferences until her sudden death. DVAEYC established a scholarship in her honor when she stepped down as national president, and she awarded the first one in person.

One of Ward's major contributions to NAEYC, and to the profession, was the development of the first formal Code of Ethics for the early childhood profession. An initial draft was shared at the 1976 DVAEYC Annual Conference. Those in attendance were challenged to share Ward's personal and professional "inquiry into the beginnings of a code of ethics for early childhood education."[73] A later draft of the code was shared in commemoration of Kenneth Wann, "an ethical man."[74]

In collaboration with Lilian Katz, she wrote about the importance of ethical responsibility and standards in the NAEYC publication *Ethical Behavior in Early Childhood Education*. This "Initial Code of Ethics for Early Childhood Educators" called upon members of the profession to respect the child, the parents, and family members; to admit biases on the way to becoming a conscious professional; to recognize their capacity to continue to learn throughout life; and to cooperate with persons and organizations to improve opportunities for children and families. The Code called upon administrators and directors with major responsibilities for a total program of services to "maintain the program by the highest known standards as if my own children were being served."[75] It called upon them to keep abreast of current and projected developments in the field, and to provide advancement opportunities for both self and staff members. A separate section for policy and decision makers reminded them to value ethical practices; to draw heavily on the opinions of parents and community leaders; and to "contribute to the ongoing review, evaluation, and modification of services as needed by the community, families and children."[76] This work was the precursor of both the current NAEYC Statement of Commitment and Code of Ethical Conduct and the current position statements and publications relating to Developmentally Appropriate Practices in Programs for Young Children.[77]

The World Organization or Early Childhood Education (OMEP)

Ward was an active participant in the United States National Committee (USNC) of OMEP, serving as Second Vice President and membership chair during the 1977–1978 academic year, and Vice President and President Pro Tempore from 1979 to 1980. She was the U.S. National President for 1980–1981 and became Past President during the next year. She was elected to the World Executive Council in 1982 and served as World Vice President. She remained a member of the World Executive Council until the day of her demise. One reason for her involvement with the World Organization was "to be sure that they know black people exist. I am an unofficial representative for blacks on the World Council."[78]

Education for Peace

Toward the end of her life, Ward began to speak about peace and social justice. Her papers contain notes on definitions of, quotes about, and poetry describing peace. She wrote that peace-making requires empathy for others, and that we can begin to train a generation for peace when people recognize the urgency of helping children to develop these attitudes and skills.[79]

Publications

Ward authored a variety of publications. Her earliest works discussed such practical topics as classroom space, materials, program ideas, and curriculum.[80] A later publication[81] focused on cultural context. Her expertise in teacher education was shared in "The Making of a Teacher: Many Disciplines." Ward utilized Soltis's idea of "unpeeling an onion," to conceptualize discovering meaning through in-depth exploration, as a mode for adult learning. She also highlighted teaching as an aesthetic experience, involving style, imagination, animation, and a feeling of unity.[82] As discussed above, her last professional work focused on ethical and peace issues.

Evangeline Ward died as she lived, a true professional. She had presented the keynote speech at the annual Australian Early Childhood Education Conference in Canberra on the day of her sudden death, October 10, 1985.[83] Memorial tributes flowed into Philadelphia and Washington, D.C., from around the globe. It can be said of Evangeline Howlett Ward, as she said of Kenneth Wann, that the professional lives of others are a perpetual memorial.

WORLD ORGANIZATION FOR EARLY CHILDHOOD EDUCATION (ORGANISATION MONDIALE POUR L'EDUCATION PRESCOLAIRE) (OMEP)

OMEP has been in existence since 1948. It is an international nongovernmental organization (NGO) that cooperates with other NGOs with similar aims. Its aim is to promote for every child, from birth to eight years, optimum conditions for his well-being, in the family and society. Many professionals from education, medicine, law, psychology, and social work belong to OMEP, as well as parents. A brief history of its creation follows.[84]

Creation of the Organization

Shortly after World War II, a conference was held in Zurich, Switzerland (1945), to discuss what should be done with the destitute and war-stricken children of Europe. Among the participants was Lady Majory Allen of Hurt-wood, Great Britain. She was a landscape architect by training, but her work for the children made her chairman of the British Nursery School Association. Through her marriage, to Lord Allen, Foreign Secretary, she had access to many influential persons all over the world.

Lady Allen was concerned that UNESCO, the new international organi-zation for education, science, and culture, did not intend to include the preschool age child in its field of activities. She advanced the idea that a new organization had to be founded, whose task should be to press UNESCO to include the preschool age in its activities.

Alva Myrdal of Sweden and Lady Allen invited like-minded persons to a meeting, in July 1946, to discuss the possibility for such an international orga-nization, for early childhood education. They felt that the formative years of the child must be one of the prime concerns of UNESCO working for devel-oping an international democratic culture. A Working Committee was formed, and a second meeting took place in November 1946. It was decided to invite more countries to participate, and the planned organization was named the World Council for Early Childhood. Dr. George Stoddard repre-sented the United States.

A series of preparatory meetings followed in various European cities to decide what kind of an organization they wanted to form. They also had talks with UNESCO. It was decided the organization was neither for professional teachers (they already had their unions) nor benevolent in character. It was to be an organization "for all organizations or people who are interested, or engaged in nursery school work."[85] It was also decided that no definition of the term "early childhood education" be given by the organization, since the term was defined differently in different countries, particularly what years it is supposed to include. At that time, there was a disparity of standards in early childhood education in different countries. Countries who attended these pre-liminary meetings were asked to send representatives to the organization. Meetings were held between UNESCO and the Working Committee, which became the Interim International Council on Early Childhood Education.

In the spring of 1947, the group was informed that UNESCO would hold a World Seminar on Early Childhood Education in July/August 1948 in Pode-brady, near Prague. The new organization planned to hold its first world meeting immediately after the UNESCO Seminar. The participants paid for their own expenses. Invitations to the first World Conference were sent to all countries including those who were not members of UNESCO, for six dele-gates. The draft of the organizational constitution was written during the first conference of the World Council for Early Childhood Education in August 1948. It was updated through the work of the Constitutional Commission headed by Dr. Evangeline Ward, at the World Assembly in Geneva, Switzer-land, in 1983.

Ever since that first meeting in 1948, OMEP has been organizing biennial and triennial World Assemblies and Congresses throughout the World. These have provided an international forum for the sharing of knowledge, ideas, and values that lead to recognition of the importance of the early years of childhood in building a strong foundation for peaceful international relations.

The World Council is the decision-making body composed of the presidents of the fifty-eight National Committees of OMEP. It also has a constitution.

National Committees

The National Committees are subgroups of OMEP. They are a diversified group. Some come under the leadership of government officials, and others are run entirely by volunteers (the U.S. National Committee is an example), or by independent/private groups. The main requirement is that membership should be representative of all aspects of work for the care and education of young children. There is only one National Committee in each country. There is a preparatory period before a National Committee becomes final and representative of the country. No member shall be excluded for the reason of race, creed, nationality, or political opinion.[86]

The National Committees report to the World Council and share their information and products at the World Assembly. OMEP also publishes the *International Journal of Early Childhood Education* twice a year.

OMEP/U.S. National Committee

The United States National Committee was established in 1948. It consists of individuals and organizations who are interested in the education and well-being of young children from birth to eight years. It contributes professional leadership at the local, state, and national levels. It holds national and regional meetings in conjunction with other early childhood conferences. It prepares and distributes publications, and a newsletter. It promotes special projects for the benefit of children. It is governed by bylaws reflecting the goals of OMEP. The board is made up of six officers and eight regional representatives.

Past and present activity committees include: development, history/archives, send a book, newsletter, and membership. In recent years, members of the U.S. National Committee have represented OMEP in the NGO meetings of the United Nations in New York City.

The United States was involved in the founding and is participating in the evolution of the World Organization for Early Childhood Education.

NOTES

1. Evangeline Ward, *For the Children's Tomorrow: Educate for Peace* (U.S. National Committee of the World Organization for Early Childhood Education, November 1985), 6.

2. In pamphlet, Association for Childhood Education International, *Celebrating a Century of Concern for Children: Centennial Celebration Program [October 1–4, 1992]* (Saratoga Springs, NY: Author).

3. "First Report of the International Kindergarten Union Organized at the 32d Annual Meeting of the National Educational Association at Saratoga Springs, July, 1892," in pamphlet, Association for Childhood Education International, *Celebrating a Century of Concern for Children: Centennial Celebration Program [October 1–4, 1992]* (Saratoga Springs, NY: Author); and Ira L. Smith, *Half a Century of Progress, 1892–1942* (Washington, DC: Association for Childhood Education, 1942), 84, 94.

4. Smith, *Half a Century of Progress, 1892–1942,* 87, 94.

5. Ibid., 94–95; Patty Smith Hill, "Kindergarten: History of the Association for Childhood Education," in *The American Educator Encyclopedia* (Chicago: United Educators, Inc., 1941; reprint, Washington, DC: ACEI, 1967), 1973–1976 (page citations are to the reprint edition); and Evelyn Weber, *The Kindergarten: Its Encounter with Educational Thought in America* (New York: Teachers College Press, 1969), 69.

6. Winifred Bain [& L. Hooper], *75 Years of Concerns for Children: A History of the Association for Childhood Education International* (Washington, DC: CEI, 1967), 78.

7. Smith, *Half a Century of Progress, 1892–1942,* 90.

8. Bain, *75 Years of Concerns for Children,* 78.

9. Sue Wortham, *Childhood, 1892–1992* (Wheaton, MD: Association for Childhood Education International, 1992), 38–39.

10. Bain, *75 Years of Concerns for Children,* 27.

11. Ibid., 30.

12. Ibid., 47.

13. Edmund Wehrle, *Back to Saratoga, 1892–1992: An Exhibit Celebrating One Hundred Years of the Association for Childhood Education* (College Park, MD: Historical Manuscripts and Archives Department, University of Maryland at College Park Libraries, 1992), 1.

14. Mary Dabney Davis, "How NANE Began," *Young Children* 20 (November 1964): 106–109. Eliot reported on the Ruggles Street Nursery School and Training Centre.

15. Dorothy Hewes, "NAEYC's First Half Century: 1926–1976," *Young Children* 31 (September 1976): 461–476. Article gives a detailed account of the NANE/NAEYC history.

16. Ibid., 472.

17. Sue Bredekamp, "Defining Standards for Practice: The Continuing Debate," in *Continuing Issues in Childhood Education,* 2d ed., ed. Carol Seefeldt and Alice Galper (Columbus, OH: Merrill, 1998), 179, 181–185.

18. Sue Bredekamp and Carol Copple, eds., *Developmentally Appropriate Practice in Early Childhood Programs,* rev. ed. (Washington, DC: National Association for the Education of Young Children, 1997), 8–9.

19. Ibid., 16–22.

20. Ibid., 23.

21. See, for example: Jan Jipson, "Developmentally Appropriate Practice: Culture, Curriculum, Connections," *Early Education and Development* 2, no. 2 (1991), 120–136; and Shirley A. Kessler and Beth Blue Swadener, eds., *Reconceptualizing the Early Childhood Curriculum: Beginning the Dialogue* (New York: Teachers College Press, 1992).

22. Craig Hart, Diane C. Burts, and Rosalind Charlesworth, eds., *Integrated Curriculum and DAP: Birth to Age Eight* (Albany: State University of New York Press, 1997), 2; and Gaye Gronlund, "Bringing the DAP Message to Kindergarten and Primary Teachers," *Young Children* 50, no. 5 (July 1995): 4–13.

23. Diane C. Burts and Teresa K. Buchanan, "Preparing Teachers in Developmentally Appropriate Ways to Teach in Developmentally Appropriate Classrooms," in *Continuing Issues in Childhood Education,* 2d ed., ed. Carol Seefeldt and Alice Galper (Columbus, OH: Merrill, 1998), 129–158.

24. Marcy Whitebook and Millie Almy, "NAEYC's Commitment to Good Programs for Young Children: Then and Now: A Developmental Crisis at 60?," *Young Children* 41, no. 6 (September 1986): 37.

25. Ibid., 38–39.

26. Ibid., 39.

27. Sue Bredekamp and Stephanie Glowacki, "NAEYC Accreditation: The First Decade of NAEYC Accreditation: Growth and Impact on the Field," *Young Children* 51, no. 3 (March 1996): 3 8; and Sue Bredekamp and Barbara A. Willer, ed., *NAEYC Accredi-*

tation: A Decade of Learning and the Years Ahead (Washington, DC: National Association for the Education of Young Children, 1996), 1.

28. Both personnel certification via the CDA credentialing process, and endorsement of college and university teacher preparation programs (through the folio review process of NCATE), occurred during other time periods.

29. Bredekamp and Glowacki, "The First Decade of NAEYC Accreditation: Growth and Impact on the Field," 2; and National Association for the Education of Young Children, *Accreditation Criteria & Procedures: Position Statement of the National Academy of Early Childhood Programs, A Division of the National Association for the Education of Young Children* (Washington, DC: Author, 1991), 11.

30. Bredekamp and Glowacki, "The First Decade of NAEYC Accreditation: Growth and Impact on the Field," 39.

31. Ibid., 40; Sue Bredekamp and Stephanie Glowacki, "The First Decade of NAEYC Accreditation: Growth and Impact on the Field," in *NAEYC Accreditation: A Decade of Learning and the Years Ahead,* 2.

32. National Association for the Education of Young Children, "National Voluntary Accreditation for Early Childhood Programs," *Young Children* 40, no. 6 (September 1985): 30.

33. NAEYC, *Accreditation Criteria & Procedures,* 1.

34. NAEYC, "National Voluntary Accreditation for Early Childhood Programs," 30.

35. Centers in Alaska, California, Georgia, Indiana, Kansas, Michigan, New Jersey, New York, Ohio, Texas, Washington, D.C., Virginia, and Washington were accredited. National Association for the Education of Young Children, "NAEYC Accredits Early Childhood Programs," *Young Children* 41, no. 5 (July 1986): 43.

36. See: National Association for the Education of Young Children, "Attention: Early Childhood Professionals: *Are You Interested in Becoming a Validator for NAEYC's National Academy of Early Childhood Programs?,*" *Young Children* 40, no. 6 (September 1985): 32; National Association for the Education of Young Children, "What Directors Need to Know About National Association for the Education of Young Children, *Guidelines for Preparation of Early Childhood Professionals: Guidelines Developed by the National Association for the Education of Young Children and the Division for Early Childhood of the Council of Exceptional Children and by the National Board for Professional Teaching Standards* (Washington, DC): National Association for the Education of Young Children, 1996)'s Accreditation System," *Young Children* 41, no. 3 (March 1986): 35–36; Sue Bredekamp and Peggy L. Apple, "How Early Childhood Programs Get Accredited: An Analysis of Accreditation Decisions," *Young Children* 42, no. 1 (November 1986): 34–37; Barbara Willer and Sue Bredekamp, "A 'New' Paradigm of Early Childhood Professional Development," *Young Children* 48, no. 4 (May 1993): 63–66; Blakely Fetridge Bundy, "*National Academy:* Achieving Accreditation: A Journal of One Program's Experience," *Young Children* 43, no. 6 (September 1988): 27–34; N. Catherine Norris, "The NAEYC Accreditation Process Isn't Really So Scary—Why Not Try It?," *Young Children* 49, no. 6 (September 1994): 72–74; National Association for the Education of Young Children, "*National Academy:* Accreditation: Who? What? When? Where? Why?," *Young Children* 42, no. 5 (July 1987): 57; and Roberta Recken, "*National Academy:* Accreditation Update: Who Gets Accredited?," *Young Children* 44, no. 2 (January 1989): 11.

37. National Association for the Education of Young Children, "*National Academy:* Academy Reviews Accreditation Criteria," *Young Children* 44, no. 6 (September 1989): 67–69.

38. Early research included the doctoral dissertation of Sue Bredekamp (Sue Bredekamp, "The Reliability and Validity of the Instruments Used in a National Accreditation System for Early Childhood Programs" [Ph.D. diss., University of Maryland, 1985]), and a 1986 study conducted by Bredekamp and Apple, "How Early Childhood Programs Get Accredited: An Analysis of Accreditation Decisions," 34–37.

39. Judy Herr, Renee Demars Johnson, and Karen Zimmerman, "Benefits of Accreditation: A Study of Directors' Perceptions," *Young Children* 48, no. 4 (May 1993): 32–35.

40. Bredekamp and Apple, "How Early Childhood Programs Get Accredited," 35–37.

41. Karen Talley, "National Accreditation: Why Do Some Programs Stall in Self-Study?," *Young Children* 52, no. 3 (March 1997): 32–33, 35–36.

42. National Association for the Education of Young Children, "*National Academy: Reaccreditation: A Snapshot of Growth and Change in High-Quality Early Childhood Programs*," *Young Children* 45, no. 2 (January 1990): 61.

43. Gwen Morgan, "Licensing and Accreditation: How Much Quality Is *Quality?*," in *NAEYC Accreditation: A Decade of Learning and the Years Ahead,* 130–131.

44. Jerlean Daniel "*From Our President:* Reflections on a Decade of NAEYC Accreditation," *Young Children* 51 no. I (November 1995): 2.

45. Barbara A. Willer, "Preface," in *NAEYC Accreditation: A Decade of Learning and the Years Ahead,* ed. Sue Bredekamp and Barbara A. Willer (Washington, DC: National Association for the Education of Young Children, 1996), v.

46. Whitebook and Almy, "NAEYC's Commitment to Good Programs for Young Children: Then and Now," 39.

47. National Association for the Education of Young Children, "NAEYC to Launch New Professional Development Initiative," *Young Children* 46, no. 6 (September 1991): 37.

48. Ibid., 38.

49. Ibid.

50. National Association for the Education of Young Children, *Guidelines for Preparation of Early Childhood Professionals: Guidelines Developed by the National Association for the Education of Young Children and the Division for Early Childhood of the Council of Exceptional Children and by the National Board for Professional Teaching Standards* (Washington, DC: National Association for the Education of Young Children, 1996).

51. National Association for the Education of Young Children, "Early Childhood Teacher Certification: A Position Statement of the Association of Teacher Educators and the National Association for the Education of Young Children," *Young Children* 47, no. 1 (November 1991): 16–21.

52. All of these documents appear in the 1996 NAEYC publication *Guidelines for the Preparation of Early Childhood Professionals.*

53. Sue Bredekamp, "The Early Childhood Profession Coming Together," *Young Children* 47, no. 6 (September 1992): 36.

54. Ibid., 37.

55. Julienne Johnson and Janet B. McCracken, ed., *The Early Childhood Career Lattice: Perspectives on Professional Development* (Washington, DC: National Association for the Education of Young Children, 1994), 157.

56. Bredekamp, "The Early Childhood Profession Coming Together," 37.

57. Ibid., 38; and Johnson and McCracken, ed., *The Early Childhood Career Lattice,* 55–88.

58. NAEYC, *Guidelines for Preparation of Early Childhood Professionals;* and National Association for the Education of Young Children, *National Institute for Early Childhood Professional Development Background Materials for "The Early Childhood Profession Comes Together . . . Again": Second Annual Conference of NAEYC's National Institute for Early Childhood Professional Development [Minneapolis, Minnesota, June 2–5, 1993]* (Washington, DC: National Association for the Education of Young Children, 1993).

59. National Black Child Development Institute, "Constraints and Opportunities for African American Leadership in Early Childhood Education," *Young Children* (May 1994): 32–36; National Institute for Early Childhood Professional Development, *"Nurturing Leaders through Professional Development" [Minneapolis, Minnesota, June 5–8, 1996]* Washington, DC: National Association for the Education of Young Children, 1996); and National Institute for Early Childhood Professional Development, *"For Leaders . . . By Leaders . . . To Create New Leaders . . ." Background Readings Third Annual Conference of NAEYC's National Institute for Early Childhood Professional Development [Chicago, Illinois, June 2–5, 1994]* (Washington, DC: National Association for the Education of Young Children, 1994).

60. Sharon L. Kagan and Barbara T. Bowman, eds., *Leadership in Early Care and Education* (Washington, DC: National Association for the Education of Young Children, 1997).

61. National Institute for Early Childhood Professional Development, *Sixth Annual Conference "Transforming Ideas into Action" [Seattle, Washington, June 18–25, 1997]* (Washington, DC: National Association for the Education of Young Children, 1997).

62. Sharon L. Kagan and Michelle J. Neuman, "Highlights of the Quality 2000 Initiative: *Not By Chance* [An Approach to Licensing Individuals: Requirements for Early Care and Education Staff]," *Young Children* 52, no. 6 (September 1997): 55.

63. Ibid., 57–58.

64. Ibid., 57.

65. "Dr. Evangeline Howard [sic] Ward, Divorcee" TMs (Photocopy), P. 207, Evangeline Ward Papers [uncatalogued].

66. Ibid., 212.

67. Ibid. 213, 216; and *Who's Who of American Women,* 8th ed. (1974–1975), 1006.

68. "Dr. Evangeline Howard [sic] Ward, Divorcee," 216.

69. Ibid., 219–220.

70. Evangeline Ward, Untitled speech at Follow Through Parent Involvement Workshop (College Station, Arkansas: Elementary School, September 21, 1968), unpaged; Evangeline Ward Papers [uncatalogued].

71. Roberta Wong Bouverat and Harlene Lichter Galen, *The Child Development Associate National Program: The Early Years and Pioneers* (Washington, DC: Council for Early Childhood Professional Recognition, 1994), 67.

72. "Dr. Evangeline Howard [sic] Ward, Divorcee," 218–219.

73. Some of the questions posed were: "If you agree with me that each child is born with unknown and limitless potential . . . What is your *ethical* commitment to encourage its emergence?

Do you really believe that parents and family members are the single most important continuing influences in a child's educational or learning style?

Do you know more about options—for early childhood curriculum than you *use* in your center? . . . *all* children need openness—freedom of choice—SOME OF THE TIME . . . *all* children need parameters that will not bend or move back—*SOME OF THE TIME.* Is it ever ethical to assume that one model works all the time?" Evangeline Ward, "DVAEYC Speech" Ms (speech presented at the annual meeting of the Delaware Valley Association for the Education of Young Children, Philadelphia, Pennsylvania, Spring, 1976), 3–7, Evangeline Ward Papers [uncatalogued].

74. Evangeline H. Ward, "Through the Lives of Others: A Perpetual Memorial" (Coral Gables, Florida: Kenneth Wann Memorial Conference, July 2, 1976), 13.

75. Lilian G. Katz and Evangeline H. Ward, *Ethical Behavior in Early Childhood Education* (Washington, DC: National Association for the Education of Young Children, 1978), 20–24.

76. Ibid., 24–25.

77. Carol Brunson Phillips, ed., *Essentials for Child Development Associates Working with Young Children* (Washington, DC: CDA Professional Preparation Program, Council for Early Childhood Professional Recognition, 1991), 30–36; and Bredekamp and Copple, eds., *Developmentally Appropriate Practice,* rev. ed.

78. "Dr. Evangeline Howard [sic] Ward, Divorcee," 220.

79. Ward, *For the Children's Tomorrow: Educate for Peace,* passim.

80. Dr. Evangeline H. Ward, *Early Childhood Education* (Dansville, NY: F. A. Owen Publishing Company, 1968); Evangeline H. Ward, *Places and Spaces* in *Nursery School Portfolio* (Washington, DC: Association for Childhood Education International, 1969); and Evangeline Ward, "A Child's First Reading Teacher: His Parents," *The Reading Teacher* (May 1970).

81. Dr. Evangeline H. Ward in cooperation with Muriel Hamilton and John R. Dill, *The Young Black Child: His Early Education and Development,* Monograph #3 (a position paper prepared for the Educational Policy and Information Center, National Urban League, Inc., July 1972).

82. Evangeline H. Ward, "The Making of a Teacher: Many Disciplines," in *Teacher Education of the Teacher, by the Teacher, for the Child: Proceedings from a Conference Sponsored by the National Association for the Education of Young Children,* ed. Bernard

Spodek (Washington, DC: National Association for the Education of Young Children, 1974), 48, 50–51.

83. "In Memoriam," *Young Children* 41, no. 1 (November 1985), 56.

84. Most of the information in this section comes from *World Organization for Early Childhood Education: The First Ten Years, 1948–1958,* ed. Margaret Roberts (no place of publication: [1988?]), 1–10. The book presents in great detail the trials and accomplishments of these years.

85. OMEP, *World Organization for Early Childhood Education: The First Ten Years, 1948–1958,* 5.

86. Ibid., 91. A second volume of the History of OMEP was published recently. *The History of OMEP, 1959–1971,* co-eds. Vera Miśurková OMEP Archivist, Czech Republic, and Margaret Roberts, United Kingdom (no place of publication: OMEP, 1998).

Chapter 21

Conclusions

The roads you travel so briskly lead out of dim antiquity,
and you study the past chiefly because of its bearing on
the living present and its promise for the future.
—James G. Harbord (1866–1947)[1]

Early childhood education has a professional identity today as a result of the work of the caregivers, educators, theoreticians, and teacher-educators of the past. The purpose of this volume was to trace the evolution of early childhood education and the influences that shaped it over the centuries. A synchronous picture of several themes relating to child care and the education of young children from antiquity to the present time has been presented.

Several of the themes identified in Chapter 1 recur throughout the book, tying the chapters together. Additional topics that appear to have relevance include: theoretical, philosophical, and psychological foundations of schools and programs; parent involvement in the school; classroom and group organization; the role of the teacher and teacher autonomy; and aspects of diversity. A brief review of the themes appear below.

THE IMPORTANCE OF CHILDREN

Every society, cultural, and ethnic group discussed in this book held that children were and are important. However, many societies, such as the ancient Greeks and the Romans practiced infanticide. Although the Roman emperors under the Christian influence made it a capital offense, the non-Jewish communities of the Middle Ages and on into the eighteenth century in Germany and Switzerland continued to practiced infanticide and abandonment. Jewish religious law and practice forbade infanticide and abortion.

Some of the views, practices, and customs that were prevalent in the Dark Ages (400 to 900) and the Middle Ages (900–1400) became unpopular in Western society, but are now returning to acceptance. Among them are: fostering a gradual transition from the environment of the womb to the outside world, by avoiding exposing the infant to strong sunlight and rough handling; delay in cutting the umbilical cord for several minutes; suckling the infant on demand and not on a rigid schedule; and carrying the child in a sling attached to the parent's chest or back.

In the thirteenth century, instruction manuals on child rearing began to appear in Europe. The availability of schooling was expanded. Children were at first tolerated, and then regarded as individual, independent human beings.

They were the beginning of changes that grew in the Renaissance and Reformation periods that followed.

After the Middle Ages, several reformers developed/devised and described programs to educate the mother and the young child, for example, Comenius, Rousseau, Locke, and Pestalozzi. Some of these programs came to the United States.

During the colonial period in the United States, and into the eighteenth century, infanticide and abandonment took place. During the Industrial Revolution and Post–Industrial Revolution periods, young children, particularly orphans and those from poor families, were forced to work in the factories for up to eighteen hours a day. The Factory Acts in England gradually led to effective child labor law enforcement and the implementation of infant schools modeled on that opened by Robert Owen at New Lanark, Scotland. Child labor was also a problem in the United States in the nineteenth and early twentieth centuries. Beginning with the mechanization of the shoe industry and the opening of Slater's mill in Rhode Island, American children became mill workers. Dame schools, and later infant schools, based on Owen's school in Harmony, Indiana, appeared, and began to meet the needs of parents who worked.

The first child labor laws in the United States were passed in Massachusetts in 1836. They prohibited children under fifteen years of age from working in factories unless they had three months of schooling during the previous year, but as in England, the laws were seldom enforced. The first federal labor law, which was administered by the Children's Bureau, was passed by Congress in 1916, but was declared unconstitutional shortly thereafter. It took another twenty years before federal standards for the employment of young people were set. Eventually this removed the need for dame schools. Later, some infant schools became day care centers.

Maria Montessori opened the Casa dei Bambini to meet both the needs of the working poor and the owners of the housing. She viewed children as independent thinkers who could construct their own knowledge through the use of the didactic materials. Montessori believed that children had rights. She saw in them the possibilities for forming the foundation of a world at peace. In a later time period, kindergartners and other early childhood professionals fought for children's rights, for example, Wiggins in 1892, and the federal government in 1930 with the *Children's Charter*, leading to the United Nations Declaration of the Rights of the Child in 1959 and the Convention on the Rights of the Child thirty years later (1989).

THE CARE AND EDUCATION OF CHILDREN: PARENTAL TEACHER ROLE

In many of the societies studied, particularly those of antiquity, all children were left in the care of their mother (sometimes their nurse and their mother) until the age of six or seven. At that time, boys went to some type of school, while girls remained under their mother's tutelage. Several societies developed rituals for the child's initial school experience. For example, Locke suggested the practice drawn from the Middle Ages of teaching the alphabet with apples, raisins, almonds, and dice.[2]

In every time period discussed, parents had the first and continuing responsibility for teaching their children about life in the society they were about to enter, as well as providing them with the skills to make their way in that society. Nurses, tutors, and teachers had delegated responsibility for teaching children.

DIFFERENTIATION BETWEEN CHILDREN AND ADULTS

All of the societies studied made distinctions between children and adults, albeit in different ways. There was a concept of childhood dating back to ancient Israel and Greece. Among the ways in which societies differentiated between children and adults were baby-naming ceremonies (found in ancient Athens, Judea, through the colonial times to the Native Americans and the blacks). This practice continues in modern times, as do coming-of-age ceremonies practiced by almost every society.

IMPORTANCE OF PLAY

Children have always played. When they did not have toys, they found objects in nature or in their surroundings. The Athenians saw child play as important, as did the Romans, who saw it as practice for future roles. Native American fathers made toys for their children, like bows and arrows. The Romans, like societies in the Middle Ages and later, believed that free and rough play was more suited to boys. Jewish children of the Talmudic and Mishnaic Periods and the Middle Ages had toys, as did the children in classical Athens. In some societies, fathers made toys for their children. In the nineteenth century, toys were manufactured. Children's books were introduced by Comenius. The *Orbis Pictus,* the first picture book, was followed by an expanding literature for children.

Robert Owen, the enlightened factory owner, found play both important and beneficial. Even the Puritans said that children could play games and play with their toys, as long as it did not interrupt the Sabbath. In the early nineteenth century, all boys played games involving strength and motor skills, while girls engaged in dramatic play and hopscotch. One toy that has been utilized by children from ancient times to the present is the ball, which is the first of the Froebelian gifts. Froebel felt that play is serious and of deep significance because it develops the mind through self-activity. He used it as a method for educating the young. Later educators and theoreticians continued this theme. Montessori believed that only those forms of play that had an adaptive, preparatory function were appropriate. Piaget viewed play as the basis for the self-initiated activity from which the child constructs characteristic ways of thinking and acting (assimilation).

AIM, GOAL, AND PURPOSE OF EDUCATION

Over the centuries, there have been a series of differentiated goals, aims, and purposes for educating children. Each society shaped the goal of education. With the exception of the limited education during the Middle Ages, the goals of education from antiquity on was to develop competent citizens who were able to participate and act intelligently.

Beginning with Comenius and Locke in the seventeenth century, through Rousseau in the eighteenth century, and continuing with Pestalozzi and Froebel in the nineteenth century, there was a definite effort to reform elementary education based on the natural development of children. The methodology of teaching various subjects is portrayed in terms of its relationship to child development, philosophical roots, as well as its palatability to the child.

The early settlers in America brought with them the educational practices from their home countries. Many of the colonists on the East Coast had come to the United States to escape religious persecution; therefore, they saw education as salvation from original sin. The church became a major influence in colonial life. On the West Coast, Spanish missionaries brought a different religious flavor to their schools, to Christianize the Native Americans. They too set up a framework for the education of children based on religious teachings.

Strong educational links were forged between Europe and the United States during the seventeenth and eighteenth centuries. Professionals from both sides of the Atlantic traveled back and forth. Europeans brought knowledge of early education practices to the United States, and Americans learned about the latest facilities and programs in Europe. This custom continues to the present time.

The American educational reformers, like their earlier European predecessors, wanted universal education. Mann created a "common school," which would lay the foundation for the responsible exercise of citizenship. He also introduced teacher training in the United States.

The kindergarten, an institution developed specifically for children under seven years of age in Germany by Froebel, successfully made its way to the United States. It was followed by the nursery school, which came from England fifty years later. The first kindergartens in the United States were private schools for children from the upper classes. The kindergartens were incorporated into public school systems in St. Louis in the 1870s and spread to the rest of the country. With the influx of immigrants between the 1880s and 1920s, the kindergartens were opened for poor and immigrant children who needed to be "Americanized." Universal education for boys and girls, poor and rich, from diverse backgrounds and with diverse needs, which began in the kindergartens and the common schools, has gradually become the accepted practice across the United States and around the world.

Literacy for all people became an educational goal during the eighteenth century for several reasons. Initially the purpose was to teach them to read the Bible and other religious tracts. Later, reading and writing became necessary for communication and business, although in many societies it was limited to males. Education was used to improved health and other child-rearing practices. This continued in the kindergartens, and nursery schools, and is found in many early education programs today. Head Start, because of its conceptualization as a child development program designed to address the needs of the *whole* child and his or her family, provides health and nutrition, education, and social services. The goal is to prepare children who are sound in mind, body, and spirit.

DIVERSITY

The United States continues to have great cultural, ethnic, and language diversity. The indigenous Native American populations were overwhelmed by colonizers. Many tribes maintained their own schools. Schooling provided by the federal government was for assimilation. It took many years before Native Americans were able to partake of the educational opportunities available to other people— since the Civil Rights Act of 1964, the Bilingual Education Act, and the Self-determination Act. Their child-rearing practices prior to contact with the Europeans were somewhat reminiscent of the ancient Spartan ways. It is only in recent decades that schools and government agencies have begun to appreciate and support Native American child-rearing and educational practices.

Black Americans had a very unique experience. They came to the United States involuntarily. Their child-rearing practices were what they knew in their lands and were purely for survival during slavery. Initially, they were forbidden to have education. After emancipation, they created their own institutions. Later, they had to fight for educational, as well as for civil, equality.

Asian- and Hispanic-Americans faced discrimination and worse when they immigrated to U.S. shores. When they first came, they were forced to accept low-paying jobs and poor educational opportunities for their children. In the past thirty years, great strides have been made in providing developmentally appropriate curricula, materials, and learning modalities that address the needs of these children.

Bilingualism has existed since the Roman times. It was practised in Europe during the time of Comenius and of Pestalozzi. For the most part it is an advantage to know more than one language. In early childhood, learning of a second language does not interfere with maintaining the mother language, provided certain conditions are met. Current bilingual education practice seeks to provide culturally and linguistically diverse educational opportunities for young children of all backgrounds.

The differentiation in the education of boys and girls was a consistent theme throughout the periods studied. Boys were encouraged to read and write, both in the vernacular and in Greek and Latin. They studied science, history, and geography, and classical subjects. They participated in vigorous sports activities designed to keep them physically fit. Most girls, particularly before the nineteenth century, learned the skills and tasks of keeping a house.

Some of them studied music and dance, in order to participate in community gatherings and events. Equality in education grew as a goal during the Reformation.

Children with special needs were not an early priority of the education system in the United States. Those were the children killed, locked away in the house, or institutionalized. Following the enactment of federal legislation which mandated that educational opportunities be provided for all children, in the least restrictive setting possible, early education programs, schools, school systems, and state and local governments began to address their needs. Head Start incorporated programs for children with special needs beginning in 1975. Currently, there are federal, state, and locally funded programs for children and young people with special needs from birth to age twenty-one.

Overseas influences on early childhood education programs in the United States were not limited to the eighteenth and nineteenth centuries. In modern times, the *kibbutz* Children's Houses of Israel and the British Open Education model have made an impact on educational programs. These influences, combined with that of the progressive movement, and the work of Piaget and Vygotsky, led to today's constructivist educational orientation.

CONTENT TAUGHT AND CLASSROOM ORGANIZATION

The content taught in schools was a function of the societal goals and aims, as well as those of the community and school. Sparta gave priority to physical education and engaged in military exercises; classical Athens strove for a balance between body and mind development; and for Jewish children, intellectual development was emphasized. Locke encouraged boys to learn to read, and to study the sciences of the time, history, French (his mother tongue), gardening, and woodworking. From the Renaissance on, girls were encouraged to take up dancing. In Pestalozzi's schools, all teaching started from the elements of language, number, and form, and progressed to geography, history, gymnastics, handwork, and religious instruction. Pestalozzi began experimenting with observation/perception and description of objects—self-activity, as a way of teaching, instead of using books and memorization that was the custom. This observation/perception was part of naturalism in education. Children were guided to discover things for themselves, to describe them accurately, and to say what they understood.

Children in eighteenth-century Europe learned languages; however, it was the practice in many cultures and societies of the sixteenth through the eighteenth centuries that only boys could learn Greek and Latin, which was needed for further education and commerce. Children of both sexes could learn their mother tongue and other vernacular languages, such as German, French, or English.

Students in Robert Owen's school learned reading through storytelling and accounts of voyages, and writing by copying letters as their ancestors had done before them. History, geography, and nature study involved the use of charts and natural objects. Froebel advocated in learning by self-activity and developed the gifts and occupations to assist in this type of activity. Montessori's work focused on the individual child's interactions with her didactic materials, which were designed to be self-selected, self-paced, and often self-correcting. McMillan's open-air nursery school stressed the health and nutrition of the children, provided gardening experiences, and emphasized the importance of aesthetics in the curriculum. Dewey used both Pestalozzi's and Froebel's ideas, to develop a curriculum for each subject based on the interests and activities of children. He emphasized learning by doing, another form of self-activity. Kilpatrick extended the work through his codification of the Project Method.

In the early U.S. colonies, focus in the schools was on reading, using the Bible, the few primers that were available, and the hornbook, and writing and ciphering (arithmetic). During the mid-1800s, gymnastic exercises, dancing, and music, as well as free manipulation of materials, entered some schools' curricula. Some of today's early childhood education curriculum reflects the progressive movement, including the work of Dewey and Kilpatrick among others.

Some of the ideas that have come down to us through the ages began in ancient times, such as the use of toys modeled on real implements. Montessori's practical life exercises continued this thread. Teaching aids, such as the wax slate and stylus were used by Athenian, Roman, and Jewish children.

PROFESSIONAL DEVELOPMENT OF TEACHERS

The (male) teachers of the Talmudic academies and the masters of ancient Greece, and to some extent, Rome, were greatly respected. Throughout the fifteenth and sixteenth centuries, that was the case. However, by the seventeenth century, according to Locke, teaching was not a reputable profession. The advent of women as teachers occurred with the development of the kindergarten. Froebel tied the interests of children to the interests of women who were seeking professional emancipation at the time. He believed that female teachers could become "mothers through their work," leading to the later statement by Elizabeth Peabody—his foremost interpreter in the United States—that kindergarten teaching was the epitome of womanliness. Teachers in the early nursery schools and child care centers were also women. Often they were young girls whom Froebel, Montessori, and McMillan trained in their methods and in the use of their materials. In the first years of early childhood education in both England and the United States, teacher training was a combination of concurrently apprenticing in a kindergarten or nursery school in the morning and taking teacher training courses in the afternoon. Sometimes they had to persuade the director of the program to admit them as an apprentice.

The common schools needed teachers, so state normal schools were created to prepare them. Horace Mann opened several of the first normal schools in the United States. Over the decades, these state- and city-sponsored institutions prepared many professional early childhood educators who became licensed teachers of kindergarten and primary classes. In the 1970s, systems for credentialing paraprofessionals were developed. Today, systems exist in the United States for state licensing of early childhood teachers and national certification of both teachers and paraprofessionals.

TRENDS

The following trends appeared to some degree throughout the reviewed periods:

1. Children were deemed important in every society, but for very different reasons.
2. Children were loved by their mother; however, their treatment varied from society to society and age to age. In some societies the child was reared by another party, such as a nurse, nanny, or the state, as in Sparta. In other cases, the mother was in charge of her child's rearing, as in Rome.
3. All societies differentiated between child and adult; however, this also varied according to the time period and societal practice.
4. Throughout the centuries, the nature/nurture controversy has continually come to the fore. It has been debated by philosophers, educational and psychological theorists, parents, and education practitioners from ancient times, and through philosophers such as Locke, Rousseau, and Pestalozzi, up until the present day.
5. Children's play was important to all societies studied. It was used for different purposes depending on the goals and philosophy of the society.
6. All societies studied exhibited an expressed need for some childhood education prior to the age of seven, when formal education begins. This ranged from mother play and informal child play and play groups, to dame schools, kindergartens, nursery schools, "day care" centers, back to home-based child care for other people's children.
7. The content of education was not amorphous. It was divided into subjects.
8. Diversity of culture, ethnicity, language, gender, and special needs of children has been prevalent throughout the ages. The diverse needs of children and families have been addressed in a variety of ways.
9. Parent education appeared as a need in the latter part of the Roman Empire and continues as a trend to the present time. The education of the mother for child rearing and education led to discussion groups, periodical literature, and courses. In later decades, there was a definite effort to educate the mother for her role. Comenius and Froebel, among others, identified the mother as the child's first teacher. Eventually, this educational function of the mother opened possibilities for women's education at the secondary and tertiary levels. The parent cooperative nursery schools in the United States presented many opportunities to women for upward mobility.
10. Professional education in the modern era began with kindergarten training courses and later nursery teachers' courses. Teacher education gradu-

ally was accepted into the normal schools and later colleges and universities. Today, early childhood professional development is fostered by departments of child study, family studies and consumer sciences (formerly home economics), child care, and early childhood education at institutions of higher education around the country.

The Long View Back

In reviewing the depth and breadth of early childhood education history, one gains great respect for the people who made it happen and continue to make it happen today. They are people of varied cultural, ethnic, and language backgrounds, with differing concepts of child development, philosophy, curriculum, and program implementation, but they all share an abiding love for children and the desire to provide the most stimulating and beneficial program possible for children and families. We are humbled by their work and honored to be able to share it with you the reader. Our hope is that you will, as we will, make a difference in the lives of children and families using the lessons of history to guide us.

Notes

1. Lieutenant General James G. Harbord in Shea, James, J. Jr., *The Milton Bradley Story.* (New York: The Newcomen Society in N. America, 1973), back cover of pamphlet.

2. E. S. deBeer, ed., *The Correspondence of John Locke,* vol. I, Letters Nos. 1–461 (London: Oxford University Press, 1976), 807: 682 (24 January 1685?).

APPENDIX I
DAILY SCHEDULES OF NURSERY SCHOOLS

THE PROGRAM OF ACTIVITIES AT IOWA STATE COLLEGE NURSERY SCHOOL[1]

8:45–9:00	Children arrive, remove wraps
9:00–9:10	Domestic activities: dust, fold napkin, care of animals and pets
9:10–9:40	Quiet free play. Blocks, crayons, paper cutting, writing, marking, drawing, peg boards, wood beads, painting
9:40–10:00	News, rhythm, dramatization, finger plays
10:00–10:15	Toilet and washing of hands
10:15–10:30	Mid-morning lunch of fruit and water
10:30–10:40	Rest period
10:40–11:40	Outdoor play
11:40–12:00	Setting of tables and story period
12:00–12:45	Lunch
12:45–1:00	Toilet
1:00–2:45	Sleep
2:45–3:00	Put on shoes, toilet, go home

DAILY SCHEDULE AT RUGGLES NURSERY SCHOOL[2]

8:30	School opens
8:30–9:30	Nurse's examination, toilet, gargle, free play outdoors
9:30–10:00	Music period, tone marching, rhythms, posture training
10:00–10:15	Rest
10:15–10:25	Toilet, wash hands for lunch
10:25–10:45	Mid-morning lunch
10:45–11:10	"Occupational" or constructive handwork period
11:10–11:45	Free play outdoors
11:45–12:00	Toilet, preparation for dinner
12:00–1:00	Dinner, toilet, brush teeth, remove shoes
1:00–3:00	Afternoon nap
3:00–4:00	Put on shoes, drink milk, orange or tomato juice, free play until parents call from 3:15 to 4:00
4:00	School closes

Notes

1. National Society for the Study of Education, "The Nursery School of the Iowa State College of Agriculture and Mechanic Arts," *Twenty-Eight Yearbook: Early Childhood and Parental Education,* ed. Guy M. Whipple (Bloomington, IL: Public School Publishing Co., 1929), 181.

2. Ibid., "The Nursery School Training School of Boston," 201–202; and Abigail A. Eliot, "Two Nursery Schools," *Child Health Magazine* 5 (March 1924): 98.

Appendix 2
Materials and Equipment

Materials and equipment to be found in the early childhood education classroom.[1]

I. *Indoor Equipment*
   A. Floor Play Materials
      1. cars, airplanes, boats, fire engines, wagons, tractors, trains of assorted sizes
      2. rubber, plastic, or wooden figures of farm and domestic animals; community workers: policemen, firemen, postmen; family members: mother, father, boy, girl, baby, grandparents
      3. rocking boat
   B. Household and Dramatic Play
      1. rubber dolls; doll clothes; chest for doll clothes, doll carriages; doll beds, blankets, mattresses, pillows for dolls
      2. furniture for household play: wooden stove, cupboard for dishes, sink, small table, and chair
      3. kitchenware: dishes, tea set, small cooking utensils, silverware
      4. housekeeping equipment: broom, mop, dustpan, brush, iron, ironing board, clothesline, clothespins, full-length mirror
      5. dress-up clothes: for men and women, shoes, pocketbooks, jewelry, hats, belts other: office equipment, doctor's bags, etc.
   C. Block Building
      1. hardwood unit blocks, including shapes of units, half units, double units, quadruple units, pillars, large and small cylinders, curves, triangles, rumps, Y switches, X switches, floor boards, roof boards, large "brick" blocks, and order blocks
   D. Table Activities
      1. wooden inlay puzzles of varying degrees of difficulty, puzzle rack
      2. pegs and pegboards
      3. matching games, e.g., Lotto
      4. sets of small blocks (cubes, parquetry, interlocking, snap in)
      5. large table dominoes: picture sets, number sets, nested blocks, color cones, pounding pegboard
   E. Art Activities
      1. easels
      2. easel paint brushes with long handles
      3. tempera of various colors
      4. manila paper and newsprint
      5. paste

      6. finger paints and finger-paint paper

      7. clay

      8. construction paper of various colors

      9. blunt scissors

    10. aprons or smocks

    11. crayons and colored chalk

    12. "beautiful junk": cans, string, pieces of materials, wallpaper, macaroni, pipe cleaners, etc.

F. Music

      1. phonograph and records

      2. drums, triangles, tambourines, tom-toms

      3. sleigh bells, shakers, maracas, cymbals, rhythm sticks

      4. we had a piano

G. Literature picture story-books appropriate to the age of children including poetry, prose, humor

H. Science

      1. magnets

      2. magnifying glass

      3. thermometers

      4. tape measure, yardstick, rulers

      5. measuring cups and spoons

      6. aquarium; plants

      7. scales

I. Water Play

      1. small pitchers, watering cans, bowls of varying sizes

      2. plastic squeeze bottles, eye droppers, funnels, strainers, egg beaters, straws, brushes, soap

      3. newspapers and plastic aprons

J. Woodwork

      1. workbench

      2. hammers, nails, screws

K. Furniture

      1. child-size tables and chairs

      2. lockers or cubby holes where children hang coats and keep extra change of clothes

      3. a rug or two for story time

      4. cots for nap, all-day programs

      5. low open shelves for general storage that can be used for room dividers accessible to children

      6. cupboard or high shelves for teacher's use and for storage of supplies, art materials

II. *Outdoor Equipment*

      1. sandbox, cans, buckets, spades, spoons, etc.

      2. jungle gym

3. monkey bars

4. auto tire swings, swings, see-saws

5. slides, large and small

6. tricycles

7. wagons to pull

8. walking boards

9. balls

10. garden spot and dirt

The playground should have both concrete areas for bikes and dirt and grass for children to dig and plant.

NOTES

1. The references that follow are arranged chronologically. Christine Heinig, "Nursery School Equipment," *Childhood Education* 5 (February 1929): 302–306; National Society for the Study of Education (NSSE), *Twenty-Eighth Yearbook: Early Childhood and Parental Education,* ed. Guy M. Whipple (Bloomington, IL: Public School Publishing Co., 1929), 235–238; Federal Emergency Relief Administration, *Emergency Nursery Schools during the Second Year, 1934–1935* (Washington, DC: National Advisory Committee on Emergency Nursery Schools, [1936?]), 54–59; Arnold Gesell and Frances L. Ilg, *Infant and Child in the Culture of Today,* 21st ed. (New York: Harper & Brothers, 1943), Appendix C Toys, Play Materials, and Equipment, 372–377. They are organized according to age; Office of Economic Opportunity, Project Head Start, *Equipment and Supplies,* no. 9 (Washington, DC: Office of Economic Opportunity, n.d.), part of the rainbow series.

APPENDIX 3
THE CHILDREN'S CHARTER

1. For every child, spiritual and moral training to help him to stand firm under the pressure of life.

2. For every child, understanding and the guarding of his personality as his most precious right.

3. For every child, a home and that love and security which a home provides; and for that child who must receive foster care, the nearest substitute for his own home.

4. For every child, full preparation for his birth, his mother receiving prenatal, natal, and postnatal care; and the establishment of such protective measures as will make childbearing safer.

5. For every child, health protection from birth through adolescence, including: periodical health examinations and, where needed, care of specialist and hospital treatment; regular dental examination and care of the teeth; protective and preventive measures against communicable diseases; the issuing of pure food, pure milk, and pure water.

6. For every child, from birth through adolescence, promotion of health, including health instruction and a health program, wholesome, physical and mental recreation, with teachers and leaders adequately trained.

7. For every child, a dwelling place, safe, sanitary, and wholesome, with reasonable provisions for privacy, free from conditions which tend to thwart his development; and a home environment harmonious and enriching.

8. For every child, a school which is safe from hazards, sanitary, properly equipped, lighted, and ventilated. For younger children, nursery schools and kindergartens to supplement home care.

9. For every child, a community which recognizes and plans for his needs; protects him against physical dangers, moral hazards and diseases; provides him with safe and wholesome places for play and recreation; and makes provision for his cultural and social needs.

10. For every child, an education which, through the discovery and development of his individual abilities, prepares him for life; and through training and vocational guidance prepares him for a living which will yield him the maximum of satisfaction.

11. For every child, such teaching and training as will prepare him for successful parenthood, homemaking, and the rights of citizenship; and, for parents, supplementary training to fit them to deal wisely with the problem of parenthood.

12. For every child, education for safety and protection against accidents to which modern conditions subject him—those to which he is directly

exposed, and those which, through loss or maiming, of his parents, affect him indirectly.

13. For every child who is blind, deaf, crippled, or otherwise physically handicapped, and for the child who is mentally handicapped, such measures as will early discover and diagnose his handicap, provide care and treatment, and so train him that he may become an asset to society rather than a liability. Expenses of these services should be borne publicly where they cannot be privately met.

14. For every child who is in conflict with society, the right to be dealt with intelligently as society's charge, not society's outcast; with the home, the school, the church, the court and the institution when needed, shaped to return him whenever possible to the normal stream of life.

15. For every child, the right to grow up in a family with an adequate standard of living and the security of a stable income as the surest safeguard against social handicaps.

16. For every child, protection against labor that stunts growth, either physical or mental, that limits education, that deprives children of the right of comradeship, of play and of joy.

17. For every rural child, as satisfactory schooling and health services as for the city child, and an extension to rural families of social, recreational and cultural facilities.

18. To supplement the home and the school in the training of youth, and to return to them those interests of which modern life tends to cheat children, every stimulation and encouragement should be given to the extension and development of the voluntary youth organizations.

19. To make everywhere available these minimum protections of the health and welfare of children, there should be a district, county or community organization for health, education and welfare, with full-time officials, coordinating with a state-wide program which will be responsible to a nation-wide service of general information, statistics and scientific research. This should include: (a) Trained full-time public health officials with public health nurses, sanitary inspection, and laboratory workers. (b) Available hospital beds. (c) Full-time public welfare service for the relief, aid, and guidance of children in special need due to poverty, misfortune, or behavior difficulties, and for the protection of children from abuse, neglect, exploitation or moral hazard.

For every child these rights, regardless of race, or color, or situation, wherever he may live under the protection of the American Flag.[1]

NOTE

1. Robert H. Bremner, ed., *Children and Youth in America: A Documentary History,* 3 volumes in 5 (Cambridge: Harvard University Press, 1971, 1974), 2:106–108. Note that the Children's Charter is very reminiscent of Kate Wiggin's *Children's Rights* (1894), mentioned in Chapter 9.

Appendix 4
Chronology of Educational
Pioneers and Their Countries/States

European

Plato (427–347 B.C.) (Athens)

Aristotle (384–322 B.C.) (Athens)

Cicero (106–43 B.C.) (Rome)

Quintilian (A.D. 35–100) (Rome)

St. Augustine (A.D. 354–430) (Roman Empire)

Jan Amos Komensky Comenius (1592–1670) (Bohemia)

John Locke (1632–1704) (England)

Jean-Jacques Rousseau (1712–1778) (France)

Johann Heinrich Pestalozzi (1746–1827) (Switzerland)

Robert Owen (1771–1858) (Wales)

Friedrich Wilhelm Froebel (1782–1852) (Germany)

Rachel McMillan (1859–1917) (England)

Margaret McMillan (1860–1931) (England)

Maria Montessori (1870–1952) (Italy)

Grace Owen (1873–1965) (England)

Jean Piaget (1896–1980) (Switzerland)

American

Horace Mann (1796–1859) (Massachusetts)

Elizabeth Palmer Peabody (1804–1894) (Massachusetts)

Mary Tyler Peabody Mann (1806–1887) (Massachusetts)

Henry Barnard (1811–1900) (Hartford, Connecticut)

Frederick Douglass (1817–1895) (Born slave in Maryland)

Eudora Hailmann (1835–1904) (Indiana)

William T. Harris (1835–1909) (Connecticut)

Maria Kraus Boelte (1836–1918) (Germany/New York*)

William N. Hailmann (1836–1920) (Switzerland/U.S.*)

Susan E. Blow (1843–1916) (St. Louis)

Sarah Winnemucca (1844–1891) (Native American) (Western Nevada)

Granville Stanley Hall (1844–1924) (Massachusetts)

Kate Douglas Wiggin (1856–1923) (Maine)
Josephine Silone Yates (1859–1912) (Long Island, New York)
John Dewey (1859–1952) (Vermont)
Mary Church Terell (1863–1954) (Tennessee)
Booker T. Washington (1856–1915) (Born slave in Virginia)
Harriet M. Johnson (1867–1934) (Maine)
Caroline Pratt (1867–1954) (New York)
Patty Smith Hill (1868–1946) (Kentucky)
Alice Temple (1866–1946) (Chicago)
William H. Kilpatrick (1871–1965) (Georgia)
Bird T. Baldwin (1875–1928) (Pennsylvania)
Edna Noble White (1879–1954) (Illinois)
Arnold Gesell (1880–1961) (Wisconsin)
Margaret Naumberg (1890–1983) (New York City)
Lawrence Frank (1890–1968) (Ohio)
Abigail Adams Eliot (1892–1992) (Boston)
James L. Hymes, Jr. (1913–1998) (New York City)
Evangeline Ward (1920–1985) (Virginia)
D. Keith Osborn (1927–1994) (St. Louis)
Edward Zigler (1930–) (Missouri)
Carol Brunson Phillips Day (1947–) (Chicago)

*These two pioneers were born in Europe but lived and contributed in the U.S.A.

INDEX